lonely planet

Ireland

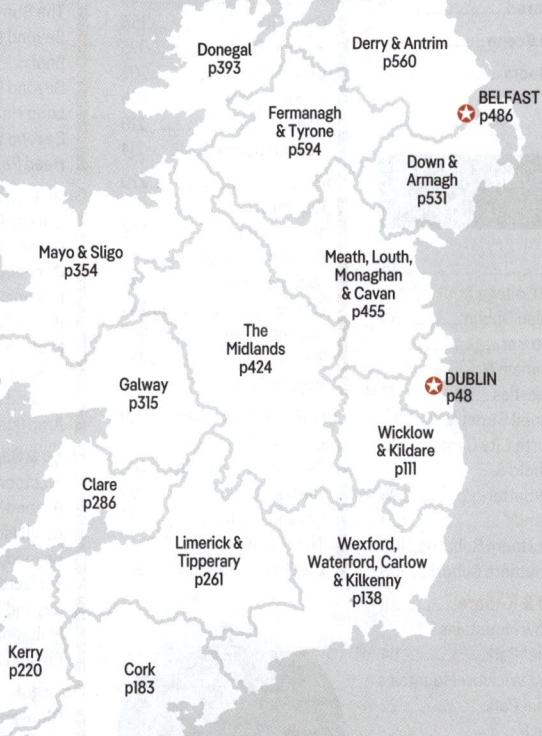

- Donegal p393
- Derry & Antrim p560
- Fermanagh & Tyrone p594
- BELFAST p486
- Down & Armagh p531
- Mayo & Sligo p354
- Meath, Louth, Monaghan & Cavan p455
- The Midlands p424
- Galway p315
- DUBLIN p48
- Wicklow & Kildare p111
- Clare p286
- Limerick & Tipperary p261
- Wexford, Waterford, Carlow & Kilkenny p138
- Kerry p220
- Cork p183

**Catherine Le Nevez, Isabel Albiston,
Fionn Davenport, Kathy Donaghy, Neil Wilson**

CONTENTS

Plan Your Trip

The Journey Begins Here 4
Ireland Map 6
Our Picks 8
Regions & Cities 22
Itineraries 26
When to Go 36
Get Prepared 38
The Food Scene 40
The Outdoors 42

The Guide

Dublin 48
  Trinity College & Georgian Dublin 54
  Temple Bar 70
  Kilmainham & the Liberties 77
  O'Connell Street & the North City Centre 86
  Smithfield & Stoneybatter 95
  Docklands 100
  The Northern Suburbs 103
  The Southern Suburbs 106

Wicklow & Kildare 111
  Wicklow Mountains National Park 114
  Beyond Wicklow Mountains National Park 122
  Kildare & Horse Country 128
  Beyond Kildare & Horse Country 133

Wexford, Waterford, Carlow & Kilkenny 138
  Wexford Town 144
  Beyond Wexford Town 149
  Waterford City 154
  Beyond Waterford City 159
  Carlow Town 165
  Beyond Carlow Town 168
  Kilkenny City 171
  Beyond Kilkenny City 177

Cork 183
  Cork City 188
  Beyond Cork City 195
  Clonakilty 202
  Beyond Clonakilty 205
  Bantry 210
  Beyond Bantry 214

Kerry 220
  Killarney National Park 226
  Beyond Killarney National Park 235
  Dingle 244
  Beyond Dingle 248
  Tralee 253
  Beyond Tralee 256

Limerick & Tipperary 261
  Limerick City 264
  Beyond Limerick City 268
  Cashel 272
  Beyond Cashel 277
  The Galtees & the Glen of Aherlow 281

Mullaghmore Head (p385)

Kylemore Abbey (p334)

Clare 286
  The Burren 290
  Beyond the Burren 297
  Ennis 301
  Beyond Ennis 304
  Loop Head Peninsula 307
  Beyond Loop Head Peninsula 311

Galway 315
  Galway City 320
  Beyond Galway City 325
  Connemara National Park 330
  Beyond Connemara National Park 334
  Clifden 337
  Beyond Clifden 343
  Aran Islands 348

Mayo & Sligo 354
  Westport 360
  Beyond Westport 363
  Achill Island 367
  Beyond Achill Island 372
  Enniscrone 377
  Beyond Enniscrone 380
  Mullaghmore 387
  Beyond Mullaghmore 385

Donegal 393
  Glenveagh National Park 396
  Beyond Glenveagh National Park 401
  Malin Head 405
  Beyond Malin Head 410
  Slieve League Cliffs 414
  Beyond the Slieve League Cliffs 417

The Midlands 424
- Athlone 428
- Beyond Athlone 433
- Strokestown 439
- beyond Strokestown 442
- Belvedere House & Gardens 448
- Beyond Belvedere House & Gardens 450

Meath, Louth, Monaghan & Cavan 455
- Brú na Bóinne 460
- Beyond Brú na Bóinne ... 466
- Trim 473
- Beyond Trim 476
- County Cavan 478
- Beyond County Cavan ... 481

Belfast 486
- City Centre 492
- Cathedral Quarter 500
- Titanic Quarter & East Belfast 506
- Holywood 513
- Queen's Quarter & South Belfast 516
- West & North Belfast 522

Down & Armagh 531
- Newcastle 536
- Beyond Newcastle 542
- Armagh City 553
- Beyond Armagh City 557

Derry & Antrim 560
- Derry City 566
- Beyond Derry City 572
- Bushmills 575
- Beyond Bushmills 578
- Ballycastle 584
- Beyond Ballycastle 587

Fermanagh & Tyrone 594
- Enniskillen 598
- Beyond Enniskillen 602

FROM LEFT: MNSTUDIO/SHUTTERSTOCK, NORADOA/SHUTTERSTOCK, SCHAGER/SHUTTERSTOCK

Musicians at Cobblestone (p99), Dublin

Toolkit

- **Arriving** 614
- **Getting Around** 615
- **Money** 616
- **Accommodation** 617
- **Family Travel** 618
- **Health & Safe Travel** ... 619
- **Food, Drink & Nightlife** ... 620
- **Responsible Travel** 622
- **LGBTIQ+ Travellers** 624
- **Accessible Travel** 625
- **Drive the Wild Atlantic Way** 626
- **Nuts & Bolts** 627
- **Language** 628

Storybook

- **A History of Ireland in 15 Places** 632
- **Meet the Irish** 636
- **Gaelic Games: More Than Sport** 638
- **William Butler Yeats** 641
- **Ireland's Red Deer** 644

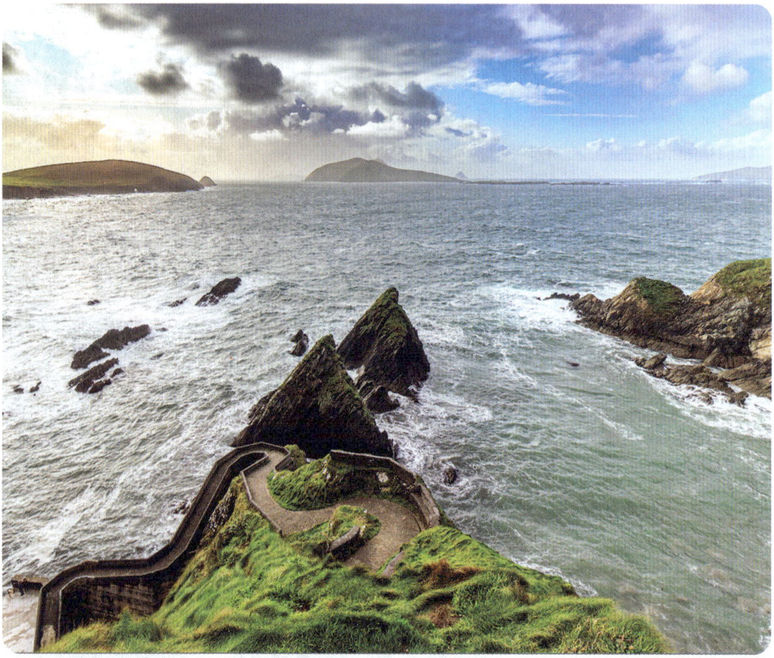

IRISH DRONE PHOTOGRAPHY/SHUTTERSTOCK

Dunquin (p249), Slea Head

IRELAND

THE JOURNEY BEGINS HERE

In small and in really profound ways, Ireland has transformed in the two decades I've been travelling through and writing about these 32 counties for Lonely Planet. Even travelling here itself has changed over that time – motorways have made getting around infinitely quicker than being stuck behind tractors, and the expanding greenways are a spectacular way to avoid the traffic altogether. There's also been a fundamental shift in Ireland's food and drink scene that makes the most of its fantastic produce and traditions (farmhouse cheeses, farm-to-fork dining, fresh-off-the-boat seafood and more than a dozen times as many whiskey distilleries), and a huge resurgence in the Irish language.

Yet so many aspects of this compelling place – the wild and raw natural landscapes, ancient sites, deep mythology and folklore, the love of literature, cosy pubs, rousing trad sessions, and above all the spirited people – haven't changed at all. And I hope they never do.

Catherine Le Nevez

lonelyplanet.com/authors/catherine-le-nevez

A Lonely Planet author since 2004, Catherine has a Doctorate in Creative Arts in Writing and insatiable wanderlust. She wrote the Cork, Kerry, and Wexford, Waterford, Carlow & Kilkenny chapters.

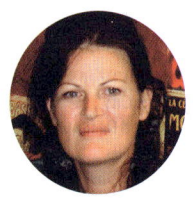

My favourite experience is **Slea Head** (p252), a journey through history – beehive huts, ringforts, inscribed stones, early Christian sites – along a spectacular edge-of-the-world coastline, ending in a music-filled Dingle pub.

WHO GOES WHERE

Our writers and experts choose the places which, for them, define Ireland.

The **Mourne Mountains** have appeared in various works of art, including a ballad by Don McLean. The lulling melody and the narrator's longing for the familiar landscape of home capture the romance of these rolling hills that 'sweep down to the sea'. My favourite access point is Kilbroney Park (p543); its foothills were the inspiration for CS Lewis' Narnia.

Isabel Albiston
@isabel_albiston
After 20 years away, Isabel is living in Belfast again. She wrote the Belfast, Down & Armagh, Derry & Antrim, and Fermanagh & Tyrone chapters.

Ireland is famous for breeding world-class racehorses, and you can meet some of them at the **Kildangan Stud** (p131) in County Kildare. Even if you're not into horse racing, the sight of these magnificent creatures up close is a profoundly moving experience, and if you take part in the 'foal to fame experience', you can meet their babies when they've still got wobbly legs. Magic stuff.

Fionn Davenport
@fionndavenport
Fionn has been writing travel guides about Ireland since the pre-internet age. He wrote the Dublin and Wicklow & Kildare chapters.

An Port (p419) or the abandoned village of Port in southwest Donegal is one of the most awe-inspiring places I've ever been. Sit awhile on the pier and watch the Atlantic roll in, or visit the *clahan* or cluster of houses where people once eked out a living in this wild place. It's impossible not to be inspired by its beauty, majesty and otherworldly wildness.

Kathy Donaghy
@missoulakate_kathydonaghy
Kathy wrote the memoir Finding My Wild. *She lives on the Inishowen Peninsula in County Donegal. Kathy wrote the Mayo & Sligo and Donegal chapters.*

The first time I visited the **Wormhole** (p350) on Inishmore, it was hard to believe this was a natural feature – the huge, rectangular rock pool looks like it has been fashioned by human hands. But natural it is, and wildly impressive. To then learn that it had been used as a venue for the Red Bull Cliff Diving Championships just added to the aura of the place – search for it on YouTube and prepare to have your mind blown!

Neil Wilson
@neil3965
Neil is a travel writer living in Scotland. He wrote the Limerick & Tipperary, Clare, Galway, Midlands, and Meath, Louth, Monaghan & Cavan chapters.

ANCIENT MONUMENTS

Thanks to the pre-Celts, Celts and early Christians, some of Europe's most significant ancient and monastic sites are a feature of the Irish landscape. Many enigmatic monuments are located in atmospheric but rarely visited rural locations. The significance of some of the stone figures and formations remains uncertain, which makes them all the more intriguing, prompting speculation and allowing for imaginative interpretations. At some sites, the process of discovery is ongoing as archaeologists continue to excavate.

Winter Solstice

At Newgrange (p463; pictured) – one of the 40-plus passage tombs at Brú na Bóinne – the sunlight precisely aligns with the roof-box at sunrise during the winter solstice.

Dolmens

Ireland has almost 200 dolmen portal tombs. The oldest is the Burren's Poulnabrone (p296; pictured), from the Neolithic period, between 4200 and 2900 BCE.

Round Towers

An Irish architectural innovation, free-standing medieval round towers were symbols of prestige, power and wealth. Around 65 stone towers remain intact, mostly at former monastic sites.

Little Skellig, from Skellig Michael and its monastery (p243)

BEST ANCIENT MONUMENT EXPERIENCES

Visit the remnants of the ❶ **Glendalough** (p119) monastic settlement, located in a forested valley on the edge of a glacial lake in County Wicklow.

Discover the impressive cluster of medieval buildings, including a round tower and Romanesque frescoes, at County Tipperary's ❷ **Rock of Cashel** (p274).

Take a boat trip out to the remains of an ancient monastery perched on the rocky island of ❸ **Skellig Michael** (p242) in County Kerry.

Avoid the crowds and visit the moody and evocative Stone Age passage graves strewn about the ❹ **Loughcrew Hills** (p471) of County Meath.

Marvel at the immense round stone walls topped by a grass dome at ❺ **Newgrange** (p463), part of the vast Neolithic necropolis of County Meath's Brú na Bóinne.

INTO THE WILD

Ireland's moody mountains, rolling hills, blanket bogs, inland loughs and gushing rivers are home to a range of wildlife. A variety of marine life visits Irish waters and can be spotted on boat trips, or from the shoreline. Ireland is also an important breeding area for seabirds, and a destination or stop-off point for many migrating birds. Seven of Ireland's wildest and most untouched areas are national parks, where the ecosystem is protected and nature thrives.

FROM LEFT: JOOST VAN UFFELEN/SHUTTERSTOCK, GABRIEL12/SHUTTERSTOCK, NICOLA_K_PHOTOS/SHUTTERSTOCK

Marine Life

Basking sharks and humpback, minke, fin and killer whales are among the visitors to Ireland's waters. Bottlenose dolphins inhabit the island's coast and inlets, including the Shannon Estuary.

Red Deer

The red deer in Killarney National Park (p225) are thought to be the only herd of indigenous deer in Ireland. Elsewhere, red deer were introduced from Britain.

Irish Hares

Hikers often spot the Irish hare on the trails – a legacy of the last ice age and a unique subspecies of mountain hare found only on the island of Ireland.

Puffins, Saltee Islands (p151)

BEST WILDLIFE EXPERIENCES

Spot seals, golden hares, puffins, fulmars, guillemots and kittiwakes on ❶ **Rathlin Island** (p587) in County Antrim.

Explore County Mayo's ❷ **Wild Nephin National Park** (p372), home to a range of wildlife, including otters, mountain hares, red deer and rare birdlife.

Take a boat trip to see the bird sanctuary of ❸ **Little Skellig** (p243) in County Kerry, home to the second-largest colony of breeding gannets in the world.

Look out for red deer, badgers, foxes and otters, as well as a variety of birdlife, in ❹ **Glenveagh National Park** (p396) in County Donegal.

Hear the squawks of puffins, gannets, Manx shearwaters, razorbills and guillemots – just some of the 220 species recorded at the ❺ **Saltee Islands** (p151) in County Wexford.

PINTS & TRAD SESSIONS

Finding yourself swept up in a spirited trad-music session in a character-filled pub is a quintessential experience of visiting Ireland. The trad scene is most active on the west coast, but you can catch sessions all over the country. At pubs often warmed by crackling open turf fires, local musicians play, others pick up the tune and the energy becomes electrifying. As the Guinness flows, you'll be joining in by the end of the night.

Oral Traditions

In the past, trad music was never written down but instead passed on from one musician to another, with each player adding their own personal flair.

Instruments

At trad sessions, instruments often include the flute, tin whistle, accordion, fiddle, bodhrán (hand-held goatskin drum) and uilleann pipes (bagpipes; pictured).

Trad Recordings

Ensemble group Ceoltóirí Chualann was the first to reach a wider audience in the 1960s. From these pioneers came the Chieftains, perhaps Ireland's most important traditional music group.

Matt Molloy's (p360)

BEST TRAD EXPERIENCES

Head out on a ❶ **traditional music pub crawl** (p320) in Galway city, where several pubs with daily trad sessions are located within stumbling distance of one another.

Catch an impromptu trad session at pubs in ❷ **Doolin** (p294) in County Clare, where local musicians gather in corner snugs to play.

Join locals and musicians crammed in for trad sessions at ❸ **Matt Molloy's** (p360), the Westport pub that's owned by a member of the Chieftains.

Tap your feet to trad music in the world-famous pubs of Dublin's ❹ **Temple Bar** (p70).

Discover why the family-run ❺ **De Barra's** (p202) in Clonakilty, County Cork, has gained a reputation as one of Ireland's best folk music venues.

BEACH LIFE

Ireland's coastline combines rugged cliffs with stretches of white and golden sands. All around the country, you'll find sheltered beaches suitable for bathing, patrolled by lifeguards in summer. The water might be cold, but Ireland is a top surfing destination, offering excellent surf schools, gentle beginner breaks and more challenging swells. Surfboards, wetsuits, paddleboards, snorkelling gear and kayaks can usually be rented at or near popular beaches.

Blue Flag Beaches

Each summer season (1 June to 15 September), Irish beaches awarded a Blue Flag rating have adhered to a strict criteria that includes water quality and safety.

Sand Dunes

Ireland's north and west coasts are home to the country's most extensive sand dune systems, in which Neolithic and Bronze Age artefacts have been discovered.

Wheelchair-Accessible Beaches

Beach wheelchairs are available free of charge at certain beaches (book ahead). County Wexford (wexfordcoco.ie) is especially well equipped, with reservations available at eight different beaches.

Malin Beg Beach (p416)

BEST BEACH EXPERIENCES

Descend steep steps from the cliffs to reach the soft sands of ❶ **Malin Beg Beach** (p416), an off-the-beaten-track beach in County Donegal.

Surf the exposed beach break, with both left-hand and right-hand waves, and catch the sunset at ❷ **Lahinch** (p300) in County Clare.

Sink into fine white sand flanked by grassy hills at County Mayo's ❸ **Keem Bay** (p367), one of the most beautiful beaches in Ireland.

Spot butterflies and rabbits among the wildflower-strewn dunes, and listen for the hum of the sands at ❹ **White Park Bay** (p582) in County Antrim.

Join in the seaside fun, take a surf lesson or relax on the sands of ❺ **Tramore Strand** (p160), County Waterford's summer playground.

CASTLES & COUNTRY HOUSES

Ireland's castles and country houses are a window into its past, from the fortified homes of Irish earls and Anglo-Norman knights to those built post-plantation. These days, many of the country's finest properties are open to the public to explore on tours, and the grounds often include outstanding gardens and walking paths. You'll usually find an on-site cafe and sometimes cycling trails and other activities, making for a great day out.

Northern Estates

In Northern Ireland, the National Trust manages a number of the area's grand country houses, which are mostly open for guided tours and have expansive grounds.

The Gardens of Ireland

County Wicklow's grand estates have some of the country's best gardens. County Carlow's estates are also renowned for their gardens, linked along the Garden Trail (p168).

Stay in a Castle

Complete with turrets, some of Ireland's grand historic castles are now luxurious hotels where you can live out your fairy-tale fantasies on an overnight stay.

Dunluce Castle (p580)

BEST CASTLE & COUNTRY HOUSE EXPERIENCES

Take a tour to learn the dark history of County Donegal's ❶ **Glenveagh Castle** (p397) and then explore the gardens and parkland.

Discover *Game of Thrones* filming locations on the grounds of ❷ **Castle Ward** (p548), a grand country house in County Down built in two architectural styles.

Explore the magnificent country estate of Wicklow's ❸ **Powerscourt** (p117), where the main draw is the impressive gardens with views of the Great Sugarloaf mountain.

Roam the richly decorated rooms of ❹ **Kilkenny Castle** (p172), located in splendid grounds at the gateway to Kilkenny city's 'medieval mile'.

Clamber over the ruins of ❺ **Dunluce Castle** (p580) and marvel at its spectacular setting on Antrim's Causeway Coast.

HAPPY HIKING

Ireland's wild beauty is constantly in motion, from the ripples in the water of inland loughs, to the still or stormy seas, to the ever-shifting light and rolling mists. One of the best ways to experience the changing scenery is on foot, hiking along coastal trails, parkland walks, greenways, and inland river and canal paths. Whether you're seeking dramatic clifftop walks or gentle woodland strolls, Ireland has a trail for everyone.

Accessible Trails

Ireland has a number of wheelchair-accessible trails and paths, such as the Cliffs of Moher (pictured), as well as forest park trails, canal towpaths and greenways along former rail lines.

Changeable Weather

Trails that seem straightforward in sunny conditions can quickly become treacherous in mist and rain. When hillwalking, bring a map, a compass and warm clothes.

Ireland's Highest Mountain

In County Kerry, Carrauntoohil (p232; 1039m) in the Macgillycuddy's Reeks mountain range is Ireland's highest peak. Several routes go to the top, and guiding companies lead ascents.

Slieve League Cliffs (p414)

BEST HIKING EXPERIENCES

Hike the trails that traverse the spine of the ❶ **Wicklow Mountains** (p116), marvelling at the wild topography and glacial valleys.

Explore the remarkable hexagonal rocks of Antrim's ❷ **Giant's Causeway** (p618) and visit a host of nearby attractions on a coastal hike.

Pull on your walking boots to explore the rugged wilderness atop the soaring sea cliffs of Donegal's ❸ **Slieve League Cliffs** (p414).

Take the so-called 'stairway to heaven', the ❹ **Cuilcagh Boardwalk Trail** (p606), over the blanket bogs of Cuilcagh Mountain, with views over the Fermanagh lakes.

Tackle the ❺ **Diamond Hill Trail** (p332) for panoramic views of the moody mountains and Galway coastline.

A NATION OF STORYTELLERS

The Irish love of language has contributed to an extraordinary legacy of writers and storytellers that includes four Nobel Prize for Literature laureates: William Butler Yeats, George Bernard Shaw, Samuel Beckett and Seamus Heaney. Ireland is one of the world's most notable heavyweights of the written word – a tradition that continues to thrive with new generations.

EXPERIENCES

Wander the evocative exhibits at the ❶ **James Joyce Centre** (p90) before heading on a Joycean walking tour of Dublin's streets.

Starting from the ❷ **Patrick Kavanagh Centre** (p482), follow in the footsteps of Patrick Kavanagh in and around Inniskeen, County Monaghan.

See nostalgic items that belonged to the poet at the ❸ **Seamus Heaney Home Place** (p572) arts and exhibition centre in his home village of Bellaghy, located between Belfast and Derry.

Discover the works of celebrated local writers such as John B Keane and Peig Sayers at the ❹ **Kerry Writers' Museum** (p257) in Listowel, also renowned for its literary festival.

Make a pilgrimage to ❺ **Benbulben** (p389), at the heart of the Sligo landscape known as Yeats country, which inspired the lyrical works of William Butler Yeats.

FROM LEFT: ALEX_MASTRO/SHUTTERSTOCK, MCCARTHY'S PHOTOWORKS/SHUTTERSTOCK

City of Literature

A UNESCO City of Literature, Dublin is the vanguard for Irish writing: discover its progression, richness and breadth at the Museum of Literature Ireland (p61).

Browsing the Shelves

Ireland is spoilt for independent bookshops and libraries; Dublin's National Library of Ireland (p66) has a domed reading room and 12 million documents, photographs and books.

Literary Festivities

Readings, book launches, screenings and more take place at literary festivals Ireland-wide. County Cork's Cape Clear International Storytelling Festival (p209) keeps Irish storytelling traditions alive.

Titanic Belfast (p508)

BEST MUSEUM EXPERIENCES

Learn about the ❶ **Titanic** (p508) at the impressive multimedia museum in the former Belfast shipyards where the 'unsinkable' ship was built.

Uncover the dark history of ❷ **Cork City Gaol** (p190), a foreboding Victorian-era prison that is now a fascinating museum.

Wander Waterford city's ❸ **Viking Triangle** (p156) to find a slew of diverse museums. The 12th-century Reginald's Tower chronicles Waterford's Viking history.

Step into the ❹ **Galway City Museum** (p323) to discover Galway's story – spanning from ancient to modern times – and its marine biology.

Understand the capital at the quirky ❺ **Little Museum of Dublin** (p55) through memorabilia, photographs and artefacts donated by the general public.

INTERPRETING THE PAST

The nation's vast back catalogue of stories is found at its museums. From local collections in small villages to high-tech immersive experiences in big cities, these spaces reveal facets of Ireland's long history through its experiences, achievements and advancements – as well as the people who shaped them. Dive in for a deeper understanding of the country.

National Museums of Ireland

Dublin has some of Ireland's most important archaeological artefacts and artworks, many housed in the capital city's three branches of the free National Museum (museum.ie).

Museum Tours

Plan ahead to get the most from your visit: numerous museums offer guided and/or audio tours, sometimes via downloadable apps (remember to bring earbuds).

REGIONS & CITIES

Find the places that tick all your boxes.

Donegal

IRELAND'S UNMISSABLE YET FORGOTTEN COUNTY

Quietly dramatic, Ireland's most northerly county is home to the country's highest cliffs, broad sandy beaches and an active surf scene, as well as heather-covered mountains, isolated castles, red deer and golden eagles. Donegal's Irish-speaking areas have a rich culture of trad music.

Mayo & Sligo

IDYLLIC ISLANDS, BREATHTAKING BEACHES AND OUTDOOR ADVENTURES

Remote mountain passes, spirited towns, crumbling castles and islands rich in folklore await in counties Mayo and Sligo. Here you can watch big-wave surfers at Mullaghmore and then visit the tombs of Carrowmore Megalithic Cemetery and the 5000-year-old stone enclosures preserved beneath the bogs at the Céide Fields.

The Midlands

THE IRISH HEARTLAND

Many visitors to Ireland skip the Midlands, but they miss out on experiencing a taste of authentic rural life in unhurried villages surrounded by verdant fields and grand country houses. There are sacred monastic sites to visit and waterways to cruise at a delightfully relaxed pace.

Fermanagh & Tyrone

ANCIENT LANDSCAPE OF LAKELANDS AND HILLS

In County Fermanagh, Lough Erne's islands are home to an array of wildlife, mysterious stone figures and the remains of a monastery. The starry dark skies of neighbouring County Tyrone can be observed through telescopes at Davagh Forest, which is connected by a boardwalk trail to the Beaghmore Stone Circles.

Donegal p393

Mayo & Sligo p354

The Midlands p424

Derry & Antrim

HOME OF THE CAUSEWAY COAST

The remarkably beautiful stretch of coast between Belfast and Derry has numerous attractions, including the undulating Glens of Antrim, the seabird colonies of Rathlin Island, the dramatic hexagonal rocks of the Giant's Causeway, the world's oldest licensed whiskey distillery and the walled city of Derry itself, to name just a few.

Belfast

CHARACTERFUL PORT CITY

Belfast has lived through dark times, but these days, the focus is on fun: coming together for a meal in one of the city's restaurants, catching a gig or attending an arts event. The city's history, including its links to the RMS *Titanic*, is explored in a number of worthwhile museums.

Derry & Antrim
p560

BELFAST
p486

Fermanagh & Tyrone
p594

Down & Armagh
p531

Meath, Louth, Monaghan & Cavan
p455

Down & Armagh

COASTLINE, MOUNTAINS AND LEGENDS

County Down's coastline and Armagh city's religious sights are reachable on day trips from Belfast, but don't rush through. The Mournes, Strangford Lough and the Ring of Gullion are designated areas of natural beauty, and historical sites date from as far back as the Stone Age.

Meath, Louth, Monaghan & Cavan

THE STORY OF IRELAND

Ireland's earliest inhabitants lived in Meath and Louth, in an area that is now a commuter belt for Dublin. The tombs at Brú na Bóinne and Loughcrew are their legacy. Nearby, the Hill of Tara was the seat of Ireland's high kings. Monaghan and Cavan offer walking trails through unspoilt landscapes.

Galway

FESTIVALS, RUGGED LANDSCAPES AND WINDSWEPT ISLANDS

Ireland's largest Gaeltacht (Irish-speaking area) is found in County Galway, home of the country's finest oysters, and wild and moody Connemara National Park. Galway city is a cultural hotspot with a packed schedule of festivals and a vibrant trad-music scene.

Clare

CAVES, CLIFFS, COAST AND CRAIC

County Clare is home to Ireland's famous Cliffs of Moher, as well as the wildflower-strewn lunar landscapes of the Burren. But it isn't just Clare's natural beauty that brings the crowds. Come evening, the county's pub floors shudder under the weight of feet tapping to the beat of trad sessions.

Kerry

THE JEWEL IN IRELAND'S SCENIC CROWN

Kerry is home to Ireland's highest mountains, wildlife-rich Killarney National Park and a number of charming peninsulas to explore. Remote islands, including the remarkable Skellig Michael, sit amid the crashing waves. Given its natural beauty, it's no wonder Kerry is a popular destination, but it's always possible to escape the crowds.

Cork

URBAN BUZZ, ARTISAN PRODUCERS, WILD COASTLINE

Ireland's largest county is where you'll also find its second city and its best food, from artisan producers and suppliers to markets and restaurants. The county's wild west has outstanding scenery, where narrow roads traverse enchanting headlands, passing picture-perfect fishing villages.

Dublin

IRELAND'S CAPITAL OF COOL

Ireland's capital city has no shortage of museums and galleries to visit, but beyond the major sights, there are vintage shops and neighbourhood brunch cafes to discover, not to mention elegant Georgian architecture, distilleries and breweries, and Dublin's legendary nightlife. The city's rich literary heritage is celebrated at a number of sites.

DUBLIN p48

Wicklow & Kildare p111

Wicklow & Kildare

HIGH TRAILS AND FAST HORSES

South of Dublin, the Wicklow Mountains form a bracken-covered spine replete with gushing waterfalls, deep glacial valleys and important early Christian sites, including Glendalough. On the fringes are spectacularly located aristocratic houses with landscaped gardens to visit. The paddocks of neighbouring County Kildare are home to Ireland's finest racehorses.

Limerick & Tipperary p261

Wexford, Waterford, Carlow & Kilkenny p138

Wexford, Waterford, Carlow & Kilkenny

SWEEPING BEACHES, WOODED VALLEYS, VIBRANT STREETLIFE

Known as the 'sunny southeast' because of the warm and dry weather, this sheltered corner of Ireland offers outdoor activities ranging from gentle riverside walks to kitesurfing. History abounds in the mystical standing stones, castles, abbey ruins and medieval buildings, while the county towns are burgeoning creative centres.

Limerick & Tipperary

HEARTLANDS, HISTORY AND CULTURE

At the mouth of the River Shannon, Limerick, Ireland's third city, is rich in history. Nearby are the thatched cottages of Adare, the medieval structures of the Rock of Cashel and dairies that produce the famed Cashel Blue cheese. The surrounding hills of Tipperary are home to castles, ancient abbeys and walking trails.

ITINERARIES

Wild West Coast

Allow: 6 days **Distance:** 809km

Ireland's wild Atlantic coast offers windswept adventures and craggy islands. This route will have you gazing over towering sea cliffs, surfing wild waves, relaxing on pristine beaches, feasting on oysters and Guinness, and catching trad sessions performed by some of the country's best musicians.

Cliffs of Moher (p298)

❶ BANTRY ⏱1 DAY

Start your wild west adventure in **Bantry** (p210), where you can visit 18th-century **Bantry House** (p210) and its spectacular gardens, and dine on Bantry Bay mussels. If you're up for a challenge, you can drive, cycle or climb the single-track road up to **Priest's Leap** (p212) for sweeping bay views. Next, take an afternoon drive to the scenic peninsula of **Mizen Head** (p214).

🚗 **Detour:** Book well ahead for a boat trip to the remarkable early Christian monastic island of **Skellig Michael** (p242) while en route to Dingle. ⏱3hr

❷ DINGLE ⏱1 DAY

Make a stop in the colourful harbour town of **Dingle** (p244), one of Ireland's largest Gaeltacht (Irish-speaking) spots. Sample artisan products, take a seal-spotting boat trip (pictured) or head out in a kayak or stand-up paddleboard before retiring with a pint in one of Dingle's pubs.

❸ CLIFFS OF MOHER ⏱1 DAY

To beat the crowds, arrive early at the **Cliffs of Moher** (p298) for walks along a narrow path high above the Atlantic Ocean. Next, view the sheer cliff face from the water on a boat trip. In the evening, head to nearby **Doolin** (p294) to hear trad music and eat seafood.

🚗 **Detour:** Walk through the wildflowers, wildlife and karst limestone landscapes of the **Burren** (p290). ⏱3½hr

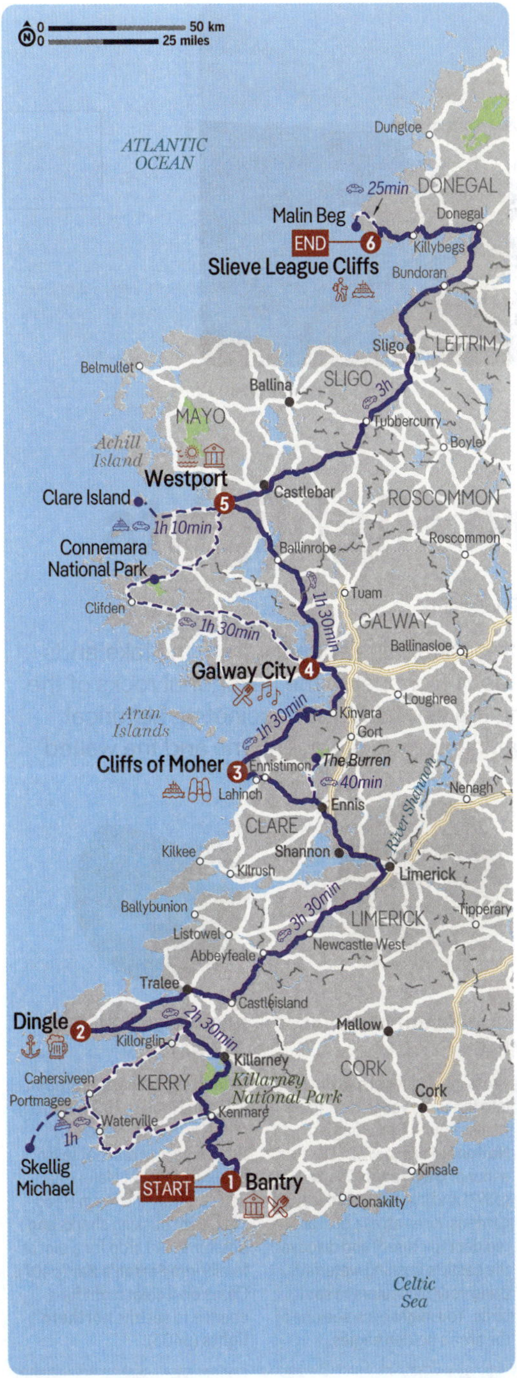

④ GALWAY CITY ⏱ 1 DAY

Start your day next to Galway city's **Spanish Arch** (p323), an extension of the medieval city walls. Uncover its history at the **Galway City Museum** (p323), before exploring on foot. Later, head out for oysters and other freshly caught seafood. In the evening, experience Galway's trad-music scene on a **pub crawl** (p320).

🚗 *Detour:* Take in the savage beauty of the landscape on a road trip through **Connemara National Park** (p330). ⏱ 1½hr

⑤ WESTPORT ⏱ 1 DAY

The picturesque planned town of **Westport** (p360) in County Mayo is packed with pubs and near to some beautiful beaches. Stroll its Georgian architecture and then visit the town's boutiques. Alternatively, start your day with a hike up the nearby holy mountain of **Croagh Patrick** (p365) before catching a trad session in **Matt Malloy's** (p360).

🚗 *Detour:* Take a 10- to 20-minute ferry to **Clare Island** (p364) for peaceful hill walks. ⏱ 1 day

⑥ SLIEVE LEAGUE CLIFFS ⏱ 1 DAY

Head west to the soaring cliffs of **Slieve League** (p414; pictured), which are Ireland's highest. Put on your walking boots to tackle the trails, from which you can spot sure-footed sheep grazing near the sheer drop. Hear stories about the area and gaze up at the cliffs from below on a boat trip.

🚗 *Detour:* Catch the sunset on **Malin Beg Beach** (p416). ⏱ 1hr

Giant's Causeway (p581)

ITINERARIES

Northern Highlights

Allow: 4 days   **Distance:** 324km

The North is packed with outstanding scenery, from the lakelands of Fermanagh to the wilds of Donegal to the hexagonal rocks of the Giant's Causeway. Along the way, discover fascinating historical sites, including the intriguing islands of Lough Erne and the walled city of Derry.

❶ ENNISKILLEN ⏱1 DAY

Start in **Enniskillen** (p598), gateway to adventures on Lough Erne (pictured). After checking out the town's **Castle Museums** (p598), take a boat trip to explore the monastic ruins and round tower of **Devenish Island** (p602), or paddle out by kayak to see the mysterious stone figures of **White Island** (p603). Sample the local produce, which includes meat from livestock that graze on the islands.

❷ GLENVEAGH NATIONAL PARK ⏱ ½ DAY

Cross into Donegal and drive into the Derryveagh Mountains that surround **Glenveagh National Park** (p396). Take a tour of **Glenveagh Castle** (p397) and stroll the landscaped gardens. Keep an eye out for red deer (pictured) and discover the castle's gushing waterfalls. Bring your binoculars to spot birds. You might even see one of the area's golden eagles.

❸ INISHOWEN PENINSULA ⏱ ½ DAY

Ireland's most northerly point is **Malin Head** (p405; pictured), at the tip of the Inishowen Peninsula and reachable by car or by bike. At Malin Head, you can walk the Malin Head Trail, spot basking sharks and dolphins, and stop for a pint at family-run **Farren's Bar** (p407). Come on a clear night for a chance to see the **northern lights** (p406).

❹ DERRY CITY ⏱ 1 DAY

Spend a day in **Derry city** (p566). Get your bearings by strolling the **city walls** (p569) and then explore the murals of the **People's Gallery** (p570) and the **Museum of Free Derry** (p568). Next, cross the Peace Bridge (pictured) to Ebrington Sq, where you can sample the beer at the **Walled City Brewery** (p571). In the evening, catch some live music in one of the city's bars.

❺ GIANT'S CAUSEWAY ⏱ ½ DAY

One of the best ways to take in the scenery of the north Antrim coast is to hike a section of the **Causeway Coast Way** (p583). Allow time to explore the dramatic hexagonal rocks of the area's star attraction, the **Giant's Causeway** (p618).

↪ *Detour:* A 5km walking and cycling trail leads to the **Old Bushmills Distillery** (p575), which is open for tours and tastings. ⏱ 2½hr

❻ BALLYCASTLE ⏱ ½ DAY

Seaside **Ballycastle** (p584) has a sandy beach, pier-side fish and chips, and pubs with trad music to enjoy. Nearby is the **Carrick-a-Rede Rope Bridge** (p588; pictured), which links the mainland to a small island; cross it if you dare.

↪ *Detour:* From Ballycastle, a ferry transports you to wildlife-rich **Rathlin Island** (p587), where nesting puffins and their chicks can be spotted on nearby sea stacks in summer. ⏱ 1 day

ITINERARIES

East Coast Cities & Sights

Allow: 6 days **Distance:** 332km

If you love to combine days hiking and biking in the hills with urban culture and nightlife, this itinerary is for you. Ireland's two largest cities sit just two hours apart by road or rail, each packed with museums, restaurants and pubs. To the south of both are scenic mountain ranges.

Temple Bar (p70), Dublin

① BELFAST ⓒ 1 DAY

Begin in **Belfast** (p486), where you can learn about the *Titanic* at a number of attractions in the **Titanic Quarter** (p506; pictured). Next, head to the city centre for a spot of **shopping** (p495) and take a look at the street art in the **Entries** (p497) and **Cathedral Quarter** (p502). Make a reservation to eat at one of the city's top restaurants in the evening. End the day with a pint in the **Crown Liquor Saloon** (p492).

② NEWCASTLE ⓒ 1 DAY

Take the scenic route from Portaferry via the Ards Peninsula and the Strangford Lough ferry to **Newcastle** (p536). Walking trails through the Mournes start from town, including up **Slieve Donard** (p539), the North's highest peak. You can also hire an e-bike and hit the hills on two wheels.

Detour: It's a 40-minute drive to catch some folk or trad music in one of several pubs in the village of **Rostrevor** (p543). ⓒ 2½hr

③ BRÚ NA BÓINNE ⓒ 1 DAY

Arrive early to secure a spot on the passage tomb tours and spend the day exploring the remarkable collection of prehistoric burial sites and museum at **Brú na Bóinne** (p460), including **Newgrange** (p463) – which dates from around 3200 BCE – and **Knowth** (p463), with an impressive collection of passage-grave art.

Detour: Drive west to explore the lesser visited Stone Age passage graves at **Loughcrew** (p471). ⓒ 4hr

FROM LEFT: VANDERWOLFIMAGES/SHUTTERSTOCK, JURAJ KAMENICKY/SHUTTERSTOCK

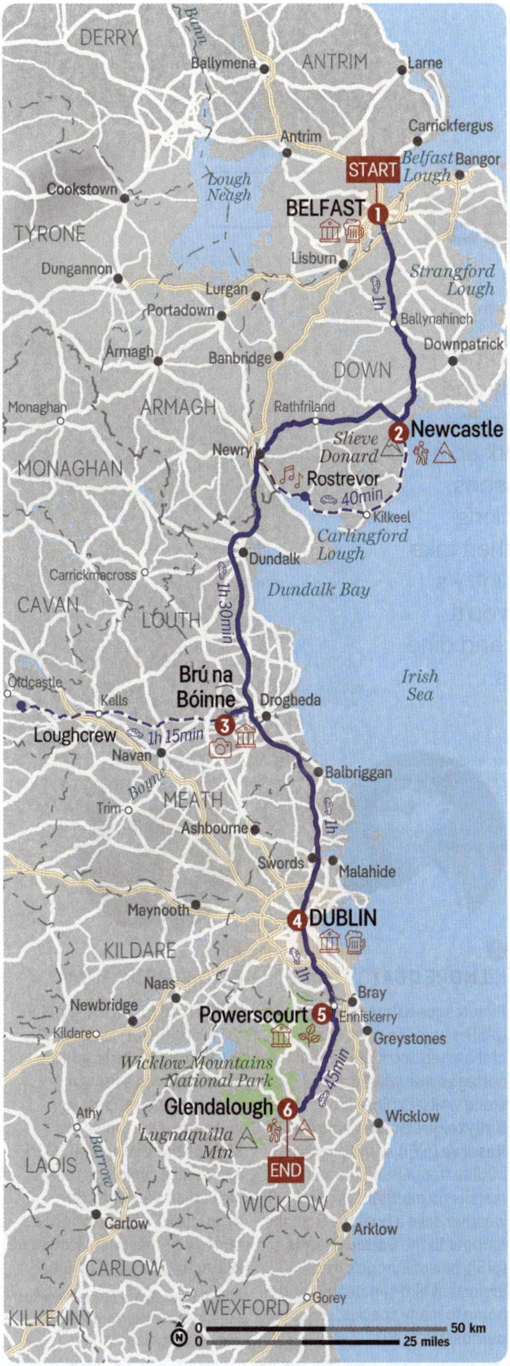

④ DUBLIN ⏱ 2 DAYS

Two days in **Dublin** (p48) gives you enough time to see the major sights. Stroll through **Trinity College** (p54) and take a look at the artefacts in the **Chester Beatty** (p60). Visit the **Archaeology** (p61) and **Natural History** (p62) museums or the **National Gallery** (p54), and then hit the pubs of **Temple Bar** (p70). On day two, learn how the black stuff is brewed at the **Guinness Storehouse** (p80), and then visit more museums and parks.

⑤ POWERSCOURT ⏱ ½ DAY

The main attraction at the **Powerscourt Estate** (p117) is the magnificent gardens; the grand house is closed to the public. Take time to explore the Japanese Gardens and Pepperpot Tower, and stop at the cafe and gift shops before driving out to view the 121m-high **Powerscourt Waterfall** (p117), Ireland's highest. From here, nature trails lead through giant redwoods and ancient oak trees. Nearby are two par-72 golf courses.

⑥ GLENDALOUGH ⏱ ½ DAY

You have plenty to do and see at the ancient monastic site of **Glendalough** (p119). With half a day to spend, wander around the ruins, including the 10th-century round tower and St Kevin's Kitchen, a classic early-Irish church. Afterwards, walk to the Upper Lake (pictured) and back. If you have more time, you can hike the 19km **Miners' Way** (p118) through the Wicklow Mountains.

ITINERARIES

Sunny Southeast

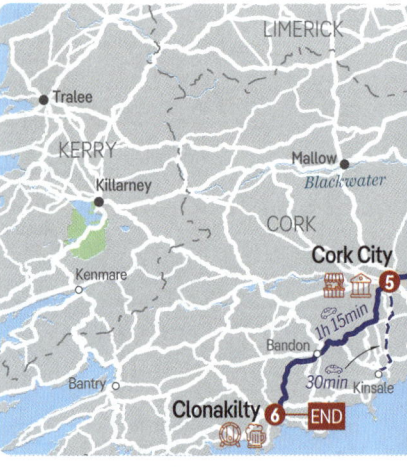

Allow: 4 days **Distance:** 258km

Ireland's southeastern corner enjoys a (relatively) sunny and dry climate and serves up the country's best food. Work up an appetite with surfing lessons, bike rides and visits to Viking-themed museums, and then take a culinary tour of the country's foodie hotspots, where you'll graze at artisan markets and dine at acclaimed restaurants.

❶ WEXFORD ½ DAY

Start with a walk around the historic buildings of **Wexford town** (p144) and then head to Gothic Revival **Johnstown Castle** (p146; pictured), set in monumental gardens; the stable yard houses the **Irish Agricultural Museum** (p146). Also on Wexford's outskirts is the **Irish National Heritage Park** (p147), the site of the first Anglo-Norman settlement in Ireland, as well as reconstructed sites from other historical periods.

❷ KILMORE QUAY ½ DAY

Picturesque **Kilmore Quay** (p151) is home to narrow lanes of thatched and slate-roofed cottages with whitewashed stone walls. Explore the coastal **Ballyteigue Burrow Nature Reserve** (p151), with abundant birdlife frequenting the salt marsh and mudflats. In good weather, take a boat trip from the harbour to the **Saltee Islands** (p151), one of Europe's most important bird sanctuaries and home to many species, including puffins (pictured).

❸ WATERFORD 1 DAY

Waterford (p154) is the place for Viking history. Start in the **Viking Triangle** (p156; pictured), with a replica longboat and fascinating museums. Don't miss the **King of the Vikings** (p156) VR experience, which recreates life in then Vadrarjfordr. After, check out Waterford's famous crystal at the **House of Waterford Crystal** (p154).

Detour: Rent a bike in Waterford and cycle the **Waterford Greenway** (p160) to Dungarvan. 4hr

④ DUNGARVAN ½ DAY

See the boats and colourful pubs of the **Dungarvan** (p162; pictured) quayfront and sample seafood, farmhouse cheeses and other artisan produce at the **farmers market** (p162). Also worth a visit is the Anglo-Norman **castle** (p162) that guards the harbour. Hopheads can book a tour of **Dungarvan Brewing Company** (p162).

🚗 *Detour:* Take in spectacular scenery along the Copper Coast on a one-hour drive to the surf town of **Tramore** (p160). ⏱ 4hr

⑤ CORK CITY 1 DAY

Arrive in **Cork city** (p188) ready to eat. Begin grazing at the **English Market** (p192; pictured) and then browse the artisan vendors at the **Marina Market** (p191). Next, stroll the university campus and discover the grim history of **Cork City Gaol** (p190), a foreboding Victorian-era prison. End the day at one of the city's excellent restaurants.

🚗 *Detour:* Make the quick hop over to **Kinsale** (p195) to stroll its charming harbour, galleries and standout eateries. ⏱ 2hr

⑥ CLONAKILTY ½ DAY

In the market town of **Clonakilty** (p202), you can sample the famous Clonakilty black pudding and taste triple-distilled whiskey at **Clonakilty Distillery** (p204). Learn about local independence hero Michael Collins (pictured) at a museum in what was once his **home** (p203), and at the **Michael Collins Centre** (p203) on the outskirts of town. Finally, catch a folk music session at **De Barra's** (p202).

FROM LEFT: ROY HARRIS/SHUTTERSTOCK, D. RIBEIRO/SHUTTERSTOCK, MICK HARPER/SHUTTERSTOCK

Kilkenny Castle (p174)

ITINERARIES

Inland Ireland

Allow: 4 days **Distance:** 304km

Heading inland offers an alternative insight into Irish life, from horse racing to hurling to dairy farming, with stops at thriving towns that are home to vibrant arts scenes and lively pubs. Travel along quiet rural roads leading to impressive medieval castles and monastic sites on this route through the Irish heartlands.

1
KILDARE ½ DAY

The biggest attraction in **Kildare** (p128) is the **Irish National Stud** (p130), 1.5km south of town, where you can wander the paddocks and see the thoroughbreds. If you are in town for race day, don your finest hat and take the shuttle bus from Kildare to the **Curragh Racecourse** (p128; pictured). At other times, you can see the racecourse on a behind-the-scenes tour.

2
CARLOW TOWN ½ DAY

The main sights of **Carlow town** (p165) are in the town centre. Start at **Carlow Castle** (p166; pictured), then check out the **cathedral** (p166). Visit the **museum** (p166) for intriguing archaeological finds. Dip into Carlow's thriving arts scene at the **Visual Centre for Contemporary Art** (p167). If time allows, visit a few gardens near the town, including the **Delta Sensory Gardens** (p622).

3
KILKENNY CITY 1 DAY

With a day to spend in **Kilkenny city** (p171; pictured), begin by exploring the **medieval mile** (p171) that connects the cathedral and castle. Stop to browse Irish crafts and designs in the **Castle Yard** (p175) and then walk along the riverbanks or take a boat trip. While in town, try to catch a hurling game. In the evening, head to the city's legendary pubs for live music.

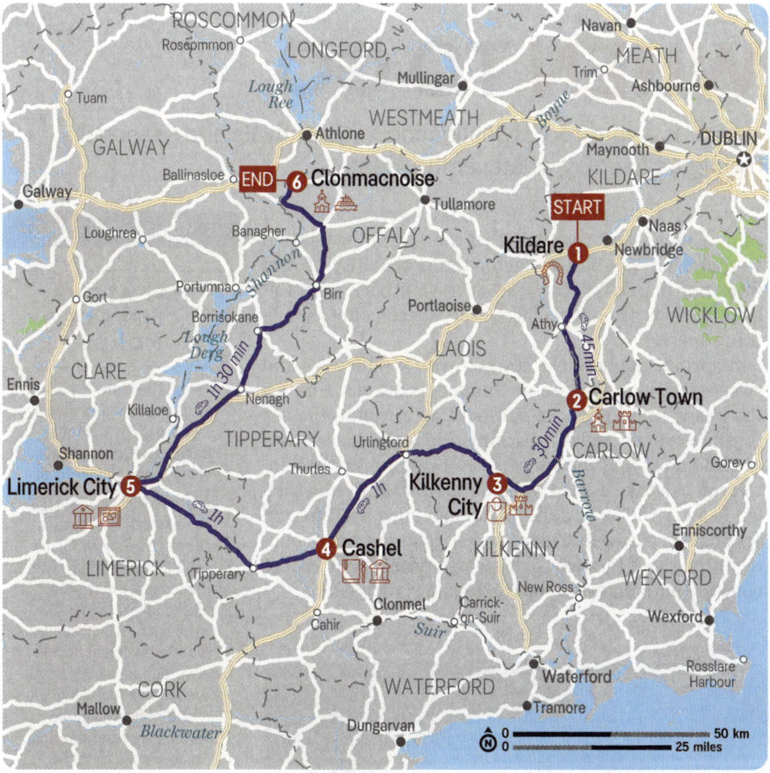

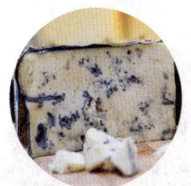

4

CASHEL 1 DAY

Head straight to the most important sight in **Cashel** (p272), a cluster of medieval buildings on a limestone bluff known as the **Rock of Cashel** (p274). Afterwards, go to the ruins of **Hore Abbey** (p275), from where you can snap photos of the Rock of Cashel. Afterwards, spend some time exploring the museums of pretty Cashel town and sample some Cashel Blue cheese (pictured).

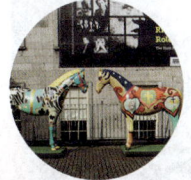

5

LIMERICK CITY ½ DAY

Stop in the city of **Limerick** (p264) to see the Georgian architecture and visit the **Hunt Museum** (p265; pictured). On Saturday mornings, the **Milk Market** (p266) is crammed with stalls selling artisan produce and local cheeses. You can also take an *Angela's Ashes* **walking tour** (p267), which includes places mentioned in the book by Frank McCourt.

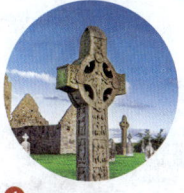

6

CLONMACNOISE ½ DAY

The monastic ruins of **Clonmacnoise** (p430) are located in a bucolic setting. Ireland's most significant monastic site attracts scholars from around the world. Allow a couple of hours to explore the ruins, which include early Christian tombstones, two round towers, three high crosses and nine churches. You can also reach the ruins by boat along the **River Shannon** (p432).

FROM LEFT: STEPHEN BARNES/SHUTTERSTOCK, TOHUWABOHU 1976/SHUTTERSTOCK, BORISB17/SHUTTERSTOCK

WHEN TO GO

Ireland is a year-round destination, with festivals and seasonal highlights to enjoy whatever the month.

There's no getting around it: Ireland is green because it rains a lot, all year-round. Rather than planning to avoid wet weather, it's best to factor the probability of rain into your plans. With a raincoat in your backpack, Ireland really is a country where every season offers something special.

In spring, the hills are covered with wildflowers and sweet-smelling yellow gorse. Summer is the best time for the beach and long days outdoors. In autumn, the sea is still warm enough for bathing, the forest leaves turn red and gold, and the sunsets can be stunning. In winter, you can take a crisp walk in the frosty hills and then while away the long, dark night enjoying a fireside trad session in a cosy pub. There are festivals across the country throughout the year, so it's worth timing your visit to coincide with an event that takes your fancy.

ⓘ I LIVE HERE

MAY AT THE CLIFFS OF MOHER

Michelle Moroney is a yoga teacher and owner of the Cliffs of Moher Retreat in County Clare. @cliffsofmoher.retreat

In late spring, we often get good weather. It always seems to be sunny for my son's birthday in May. The beaches are quiet, too; I like to take sunset walks in Lahinch. In Ennistimon woods, the forest floor is covered with a blanket of bluebells, yellow celandine and white wild garlic flowers. There is hope and magic in the air in May.

Valentia Island (p237)

WET WEST

Over the last few years, weather stations in Kerry and Mayo have topped annual lists of Ireland's wettest places. Valentia Island in Kerry gets almost twice as much annual rainfall as Dublin.

Weather Through the Year (Dublin)

JANUARY	FEBRUARY	MARCH	APRIL	MAY	JUNE
Avg. daytime max: **8°C**	Avg. daytime max: **8°C**	Avg. daytime max: **9°C**	Avg. daytime max: **11°C**	Avg. daytime max: **13°C**	Avg. daytime max: **16°C**
Days of rainfall: **8**	Days of rainfall: **7**	Days of rainfall: **8**	Days of rainfall: **8**	Days of rainfall: **8**	Days of rainfall: **8**

NORTH ATLANTIC DRIFT

Ireland's temperate climate is a result of the North Atlantic Drift. This warm ocean current extends from the Gulf Stream, which brings warm water from the Gulf of Mexico. The Gulf Stream is predicted to weaken in the coming years, causing temperatures in Ireland to drop.

Big Festivals, Events & Parades

Ireland's most famous festivity is St Patrick's Day. It's celebrated all over the country, but the biggest party is in Dublin, with the multiday **St Patrick's Festival** (p61) featuring a programme of events and a famous parade attended by hundreds of thousands of spectators. ☁ **March**

The **Galway International Arts Festival** (p324) is the country's most important cultural festival, with music, dance performances and comedy events. ☁ **July**

In Ireland's second city, Cork, concert halls, underground venues, churches and even harbour cruises are filled with jazz during the fabulous five-day **Cork Jazz Festival** (p191). ☁ **October**

Ireland is the home of Halloween. It originated over 2000 years ago from Samhain (pronounced 'sow-wen'), the harvest celebration of the ancient Celts. Festivities take place throughout the country; Meath's **Púca Festival** (p475) is a mystical, atmosphere-filled spectacle. ☁ **October**

Local Festivals & Sporting Events

Forest bathing, lakeside saunas, sunrise swims and storytelling sessions are among the invigorating events of spring's **Wander Wild Festival** (p233), held in the glorious surrounds of Kerry's Killarney National Park. ☁ **April**

Fiddlers, accordionists, drummers, singers, flautists and whistle players gather in Ennis, County Clare, for the **Fleadh Nua** (p302) trad music festival. Events include ticketed concerts, free singing sessions and walking tours in the town's streets. ☁ **May**

Kilkenny fills with comedians who have their audiences in stitches during the **Cat Laughs Comedy Festival** (p176), a fixture since 1994. Come for hilarious performances of improv, sketch and stand-up comedy. ☁ **June**

Swimmers take to the bracing waters around Ireland for a chilly **Christmas Day dip** to raise money for charity. Locations include the **Forty Foot** pool (p107) in the Dublin suburb of Sandycove. 🌧 **December**

⊛ I LIVE HERE

SUMMER ON LOUGH ERNE

Barry Flanagan is a tour guide and owner of Erne Water Taxi in County Fermanagh.
@ernewatertaxi

It's a different world out on the lough, and no two days are the same. The ever-changing wind affects how the boat moves and the way that the light is reflected on the water. In summer, the islands are a luscious green. I love to catch a glimpse of a kingfisher near the banks of the River Erne and listen for the call of curlews on Devenish Island.

Lough Erne (p607)

SUNNY SOUTHEAST

The driest, sunniest part of the country is the southeastern corner, which includes counties Carlow, Kilkenny, Tipperary, Waterford and Wexford. This part of Ireland gets an average of seven hours of sunshine a day in early summer.

	JULY	AUGUST	SEPTEMBER	OCTOBER	NOVEMBER	DECEMBER
Avg. daytime max	**18°C**	**17°C**	**16°C**	**14°C**	**11°C**	**8°C**
Days of rainfall	**9**	**9**	**8**	**9**	**9**	**9**

GET PREPARED FOR IRELAND

Useful things to load in your bag, your ears and your brain.

Clothes

Raincoat In summer, bring a light jacket that you can carry in your day bag in case of showers. In winter, you'll need a warm coat that's also waterproof. Umbrellas are useful only when there's no wind.

Layers Sunny spring and summer days can look like T-shirt weather, but if the sky clouds over, it can suddenly feel cool. It's always a good idea to carry an extra layer, especially for the evening.

Boots If you plan on hiking, bring waterproof trail shoes or boots. You'll be glad of them on muddy trails.

Denim Jeans are fine pretty much everywhere. In smarter restaurants and bars, you can wear a more dressed-up top or shirt with jeans.

Shoes Some nightclubs require that you wear shoes and not runners (trainers/sneakers).

> ### Manners
>
> **Most Irish people are friendly** and inclined to stop for a chat. It's polite to greet the people you pass by, especially in rural areas.
>
> **Avoid discussing religion and politics in Northern Ireland**, unless you're sure the topic won't cause offence. Some people in Northern Ireland identify as Irish, some as British and others as Northern Irish, so try not to make assumptions or assertions.

📖 READ

Ulysses (James Joyce; 1922) Joyce's experimental, modernist masterpiece takes place over the course of a single day in Dublin.

Milkman (Anna Burns; 2018) A darkly funny perspective on life in West Belfast during the Troubles, which won the Man Booker Prize.

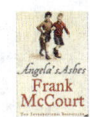

Angela's Ashes (Frank McCourt; 1996) Pulitzer Prize–winning story of a poverty-stricken childhood in Limerick.

Let Me Go Mad in My Own Way (Elaine Feeney; 2025) Poignant multigenerational story set in the writer's native west of Ireland.

Words

What's the craic? Can be used to ask what's happening in general, to ask for gossip or find out what's going on with a particular situation.

Great craic A situation, place or person that is fun, jolly or good company ('She's great craic').

Bout ye? How are you?/what's happening? Common in Northern Ireland.

Eejit (ee-jit) Idiot/fool. Often used affectionately.

Bold Naughty. Usually used with children.

Banjaxed Broken beyond repair ('The car's banjaxed') or if someone is very drunk ('He got banjaxed last night').

Bang on Just right/accurate/correct.

Fair play Well done/good for you.

Gas Funny. Can be used to describe a person ('She's gas') or situation ('That's gas').

Grand Great/fine/good. 'You're grand' means it's fine; don't worry.

So Often used at the end of a sentence, particularly in the west of Ireland ('It'll be grand, so').

So it is Sometimes used in Northern Ireland at the end of sentences ('That's the last train, so it is').

Sure look Ah well/so it goes/that's how it is. Often used to wrap up a conversation.

No bother Not a problem/you're welcome.

Take a dander To go for a walk or explore ('Take a dander to the shops').

Wee Small.

The jacks Slang for bathroom/toilet.

Yoke Any nearby object.

Giving out Scolding, criticising or complaining.

Deadly Fantastic/awesome.

Class Excellent/fun ('She's class').

▷ WATCH

The Banshees of Inisherin (Martin McDonagh; 2022) Colin Farrell and Brendan Gleeson play longtime best mates whose friendship is thrown into crisis. (Pictured: Keem Bay, p367, a filming location.)

Derry Girls (Michael Lennox; 2018–22) This comedy TV series follows the high jinks of four schoolgirls in 1990s Derry.

Michael Collins (Neil Jordan; 1996) Liam Neeson stars in this Oscar-winning biopic about the Irish fight for independence.

The Secret of Kells (Tomm Moore and Nora Twomey; 2009) The first in a trilogy of animated films of Irish folklore.

The Spin (Michael Head; 2025) Comedy about two record-shop owners' road trip from Omagh to Cork to save their failing business.

🎧 LISTEN

The Blindboy Podcast (2017–present) Hosted by Blindboy (of comedy hip-hop duo the Rubberbandits), this podcast features interviews, fiction and comedy.

Shapeshifter (Alannah Thornburgh; 2025) Debut album by the Mayo multi-instrumentalist/composer, inspired by rural Ireland's fairy folklore and mythology.

Sunday Bloody Sunday (U2; 1983) This song depicts the horror of the Bloody Sunday killings in Derry during the Troubles.

Salt of the Lee (Cliffords; 2025) Mighty four-track EP from an up-and-coming Cork-based indie rock/pop band that showcases the powerhouse vocals of Iona Lynch.

Seafood chowder with soda bread

THE FOOD SCENE

Ireland's groundswell of artisan producers, its lush pastures, fields and woodland, and its rivers, lakes and coastline make dining a treat.

Ireland's culinary scene has gone from strength to strength in recent decades, with a focus on quality local produce. Farms and suppliers are regularly name-checked on menus, and there is a move towards embracing seasonal produce and organic farming. Throughout the country, you'll find artisans creating everything from specialist breads to farmhouse cheeses, handmade chocolates, 'cow-to-cone' ice-creams, craft beers, and gins made from local botanicals.

Irish Cuisine

Traditional Irish cuisine involves simply prepared staples, such as potatoes and root vegetables served with lamb, beef or pork. Today, these ingredients are treated with creativity to produce innovative dishes in the best restaurants, helmed by talented chefs from Ireland and around the world.

For many, enjoying fresh, local seafood within view of the ocean is a highlight of a trip to Ireland. Numerous fishing ports are superb places to dine; Kilmore Quay in Wexford is known across the country for its crab, mussels, scallops and prawns. For oysters, head to Galway.

Finding vegetarian and vegan food, as well as gluten-free options, is no problem in most places in Ireland, though quality varies.

Time for Tea

Irish people tend to drink a lot of tea, and you'll certainly be offered a cup if you visit a local's home. It's usually taken with milk and accompanied by biscuits. (Dunking them in the tea is optional.) Coffee is increasingly popular, and in most areas of the country, it's possible to find coffee shops that use high-quality, locally roasted beans.

For a midmorning or late afternoon snack, head to a cafe for a freshly baked scone or tray bake (sweet cakes or biscuits that are baked in the oven on a flat tray and then cut into small rectangular slices).

Whiskey & Stout

In the 1990s, Ireland had only three working distilleries: Jameson's, Bushmills and Cooley's. But an explosion in artisan distilling saw the number grow to 50 in 2025 and a range of aged whiskeys produced. The Irish call whiskey *uisce beatha* (water of life).

Guinness (the 'black stuff') is not the country's only stout. Murphy's and Beamish are both brewed in Cork city, and many breweries across the country produce their own stouts. Some of the most highly rated are the Porterhouse Brewing Company's Oyster Stout and Dungarvan Brewing Company's Black Rock Irish Stout.

Local Specialities

Irish Dishes

Abernethy butter A slow-churned butter produced in County Armagh.
Boxty A savoury potato pancake patty.
Champ and Colcannon Mashed-potato dishes made with spring onion and cabbage, respectively.
Seafood chowder Creamy seafood soup, usually accompanied by soda bread.
Clonakilty black pudding This County Cork blood sausage has its own dedicated museum.
Irish stew Comforting dish made with meat, potatoes and root vegetables.
Oysters Irish waters produce exceptional, subtly flavoured oysters.
Soda bread Made with buttermilk and bicarbonate of soda. Guinness is sometimes added, giving the loaf a rich, malty taste.
Waterford blaa A doughy white bread roll.
Wexford strawberries Widely considered the country's best.

Seaweed

Carrageen moss A reddish seaweed that can be found in dishes as diverse as salads and ice cream.
Dulse A purple seaweed that is dried and eaten as a snack or as a seasoning; also known as *dillisk*.
Kelp A nutritious seaweed that can be cooked and eaten.

Irish Cheeses

Ardrahan Farmhouse pasteurised cow's cheese with an earthy taste.
Corleggy Handmade raw goat's cheese.
Gubbeen Cow's cheese; includes a crumbly, oak-smoked variety.
Durrus A creamy, fruity farmhouse cheese made using traditional techniques.
Cashel Blue Creamy blue cheese from County Tipperary.
Cooleeney Soft cheese made from the raw and pasteurised milk of a Friesian dairy herd.
Cratloe Hills Semi-firm sheep's cheese from County Clare with a subtle, nutty taste.

FOOD FESTIVALS

Waterford Festival of Food (p162; late April) In Dungarvan, this festival includes foraging trails and themed food markets.
Baltimore Seafood & Wooden Boat Festival (p208; late May) A celebration of local seafood and other West Cork produce, plus traditional wooden boat races.
Cork on a Fork (p191; August) Many food events, including food trails, and cooking demos and classes.
Galway International Oyster & Seafood Festival (p324; late September) Huge festival with oyster-eating championships and piles of fresh seafood.
Dingle Food Festival (p247; early October) Charming Dingle teems with food markets, tastings, demonstrations and more.
Savour Kilkenny (p176; October) Cookery demonstrations, market stalls, and a craft brewery and distillery marquee are among the harvest celebrations.

THE YEAR IN FOOD

SPRING

Market stalls overflow and restaurant chefs get creative with seasonal asparagus, spinach, broccoli, spring onions and rhubarb. Woodland areas carry the scent of abundant wild garlic.

SUMMER

The early crops of potatoes are ready for harvesting. It's the best time of year for crustaceans, including langoustines, lobster and crab. In late summer, hedgerows offer juicy blackberries for picking.

AUTUMN

In September, apples are picked to be sold in markets or brewed into cider. Seasonal vegetables include parsnips, squash, turnip and pumpkin. September and October are best for mushrooms.

WINTER

Wild game, including venison, rabbit and pheasant, features prominently on menus. The native oyster season runs from September to April. Look out for winter cabbage, sprouting broccoli and carrots.

Mt Errigal (p401)

THE OUTDOORS

One of the best ways to experience Ireland's wild beauty is to embrace the outdoors, be it on foot, by bike or on horseback.

Gentle hills, rocky ridges, wild boglands, soaring sea cliffs, remote islands and unpredictable weather are all part of experiencing the great Irish outdoors. There are several scenic mountain ranges to hike, including the Wicklow Mountains in the east, the Mournes in the north and the mountains of Kerry in the southwest, while Ireland's coastal waters, rivers and lakes can be explored by canoe, kayak or stand-up paddleboard (SUP). Ireland's wild Atlantic waves are popular with surfers, who don thick wetsuits and brave the waters year-round.

Walking & Hiking

Ireland's coastline, hills and inland waterways are traversed by a network of walking trails, with options ranging from gentle strolls to multiday hikes. The country's forest parks have graded waymarked trails that are excellent for short walks. These trails often include options that are wheelchair- and pushchair-accessible and ideal for families, especially the interpretative and themed trails with carvings of woodland characters to spot along the way. Many hill and mountain walks are also waymarked, but you'll need to bring a compass and a map. In areas of blanket bog, boardwalks have been constructed to protect the delicate natural habitat, adding an element of fun – and making for drier feet, too. Two useful websites for finding local hiking routes are **Sport Ireland** *(sportireland.ie/outdoors)* and **Walk NI** *(walkni.com)*.

Long-distance walking trails include the Ulster Way, a 1024km circular route

---

Popular Sports

GOLF
Tee off at the spectacularly situated links courses of **Royal Portrush Golf Club** (p579), with views over the North Atlantic.

BIRDWATCHING
Sail from Kilmore Quay to the **Saltee Islands** (p151) to spot some of the bird sanctuary's 220 species, including puffins.

CANOEING & KAYAKING
Go midnight kayaking on **Lough Hyne** (p205), where you're likely to experience marine phosphorescence.

FAMILY ADVENTURES

Do a treetop walk at **Beyond the Trees** (p122) in Avondale Forest Park in County Wicklow.

Go surfing at **Tramore Strand** (p160) in County Waterford. A great spot for beginner surfers is **Rossnowlagh Beach** (p422) near Bundoran in County Donegal.

Meander around the islands and inlets of County Fermanagh's Upper Lough Erne with **Share Discovery Village** (p602).

Pan for gold and enjoy falconry demonstrations on a visit to Wexford's 14-hectare **Irish National Heritage Park** (p147).

Pet piglets, lambs, ducklings and chicks at **Muckross Traditional Farms** (p227) in County Kerry, where 1930s' farming practices are recreated.

---

through Northern Ireland. It has a 50km section known as the **Causeway Coast Way** (p583) on the north Antrim coast and the 37km Mourne Way trail across the Mourne Mountains in County Down. In the Republic, the 650km Coast to Coast Walk is made up of five linked sections, beginning in Dublin with the Wicklow Way and ending with the Kerry Way.

Ireland's mountains and hills can be climbed on day hikes. **Carrauntoohil** (p232) in County Kerry and the **Twelve Bens** (p333) in Connemara are the most challenging. In County Down, **Slieve Donard** (p539) is a straightforward climb. Other peaks include **Mt Errigal** (p401) in County Donegal and **Mt Brandon** (p249) in County Kerry.

Surfer, Bundoran (p421), Donegal

Cycling

There's a huge network of minor roads that are perfect for exploring by bike – with the help of a good map. Waymarked routes include the **Kingfisher Trail**, which extends 370km along the back roads of counties Fermanagh, Leitrim, Cavan and Monaghan. Looped cycle routes run from Clifden Cycle Hub in Connemara, County Galway, and through **Killarney National Park** (p225) in County Kerry. **Sustrans** (*sustrans.org.uk*) has maps of signed cycling routes in the North, including traffic-free rides.

A growing network of predominantly off-road greenways, many following old railway lines, offer gentle adventures; check **Greenways Ireland** (*greenwaysireland.org*) for existing and upcoming routes.

A number of forest parks have purpose-built, graded mountain-biking trails; several have bike rental and uplift services. Some of the best include **Davagh Forest** (p608) and **Kilbroney Park** (p543).

Surfing

Ireland is an increasingly popular destination for surfing and is considered by many to have some of the best waves in the world. Surf schools offer lessons and equipment hire at the major surf spots in counties Donegal, Sligo, Clare, Antrim, Derry and Waterford. Expert surfers test their skills with the towering waves at **Mullaghmore** (p385) in County Sligo.

STAND-UP PADDLEBOARDING
Paddle out to see the **Samson Wreck** (p164) in the waters around Ardmore, County Waterford.

MOUNTAIN CLIMBING
Climb Ireland's highest summit, mighty **Carrauntoohil** (p232), in the country's tallest mountain range, the Macgillycuddy's Reeks.

HORSE RIDING
Canter along a sandy beach, with the Atlantic on one side and the hills of Connemara on the other, with **Point Pony Trekking** (p345).

DIVING
Discover wrecks in the waters near Rathlin Island in County Antrim on a dive with **Aquaholics** (p578).

ACTION AREAS

Where to find Ireland's best outdoor activities.

National Parks

1. Killarney National Park (p226)
2. Burren National Park (p290)
3. Connemara National Park (p330)
4. Wild Nephin National Park (p372)
5. Glenveagh National Park (p396)
6. Páirc Náisiúnta na Mara, Ciarraí (p250)

Beach

1. Portstewart Strand (p578)
2. Murlough National Nature Reserve (p542)
3. Rosslare Strand (p50)
4. Ballymastocker Bay (p408)
5. Enniscrone Beach (p377)

THE GUIDE

IRELAND
THE GUIDE

Donegal p393

Derry & Antrim p560

★ BELFAST p486

Fermanagh & Tyrone p594

Down & Armagh p531

Mayo & Sligo p354

Meath, Louth, Monaghan & Cavan p455

Galway p315

The Midlands p424

★ DUBLIN p48

Wicklow & Kildare p111

Clare p286

Limerick & Tipperary p261

Wexford, Waterford, Carlow & Kilkenny p138

Kerry p220

Cork p183

Chapters in this section are organised by hubs and their surrounding areas. We see the hub as your base in the destination, where you'll find unique experiences, local insights, insider tips and expert recommendations. It's also your gateway to the surrounding area, where you'll see what and how much you can do from there.

Fanad Lighthouse (p408)
LUKASSEK/SHUTTERSTOCK

Researched by
Fionn Davenport

Dublin

IRELAND'S CAPITAL OF CHARACTER

A small city with a huge reputation, Dublin has a mix of heritage and hedonism that won't disappoint.

Dublin has been making noise since around 500 BCE, when Celtic settlers set up camp at a crossing on the River Liffey. They called it Áth Cliath – the 'Ford of the Hurdles' – and the name lives on today as the Irish for Dublin, Baile Átha Cliath. A lot has happened since then, from Viking raids to Norman rule to full-blown rebellion, but modern-day Dublin is more about craic than conflict.

It's still Ireland's busiest hub, with over a quarter of the country's population living in or around the capital. As you'd expect, it offers the most choice when it comes to hotels, restaurants, shops and things to do. If you want services, this is where you'll find them – from Michelin-starred tasting menus to late-night chippers to plush spas and live trad sessions.

Though the city centre is fairly small, Dublin spreads wide. It's a city of neighbourhoods, each with its own personality. Head south for elegant streets and coastal cafes, or north for lively markets and pockets of grit and grandeur. Some of the best experiences are found beyond the city centre, whether it's a boozy brunch in Stoneybatter or a dip in the oh-so-chilly Irish Sea in Sandycove.

It's not the prettiest capital, and Dubliners won't pretend otherwise. But they'll also tell you that charm beats beauty, and they'll point you towards the show-stopping Georgian squares or the Victorian shopfronts with a look that says: see? They'll also remind you that it's easy to love a city that's lovely, but real affection is rooted in character. Dubliners themselves are one of the city's great joys. Garrulous, sarcastic and quick to laugh, they wear their opinions like badges and their hearts close to the surface. They'll be the first to complain about the city's flaws and the last to let an outsider get away with it. And when they say it's the greatest city in the world – 'if you ignore all the others' – there's enough twinkle in the eye to make you believe it.

Spend a few days here, and you might just find yourself joining in.

SHAWNWIL23/SHUTTERSTOCK

THE MAIN AREAS

TRINITY COLLEGE & GEORGIAN DUBLIN
Historic heart of the city. **p54**

TEMPLE BAR
Nightlife central. **p70**

KILMAINHAM & THE LIBERTIES
Distilleries and breweries. **p77**

O'CONNELL STREET & THE NORTH CITY CENTRE
Grandeur of old Dublin. **p86**

For places to stay in Dublin, see p109

THE GUIDE

DUBLIN

DAVID SOANES/SHUTTERSTOCK

Left: Guinness Storehouse (p80); right: Docklands (p100)

SMITHFIELD & STONEYBATTER
Twin hipster 'hoods
p95

DOCKLANDS
Dublin's tech hub. **p100**

THE NORTHERN SUBURBS
Beaches and stadiums.
p103

THE SOUTHERN SUBURBS
Coastal dips and art deco cinema. **p106**

49

Find Your Way

Dublin is compact and flat, with most major sights within walking distance. The city offers a rent-and-ride Dublin Bikes scheme, a two-line light-rail system called the Luas, a suburban DART train that runs along the coast, and an extensive bus network for getting to those spots beyond the centre.

The Northern Suburbs
p103

Phoenix Park

Smithfield & Stoneybatter
p95

TRAM & TRAIN
The **Luas** *(luas.ie)* tram system has two lines, Red and Green, which run through the city centre. The **DART** *(irishrail.ie)* suburban rail line skirts the coastline between Howth in County Dublin and Greystones in County Wicklow. You can buy a ticket at the stations or use a Leap Card.

National Museum of Ireland– Decorative Arts & History

Guinness Storehouse

Kilmainham & the Liberties
p77

BUS
Dublin Bus covers most areas in the city, with Nitelink (the night bus) running 12 routes at the weekend. The easiest way to pay for public transport in Dublin is with a prepaid **Leap Card** *(leapcard.ie)*. Leap Visitor Cards can be purchased for one, three or seven days.

FROM THE AIRPORT
The best way to get into town is by bus. Journeys take around 30 minutes. **Aircoach** *(aircoach.ie)* and **Dublin Express** *(dublinexpress.ie)* have regular services to the city centre and the suburbs, or you can hop on the cheaper but slower **Dublin Bus** *(dublinbus.ie)*.

WALK
Dublin's city centre is flat and eminently walkable. It's less than 2km from one end of the city centre to the other. An increasing number of roads are pedestrianised, particularly in the summer, which makes the whole experience even more pleasant.

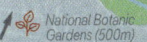
National Botanic Gardens (500m)

0 1 km
0 0.5 miles

Chapter One

O'Connell Street & the North City Centre
p86

General Post Office

Temple Bar

Temple Bar
p70

Docklands
p100

Christ Church Cathedral

Trinity College Dublin

National Gallery of Ireland

St Patrick's Cathedral

Trinity College & Georgian Dublin
p54

The Southern Suburbs
p106

Stella Cinema

Plan Your Days

It's easy to fill a day in Dublin, whether you're hitting up the museums and galleries or making the most of the city's thriving food scene.

Deer, Phoenix Park (p103)

Day 1

Morning
● Start with a stroll through the grounds of **Trinity College** (p58) before ambling up Grafton St to **St Stephen's Green** (p55). To see some beautiful books and artefacts up close, drop into the **Chester Beatty** (p60).

Afternoon
● Choose your cultural fix, or take in the full trio: the **National Museum of Ireland – Archaeology** (p61), the **National Gallery** (p54) and the **Museum of Natural History** (p62) are all in the same neighbourhood.

Evening
● It wouldn't be a night in Dublin without a pint and a bit of trad music. Hit up one of the pubs in **Temple Bar** (p70) to get acquainted.

You'll Also Want to...
Soak up the spirit of the city with a visit to distilleries and design boutiques, and then take a jaunt along the coast.

VISIT THE DISTILLERIES
Dublin's whiskey scene has seen a resurgence in recent times, with cool distilleries such as **Teeling** (p83) and **Roe & Co** (p84) opening their doors to visitors.

HIT THE BEACH
A short trip on the DART train gets you to coastal **Sandycove** (p106) – home to a **Joyce museum** (p108) and the **Forty Foot** (p107), the most famous sea-swimming spot in Dublin – or the fishing village of **Howth** (p105).

CATCH A MATCH
Gaelic sports are at the heart of Irish culture. Whether hurling or football, matches are fast, thrilling and ferocious. See them for yourself at **Croke Park Stadium** (p105).

Day 2

Morning
- Begin with a little penance at either (or both) of Dublin's medieval cathedrals, **St Patrick's** (p77) and **Christ Church** (p70), before pursuing pleasure at Dublin's most popular tourist attraction, the **Guinness Storehouse** (p80).

Afternoon
- Head north of the river, starting with a walk up O'Connell St to see the **General Post Office** (p86). Afterwards, explore the complex story of the Irish diaspora at **EPIC The Irish Emigration Museum** (p88). Take a break for lunch along **Capel Street** (p91).

Evening
- Check out the restaurant and bar scene in **Stoneybatter** (p95), whether you fancy a traditional pub or a hipster bistro.

Day 3

Morning
- Go west to **Kilmainham** (p77), visiting first the fine collection at the **Irish Museum of Modern Art** (p82) before going out the back entrance and stepping into **Kilmainham Gaol** (p85). If the weather is good, take a stroll around the **War Memorial Gardens** (p83).

Afternoon
- Explore the excellent collection of the **National Museum of Ireland – Decorative Arts & History** (p95) and then head to **Phoenix Park** (p103).

Evening
- Take a thematic tour – either a **literary walk** (p64) or a **musical saunter** (p73); either way, they both involve drinking.

UNDERSTAND DUBLIN
Dubliners tell the story of their city at the **Little Museum of Dublin** (p55), the collection of which is made up of local contributions from the public.

GO GREEN
Phoenix Park (p103), one of the world's largest city parks, is home to the Irish president, the US ambassador, the zoo – and a herd of wild deer.

SHOP UNTIL YOU DROP
Hit up the design shops and indie boutiques of the wonderfully elegant **Powerscourt Townhouse** (p66), once the city dwelling of the viscounts of Powerscourt, now an arcaded shopping centre.

VISIT A GEORGIAN TOWNHOUSE
One of the city's best museum experiences is **14 Henrietta Street** (p90), where 250 years of history are laid bare.

Trinity College & Georgian Dublin

HISTORIC HEART OF THE CITY

GETTING AROUND

Flat and full of eye-catching distractions at every turn, this is a neighbourhood best explored on foot. For public transport, both buses and the Luas run right through the heart of it.

☑ TOP TIP

The area around Grafton St is easily the most popular neighbourhood in Dublin, which means big crowds and high hotel prices. East of St Stephen's Green, things are quieter, and calmer.

If you had to pick just one pocket of Dublin to dive into (though honestly, why limit yourself?), make it the area in and around Trinity College. Ireland's most prestigious university – all elegant courtyards and ivy-clad buildings – sits at the top of pedestrianised Grafton St, which leads to the centrepiece of Georgian Dublin, the beautifully landscaped St Stephen's Green, dotted with statuary to provide a veritable who's who of Irish history.

East of here is where much of moneyed Dublin works and plays, amid neoclassical beauties thrown up during Dublin's 18th-century prime. These include the home of the Irish parliament at Leinster House and the National Gallery, the main branch of the National Museum of Ireland, and the Museum of Natural History.

West of Grafton St is a warren of narrow lanes and streets – think funky boutiques, great restaurants and a huge choice of bars and cafes. Further west again are Dublin Castle and Chester Beatty, both of which can be explored in half a day.

Classic to Contemporary Art

World-class collection

A magnificent Caravaggio and a breathtaking collection of works by Jack B Yeats are the main reasons to visit the **National Gallery of Ireland** *(nationalgallery.ie; free)*, but not

EATING: OUR PICKS

Pickle: Exceptional Indian food with a difference – tandoori guinea fowl or wild boar vindaloo, anyone? *5-10pm Mon-Fri, from 3pm Sat & Sun* €€

Library Street: Sophisticated, superb sharing plates from Michelin-trained Kevin Burke. *5-11.30pm Tue-Thu, from 2.30pm Fri & Sat* €€

Uno Mas: A chichi tapas joint with dishes such as ham croquettes and octopus with kale. *5.30-9.30pm Tue, 12.30-2.30pm & 5.30-9.30pm Wed-Sat* €€

Comet: A future Michelin star; book well in advance to sample the Scandi-Irish cuisine. *5.30-9pm Wed & Thu, 12.30-2pm & 5.30-9.30pm Fri & Sat, 12.30-3.30pm Sun* €€€

the only ones. The gallery's excellent collection is strong in Irish art, and there are also high-quality collections of every major European school of painting.

You'll find works by Rembrandt and his circle; paintings by El Greco, Goya and Picasso; and a well-represented display of Italian pieces from the early Renaissance to the 18th century.

The Green
Dublin's favourite park

Dublin's most beloved green space, **St Stephen's Green** *(ststephensgreenpark.ie; dawn-dusk)* was once a grim site of public executions – now it's all sunbathers, picnics and swans. Landscaped in the 18th century, the green became a Georgian showpiece, its northern side (where you'll find the Shelbourne hotel; p109) is dubbed the Beaux Walk.

The main entrance is via the Fusiliers' Arch, built in memory of Dubliners who died in the Boer War. Scattered throughout the park are monuments to Wolfe Tone, James Joyce and victims of the Famine, along with a bandstand from Queen Victoria's jubilee and a lively playground. It's free to enter thanks to Arthur Edward Guinness (great-grandson of Arthur Guinness and one of the protagonists of Netflix' *House of Guinness*), who, in 1877, pushed to open it to the public and funded its gardens and ponds. Just don't trample the flowerbeds – that still gets you kicked out.

The Story of the City
Artefacts sourced by citizens

The award-winning **Little Museum of Dublin** *(littlemuseum.ie; €18)* tells the city's story via quirky memorabilia, photographs and artefacts donated by the general public. The collection includes a lectern used by JFK on his 1963 visit to Ireland and a whole room on the 2nd floor devoted to the history of U2, as well as the personal archive of Alfred 'Alfie' Byrne (1882–1956), mayor of Dublin a record 10 times and known as the 'Shaking Hand of Dublin'. All visits are by a 29-minute guided tour, which must be prebooked.

Cobbles & Courtyards
A hotchpotch of history

If you're expecting turrets and drawbridges, **Dublin Castle** *(dublincastle.ie; adult/child €8/4)* might throw you. This is no fairy-tale fortress, but rather a layered patchwork of architecture, with only the 13th-century **Record Tower** surviving from the original Anglo-Norman stronghold built by order of King John in 1204. For over 700 years, it served as the centre of British rule in Ireland.

Today, you can only explore the castle via the guided tour (included in admission), which covers the opulent, if sometimes questionably decorated, **State Rooms**. Expect gilded rococo ceilings, lush Irish carpets and the throne used by King

Continues on p60

A SHY PAINTING

One of the National Gallery of Ireland's most beloved yet least-seen treasures is FW Burton's exquisite 1864 watercolour, *Hellelil and Hildebrand, the Meeting on the Turret Stairs*. Inspired by a Danish ballad, it captures a brief, heart-stopping moment as two doomed lovers share a final embrace before parting forever. The tenderness of the scene, combined with Burton's extraordinary attention to detail, has made it one of the gallery's most important works.

Yet it is also one of the most fragile – the pigments are so sensitive that even minimal light exposure could cause damage. To preserve it, the painting is shown only twice a week, for one hour at a time: Thursdays at 11.30am and Sundays at 2pm, always in Room 20.

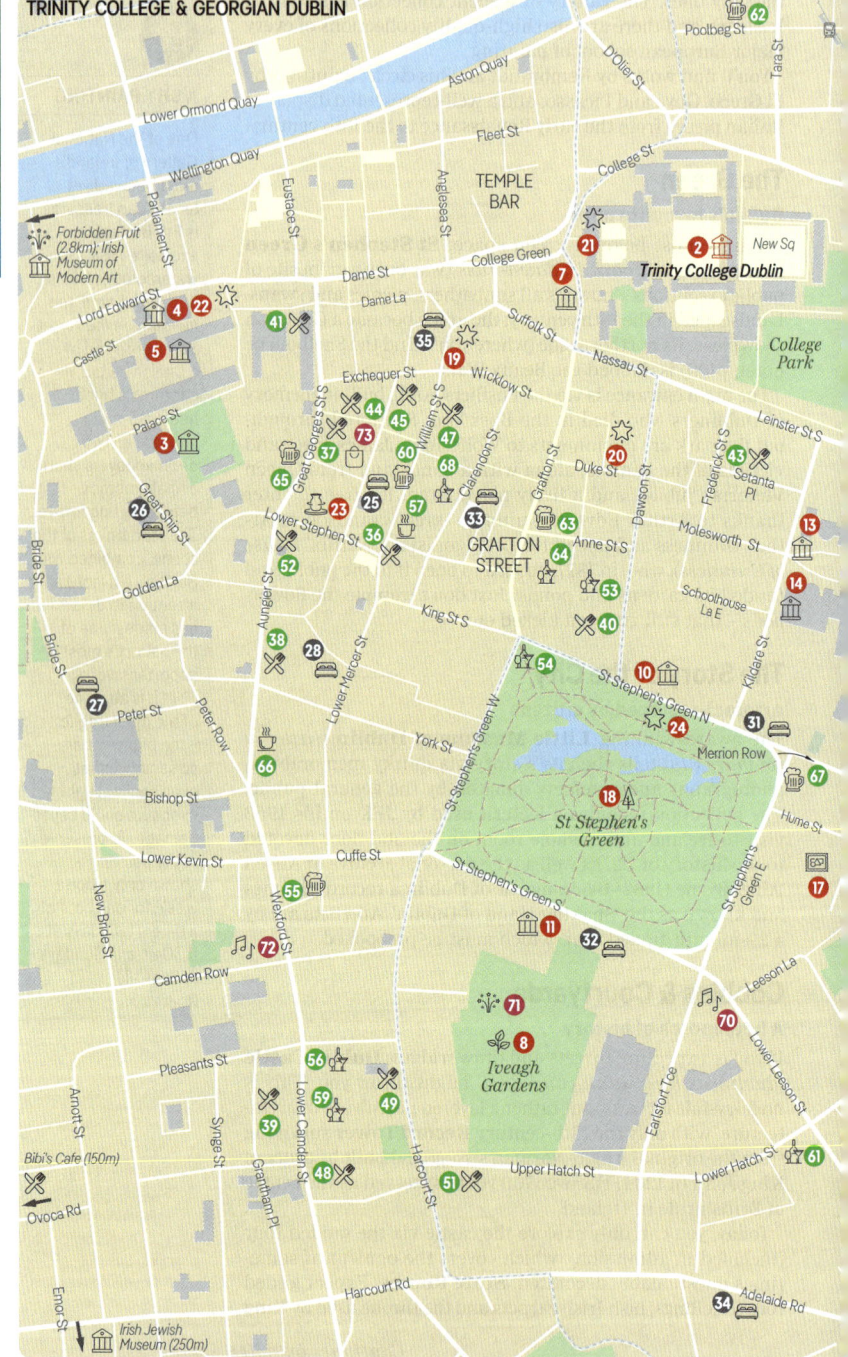

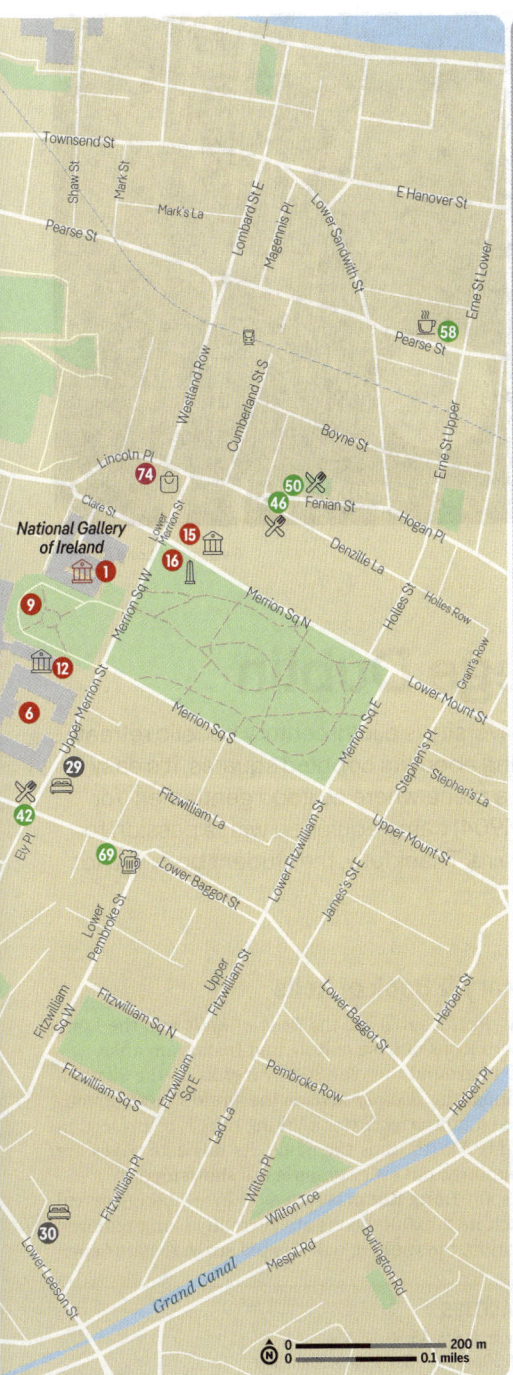

HIGHLIGHTS
1. National Gallery of Ireland
2. Trinity College Dublin

SIGHTS
3. Chester Beatty
4. City Hall
5. Dublin Castle
6. Government Buildings
7. Irish Whiskey Museum
8. Iveagh Gardens
9. Leinster House
10. Little Museum of Dublin
11. Museum of Literature Ireland
12. Museum of Natural History
13. National Library of Ireland
14. National Museum of Ireland – Archaeology
15. Oscar Wilde House
16. Oscar Wilde Statue
17. Royal Hibernian Academy of Arts
18. St Stephen's Green

ACTIVITIES
19. 1916 Rebellion Walking Tour
20. Dublin Literary Pub Crawl
21. Historical Walking Tour
22. Sandeman's New Dublin Tour
see 23 Sightseeing Bike Tours
23. Silver Works
24. Viking Splash Tours

SLEEPING
see 50 Alex
25. Brooks Hotel
26. Chancery
27. Citizen M
28. Marlin
29. Merrion
30. Number 31
31. Shelbourne
32. Staunton's on the Green
see 49 The Dean
33. Westbury Hotel
34. Wilder Townhouse
35. Wren Urban Nest

EATING
36. Bambino
37. Blazing Salads
38. Bow Lane Social Club
39. Cake Café
40. Comet
41. Doom Slice
see 42 Ely Wine Bar
42. Etto
43. Library Street
44. Loose Canon
45. Mani
see 17 Margadh @ RHA
46. Note
47. Pepper Pot
48. Pickle
49. Sophie's @ The Dean
50. Tang
51. Tír
52. Uno Mas

DRINKING & NIGHTLIFE
53. 37 Dawson Street
54. 9 Below
55. Against the Grain
see 23 Amy Austin
56. Anseo
57. Clement & Pekoe
58. Creed Coffee Roasters
59. Frank's
60. Grogan's Castle Lounge
61. House
62. John Mulligan's
see 44 Kaph
63. Kehoe's
64. La Cave
65. Long Hall
see 66 Lucky Duck
66. Network
67. O'Donoghue's
see 40 Peruke & Periwig
68. Row Wines
see 20 The Duke
69. Toners

ENTERTAINMENT
70. Sugar Club
71. Taste of Dublin
72. Whelan's

SHOPPING
see 45 Industry
see 45 Irish Design Shop
73. Om Diva
see 47 Powerscourt Townhouse
74. Sweny's Pharmacy

Gaia, in the Long Room

TOP EXPERIENCE

Trinity College Dublin

Ireland's most prestigious university is a 16th-century bucolic retreat in the heart of the city. Ambling about its cobbled squares, it's easy to imagine Trinity College as a place where all good gentlemen (for only men were allowed until 1904) came equipped with a passion for philosophy and a love of empire. Thankfully, the student body is a lot more diverse these days.

DON'T MISS
- Old Library & *Book of Kells*
- Book of Kells Experience
- Trinity Trails walking tour
- Museum building
- Douglas Hyde Gallery of Contemporary Art

Old Library & Book of Kells

Trinity's twin treasures are the *Book of Kells* and the Long Room – both icons of Irish culture and Instagram alike.

Created in around the year 800 by monks on the Scottish island of Iona, the *Book of Kells* is the world's most famous illuminated manuscript. After a Viking raid, it resurfaced in Kells, County Meath, thus the name. Its intricate pages are rotated regularly, but every glimpse is a showstopper.

Upstairs, the **Long Room** is even more breathtaking in real life. Though its 200,000 books are currently being removed for restoration, the vaulted, oak-scented space remains open

PRACTICALITIES
- visittrinity.ie ● €16-33.50
- 8.30am-6.30pm Mon-Sat; from 9.30am Sun

until at least the end of 2027. Instead of the books, you get to see *Gaia,* a glowing globe of Earth suspended mid-air, offering a magical new focal point to this already majestic hall.

Book of Kells 360

Book of Kells 360, housed in the sleek Red Pavilion, offers an immersive stand-in while the Long Room undergoes renovation. It begins with The Secret Life of the Collections, where digital avatars such as Jonathan Swift guide you through Trinity's lesser-known treasures. From QR-coded artefacts to animated musical scores, it's engaging and clever. But it's the sweeping, cinematic reveal of the *Book of Kells* that really stuns – bringing its beauty to life in a way that panels never could. The finale – a digital homage to the Long Room – is dazzling enough to make you forget, briefly, that you're not in the real thing.

Trinity Trails Walking Tour

Every 45 minutes, a student guide swings into action beneath the Campanile in Front Sq, ready to whisk you through Trinity's living history. Over three-quarters of an hour, you'll pick up campus gossip, eyebrow-raising legends and the odd scandal involving the college's brightest alumni – including an attempted murder. You'll pass by the rooms once occupied by Jonathan Swift, Oscar Wilde and Sally Rooney. Your guide peppers the stroll with personal tips and tongue-in-cheek asides that turn arcane dates into memorable sound bites. The finale is access to the Museum Building, its russet stone and Byzantine flourishes usually off-limits to casual wanderers.

Museum Building

A contender for Trinity's most beautiful building is the lesser-known Museum Building in New Sq. Built in the 1850s and inspired by Byzantine Venice, it's a riot of stone and story, with 22 types of stone (13 Irish), floral carvings plucked from campus gardens and animals including a famously dodgy monkey. Inside, 11,000-year-old deer flank a kaleidoscopic domed hall of Irish marble, making this a true hidden gem of the university. You can only visit the building if you're a student or as part of the Trinity Trails walking tour.

Douglas Hyde Gallery of Contemporary Art

One of Dublin's best contemporary art galleries, the Douglas Hyde is tucked away in the Arts & Social Science Building. Its ambitious contemporary programme stays firmly in the cutting-edge camp; exhibitions here are often 'enhanced' with film, live music or performance-driven sideshows.

NO NORMAL STUDENT

Trinity's most famous alum of recent years may well be literary sensation **Sally Rooney**, author of *Conversations with Friends* (2017) and *Normal People* (2018). In 2011 she aced the notoriously tough Scholar's exam, earning lifelong academic perks including free accommodation – her room was in the GMB Building. Her time at Trinity deeply shaped her writing, not least the sharp, emotionally charged dialogue she's now known for.

TOP TIPS

● The best way to experience the best of Trinity is to combine a Trinity Trails walking tour with the Book of Kells Experience, which gives you access to both the Long Room and the Red Pavilion.

● If you just want to see the *Book of Kells* and Long Room, book a fast-track ticket online to get cheaper and speedier access.

● The Pavilion Bar (aka the Pav), located at the far end of the playing fields, is a great spot for a summer alfresco drink, especially if there's a cricket match on.

Dublin Castle (p55)

A LONG WAIT

Dublin Castle, long the seat of British administration in Ireland, symbolised centuries of colonial authority and was deeply resented by those seeking independence. On 16 January 1922, it was formally handed over to Michael Collins, the leader of the Provisional Government.

Popular lore has it that when arriving to the castle, Collins replied to a scolding about his lateness with the quip: 'We've been waiting 700 years. You can have the seven minutes.' In reality, Collins was more than an hour late.

The likeliest exchange came when a functionary greeted him with, 'We're glad to see you, Mr Collins,' to which Collins allegedly retorted, in his Cork accent, 'Ye are like hell, boy!'

Continued from p55

George V. One sombre highlight is the room where a wounded James Connolly was kept after the 1916 Rising, nursed back to health just to face execution.

Even without a tour, the cobbled courtyard is worth a wander, especially during the festive season when it transforms into a charming **Christmas market**.

The Rarest Objects

A treasure trove

On the grounds of Dublin Castle, the world-famous **Chester Beatty** *(chesterbeatty.ie; free)* has a breathtaking assembly of more than 20,000 manuscripts, including the world's second-oldest biblical fragment and a collection of Qurans (from the 9th to the 19th centuries) considered among the best examples of illuminated Islamic texts in the world.

Other treasures include ancient Egyptian texts on papyrus, intricately designed little medicine boxes and perhaps the finest selection of Chinese jade books on the planet. Keep an eye on the calendar of events – the museum regularly runs qigong workshops on the rooftop garden, as well as sound baths and meditation sessions.

 EATING: BEST FOR BRUNCH

| **Bow Lane Social Club**: Did somebody say drag brunch? Weekends here are boozy, raucous and oh-so-fun. *4-11.30pm Wed & Thu, 2pm-3am Fri, from 11.30am Sat, noon-11.30pm Sun* €€ | **Cake Café**: House-made baked beans, avocado toast and towering slices of cake – need we say more? *10am-5pm Mon-Sat* € | **Bibi's Cafe**: This neighbourhood favourite is perfect for a languid Saturday morning with pancakes or poached eggs. *9.30am-3.30pm Mon & Wed-Sun* €€ | **Sophie's @ The Dean**: Sophie's at The Dean serves pancakes, burgers and eggs with skyline panoramas. *7am-11.30pm Mon-Thu, to 12.30am Fri & Sat, 8am-11pm Sun* €€ |

Traditional HQ

An evening of trad

For one of the most fun nights out in Dublin, head straight to **O'Donoghue's** *(odonoghues.ie; free)* – a rollicking crash course in trad and folk that kicks off around 9pm every night. This is where The Dubliners got their start, and the spirit of spontaneous, foot-stomping sessions still lives on. Even when no one's playing, the place hums with energy. Inside, the old bar oozes character; outside, the covered coach yard fills fast with chat, laughter and the clink of some of the best-poured pints in town. Whether you're here for the music, the Guinness or just the buzz, it's pure craic from the first sip.

Go Back in Time

Historical treasures

Established in 1877, the **National Museum of Ireland – Archaeology** *(museum.ie; free)* is the country's leading institution for cultural and archaeological treasures. Housed in a grand building that dates from the 1890s, it holds some of Ireland's most iconic artefacts, including the 12th-century Ardagh Chalice and the 8th-century Tara Brooch – both masterpieces of Celtic metalwork.

The **Ór – Ireland's Gold** exhibit showcases exquisite Bronze and Iron Age artisanship, including the intricate gold boat from the Broighter Hoard and a ceremonial collar that is unrivalled in all of Europe. Another standout is the Loughnashade trumpet, an ornate war instrument from the 1st century BCE.

The **Kingship and Sacrifice** gallery features haunting Iron Age 'bog bodies' recovered from the midlands – eerily well-preserved figures believed to be victims of ritualistic sacrifice.

Upstairs, explore **Viking Ireland** (with finds from Dublin's Wood Quay), **Medieval Ireland 1150–1550** and **Ancient Egypt**, which features artefacts from excavations carried out between 1890 and 1930.

Literary Legends

The epicentre of Irish writing

The **Museum of Literature Ireland** *(MoLI; moli. ie; adult/child €14.50/12)* is a vibrant tribute to Ireland's literary legacy, set in the elegant Georgian surrounds of Newman House – once home to the Catholic University of Ireland, alma mater of James Joyce, Pádraig Pearse and Éamon de Valera.

Inside, Irish writing is celebrated, from medieval manuscripts to modern masterpieces, with standout exhibits including Joyce's *Ulysses* notebooks and first edition. Rotating displays spotlight contemporary voices such as Claire-Louise Bennett and Patrick McCabe.

Visit on the first Friday of the month for a free, late-night literary bash featuring readings, music and

BEST FESTIVALS IN DUBLIN

Dublin International Film Festival: Two weeks of screenings, premieres and celebrities around the city.

St Patrick's Festival: As well as the parade, the Festival Quarter is the hub of live music, DJs and comedy, usually held at Collins Barracks (p95).

Pride: Pride is a big deal in Dublin, and the LGBTIQ+ festival is only growing. Expect gigs, parties and one hell of a march.

Forbidden Fruit: The city's foremost music festival, with huge acts playing on the grounds of the Royal Hospital Kilmainham (p82).

Dublin International Literature Festival: Merrion Sq goes literary for 10 days in May, with readings, interviews and food trucks.

MORE OF THE NATIONAL MUSEUM

The museum's sister institutions are made up of the stuffed beasts of the **Museum of Natural History** (p62), the decorative arts section at **Collins Barracks** (p95) and a **Country Life** museum in County Mayo, on Ireland's west coast.

JOYCEAN PILGRIMAGE

Every year on 16 June, Dublin transforms into a living tribute to James Joyce, as fans in boater hats, round spectacles and petticoats celebrate Bloomsday – the date on which *Ulysses* is set. One of the day's highlights is **Sweny's Pharmacy** *(sweny.ie)*, which is featured in the novel and preserved exactly as it appeared in 1904, the year Joyce first met Nora Barnacle, his lifelong partner.

The shop hosts intimate readings and performances of Joyce's celebrated (and occasionally confusing) words. If you miss the celebrations, Sweny's remains open year-round, with Thursday-evening readings for visitors. You can even buy a bar of lemon soap, just like Leopold Bloom, or browse the antique cabinets packed with old remedies, photographs and timeworn editions of *Ulysses*.

discussion. Grab a bite at the **Commons Café**, or escape to the leafy **Readers Garden**, where Joyce posed for his graduation photo under the ash tree.

The Dead Zoo
The weird and the wonderful

Affectionately known as the 'Dead Zoo', the **Museum of Natural History** *(museum.ie; free)* is a wonderfully strange throwback to Victorian curiosity. Opened in 1857 by explorer Dr David Livingstone, its collection of taxidermised animals and labelled specimens has remained almost unchanged ever since.

The ground-floor **Irish Room** showcases native mammals, sea creatures and birds, plus three towering skeletons of 10,000-year-old Irish elk. Upstairs, the **Mammals of the World** gallery features everything from zebras and giraffes to one rather cross-looking hippo. Evolution fans can admire the line-up of primate skeletons – orangutan to human – that's perfect for a thought-provoking photo.

Floating above it all, and stealing the show, is a 20m-long skeleton of a fin whale, discovered beached in Sligo, now suspended mid-air like something out of a natural history dream.

Quintessential Boozer
Dublin's best pub?

John Mulligan's of Poolbeg St isn't just a pub – it's a Dublin institution, with history, swagger and a healthy disdain for fuss. Though only licensed since 1852, it began life as a spirit grocer's back in 1782, when Poolbeg St teemed with oddballs, biscuit makers and a porcelain seller dubbed the 'Emperor of China'.

The pub itself has barely changed since, which is a big part of its charm. James Joyce was a regular and set a scene from *Dubliners* in the back room, later home to Judy Garland's week-long poker sessions in 1951 during her run at the nearby (now demolished) Theatre Royal. John F Kennedy once called in for a pint – long before he was president – and sat in Joyce's favourite spot. As for fame? Mulligan's famously doesn't care: they once silenced balladeer Liam Clancy with a deadpan 'There's no singing here'.

The house rules may have softened, but Mulligan's old-school soul remains. The best bar in Dublin? Quite possibly.

EATING: WINE WITH DINNER

Note: An uber-cool wine bar where you can enjoy a languid dinner or just a few snacks. *12.30-2.30pm & 5-9.30pm* €€

Etto: Award-winning restaurant and wine bar that does contemporary versions of classic Italian cuisine. *5-9.30pm* €€€

Ely Wine Bar: Choose between the dinner menu or 'bites and flights', with small plates and sampler glasses of wine. *5-11.30pm Tue-Sun* €€

Loose Canon: Grab a cheeseboard or a buttery toasted sandwich at this wine and cheese shop. *11am-11.30pm Mon-Sat, from 12.30pm Sun* €

Oscar Wilde House

Wilde's Homeplace
Behind the curtain

Blue plaques mark many houses on Merrion Sq, but none more significant than 1 Merrion Sq, the childhood home of Oscar Wilde. Raised alongside his siblings by two remarkable parents, Wilde's father was a renowned surgeon and his mother, Jane, a revolutionary poet.

Today, the **Oscar Wilde House** *(oscarwildehouse.com; tour €25)* belongs to the American College Dublin, and guided tours lead visitors through its grand rooms, from the library to a balcony overlooking the park. Along the way, you'll hear tales of Wilde's dazzling wit, personal struggles and unconventional upbringing.

From the drawing room, you can spot the flamboyant **statue** of Wilde lounging in the square below, where admirers gather to photograph him and read the witty quotes inscribed around the surrounding granite pillars.

Dublin's HQ
You can't fight city hall

Built as the Royal Exchange between 1769 and 1779, Dublin's **City Hall** *(dublincity.ie/dublincityhall; free)* is a grand Georgian structure that was restored to its former glory in 2000. Its centrepiece is the rotunda – a soaring, columned space crowned by a statue of Daniel O'Connell. Nationalist icons Charles Stewart Parnell and Michael Collins both lay in state here.

Before City Hall, the site hosted the Eagle Tavern – birthplace of the scandalous Hellfire Club. Today, visitors can explore the rotunda (when not booked for weddings) and attend occasional free history talks.

A SLICE OF AMERICA

The biggest food trend to hit Dublin in recent years is New York-style pizza slices – quick, easy and, crucially, a budget-friendly alternative to a full sit-down meal. Leading the charge is **Bambino** on Stephen St Lower, a viral TikTok hit that's now a magnet for queues and phone-wielding foodies. Be warned: no matter what time of day it is, you'll have to wait for a slice.

Just around the corner on Drury St, **Mani** serves up thick, square slices – don't miss the carbonara, it's outrageously good. Meanwhile, **Doom Slice** on Dame Lane dishes out Detroit-style slabs straight from a tiny hole in the wall, proving that big flavour doesn't need big floorspace. And the queues aren't that long.

TRINITY'S FIRST FEMALE STUDENT

Founded in 1592, Trinity College Dublin (p58) barred women until 1904, when King Edward VII authorised their admission, overruling the board's resistance. Provost George Salmon, who swore women would be admitted 'over his dead body', died days after the authorisation letter arrived. **Isabel Marion Weir Johnston** was the first woman officially enrolled (studying English and French), but was excluded from lectures, the dining hall, campus after 6pm and most societies. In response, she founded the Elizabethan Society. Sadly, ill health forced her departure from the university before she completed her degree. Most restrictions endured until the 1960s, yet today, women form the majority at Trinity – a striking contrast to the barriers faced by its earliest female students.

Iveagh Gardens

Secret Garden
Smell the roses

St Stephen's Green might get all the glory, but the **Iveagh Gardens** *(free)* are every bit as lovely (and half as crowded). Ninian Niven designed them in 1863 as the private grounds of Iveagh House, and they include a rustic grotto, cascade, fountain, maze and rosarium, with a plethora of rose varieties that smell heavenly in the spring. Regular big-ticket gigs take place here in the summer, along with the **Comedy Festival** *(ppcomedyfestival.com)* and **Taste of Dublin** *(tasteofdublin.ie)*. Enter the gardens from Clonmel St (off Harcourt St) or from Upper Hatch St, which brings you straight into the rose garden.

Walk with the Writers
An upmarket pub crawl

How do you justify an evening of drinking? By calling it the **Dublin Literary Pub Crawl** *(dublinpubcrawl.com; adult/student €20/18)*, of course. On this two-hour performance tour, two actors lead you on a jaunt of pubs associated with

DRINKING: CONTEMPORARY BARS

| **Anseo**: The closest Dublin has to a proper dive bar, with cool customers and an even cooler soundtrack. *4-11.30pm Mon-Thu, to 12.30am Fri & Sat, to 11pm Sun* | **Against the Grain**: A craft-beer bar run by Galway Bay Brewery, with a dizzying selection of beers on tap. *noon-midnight Mon-Thu, to 2am Fri & Sat, 12.30pm-midnight Sun* | **House**: An elegant bar spread across two Georgian townhouses, with a nightclub vibe at weekends. *8am-midnight Mon, to 2am Tue & Wed, to 3am Thu & Fri, noon-3am Sat, to 11pm Sun* | **Sugar Club**: A top music venue for gigs, live DJ sets and 'story slam' nights. *7pm-late* |

famous Dublin writers, including Samuel Beckett, Oscar Wilde and Brendan Behan. (Just don't try to match Behan's drinking prowess.)

Along the way, the actors recite the words of these famous poets and writers, and tell the stories of the pubs and the city itself. The tour leaves from **The Duke** on Duke St, where you can grab a bite beforehand to line your stomach. If you don't drink, join the Monday-morning tour, which has all of the lit without getting you lit.

Whiskey a Go-Go
Sink a dram

If there's one thing Dublin's not short of, it's whiskey distilleries. The industry underwent something of a resurgence, and now numerous distilleries are on the go, most of which are spread around the Liberties (p83). But if you want to taste a few different spirits and not just one brand, head to the **Irish Whiskey Museum** *(irishwhiskeymuseum.ie; tours €23-35)* near Trinity College.

You'll learn all about the history of Irish whiskey on a guided tour before tasting a few different varieties at the end. Serious fans will want to book the premium tour for more exclusive sips, or the blending experience, where you can create your own whiskey. However, you don't have to do a tour to have a taste – just head straight to the bar and order a whiskey flight from the knowledgeable barkeeps.

Musical Magnet
The musician's favourite venue

Whelan's *(whelanslive.com)* isn't just a pub – it's many an Irish musician's spiritual home. From the outside, it looks like a run-of-the-mill bar on Wexford St, but the venue inside has played host to an incredible array of visiting artists over the years, from Jeff Buckley to David Gray.

They don't just come to perform. You'll often see a famous face milling around the back of the crowd, checking out their competition. The main stage is in a midsized room attached to the bar, and when the show is done, you can often find the acts filling up in the bar, along with their fans. In the smaller room upstairs, you might see an up-and-coming band or an act trying out new material.

DUBLIN'S BEST TOURS

Historical Walking Tour: Multi-thematic walking tours led by experts covering the Famine, the Easter Rising and Partition.

1916 Rebellion Walking Tour: Superb two-hour tour starting in the International Bar and led by Trinity graduates; covers all manner of historical goings on.

Sandeman's New Dublin Tour: A high-energy and thoroughly enjoyable free three-hour walking tour of the city's greatest hits; tip only if you enjoyed the tour.

Viking Splash Tours: A 1¼-hour semi-amphibious tour with a Viking helmet on your head. Go on, you know you want to.

Sightseeing Bike Tours (p68): Two-and-a-half-hour tours on bike or ebike that take in the city's highlights.

DRINKING: CLASSIC PUBS

Grogan's Castle Lounge: A city institution, Grogan's has long been a favourite haunt of Dublin's writers and artists. *10.30am-11.30pm Mon-Thu, to 12.30am Fri & Sat, 12.30-11pm Sun*

Long Hall: One of the oldest pubs in Dublin, with a decor that's barely changed since the 1860s. Springsteen's favourite when town. *noon-11.30pm Mon-Thu, to 12.30am Fri & Sat, 12.30-11pm Sun*

Kehoe's: A Victorian stunner with a gorgeous snug and an upstairs extension – in what was once the publican's house. *11am-11.30pm Mon-Thu, to 12.30am Fri & Sat, 12.30-11pm Sun*

Toners: The closest thing to a country pub in the city, with an award-winning snug. *10.30am-11.30pm Mon-Thu, to 12.30am Fri & Sat, 11.30am-11.30pm Sun*

Live Like a Viscount
Shop in style

On sunny days, the wide stone steps of **Powerscourt Townhouse** *(powerscourtcentre.ie)* fill with Dubliners sipping coffee and chatting. Fitting, really, as this elegant Georgian mansion was built in the 18th century for entertaining by Richard Wingfield, 3rd Viscount Powerscourt, during Parliament season.

Today, it's a chic shopping centre, home to boutiques selling everything from vintage gems to wedding dresses and upscale interiors.

If you're after a special keepsake, stop by **Chupi** or **MoMuse** for dainty gold jewellery. **Cloon Keen** offers beautifully packaged Irish-made candles and perfumes. Just around the corner, Drury St continues the stylish streak with vintage finds at **Om Diva**, smart design pieces at **Industry** and local treasures in the **Irish Design Shop**.

Ireland's Library
The ultimate archive

The **National Library of Ireland** *(nli.ie; free)*, on Kildare St, holds over 12 million items and serves as Ireland's library of record. Built between 1884 and 1890, its design mirrors that of the neighbouring National Museum, most notably in the stunning dome of its reading room – the very spot where Stephen Dedalus mused on Shakespeare in *Ulysses*.

Highlights include a vast permanent exhibition on WB Yeats – featuring manuscripts of 'The Lake Isle of Innisfree' and 'Easter, 1916', alongside photos, school reports and even his Nobel Prize for Literature medal. The 2nd floor houses a free Genealogy Advisory Service for those tracing their Irish roots. Occasional tours, sometimes led by the library's director, round out this literary gem.

People & Politics
Home of the government

Stroll along Upper Merrion St and you'll likely spot a few *gardaí* (Irish Republic police) stationed outside **Government Buildings** *(taoiseach.gov.ie; free)*, home to the Department of the Taoiseach (Prime Minister). This impressive Edwardian structure opened in 1911 as the Royal College of Science and was repurposed as government offices in 1989. Free 40-minute

---

ANY RESERVATIONS?

Dublin has a thriving food scene, but that means it's often tricky to nab a dinner reservation, particularly in the popular spots around the Grafton St area. Tables are even harder to find at the weekend when it feels like the whole city is out for dinner.

If you haven't secured your reservations weeks in advance, don't panic. It's always worth ringing or stopping by to see if there have been any last-minute cancellations. You can also follow @*lastminutetabledublin* on Instagram to keep track of 11th-hour availability or check out **EarlyTable** *(earlytable.ie)*, which gets you up to 50% off your bill if you book an early sitting. Hooray for the early birds!

 DRINKING: BEST FOR COFFEE

Clement & Pekoe: A cool version of an Edwardian tearoom, with carefully made drip coffees and cold brews. *8am-7pm Mon-Fri, 9am-6.30pm Sat, 11am-6pm Sun*

Kaph: A magnet for caffeine fiends, with homemade cakes and coffee as strong as rocket fuel. *8am-7pm Mon-Sat, 11am-6pm Sun*

Network: A tiny cafe with swoon-worthy latte art and all kinds of coffee paraphernalia. *7.30am-6pm Mon-Fri, from 9am Sat, 10am-5pm Sun*

Creed Coffee Roasters: Superb outpost of a Kildare-based microroastery – the Colombian Popayan reserve is excellent. *7.30am-4pm Mon-Sat, 9am-2pm Sun*

Powerscourt Townhouse

tours (when available) include a look inside the Taoiseach's office, the Cabinet Room and a striking ceremonial staircase featuring a stained-glass window by Evie Hone, originally created for the 1939 New York Trade Fair. **Tours** *(free)* generally run on Saturdays only, usually with between three and five slots from 10.30am to 4pm. Tickets are first-come (from 9.30am), first-served at the Clare St entrance of the National Gallery.

Behind Government Buildings sits **Leinster House** *(oireach tas.ie)*, a grand Palladian mansion designed by Richard Cassels in the 1740s for James Fitzgerald, Duke of Leinster. It now houses Oireachtas na Éireann (parliament of the Republic of Ireland), though public tours are currently only possible via sponsorship from a senator or Teachta Dála (TD; member of the lower house of the Irish parliament).

Contemporary Art

Fine art and fine dining

The **Royal Hibernian Academy of Arts** *(rhagallery.ie; free)*, aka the RHA Gallery, has an exalted reputation as one of Ireland's most prestigious exhibition spaces for modern and contemporary art. The gallery is run by a council of academicians – their name for member artists. Notable names associated with the

PICTURE-PERFECT FOOD

What makes the RHA Gallery really special is its cafe and wine bar, **Margadh** *(margadh-rha.ie; tasting menu €56)*. During the week, there's a casual lunch menu of soup, salads and sandwiches, made with well-sourced ingredients such as crab, crayfish or fresh burrata. But in the evenings, the space turns into a fancy wine bar with a curated list of bottles from around the world, along with an excellent selection of wines by the glass. You can order food à la carte, but doing so would be a shame, as the tasting menu is one of the best in the city. Expect to see dishes such as kingfish with kumquat and chilli, or a baked Flaggy Shore oyster with nduja sausage and lime.

 DRINKING: BEST FOR COCKTAILS

Peruke & Periwig: This teeny little Tardis of a bar has an eccentric apothecary vibe, with hipster mixologists and a lengthy menu. *noon-midnight Sun-Thu, to 2.30am Fri & Sat*

9 Below: On the edge of St Stephen's Green, this basement bar is the epitome of luxury, with table service and high-end liquors. *5-11.30pm Tue-Thu, to 12.30am Fri & Sat*

37 Dawson Street: Antiques, eye-catching art and elegant bric-a-brac adorn this bar – a favourite with the trendy crowd. *noon-2.30am Tue-Sun, to 11.30pm Mon*

Lucky Duck: This Aungier St boozer pairs Victorian pub charm with superb cocktails, plush armchairs and Indian-style tapas upstairs. *11am-12.30am Mon-Thu, to 1am Fri & Sat, 11.30am-12.30am Sun*

Irish Jewish Museum

PUB HOURS

First introduced in 1914, Ireland's pub opening hours were a direct response to wartime productivity concerns. During WWI, authorities feared that excessive drinking among munitions workers was affecting morale and efficiency, so strict licensing laws were brought in – and they've been tightly monitored ever since.

While the rules have relaxed slightly over the past century, change has come slowly. One major update was the abolition of the 'holy hour' in 2000, when pubs were once required to close between 2pm and 4pm on Sundays. Today, last orders are 11.30pm Monday to Thursday, 12.30am Friday and Saturday, and 11pm on Sunday, with half an hour's drinking-up time. Many city-centre pubs now operate under late licences, serving until 1.30am or even 2.30am.

gallery include Jack B Yeats, Sir John Lavery and Sarah Purser, the first woman to be elected to the council. Its current president is Abigail O'Brien – the first female to serve in the role.

The biggest event of the year is the **RHA National Exhibition**, which usually runs from May to the end of July and shows the work of those artists deemed worthy enough to be exhibited by the selection committee (made up of members of the Royal Hibernian Academy).

Dublin on Two Wheels

On yer bike

Want to tick off a load of sights in one go? Join **Sightseeing Bike Tours** *(sightseeingbiketours.com; €35)*, where guides take you between all the big attractions without you having to worry about plotting a route or navigating Dublin's one-way streets. The tours cover a big chunk of the city, from Dublin Castle and the surrounding neighbourhoods to Christchurch and the Liberties. The best bit? You can choose to cycle an e-bike to make your spin that little bit easier.

The outfit is based in the bike storage area on the ground floor of the Drury St car park, and you can also rent a bike here if you want to explore on your own.

 EATING: BEST FOR A QUICK LUNCH

Pepper Pot: In the Powerscourt Townhouse (p66); a cute cafe best known for its pear, bacon and cheddar sandwich. *10am-6pm Mon-Fri, from 9am Sat, noon-6pm Sun* €

Tang: Hop in for quick, on-the-go Middle Eastern food, such as Lebanese flatbreads and spicy rice bowls. *8am-3.30pm Tue-Sun* €

Blazing Salads: If you want to be virtuous, this is the place to be – this Californian-style salad bar is the epitome of wellness. *9am-6pm Mon-Sat* €

Tír: A cool deli on Hatch St, open for breakfast baps, and artisan sandwiches at lunchtime. *8am-3pm Mon-Fri* €

Foodie Rambles
Eat your way through Dublin

Feeling peckish? Join a foodie tour of the city with **Fab Food Trails** (*fabfoodtrails.ie; €80*). The tasting walks last between 2½ to three hours and take in some of the city centre's choicest independent producers, with plenty of nibbles along the way. You'll visit up to eight bakeries, cheesemongers and delis, learning about the food culture of each neighbourhood that you explore – you might tuck into an artisan toasted cheese sandwich or a little tub of gelato. The guides keep well up to speed with Dublin's ever-changing food trends, and the tours all start in the city centre. The company also runs Food & Fashion tours.

Historic Neighbourhood
Dublin's Jewish past

Housed in an old synagogue, the **Irish Jewish Museum** (*jewishmuseum.ie; free*) tells the story of the country's Jewish community over the last 150 years through a wealth of materials. Amid the old photos and artefacts is memorabilia from WWII, including a Star of David arm patch and the marriage certificate of Ester Steinberg, the only known Irish victim of the Holocaust.

Unless you were looking for it, you might walk straight past its door. The original synagogue consisted of two adjoining terraced houses on a quiet street in Portobello, so the entrance seamlessly blends in with the surroundings. The museum is only open on Sundays, from 10.30am to 2.30pm.

Crafting Silver
Creative workshop

Tucked away on Drury St, **Silver Works** (*silverworks.ie; from €85*) looks like your typical jeweller from the outside, but step inside and you'll find a hands-on workshop space keeping Dublin's centuries-old silversmithing tradition alive.

The two-hour beginner workshop is the most popular, where you're guided through the process of creating a piece of jewellery – and you finish with a shiny souvenir that you actually made yourself. They also host Claddagh ring (crowned-heart ring) and metal clay classes, as well as full-day workshops on setting gemstones or forging a spinner ring. Highly recommended if you're after a creative evening that doesn't involve yet another pub.

OPEN DAYS

If you're the kind of person who loves a glimpse behind closed doors, plan your Dublin visit around two standout annual events.
 Culture Night (*culturenight.ie*) takes place across the island, usually on the third Friday in September, and transforms the city into an open house of creativity. Expect hundreds of free events, pop-up performances, exhibitions and tours in venues that are often off-limits to the public – from historic institutions to contemporary studios.
 A few weeks later comes **Open House Dublin** (*openhousedublin.com*), a free architecture festival every October that celebrates the city's built heritage. It offers guided tours of remarkable buildings, fascinating private homes and innovative new spaces, giving curious visitors a rare chance to explore Dublin's architecture from the inside out.

 DRINKING: WINE BARS

Amy Austin: Uber-cool wine bar inside a car park (trust us, it works). It's dog friendly, too. *5-10.30pm Mon-Wed, from 12.30pm Thu-Sat*

Frank's: Looks like an old butcher, but inside it's a sleek wine bar with communal vibes and Pet Nat. *4-10pm Tue & Wed, to 11pm Thu-Sat, 5-10pm Sun*

La Cave: An old-school basement bar that will transport you to Paris. *noon-1am Mon-Sat, 2pm-midnight Sun*

Row Wines: Small plates, excellent wine and a superb soundtrack make this spot very popular. *5-11.30pm Tue-Thu, to 1.30am Fri & Sat, noon-11pm Sun*

Temple Bar

NIGHTLIFE CENTRAL

GETTING AROUND

Temple Bar is compact and easy to navigate on foot, with cobbled, pedestrianised streets that are perfect for wandering. At the western edge, the ground gently slopes upward towards Christ Church Cathedral.

Temple Bar is Dublin's most infamous playground – a cobbled maze of pubs, pints and late-night singalongs. Come evening, it descends into (mostly) good-natured chaos, the kind that spills from doorways and draws you in whether you planned to stay or not.

By day, though, the mood shifts. It leans more boho than boozy, with vintage shops, art-house cinemas, indie galleries and piercing studios tucked along its lanes, along with one of Dublin's best-loved bookshops. Sushi bars and record stores round out the mix. Looming over its western edge is Christ Church Cathedral, a reminder that even in the city's most spirited quarter, history is always close at hand.

You could blitz through Temple Bar in an hour, but that's missing the point. It isn't a checklist – it's a vibe. Linger, wander, let the music guide you, and see where the night (or day) takes you.

Cathedral Quarter

An iconic structure

Christ Church (*christchurchcathedral.ie; adult/child €12/4*) is one of Dublin's most striking landmarks, thanks to its hilltop perch and dramatic flying buttresses. It was founded by the Vikings in 1030 and rebuilt from 1172, mostly under the impetus of Anglo-Norman noble Richard de Clare, Earl of Pembroke (better known as Strongbow), who invaded Ireland in 1170 and whose monument has pride of place inside.

☑ TOP TIP

Keep an eye on your receipts if you're drinking in the evening. In some bars, the price of a pint sneaks up at 11pm or midnight (or both), when the bar owners assume people stop paying attention. Our advice? Take your business elsewhere if you see it happen.

After the original wooden church was replaced by the building you see today, the cathedral vied for supremacy with nearby St Patrick's (p77), but like its sister church, it fell on hard times in the 18th and 19th centuries – the nave had been used as a market and the crypt housed taverns. It was virtually derelict by the time restoration took place in 1878, courtesy of funds provided by distiller Henry Roe, rivals of the Guinness family, who had paid for the restoration of St Patrick's. Today, both these Church of Ireland cathedrals are outsiders in a largely Catholic nation.

TEMPLE BAR

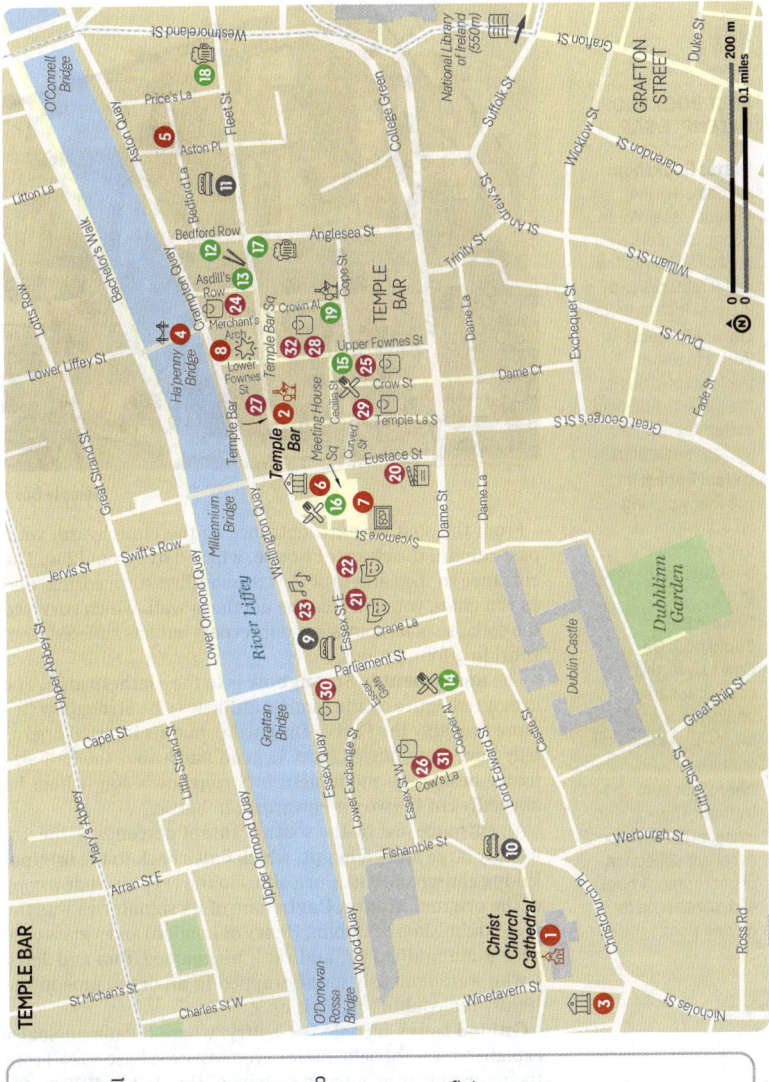

HIGHLIGHTS
1 Christ Church Cathedral
2 Temple Bar

SIGHTS
3 Dubhlinn: Experience Viking & Medieval Dublin
4 Ha'penny Bridge
5 Icon Factory
6 National Photographic Archive
7 Photo Museum Ireland

ACTIVITIES
8 Dublin Musical Pub Crawl

SLEEPING
9 Clarence Hotel
10 Kinlay House
11 Morgan Hotel

EATING
12 Banyi Japanese Dining
13 Elephant & Castle
14 Sano Pizza
15 Seafood Cafe
16 Temple Bar Food Market

DRINKING & NIGHTLIFE
17 Auld Dubliner
18 Palace Bar
19 Vintage Cocktail Club

ENTERTAINMENT
20 Irish Film Institute
21 New Theatre
22 Project Arts Centre
23 Workman's Club

SHOPPING
24 Big Smoke Vintage
see 21 Connolly Books
25 Flip, Sharpsville & Helter Skelter
26 Gutter Bookshop
27 Library Project
28 Lucy's Lounge
29 Nine Crows
30 Oxfam Books
31 Temple Bar Bookshop
32 Tola Vintage

THE GUIDE · DUBLIN TEMPLE BAR

71

Temple Bar

BEST BOOKSHOPS IN TEMPLE BAR

Gutter Bookshop: Named after the famous Oscar Wilde quote, this indie bookshop has all the latest releases and loads of Irish authors.

Library Project: With a focus on photography, this is the place to find thick coffee-table books and art magazines.

Oxfam Books: If you fancy picking up a cheap read, this secondhand bookshop is the place to go.

Temple Bar Bookshop: On Cow's Lane, this cosy antiquarian bookshop specialises in rare books and first editions.

Photo Museum Ireland: The museum (p74) has an excellent collection of photography books and manuals on the ground floor.

From the southeastern entrance to the churchyard, walk past ruins of the **chapter house**, which dates from 1230. The entrance to the cathedral is at the southwestern corner, and as you enter, you will face the northern wall, which survived the collapse of its southern counterpart but has suffered from subsiding foundations.

The **monument to Strongbow** is in the southern aisle. The armoured figure on the tomb is unlikely to be Strongbow (it's more probably the Earl of Drogheda), but his internal organs may have been buried here. Legend has it that the half-size figure beside the monument is Strongbow's son, whom he allegedly cut in two for cowardice in battle.

An entrance just by the south transept descends to the unusually large arched **crypt**, which dates back to the original Viking church of 1030. Curiosities in the crypt include a copy of the original **Magna Carta** (one of its signatories was the then Archbishop of Dublin, Henry of London) and a glass case with a mummified cat and rat – nicknamed Tom and Jerry – who were famously found trapped in an organ pipe in the 1860s. You couldn't make it up.

Guided tours include the belfry, where a campanologist explains the art of bell-ringing (you can even have a go). From the main entrance, a bridge – part of the 1871 to 1878 restoration – leads to Dublinia (p75).

EATING IN TEMPLE BAR: OUR PICKS

Elephant & Castle: Feeling delicate? A giant plate of spicy chicken wings will cure what ails you. *10am-9pm* €€

Sano Pizza: Excellent Neapolitan pizza at an even better price, and you don't need to book in advance. *noon-11pm* €

Banyi Japanese Dining: This compact restaurant has arguably the best Japanese cuisine in Dublin. *12.30-9.30pm* €€

Seafood Cafe: Sustainable, locally sourced seafood served in a variety of ways. *12.30-9.30pm* €€

A Photogenic Pub
Popular pints
The most photographed pub facade in Dublin, perhaps the world, the **Temple Bar** *(thetemplebarpub.com)* is smack bang in the middle of the tourist precinct and is usually chock-a-block with visitors. But despite its enduring popularity (and long lines on busier days), it still presses all the right buttons. There's live music every day, starting at 10.30am and going right through until the wee hours, with traditional musicians playing on the tiny stage in the middle of the bar. There's a beer garden with a retractable roof, and you can get a bite to eat during the day and early in the evening – just don't expect to get grub once the hardy drinking kicks off after 8pm.

Lost in Music
Pints and trad
Want to get a taste of the traditional music scene but not sure where to start? Head off on a **Dublin Musical Pub Crawl** *(musicalpubcrawl.com; adult/child €22/16)*. Kicking off at the Ha'penny Bridge Inn, the 2½-hour tour is led by two professional musicians who play a few tunes while they talk about the history, culture and heritage around trad.

The tour finishes in Flanagan's on O'Connell St, and you can have a bite before you depart (sandwiches or pizza) or a proper meal in Flanagan's when you finish – you have the option of booking a table online when you buy your tour ticket.

Be warned, though – this isn't a tour for those who want a bit of rowdiness. In the spirit of a proper session, it's described as a 'listening tour', designed for you to take in the music without a load of chatter in the background.

Sample Market Goodies
Weekend eats
The **Temple Bar Food Market** is one of the longest-running in town. Held in Meeting House Sq every Saturday, the market sees various stallholders setting up shop to sell everything from Gruyère-stuffed crêpes to apple pies. You'll usually find the longest line in front of the van with the sizzling artisan sausages being grilled. But it's not the only resident of the square – in the summer months, there are often screenings of outdoor movies, as well as circus performances and family fun days.

Cutting-Edge Theatre
Fringe performances
The **Project Arts Centre** *(projectartscentre.ie)* is the city's most interesting venue for challenging new work, be it drama, dance, live art or film. You never know what to expect, which makes it all that more fun. We've seen some awful rubbish here, but we've also caught some of the best shows in town.

The arts centre is worth a visit if only to see the hint of the mural (2016) by Dublin artist Maser. The artwork was created

PICTURESQUE BRIDGE

Dublin's most famous bridge, the **Ha'penny**, was built in 1816 and remains one of the oldest cast-iron bridges in the world. It replaced the seven ferries that once carried passengers back and forth across the River Liffey, providing a safer and more reliable crossing between the city's north and south banks.

Officially named the Liffey Bridge, it soon became known by its more charming nickname, taken from the ha'penny (halfpenny) toll that pedestrians were charged to cross it until 1919. For a short time, when the fare was increased to one and a half pence, Dubliners wryly dubbed it the 'Penny Ha'penny Bridge'. Today it's one of Dublin's most photographed landmarks, a symbol of the city that's as recognisable as the Guinness harp.

in support of Repeal the 8th, Ireland's movement for abortion reform. The mural was partially painted over in July of that year to avoid the centre losing its charitable (and therefore politically neutral) status.

Photography Exhibitions
Worth a thousand words

Photo Museum Ireland *(photomuseumireland.ie; free)* is a gallery celebrating the best in – you guessed it – photography. The exhibitions change fairly regularly and feature homegrown talent or international artists, with the work displayed in small spaces on the upper floors.

The gallery also runs photography classes and workshops led by renowned photographers, and the bookshop downstairs is well stocked with all manner of photographic tomes and manuals, as well as a hefty supply of arty postcards. At the other end of Meeting House Sq, the **National Photographic Archive** *(nli.ie; free)*, a branch of the National Library of Ireland (p66), has a rotation of works on display from its extensive collection, which changes a few times a year.

Views from the Left
Marxism is alive and well

Not quite so new anymore, the **New Theatre** *(thenewtheatre.com)* was established in 1997 to showcase experimental, challenging works (read: plays by unknown artists bent on being provocative). Nearly three decades later, this 66-seat space is still going strong and still 'giving a voice to the unheard' (to quote its own website).

Any doubts about its political affiliations are quickly dispelled when you see that it's above Dublin's only truly leftist bookshop, **Connolly Books** *(connollybooks.org)*, which was, for a long time, connected to the Communist Party of Ireland, whose members held meetings in the room now occupied by the theatre. The bookshop is open from 10am to 5.30pm, Tuesday to Saturday.

Swing by the Icon Factory
A gallery of fame

In the heart of the neighbourhood, the **Icon Factory** *(iconfactorydublin.com; free)* is a not-for-profit, artist-run gallery celebrating Irish legends through bold, vibrant portraiture.

A SAUCY PAST

Temple Bar may never have quite fulfilled its early promise as Dublin's official cultural quarter, but in truth, it has always been true to itself. In 1742 Handel premiered his *Messiah* on Fishamble St, while just around the corner on Bagnio Slip (now Lower Fownes St), gentlemen queued for a rather different kind of performance.

The word bagnio (originally Italian for 'bathhouse') had by then become slang for brothel, and Temple Bar had more than a few. It seems fitting, then, that mind and body, high art and low vice, have always coexisted here. The neighbourhood's appetite for pleasure runs deep, and across all forms – a place where Dublin's history of indulgence, entertainment and expression has always found a willing stage.

 DRINKING IN TEMPLE BAR: TOP SPOTS

Palace Bar: With its mirrors and wooden niches, the Palace is one of Dublin's great 19th-century pubs. *10.30am-11.30pm Mon-Thu, to 12.30am Fri & Sat, 12.30-11.30pm Sun*	**Workman's Club**: This cool music venue is the place to be for a post-gig beer or a late-night bop. *5pm-3am*	**Vintage Cocktail Club**: A not-so-secret speakeasy with dark, cosy rooms and a rooftop terrace. Booking essential. *5pm-1.30am Mon-Fri, from 12.30pm Sat & Sun*	**Auld Dubliner**: Sure, it's a tourist favourite, but it's still a reliable place for a singsong and a laugh. *10.30am-11.30pm Mon & Tue, to 2.30am Wed-Sat, 12.30-11pm Sun*

Icon Factory

The 'legends' are pretty much anyone who has made a name for themselves: think musicians, sports stars, writers and rebels, all reimagined in striking graphic form. The artworks spill out into the surrounding streets via the **Icon Walk**, Ireland's largest open-air art installation.

Inside the gallery, you'll find original prints, T-shirts and posters for sale, all supporting the project and the local artists behind it. Artists can exhibit commission-free, and those who contribute works inspired by Irish icons are offered solo exhibitions. It's arty, passionate, a bit punk – and a bold effort to embody the original spirit of Temple Bar.

Art-House Cinema
Catch a film

The cinephile's movie theatre of choice, the **Irish Film Institute** *(ifi.ie)* is the place to watch both artsy new releases and old movies from the archive. The institute is housed in what was once an 18th-century Quaker meeting house and frequently hosts premieres and film festival screenings.

The cafe-bar is a great spot for a pre-movie bite, and it does a well-priced combo deal with a ticket and a meal. During the day, it shows free movies as part of the Archive at Lunchtime series, where you can see short films from the IFI Irish Film Archive.

The Viking Past
Family-friendly history

Housed in the old Synod Hall adjoining Christ Church Cathedral, **Dublinia: Experience Viking & Medieval Dublin** *(dublinia.ie; adult/child €16/9.50)* is a lively, slightly kitsch,

BEST VINTAGE SHOPS IN TEMPLE BAR

Lucy's Lounge: This colourful, jam-packed shop has been trading for decades and is well and truly part of the furniture.

Big Smoke Vintage: Boutique in Merchant's Arch with old band T-shirts and battered motorcycle jackets.

Nine Crows: A favourite among Dublin's cool kids, with pieces organised by theme.

Tola Vintage: Stock up on loads of secondhand gear and pay by the weight, not the label.

Flip, Sharpsville & Helter Skelter: Three shops in one, all selling the same vintage male-fashion moods of the 1950s.

STAYING IN TEMPLE BAR

Unless you're in for a no-holds-barred, knees-up weekend and don't care too much about sleeping, we don't recommend that you overnight in Temple Bar – you'll pay above the odds for a hotel room that is generally more cramped and noisier than elsewhere, and you won't win any arguments (or friends) trying to shush gangs of rowdy revellers intent on keeping the party going until the small hours. If you do insist on overnighting here, ask for a room on an upper floor or away from the street.

The good news is you don't have to stay to enjoy a night here: Temple Bar's central location and Dublin's size mean you can get in and out of the neighbourhood with relative ease.

Dublinia: Experience Viking & Medieval Dublin (p75)

but hugely enjoyable dive into the city's Viking and medieval past. It's especially popular with families – the exhibits may feel a bit old-school, but kids love the hands-on displays, models and immersive streetscapes.

Highlights include a detailed medieval quayside, a cobbler's shop and a brilliant scale model of the city. Upstairs, **Viking Dublin** showcases artefacts recovered from Wood Quay, the world's largest Viking dig site. You can try on a helmet, wield a sword and explore a recreated longboat.

Don't miss the climb up **St Michael's Tower** for grimy-window views over the rooftops to the Dublin hills. There's also a decent little cafe and, of course, a gift shop on your way out.

Kilmainham & the Liberties

DISTILLERIES AND BREWERIES

Stretching westward along the Liffey, the Liberties and Kilmainham are two of the oldest neighbourhoods in Dublin. First up is the Liberties, where St Patrick's Cathedral looms and, just behind it, the vellum-scented Marsh's Library lurks. The once blue-collar lanes now trade smoke breaks for flat whites, their 19th-century whiskey swagger reborn in avant-garde cafes and restaurants, new hotels and a new generation of distilleries.

On the Liberties' western edge is Dublin's most famous landmark, the Guinness Storehouse – seven floors of stout lore crowned by the selfie-magnet that is Gravity Bar. Further west and you're in Kilmainham, where the Irish Museum of Modern Art sees tomorrow's ideas splashed on 17th-century walls. Beyond its western gate is Kilmainham Gaol, where echoing stone corridors mutter tales of revolution, even as the neighbourhood plots its next craft-beer bash.

A Storied Cathedral

Ireland's largest church

St Patrick's Cathedral *(stpatrickscathedral.ie; adult/child €11/5.50)* is Ireland's largest church and the final resting place of Jonathan Swift, author of *Gulliver's Travels* (1726). According to legend, St Patrick baptised local chieftains here in the 5th century. Whether true or not, it's sacred ground.

The cathedral was built between 1191 and 1270, and like Christ Church Cathedral (p70), it endured storm and fire damage, and has been altered several times (most questionably in 1864 when flying buttresses were added during the neo-Gothic craze). Oliver Cromwell, during his 1649 visit, converted St Patrick's to a stable for his horses – an indignity he inflicted on many Irish churches. Jonathan Swift was dean from 1713 to 1745, but the cathedral was neglected after his tenure until the 1860s, when it was restored, courtesy of the Guinness family. Also like Christ Church, St Patrick's is a

GETTING AROUND

While Kilmainham is within walking distance of the city centre (with the furthest attraction roughly an hour's stroll away), you can make life easier by catching the bus. The hop-on, hop-off services stop at all the major attractions in the neighbourhood, and some include discounted entry. Alternatively, hop on a **Dublin Bike** *(dublinbikes.ie)* – there are three stations in Kilmainham.

☑ **TOP TIP**

The Guinness Storehouse (p80) can get pretty busy, so your best bet for a relaxed experience is to prebook your tickets and visit on a midweek morning – Tuesdays, Wednesdays and Thursdays are usually quieter.

BEST SHOPS IN KILMAINHAM & THE LIBERTIES

Hopeless Botanics: You may not be in the market for a giant houseplant, but the pots and candles in this botanic shop are beautiful. *10am-6pm Tue-Sat, 11am-5pm Sun*

Betty Bojangles: This vintage store is jam-packed with clothes, from smoking jackets to sequinned dresses. *11am-6pm Mon-Sat*

Space Out Sister: A beautiful boutique on Francis St selling vintage and handmade lingerie. *11am-5pm Tue-Sat*

Marrowbone Books: This homely little shop is packed with secondhand books, and it sometimes puts on gigs. *noon-7pm Wed-Sun*

Irish Museum of Modern Art Gift Shop: Elegant keepsakes from the art museum's collection. *11.30am-5.30pm Tue-Fri, from 10am Sat, from noon Sun*

Church of Ireland cathedral – meaning that overwhelmingly Catholic Dublin has two Anglican cathedrals.

Entering the cathedral from the southwestern porch, you come almost immediately, on your right, to the **tombs of Swift** and his longtime companion **Esther Johnson**, aka Stella. On the wall nearby are Swift's own (self-praising) Latin epitaphs to the two of them, and a bust of Swift.

The huge and dusty **Boyle Monument** to the left was erected in 1632 by Richard Boyle, Earl of Cork, and is decorated with numerous painted figures of members of his family. The figure in the centre on the bottom level is the earl's five-year-old son Robert Boyle (1627–91), who grew up to become a noted scientist. His contributions to physics include Boyle's Law, which relates to the pressure and volume of gases.

The interior stuns with its soaring ceilings, stained glass and elegant pillars. Guided tours run daily, or you can attend the **Choral Evensong**, which is particularly magical at Christmas during candlelit carol services.

The park adjacent to St Patrick's Cathedral was once a slum, but it's now a lovely garden to sit in and catch some sunshine. There's a small wooden playground for kids, loads of colourful flowerbeds and people lounging on the grass. On Sundays, there's a small market, with stalls selling secondhand books, antique maps and bric-a-brac. It's not particularly large, but it's a pleasant way to spend an hour or so. A small cafe sells coffee, too.

Old-World Library

Step back in time

Marsh's Library (*marshlibrary.ie; adult/child €7/4*) is a beautifully preserved 18th-century library tucked beside St Patrick's Cathedral. Founded in 1701 by Archbishop Narcissus Marsh and opened in 1707, it was designed by Sir William Robinson. Inside are 25,000 books from the 16th to the early 18th century, including rare maps, manuscripts and incunabula.

Creaking floors, oak bookcases and ghost stories add to the charm, while bullet holes from the 1916 Rising remain visible in the shelves. Chat to the librarians, explore the glass displays and soak up the silence – this atmospheric space is an evocative window into Dublin's scholarly past.

EATING IN KILMAINHAM & THE LIBERTIES: OUR PICKS

Leo Burdock's: Dublin's most famous fish and chips shop is a rite of passage for many. *11.30am-midnight Sun-Thu, to 1am Fri & Sat* €

Coke Lane Pizza: Excellent sourdough pizzas served fresh from the hatch on the terrace of Lucky's bar. Another branch is at the Circular Bar in Rialto. *5-11pm Sun-Fri, from 2pm Sat* €

Spitalfields: Gastro-pub with an elevated menu of Iberian-influenced dishes. Recommended. *5-9pm Tue-Sat* €€

Variety Jones: This edgy restaurant was awarded a Michelin star in 2020. World class. *5.30-10pm Tue-Sat* €€€

KILMAINHAM & THE LIBERTIES

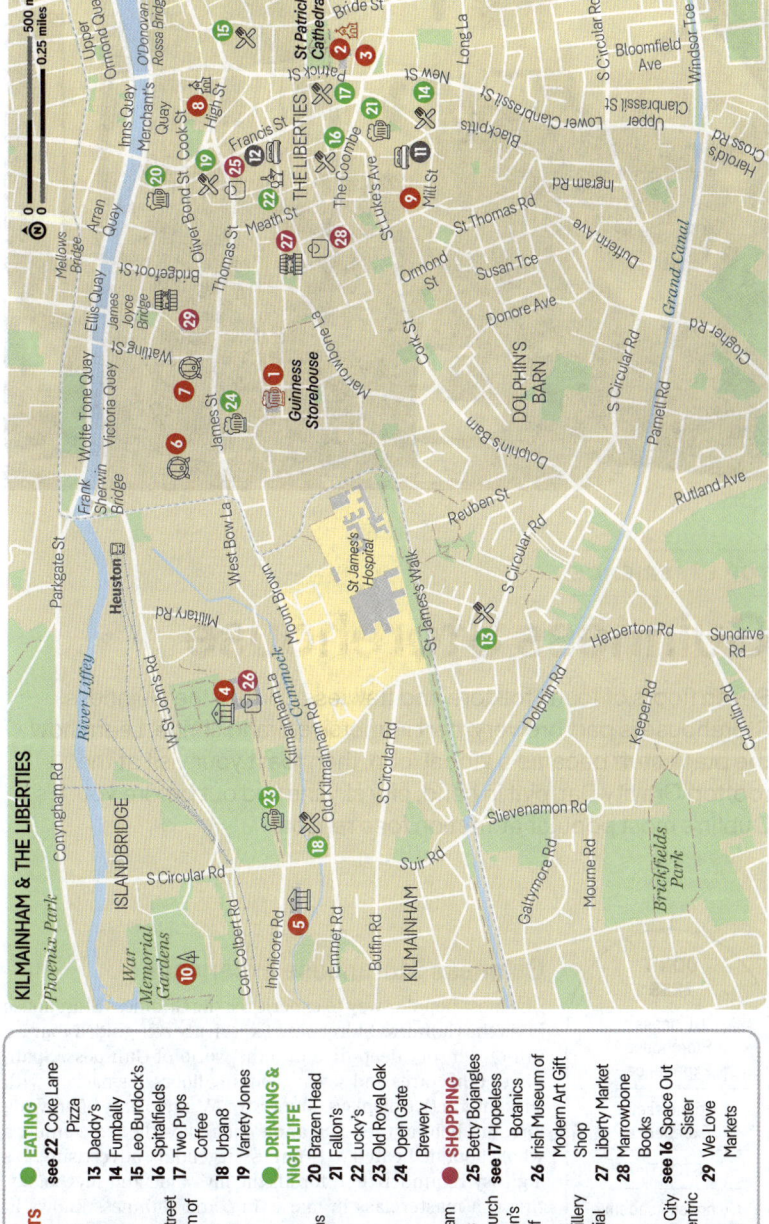

★ HIGHLIGHTS
1. Guinness Storehouse
2. St Patrick's Cathedral

SIGHTS
3. 35a Kevin Street
4. Irish Museum of Modern Art
5. Kilmainham Gaol
see 3 Marsh's Library
6. Pearse Lyons Distillery
7. Roe & Co Distillery
see 4 Royal Hospital Kilmainham
8. St Audoen's Catholic Church
see 8 St Audoen's Church of Ireland
9. Teeling Distillery
10. War Memorial Gardens

● SLEEPING
11. Aloft Dublin City
see 21 Hyatt Centric
12. StayCity Aparthotels

● EATING
see 22 Coke Lane Pizza
13. Daddy's
14. Fumbally
15. Leo Burdock's
16. Spitalfields
17. Two Pups Coffee
18. Urban8
19. Variety Jones

● DRINKING & NIGHTLIFE
20. Brazen Head
21. Fallon's
22. Lucky's
23. Old Royal Oak
24. Open Gate Brewery

● SHOPPING
25. Betty Bojangles
see 17 Hopeless Botanics
26. Irish Museum of Modern Art Gift Shop
27. Liberty Market
28. Marrowbone Books
see 16 Space Out Sister
29. We Love Markets

TOP EXPERIENCE

Guinness Storehouse

Seven floors of foam, folklore and flawless pours – the Guinness Storehouse is part brewery, part immersive brand shrine. Learn how the black stuff became a global icon, then toast your visit at the rooftop Gravity Bar, pint in hand, city skyline laid out before you. It's Dublin's most popular attraction for a reason.

Guinness Storehouse Experience

The most popular way to experience the Guinness Storehouse is via the Guinness Storehouse Experience self-guided tour – a full-on sensory deep-dive into the world of Guinness. Spanning 1.6 hectares and seven gleaming floors, it's packed with slick interactive displays, immersive AV and plenty of brewing lore. But behind the foam and folklore lies the real genius: a whole floor dedicated to Guinness' legendary advertising. It's a glossy reminder that, for all the mystique and mythology, this is a masterclass in marketing, and Guinness knows it.

DON'T MISS
- Guinness Storehouse Experience
- Connoisseur Experience
- STOUTie
- Guinness Academy
- Guinness Brewery Experience

PRACTICALITIES
- guinness-storehouse.com
- €26-350
- 10am-5pm Mon-Fri, 9.30am-6pm Sat, 9.30am-5pm Sun

You finish your tour with a freshly poured pint of Guinness (or its zero-alcohol Guinness 0.0) in the rooftop Gravity Bar.

Connoisseur Experience

As a premium add-on, the 90-minute Connoisseur Experience whisks you up to a private bar on the 4th floor, where a Guinness expert guides you through four key brews: Draught, Original, Foreign Extra Stout and the Brewers' Project. You'll learn, for example, how the slightly sweeter Foreign Extra Stout began life as 'West India Porter' and now makes up 45% of global Guinness sales, thanks to its huge popularity in Africa and Asia. After tasting each variant, you'll be shown how to master the iconic Guinness pour before rounding off the experience with a full pint of your top pick.

STOUTie Experience

Ever fancied seeing your face in a pint of Guinness? The STOUTie Experience lets you do just that – for an extra fee, your portrait is printed onto the frothy head of a freshly poured pint. It's definitely on the gimmicky side, but the printing tech is impressively precise – far more flattering than your average beach caricature.

Guinness Academy

If you're determined to master the art of the perfect Guinness pour, the Guinness Academy is the add-on for you. In this hour-long session, you'll be guided through all five steps – you'll start by holding a clean, dry tulip glass at a 45-degree angle, filling it three-quarters of the way up, letting it settle, topping it off and then watching that iconic surge and settle. It's a hands-on bit of fun, and you'll walk away with a certificate, a pint and the bragging rights of having poured a Guinness at the source.

Guinness Brewery Experience

For the ultimate Guinness deep dive, the small-group Brewery Experience takes you behind the scenes to parts of St James' Gate that are off-limits to regular visitors. The expert guides deliver a rich, story-packed tour of the brewery's history, followed by a gourmet four-course meal (with Guinness pairings, naturally) at the excellent **1837 Brasserie & Bar**. The grand finale is a couple of well-earned pints in the **Gravity Bar** with panoramic city views. It's a half-day affair and definitely a splurge that's best suited to true Guinness devotees.

OPEN GATE BREWERY

Less tourist trap, more insider hangout, Guinness' Open Gate Brewery is a slick alternative to the Storehouse experience – perfect if you want the Guinness creds without the full-on fanfare. The industrial-chic space ticks all the taproom boxes: sleek taps, camera-friendly corners and a peek at the brewing action. Expect core pours plus playful experiments (Nitro Milk Chocolate Stout, anyone?). Another treat is the excellent selection of snacks, including a proper pretzel.

TOP TIPS

● Book your tickets online in advance to take advantage of a 10% discount on the price of admission.

● If you can, visit early in the week (Monday to Wednesday) – typically the quieter days in what is Dublin's most popular tourist experience.

● Give yourself plenty of time: you can tour the whole place in 90 minutes, but plan on two to three hours to make the most of all the exhibits (and the Gravity Bar).

● Use your senses in the Tasting Room on the 2nd floor: inhale the different scents and enjoy your bonus mini pint before heading up to the Gravity Bar.

GIGS & EVENTS

For most Dubliners, a trip to Kilmainham means one thing: an epic gig. The Royal Hospital Kilmainham is the home of IMMA, but on select evenings in summer it becomes a hub of live music, with everyone from Patti Smith to Primal Scream taking to the stage. It's a special setting – the gentle slope makes it a natural amphitheatre (of sorts), and if it's a nice day, the sun sets opposite the main stage, bathing it in a golden light.

As well as the one-off gigs, this is also where Forbidden Fruit (p61) takes place every June. The museum's summer programme also features lots of family events as well as **foraging classes** and morning and lunchtime **yoga**.

Royal Hospital Kilmainham

Modern Art
A stellar collection

The **Irish Museum of Modern Art** *(IMMA; imma.ie; free)* might be a bit of a trek from town, but it's definitely worth the effort. The gallery is home to Ireland's most important collection of modern and contemporary Irish and international art, and it's housed in the elegant, airy expanse of the **Royal Hospital Kilmainham**, designed by Sir William Robinson and built between 1684 and 1687 as a retirement home for soldiers.

Inside the gallery, you'll find a mix of contemporary pieces from Irish artists and works from heavy hitters such as Pablo Picasso and Joan Miró in the permanent collection. Temporary exhibitions change regularly and feature homegrown talent or work loaned by international galleries. New pieces are added to the collection every year.

In the summer months (between June and September), a huge array of outdoor activities and exhibitions are staged as part of **IMMA Outdoors**, from curator talks and guided walks to sound baths and open studios. There's also live music in the courtyard.

DRINKING IN KILMAINHAM & THE LIBERTIES: OUR PICKS

Brazen Head: Reputedly Dublin's oldest pub, the Brazen Head has been serving thirsty patrons since 1198. *10.30am-midnight Mon-Thu, to 12.30am Fri & Sat, 12.30pm-midnight Sun*

Fallon's: A fabulously old-fashioned bar with a wood-burning stove and a great snug. *10.30am-11.30pm Mon-Thu, to 12.30am Fri & Sat, 12.30-11pm Sun*

Old Royal Oak: Kilmainham locals are fiercely protective of this gorgeous traditional pub, which opened in 1845. *5pm-midnight Mon-Thu, 3pm-1am Fri, 12.30pm-1am Sat, to 11pm Sun*

Lucky's: A favourite of art students from the nearby National College of Art and Design; craft beer and wine on tap. *11.30am-midnight Mon-Thu, to 1am Fri, from 1pm Sat, 1-11.30pm Sun*

Garden Stroll
Kilmainham's finest
Most visitors rarely venture this far west, but they're missing a lovely bit of landscaping in the shape of the **War Memorial Gardens** (*heritageireland.ie; free*) – by our reckoning, as pleasant a patch of greenery as any you'll find in the heart of the Georgian centre. Designed by Sir Edwin Lutyens, the memorial commemorates the 49,400 Irish soldiers who died during WWI. Their names are inscribed in the two huge granite bookrooms that stand at one end.

A Taste of Teeling
Traditional whiskey distillery
Dublin's first new distillery in more than 125 years, **Teeling** (*teelingwhiskey.com; tours €20-35*) only began production in 2015, with its Single Pot Still bottling, released in 2018, the first Dublin-distilled whiskey to reach the market for over 50 years. At the distillery, you can explore the visitor centre and take a tour of the production process before ending with a tasting of their small-batch whiskey and a whiskey cocktail.

You'll get a taste of whiskey at the end of the tour, but to try the really good stuff, you'll have to upgrade to one of the organised tastings, which range from the **Teeling Tasting** (*€20*) to the **Distillery Select Tasting Tour** (*€35*), where you'll indulge in three special whiskeys, including the exceptional, award-winning, 21-year-old Reserve Single Malt. There's also an excellent cafe on the premises.

Five for Twenty!
Traditional market
As traditional markets go, it doesn't get more authentic than the **Liberty Market** (*libertymarket.ie; free*), which has been going strong on Meath St since 1973. As everything around it yields to the inevitable forces of gentrification, this local market remains defiantly unaffected, offering deals on all manner of items, from clothing and jewellery to toys and gardening supplies. Even if you don't buy anything, it's great for a browse and remains a colourful reminder of the traditional spirit of the Liberties, where bargaining is an art form, and stallholders know most of their customers by name. It's open from 10.30am to 4pm Thursday and Friday, and to 5pm on Saturday.

THE CAPITAL OF WHISKEY

In the early 1800s Dublin had 37 whiskey distilleries, with the Liberties at its heart, thus earning it the nickname the 'Golden Triangle'. Four great names dominated production: John Jameson, William Jameson, John Power and George Roe. Roe's 7-hectare distillery was the largest in the world, producing two million gallons a year, while even Power's smallest operation outproduced Scotland's Glenlivet five times over.

By 1887 Irish whiskey accounted for 70% of global sales, with two of every three bottles in London being Irish. But in the 20th century, Prohibition in the US, a trade war with Britain and failure to modernise production brought the industry to its knees – a collapse from which it is only now beginning to recover.

 EATING IN KILMAINHAM & THE LIBERTIES: BEST FOR BRUNCH

Two Pups Coffee: A beloved neighbourhood joint serving French toast, Turkish eggs and excellent coffee. *8.30am–3.30pm Mon-Fri, from 9am Sat & Sun* €

Fumbally: A bright, airy warehouse cafe that serves healthy dishes and homemade kombucha. *8am-5pm Tue-Fri, from 10am Sat, plus 7-9.30pm Wed* €

Urban8: A Dublin 8 favourite serving stylish Irish dishes and brilliant breakfasts in a warm, community-focused space. *10am-9.30pm Mon-Sat, 10.30am-8pm Sun* €

Daddy's: Brunch-focused spot in Rialto serving modern Irish dishes – don't miss the croissandwich or the Turkish eggs. *8.30am-3pm Mon-Sat, from 10am Sun* €

THE LIBERTIES

The Liberties takes its name from medieval times, when the area lay just outside Dublin's city walls under the control of the Abbey of St Thomas the Martyr. The abbey was granted a special 'liberty', allowing tax-free land and local control over trade – a privilege that gave the district its name.

Centred on the ancient Sligh Mór (or 'Big Road') – today's Thomas St, Meath St and Cornmarket – the Liberties flourished as a hub of brewing, distilling and craftsmanship.

In the 17th century, French Huguenots introduced weaving, tanning and tailoring, as well as the 'Dutch Billy' gable-fronted houses that once defined its skyline. Most were later replaced by Georgian terraces, though a rare example survives at **35a Kevin Street**, with its distinctive tapered facade.

Kilmainham Gaol

Craft Whiskey
Boutique distillery

The boutique **Pearse Lyons Distillery** *(pearselyonsdistillery.com; tour €22-32)* opened in the former St James' Church in 2017, with a cool glass spire on the old building. They distil small-batch, craft Irish whiskey, and their tours include a history of distilling in the Liberties and a range of cocktail experiences, as well as the obligatory tasting. They also make gin – and you can blend your own in the **Gin School Experience**.

Places of Worship
Two churches, same saint

On High St, two neighbouring churches honour St Audoen, the 7th-century bishop of Rouen and patron saint of the Normans. The older, **St Audoen's Church of Ireland**, built between 1181 and 1212, is Dublin's only medieval church that is still in use. Step through its Romanesque doorway to touch the 9th-century 'lucky stone' and see the early Christian slabs that suggest even older foundations.

Inside, Cromwell-era damage is visible on the funerary monuments, and the architecture blends 12th-, 15th- and 19th-century elements. Enter via St Audoen's Arch, which was once part of the city walls.

Beside it stands the larger, 19th-century **St Audoen's Catholic Church**, home to Ireland's Polish chaplaincy since 2006.

Art Deco Whiskey
Guinness' own whiskey

Roe & Co *(roeandcowhiskey.com; from €25)* may have reopened in 2019, but its name is steeped in Liberties whiskey history. Founded in the 18th century, within 100 years, George

Roe's distillery became the world's largest single whiskey producer – and a fierce rival to Guinness. By 1926 Irish whiskey's decline forced its closure, and Guinness bought the site in 1946.

The new distillery, housed in the art deco **Guinness Power Station** that once powered the whole brewery, does the usual distillery tour, but the emphasis is on cocktails: after a traditional tasting, you learn about flavour profiles in a mixology workshop before heading to the bar to sample the bartender's wares. Book ahead.

A Most Historic Prison
The stark sight of Kilmainham Gaol

If you want to understand Ireland's struggle for independence, a visit to **Kilmainham Gaol** (*kilmainhamgaolmuseum.ie; adult/child €8/4*) is essential. This grim prison, built in 1796 and closed in 1924, played a pivotal role in nearly every chapter of the country's long resistance to British rule – and it still exudes an eerie power.

The uprisings of 1798, 1803, 1848, 1867 and 1916 ended with the leaders' confinement here. Robert Emmet, Thomas Francis Meagher, Charles Stewart Parnell and the leaders of the 1916 Easter Rising were all visitors, but it was the executions in 1916 that most deeply etched the jail's name into the Irish consciousness. Of the 15 executions that took place between 3 May and 12 May 1916, 14 were conducted here. As a finale, prisoners from the Civil War were held here from 1922.

Browsing the **museum** provides excellent context and access to some of the former prisoners' personal belongings and letters. The enthusiastic guides provide a thought-provoking tour of the eerie prison, which is the largest unoccupied building of its kind in Europe. The tour finishes in the gloomy yard where the 1916 executions took place.

Visits are by guided tour only, and the group sizes are kept small. If you want to visit, you'll need to book as far in advance as possible, as time slots sell out quickly, particularly during the summer and on weekends.

Try 'We Love Markets'
Flea market

At the Digital Hub on Thomas St, **We Love Markets** (*welovemarkets.ie; free*) brings a lively mix of vintage, secondhand and local finds to the heart of Dublin on the last Sunday of every month. Expect everything from antique treasures to rails of retro clothing and personal bits from Dubliners clearing out their wardrobes. The atmosphere is always buzzing – a resident vinyl van spins tunes while food trucks dish up crowd-pleasers such as loaded baked potatoes and lobster rolls.

WHY I LOVE THE LIBERTIES

Nicola Brady, travel writer
@nicola_brady

Anything you could want from a day in Dublin can be found in the Liberties. You've got the big attractions like the Guinness Storehouse and the neighbouring distilleries, as well as historical sights like St Patrick's Cathedral and the old city walls. The food scene here is the best in the city, with everything from Michelin-starred dining to casual brunch cafes, but it also feels like it's got a sense of the proper, old-school Dublin to it, from the women selling flowers off Thomas St to the fellas propping up the bar in an old pub. It feels like a neighbourhood with a soul.

O'Connell Street & the North City Centre

GRANDEUR OF OLD DUBLIN

GETTING AROUND

O'Connell St and its attractions are pretty straightforward and can be explored with ease on foot, with the biggest demand on your time being a visit to big three attractions (the Hugh Lane Gallery, EPIC and the *Jeanie Johnston*) or choosing where to eat along Parnell St and Capel St.

Edgier and more lived-in than its southside counterpart, the area just north of the River Liffey blends faded Georgian elegance with classic Dublin grit and a vibrant multicultural edge. At its heart is O'Connell St – Ireland's widest boulevard – once the pride of Georgian Dublin and still a vital artery of city life.

Here, history is everywhere: the EPIC Irish Migration Museum vividly tells the story of Ireland's global diaspora, while the *Jeanie Johnston* famine ship offers a moving insight into 19th-century migration. On O'Connell St, the GPO Museum is in the post office where the 1916 Rising began.

The neighbourhood is also brimming with a rich, international food scene. From a two-Michelin-star restaurant showcasing modern Irish excellence to Palestinian falafel stalls, Filipino bakeries and Korean fried chicken joints, the northside's mix of flavours perfectly reflects Dublin's own evolving, multicultural identity.

Going Postal
Emblem of independence

If you're looking for a quintessential Dublin landmark, this is it. The **General Post Office** is at the heart of Ireland's struggle for independence. It served as command HQ for the rebels during the 1916 Easter Rising, and you can still see the pockmarks of the struggle in the Doric columns outside.

As a result, the GPO has become the focal point for all kinds of protests, parades and remembrances; it's also home to an interactive visitor centre: **GPO Witness History** *(gpomuseum.ie; adult/child €15/7.50)*. This wonderful museum serves as a fitting tribute to the 1916 Easter Rising and its key role in the creation of the Irish state. Interactive and full of touchscreens, the exhibit explores all facets of the Rising, from its origins to its aftermath. If you see only one thing, watch the melodramatic film that recounts the events of Easter Week 1916.

☑ TOP TIP

By day, O'Connell St is a bustle of activity, with shoppers, hawkers, walkers and others going about their business. At night, however, it can be a different story, as alcohol and drugs can give the street an air of menace and, sadly, the odd spot of trouble. Give it a wide berth after dark.

O'CONNELL STREET & THE NORTH CITY CENTRE

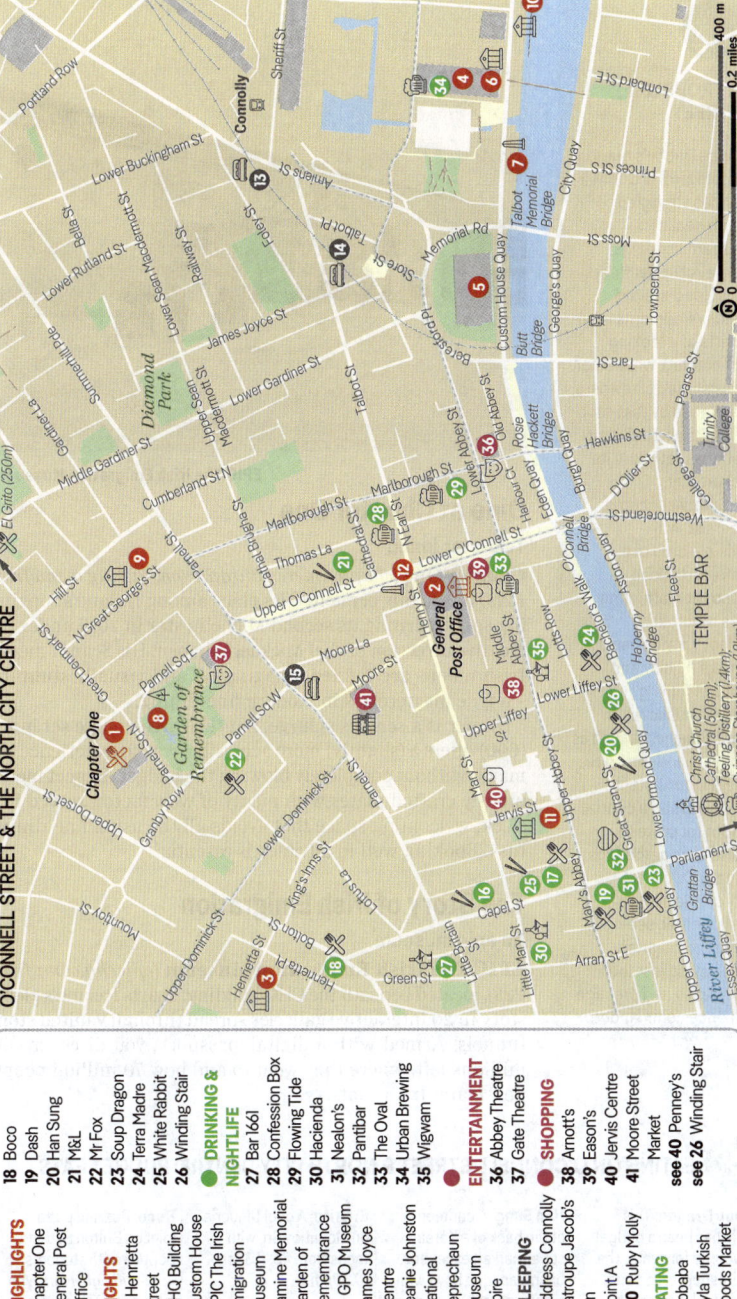

★ HIGHLIGHTS
1. Chapter One
2. General Post Office

● SIGHTS
3. 14 Henrietta Street
4. CHQ Building
5. Custom House
6. EPIC The Irish Emigration Museum
7. Famine Memorial
8. Garden of Remembrance
   see 2 GPO Museum
9. James Joyce Centre
10. Jeanie Johnston
11. National Leprechaun Museum
12. Spire

● SLEEPING
13. Address Connolly
14. Latroupe Jacob's Inn
15. Point A
    see 30 Ruby Molly

● EATING
16. Aobaba
17. Ayla Turkish Foods Market
18. Boco
19. Dash
20. Han Sung
21. M&L
22. Mr Fox
23. Soup Dragon
24. Terra Madre
25. White Rabbit
26. Winding Stair

● DRINKING & NIGHTLIFE
27. Bar 1661
28. Confession Box
29. Flowing Tide
30. Hacienda
31. Nealon's
32. Pantibar
33. The Oval
34. Urban Brewing
35. Wigwam

● ENTERTAINMENT
36. Abbey Theatre
37. Gate Theatre

● SHOPPING
38. Arnott's
39. Eason's
40. Jervis Centre
41. Moore Street Market
    see 40 Penney's
    see 26 Winding Stair

A TROUBLED STREET

Once Dublin's grand boulevard, O'Connell St has struggled with decline. Vacant buildings, derelict upper floors and long-stalled redevelopments leave parts of it looking neglected, while retail has shifted elsewhere, replaced by fast-food outlets and low-rent shops that dilute its character.

Safety concerns persist, with visible drug use, street drinking and theft affecting its reputation. Heavy traffic can make it noisy and unwelcoming, while public realm improvements such as paving and the Spire feel inconsistent. Though still a central spot for protests and civic gatherings, many Dubliners prefer to avoid it altogether, seeing the thoroughfare as having lost the vibrancy and prestige it once commanded.

EPIC The Irish Emigration Museum

Dine at Chapter One

Two-star lunch

Chapter One *(chapteronerestaurant.com; tasting menu from €215)* has firmly cemented its place among Ireland's top dining spots, earning its second Michelin star in 2019 under the creative direction of chef Mickael Viljanen. His Scandi-meets-Irish menus are refined, imaginative and visually stunning – a true masterclass in modern fine-dining.

Dinner is a serious splurge, but the three-course set lunch (€90) offers a (slightly) more accessible way to experience the magic without completely blowing the budget. Expect meticulously crafted plates with plenty of wow factor, served in a sleek, welcoming space that avoids all the usual fine-dining fuss. Booking well in advance is essential.

The Story of Irish Emigration

An epic museum

EPIC The Irish Emigration Museum *(epicchq.com; from €28)*, located beneath the CHQ building, charts Ireland's global story in 20 interactive galleries spread through vaulted stone tunnels. Armed with a digital 'passport', you discover why millions left, where they went to and how 70 million people now claim Irish roots.

 EATING ON O'CONNELL STREET & NORTH CITY CENTRE: BUDGET EATS

Soup Dragon: This cafe has been a budget favourite for years. The daily soup, bread and fruit deal is a bargain. *8am-5pm Mon-Fri* €

Han Sung: A canteen at the back of a Korean supermarket; excellent bibimbap (rice bowl with meat, vegetables and egg). *10am-9pm Mon-Sat, 11.30am-8.30pm Sun* €

El Grito: A cool taqueria on Mountjoy Sq, with tacos from €3. *11.30am-10.30pm* €

Boco: Buzzing pizza joint on Bolton St that's popular with students. *4pm-midnight Mon-Wed, from noon Thu, to 1am Fri, 2pm-1am Sat, to 11.30pm Sun* €

Inside, the **Irish Family History Centre** lets you trace your own clan for free via surname databases, or book 30-, 60- or 90-minute one-to-one sessions with professional genealogists (extra fee, advance booking advised).

EPIC's basement setting adds atmosphere, and rotating campaigns such as **This Is Not Us** tackle tired leprechaun clichés with CGI installations and St Patrick's Day pop-ups.

After your visit, the cafes in the CHQ handle everything from flat whites to sushi, so you can refuel without leaving the building.

The Industrial CHQ Building
Converted warehouse

The highlight of Dublin's modern Irish Financial Services Centre is the 19th-century **CHQ Building** (chq.ie; free) – an industrial masterpiece with the largest clear-span floor space of any pre-20th-century structure in the city.

Designed in 1820 by Scottish engineer John Rennie, it was built as a bonded warehouse for tobacco, tea and spirits, originally known as the Tobacco Store and later as Stack A. Its Georgian brick walls enclose more than 8000 sq metres beneath a slate roof supported by an entirely cast-iron frame – a pioneering, fireproof design with not a single piece of wood used. The building still retains most of its nine original vaults, though half of one was removed in 1884 to widen Custom House Quay. Today, those vaults are taken up by EPIC The Irish Emigration Museum, which remains CHQ's primary tenant.

The rest of the building is taken up by a disappointingly small selection of food outlets, but they do include the excellent **Urban Brewing** (urbanbrewing.ie) microbrewery. Still, it all feels a little under-utilised and a far cry from 1856, when the building hosted a banquet for 3000 returning soldiers of the Crimean War.

Note that as EPIC's founder is a former CEO of the Coca-Cola Company, you'll find no Pepsi products on sale in the building.

Famine Ship
Replica sailing boat

One of Dublin's most striking attractions, the ***Jeanie Johnston*** (jeaniejohnston.ie; adult/child €15/10) is a faithful working replica of a 19th-century 'coffin ship' – the grim nickname given to the vessels that carried starving Irish emigrants across the Atlantic during the Great Famine (1845–51). Remarkably, the original *Jeanie Johnston* saw no deaths across its 16 crossings between 1848 and 1855, with it safely transporting over 2500 passengers.

The guided tour begins on the open deck, where you can admire the traditional artisanship and towering rigging. Below deck, the atmosphere shifts as you step into the dark, claustrophobic quarters where up to 250 people would have endured 47-day voyages, with only 30 minutes of fresh air daily.

FLEXIBLE TICKETING

Ticketing at EPIC The Irish Emigration Museum is designed to be flexible and good value. The basic self-guided admission can easily be bundled with other attractions, letting visitors tailor their experience to their interests. One of the most popular options is the EPIC and *Jeanie Johnston* combo, which pairs the museum visit with a guided tour of the famine ship moored just five minutes away.

There are also hop-on, hop-off bus packages, giving you 24- to 72-hour access to Dublin's main sightseeing routes alongside your museum entry. For those keen to explore further, tickets can be combined with other city heavy-hitters such as the Guinness Storehouse or Jameson Distillery, making EPIC an easy starting point for discovering Dublin's wider story.

HAUNTED SCULPTURES

Just east of the Custom House stands one of Dublin's most haunting and photographed pieces of public art: the set of life-size bronze figures known simply as **Famine**.

Created in 1997 by sculptor Rowan Gillespie, the installation commemorates the devastating years of the Great Famine (1845–51), when more than one million Irish people died and another million were forced to emigrate. The gaunt, emaciated figures, their faces marked by despair and determination, symbolise that desperate exodus.

They stand on the very spot where the first so-called 'coffin ship', the *Perseverance*, departed for New York on St Patrick's Day 1846. In a rare glimmer of hope amid tragedy, every passenger on that voyage survived – a poignant reminder of endurance in the face of unimaginable loss.

Famine

As you move through the space, the stories of real passengers bring the experience vividly to life – a sobering glimpse into the desperation, courage and resilience of those who left Ireland in search of something better.

It can be visited on a joint ticket combining EPIC (p88).

All Things Joyce
Georgian Joyce

The **James Joyce Centre** *(jamesjoyce.ie; adult/child €7/5)* is in a beautifully restored house, with exhibits of furniture from Joyce's Paris apartment, a life-size recreation of a typical Edwardian bedroom and the original door of 7 Eccles St – the home of Leopold and Molly Bloom in *Ulysses* (1922). The centre also runs two walking tours, **Introducing Joyce's Dublin** and **Footsteps of Leopold Bloom**. The house was once the residence of dancing master Professor Denis J Maginni, who features in *Ulysses*.

A House with History
Dublin's Georgian past

Dublin has its fill of Georgian townhouses, but most are a symbol of grandeur and pomp. That's not the case at **14 Henrietta Street** *(14henriettastreet.ie; adult/child €10/6)*, which has been carefully restored to gently peel back layers of complex social history over a period of 250 years. Part museum, part community archive, it spans the magnificent elegance of upper-class life in the 1740s to the destitution of the early 20th century, when the house was occupied by 100 tenants living in near squalor.

You can only visit on a 75-minute guided tour, which is also offered in Irish Sign Language. The museum also runs guided walking tours of the local neighbourhood, as well as themed talks (and the occasional singalong) led by former residents or social historians.

A Glutton's Delight
Haven of world cuisine

Ask any Dublin foodie for their favourite neighbourhood, and the recently pedestrianised Capel St is likely to top the list. Not only is it the longest traffic-free street in the city – it's also likely the tastiest. Stroll along and you'll find a smorgasbord of restaurants, cafes and shops representing cuisines from around the world.

White Rabbit *(@white.rabbit.hq)*, tucked at the back of the Super Asia Foods supermarket, serves knockout Korean dishes such as pork belly *cupbap* and platters of spicy fried chicken. Don't miss the corn dogs – sausage and mozzarella deep-fried, sugar-dusted and topped with mustard and ketchup. Further up, **Ayla Turkish Foods Market** *(ayla.ie)* tempts with syrup-soaked baklava and rows of flaky *börek* stuffed with tangy feta – perfect for snacking on the go.

Aobaba *(facebook.com/aobabadublin)* might look like just another bubble-tea joint, but its Vietnamese food is the real draw – fresh summer rolls, *banh mi* and steaming bowls of *pho*. Craving comfort food? **Dash** *(dashburger.ie)* dishes up indulgent smash burgers, pressed on the grill with onions and dripping in truffle butter or chipotle sauce.

Cap the evening with a pint at **Nealon's** *(jacknealons.ie)*, a cosy, old-school pub near the Liffey end of the street. No frills, just good vibes.

James Gandon's Masterpiece
Neoclassical building

One of the most striking sights along the River Liffey, the **Custom House** is a neoclassical masterpiece that long stood as a grand but inaccessible symbol of government. That changed in 2021, when the **Custom House Visitor Centre** *(heritageireland.ie; free)* opened, allowing the public inside this 18th-century icon.

Designed by James Gandon (1743–1823) and built between 1781 and 1791, its interior now features interactive exhibits, AV projections and detailed models that trace its turbulent 200-year history. Look for the sculpted river heads, globe-trotting statues and the statue of Hope high above the dome's four clocks.

A GEORGIAN STREET

Laid out in the 1720s by developer Luke Gardiner, **Henrietta St** was Dublin's first great example of Georgian urban planning. Wider than most streets of its time, it was lined with red-brick Palladian mansions built for the city's wealthiest families. Gardiner himself lived at No 10, designed by Richard Cassels. Originally known as Primate's Hill (after the Archbishop of Armagh's residence), it was later renamed in honour of one of two possible Henriettas from the British aristocracy.

The street's fortunes declined after the Act of Union (1801), when many of Dublin's elite left for London. By the late 19th century, the once-luxurious houses had become overcrowded tenements, home to hundreds. Today, 14 Henrietta Street tells this story of privilege, poverty and transformation.

 EATING ON O'CONNELL STREET & THE NORTH CITY CENTRE: OUR PICKS

M&L: The best Chinese restaurant in Dublin, with spicy Szechuan-style cuisine. *11.30am-10pm Mon-Sat, from noon Sun* €

Terra Madre: Contender for most authentic Italian restaurant in Dublin. *12.30-3pm & 5-10pm* €€

Winding Stair: Contemporary Irish cuisine in an elegant 1st-floor dining-room. *noon-3.30pm & 5.30-10.30pm* €€

Mr Fox: Fine dining in a gorgeous setting on Parnell Sq. *noon-2pm & 5-9.30pm Tue-Sat* €€€

A NIGHT AT THE THEATRE

Two of the country's top theatres are within a stone's throw of O'Connell St. The **Abbey Theatre** (abbeytheatre.ie) is Ireland's national theatre. Founded in 1904 by WB Yeats, it played a central role in the development of a consciously native cultural identity. Expect to see a mix of homegrown theatre from Irish playwrights, as well as touring performances from around the world.

Just north of O'Connell St, the **Gate** (gatetheatre.ie) is Dublin's most elegant theatre, housed in a late-18th-century building. It features a generally unflappable repertory of classic Irish, American and European plays; both Orson Welles and James Mason acted here early in their careers.

Moore Street Market

Market Days
Old-school Dublin

Make your way up Moore St, and your walk will be accompanied by the calls of the **Moore Street Market** traders shouting out their daily deals. You might not want a sackful of apples, but you can't hear the shout of 'Ten for a euro!' without thinking it sounds like a deal. The market may not be as vibrant as it once was, but it's still going strong, and the permanent buildings on the street have brought an air of multiculturalism to this corner of the city. You'll find Brazilian restaurants, Asian markets and Indian spices.

For a real culinary adventure, head to the **Moore Street Mall** next to Lidl. It may not look like much, but this food court offers options from all over the world, from Balkan cafes and Bolivian restaurants to noodle and curry vendors. The prices are fantastic.

Dublin's Coolest Bar
Hedonistic hideaway

From the outside, **Hacienda** (at 15 Little Mary St) could almost pass for an abandoned Spanish farmhouse – whitewashed walls, shuttered windows and not a soul in sight. It rarely stirs

DRINKING ON O'CONNELL ST & NORTH CITY CENTRE: OUR PICKS

Hacienda: Dublin's coolest bar is hidden inside an unmarked Spanish-style cottage and only accessible via a doorbell. *8-11.30pm Mon-Thu, to 12.30am Fri & Sat, 8-11pm Sun*

Bar 1661: Ireland's moonshine, poitín, is transformed into excellent cocktails at this world-class bar. *5-11.30pm Mon-Thu, 2pm-12.30am Fri & Sat, to 11pm Sun*

Pantibar: A raucous and fun gay bar owned by 'gender discombobulist' Rory O'Neill, aka Panti Bliss. *4-11.30pm Mon-Thu, to 12.30am Fri & Sat, to 11pm Sun*

Wigwam: Loads of craft beers, loads of cocktails and a raucous bottomless brunch at weekends. *11am-11.30pm Mon-Thu, to 2.30am Fri & Sat*

before 8pm, and the facade gives no hint of life within, with the doors firmly closed.

It seems dormant until well past nightfall. Even then, there's no strolling in. To enter, you press the buzzer marked 'bar' and hope that Shay Duignan, the owner (and uncanny Doc Brown lookalike), decides you're worth admitting.

If you're in luck, you'll step into a warren of shadowy nooks and sci-fi-set-worthy rooms, their walls crammed with photographs of celebrity patrons – this is the bar that visiting stars come to when they want to celebrate in Dublin (and if you're famous like Taylor Swift, Shay will give you and your friends exclusive run of the place).

It's elusive, eccentric and effortlessly cool – without doubt the most intriguing bar in Dublin.

Dublin's Disney
One for the kids

Billed as a child-friendly museum of Irish folklore, the **National Leprechaun Museum** (*leprechaunmuseum.ie; from €11*) is really a romper room for kids sprinkled with bits of fairy tale. Which is no bad thing, even if the picture of the leprechaun painted here is more Lucky Charms and Walt Disney than sinister creature of pre-Christian mythology. On weekend nights, the tone shifts, with adults-only sessions that delve into the creepier corners of Irish mythology.

Sky-High Sculpture
Prominent landmark

The city's most visible landmark soars over O'Connell St and is an impressive bit of architectural engineering that was erected in 2001. From a base only 3m in diameter, the **Spire** soars more than 120m into the sky and tapers into a 15cm-wide beam of light…it's tall and shiny, and it does the trick rather nicely.

The brainchild of London-based architect Ian Ritchie, it's apparently the highest sculpture in the world, but much like the Parisian reaction to the construction of the Eiffel Tower, Dubliners are divided as to its aesthetic value and have regularly made fun of it. Among other names, we like 'the erection in the intersection', the 'stiletto in the ghetto' and the altogether brilliant 'eyeful tower'.

GO CITY PASS

If you plan to tick off several major attractions, a pass from **Go City Dublin** (*gocity.com; from €69*) can save you money. Choose between the All-Inclusive Pass or the Explorer Pass, where you decide how many sights to see.

The All-Inclusive option is simplest; it's valid for between one and five days and covers everything from headline draws like the Guinness Storehouse (p80), Christ Church Cathedral (p70) and EPIC The Irish Emigration Museum (p88) to smaller gems like the Teeling Distillery (p83) and 14 Henrietta Street (p90). It also includes extras such as hop-on, hop-off bus tours, guided food walks and even excursions to the Game of Thrones Studio Tour (p544) in Northern Ireland.

 DRINKING ON O'CONNELL ST & THE NORTH CITY CENTRE: OUR PICKS

Confession Box: This historic pub is popular with tourists and locals. It used to be a favourite spot of Michael Collins, a leader in the fight for Irish independence. *11am-11pm Mon-Fri, 10am-midnight Sat & Sun*

Flowing Tide: A longtime stalwart of Dublin's theatre-going community – the Abbey is directly across the street. *10.30am-11.30pm Mon-Thu, to 12.30am Fri & Sat, 12.30-11pm Sun*

The Oval: A great little pub where young and old come together in conversation, and the rich, creamy pints go down a treat. *10.30am-12.30am Mon-Thu, to 1am Fri & Sat, to midnight Sun*

Nealon's: Traditional pub with exceptionally friendly staff and a gorgeous cocktail lounge on the 1st floor. *2-11.30pm Mon-Thu, to 12.30am Fri, 12.30pm-12.30am Sat, 12.30-11pm Sun*

BEST SHOPPING AROUND O'CONNELL STREET

Arnott's: Arguably the best of Dublin's department stores, Arnott's stocks virtually everything from garden furniture to high fashion.

Penney's: Ireland's cheapest department store is a place to find all kinds of everything without paying a fortune for it.

Jervis Centre: Modern, domed mall that is a shrine to the British chain store. Boots, Topshop, New Look, M&S and Superdrug all get a look in.

Eason's: Huge bookshop on O'Connell St with a great selection of magazines and foreign newspapers.

Winding Stair: Handsome old bookshop with a limited but excellent selection of quality new and old books.

Spire (p93)

Memorial Garden
Peaceful and quiet

On the northeastern corner of Parnell Sq, the **Garden of Remembrance** *(heritageireland.ie; free)* is a rather austere little park, but it's a tranquil space to clear your head for a little while.

It was opened by President Éamon de Valera in 1966 for the 50th anniversary of the 1916 Easter Rising and is dedicated to all those who gave their lives to the cause of Irish liberty. There's a pool in the centre and a bronze statue of the **Children of Lir** by Oisín Kelly. According to Irish legend, the children were turned into swans by their wicked stepmother.

Smithfield & Stoneybatter

TWIN HIPSTER 'HOODS

West of O'Connell St along the Liffey, Smithfield and neighbouring Stoneybatter are a twin-pack of urban cool. Traditional Smithfield was once a rough-and-tumble warehouse district, but it has swapped pallets for penthouses, with sleek glass towers looking down on the cobbles of the main square. Amid the modernity, though, are some pulsing flavours of old-school Dublin, including the best trad bar in town.

Neighbouring Stoneybatter has seen some changes, too. Once upon a time, a builder's breakfast roll was the closest thing you'd get to artisanal, but then the creatives moved in looking for cheaper rents close to the city centre. Two decades on, and Dublin's unofficial 'gayborhood' is all about vinyl-spun beats, candlelit small plates and craft brews.

While Stoneybatter remains a largely residential neighbourhood, it's a great destination for a night out, while Smithfield has a couple of heavyweight attractions.

GETTING AROUND

From the city centre, the Luas Red line takes you through Smithfield and on to the National Museum of Ireland before cutting across the river. From the Museum stop, it's only a 10-minute walk to the heart of Stoneybatter; otherwise, your best bet is to hop on a **Dublin Bike** *(dublinbikes.ie)*.

History, Home & Heritage
Converted 18th-century barracks

Collins Barracks, once the world's largest military barracks, is a vast grey-stone complex that's now home to the **National Museum of Ireland – Decorative Arts & History** *(museum.ie; free)*.

The museum houses a rich and varied collection, spanning centuries of Irish design, political history and daily life. A highlight is the **Soldiers & Chiefs** exhibition, which traces the story of Irish soldiers from the 16th century to the present day. Among the many artefacts is the army coat of Michael Collins, worn during the Irish War of Independence. He was assassinated in 1922, and the barracks were renamed in his honour, hence why many Dubliners still call it Collins Barracks.

Elsewhere, the museum explores Ireland's decorative heritage, from intricate silver and glass pieces to furniture, weaponry and folk-life displays. The **Way We Wore** offers a stylish look

☑ TOP TIP

Stoneybatter is a largely residential neighbourhood with virtually no hotels (but plenty of AirBnB listings), whereas Smithfield has more sleeping options – and it's closer to the city centre.

SMITHFIELD & STONEYBATTER

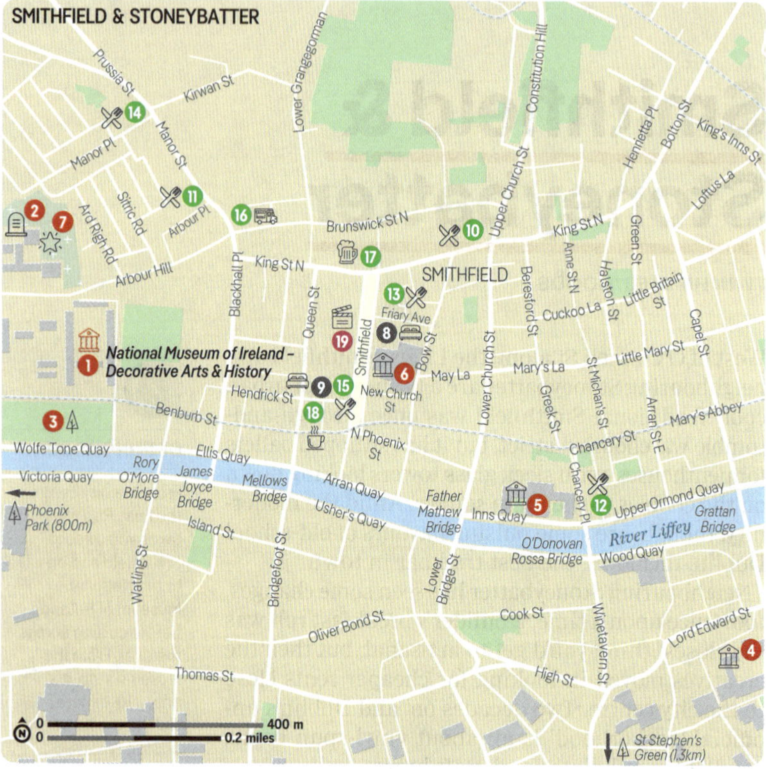

HIGHLIGHTS
1. National Museum of Ireland – Decorative Arts & History

SIGHTS
2. Arbour Hill Cemetery
see 1 Collins Barracks
3. Croppies' Acre
4. Dublin Castle
5. Four Courts
6. Jameson Distillery Bow St

ACTIVITIES
7. Arbour Hill Guided Tours

SLEEPING
8. Generator Hostel
9. Hendrick

EATING
10. Bonobo
11. Grano
12. Legal Eagle
13. Oxmantown
14. Slice
15. Third Space
16. Vietnom

DRINKING & NIGHTLIFE
17. Cobblestone
18. Proper Order

ENTERTAINMENT
19. Lighthouse Cinema

EATING IN SMITHFIELD & STONEYBATTER: OUR PICKS

Grano: An exceptional Italian restaurant in Stoneybatter, with homemade pasta and killer tiramisu. *5-10pm Mon-Fri, 12.30-10pm Sat & Sun* €€

Bonobo: Come here for Neapolitan-style pizza and a lovely beer garden – the ideal ingredients for a good night out. *4pm-midnight* €€

Legal Eagle: Top-rated gastro-pub with a daily hotpot and a fine Sunday roast; the wine list is excellent. *5-9.30pm Wed-Sat, noon-7pm Sun* €€

Vietnom: Vietnamese-fusion food truck in the beer garden of the fabulous Glimmer Man pub. *6-10pm Thu & Fri, to 9pm Sat* €

at clothing and jewellery over the last 250 years, while **Reconstructed Rooms** showcases interiors from 1600 onwards. Don't miss the **Eileen Gray** exhibit, where her groundbreaking, modernist furniture (including the iconic non-conformist chair) is given pride of place.

If you're short on time, head straight to **Curator's Choice**, where 25 standout objects are displayed with curator commentary, offering a choice snapshot of the museum's vast and eclectic holdings.

The Gritty City
A moving tour

If you want to see the realities of life in Dublin (or any major city), then a walking tour with **Secret Street Tours** (secretstreettours.org; €15) is the way to go. Led by people affected by homelessness, these tours take you around Smithfield and the surrounding neighbourhood, starting off at Collins Barracks (p95). You'll see the local cultural and historical sights through the eyes of someone who knows what it's like to live on these streets. If there's one walking tour to take while you're in Dublin, this is it.

Solemn Memorial
Historic park

Easy to overlook, the small park in front of Collins Barracks holds deep symbolic weight in Ireland's independence story. Known as the **Croppies' Acre**, it was once a soldiers' exercise ground, but local tradition claims it became a mass grave for rebels – the 'croppies' (named for their short hair) – of the 1798 Rebellion. An archaeological survey in the 1990s found no human remains, yet in 1998 the National Graves Association erected a memorial here. Fact or legend, it remains a powerful place of remembrance, honouring those who fought and fell in that doomed uprising.

Raise a Glass
Smithfield spirit

The distilleries of the Liberties (p83) might be coming for its throne, but the **Jameson Distillery** (jamesonwhiskey.com; from €26) in Smithfield has been luring in visitors for decades, despite not producing a drop of whiskey in this location since 1971. But no matter – visit the museum and get a slick tour through a recreation of the factory before sitting down for a tasting.

SMITHFIELD AS BERLIN

In the 1965 Cold War thriller *The Spy Who Came in from the Cold*, Smithfield Plaza stood in for Berlin's notorious Checkpoint Charlie, with the film set constructed on the very spot where the Generator Hostel now sits. At the time, Dubliners were thrilled to see their city appear on the big screen, rubbing shoulders (cinematically, at least) with one of the world's most famous espionage settings.

Yet the excitement came with a touch of irony: audiences quickly realised that bombed-out, post-war Berlin and 1960s' Smithfield looked convincingly similar without much effort from the set designers. Still, the production left its mark, giving Smithfield an unexpected brush with Hollywood glamour, even if the comparison wasn't exactly the kind the locals might have wished for.

SEE ANOTHER NEIGHBOURHOOD

Secret Street Tours also runs a walking tour in the **Liberties**, which kicks off on Palace St beside **Dublin Castle** (p55) and wraps up near **St Stephen's Green** (p55).

Jameson Distillery (p97)

STREET ART IN SMITHFIELD

The laneway beside Proper Order hides two striking pieces by the street art collective **Subset**, including a bold black-and-white portrait that feels both intimate and cinematic. The group, known for pushing creative boundaries in Dublin's urban spaces, has left its mark all over the city, but Smithfield boasts some of their most distinctive work.

At the other end of Smithfield Market, by the Cobblestone, a building is covered in a vivid mural of two traditional musicians, one playing the fiddle, the other the flute.

On Stirrup Lane, another Subset creation, *Horseboy*, bursts with psychedelic colour and an optical illusion effect that shifts as you move past; it's a blend of urban energy and surreal imagination.

If you're serious about whiskey, there are plenty of immersive options to explore. Go behind the scenes with the Secret Tasting, where you'll sample four premium blends exclusive to the distillery, or roll up your sleeves and blend your own whiskey straight from the barrel. There are cocktail-making classes for the mixology-curious, and a dedicated Redbreast tasting experience for fans of Ireland's most prestigious whiskey brand.

Night at the Movies
Popcorn and Pilsner

If you like independent cinema, you'll love the **Lighthouse** (*lighthousecinema.ie*; adult/child €13/10.50). This snazzy four-screener in a cool building just off Smithfield Plaza shows a mix of art-house and mainstream releases, documentaries and Irish films. The themed movie seasons are always worth checking out – you might catch the entire back catalogue of Wes Anderson's films or an all-night marathon of the *Lord of the Rings* trilogy.

It also runs Parent-and-Baby matinees and a Cinema Book Club, where a screening of a book adaptation is followed by a casual chat in the bar. Previous movies have included *Brokeback Mountain* (2005), *The Beach* (2000) and *Matilda the Musical* (2010).

EATING IN SMITHFIELD & STONEYBATTER: OUR FAVOURITE CAFES

Proper Order: A small Smithfield cafe with excellent coffee and treats from No Messin' Bakery. *7am-5pm Mon-Fri, from 10am Sat* €

Slice: This Stoneybatter joint is a local hotspot for brunch and hot chocolate. *8am-4pm Mon-Thu, to 5pm Fri, 9am-5pm Sat & Sun* €

Oxmantown: Excellent sandwiches and decadent Vietnamese iced coffees. *8am-4pm Mon-Fri* €

Third Space: A laid-back cafe in Smithfield with a neighbourhood mindset and social vibe. *7am-6pm Mon-Fri, 9am-3pm Sat & Sun* €

The Home of Trad
Best traditional music pub in town
The **Cobblestone** *(cobblestonepub.ie)* proudly calls itself 'a drinking pub with a music problem', a tongue-in-cheek nod to the constant hum of live trad sessions echoing through this beloved Smithfield haunt. Far from a problem, though, the music is the soul of the place. With multiple sessions daily, it draws some of the finest trad musicians in the country.

A Grave History
Historic cemetery
This small cemetery at **Arbour Hill** *(heritageireland.ie; free)* is the final resting place of 14 of the executed leaders of the 1916 Easter Rising. The burial ground is plain, with the 14 names inscribed in stone. Beside the graves is a cenotaph bearing the Easter Proclamation, a focal point for official and national commemorations.

The front of the cemetery, incongruously but poignantly, contains the graves of British personnel killed in the War of Independence. Here, in the oldest part of the cemetery, the toppled gravestones were lined up against the boundary walls, where they still stand solemnly today.

There are free **tours** *(phoenixparkvisitorcentre@opw.ie)* of the cemetery every Friday at 2pm between April and October; email to reserve a spot.

Admire the Four Courts
Georgian building
This masterpiece by James Gandon (1743–1823) is a mammoth complex stretching 130m along Inns Quay, as fine an example of Georgian public architecture as there is in Dublin. Despite the construction of a brand-new criminal courts building further west along the Liffey, the **Four Courts** *(courts.ie; free)* is still the enduring symbol of Irish law going about its daily business. Visitors are allowed to wander through the building, but not to enter the courts or other restricted areas.

WITTGENSTEIN IN DUBLIN

In 1947 the philosopher **Ludwig Wittgenstein** (1889–1951) – one of the most influential thinkers of the 20th century – suddenly resigned his professorship at Cambridge University and came to live in Dublin. Known for revolutionising modern philosophy with works like *Tractatus Logico-Philosophicus*, Wittgenstein sought quiet and anonymity, taking a small room at Ross' Hotel on Parkgate St (today the Ashling Hotel).

He chose Dublin because of his friendship with a consultant psychiatrist at nearby St Patrick's Hospital, and over the nine months of his stay here, he was extremely productive, writing much of what would later be published as *Philosophical Investigations* (1953). When he wasn't writing, he was known to enjoy walks in the Phoenix Park (p103) and the National Botanic Gardens (p104) in Glasnevin.

Docklands

DUBLIN'S TECH HUB

GETTING AROUND

If you want to explore the neighbourhood at a faster clip, sign up for **Dublin Bikes** *(dublinbikes.ie)* or download the app. Bikes are parked at stations all over the Docklands, and the first 30 minutes are free. You can sign up for a one- or three-day ticket, and e-bikes are also available.

The closest Dublin comes to a skyline is in the gleaming Docklands, where glass-and-steel towers stretch skywards. At 79m, the 22-storey Capital Dock is the tallest building in the Republic, looming over a cluster of global banks and tech giants.

At the centre is Grand Canal Sq, a 10,000-sq-metre plaza designed by renowned landscape architect Martha Schwartz. Dubbed the 'Silicon Docks', the area is home to some of tech's biggest names – Google, Facebook, LinkedIn, X (formerly Twitter) and Indeed all have offices here.

It's also where you'll find one of Europe's most iconic recording studios, three top-class entertainment venues and – just south of the canal in swanky Dublin 4 – the wonderful National Print Museum, one of the city's finest and most undiscovered 'little' museums.

Musical Legends
Recording studios

What do Ed Sheeran, Metallica and Lady Gaga have in common? They've all recorded at **Windmill Lane** *(windmilllane recording.com; adult/child €22/15)*, one of Dublin's most iconic studios. Originally on John Rogerson's Quay, it earned its legendary status early on when U2 recorded their first three albums there – *Boy* (1980), *October* (1981) and *War* (1983) – prompting fans to graffiti the walls in tribute.

Today, the studio welcomes visitors for behind-the-scenes tours. You can step into the recording rooms, hear stories of legendary sessions and get a sense of the creative energy that's passed through these halls. For music fans, it's as close to sacred ground as Dublin gets.

☑ TOP TIP

On the last Thursday of the month, the National Print Museum (p102) comes to life thanks to its founders, a group of retired printers known as 'the Chapel', who share stories, give live demos and flaunt the still-working machines.

Go Kayaking
Paddle the Liffey

Want to see the city from a different perspective? Then head out to explore the River Liffey with **City Kayaking** *(citykay aking.com; adult/child €59/55)*. You'll start at Custom House Quay and paddle your way towards the city centre, getting

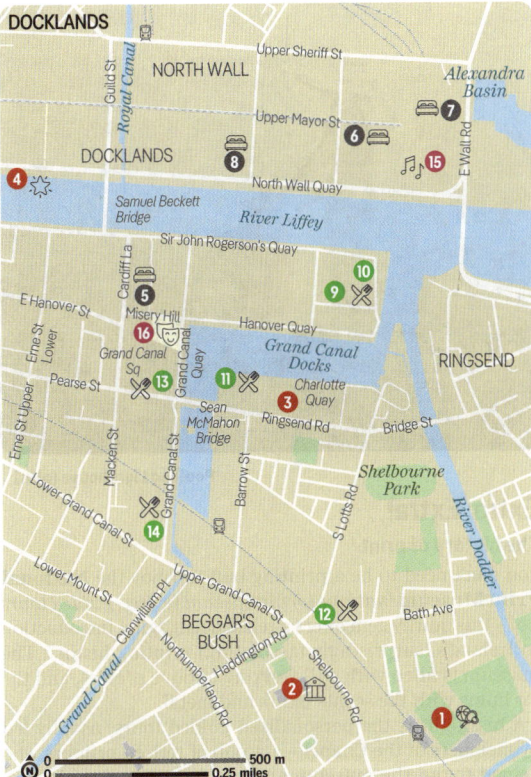

SIGHTS
1 Aviva Stadium
2 National Print Museum
3 Windmill Lane Recording Studios

ACTIVITIES
4 City Kayaking

SLEEPING
5 Anantara The Marker
6 Beckett Locke
7 Gibson Hotel
8 Mayson

EATING
9 Allta
10 Bites by Kwanghi
11 Charlotte Quay
12 Juniors Deli & Cafe
13 Nutbutter
see 12 Old Spot
14 Osteria Lucio
see 8 Ryleigh's Rooftop Steakhouse

ENTERTAINMENT
15 3 Arena
16 Bord Gáis Energy Theatre

GIGS & GAMES

The area is home to standout venues.

The **Bord Gáis Energy Theatre** (by Libeskind) is a striking glass-and-steel space hosting everything from opera to blockbuster musicals – its forecourt is best seen at dusk.

The **3 Arena** is Dublin's biggest indoor venue, drawing global stars including Billie Eilish, the Doobie Brothers and Camila Cabello.

Just south of the canal in swanky Dublin 4, the **Aviva Stadium** rises like a gleaming shell, hosting Irish rugby, football and concerts.

Buy tickets via fai.ie or irishrugby.ie, and gig tickets via ticketmaster.ie.

a unique angle on the riverside buildings on your way. The guided tours last around two hours, and at least 90 minutes are spent on the water, where you'll paddle underneath the Ha'penny and O'Connell bridges.

For something special, book the **Music Under the Bridges** tour, where musicians park up on stage boats under the bridges to perform music and spoken-word pieces while you bob around on the water.

Lighthouse Keeper
A seaside stroll

One of the city's most rewarding walks is a stroll along the Great South Wall to the **Poolbeg Lighthouse**, the stumpy red tower visible in the middle of Dublin Bay. The lighthouse dates from 1768, but it was redesigned and rebuilt in 1820. To get here, take the 47 bus from the city centre to Ringsend and then make your way past the power station to the start of the wall (it's about 1km).

It's not an especially long walk out to the lighthouse – about 800m or so – but it will give you a stunning view of the bay and the city behind you. It's best enjoyed just before sunset on a summer's evening.

BEGGARS BUSH BARRACKS

The National Print Museum is housed in the former Beggars Bush Barracks, a handsome red-brick complex built in 1827. During the Easter Rising of 1916, rebels famously overlooked the lightly defended barracks, a missed tactical opportunity.

In 1922 it became the first military barracks formally handed over to the Irish Free State following the treaty that ended hostilities (and led to the establishment of Northern Ireland). Just months later, as the country descended into Civil War, it was where Erskine Childers, an anti-Treaty leader, was executed for possessing a pistol – an irony not lost on history, as the weapon had been a gift from Michael Collins, leader of the opposing pro-Treaty forces.

Poolbeg Lighthouse (p101)

Extra, Extra!
The history of print

You don't need to be a printing buff to enjoy the **National Print Museum** *(nationalprintmuseum.ie; free, guided tours €6)* – this quirky gem offers a relaxed, engaging introduction to Ireland's (surprisingly fascinating) printing history. The museum is filled with still-working antique presses, and the air hums with the scents of ink and metal.

A highlight is the personalised guided tours, usually led by members of the Chapel – a group of retired printers who helped found the museum and are full of stories, demonstrations and charm. Tours can be tailored to your interests; history lovers, for instance, can hear about the struggles of the rebels to print the 1916 Proclamation.

There are also hands-on craft workshops for adults and children, covering everything from calligraphy to wood-type poster printing – perfect for anyone keen to get inky.

EATING IN THE DOCKLANDS: OUR PICKS

Nutbutter: Vegan-friendly cafe in Grand Canal Dock with massive salads, tacos and a great breakfast menu. *11.30am-9.30pm* €€

Allta: A chic, industrial space, home to one of Dublin's best restaurants, serving inventive meat and fish dishes. *12.30pm-midnight Thu-Sat, from 5pm Wed* €€€

Juniors Deli & Cafe: Delicious food and a buzzing atmosphere. *8.30-10.30am, noon-2.30pm & 5.30-10pm Mon-Fri, 11am-3pm & 5.30-10pm Sat, 11am-3.30pm Sun* €€

Osteria Lucio: Top-quality Italian fare from Ross Lewis, co-owner of Chapter One (p88). *5-9.30pm Wed & Fri-Sun, noon-2.30pm & 5-9.30pm Thu* €€

Old Spot: A gorgeous gastro-pub that does an excellent Sunday roast. Bookings essential. *noon-3pm & 5-9.30pm Tue-Sat, to 8pm Sun* €€

Bites by Kwanghi: A bright restaurant serving Asian street food with a contemporary twist. *noon-3pm & 5-9.30pm Mon-Fri, 2-9pm Sat* €€

Ryleigh's Rooftop Steakhouse: This place serves more than steak, with a view. *7-11am, noon-3pm & 5-10pm Mon-Fri, from 11am Sat & Sun* €€

Charlotte Quay: A lively restaurant for cocktails and beautiful plates of food in Grand Canal Dock. *4-11pm Tue, noon-11.30pm Wed-Sat, 1-9pm Sun* €€

The Northern Suburbs

BEACHES AND STADIUMS

Dublin's city centre might be compact, but just beyond what locals call 'town' lies a different side of the city entirely. You don't have to go far – a short train ride lands you in Howth, where you can stroll through a charming seaside village or follow a clifftop trail with sweeping views back towards the city.

If that sounds like too much effort, you can still get a breath of fresh air without leaving the city. In Glasnevin, the National Botanic Gardens are gorgeous – and only a short hop away from Ireland's national cemetery, while the Phoenix Park is Dublin's largest green lung. And when evening falls, head for Phibsborough – a once-sleepy neighbourhood that now buzzes with bars, restaurants and creative energy.

Dublin's Green Lung
Bucolic bliss

Phoenix Park is one of the largest enclosed city parks in the world – and stepping through the pillared gates on Parkgate St, you'd never guess you were still in Dublin. Within minutes, the hum of traffic fades, replaced by birdsong, blooming flowerbeds and sightings of the park's best-loved residents, a herd of fallow deer. Whatever you do, don't try to feed them.

Another notable resident is the Irish president, who lives in the elegant white **Áras an Uachtaráin** *(president.ie; tour only)*, a Palladian mansion that served as inspiration for James Hoban's White House in Washington, DC. Free tours run at weekends – just grab a ticket from the **Phoenix Park Visitor Centre** *(phoenixpark.ie; free)*.

GETTING AROUND

The **DART** *(irishrail.ie)* suburban train gets you to Howth in around 30 minutes from the city centre. For the Phoenix Park, hop on the Luas Red line and get off at the Museum stop – it's only a short walk to the Parkgate St entrance from there. For Glasnevin and Phibsborough, your best is the bus – there are multiple routes from the city centre.

☑ TOP TIP

If you're heading out for a hike, make sure you're prepared for all weather. The skies can shift from glorious blue to dark grey within a matter of minutes, so bring a rain jacket, even if it's sunny.

EATING IN THE NORTHERN SUBURBS: OUR PICKS

Shouk: Top-notch Middle Eastern food at a great price; the platters are made for sharing. *noon-10pm Wed-Sun €*

Baily Bites @ Kish: A strong contender for best fish and chips in Dublin. Expect fresh catch right out of the sea. *10am-5pm Mon-Fri, to 5.30pm Sat €*

Eatyard: A rotating list of excellent food vendors at the back of the Bernard Shaw pub. Top notch. *noon-10pm Thu-Sun €*

Badam: A 14-seater spot beneath the railway tracks that serves the best Indian/Nepalese food in town. Reservations essential. *4-11pm Mon & Wed-Fri, 12.30-11pm Sat & Sun €*

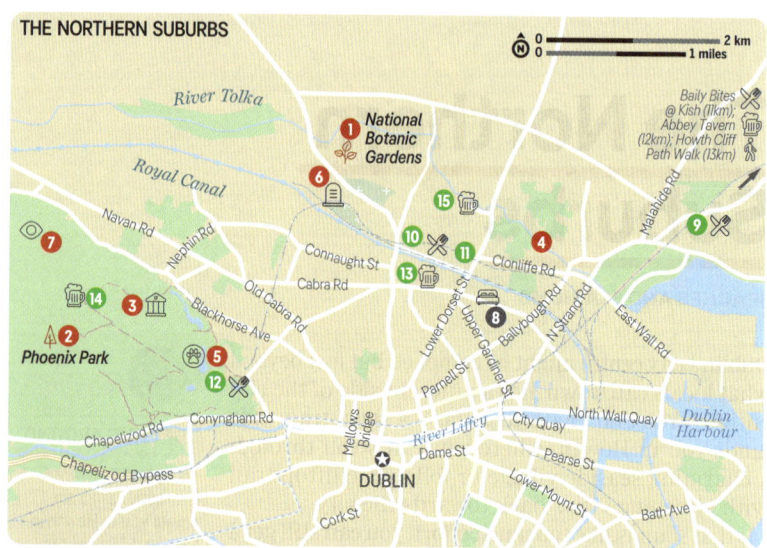

THE NORTHERN SUBURBS

HIGHLIGHTS
1. National Botanic Gardens
2. Phoenix Park

SIGHTS
3. Áras an Uachtaráin
4. Croke Park Stadium & Museum
5. Dublin Zoo
6. Glasnevin Cemetery
7. Phoenix Park Visitor Centre

SLEEPING
8. Croke Park Hotel

EATING
9. Badam
10. Eatyard
see 7 Phoenix Cafe
11. Shouk
12. Victorian Tea Rooms

DRINKING & NIGHTLIFE
13. Doyle's Corner
14. Hole in the Wall
15. John Kavanagh's

> **EATING IN PHOENIX PARK**
>
> Of the park's two **cafes** (phoenixparkcafe.ie), the best known is the **Victorian Tea Rooms**, in a pretty building off Chesterfield Ave, near the zoo. It serves the kind of fare you crave halfway through a long walk: homemade cakes, giant cookies and bowls of soup.
>
> The **Phoenix Cafe** in the visitor centre (p103) isn't as pretty, but has an excellent menu of fresh salads and scones with homemade jam. On sunny days you can eat alfresco.

Hear an unexpected roar or trumpet? That's the nearby **Dublin Zoo** (dublinzoo.ie; adult/child €25/19.50) – one of the oldest in the world, and another of the park's beloved institutions.

Dublin's Graveyard

More than a million souls

The tombstones at **Glasnevin Cemetery** (dctrust.ie; tours €15), Ireland's largest burial site, form a roll call of Irish history. Daniel O'Connell, who founded the cemetery in 1832 to allow people of all faiths a dignified burial, lies here, along with Charles Stewart Parnell and many other political and cultural figures.

The best way to explore it is on a **guided tour** – full of insight, humour and the occasional ghost story – through what locals jokingly call 'Croak Park'. Don't miss the **Glasnevin Cemetery Museum**, or the chance to climb **O'Connell Tower** for sweeping views across the city.

Botanical Delights

Garden central

If you want to stop and smell the roses, there's no better place than the **National Botanic Gardens** (botanicgardens.ie; free). While there are acres of pretty flowers and plants outside, a highlight is the series of curvilinear glasshouses, dating from 1843 to 1869 and created by Richard Turner, who was also responsible for the glasshouse at Belfast's Botanic Gardens (p516) and the Palm House in London's Kew Gardens. Within these Victorian masterpieces, you'll find the latest in botanical technology, including a series of computer-controlled climates reproducing environments from different parts of the world.

If you're visiting from Glasnevin Cemetery, a little gate links the two places from the northeastern part of the cemetery.

Stadium Tour
Home of the GAA

For fans of the GAA (Gaelic Athletic Association), **Croke Park Stadium** (crokepark.ie; guided tours from adult/child €18/12) is sacred ground. But even if you're not a GAA fan, a tour of the stadium is excellent, particularly the moment when you can run through the tunnel and out towards the pitch. Take it up a notch by booking a walk on the **Skyline** (€24) for a guided tour along the top of the building's roof. You can also do this at dusk for an even better view of the city at sunset.

There's also the **GAA Museum** (adult/child €10/8), where you can learn about the history and importance of Gaelic sports in Ireland. Test your skills in the Interactive Games Zone to see what you're like with a hurley (flat ashen stick used in the game of hurling).

Hilltop Hike
Walking Howth's headland

Tidily positioned at the foot of a bulbous peninsula, the pretty port village of **Howth** (the name rhymes with 'both') is a major fishing centre, a yachting harbour and one of the most sought-after addresses in town.

A Howth highlight is the 6km looped **cliff path walk** around the headland that begins at Howth DART station. From here, follow the green arrow along the promenade and then turn right onto the cliff path. The walk takes you up to the summit (from which there are gorgeous views over the grassy slopes to the sea) before looping back down again. There are other, longer walks marked by blue, red and purple arrows (which partially overlap the green route) that lead to the Baily Lighthouse and back over rougher, mountainous terrain.

And if you're visiting at the weekend, when you're done you can pop into **Howth Market** (howthmarket.ie) on Saturdays and Sundays (from 9am to 6pm) for a coffee and a bun.

A DESIRABLE ADDRESS

A quick glance at Howth – perched at the foot of a headland that juts into the Irish Sea – makes it clear why this is one of Dublin's most desirable places to live.

Over the past century, countless notable figures have called it home. WB Yeats lived here in the 1890s and wrote 'The Lake Isle of Innisfree' while gazing across the water, while James Joyce immortalised Howth in *Ulysses* and proposed to Nora Barnacle on Howth Head in 1904.

In more recent decades, the area has drawn residents such as Dolores O'Riordan, Enya and Brendan Gleeson. Yet even within Howth, there's a quiet hierarchy – and as locals will remind you, the higher up the hill you live, the fancier the view and the address.

 DRINKING IN THE NORTHERN SUBURBS: OUR PICKS

| **John Kavanagh's**: One of Dublin's most famous bars backs on to Glasnevin Cemetery. 10.30am-11.30pm Mon-Thu, to midnight Fri & Sat, to 11pm Sun | **Hole in the Wall**: Longest pub in Ireland, with cosy snug and great bar food. On the edge of Phoenix Park. noon-11.30pm Mon-Thu, to 12.30am Fri & Sat, 11am-11.30pm Sun | **Abbey Tavern**: An old-style pub in Howth, with live music out the back. 12.30-11.30pm Mon-Thu, to 12.30am Fri & Sat, to 11pm Sun | **Doyle's Corner**: Popular pub in Phibsborough that's owned by Gavin James. 3-11.30pm Mon-Wed, from 12.30pm Thu, 12.30pm-12.30am Fri & Sat, to 11pm Sun |

The Southern Suburbs

COASTAL DIPS AND ART DECO CINEMA

GETTING AROUND

For Sandycove and Dalkey, hop on the **DART** *(irishrail.ie)* and you'll be there in around 40 minutes. Rathmines is on a bunch of bus routes that will deposit you in the heart of the action in around 15 minutes.

Dublin's southern suburbs stretch out from the edge of the city centre into a series of village-life neighbourhoods that are among the city's most desirable places to live. Rathmines – just beyond the Grand Canal – has graduated from student burg to place for professionals on the move, its pretty red-brick terraces and Georgian standalones now as pricey as those in adjoining Ranelagh, which has always been fancy. There are no sights as such here, but Dublin's most beautiful cinema is located in the middle of Rathmines village.

The suburban sprawl extends southward down to the seaside villages of Sandycove and Dalkey, where you can take a dip in the sea, visit a Joycean Martello tower and even spot a celebrity or two.

A Night at the Movies
Art deco classic

The **Stella** *(stellacinemas.ie; from €21)* in Rathmines is Dublin's most elegant cinema – a beautifully restored art deco gem that first opened in 1923. While the films have moved on from silent classics starring Clara Bow and Rudolph Valentino, the cinema itself remains a throwback to a more glamorous age. Moviegoers sink into plush armchairs and velvet couches, complete with little tables for cocktails and snacks – delivered straight to your seat. For an extra splash of style, head upstairs to the **Stella Cocktail Club** for a pre-film drink.

☑ **TOP TIP**

If you're planning an evening at the Stella Cinema, prebook your seats to get the best selection; you can also prebook your drinks and snacks from their (pretty) extensive menu.

On the Coast
Sea walks

Just south of Sandycove is **Dalkey,** a well-to-do enclave favoured by resident celebrities such as Bono and Enya; during the Covid-19 lockdown, Matt Damon was happily stuck here for months.

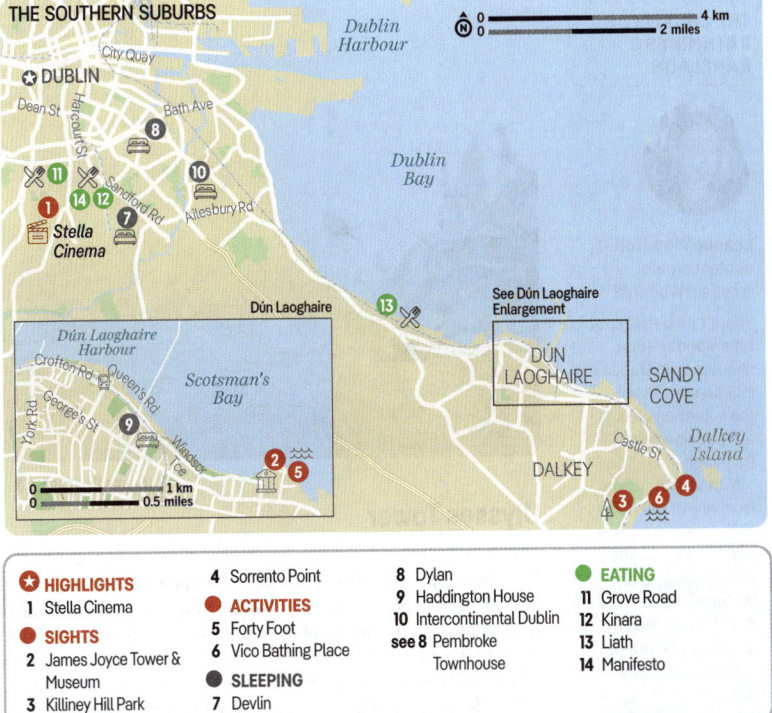

- ★ **HIGHLIGHTS**
- 1 Stella Cinema
- ● **SIGHTS**
- 2 James Joyce Tower & Museum
- 3 Killiney Hill Park
- 4 Sorrento Point
- ● **ACTIVITIES**
- 5 Forty Foot
- 6 Vico Bathing Place
- ● **SLEEPING**
- 7 Devlin
- 8 Dylan
- 9 Haddington House
- 10 Intercontinental Dublin
- see 8 Pembroke Townhouse
- ● **EATING**
- 11 Grove Road
- 12 Kinara
- 13 Liath
- 14 Manifesto

Begin your exploration in the village, wandering between the chichi food stores and bookshops before heading out to the coast and the small park at **Sorrento Point**, where you'll get some great views.

If you want to head off on a longer walk (and you should), make your way along the Vico Rd, stopping for a dip at the **Vico Bathing Place**, where you'll see swimmers almost every day of the year. Climb the 'Cat's Ladder' steps and you'll soon be in **Killiney Hill Park**, where you can stand on the top of the Pyramid of Dublin and feel like the king of the world.

Dive In

Cold-water dip

These days, it feels like half of Dublin has a sea-swimming habit and the dry robe to match. One of the most popular spots for a dip is the **Forty Foot** *(free)* in the south Dublin suburb of **Sandycove**. This open-air seawater bathing pool is usually full of eager swimmers, but be warned: the waves can get fairly wild on windy days, and you'll likely have to wait your turn when the sun is shining. Sharon Horgan shot a scene from *Bad Sisters* here.

THE FORTY FOOT GENTLEMEN

The 40th Regiment of Foot, a British Army unit once stationed in Sandycove, would prove their toughness by leaping naked into the cold natural pool.

The Forty Foot became a local institution, famed for its bracing year-round swims and hardy regulars. It remained men-only until the 1970s, when women could join on one condition: that they wear bathing suits. Today, the Forty Foot welcomes everyone brave enough to take the plunge, clothed or not.

THE CHARMS OF RATHMINES & RANELAGH

Leanne Woodfull, content creator
@LeanneWoodfull

There's no better spot for a wander – just minutes from Dublin's city centre – than the suburban bliss of Rathmines and Ranelagh.

With a cuppa-to-go from one of the many quirky cafes on every corner, you can stroll through streets of Victorian red-brick that once housed Irish greats like Maureen O'Hara and James Joyce.

The cool kids of Dublin flock to this area for a reason – whether it's endless thrifting along Rathmines Rd, arty hotspots like the **MART Gallery** and the Stella Cinema (p106), or the pocket of award-winning foodie havens in Ranelagh, there's truly something for all tastes, and all budgets.

Forty Foot (p107)

Ulysses Tower
Joyce museum

This Martello tower is where the action begins in Joyce's epic novel *Ulysses* (1922). The tower is the home of Buck Mulligan, who at the end of the chapter heads to the nearby Forty Foot (p107) for a morning swim.

The **museum** *(joycetower.ie; free)* was opened in 1962 by Sylvia Beach, the Paris-based publisher who first dared to put *Ulysses* into print, and has photographs, letters, documents, various editions of Joyce's work and two death masks of Joyce on display.

 EATING IN THE SOUTHERN SUBURBS: OUR PICKS

Grove Road: This brunch and breakfast spot in Rathmines serves one of the best avo toasts in town. *8am-4pm Mon-Fri, from 9am Sat, from 9.30am Sun* €€	**Manifesto**: Classic pizzeria in Rathmines, with expertly charred pizzas and an inventive wine list. *5-10pm* €€	**Kinara**: Impeccable Pakistani restaurant in Ranelagh serving unusual curries. *5-11pm daily, plus noon-3pm Thu & Fri, 1-5pm Sun* €€	**Liath**: You'll need to book well in advance to secure a seat at this two-Michelin-star restaurant in Blackrock Market. *7.30-9.30pm Wed-Sat, plus 1-4pm Sat* €€€

Places We Love to Stay

€ Budget €€ Midrange €€€ Top End

Trinity College & Georgian Dublin MAP p56

Brooks Hotel €€ A boutique, family-run hotel with huge beds and a cosy residents' lounge.

Marlin €€ The rooms are small but functional in this 2019-opened hotel, and the prices are great.

The Dean €€ Funky rooms, Smeg fridges and a hopping rooftop bar – light sleepers, beware.

Staunton's on the Green €€ This handsome Georgian house has charming bedrooms and a beautiful garden.

Wren Urban Nest €€ With eco-credentials and calming decor, this is a great base for exploring the neighbourhood.

Number 31 €€ The former home of modernist architect Sam Stephenson, with elegant rooms and a cool sunken lounge.

Citizen M €€ The trendy hotel chain debuted in Ireland in 2025; located across from St Patrick's Cathedral.

Alex €€ A beautifully sleek hotel where gorgeous design meets comfort. The lobby has a cool co-working space.

Wilder Townhouse €€ Set in a striking red-brick building, the Wilder has a delightfully quirky vibe.

Chancery €€€ Quietly elegant hotel that blends modern comfort with low-key, luxe vibes.

Shelbourne €€€ Dublin's most famous hotel was founded in 1824 and is the height of old-school luxury.

Merrion €€€ A resplendent five-star hotel in a terrace of beautifully restored Georgian townhouses.

Westbury Hotel €€€ Pricey Dublin stalwart, but it's worth it for the sheer quality. Some suites have terraces.

Temple Bar MAP p71

Kinlay House € This huge hostel has basic rooms in a former boarding house.

Clarence Hotel €€ Refurbished in 2022, this slick hotel has a great cocktail bar.

Morgan Hotel €€ A hotel right in the middle of the action; some rooms have balconies.

Kilmainham & the Liberties MAP p79

Aloft Dublin City €€ This sleek hotel is right by the Teeling Distillery (p83) and has a great rooftop bar.

Hyatt Centric €€ Clean, modern rooms close to St Patrick's Cathedral (p77).

StayCity Aparthotels €€ A range of one- and two-bedroom apartments; ideal if you're travelling in a group.

O'Connell St & the North City Centre MAP p87

Latroupe Jacob's Inn € A modern hostel with pod-style bunks and private rooms.

Ruby Molly €€ A 'lean luxury' hotel with elegantly minimalist rooms and fabulous amenities.

Address Connolly €€ Snazzy rooms and a tiny rooftop lounge beside Connolly Station.

Point A €€ This 'budget boutique' hotel has slick rooms and a great bar.

Smithfield & Stoneybatter MAP p96

Generator Hostel € A funky, bright hostel with comfy dorms and a lively social scene.

Hendrick €€ Cosy rooms and interior street art in a great location in Smithfield.

Docklands MAP p101

Gibson Hotel €€ By the 3 Arena (p101), this modern hotel is ideal for gigs or people taking the ferry.

Mayson €€ Uber-cool boutique hotel on the river, with a tiny pool and nifty rooftop bar.

Beckett Locke €€ Chic suites and apartments with full kitchens and working areas.

Anantara The Marker €€€ This swish five-star rebranded in 2023 and is still the hotel of note in the area.

Northern Suburbs MAP p104

Croke Park Hotel €€ Just over the road from the stadium, with a lovely big terrace for alfresco dining.

Portmarnock Hotel & Golf Links €€ Beachfront hotel with huge rooms and a sensational golf course.

Southern Suburbs MAP p107

Haddington House €€ A boutique hotel on the seafront in Dún Laoghaire, with a top-notch restaurant.

Devlin €€ Sister property to the Dean in Ranelagh, with small but stylish rooms and a rooftop bar.

Pembroke Townhouse €€ An elegant boutique hotel within walking distance of town.

Dylan €€ A wonderfully quirky hotel with a buzzy bar and terrace that's a hit on sunny days.

Intercontinental Dublin €€€ This seriously plush hotel makes for a decadent getaway and has a great spa to boot.

Left: Wicklow Way (p117); right: horse race, Kildare (p128)

Researched by
Fionn Davenport

Wicklow & Kildare

HIGH TRAILS AND FAST HORSES

In two wild counties near Dublin, hike rugged mountain trails, spot soaring eagles and watch racehorses roam across wide open paddocks.

They may sit side by side on Dublin's doorstep, but the counties of Wicklow and Kildare offer two very different kinds of adventure: one climbs into wild mountains; the other gallops across lush plains. What they do have in common is that both sit firmly in Dublin's ever-expanding commuter belt.

To the south, Wicklow, aka the 'Garden of Ireland', does drama well. The Wicklow Mountains carve a bold line through the east, their granite slopes cloaked in heather and bracken, hiding glacial valleys, misty lakes and the stunning 6th-century monastic site at Glendalough – more film set than spiritual ruin.

Skirting the mountains are the grand estates of the 18th-century one percenters – Powerscourt, Russborough and Killruddery – complete with Palladian mansions and manicured gardens. Along the coast, Bray mixes classic seaside charm with a spectacular cliff walk, while inland, Avondale Forest Park's treetop walkway brings nature to new heights.

Head west, and you're in Kildare – flat, fertile and built for speed. Known as the 'Thoroughbred County', it's home to world-renowned stud farms and generations of champion racehorses, with two visitable studs providing a glimpse into this fast-paced world. But Kildare isn't all horsepower. Ireland's only motor-racing track is here, while the Bog of Allen is a conservation hub and a quiet, elemental landscape that has deep roots in Irish natural history.

THE MAIN AREAS

WICKLOW MOUNTAINS NATIONAL PARK
Gorgeous scenery and an ancient monastic settlement. **p114**

KILDARE & HORSE COUNTRY
Heartland of Irish horse racing. **p128**

THE GUIDE

WICKLOW & KILDARE

Kildare & Horse Country, p128
Ireland's most famous racecourse sits amid a lush hinterland of horse paddocks and stud farms.

Wicklow Mountains National Park, p114
Scenic granite hills harbour the cradle of Irish Christianity, as well as aristocratic estates and hiking trails galore.

Find Your Way

Bring your walking boots for Wicklow and Kildare – even the region's largest town, Bray, is easily walkable (there are no cities here). Buses and trains cover longer distances, though you'll need a car in more remote areas.

CAR
For motorists, the M4, M7 and M11 motorways provide fast and easy access to all parts of the region, except for the Wicklow Mountains and the Bog of Allen, where narrow, winding roads are the norm.

BUS & TRAIN
Both Wicklow and Kildare are easily accessed from Dublin. Frequent trains (transportforireland.ie) and **Bus Éireann** buses run to Bray, Greystones, Wicklow town, Kildare town and Newbridge, while the specialist **St Kevins Bus** (glendaloughbus.com) runs daily from Dublin to Glendalough.

Powerscourt Estate (p117)

Plan Your Time

The main sights in both Wicklow and Kildare lie within easy day-trip distance of Dublin and are well served by bus and train.

Pressed for Time

● In the morning, head straight for **Glendalough** (p119), and after a wander around the impressive ruins of this ancient monastic site, take a walk to the **Upper Lake** (p120) and back. If you got to Glendalough by bus, extend your walk to **Camaderry** (p120) before catching the return bus to Dublin. If you're driving, you'll have time in the afternoon for a visit to the gorgeous gardens at **Powerscourt** (p117).

Three Days to Explore

● If your trip doesn't coincide with a race day at the **Curragh** (p128), you can meet some expensive stallions at either the **Irish National Stud** (p130) or **Kildangan Stud** (p131). Devote a day to **Glendalough** (p119) and **Powerscourt** (p117), and another to visiting Avondale's **treetop walkway** (p122) and **Avoca Handweavers** (p125).

SEASONAL HIGHLIGHTS

SPRING
The first classic race of the horse-racing season kicks off at the Curragh with the **Irish 2000 Guineas** (p128) at the end of May.

SUMMER
Bray's **Air Display** (p125; early August) has aerobatic manoeuvres, food stalls, a fun fair, music and helicopter flights.

AUTUMN
Autumn colours put on a show, notably at **Mt Usher Gardens** (p125), **Kilmacurragh Botanic Gardens** (p125) and **Powerscourt** (p117).

WINTER
Do your Christmas shopping at **Avoca Handweavers** (p125). The gardens at **Powerscourt** (p117) still look great.

Wicklow Mountains National Park

HIKING TRAILS | MONASTIC HERITAGE | GEORGIAN MANSION

As you cross into Wicklow from Dublin, the urban sprawl gives way to wide-open moors, rolling bogland and lonely corrie (glacial) lakes tucked into the hills. From Rathfarnham, the Military Road wends its way for 40km through the spine of the Wicklow Mountains National Park – Ireland's largest at 13,000 hectares. This scenic drive is all cinematic sweeps of heather, bog and stone, along a road carved out in the early 1800s by the British, who were on the hunt for Irish rebels.

Tucked deep within this rugged beauty is Glendalough, a 6th-century monastic site turned visitor magnet. Medieval monks came here for isolation. Today, it's pilgrims of a different kind – hikers, history buffs and Instagrammers – who make the journey.

Yet despite its popularity, Wicklow still has plenty of off-grid opportunities. Lace up and tackle all or parts of the Wicklow Way, a 128km hiking trail that winds through forests, valleys and peaks to provide a front-row seat to some of the country's most epic natural scenery.

GETTING AROUND

Public transport in the Wicklow Mountains is thin on the ground, apart from **St Kevins Bus** (glendaloughbus.com), which runs twice daily (11am and 6pm; 90 min) from **St Stephen's Green** in Dublin via Bray, Kilmacanogue, Roundwood and Laragh. Day-trip timings give you five hours at Glendalough, which is enough time to explore the monastic site, have lunch and enjoy a hike to the Upper Lake.

☑ TOP TIP

The **National Park Information Office** is near the Upper Lake car park in Glendalough. The centre has info on wildlife, and a free map – *The Walking Trails of Glendalough*. Don't confuse it with the **Glendalough Visitor Centre**, which is beside the lower car park and deals only with the monastic site.

Drive the Military Road
Scenic mountain route

The **Military Road** (now the R115), built in the early 1800s by the British army to suppress Irish rebels after the 1798 Rising, winds through the remote heart of the Wicklow Mountains and offers breathtaking views.

From Rathfarnham, still within Dublin city's limits, the road provides easy access to the high moors, rounded granite hills and pretty mountain lakes that dominate the scenery. Look out for parking places that mark the starting points for many fine walks.

If you're coming from Enniskerry, join the road at Glencree and follow it south through the Sally Gap and Glenmacnass Valley to Laragh. At the Sally Gap, detour east to a spectacular

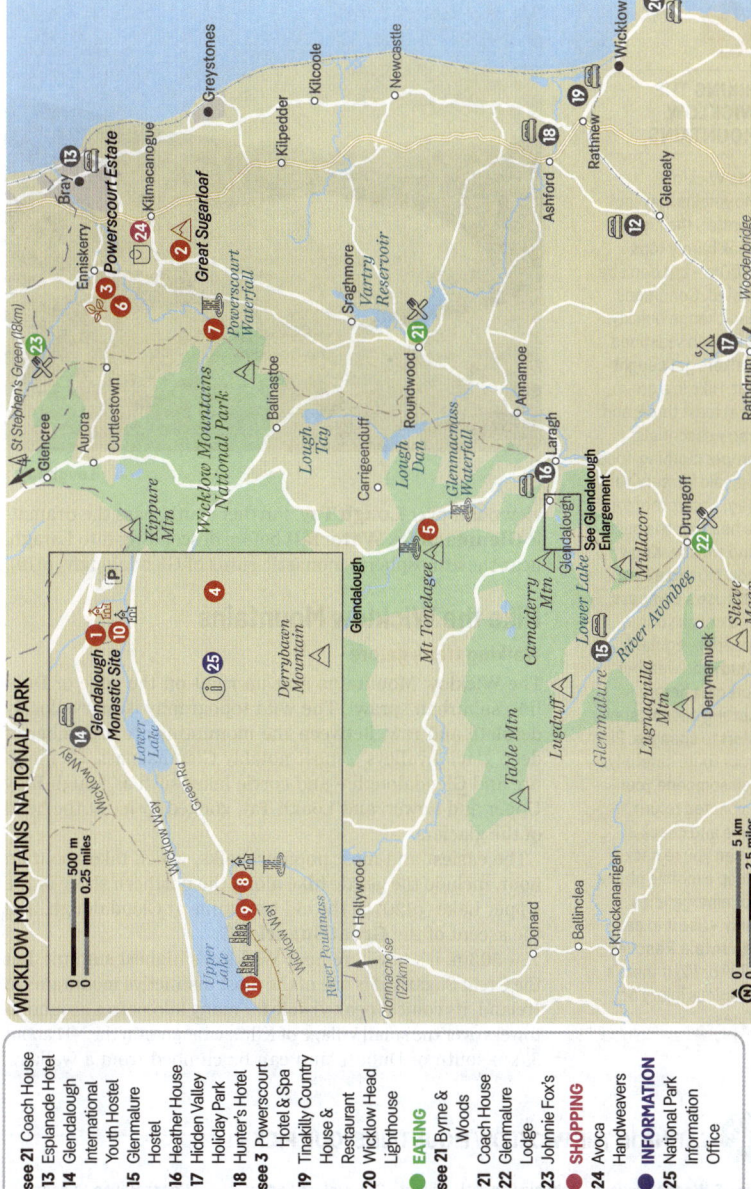

WICKLOW & KILDARE WICKLOW MOUNTAINS NATIONAL PARK

HIGHLIGHTS
1. Glendalough Monastic Site
2. Great Sugarloaf
3. Powerscourt Estate

SIGHTS
- see 1 Cathedral of St Peter & St Paul
4. Glendalough Visitor Centre
5. Glenmacnass Waterfall
6. Powerscourt Distillery
7. Powerscourt Waterfall
- see 1 Priest's House
8. Reefert Church
- see 1 Round Tower
- see 11 St Kevin's Bed
9. St Kevin's Cell
10. St Kevin's Kitchen
11. Teampall na Skellig

ACTIVITIES
- see 3 Powerscourt Golf Club

SLEEPING
12. Ballyknocken House & Cookery School
- see 21 Coach House
13. Esplanade Hotel
14. Glendalough International Youth Hostel
15. Glenmalure Hostel
16. Heather House
17. Hidden Valley Holiday Park
18. Hunter's Hotel
- see 3 Powerscourt Hotel & Spa
19. Tinakilly Country House & Restaurant
20. Wicklow Head Lighthouse

EATING
- see 21 Byrne & Woods
21. Coach House
22. Glenmalure Lodge
23. Johnnie Fox's

SHOPPING
24. Avoca Handweavers

INFORMATION
25. National Park Information Office

Lough Tay

HIKING THE WICKLOW MOUNTAINS

The Wicklow Mountains may look gentle – the highest peak barely tops 1000m – but don't be fooled. Conditions can change quickly, and even seasoned walkers get caught out. Hike in a group of at least three, and carry essentials: proper clothing, food, first aid kit, survival bag, waterproof torch (a headlamp is best) and whistle. Know how to read a map and use a compass, and check your location regularly. Study the weather forecast before setting out and stay alert to changes. Plan your route carefully, tell someone your expected return time and check in when you're back. Keep a mobile phone for emergencies only – use it to call **Mountain Rescue** *(999 or 112)* if there's a serious injury or illness.

viewpoint over **Lough Tay**. Further south, pass the dramatic **Glenmacnass Waterfall** before descending into Laragh, near the atmospheric monastic ruins of Glendalough (p119).

Hike the Wicklow Mountains

Walking trails galore

The Wicklow Mountains rear up right on the edge of Dublin's suburban sprawl. The wild topography is marvellously desolate and raw. Between the mountains are a number of deep glacial valleys – most notably Glenmacnass, Glenmalure and Glendalough – and corrie lakes such as Lough Bray Upper and Lower, and Lough Tay, gouged by ice at the head of the glaciers.

The easiest and most popular walks, which take about an hour, include the gentle hike along the northern shore of the Upper Lake (p120) to the old lead mine at Glendalough, and the ascent of the **Great Sugarloaf**.

At 503m, it's nowhere near Wicklow's highest summit, but the Great Sugarloaf is one of the most distinctive mountains in Ireland, its conical peak visible for many kilometres around. It towers over the small village of Kilmacanogue, on the N11 about 35km south of Dublin, and can be climbed from a walkers'

EATING IN THE WICKLOW MOUNTAINS: OUR PICKS

Byrne & Woods: Elegant restaurant in an old cottage in Roundwood serving locally sourced dishes and well-chosen wines. *12.30-9pm Thu-Sat, to 8pm Wed & Sun* €€

Johnnie Fox's: Northwest of Enniskerry, this traditional 19th-century pub has a standout seafood menu. *12.30-9.30pm, bar 11am-11.30pm Mon-Thu, to 12.30am Fri & Sat, noon-11pm Sun* €€

Glenmalure Lodge: Hearty all-day pub food includes steak and Guinness pie, lamb stew and a ploughman's lunch. *7.30-10am & noon-9pm, bar 10am-11pm* €€

Coach House: Superb restaurant with a deli and bakery. Inventive takes on the classics, such as beef cheek burgers. *5.30-8.30pm Mon-Tue & Thu, from 1pm Fri, from noon Sat, to 5.30pm Sun* €€

car park on the L1031 minor road (off the R755 road, 7.5km south of Enniskerry). It's a steep but straightforward hike – allow one hour round trip.

You'll find more challenging and less busy terrain on the **Lough Bray Loop** – a 6.6km circuit from the Lough Bray car park on the Military Road – and the route up the 925m Lugnaquilla, the highest summit in the Wicklow Mountains, and for experienced hikers only.

For Lugnaquilla, drive southwest from Laragh over the mountains to Glenmalure. At Drumgoff Bridge, turn right and continue 6km up a narrow road to a car park where multiple trails begin. Just 500m beyond the car park is **Glenmalure Hostel** – a rustic, off-grid 19-bed hideaway with no electricity, no phone, and water coming from a stream only. It's all gas lamps and an open log fire. You can walk up the hidden **Fraughan Rock Glen** west of the car park and continue to the summit of **Lugnaquilla**. Allow six hours for the return trip.

The **Wicklow Way** *(wicklowway.com)* is Ireland's oldest and best-known long-distance hiking trail. The 128km route, from Marlay Park in Dublin to Clonegal in County Carlow, winds through remarkable scenery. It takes about six or seven days, but there are plenty of half- and full-day options along the way, notably the easy 11km from Roundwood to Glendalough.

Explore an Aristocratic Estate

Gorgeous gardens and stunning views

Just 500m south of the village of Enniskerry, the magnificent **Powerscourt Estate** *(powerscourt.com; adult/child €14/5.50)* lies within easy day-tripping distance of Dublin. At its heart is an elegant Georgian mansion, but the real draw is the gorgeous grounds and gardens, and the stunning views towards the Great Sugarloaf mountain.

The 20-hectare landscaped **gardens** are the star attraction, originally laid out in the 1740s but redesigned in the 19th century by Daniel Robinson, one of the foremost horticulturalists of his day. His masterpiece is a magnificent blend of sweeping terraces, elegant statuary, ornamental lakes, secret hollows, rambling walks and walled enclosures replete with more than 200 types of trees and shrubs, all designed to frame the ever-present backdrop of the Great Sugarloaf mountain.

Tickets come with a map laying out 40-minute and hour-long walks around the gardens. Don't miss the exquisite **Japanese Gardens** or the **Pepperpot Tower**, modelled on a 7.5cm-tall pepperpot owned by Lady Wingfield. The **animal cemetery** is the final resting place of the Wingfields' pets and even one of the family's favourite milking cows. Some of the epitaphs are surprisingly personal.

Powerscourt House itself is every bit as grand as the gardens. Though most of it is not open to the public, there's a fine cafe, a small exhibition and several gift and homewares shops to browse.

A 6km drive to a separate part of the estate takes you to the 121m-high **Powerscourt Waterfall** *(adult/child €7.50/3.50)*, the highest waterfall in Ireland. It's at its most impressive after

HISTORY OF POWERSCOURT ESTATE

Powerscourt Estate has existed more or less since 1300, when the LePoer (later anglicised to Power) family built themselves a castle here. In 1603, the property came into the possession of Richard Wingfield, Marshall of Ireland, and his descendants lived here for the next 350 years. In 1730, Georgian wunderkind Richard Cassels was tasked with building a 68-room Palladian mansion around the core of the old castle.

The Wingfields left in the 1950s, after which the house underwent a massive restoration. On the eve of its opening in 1974, a fire gutted the building. The estate was eventually bought by the Slazenger family, who have overseen its second restoration, and the addition of various amenities, including two golf courses and the Powerscourt Hotel.

THE POWER OF AVOCA

In recent decades, Wicklow has earned a reputation as a hub of Irish craft and design, thanks largely to one iconic brand. Founded in 1723, Avoca Handweavers really flourished in the 1920s when the Wynne sisters – Emily, Winifred and Veronica – began creating garments for the British royal family and selling their tweed to Italian designer Elsa Schiaparelli.

Now part of the Aramark retail group, Avoca sells everything from knitwear, textiles and ceramics to toys, homewares and gourmet food, alongside its own bestselling cookbooks. Every product carries a distinctive sense of 'Irishness' that's instantly recognisable – and which has been copied by plenty of other retailers. The **flagship store** is in Kilmacanogue, while the **Powerscourt Estate** (p117) has another popular Avoca outlet complete with cafe.

heavy rain. A nature trail has been laid out around the base of the waterfall – a popular picnic spot – and takes you past giant redwoods, ancient oaks, beech, birch and rowan trees. There are plenty of birds in the vicinity, including the chaffinch, cuckoo, chiffchaff, raven and willow warbler. Walking from the house to the falls is not recommended, as the route lies on narrow roads with no footpath.

Try Local Whiskey
Whiskey experience

Powerscourt has its own **distillery** *(powerscourtdistillery.com; €25)*, which has been producing whiskey under the Fercullen brand since 2018. The tour includes an explanation of the distilling experience (flavoured with plenty of storytelling) and a visit to the warehouse. It's interesting and a bit of fun, but the standout element is the pairing experience *(€45)*. Their whiskies are paired with locally sourced nibbles, from exquisite patés to charcuterie, cheese and homemade biscuits – you'll be amazed at how good they taste with a drop of the cratur.

Tee off at Powerscourt Golf Club
Championship courses

Golfers can choose between two stunning par-72 courses at **Powerscourt Golf Club** *(powerscourtgolfclub.com; green fee from €55)*, both set beneath the shapely peak of the Great Sugarloaf. The **West Course**, with streams and ravines, is slightly tougher than the more scenic **East Course**, which is framed by hedgerows, ancient oaks and beech trees. Club rental and caddies all available.

Walk the Miners' Way
Exploring industrial heritage

The granite rocks on the eastern edge of the Wicklow Mountains are laced with mineralised quartz veins that were once rich in galena and sphalerite. These ores of lead and zinc were mined extensively between 1726 and 1925, leaving the valleys of Glendasan, Glendalough and Glenmalure with a legacy of old mine workings, spoil heaps, rusting machinery and ruined buildings.

The **Miners' Way** is a 17km walking trail that links the main industrial heritage sites in the three glens. It should take around six hours to complete, and has an elevation gain of around 580m. Pick up a map and guide at the Glendalough Visitor Centre.

Round Tower (p120)

TOP EXPERIENCE

Glendalough

Tucked into a narrow valley in the Wicklow Mountains, Glendalough was made to be found slowly. One of Ireland's most important early Christian sites, it's also one of its most beautiful – with stone ruins scattered amid forest and lakes. Despite the crowds, the place exudes an otherworldly calm, and it's easy to see why monks came here in search of solitude and pine-scented silence over 1000 years ago.

Monastic Site

Glendalough was founded in the late 5th century by St Kevin, an early Christian hermit about whom there is lots of folklore.

He came to Glendalough seeking solitude to better commune with God. He settled in a former Bronze Age tomb on the southern shore of the Upper Lake, where he lived for seven years on a near-starvation diet, clothed in animal skins and befriending birds and beasts. Ironically, his retreat soon attracted followers, and over time Glendalough grew into one

DON'T MISS

Upper Lake

Round Tower

St Kevin's Kitchen

Reefert Church

St Kevin's Cell

Cathedral of St Peter & St Paul

Monastery Gatehouse

PRACTICALITIES
- glendalough.ie ● open 24hrs; visitor centre 9.30am-6pm mid-Mar-Oct, to 5pm rest of year ● visitor centre adult/child €5/3 (car parking €4, includes one admission to visitor centre)

CLIMB THE SPINC

One of the most popular waymarked hikes at Glendalough is the **Spinc**, the steep ridge running along the southern flank of the Upper Lake. You can go part of the way and turn back, or complete a circuit of the Upper Lake by following the path down to the old mine workings and returning along the north shore (6km, allow three hours).

TOP TIPS

- The monastic site is free to enter, but you have to pay €4 for the car parks.

- The visitor centre car park is more convenient for the monastic site; the Upper Lake car park is good for picnics, the lake beach and walks.

- At weekends and daily in July and August, the car parks can be full by 11am, so arrive early.

- Despite signs on the approach saying 'cash only', you can pay the fee for the Upper Lake car park by card.

- There is a large free car park by the Woollen Mills south of Laragh village, a 30-minute walk from the monastic site.

of Ireland's great monastic centres, rivaling **Clonmacnoise** by the 9th century.

During the Middle Ages, when Ireland was known as 'the Island of Saints and Scholars', Glendalough became a monastic city catering to thousands of students and teachers. Its success brought repeated Viking raids, and in 1398 English forces from Dublin almost destroyed it.

Though rebuilt in parts, the monastery lingered only until the 17th century. The site is entered through the only surviving **monastery gatehouse** in Ireland.

Round Tower

The imposing 10th-century **Round Tower** is the focus of this early Christian settlement, standing 33m tall and 16m in circumference at the base. The upper storeys and conical roof were reconstructed in 1876.

Cathedral of St Peter & St Paul

The **Cathedral of St Peter & St Paul**, just southeast of the Round Tower, has a 10th-century nave. The chancel and sacristy date from the 12th century. At the centre of the graveyard, to the southwest of the cathedral, is the **Priest's House**. This odd building dates from 1170 but has been heavily reconstructed. It may have been the location of shrines to St Kevin. Later, during penal times, it became a burial site for local priests – hence the name.

St Kevin's Kitchen

Glendalough's trademark is **St Kevin's Kitchen** or Church, located at the southern edge of the monastic site. This compact structure, with a miniature round-tower-like belfry, protruding sacristy and steep stone roof, is a medieval masterpiece. It was never actually a kitchen, though – it got its nickname because the belfry resembles a kitchen chimney. The oldest parts of the building date from the 11th century; the structure has been remodelled since, but it's still a classic early Irish church.

Upper Lake

While the most fascinating ancient structures lie in the lower part of the valley east of the Lower Lake, the best scenery is found at the Upper Lake.

Reefert Church

The considerable remains of **Reefert Church** sit above the tiny River Poulanass, south of the Upper Lake car park. This small and plain 11th-century Romanesque church has some reassembled arches and walls. Traditionally, Reefert (meaning 'Royal Burial Place') was the burial site of the chiefs of the local O'Toole family.

Climb the steps at the back of the churchyard, follow the path to the west to arrive at the top of a rise overlooking the Upper Lake, where you'll find the scant remains of **St Kevin's Cell**, which is nothing more than a small beehive hut.

Teampall na Skellig & St Kevin's Bed

The original site of St Kevin's settlement, **Teampall na Skellig**, is at the base of the cliffs towering over the southern side of the Upper Lake. The terraced shelf is home to the reconstructed ruins of a church and early graveyard. Rough wattle (woven hazel branches) huts once stood on the raised ground nearby.

Just east of Teampall na Skellig is the 2m-deep artificial cave called **St Kevin's Bed**, said to be where Kevin lived. The earliest human habitation of the cave was long before St Kevin's era, however. There is evidence that people lived in the valley for thousands of years before any monks arrived.

There's no boat service to these sites, so you'll have to settle for gazing at them from the signposted viewpoint on the trail along the lake's north shore.

Upper Lake Walk

The easiest and most popular walk in Glendalough is the gentle trail along the northern shore of the Upper Lake, leading to the abandoned lead and zinc mine workings that date back to 1800. Rather than following the road, which runs some 30m inland, the better option is to hug the lakeshore itself, where the views are far more rewarding. From the Visitor Centre, it's about 2.5km one way – a stroll suitable for most walkers. Those with energy to spare can continue beyond the mine ruins, following the path further into the valley towards its steep, dramatic head.

> **HIKE TO CAMADERRY MOUNTAIN**
>
> For a more challenging adventure, tackle **Camaderry** (700m), which rises behind the valley's northern hills. The unmarked trail begins opposite the entrance to the Upper Lake car park, beside the Wicklow Mountains National Park sign. From here, it's a steep climb through woodland until the path emerges onto open mountain slopes with superb scenery. Continue west along the ridge to reach the summit. The out-and-back covers about 7.5km (four-hour round-trip), and while the going is tough, it's a rewarding hike.

Upper Lake

Beyond Wicklow Mountains National Park

Away from the mountains, Wicklow offers lush landscaped gardens, aristocratic mansions, artisan food shops, woodland walks and coastal scenery.

Places
Avondale p122
Rathdrum p123
Vale of Avoca p125
Bray p125
Greystones p126
Blessington p127

The coastal towns and rolling valleys of eastern Wicklow play second fiddle to the mountains in terms of dramatic scenery, but they are still popular weekend destinations for Dubliners – visit midweek to avoid the crowds. Highlights include the seaside town of Bray, the gardens at Killruddery House, the treetop walkway at Avondale Forest Park and the beautiful Vale of Avoca.

West of the Wicklow Mountains, the landscape is more rural than rugged, especially when heading towards the borders of Kildare and Carlow. The wild moorland terrain gives way to rich pastures, woodland and lakes. The main attraction here is the magnificent Palladian pile at Russborough House, located just outside the town of Blessington.

Avondale

TIME FROM WICKLOW MOUNTAINS NATIONAL PARK: **30MIN**

Soar above the trees

There's a moment, halfway up the spiral tower at **Beyond the Trees** (*beyondthetreesavondale.com; adult/child €18/15*), when you stop and realise you're eye-level with the canopy. This 1.4km treetop walkway, opened in 2023, lets you wander

---

GETTING AROUND

Away from the coast, public transport is sparse, so it's better to have your own wheels.

The M11/N11 runs south from Dublin through the heart of eastern Wicklow, providing easy car and bus (*buseireann.ie*) access from the capital. A railway line (*irishrail.ie*) links Dublin to Bray, Greystones, Wicklow town, Rathdrum and Arklow, continuing to Enniscorthy, Wexford and Rosslare.

To the west of the Wicklow Mountains, the N81 runs from Dublin to Blessington and on to Tullow in County Carlow, with two minor roads linking east across the mountains via the passes of Sally Gap and Wicklow Gap.

high above Avondale Forest, floating above oaks, redwoods, larch and eucalyptus.

Built on slender timber pylons, the gently sloping path features nature displays and play zones for kids. At its heart is a 38m spiral tower with panoramic views across Wicklow's rolling hills, all the way to the distant peak of Lugnaquilla (p117).

Adventurous types can grab a mat and ride down the 90m spiral slide in seconds – it's fast, fun and wildly popular.

The entire experience is wheelchair accessible and ideal for a family day out. Allow 90 minutes for the walk, or more if you want to explore Avondale House nearby. It's forest bathing, Wicklow-style – complete with a zap of adrenaline.

The birthplace of Parnell

The fine Palladian mansion of **Avondale House** *(beyondthetreesavondale.com; adult/child €16/13)*, located at the heart of the Avondale estate, was designed by James Wyatt in 1779, and was the birthplace and Irish headquarters of Charles Stewart Parnell, one of the key figures in the Irish independence movement.

Its highlights include a stunning vermilion-hued library and the American Room, dedicated to Parnell's eponymous grandfather, admiral of the USS *Constitution* during the War of 1812.

Guided tours of the house last around 90 minutes and include the elegant dining room and a wealth of information on Irish history, as well as some poignant details on the domestic lives of the Parnells – Charles had 10 siblings, including sisters Fanny and Anna, who were remarkable in their own right: together, they founded the Ladies Land League to raise money for poor tenant farmers in Ireland.

Rathdrum

TIME FROM WICKLOW MOUNTAINS NATIONAL PARK: **45MIN**

Food festivals and foraging

The lush farmland east and west of the Wicklow Mountains is a source of quality produce for Wicklow's restaurants and a source of pride for locals, celebrated most weekends in **farmers markets** *(loveyourlocalmarket.ie/Wicklow.html)* across the county and annually during the **Taste of Wicklow Food Festival** *(tasteofwicklow.ie)*, held in Wicklow town on the last weekend in June. Along with workshops by celebrity chefs, live music, street food and kids events, the festival offers the chance to sample a wide range of artisan food producers.

If you can't make the festival, opt for a foraging walk with Geraldine Kavanagh of **Wicklow Wild Foods** *(wicklowwildfoods.com; €50)*. She'll take you on a three-hour exploration of the woods at Avondale Forest Park near Rathdrum, introducing you to the edible plants that flourish here – from dandelion and nettles to gorse flowers, meadowsweet, pennywort, wood sorrel, fir tips and wild garlic – finishing with a picnic based around foraged foods. Walks run most weekends from March to October and should be booked in advance.

CHARLES STEWART PARNELL

Between 1880 and 1890, Avondale became synonymous with the struggle for Home Rule (a limited form of self-government whereby Ireland would govern itself while remaining part of the United Kingdom). The movement was led by Charles Stewart Parnell (1846–91), the charismatic lawyer and politician hailed as the 'uncrowned king of Ireland'. His career collapsed in 1890 when fellow MP Captain William O'Shea filed for divorce from his wife, Kitty O'Shea, naming Parnell as co-respondent.

The revelation of Parnell's long affair with Kitty O'Shea scandalised Victorian Ireland, and the powerful Catholic clergy declared him unfit to lead. Though the couple married swiftly once the divorce was final, the damage was irreparable. Parnell resigned, retreated in despair to Avondale, and died there the following year.

THE MEETING OF THE WATERS

Although Avoca is best known these days for its connection to the craft empire that bears its name, in earlier times this darkly wooded valley that begins where the rivers Avonbeg and Avonmore come together was linked to the aptly named 'The Meeting of the Waters,' an 1808 poem by Ireland's national bard, **Thomas Moore** (1779–1852).

Moore celebrated the tranquillity and beauty of the spot: 'There is not in the wide world a valley so sweet / As that vale in whose bosom the bright waters meet.' While it's a sentiment very much in keeping with romantic spirit of the age, it remains a lovely spot to take a deep breath today.

Avoca Handweavers

Sample beers at Wicklow Brewery

Wicklow Brewery *(wicklowbrewery.ie; €20)*, located 7km southeast of Rathdrum, offers engaging hour-long tours of how their preservative-free beers are made using the brewery's own well water. The St Kevin's Red ale and the spicy GingerKnut IPA are standouts. The daily tours include five tastings, often featuring experimental brews. On weekends, you can stop by the brewery's beer hall for a pint; live-music concerts regularly take place amid the kettles and tanks.

Visit Parnell Memorial Park

In the centre of the village, the beautiful **Parnell National Memorial Park** *(free)* is home to ponds, sculptures and winding paths, as well as a bronze statue of Rathdrum-born Irish nationalist hero Charles Stewart Parnell (p123), and a 2016 commemorative stone inscribed with the text of the 1916 Proclamation of the Irish Republic.

The garden of Ireland

County Wicklow earns its nickname, the 'Garden of Ireland', thanks to a climate that's perfectly balanced (never too warm or too cold, never too wet or too dry), creating ideal conditions for an extraordinary range of gardens.

EATING BEYOND THE WICKLOW MOUNTAINS: OUR PICKS

Hollywood Cafe: This former post office was once home to the Irish emigrant who gave the name of his village to Hollywood, USA. *9am-5.30pm Sat-Thu, to 9pm Fri* €

Mickey Finns: Cosy pub in Redcross serving brewery-fresh food, and host to traditional music every Wednesday year-round. *12.30-9.30pm, bar to midnight* €€

Bates Restaurant: Housed in a 1785 coaching inn in Rathdrum, this restaurant is hidden down an alley beside a pub. *6-8.30pm Wed-Fri, 5.30-9.30pm Sat, 12.30-8pm Sun* €€

Strawberry Tree: Elegant organic restaurant at Brook Lodge, 12km southwest of Rathdrum. *6.30-9.30pm Wed-Sun Sep-Jun, daily Jul-Aug* €€€

One of the finest is **Kilmacurragh Botanic Gardens** *(botanicgardens.ie; free)*, located 7km east of Rathdrum. Managed by the National Botanic Gardens, this beautifully informal estate surrounds the ruins of an 18th-century mansion. First planted in 1712 and reimagined in the 19th century under the influence of Irish garden designer William Robinson, Kilmacurragh today features native woodland, hedgerows, wildflower meadows and a Chilean garden, but its most popular attraction is the springtime riot of rhododendrons and azaleas.

Further south, 14km from Rathdrum, **Mount Usher Gardens** *(mountushergardens.ie; €10)* offer a Robinson-style layout along the River Vartry. Tree Trail maps guide visitors to highlights such as the crocus-lined Palm Walk, the Azalea Walk in late May and the vividly hued Maple Walk in autumn. There's also an Avoca-run cafe, and a courtyard of boutique shops selling everything from baked goods and plants to clothes and art.

Vale of Avoca

TIME FROM WICKLOW MOUNTAINS NATIONAL PARK: **30MIN**

A cottage industry

Although today it's a multimillion-euro business (p118) with branches all over Ireland, **Avoca Handweavers** *(avoca.com; free)* began life in 1723 as a cooperative weaving mill in the picture-postcard village that gave it its name. You can wander around the whitewashed cottage-style mill buildings and take a tour of the weaving sheds. There are audio guides for hire (also available in German, French, Spanish and Italian), or you can just chat with the weavers as they work their traditional handlooms.

Bray

TIME FROM WICKLOW MOUNTAINS NATIONAL PARK: **1HR**

Walk the clifftop to Greystones

Beginning at the southern tip of Bray's seafront, a dramatic 7km **Cliff Walk** winds along the coast to Greystones. Originally built in the 1840s during the railway's construction, the trail hugs steep cliffs above the track and offers sweeping sea views, with sightings of porpoises, dolphins and basking sharks a possibility.

Landslides in 2021 forced the closure of the cliff walk, though a public campaign to reopen it continues. It may be accessible again by the time you visit.

If so, walk from Greystones to Bray for a gentler climb towards Bray Head's panoramic lookout. Along the way, keep an eye out for seabirds, kestrels and Ireland's only native reptile, the viviparous lizard.

Return by train – the journey takes around 10 minutes.

Look to the skies

Bray's famous **air show** *(brayairdisplay.com; free)* – Ireland's largest – takes place over two days in late July. Overhead you'll see flyovers and aerobatic manoeuvres, while on the ground at the seafront park on Strand Rd there are artisan

SINÉAD O'CONNOR

Bray's most famous resident was singer Sinéad O'Connor, who lived in **Montebello**, a double-fronted 1860s Victorian house facing the seafront on Strand Rd. She bought the house in 2007 and lived there until 2021.

Although Sinéad spent plenty of time abroad, she always returned to her 'beloved base', which she restored in her own unique way. This included distinctive quoin stones painted in red, yellow and green – in keeping with her passion for all things Jamaican. The singer died in 2023, aged 56; she remains one of the most loved of all Irish performers, with An Post (the Irish postal service) even issuing a stamp in her honour.

THE HAPPY PEAR

The Happy Pear began in 2004 when twins David and Stephen Flynn opened a fruit and veg shop in Greystones, with a mission to make healthy eating fun and accessible. Since then, they've built a plant-based empire, with a cafe, supermarket product range and podcast. Known for their cheerful energy and community ethos, the twins (aka 'hummus Jedward') became Ireland's best-known advocates of plant-based living.

However, their rise faltered in 2022 after claims made on their podcast linking certain foods to reduced breast cancer rates were widely condemned as misleading. A public apology followed, and they pledged to focus on what they know best – creating wholesome, plant-based food infused with their trademark message of positivity and wellness.

food, drink and craft stalls, a fun fair, music concerts, plus opportunities for helicopter flights.

Craft beers and bric-a-brac

Four former fisher's terraces make up the maze of rooms of the **Harbour Bar** *(theharbourbar.ie)*, one of the most beloved bars along Ireland's eastern seaboard. Maybe it's the vintage maritime bric-a-brac, the resident cat, or maybe it's the fine selection of local brews, with plenty of craft beers by local brewers on sale, including County Wickow's Wicklow Wolf (made in Bray), Larkin's Brewing (from nearby Kilcoole), and County Kildare's Whiplash (from Celbridge). The beer garden gets rammed on sunny days; live music plays from Wednesday to Sunday.

The gardens at Killruddery House

Closer to Dublin, **Killruddery House & Gardens** *(killruddery.com; adult/child €10.50/4)*, located just outside Bray, has been the seat of the Brabazon family since 1618. Its 17th-century gardens now sit within a 320-hectare estate that also includes a working organic farm. Stroll beneath ancient beech hedges and through a thriving walled kitchen garden filled with chickens, vegetables and flowering glasshouses. Enjoy farm-to-table dining at the Grain Store restaurant, shop for homemade produce in the farm shop, or grab a wood-fired pizza from the outdoor pizza shed (open Wednesday to Sunday).

Greystones

TIME FROM WICKLOW MOUNTAINS NATIONAL PARK: **30MIN**

Flour power: Scéal Bakery

By the water in Greystones, **Scéal** *(scealbakery.com)* feels more like a slow morning ritual than just a bakery stop. Housed in a bright, breezy space along the marina, this cult-favourite bakery (the name is pronounced *scale* and is the Irish for 'story') serves sourdoughs and outrageously good pastries, including black forest gateau Danishes, wild garlic focaccia, cream-filled brioche and their signature everything bagel croissant. Seasonal drinks such as pink jasmine iced tea or a rich Mont Blanc iced coffee are made for sipping slowly while you people-watch or catch the salty breeze.

EATING IN BRAY & GREYSTONES: OUR PICKS

Dockyard No 8: This cafe in Bray is a fantastic spot for breakfast or lunch; sit outside in good weather. *9am-4.30pm; plus 5.30-9.30pm Thu-Sat €€*

Harbour Bar: Former fishers' cottages in Bray, with maritime charm, great fish and chips, and a buzzing beer garden. *1-11.30pm Mon-Thu, to 12.30am Fri, from noon Sat, to 11pm Sun €€*

Caladh: A stylish seaside brasserie in Greystones serving classic, ingredient-led dishes with a well-priced wine list. *5-11.30pm Wed-Fri, from 10am Sat-Sun €€*

Happy Pear: Half of Greystones seems to meet at this popular cafe, deli and organic grocery. *9am-5pm Mon-Fri, to 6pm Sat & Sun €*

Russborough House

Blessington

TIME FROM WICKLOW MOUNTAINS NATIONAL PARK: **45MIN**

The magnificent Russborough House

Just 5km southwest of Blessington, **Russborough House** *(russborough.ie; adult/child €14/6)* is one of Ireland's finest stately homes, a Palladian palace built for Joseph Leeson (1705–83), later the first Earl of Milltown and, later still, Lord Russborough. The house was built between 1741 and 1751 to the design of Richard Cassels (who also designed Powerscourt Estate, p117), who was at the height of his fame as an architect. Poor old Richard didn't live to see it finished, but the job was well executed by Francis Bindon. The house remained in the Leeson family until 1931.

Since 1952, the house has been owned by the Beit family, who founded the De Beers diamond-mining company and stocked the mansion with a remarkable art collection, including masterpieces by Velázquez, Vermeer, Goya, Rubens and others. It was only after the Beits bought the pile that the drama of the **Russborough Raids** began.

Today, you can tour Russborough's lavishly decorated rooms, admire the remaining art collection, and explore its 80 hectares of grounds, complete with a walled garden, hedge maze and walking trails. The **National Birds of Prey Centre** is also based here, home to owls, hawks and falcons.

But Russborough isn't just about the past. Tucked into the old stables, a thriving creative community now calls the estate home. Visitors can drop into working studios to see Eleanor Swan's delicate ceramics, the expressive ironwork of blacksmith duo Michael Calnan and Gunvor Anhøj, and hand-cut stoneware from Hennessy & Byrne. It's craft with a pulse – and if you're feeling inspired, the **Schoolhouse for Art** *(schoolhouseforart.com)* runs a range of drawing and painting courses rooted in 19th-century French atelier traditions.

RUSSBOROUGH RAIDS

Russborough's renowned art collection has suffered four major robberies. The first came in 1974, when a gang led by English heiress-turned-IRA member **Rose Dugdale** stole 19 priceless works in a raid that made international headlines. Although the paintings were recovered, the heist inspired Dublin gangster **Martin 'The General' Cahill** to strike in 1986. (Cahill was so notorious that John Boorman even made a film about his life, *The General*, starring Brendan Gleeson in the title role.)

Cahill's gang stole 18 works in a bungled raid that left some pieces badly damaged; thankfully, all but two were eventually recovered. Further thefts in 2001 and 2002 prompted major upgrades in security and, ultimately, the decision to sell off much of the collection.

Kildare & Horse Country

WORLD-CLASS STUD FARMS | GEORGIAN HERITAGE | SHOPPING

GETTING AROUND

County Kildare is within easy reach of Dublin via the M4 and M7 motorways, with fast, frequent train and bus services *(transportforireland.ie)* to Newbridge and Kildare town. To visit attractions beyond the main towns – including Kildangan Stud – you'll need a car.

You can walk from Kildare town train station to the Irish National Stud in 30 minutes, and from Newbridge station to Newbridge Silverware in 20, but the Curragh Racecourse requires a taxi or shuttle bus.

County Kildare, known for its lush pastures, remains the beating heart of Ireland's horse-racing world. Its landscape is dotted with elegant stud farms where champion racehorses are bred and trained. Though Dublin's commuter belt now reaches deep into the county, Kildare still retains its rural charm and equestrian prestige.

While not packed with major tourist sights, Kildare makes for a rewarding day-trip. The Curragh, a vast stretch of open grassland between Kildare town and Newbridge, is Ireland's most iconic training ground. Visit early in the morning or at dusk to watch thoroughbreds galloping across it.

At the Irish National Stud and the exclusive Kildangan Stud, visitors can get close to world-class horses. For something different, Castletown House in Celbridge offers Palladian grandeur, while Newbridge's Museum of Style Icons displays film and fashion memorabilia. Kildare Village, with over 120 designer outlets, adds a stylish finish.

A Day at the Races

Home of Irish horse racing

The **Curragh Racecourse** *(curragh.ie; from €20)*, located 3km southwest of central Newbridge, is among the oldest, most famous and most prestigious racecourses in the world. It hosted its first recorded race in 1727 and was inaugurated as an official racing facility in 1868, but it had been a favoured place with the Irish nobility for hawking, hunting and horse racing since at least 1682, and chariot races took place here as long ago as the 3rd century CE. Its name comes from the Gaelic *cuirreach,* meaning 'the place of the running horse'.

Each year sees more than 20 race days, including the five Irish Classics, from the Irish 2000 Guineas in May to the Irish St Leger in September. But race days are not just about the ponies: these are grand social occasions, with people dressed to the nines cramming the terraces, restaurants and champagne

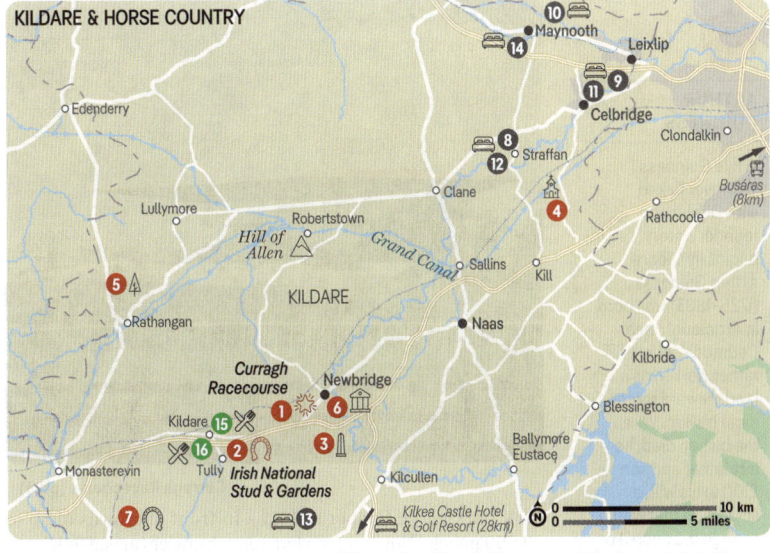

KILDARE & HORSE COUNTRY

- ★ **HIGHLIGHTS**
  1. Curragh Racecourse
  2. Irish National Stud & Gardens
- ● **SIGHTS**
  3. Donnelly's Hollow
  4. Grave of Arthur Guinness
  5. Killinthomas Wood
  6. Museum of Style Icons
  see 6 Newbridge Silverware
- ● **ACTIVITIES**
  7. Kildangan Stud
- ● **SLEEPING**
  8. Barberstown Castle Hotel
  9. Batty Langley Lodge
  10. Carton House
  11. Castletown Gate House
  see 15 Firecastle
  12. K Club
  13. Martinstown House
  14. NUI Maynooth
  see 15 Silken Thomas
- ● **EATING**
  see 6 Domo's Emporium
  15. Firecastle
  see 15 Hartes of Kildare
  16. L'Officina by Dunne & Crescenzi
- ● **SHOPPING**
  see 16 Kildare Village

bars; there are sometimes live music performances after the racing. Even if you're not the horsey type, it's worth experiencing for the passion and atmosphere alone.

The racecourse was redeveloped in 2019 and now sports a magnificent modern grandstand with a vast, floating, copper-coloured roof that reflects the horizontality of the surrounding grasslands. If you can't make a race day, guided **behind-the-scenes tours** (€50) of the racecourse take place on Wednesdays and Thursdays from April to October, during which you get to see the jockeys' changing rooms, the saddling areas and other places that are normally off-limits to the public.

Boxing Lore
A famous boxing bout

In the quiet hollow of the Curragh stands the solitary, unimpressive obelisk of **Donnelly's Hollow** (free) – an unlikely monument marking one of Ireland's most storied sporting victories. It was here that Dan Donnelly, Ireland's greatest bare-knuckle fighter and the 'King of the Curragh', won two decisive bouts against two English champions – Tom Hall in

> ☑ **TOP TIP**
>
> On all race days, free shuttle buses run to the Curragh from Kildare and Newbridge train stations. On the five Irish Classics race weekends – the 1000 Guineas, 2000 Guineas, Derby, Oaks and St Leger – **Bus Éireann Expressway** (expressway.ie) operates a bus from Dublin's **Busàras** (Dublin's main bus station) direct to the racecourse.

ARTHUR GUINNESS

While Guinness is forever linked with Dublin, its founder's story begins in Kildare. Arthur Guinness (1725–1803) was born in Ardclough, near Celbridge, where his father worked as a land steward for the local bishop. When the bishop died, he left father and son £100 in his will, a small sum that would change the course of Irish history.

Arthur used the money to found a brewery in Leixlip in 1755. Four years later, he took advantage of depressed property prices in Dublin to lease the now-famous St James's Gate site for 9000 years (paying £45 a year). Though he built his fortune in Dublin, Arthur and his family are buried at **Oughterard Cemetery**, 10km south of Celbridge.

Curragh Racecourse (p128)

1814 and George Cooper in 1815 – in front of crowds of up to 30,000 people. Not bad for a bar-room brawler turned folk hero.

Legend has it that after Donnelly beat Hall (in 20 minutes), he celebrated for five days in a pub in Kilcullen.

Admire the Art of Breeding

Stallions, fillies and foals

The **Irish National Stud** *(irishnationalstud.ie; adult/child €19/11)*, located 1.5km south of Kildare town, is the big attraction in Kildare, with notable visitors including the late Queen Elizabeth II. Owned and managed by the Irish government, the immaculately kept centre breeds stallions to mate with mares from all over the world. You can wander the paddocks and go eye-to-eye with famous stallions, or take a 45-minute **guided tour** *(four daily, two Oct–Mar; included in admission)*.

The stud was founded in 1900 by Colonel Hall Walker (of Johnnie Walker whisky fame). He was remarkably successful with his horses, but his eccentric breeding techniques relied heavily on astrology: the fate of a foal was decided by its horoscope, and the roofs of the stallion boxes opened on auspicious occasions to reveal the stars above and hopefully influence the horses' fortunes.

EATING IN KILDARE TOWN & HORSE COUNTRY: OUR PICKS

Firecastle: Mouthwatering Kildare town deli serving inventive salads, vegan dishes and black-pudding sausage rolls. *7.30am-6pm Mon-Sat, 8am-5pm Sun* €

Hartes of Kildare: Hotspot Hartes has plush green banquettes, gleaming timber furniture and brilliant gastro-pub fare. *noon-3.45pm & 5-9pm Tue-Thu, to 9.45pm Fri & Sat, noon-8.30pm Sun* €€

Domo's Emporium: Excellent coffee and a tempting breakfast menu at this popular cafe in the Newbridge Silverware showroom. *9am-5.30pm Mon-Sat, from 10am Sun* €€

L'Officina by Dunne & Crescenzi: Kildare Village outpost of the authentic Italian restaurant located in the heart of Dublin. *8.30am-8pm Mon-Fri, from 9.30am Sat-Sun* €€

Guided tours include access to the intensive-care unit for newborn foals. Visit between February and June, and you might even witness a foal being born; otherwise, the foaling unit screens a 10-minute video of the process. Each spring afternoon at 3pm, foals are walked back to their stables. Most of these future geldings will never revisit the Teasing Shed – where stallions are 'encouraged' before 'covering' a mare. The stud's top sires can command insemination fees of up to €120,000.

Other attractions include lakeside walks, a 'fairy trail' for kids and the **Irish Horse Museum** *(included in admission)*, which celebrates championship horses and the history of horse racing. You can also visit Colonel Hall Walker's **Japanese Gardens** *(included in admission)*, considered the best of their kind in Europe. Created between 1906 and 1910, they trace the journey from birth to death through 20 landmarks, including the Tunnel of Ignorance, the Hill of Ambition and the Chair of Old Age.

Meet a Million-Dollar Foal
A sheikh's magnificent folly

About 10km southwest of Kildare town, **Kildangan Stud** *(horsecountry.ie; €35)* stretches across 647 hectares of pristine farmland and cutting-edge facilities, part of Sheikh Mohammed bin Rashid Al Maktoum's Godolphin empire. While his reputation has taken on a sinister edge due to his involvement in the kidnapping and forced imprisonment of one of his daughters and allegations of being complicit in the murder of his brother's wife, his standing in the horse-racing world remains curiously untarnished. On the contrary, he remains one of the most powerful figures in the equine industry.

This powerhouse of the racing world invites visitors behind the scenes with its 'Foal to Fame' experience – a 1½-hour guided tour through immaculate yards, lush paddocks and training grounds. Along the way, there's the chance to meet prized stallions and, in late spring or early summer, glimpse a wobbly-legged newborn foal finding its feet.

Among the resident superstars are Night of Thunder and Bluepoint, two champions turned elite sires, with covering fees of €100,000 and €60,000, respectively – proof that in the world of racing bloodlines, greatness comes at a price. Advance bookings only.

Bluebells & Fairytales
Beautiful woodland walk

A couple of kilometres north of Rathangan, **Killinthomas Wood** is a 70-hectare forest that may well be home to one of the loveliest walks in Ireland. Popular with walkers and nature lovers, it has five waymarked trails totalling around 10km, ranging from short strolls of just over 1km to longer loops just shy of 5km.

Beginning and ending at the car park, each weaves its way through a mix of conifer and broadleaf woodland – the lack

THE SHERGAR TRAGEDY

If Arkle (p132) was Ireland's most beloved steeplechaser, then Shergar is surely the country's most famous horse – though not solely because of what he achieved on the track. His record was remarkable: in 1981, the three-year-old won the Epsom Derby by 10 lengths, the largest margin in history, and followed up with victory in the Irish Derby. Later that year, his owner, the Aga Khan, retired him to stud in Kildare, where he was paraded through Newbridge like a national hero. But on 8 February 1983, Shergar was stolen from Ballymany Stud by a gang believed to be linked to the IRA. Negotiations dragged on for three days before contact ceased. Shergar was never found, and his disappearance remains one of Ireland's great unsolved mysteries.

AWESOME ARKLE

Inside the National Stud's Irish Horse Museum stands the skeleton of Arkle (1957–70), still revered as the greatest steeplechaser of all time. Through the 1960s, he dominated National Hunt racing, winning three consecutive Cheltenham Gold Cups (1964–66), a feat achieved by only four horses in history.

His death in 1970 provoked an extraordinary outpouring of grief: television and radio led with the news, tributes were paid in Dáil Éireann (the lower house of the Republic of Ireland's parliament), and many spoke of him as if he were a head of state. More than half a century on, his Timeform rating of 212 remains unmatched – the ultimate benchmark of greatness.

---

of gradient and plenty of picnic tables means it's the ideal spot for families to get a bit of gentle exercise in gorgeous surroundings. Each of the walks is lovely, but the best of the lot is the **Bluebell Walk,** where each spring and early summer the forest floor transforms into a carpet of bluebells and wild garlic. Killinthomas Wood is 10km north of Kildare town.

Stars of the Silver Screen
Two museums, one big surprise

The otherwise unassuming town of **Newbridge**, just off the M7, is home to one of Ireland's best-known silverware manufacturers – and one of its most surprising museums. Founded in 1934, **Newbridge Silverware** *(newbridgesilverware visitorcentre.com; guided tour adult/child €15/9)* produces a vast array of silver jewellery, silver-plated cutlery, homewares and engravable gifts, all of which are on sale in the onsite store. Thirty-minute guided factory tours take place Monday to Wednesday at 11am and 2.15pm. You can also indulge in afternoon tea at the Silver Restaurant, served, naturally, on Newbridge silverware.

Upstairs, the mood shifts from silver to stardust. The **Museum of Style Icons** *(free)* dazzles with original dresses, suits and stage costumes once worn by a glittering cast of cultural icons. It all began in 2006, when the owners acquired Audrey Hepburn's dress from *Charade* (1963). That first purchase sparked a remarkable collection, now featuring pieces worn by Marilyn Monroe, Princess Diana, Elizabeth Taylor, Angelina Jolie and more.

Photographs, letters and background stories bring the garments to life. Look out for Tippi Hedren's green suit from Alfred Hitchcock's *The Birds* (1963) – the exhibit text doesn't shy away from detailing the director's troubling behaviour towards her on set.

Retail Glam
Popular shopping outlet

Shoppers from all over the country come to **Kildare Village** *(kildarevillage.com)*, an outlet mall 1.5km south of Kildare town. It's Ireland's biggest shopping centre, with the brick and timber architecture designed to reflect the county's stud farms.

The boutiques are laid out like a designer high street, with names like Michael Kors, Mulberry, Samsonite, ECCO and Calvin Klein among the mix. Most of the wares are from last season's collections, but there are some good bargains to be had. There are also cafes and restaurants.

The easiest way to get here is by car via the M7. Alternatively, **Iarnród Éireann** *(irishrail.ie)* trains run to Kildare town, and **Dublin Coach** *(dublincoach.ie)* offers a direct service from Burgh Quay every 30 minutes, taking about an hour.

Beyond Kildare & Horse Country

Rural County Kildare preserves contrasting legacies: of the Anglo-Irish aristocracy on one hand and large-scale industrial peat extraction on the other.

Places
Celbridge p133
Donore p134
Ballitore p134
Lullymore p135

Kildare's lush landscape and proximity to Dublin have always made it attractive to those with money who want to be close to the capital. In the past, that meant aristocratic estates and mansions, exemplified by the splendours of Castletown House; today it manifests as commuter belt communities, upmarket dormitory towns, luxury country hotels and golf resorts – not to mention world-class golf at Carton House and the K Club, and high-octane thrills at Mondello Park.

But the far west of the county is characterised by a very different landscape. The Bog of Allen – the largest area of raised bog in Ireland – was subject to large-scale peat extraction for 100 years and provides a lesson in ecological destruction.

Celbridge
TIME FROM KILDARE TOWN: **35MIN**

A Palladian masterpiece

Magnificent **Castletown House** *(castletown.ie; free)* is Ireland's most imposing Georgian estate and a grand reminder of the wealth and influence wielded by the Anglo-Irish elite in the 18th century. **Guided tours** *(free; Jul-Nov only)* at noon and 3pm offer a glimpse into the extravagant world of the Georgian one-percent; otherwise, you're free to roam the grounds at your own pace. Don't skip the riverside path – the view back towards the house is cinematic.

The house was built between 1722 and 1732 for William Conolly (1662–1729), speaker of the Irish House of Commons and, at the time, the richest man in Ireland. Born in Ballyshannon, County Donegal, to modest means, Conolly made his fortune through strategic land acquisitions following the Battle of the Boyne in 1690. He commissioned architect Sir Edward Lovett Pearce to craft a palace worthy of a prince, expanding on an earlier design by Italian architect Alessandro Galilei. The result was a neoclassical triumph crowned by the Long Gallery, adorned with portraits and delicate stucco work by the Francini brothers.

GETTING AROUND

It's best to have a car when exploring beyond Kildare town and the Curragh. You'll certainly need one to reach the Bog of Allen.

There are frequent bus and train services *(transportforireland.ie)* to Maynooth, Celbridge and Newbridge, but you'll need your own car to explore beyond them. **Dublin Bus** *(dublinbus.ie)* runs the C4 every 30 minutes from Aston Quay in Dublin city centre to Celbridge Main St *(1hr)*, where you'll find the main gate to Castletown House. The bus then goes on as far as Maynooth.

WORLD-CLASS GOLF

Kildare is home to two outstanding golf resorts, located just 13km apart. In Straffan, the **K Club** *(kclub.ie)* offers two championship courses, most famously the Palmer North, which hosted the Ryder Cup and remains one of Ireland's premier parkland layouts.

In Maynooth, you have **Carton House** *(cartonhouse.com)*, where golfers can choose between the picturesque, tree-lined O'Meara Course and the more demanding Montgomerie, known for its linksy style and deep bunkering.

Both estates combine world-class golf with historic settings, luxury facilities and scenic beauty, making them perennial favourites for visiting players seeking memorable rounds in Ireland's horse and golf country.

Conolly died before the house was completed, but his widow, Katherine, carried on the vision, adding the curious 42.6m **Conolly Folly** and the whimsical, corkscrew-shaped **Wonderful Barn** just outside Leixlip (closed to the public, but best described as Georgian eccentricity turned up to eleven).

In the 20th century, the house passed from the Conolly family to conservationist Desmond Guinness (of the Guinness beer-making family), whose restoration efforts were later continued by the Castletown Foundation and, from 1994, by the Office of Public Works.

Castletown is signposted from Junction 6 on the M4.

Donore

TIME FROM KILDARE TOWN: **25MIN**

Petrol-head experience

Kildare's other great racing passion swaps hooves for horsepower. On the edge of Donore, **Mondello Park** *(trackdays. ie; half/full-day from €155/225)* is Ireland's only international motorsport venue, hosting year-round races across a mix of disciplines – from karting to superbike championships. On race days, you can check out rare racing cars, including a Jordan F1, at its small museum.

On non-race days, the track opens up to the public for a variety of high-octane driving experiences. You can slip behind the wheel of a single-seat Formula car, test out a Ferrari or a Porsche, or learn to drift like a pro. There's even the option to bring your own car onto the track – just be sure to book ahead.

Ballitore

TIME FROM KILDARE TOWN: **25MIN**

'Inward Light' in Ireland

Low-key Ballitore is the only planned and permanent Quaker settlement in Ireland, founded by settlers from Yorkshire in 1726.

Set in a tiny, restored Meeting House of the Society of Friends (which also houses the local library), this small **museum** *(quakers-in-ireland.ie; free)* documents the lives of Ballitore's Quaker community, including the former owner, Mary Leadbeater, who was known for her aversion to war.

On the southern edge of the village, there is a Quaker cemetery.

Iron Age remains

About 4km west of Ballitore village is the **Rath of Mullaghmast** *(free)*, an Iron Age hill fort and standing stone that was the site of an infamous massacre of up to 400 Gaelic nobles by English forces at some point between late 1577 and early 1588. The nobles were lured there under the false pretence of performing military service, but were then slaughtered – records suggest some were also burnt at the stake.

In 1843, Daniel O'Connell, a champion of Catholic emancipation who was known as the 'Liberator', held the last of his famous 'monster meetings' here – large-scale, peaceful meetings aimed at promoting the repeal of the 1800 Act of Union and the re-establishment of an Irish parliament. It's

Carton House

reputed that upwards of one million people showed up to hear him speak.

Lullymore

TIME FROM KILDARE TOWN: 20MIN

Ireland's largest raised peat bog

Covering more than 950 sq km across six counties, the Bog of Allen is the largest raised peat bog in Ireland, but centuries of exploitation have removed 90% of its 10,000-year-old peat reserves.

Run by the nonprofit Irish Peatland Conservation Council (IPCC), the **Bog of Allen Nature Centre** *(ipcc.ie; adult/child €7/free)*, at Lullymore in eastern Kildare, celebrates the biodiversity of Ireland's bogs and traces the history of peat extraction and its threat to wildlife and the environment.

The garden at the back of the visitor centre has Ireland's largest carnivorous plant collection – sundews, butterworts and pitcher plants – and ponds filled with frogs and newts. A nearby boardwalk extends into Lodge Bog, one of the last untouched fragments of the Bog of Allen.

PUNCHESTOWN RACING

You don't need to know your steeplechases from your staying hurdles to enjoy a day out at **Punchestown Racecourse**, the home of Irish jump racing. A cornerstone of the sport since 1824, Punchestown is the only course in Ireland with a dedicated cross-country banks track, complete with brush fences, stone walls, hurdles and rolling grass embankments that test both horse and rider.

While races are held throughout the season, the highlight is the six-day Punchestown Festival in late April or early May, a major event in the National Hunt calendar. The atmosphere is electric: think live music, great food, style competitions and plenty of people-watching.

 EATING BEYOND KILDARE & HORSE COUNTRY: OUR PICKS

| **Life Cafe**: Rich breakfasts and succulent cakes beneath raked timber ceilings in the Straffan Antiques & Design Centre. *8.30am-5pm Mon-Sat, from 9.30am Sun* € | **Koshiba**: The best Japanese restaurant in Leinster is in the Riverfront Shopping Centre in Leixlip; dishes are as authentic as if you ordered them in Tokyo. *12.15-1pm Mon-Sat, from 1pm Sun* €€ | **Bistro 53**: Chesterfields, timber beams and bistro classics set the tone at this Maynooth spot, with weekend acoustic sets adding extra flair. *noon-3pm & 5-9.30pm, bar to 11.45pm* €€ | **Morrison Room**: Michelin-starred, French-inflected cuisine served beneath a gold leaf-flecked ceiling in the old ballroom of Carton House. *6-9pm Thu-Sat, 12.30-1pm Sun* €€€ |

Brigid's Cross

ST BRIGID

In 2023, Ireland introduced a new bank holiday on the first Monday of February to honour Brigid of Kildare, the nation's *other* patron saint. Associated with fugitives, bees, poetry and learning, Brigid was venerated in Kildare, where a perpetual fire once burned in her name.

Many, however, see her as a Christianised version of the pagan goddess Bríd, whose feast day on 1 February coincides with Imbolc, the ancient festival celebrating spring's arrival and the renewal of life. Generations of Irish children have learnt to make the woven **Brigid's Cross** from reeds, rushes or straw – traditionally hung on 1 February to ward off evil spirits and invite protection, blending pagan ritual and Christian devotion in one enduring Irish tradition.

Entertainment and preservation

The **Lullymore Heritage & Discovery Park** *(family ticket €26–49)* is an an award-winning, family-oriented park that does a fabulous job of entertaining while promoting the importance of preservation. The park was built on an area of cutaway bog where peat was once extracted for commercial purposes, but the whole area has now been given over to conservation.

A woodland trail leads through a 200-year-old forest, past various points of interest including a recreation of an Iron Age hut and an enchanting fairy village. Boardwalks lead out over the half-drowned bog to wildlife hides. There's also a pet farm, crazy golf, an adventure playground and a heritage railway providing 15-minute rides.

If the weather isn't great, there's the Funky Forest Indoor Play Centre, which mixes hard play areas for older kids (climbing nets, rope bridges and a cable run) with softer play for the little 'uns, including a ball pool. You could easily spend half a day here.

Places We Love to Stay

€ Budget €€ Midrange €€€ Top End

Wicklow Mountains
MAP p115

Glendalough International Youth Hostel € Modern hostel conveniently situated near the Glendalough monastic site; all dorms are en suite.

Heather House €€ Understated country-house elegance radiates from the luxurious bedrooms at this superb-value B&B in Laragh.

Coach House €€ The rooms above this historic inn in Roundwood are small but beautiful, while the restaurant and pub are exceptional.

Powerscourt Hotel & Spa €€€ On the grounds of the Powerscourt Estate, Wicklow's most luxurious hotel has massive rooms and a gourmet restaurant.

Wicklow Town & Around
MAP p115

Hunter's Hotel €€ One of Ireland's oldest coaching inns has 16 beautifully appointed rooms. Just outside Wicklow town, close to Rathnew.

Ballyknocken House €€ Ballyknocken has 10 individually appointed rooms (most with roll top baths) split between a beautiful 19th-century farmhouse and a former milking parlour outside Wicklow town.

Wicklow Head Lighthouse €€€ This 1781 lighthouse just south of Wicklow town has octagonal rooms with excellent views. Two-night minimum stay.

Tinakilly Country House €€€ Magnificent Victorian Italianate house that's now an elegant B&B, located 4km northwest of Wicklow town.

Rathdrum & Around

Hidden Valley Holiday Park € The River Avonmore flows through this family camping ground in Rathdrum, with riverside pitches and safe swimming.

Woodenbridge Hotel €€ Dating from 1608, this hotel 13km south of Rathdrum has hosted Sir Walter Scott, among other notables.

Bray

Strand Hotel €€ Period property once owned by Oscar Wilde. Reach the 1st-floor rooms via a sweeping timber staircase.

Esplanade Hotel €€ Red-bricked Victorian landmark topped by turrets; rooms divided between (preferred) original seafront building and a modern extension.

Kildare Town
MAP p129

Silken Thomas €€ A standout pub stay, with stylish rooms in the main building and in the old Postmaster's House.

Firecastle €€ Find 10 exquisite rooms decorated in blush pink and teal above the excellent bakery and deli; all have views over St Brigid's Cathedral.

Martinstown House €€€ A gorgeous 18th-century country manor on a big estate with seven antique-filled rooms and an elegant restaurant. Adults only.

Kilkea Castle Hotel & Golf Resort €€€ This 1180-built castle was a stronghold of the Fitzgerald family before being turned into a luxury hotel set over 73 hectares; mix of castle suites and self-catering lodges.

Celbridge

Castletown Gate House €€ Castletown's original gate lodge and the adjoining roundhouse have been transformed into comfortable lodgings administered by the Irish Landmark Trust. Two-night minimum stay.

Batty Langley Lodge €€ This two-storey, neo-Gothic Irish Landmark Trust-managed bolthole is beside the old gate into Castletown Estate and is perfect for a romantic getaway (it only sleeps two). Two-night minimum stay.

Maynooth
MAP p129

NUI Maynooth € Summer campus accommodation ranging from college rooms to self-catering apartments in dedicated village.

Carton House €€€ Once a Fitzgerald manor, this elegant Fairmont hotel offers grand rooms in the main house, simpler annex rooms and superb dining at the Michelin-starred Morrison Room.

Straffan

Barberstown Castle €€ Grand castle hotel once owned by Eric Clapton. Rooms are split between buildings that represent four separate centuries; located just outside Straffan.

K Club €€€ Luxury accommodation in a magnificent 19th-century house, plus three elegant restaurants and two world-class golf courses.

Researched by
Catherine Le Nevez

Wexford, Waterford, Carlow & Kilkenny

SWEEPING BEACHES, WOODED VALLEYS, VIBRANT STREET LIFE

Fringed by beaches and threaded by rivers, Ireland's southeast encompasses ancient castles, flower-filled gardens, charming villages and charismatic cities.

Protected from the wild Atlantic weather, these four counties – coastal Wexford and Waterford, and inland Carlow and Kilkenny – comprise Ireland's 'sunny southeast', as it's locally known. Blessed by what is typically the warmest and driest climate in the country, this is an outdoorsy paradise. Walking and cycling routes wind across the landscape, including trails in the region's flourishing gardens and gentle paths along the banks of its rivers. Getting out on the waterways with a kayak or SUP or aboard a cruise provides a different perspective as you see the scenery float past. Along the coast's secluded coves and broad beaches, activities range from surfing and kitesurfing to fishing trips from ports hauling in super-fresh seafood.

Rich seams of history run through this segment of Ireland's ancient east. Mystical standing stones, imposing castles and religious relics – including magnificent ruined abbeys – are scattered across the region, along with churches and cathedrals. At the heart of each of these four counties, their eponymous county towns – Wexford town, Waterford city, Carlow town and Kilkenny city – also chronicle the past: the Vikings founded Wexford, and Ireland's oldest city, Waterford. Carlow's ruined castle once guarded its river, and Kilkenny's medieval mile brings its Middle Ages heritage to life. Throughout the region, new stories continue to be written through tech innovations and creativity across food, music, design and art.

NICOLAS D'HOEDT/LONELY PLANET

THE MAIN AREAS

WEXFORD TOWN
Atmospheric, cultural harbour town. **p144**

WATERFORD CITY
Age-old heritage, contemporary street art. **p154**

CARLOW TOWN
Artistic gateway to picturesque countryside. **p165**

KILKENNY CITY
Magnificent castle, cathedral and nightlife. **p171**

For places to stay in Wexford, Waterford, Carlow and Kilkenny, see p181

THE GUIDE

WEXFORD, WATERFORD, CARLOW & KILKENNY

SUE BURTON PHOTOGRAPHY/SHUTTERSTOCK

Left: Waterford Greenway (p160); **right:** Tramore beach (p160)

Find Your Way

Covering just 7192 sq km, Ireland's southeasternmost corner is within two hours' drive of international airports north in Dublin and west in Cork. Ferries sail between Rosslare in County Wexford and Britain, France and Spain.

WEXFORD, WATERFORD, CARLOW & KILKENNY

THE GUIDE

Kilkenny City, p171
Kilkenny's medieval castle, cathedral and tangle of pub-lined streets make the county's flagship city a magnet for visitors.

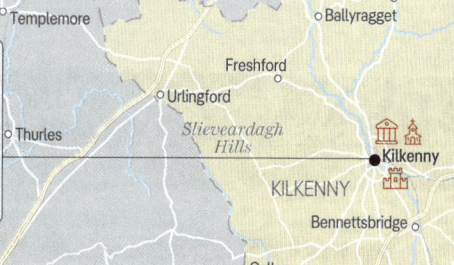

Waterford City, p154
Alongside its riverside quays, Ireland's oldest city is awash with Viking history, glassmaking heritage, gleaming museums and extraordinary street-art murals.

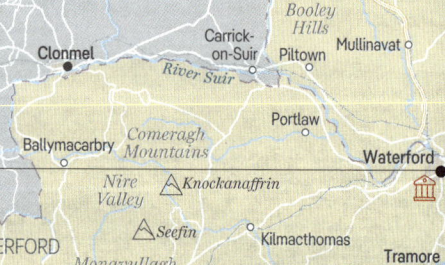

WEXFORD, WATERFORD, CARLOW & KILKENNY

THE GUIDE

Carlow Town, p165
The country's second-longest river, the beautiful River Barrow, flows through the history-rich, strategically important main town of Ireland's second-smallest county.

Wexford Town, p144
Wexford anchors its namesake county with its boat-filled waterfront and narrow streets lined with lively bars, restaurants, galleries and boutiques.

CAR
Driving is the ultimate way to reach out-of-the-way sights and make serendipitous discoveries. Main roads link larger destinations. On narrow, often single-lane backroads, go slow in anticipation of oncoming vehicles, including tractors.

BUS
Public transport is viable for many destinations across these four counties, with transit hubs in the main towns/cities. Buses tend to offer the greatest coverage, running more frequently and serving a greater number of smaller regional locales.

TRAIN
Rail services run from Dublin Connolly via Enniscorthy, Wexford town and Rosslare Strand to Rosslare Europort; and from Dublin Heuston via Carlow town, Muine Bheag (Bagenalstown), Kilkenny city and Thomastown to Waterford city.

Plan Your Time

Soak up history and culture in Waterford and Kilkenny cities, set out into the rolling countryside on a driving, cycling or walking trail, and stroll wide sandy beaches along the coast.

St Canice's Cathedral (p172)

If Time is Tight

● With just a couple of days, heading to County Kilkenny will give you a dose of history, culture and adventure. Start in architectural treasure **Kilkenny city** (p171), known as the Marble City, along its famous medieval mile, which links its landmark **cathedral** (p174) and **castle** (p172). Browse Irish crafts and design in the castle stables, stroll the riverbanks or board a cruise, cheer on a lightning-fast hurling game, and catch live music in the city's legendary pubs. Chances are there will be a festival or event on during your visit.

● Take a day trip via colourful **Thomastown** (p178), with enticing cafes and shops, and outlying sights like the splendid medieval ruins of Cistercian **Jerpoint Abbey** (p178), to the exquisite village of **Inistioge** (p178) and magical, wooded **Woodstock Gardens** (p179).

Seasonal Highlights

Make use of the warmer weather for enjoying the greenway network, and wildlife spotting along the coast. Festivals peak mid-summer.

MARCH
St Patrick's Day festivities liven up the often-chilly month of March throughout the region; Kilkenny city celebrates with a four-day **festival** (p176), with trad music spilling out of pubs during the parallel Trad Fest.

MAY
Spring is a glorious time to visit before the summer crowds descend, with long, warm days, bloom-filled gardens and festivities such as the **Blackwater Valley Opera Festival** (p163) at locations throughout the Blackwater Valley.

JUNE
June is a vibrant month, with days at their longest and a cornucopia of activities and events indoors and out. Kilkenny city is especially animated when it hosts the sidesplitting **Cat Laughs Comedy Festival** (p176).

Four Counties in Four Days

● Four full, action-packed days are just enough to get a taste of all four counties. After exploring Kilkenny, traverse the beautiful **Blackwater Valley** (p163), via heritage-steeped Lismore and Cappoquin to seaside **Ardmore** (p164) with Ireland's oldest Christian settlement's monastic ruins and sweeping beaches. Continue to food-famed harbourside **Dungarvan** (p162) before taking in spectacular scenery along the **Copper Coast** (p161) to surf hangout **Tramore** (p160), ideally suited for learning to ride the waves.

● Discover the Viking backstories of **Waterford city** (p154), especially in its museum-filled Viking Triangle; and of **Wexford town** (p144), and 1798 Rising history in **Enniscorthy** (p149). Finish by following the meandering River Barrow to garden-surrounded **Carlow town** (p165).

Southeast in a Week

● Stretching the four-day itinerary out to a week allows you to slow down, splice in some more destinations and activities, and get further off the beaten track. West of Waterford city, there are glorious walking trails in the **Nire Valley and Comeragh Mountains** (p163). Cycling between Dungarvan and Waterford city is idyllic along the **Waterford Greenway** (p160).

● To Waterford city's southeast, 19th-century steamer port **Dunmore East** (p159) has pretty parks and swimming coves and appealing pubs. Just north, make the five-minute car-ferry crossing from Passage East to Ballyhack – the jumping-off point for discovering County Wexford's **Hook Peninsula** (p153), capped by its remote lighthouse at Hook Head. Further east, extraordinary wildlife-spotting trips to the **Saltee Islands** (p151) set sail from quaint fishing port **Kilmore Quay** (p151).

JULY
By July, the southeast is getting busy, especially along the coast, but there are enough sweeping beaches to escape crowds. Inland, the countywide **Carlow Garden Festival** (p169) has open gardens, workshops, tours and picnics.

AUGUST
Summer sees festivities in full swing. Waterford city is filled with parties, peaking with **Spraoi** (p157), pronounced 'spree' and meaning 'play', featuring street performers, a parade and fireworks during the August bank holiday weekend.

OCTOBER
With cooler weather and shorter days, pubs make cosy refuges. Wexford town's world-famous **Wexford Festival Opera** (p147) includes peripheral festivities like the wonderful Wexford Spiegeltent Festival.

DECEMBER
Heading into winter, cold, dark days are brightened by Christmas magic during festivities in places such as Waterford city, hosting illuminations and ice skating during **Winterval** (p157).

Wexford Town

HISTORY | MUSEUMS | FESTIVALS

GETTING AROUND

Trains on the Dublin Connolly–Rosslare Europort line pull into Wexford's **O'Hanrahan Station**, centrally located at Redmond Sq near the waterfront; buses stopping here include direct Dublin Airport services.

Sloping gently towards the harbour, Wexford's compact town centre is easily walkable. Parallel to the quayside promenade, North Main St is the main shopping thoroughfare. Public car parks are plentiful, including by the waterfront. Buses serve the main outlying sights; Kilmore Quay via Johnstown Castle services run Monday to Saturday only. **Bolt** *(bolt.eu)* rents e-bikes (90km range) and e-scooters (40km range); payment per minute is via the app.

Set back from the fishing trawlers and shipping-container dining venues along its quays, Wexford's engaging county town spills over with vibrantly hued buildings. Locally made art and crafts abound in Wexford's knot of narrow streets, which are crammed with independent shops, restaurants and bars, along with entertainment venues, including its renowned opera house.

Today home to 21,524 inhabitants, Wexford (Irish: Loch Garman) has a tempestuous history. Vikings raided a monastery on this estuary of the River Slaney in 819 CE, naming the area Veisafjǫrðr ('inlet of the mudflats'). At the request of the deposed Irish King of Leinster, Diarmuid MacMurrough, sanctioned by England's King Henry II, the Anglo-Normans conquered in 1169. Oliver Cromwell's forces stormed and sacked the Irish Royalist city in 1649, wiping out three-quarters of Wexford's population. Rebels made a robust stand against British rule during the 1798 Rising. These epoch-defining events are explored at sights in and around the town and county.

Walk Through Wexford's Past
Historic structures and streetscapes

Vestiges of Wexford's history remain in its winding streets laid out by the Vikings. Notable sites in the town centre include the Cromwell-inflicted ruins of 1190-founded **Selskar Abbey**, where King Henry II did penance for murdering former ally Thomas Becket; and the sister of Richard Fitz Gilbert de Clare, aka Strongbow, Basilia, is believed to have wed one of Henry II's lieutenants. Now a national monument, the structure (no internal access) occupies the site of a Viking temple dedicated to Odin. Nearby, the squat **Westgate** tower, constructed around 1300, is the only survivor of seven gates that accessed the walled town.

The **Cornmarket**, dating from 1775, was once Wexford's central marketplace. During medieval times, bull baiting took

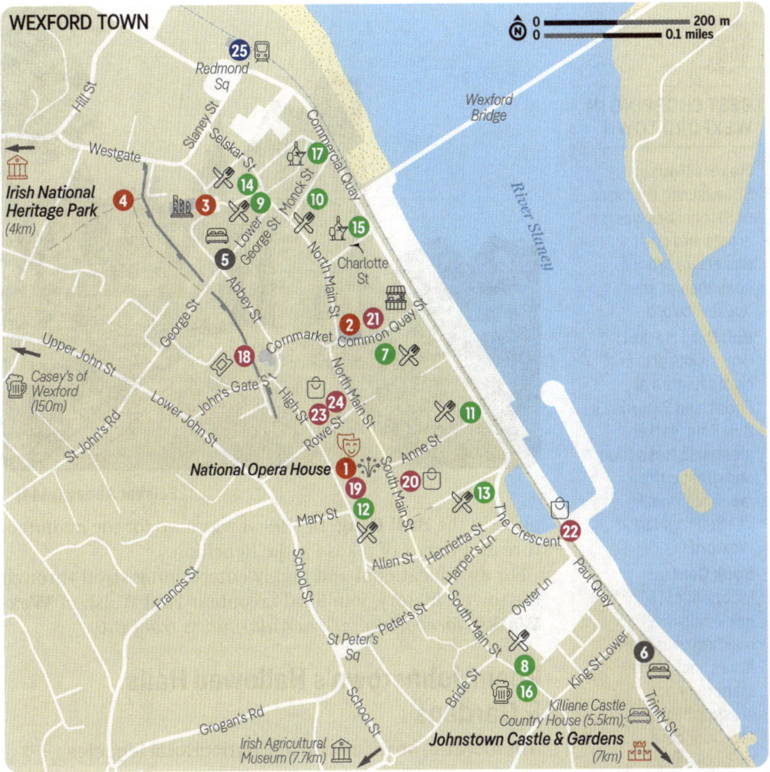

WEXFORD TOWN

★ HIGHLIGHTS
1. National Opera House

● SIGHTS
2. Bull Ring
3. Selskar Abbey
4. Westgate

● SLEEPING
5. Blue Door

6. Talbot Hotel

● EATING
7. Clovelly
8. Crust
9. Greenacres
10. Jasper's
11. La Côte
12. La Vista
13. Trough
14. Wexford Coffee Roasters

● DRINKING & NIGHTLIFE
15. CorkBuzz
16. Sky & the Ground
17. T Morris Bar

● ENTERTAINMENT
18. Wexford Arts Centre
19. Wexford Festival Opera

● SHOPPING
20. Book Centre
21. Bull Ring Market
22. Makers House
23. Martins Jewellers
24. Pádraig Grant Gallery

● TRANSPORT
25. O'Hanrahan Station

EATING IN WEXFORD TOWN: OUR PICKS

Jasper's: Buzzing bar-restaurant in Crown Quarter hotel. Vivid decor, pub fare. *5-9.30pm Wed & Thu, 10am-3pm & 5-9.30pm Fri-Sun* €€

Crust: Wood-fired pizzas topped with artisan Irish meats and cheeses (Coolea farmhouse cheddar) by a Naples-trained chef. *5-9.30pm Mon-Fri, from 1pm Sat & Sun* €€

Greenacres: Epicurean bistro, bakery, deli and gallery space serving modern Irish twists such as Guinness-bread crumbed scallops. *9am-9pm Mon-Sat* €€

La Côte: Daily caught seafood like Rosslare lobster, lemon sole and mussels at this harbour-front restaurant. *5.30-10pm Wed-Sat, from noon Sun* €€€

BEST SHOPPING IN WEXFORD TOWN

Makers House: Showcasing the work of 10 local designers, artists and craft makers. *facebook.com/themakershousewexford*

Bull Ring Market: Grassroots arts and crafts feature at Friday and Saturday's Bull Ring Market, alongside fresh food and great coffee. *facebook.com/TheBullringMarketWexford*

Book Centre: Independent bookshop in a 1775 building over three floors, including stationery and art supplies, and top-floor cafe. *thebookcentre.ie*

Martins Jewellers: Third-generation, 1947-established jewellers with traditional handmade jewellery. *martinsjewellers.ie*

Pádraig Grant Gallery: Stunning, mainly B&W local and international photography handprinted in the acclaimed Wexford photojournalist's on-site darkroom. *padraiggrant.com*

Selskar Abbey (p144)

place in the **Bull Ring**; in 1798, it was used for the manufacture and repair of pikes for the Rebellion.

For an educational and highly entertaining stroll through the town's history, join local raconteur Paul Walsh of **Wex-Walks** *(facebook.com/WexWalks; tours from €10)*.

Roam Johnstown's Hallowed Halls & Gardens

Aristocratic, horticultural and agricultural legacies

See how the aristocracy lived at **Johnstown Castle** *(johnstowncastle.ie, museum & gardens adult/child €10.50/4.50, castle tour additional €5.50/2.50)*, 7km southwest of Wexford's centre. First established by the Esmonde family following the Anglo-Norman invasion and later expelled by Cromwell, this turreted Gothic Revival masterpiece was created between 1836 and 1872 by the Grogan family, who went on to marry into the powerful Fitzgerald dynasty. Highlights include the Apostles Hall, named for its elaborately carved sculptures; the dining room with a Grogan family portrait; the grand drawing room with its original French mirrors; the library; and its last resident Lady Fitzgerald's chamber, as well as the 86m-long servants' tunnel that concealed castle workers from view. After Lady Fitzgerald's death in 1942, it was donated to the state, becoming an agricultural college and research facility until its 2019 restoration, when the castle first opened to the public. It's worth prebooking 75-minute guided castle tours online.

In the stable yard, the **Irish Agricultural Museum** depicts the changes to rural Irish life brought about by the Industrial Revolution, such as the shift from horse-drawn machinery to engine-powered equipment, through exhibits such as tractors, bicycles and farming manuals and implements.

Surrounding the castle, the magnificent **Johnstown Castle Gardens** incorporate three lakes, a walled garden, hay meadows, woodland, follies, resident otters, waterfowl and iridescent peacocks, along with a visitor centre and cafe.

Get a Cultural Fix
Visual and performing arts

The heart of Wexford's creative community, the **Wexford Arts Centre** *(wexfordartscentre.ie)*, on the Cornmarket, hosts a huge range of free contemporary art exhibitions and hands-on workshops, as well as film screenings, concerts, album launches, comedy, storytelling and diverse events; check the agenda and book tickets online. There's a daytime cafe.

Wexford's striking **National Opera House** *(nationalopera house.ie)*, Ireland's first custom-built opera house, with two performance spaces in a multi-award-winning building on the site of the old Theatre Royal, which was unveiled in 2008, presents opera as well as comedy, concerts, dance, musicals, theatre, workshops and educational events throughout the year. On the top floor, its cafe/restaurant, La Vista, overlooks the town and harbour.

The opera house is the centrepiece of the town's famous opera festival. Every autumn, Wexford is in the international spotlight when it presents the acclaimed **Wexford Festival Opera** *(wexfordopera.com)*. Established in 1951, it focuses on revitalising forgotten masterpieces, with a different theme each year (such as 2025's 'Myths & Legends'). The festival runs over 16 days from late October to early November each year. Ticket sales open in May.

Running in parallel alongside the main festival is the open-access **Wexford Fringe Festival**, with a programme packed with everything from art and photography to jazz and classical recitals and trad sessions, as well as the **Wexford Spiegeltent Festival** *(wexfordspiegeltent.com)*, hosting trad, retro big-name performances and contemporary music in its century-old wood, velvet and mirrored pavilion venue set up on the quays.

Dive Deep into Irish History
Open-air heritage museum

For the full sweep of Irish history, head 5.5km west of Wexford's town centre to the **Irish National Heritage Park** *(irishheritage.ie; adult/child €14/8)* at Ferrycarrig. Sprawled

BIRTHPLACE OF THE GUINNESS BOOK OF RECORDS

During a wildfowling trip to the Slobs wetlands just north of Wexford's harbour in 1951, the chairperson of Guinness Brewery, Sir Hugh Beaver, shot at but missed a golden plover. This provoked a debate over whether it, or the red grouse, was Europe's fastest game bird. Sir Hugh realised that publishing definitive answers could prove profitable. He was right – the first *Guinness Book of Records* was a bestseller when published in 1955, and today the reference book is itself a recordholder, as the world's biggest-selling copyrighted book – but wrong about Europe's fastest game bird (the *Guinness Book of Records* records it as the red-breasted merganser, which averages 130km/h).

EATING IN WEXFORD TOWN: BEST CAFES

Trough: Scandi-style spot for house-baked pastries and coffee, matcha, loose-leaf teas and hot chocolate. *7.30am-4pm Mon-Sat, from 9am Sun* €

Wexford Coffee Roasters: Serves own-roasted Fair Trade coffee, filled croissants, savoury/sweet scones, cookies, slices. *8.30am-4pm Mon-Fri, 9am-4pm Sat* €

Clovelly: Laneway cafe with acai bowls, soaked oats, cheese toasties, custard-filled pastries. French/AeroPress coffee. *7am-4pm Mon-Fri, from 8am Sat, 9am-3pm Sun* €

La Vista: National Opera House's top-floor cafe for panoramic views over the town and harbour, and breakfast and lunch favourites. *9.30am-4.30pm Mon-Sat* €€

Irish National Heritage Park (p147)

over 14 hectares of native woodland, marsh and banks of the River Slaney, it encompasses the site of the first Anglo-Norman settlement in Ireland. Ongoing archaeological excavations have unearthed stone foundations of the castle that replaced the original wooden fortifications, along with pottery and arrowheads.

Among the open-air museum's reconstructed sites are a Mesolithic camp, portal dolmen, monastic site, medieval ringfort and Viking harbour. Various activities and events range from panning for gold to blacksmithing and falconry demonstrations, and character-dressed guides lead themed tours ('prehistoric Ireland', 'early Christian Ireland' or 'age of invasion'). The cafe/restaurant has outdoor seating overlooking the *crannog* (fortified artificial island).

☑ TOP TIP

Wexford's accommodation fills up quickly during the summer months, thanks to its proximity to the coastline and ferry port, and especially in autumn during its renowned opera festival.

 DRINKING IN WEXFORD TOWN: OUR PICKS

Sky & the Ground: Classic pub with a roaring fire, a heated beer garden and live trad-music sessions on Sundays. *4-11.30pm Tue-Thu, 3pm-late Fri-Sun*

CorkBuzz: Stone-floor, brick-walled space serving wines by the glass or bottle with cheese and charcuterie platters. *5-9pm Wed, noon-10.30pm Thu-Sun*

Casey's of Wexford: Local and international live-music acts play every night of the week at this pub on the hill 500m west of the centre with a huge beer garden. *noon-late*

T Morris Bar: Refurbished pub-turned-bar with cocktails, stylish interiors, flagstone courtyard. *2-11.30pm Mon-Thu, noon-12.30am Fri & Sat, noon-11.30pm Sun*

Beyond Wexford Town

History is etched across the landscapes of County Wexford, from ancient and ecclesiastical remains to strategic defensive and seafaring sites.

North of Wexford town, Enniscorthy, the county's second-largest town, is home to the National 1798 Rebellion Centre and the battlefield of Vinegar Hill. Birdlife flocks to the beaches along the east coast. To Wexford's south, Rosslare is synonymous with its ferry port; its strand is a popular summer holiday spot. On the southern coast, Kilmore Quay, with its quaint thatched cottages, has a picturesque marina with a busy fishing fleet and access to the Saltee Islands bird sanctuary. Straddling the River Barrow as it flows to the sea, New Ross, with its Anglo-Norman heritage and replica Famine ship, is a gateway for a fascinating drive along the Hook Peninsula to the world's oldest working lighthouse.

Places
Enniscorthy p149
Rosslare p150
Kilmore Quay p151
New Ross p152

Enniscorthy

TIME FROM WEXFORD TOWN: **25MIN**

Relive Rebellion history

On the River Slaney 24km northwest of Wexford town, Enniscorthy (Inis Córthaidh) is County Wexford's second-largest town. At its heart, 13th-century **Enniscorthy Castle** *(enniscorthycastle.ie; adult/child €10/6)* was occupied over the centuries by British armies, Irish rebels, prisoners and local merchant families. Today it houses an exhibition exploring the castle's Anglo-Norman origins and Enniscorthy's expansion in the 1600s as a prosperous market town. Self-guided tours include the dungeon and rooftop battlement looking over the town and across to Vinegar Hill.

Under 1km south of the castle, the **National 1798 Rebellion Centre** *(1798centre.ie; adult/child €10/8)* powerfully relates Wexford's ill-fated uprising against British control in Ireland, emboldened by the French and American revolutions. An audiovisual presentation gives you the sense of being present at the Battle of Vinegar Hill, which saw the massacre of 1500 Irish men, women and children, whose pikes and knives were no match for the British muskets and cannons.

Afterwards, contemplate the struggle while walking on windswept **Vinegar Hill**, 2km east of the castle, with views across Enniscorthy.

GETTING AROUND

Trains between Dublin and Rosslare Europort stop in Enniscorthy, Wexford town and Rosslare Strand. Buses serve the county's main towns, but you'll need your own wheels (car or bike) to access smaller, off-the-beaten-track destinations (and, May to October, roadside stalls selling Wexford strawberries). Car ferries *(passageferry.ie; one-way car & passengers €10, pedestrian/cyclist €1.50)* yo-yo between Ballyhack and Passage East, County Waterford, saving a large detour via New Ross. Journey time is just five minutes; pay on board.

Rosslare

TIME FROM WEXFORD TOWN: **25MIN**

Stroll Rosslare's strand

Rosslare (Ros Láir) is more than a busy port. It's best known for **Rosslare Europort** *(rosslareeuroport.ie/en-ie)* 19km south of Wexford town, which has passenger ferries to Britain, France and Spain, as well as freight routes. A major expansion is in the pipeline, with the port also set to become a major offshore renewable energy hub to meet Ireland's target of generating 7 gigawatts of offshore wind power by 2030, but it will remain operating throughout.

For visitors, Rosslare's biggest draw is its sandy, 4.5km-long beach, **Rosslare Strand**, which begins 8km northwest of the port. It's invigorating to stroll throughout the year and to swim during summer when it's patrolled by lifeguards. At its northern tip, the 1905-established par-72, 18-hole links course at the **Rosslare Golf Club** *(rosslaregolf.com; green fees €55-120)* follows the contours of the sand dunes.

Rosslare Strand's village centre has holiday favourites like ice cream, cafes, pubs, bars and bike hire, as well as a 'sea spa' with seaweed baths, an indoor/outdoor seawater pool and salt-infused steam room at Rosslare's historic, fifth-generation-run **Kelly's Resort Hotel & Spa** *(kellys.ie)*, which welcomes nonguests.

Journey to Our Lady's Island

South of Rosslare Harbour on a peninsula in the sedimentary lagoon Lady's Island Lake – a protected conservation area – are the early Augustinian priory ruins of **Our Lady's Island** *(ourladysisland.ie)*, a pilgrimage site from 15 August to 8 September every year. Raths (enclosures of clay mounds) show its early pre-Christian population, with a pagan shrine at Carnsore Point's natural-stone druid's altar; its Irish name, Cluain-na-mBan (the 'meadow of the women') suggests female druids may have lived here. After Christianity arrived, it was founded by St Abban in the 6th century (a papal pilgrimage coin discovered here dates from the 15th century) but didn't survive desecration by Cromwell's forces in 1649.

Outside of pilgrimage season, the 2km pilgrim path is a lovely walk, passing the priory graveyard, which blooms with wild garlic in spring. Rare roseate terns breed in the lake's brackish waters, separated from the sea by a barrier beach.

THE 1798 REBELLION

After King William III's Battle of the Boyne victory, late 17th/early 18th-century Penal Laws prohibited Catholics from owning land, voting, and entering the military or higher professions; and banned Irish culture, music and education. Unlikely opposition came from liberal Protestants: the United Irishmen, led by Theobald Wolfe Tone, attempted to reform and reduce British power (Loyalist Protestants prepared for conflict by forming what later became the Orange Order). Wolfe Tone tried enlisting French help, but France's failure to successfully land an army in 1796 left the United Irishmen exposed to retribution. They met their end in the Battle of Vinegar Hill, which would become a watershed for nationalism.

 EATING IN ENNISCORTHY: OUR PICKS

Dusty Boy: Stylish cafe within art/gift shop. Great homemade sausage rolls, cinnamon scrolls, sourdough toasties. *9am-4pm Mon-Fri, from 10am Sat & Sun* €

Casa d'Galo: Char-grilled Portuguese dishes like piri-piri chicken on colourful plates, with Douro and Beira Atlântico wines. *4.30-9pm Wed & Thu, 12.30-9pm Fri-Sun* €€

Village at Wheelocks: Strawberry farm (pick-your-own May–Oct) 4km east of town serving dishes using own produce *8.30am-4pm Mon-Fri, to 5pm Sat & Sun* €€

Via Veneto: Paolo Fresilli cooks authentic pizzas, pasta, meat and shellfish dishes, many from his home region of Lazio. *5.30-10pm Wed-Sat, to 9pm Sun* €€€

Puffins, Saltee Islands

Kilmore Quay

TIME FROM WEXFORD TOWN: **30MIN**

Explore the coast

Some of Ireland's best seafood lands 23km southwest of Wexford town at photogenic fishing port Kilmore Quay (Cé na Cille Móire), where craned trawlers fill the harbour, and thatched and slate-roofed cottages with whitewashed stone walls line its narrow lanes.

From the village, the **Ballyteigue Burrow Nature Reserve** *(npws.ie)* extends 9km northwest. Behind the beach's dunes, the salt marsh and mudflats are a winter refuge for bird species, including brent geese.

Fishing is possible from the shore, or you can charter a boat at the harbour to head out to the reefs and wrecks.

Sail to the Saltees

From April to September, the **Saltee Ferry** *(threesisters.ie/saltee-ferry; adult/child €40/20)* departs from Kilmore's harbour for one of Europe's most important bird sanctuaries, the **Saltee Islands** (90-hectare Great Saltee and 40-hectare Little Saltee), some 5km offshore of Kilmore Quay to the south. Inhabited as far back as 3500 BCE and used by marauding pirates, the islands were owned by Tintern Abbey (p153) until the monasteries' dissolution. They're now frequented by puffins, garnets, Manx shearwaters, razorbills and guillemots,

---

BEST WILDLIFE SPOTTING ON WEXFORD'S EAST COAST

Wexford Wildfowl Reserve: Mute swans, goldcrests and peregrine falcons inhabit the reclaimed land of the North Slob, with overwintering Greenland white-fronted geese.

Raven Nature Reserve: Spot red squirrels, Irish hares, pine martens, and grey and harbour seals.

Curracloe Beach: Rare little terns nest in the dunes of 11km-long white-sand Curracloe, which doubled for Omaha Beach in the opening scenes of *Saving Private Ryan*.

Seal Rescue Ireland: Orphaned/injured seals are rehabilitated at Courtown's volunteer-staffed Seal Rescue Ireland.

Kilmichael Point: Look for the song thrush and European stonechat at County Wexford's northernmost point.

 EATING IN & AROUND KILMORE QUAY: OUR PICKS

Cocoa's Cafe: Scones, cakes, cookies and warm cinnamon buns, along with breakfast burritos, bagels and sourdough toasties. *9am-3pm* €

Grounds: All-day breakfasts plus evening dinners (beetroot-and-gin-cured salmon and hake with foraged seaweed). *9am-3pm plus 6-8.30pm Fri & Sat* €€

Mary Barry's: Memorabilia-filled pub 4.5km northeast. Crackling fireplaces, seafood platters and grilled fish. *noon-10pm Mon-Sat, to 9pm Sun* €€

Lobster Pot: A traditional moss-green pub 20km east of Kilmore is the atmospheric setting for sublime seafood. *5-8pm Wed & Thu, 5-9pm Fri, 1-9pm Sat & Sun* €€€

THE KENNEDYS OF WEXFORD

Patrick Kennedy (1823–58) was born in Dunganstown at the Kennedy Homestead; now incorporating a museum), still farmed by the family today. With the Great Famine ravaging Ireland, Patrick sailed to the US in 1848, becoming a barrel-maker in Boston. Patrick's second son, Patrick Joseph, became the first Kennedy to enter politics; his son, Joseph Patrick Kennedy, was the father of US President John F Kennedy.

A life-size bronze **statue** near New Ross' *Dunbrody* Famine Ship commemorates JFK's visit in summer 1963, months before his assassination. In 1968, Irish-American societies established the 252-hectare John F Kennedy Arboretum as a living tribute to him in Wexford.

among the 220 species recorded here. Nesting season, from spring to early summer, is the best time to visit. Landings are possible only on Great Saltee (weather depending); there are no toilets or shelters, so wear waterproofs (including footwear).

New Ross

TIME FROM WEXFORD TOWN: **35MIN**

Understand Irish emigration

New Ross (Rhos Mhic Triúin), 36km west of Wexford town, is Ireland's only inland port, established by the Anglo-Normans on the River Barrow in the 12th century. As vessels outgrew it, shipping declined, but in the 19th century, it was a departure point for 'coffin ships' that left Famine-stricken Ireland for the promise of the New World.

On the quay, the moored replica **Dunbrody Famine Ship** *(dunbrody.com; adult/child €14/9)* provides an unflinching glimpse into emigrants' desperate voyages. In around one hour, you'll see a film before receiving a 'ticket' to board the ship, where costumed guides convey the grim conditions for passengers, who were allowed only an hour a day up on deck for the six weeks at sea. The cramped quarters and inadequate food and water saw many passengers perish on the harrowing transatlantic journey. Afterwards, an exhibition covers Irish successes in America. There are joint tickets (€22) with the **Kennedy Homestead** *(kennedyhomestead.ie; adult/child €11/8)*, near the **John F Kennedy Arboretum** *(heritageire land.ie; adult/child €5/3)*.

Cruise the waterways

Scenic trips with **Barrow Princess River Cruise** *(threesisters .ie/barrow-princess; adult/child one-way €25/8, return €32/11)* travel the tranquil, woodland-fringed waterways between New Ross' Quay and Waterford city (two hours one way); you can take bikes *(extra €3)* on board.

From 2027, the 24km **South East Greenway** *(newross greenway.org)* will link New Ross with Waterford city via an old railway tunnel; the same year, two quayside buildings are set to house a new Norman Centre exploring New Ross' Anglo-Norman history.

HEAD OUT ON THE HOOK PENINSULA

Between Bannow Bay to the east and Waterford Harbour to the west, County Wexford's Hook Peninsula is awash with history.

START	END	LENGTH
Ballyhack	Ballyhack	60km; 4hrs

Allow at least half a day for this loop-drive, starting in ❶ **Ballyhack**; its Knights Hospitallers stone tower house, Ballyhack Castle, dates from the mid-15th century. Travel southeast through Arthurstown to ❷ **Duncannon**, home to the star-shaped Duncannon Fort.

Continue south past Dollar Bay's caves, rock formations and pools and out onto ❸ **Hook Head**. Its black-and-white-striped lighthouse is the oldest continually operating in the world. Climb its 13th-century tower up 115 spiralling steps to spot dolphins, seals and migrating whales beyond the fossil-rich shore. Drive through patchwork-field countryside to ❹ **Fethard-on-Sea**, with the crumbling remains of a 15th-century castle with a crenellated circular tower (and sea-cave kayaking and coasteering expeditions run by Fethard-based adventure company the Irish Experience). Turn north to reach the ruins of Cistercian ❺ **Tintern Abbey**, built in the early 13th century for monks from its Welsh namesake. The abbey later became a private estate; a 350m walking path leads through woodland to the Colclough Walled Garden, laid out in 1838 and beautifully restored. Wind northwest past hedgerows and drystone walls to another ruined Cistercian abbey, 1170-founded ❻ **Dunbrody Abbey**.

Back in Ballyhack, cross by car ferry to Passage East, near the town of Crooke in County Waterford.

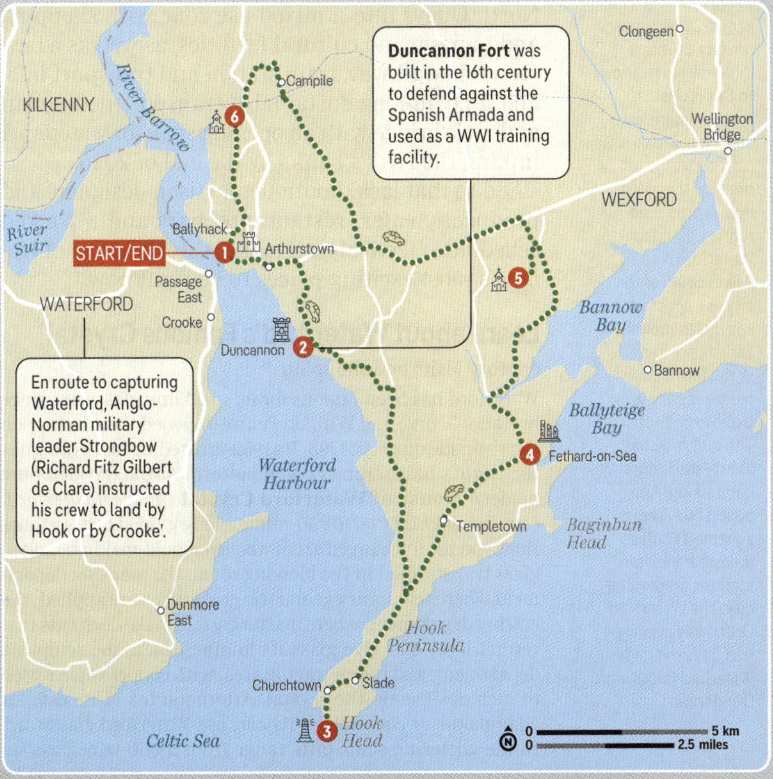

Duncannon Fort was built in the 16th century to defend against the Spanish Armada and used as a WWI training facility.

En route to capturing Waterford, Anglo-Norman military leader Strongbow (Richard Fitz Gilbert de Clare) instructed his crew to land 'by Hook or by Crooke'.

Waterford City

VIKING HISTORY | ART | FESTIVALS

GETTING AROUND

As part of Waterford's North Quays development, **Plunkett Station** will relocate 1km east of the previous station in mid-2026; trains run (via counties Kilkenny and Carlow) to Dublin Heuston, and to Limerick Junction. Buses will also converge on the new transport hub. A proposed runway extension to Waterford Airport, 9.5km south of the city, is expected to see international services resume. Waterford's city centre is easy to explore on foot. The quayside has short- and long-stay car parking. App-based bike-share scheme **TFI Bikes** *(bikeshare.ie)* has stations around the city. The Waterford Greenway cycling trail links riverside Waterford (p160) with Dungarvan.

Even in the context of more than a millennium of history (it celebrated 1111 years in 2025), Ireland's oldest city is undergoing a metamorphosis. The creative energy infusing this city of 60,079 inhabitants is visible in scores of street-art canvases splashing colour across its architecture, and a slew of sights and museums including in the city's ancient Viking Triangle. Work is advanced on a massive redevelopment of Waterford's 8-hectare former industrial North Quays into a mixed-use zone with shopping and tourism and cultural facilities, as well as a new riverside walkway, train station and transport hub, and a 207m-long sustainable-transport pedestrian and cycle bridge with an opening span for watercraft linking the river's banks by the end of 2026.

Add to that local boutiques, artisan designers and producers, cafes, restaurants, bars and a packed schedule of festivals; all make Waterford one of Ireland's most exciting places to be right now.

Learn about Waterford's Famous Crystal

Factory visits and shopping

Waterford has been famous for its sparkling glassware since brothers George and William Penrose opened their factory on the riverside quays in 1783. Its 1952-created Lismore design is the world's best-selling crystal pattern. At today's gleaming modern **House of Waterford Crystal** *(houseofwaterford.com; adult/child €18/10)*, 50-minute-long guided factory tours show you the unchanged art of wooden mould-making; molten glass transformed in the blowing room; the marking department where temporary geometric grid guides are applied; the cutting department, where master cutters make deep cuts that refract light and give glass its luminescence; the sculpting department; and the engraving area, with copper wheels used to etch designs on the crystal. Afternoon tea at its cafe, or champagne or cocktails at its bar, use Waterford glassware. In the glittering shop, gifts range from a €60 wineglass set

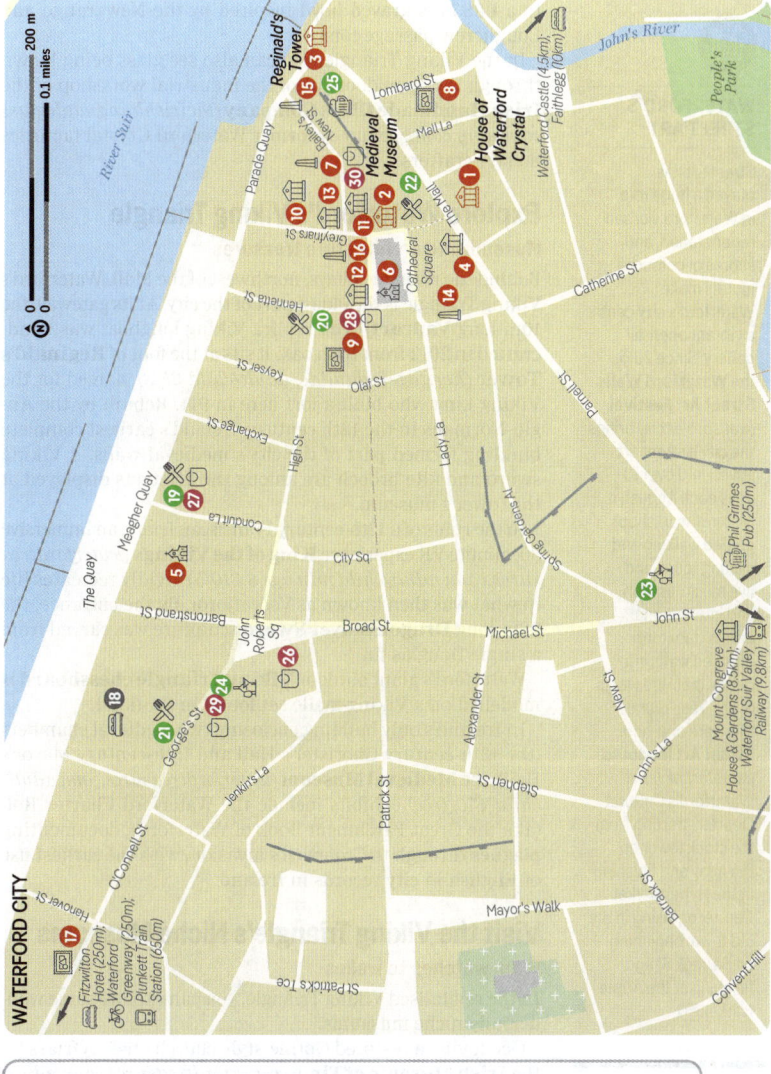

WATERFORD CITY

HIGHLIGHTS
1. House of Waterford Crystal
2. Medieval Museum
3. Reginald's Tower

SIGHTS
4. Bishop's Palace
5. Cathedral of the Most Holy Trinity
6. Christ Church Cathedral
7. Dragon Slayer Sword
8. GOMA
9. Irish Handmade Glass Company
10. Irish Museum of Time
11. Irish Silver Museum
12. Irish Wake Museum
13. King of the Vikings
14. Strongbow & Aoife sculpture
15. Vadrarfjord
16. Viking Triangle chessboard
17. Waterford Gallery of Art

SLEEPING
18. Granville Hotel

EATING
19. Berkana Bakery
20. Everett's
21. Phoenix Yard Market
22. UNioN

DRINKING & NIGHTLIFE
23. Davy Mac's
24. J&K Walsh Victorian Spirit Grocer
25. Reg

SHOPPING
26. Book Centre
27. CC Creatives
28. Gene O'Shea Irish Silver Design
29. John Palmer Music Centre
30. Magpie Collective

WATERFORD'S STREET ART

Street art has played a huge role in Waterford's urban regeneration, and scores of colourful murals make Waterford's city centre a vibrant open-air gallery. Since 2015, the **Waterford Walls Street Art Festival** *(wallsproject.ie)* brings the city's street art alive. Held over 10 days each August, it features workshops, guided walking and cycling tours, and live music, as Irish and international artists transform donated walls into larger-than-life works of art. Year-round, there are one-hour **Street Art Ink tours** *(streetartink.ie)* of Waterford's Cultural Quarter, starting from the clock tower on the quay and finishing at the Hypermarket Centre; or taking in the old town, beginning on Barrack St and finishing at the Apple Market.

☑ TOP TIP

The **Freedom of Waterford Pass** (adult/child €18/free) includes a guided Epic Walking Tour, and access to the Viking Triangle's five sights: Waterford's Medieval Museum, Christ Church Cathedral, the Irish Silver Museum, Bishop's Palace and the Irish Museum of Time.

to a €9850 engraved bowl inspired by the Newgrange and Loughcrew passage tombs.

In the Viking Triangle, you can also see glass being blown through the open doorway of the industrial workshop of the **Irish Handmade Glass Company** *(theirishhandmadeglasscompany.com)*, set up by former Waterford Crystal factories master crafters.

Explore Waterford's Viking Triangle
Museum and architecture treasures

Behind the riverside quays, northwest of the Mall, Waterford's Viking Triangle is the oldest part of the city. At its gateway, the 10m-long **Vadrarfjordr** replica Viking longboat was handcrafted in 2012 from Irish oak. It sits at the foot of **Reginald's Tower** *(heritageireland.ie; adult/child €5/3)*, named for the Viking king who built a fort here in 914. Rebuilt by the Anglo-Normans in the 12th century, Ireland's earliest complete building formed part of the city's medieval walls. A Viking sword and kite brooch are among the artefacts displayed at the tower's museum.

In the ruins of a 13th-century Franciscan friary, an immersive 30-minute VR experience **King of the Vikings** *(waterfordtreasures.com; adult/child min age 8 €10/5)* vividly recreates life in what was then known as Veðrafjǫrðr. By the entrance, the 23m-long **Dragon Slayer Sword** sculpture was carved from a single Douglas fir.

Waterford's giant outdoor **Viking Triangle chessboard** is modelled on a Viking-made set found in Scotland.

In Ireland's only building enclosing two medieval chambers (the 13th-century Chorister's Hall and 15th-century Mayor's Hall), the **Medieval Museum** *(waterfordtreasures.com; adult/child €10/free)* exhibits include the Waterford Charter Roll (aka the Great Parchment Book of Waterford), documenting plagues through to Cromwell's invasion, with the earliest use of English in city records in Ireland.

Visit the Viking Triangle's Niche Museums
From watches to wakes

In the revitalised Viking Triangle, you can explore some wonderfully niche museums.

Occupying a restored Gothic-style church on Greyfriars St, the **Irish Museum of Time** *(waterfordtreasures.com; adult/child €5/free)* spans the evolution of Irish watchmakers from the late 17th to the 20th centuries. Timepieces include longcase (grandfather) clocks, table clocks and watches.

Silver in Ireland from Viking times to 18th-century Georgian dining is displayed at the **Irish Silver Museum** *(waterfordtreasures.com; adult/child €5/free)*. The collection includes a coin minted in what's now Iraq, which arrived in 850 with Ireland's original Viking invaders.

In a 15th-century almshouse (Ireland's oldest urban domestic building), the **Irish Wake Museum** *(waterfordtreasures.com; adult/child min age 8 €11/6)*, delves into the rituals and

Reginald's Tower and Vadrarfjordr

superstitions around death. Book to experience a traditional 'Solace and Sustenance' Irish wake experience in partnership with Waterford Whisky.

Learn Waterford's Backstories

Georgian cathedrals and palace

On the site of an 11th-century Viking church, where Irish princess Aoife (daughter of Leinster King Diarmuid Mac-Murrough) married Anglo-Norman leader Strongbow the day after he invaded Waterford on 24 August 1170, Ireland's only neoclassical Georgian cathedral, the Church of Ireland **Christ Church Cathedral** *(christchurchwaterford.com)*, was built by John Roberts in 1779.

Ireland's oldest cathedral, the Catholic **Cathedral of the Most Holy Trinity** *(waterford-cathedral.com)*, on Barronstrand St in the city centre, was also designed by John Roberts and completed in 1793.

A **Strongbow & Aoife** sculpture stands on the grounds of the **Bishop's Palace** *(waterfordtreasures.com; adult/child €10/free)*, a Georgian mansion on the site of previous palaces that was designed by Richard Cassel and completed by John Roberts. Dating from 1741, the palace charts Waterford's history from the 1700s to 1970. Irish independence, World Wars

BEST EVENTS IN WATERFORD

Summer in the City: Live music, film screenings, street performers, every weekend: June–August. *waterfordarts.com*

Spraoi: Street theatre, circus acts, comedy, dance and music, plus a parade on August bank holiday weekend. *spraoi.com*

Harvest Festival: Cookery demonstrations, workshops, tours, tastings and trails over three days in early September. *waterfordharvestfestival.ie*

Imagine Arts Festival: Visual and performing arts across six days in late October. *imagineartsfestival.com*

Winterval: Illuminations, quayside ice skating, secret music gigs, storytelling and Christmas activities Fridays to Sundays from mid-November to late December. *winterval.ie*

 EATING IN WATERFORD CITY: OUR PICKS

Phoenix Yard Market: Street-food stalls spanning traditional Irish fare like bacon and cabbage to vegetarian dishes. *10am-9pm* €

Berkana Bakery: Italian bakery: gourmet sandwiches, salads, charcuterie boards. Sweets like pistachio-cream-filled cannoli. *9.30am-4.30pm Mon-Sat* €

UNioN: Sustainable ingredients at this wine bar include foraged herbs and mushrooms, wild Irish venison and line-caught fish. *12.45-2.15pm & 5.30-9.30pm Wed-Sat* €€

Everett's: Award-winning modern Irish cuisine using premium mountain-to-sea produce in atmospheric surrounds, including a vaulted cellar. *5.30-9.30pm Tue-Sat* €€€

BEST SHOPPING IN WATERFORD CITY

CC Creatives: Locally made jewellery, paintings, board games and jigsaws, body and skincare products, bags, clothing, hats, scarves. *cc-creatives.ie*

John Palmer Music Centre: Instruments include bodhrán, uilleann pipes, fiddles and tin whistles, acoustic and electric guitars plus amps. *johnpalmermusic.com*

Book Centre: Independent bookshop in a 1937, art-deco-style Savoy cinema with its original screen, stage and ceilings. *thebookcentre.ie*

Gene O'Shea Irish Silver Design: Uniquely designed, handcrafted jewellery inspired by Irish mythology/nature. *osheajewellery.com*

Magpie Collective: Fashion, jewellery, cosmetics, ceramics, prints, paintings from a local artist collective. *themagpiecollective.ie*

I and II, and Waterford sporting legends are covered on the top floor, while the ground floor is furnished as an elegant 18th-century townhouse, with the 1789 Penrose Decanter, Waterford's oldest piece of crystal.

View Visual Art
Galleries in the city

Along with Waterford's mural-splashed walls you can catch art indoors. Founded in 1939, the **Waterford Gallery of Art** *(waterfordgalleryofart.com; free)* showcases the development of Irish painting and sculpture from the 20th century in a 19th-century former bank; and hosts exhibitions, talks and workshops. The Gallery of Modern Art, aka **GOMA** *(goma waterford.ie; free)*, mounts up to nine exhibitions each year by recent graduates and emerging and established artists, with a focus on innovation.

Visit Magnificent Mount Congreve
Scented strolls in manor gardens

With a direct entrance to the Waterford Greenway, **Mount Congreve House & Gardens** *(mountcongreve.com; adult/child €12.50/free)* overlooks the River Suir 8km west of Waterford. At the splendid 1760 Georgian manor, designed by renowned Waterford architect John Roberts, you'll see an audiovisual presentation, gallery and model of the building.

Mount Congreve's greatest draw is the 28-hectare garden set amid beautiful woodland. Its 16km of trails take in 3000 types of trees and shrubs, 2000-plus varieties of rhododendrons and 600 different camellias. The 750m Fragrant Walk is a kaleidoscope for the senses. Hundreds of magnolias on the Magnolia Walk includes many raised here from seed. Walled vegetable and herb gardens provide produce for its Stables Café, serving Full Irish breakfasts, lunch and afternoon tea. From March to October, book ahead for weekly guided garden tours *(incl admission adult/child €19/6.50)* lasting 1.5 to two hours. Events during the year include June's Art in the Gardens. It's possible to stay on the property overnight in restored gatehouse lodges, forest eco-cabins and off-grid bell tents.

From mid-April to September, the charming narrow-gauge **Waterford Suir Valley Railway** *(wsvrailway.ie; adult/child €12.50/6)* passes through Mount Congreve on 40- to 50-minute tours of the old Waterford–Dungarvan railway line to/from 1878 Kilmeadan Station.

DRINKING IN WATERFORD CITY: OUR PICKS

Reg: Incorporating the medieval city walls, with six bars, a rooftop terrace, nightly live music and summer courtyard gigs. *12.30pm-midnight Sun-Thu, to 2am Fri & Sat*

J&K Walsh Victorian Spirit Grocer: An 1889 jewel with timber cabinetry, original taps. *3-11.30pm Tue-Thu, noon-12.30am Fri & Sat, noon-11pm Sun*

Davy Mac's: Vintage-fitted pub and upstairs gin bar on the canopied Apple Market entertainment quarter. *5.30pm-late Sun-Thu, 4.30pm-late Fri & Sat*

Phil Grimes Pub: Legendary live-gig lineup and ivy-clad beer garden with a wood-burning stove and a snug with its own fireplace. *5pm-midnight*

Beyond Waterford City

County Waterford's coastal highlights include Tramore, Dungarvan and Ardmore. Venture inland to explore the Blackwater and Nire valleys.

On the doorstep of Waterford city is some of the southeast's most beautiful and varied scenery. Immediately to the city's southeast is the broad natural Waterford harbour at the mouth of the 'Three Sisters' (the Rivers Nore, Suir and Barrow), where pretty village Dunmore East faces County Wexford's Hook Peninsula.

South of Waterford city, Tramore combines old-fashioned seaside funfair attractions with ideal conditions for surfing. Restaurants and pubs cluster around the boat-filled harbour in Dungarvan. Beyond the Ring Peninsula are Ardmore's beautiful beaches and Ireland's earliest Christian ruins. To the north, the Blackwater Valley leads to lovely towns like Lismore with its monumental castle. Eastwards, the Nire Valley is bounded by mountains and waterfalls.

Dunmore East   TIME FROM WATERFORD CITY: 20MIN
Discover cliffs and coves

Summertime swimming, snorkelling and sandcastle-building opportunities abound at quaint Dunmore East (Dún Mór), a 19th-century steamer port 17km southeast of Waterford city, which is perched above rose-hued sandstone cliffs with whitewashed thatched-roofed cottages and an 1825-built **lighthouse**.

Separated by the green expanse of Dunmore East's town park you'll find the once-segregated bathing spots **Mens Cove** and **Ladies Cove**. Beneath the cliffs, the largest of Dunmore's half-a-dozen cove beaches, **Lawlor's Strand**, and the adjacent **Councillor's Strand** are also great spots to seek out.

Catch Dunmore's Bluegrass Festival

Dunmore East's lively bars are split between the town's two sections. Among the Lower Village's bars, cafes and restaurants, the outdoor terrace of the **Strand Inn** *(thestrandinn. com)* overflows on sunny days. Above the fishing harbour in Dunmore's Upper Village, nautical memorabilia-filled pub **Power's Bar** *(@powersbar_dunmoreeast)* hosts legendary Tuesday-night trad sessions.

Places
Dunmore East p159
Tramore p160
Curraghmore p161
Dungarvan p162
Ardmore p164

GETTING AROUND

Buses serve most main towns, but your own wheels are best to reach destinations further afield, especially along the scenic backroads, and to allow for more flexibility in your schedule. The Waterford Greenway cycle route links Dungarvan and Waterford city, with the South East Greenway continuing to New Ross, County Wexford, from 2027. Passage East, 12km east of Waterford city, has five-minute ferries *(passageferry. ie)* for car, foot and bicycle passengers to Ballyhack, on County Wexford's Hook Peninsula.

GREENWAYS IN THE SOUTHEAST

The southeast's growing network of car-free greenways are ideal for walkers and cyclists.

Following a former railway line from Dungarvan, the **Waterford Greenway** unfolds for 48km to Waterford city's quayfront. The descent is gentlest from east to west. En route are historic ruins, gardens, farmland, three viaducts, 11 bridges and a 400m-long tunnel. Pick-up/drop-off bike rental is available in Waterford city, Dungarvan and midway at Kilmacthomas.

The 24km **South East Greenway** from Waterford city to New Ross will open in 2027. Plans are in place to link New Ross to Woodstock, near Inistioge, with the aim to extend it to Thomastown, Graiguenamanagh, and ultimately the Waterford Greenway.

Both bars are venues for the spirited **Dunmore East Bluegrass Festival** *(discoverdunmore.com)* over three days in late August – definitely catch it if you can.

Hit the water

Just north of the harbour, **Dunmore Adventure** *(dunmoreadventure.com)* has a host of watersports, from sailing and powerboating courses to kayaking and SUP, as well as Ireland's biggest inflatable **aquapark** *(adult/child €27.50/25.50)*, and zippy **sea safari boat trips** *(adult/child €45/40)* around the coastline.

Take a hike

Gentle walks wind through the 17-hectare Dunmore East Woods. To take in the clifftop scenery, the bracing **Dunmore East Coastal Walk** runs from the harbour car park trailhead at Shanoon to **Portally Cove** (1.5km one-way; 45 minutes). A more strenuous extension continues on to **Ballymacaw Cove** (additional 4km one-way, allow an extra 90 minutes each way from Portally). Driving from Dunmore East to Tramore, the most scenic route is the signposted 16km coast drive via the narrow backroads.

Tramore

TIME FROM WATERFORD CITY: **15MIN**

Ride the waves

Tramore, 13km south of Waterford city, is its summer playground. The town climbs up the hillside above its 5km-long sand-spit **strand** (Tramore's Irish name, Trá Mhór, means 'big beach'), with funfair rides and amusement arcades by the seafront promenade. Live music at Tramore's pubs in season adds to the carnival atmosphere.

The sheltered bay's slow-forming waves make Tramore a year-round magnet for surfing, especially for beginner and intermediate surfers. Surf schools such as **Tramore Surf School** *(tramoresurfschool.com; wetsuit, boots & board hire €30, lessons from €40)* get you up on the waves.

Explore the coast

At the strand's eastern end, its 30m-long, marram-grass-covered sand dunes have been evolving for more than 50,000 years and are some of the highest in Ireland. From here, you can walk to the **Back Strand** intertidal salt-marsh lagoon, a haven for wading birds. Unpredictable currents make it unsafe for swimming. Brownstown Head bookends Tramore Bay to the east, with Great Newtown Head guarding the

EATING IN TRAMORE: OUR PICKS

Seagull Bakery: Piled high with loaves, filled pizza pockets, toasties and sourdough sandwiches, plus sweet pastries. *8am-4pm Wed-Sat, 9am-1pm Sun* €

Phat Cow: Tuck into burgers, hot dogs and spicy wings on the huge covered terrace overlooking the bay. *5-9pm Wed-Fri, 4-9pm Sat, 4-8pm Sun* €

Bardoe Pizza: Wood-fired sourdough pizzas with Italian ingredients: smoked Scamorza cheese, Tuscan salami, Sicilian olives. *3-9pm Thu-Sat, 2-8pm Sun* €€

One the Waterfront: Seafood dishes including a catch of the day served on a cliffside terrace overlooking Tramore's beach. *noon-9pm Fri & Sat, to 7pm Sun* €€

Newtown Cove

western end. Nearby, off Cliff Rd, are the rocky **Newtown Cove** and staircase-accessed **Guillamene Cove** for sheltered swimming and picnics.

Go to the races

Horses once raced along the strand. Since 1912, races have taken place at **Waterford & Tramore Racecourse** *(tramore races.ie)* at Graun Hill. Famous fixtures include New Year's Day's National Hunt and the four-day August Festival, with both National Hunt and Flat races, along with fashion, food stalls and live music.

Curraghmore

TIME FROM WATERFORD CITY: **30MIN**

Tour a palatial estate

Once occupying a whopping 400 sq km, today **Curraghmore House & Gardens** *(curraghmorehouse.ie; house, gardens and shell house tour €22)* covers a 'mere' 10 sq km, accessed 1km west of the village of Portlaw (19km northwest of Waterford city). Granted by Henry II in 1177, Curraghmore (meaning 'great bog') remains the seat of Lord and Lady Waterford. Its original medieval tower was enhanced in the 18th century by Georgian architect James Wyatt, with Victorian refurbishments in the 19th century. From May to September, tours give you an insight into its architectural and ancestral history, alongside its lavish furniture and art collections, and take in the 'shell house' folly constructed in 1754 from seashells. Afterwards, stroll the formal gardens and ancient oak woodland, and stop in at its wood-panelled courtyard tearooms.

Awesome Irish acts (eg Fontaines DC; CMAT) headline massive music, art, food and wellness festival **All Together Now** *(alltogethernow.ie)* over the August bank holiday weekend.

COUNTY WATERFORD'S COPPER COAST

Designated Ireland's first UNESCO Global Geopark in 2014, the geologically rich **Copper Coast** *(coppercoastgeopark. com)* stretches around 25km between **Kilfarrasy Beach** in the east and **Ballyvoyle Beach** in the west. Some 460 million years ago, volcanoes, deserts and ice sheets shaped the rugged coastline of rocky headlands, cliffs and coves, and produced copper-rich quartz that was mined here in the 19th century. Remains include the 1824 **winding-engine house ruins at Tankardstown**. At Bunmahon, the **Geological Garden** has rocks that form the area's foundations. Nearby, a restored 1828 church houses the **Copper Coast Geopark Visitor Centre**, detailing the coast's geological and mining history.

Dungarvan

TIME FROM WATERFORD CITY: **45MIN**

Discover Dungarvan's history

With its boat-filled bay and colourful pubs along the quayfront, Dungarvan (Dún Garbhán), 47km southwest of Waterford city at the western terminus of the Waterford Greenway (p160), has immediate charm. Guarding the harbour, **Dungarvan Castle** (*heritageireland.ie; free*), with its rare polygonal shell keep and 18th-century military barracks behind its curtain wall, has witnessed pivotal points throughout the last 800-plus years of Irish history; its exhibition opens from late April to September.

Spanning the River Colligan as it flows into the bay, a single-arch stone bridge built in 1801 is a legacy of the Duke of Devonshire, who rebuilt the town centre as it is today. The county town until the 2014 merger of Waterford's county and city councils, its history is detailed in the late 18th-century former grain store housing the **Waterford County Museum** (*waterfordmuseum.ie; free*).

Savour Dungarvan's flavours

Dungarvan's fishing boats, shellfish beds and seaweed harvesting, along with the surrounding fertile farmland, make it a foodie hub. Try to catch Thursday's lively **Dungarvan Farmers Market** (p164). Throughout the week, you can pick up produce and delicacies at an array of deli-cafes around town, and dine at excellent addresses, including Paul Flynn's destination restaurant/boutique accommodation/cookery school the **Tannery** (*tannery.ie; cookery school demonstrations from €95, hands-on courses €195*).

From April to September, Marie Power of the **Sea Gardener** (*theseagardener.com; 2½-hour walk €50*) runs foraging expeditions, seaweed-cookery workshops, beach picnics and talks.

At pubs around town, try brews named for local landmarks (such as Helvick Gold Blonde Ale, Copper Coast Red Ale and Comeragh Challenger Gluten Free Ale) from the **Dungarvan Brewing Company** (*dungarvanbrew.com; tour & tasting €20*), which runs 60- to 90-minute brewery tours.

Dungarvan's epicurean celebrations peak during April's three-day **Waterford Festival of Food** (*waterfordfestivaloffood.com*), with food trails, tours, demonstrations, daily markets and more.

DUNGARVAN CASTLE

Settlement in the Dungarvan area dates back to the Stone Age, but it only received its town charter in 1215 after King John of England constructed an Anglo-Norman fortification around the late 12th/early 13th century (an early reference from 1209 recounts the Bishop of Waterford captured the Bishop of Lismore and imprisoned him in the castle's dungeons). It survived Cromwell's aggression in 1649. The British Army and Royal Irish Constabulary used the military barracks until 1922 before the castle's destruction by the Anti-Treaty IRA during Ireland's Civil War. After the Free State's Garda Síochana (police) foundation, it became the local HQ until 1987, deteriorating until reopening in 2002 as a heritage attraction.

 EATING IN DUNGARVAN: OUR PICKS

Cass & Co: Deli/cafe with breakfast *blaas* (rolls), salads, sandwiches, cakes, pastries, slices. Best coffee. *8am-5pm Mon-Sat, 10.30am-3.30pm Sun* €

Moorings: Original wood panelling, a beer garden beneath Dungarvan Castle and local seafood (platters, fish pies and seafood chowder). *noon-8pm* €€

Old Bank: Set over two floors with views of Dungarvan Harbour. Modern Irish cuisine made from local/foraged produce. *12.30-3pm & 5.30-9pm Thu-Sat* €€

Tannery: Old tannery featuring seasonal masterpieces like crab *crème brûlée*, and venison with truffled walnut pesto. *5.30-9pm Wed-Sat, 12.30-3pm Sun* €€€

TRAVERSE WATERFORD'S MOUNTAINS & VALLEYS

Wind through the Comeragh and Knockmealdown mountains and enchanting Nire and Blackwater valleys on this loop drive from Dungarvan.

START	END	LENGTH
Dungarvan	Dungarvan	180km; 1 day

Leaving Dungarvan, the Comeragh Mountains climb to the Tipperary border. ❶ **Mahon Falls** cascade over 80m-high sandstone cliffs; an easy 2km one-way gravel path leads to the base. Circumnavigating the mountains and following the Nire Valley brings you to the Knockmealdown Mountains' 1832-founded Cistercian ❷ **Mt Melleray Abbey**; its Trappist monks run a heritage centre and tearooms. At Cappoquin, the late Georgian, John Roberts–designed ❸ **Cappoquin House and Gardens** blaze with rhododendrons and azaleas in spring. Upstream, ❹ **Lismore** is dominated by its vast 1185-founded castle. Within the 17th-century defensive walls, Lismore Castle Gardens unfold over 4 hectares, with a stately yew avenue and contemporary art gallery. Head west along the Blackwater's northern riverbank to Ballyduff, where the ❺ **Blackwater Distillery** crafts gin, vodka and whiskey and runs 45-minute guided tours and tastings.

In Villierstown, take a 90-minute boat tour with ❻ **Blackwater Eco Tours** or hire kayaks, canoes or motorboats.

Rhododendrons, azaleas and rare bulbs also flourish at ❼ **Dromana House & Gardens**, with forest walking trails to the river. At the Blackwater's confluence with the River Finisk, pass under the estate's Brighton Pavilion-inspired, Indo-Gothic ❽ **Dromana Gate**. Quiet roads lined by stone walls and hedgerows return to Dungarvan.

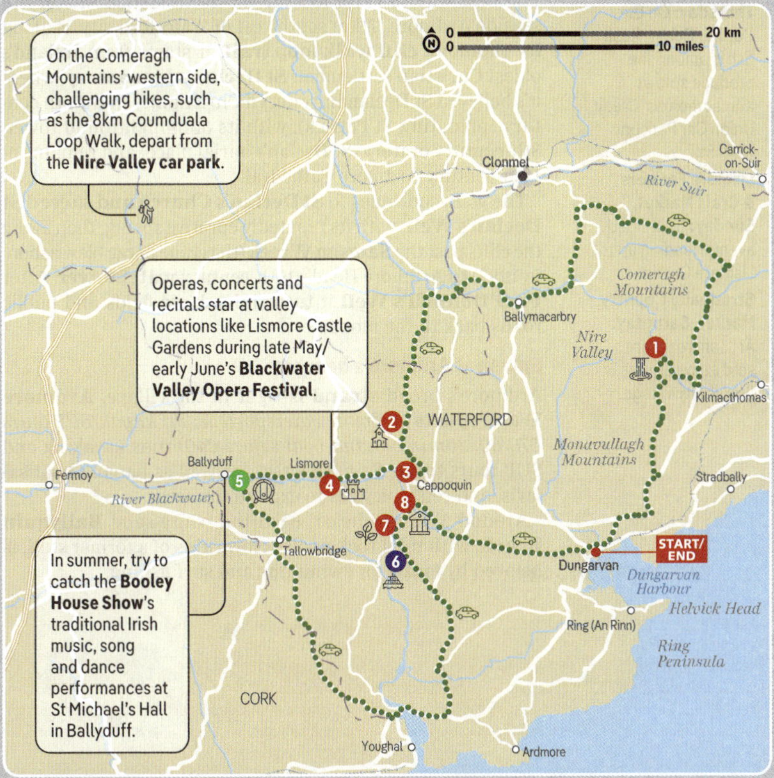

On the Comeragh Mountains' western side, challenging hikes, such as the 8km Coumduala Loop Walk, depart from the **Nire Valley car park**.

Operas, concerts and recitals star at valley locations like Lismore Castle Gardens during late May/early June's **Blackwater Valley Opera Festival**.

In summer, try to catch the **Booley House Show**'s traditional Irish music, song and dance performances at St Michael's Hall in Ballyduff.

BEST MARKETS IN COUNTY WATERFORD

Ardmore Farmers Market, Sunday: Live music during summer Sundays when stalls sell local produce, ready-to-eat dishes, art, crafts and jewellery.

Dungarvan Farmers Market, Thursday: Stalls selling breads, farmhouse cheeses, charcuterie, fruit and veggies and more, fills Dungarvan's Grattan Sq.

Kilmacthomas Farmers Market, Thursday: On the Copper Coast, fresh fish is among the produce sold at Kilmacthomas' Credit Union Car Park on Main St.

Lismore Farmers & Craft Market, Sunday: Stall-lined avenue leading up to Lismore Castle.

Stradbally Country Market, Saturday: Artisan treats are sold at the Square in Stradbally village.

Spin through the Ring Peninsula

Dungarvan is within easy reach of beaches such as sandy **Clonea Strand**, 6km east, with more on the Gaeltacht (Irish-speaking area) of the Ring Peninsula (An Rinn; 'the headland'), stretching around Dungarvan Bay to the south, with rural backroads winding through green fields.

Spirited trad-music sessions frequently take place at pubs including the **Marine Bar** *(facebook.com/MarineBarDungarvan)* and **Mooney's Tigh Tábhairne** *(facebook.com/Mooneyspub)*.

From Mooney's, it's an invigorating 7km round-trip walk along the **Helvick Head Walking Trail** to Helvick Harbour (also accessible by car), with panoramic views of the ocean and bay. By the harbour's fishing pier, wellness centre **Sólás na Mara** *(solasnamara.ie/treatments; 1hr seawater and seaweed bath single/double from €40/80)* harnesses locally harvested seaweed's naturally occurring nutrients like iodine, calcium and magnesium to ease ailments from skin conditions to stress in traditional Irish seaweed baths filled with freshly filtered, warmed seawater.

Ardmore

TIME FROM WATERFORD CITY: **1HR**

Walk Ardmore's clifftop loop trail

The best way to get a feel for the ecclesiastical history of seaside Ardmore, 71km southwest of Waterford city, is along its 4km-long **cliff walk loop trail**. It starts from Ireland's oldest Christian settlement, **St Declan's Monastery**, where it's believed St Declan introduced Christianity in the 5th century (predating St Patrick), with its 30m-high round tower, 8th-century oratory (St Declan's burial place) and remains of 12th-century Ardmore Cathedral.

The walk continues to **St Declan's Church and sacred St Declan's Well**, with its reputedly curative spring, then along the cliffs past the **Samson Wreck** (the crane barge blew ashore in 1987) to Ardmore Head's 19th-century **watchtower**. After **Fr O'Donnell's Well** it turns inland, via fields and public roads back to the monastery.

Splash at Ardmore's beaches

Ardmore's broad **strand** is right in the village. **Ardmore Watersports** *(ardmorewatersports.ie; 1hr kayak/SUP tours €70/60, 30min banana-boat safari €40)* runs kayaking and SUP tours to the *Samson* wreck, as well as banana-boat safaris, and rents bicycles to explore the area.

Around 5km northeast, beautiful white-sand **Ballyquin Beach**, with tidal rock-pools below ruins of a former stud, is beloved by locals for swimming and surf fishing.

Carlow Town

ARTS | HISTORY | MUSEUMS

The origins of Carlow's county town (Ceatharlach) stretch back into the mists of pre-written history. Winding through the town, the River Barrow was vital to Carlow's importance, evident in the remains of its castle and its military museum. While it might seem unlikely today, the town served as the capital of Ireland from 1361 to 1374 under King Edward III. Carlow's Catholic cathedral is the country's second oldest, and its college is Ireland's second-oldest tertiary education institution, established to educate Catholic men in the late 18th century. Now a non-religious, coeducational college for liberal arts and social studies, with a lively 600-strong student population, it's also the site of the town's artistic hub, the Visual Centre for Contemporary Art. Its success has catapulted Carlow's visual and performing-arts scenes to the fore and revitalised the town, which is today home to 27,351 people.

GETTING AROUND

Carlow's **train station** is on Railway Rd, situated under 1km northeast of the town centre (around a five- to 10-minute walk). Trains run north to Dublin Heuston, and south via Muine Bheag (Bagenalstown), Kilkenny city and Thomastown to Waterford city. Buses stopping at Carlow Coach Park, on the centre's southeastern edge, serve outlying areas.

Carlow's town centre is mainly flat and easily walkable. App-based bike-share service **Bolt** (bolt.eu) has bikes at 40 locations in and around town. Car parks are plentiful. Your own wheels are handy for exploring beyond the town centre and throughout the county.

Visual Centre for Contemporary Art (p167)

MAURICIO QUEVEDO/SHUTTERSTOCK

SIGHTS
1. Carlow Castle
2. Carlow Cathedral
3. Carlow County Museum
4. County Carlow Military Museum
5. Croppies Grave
6. Visual Centre for Contemporary Art

EATING
7. Caffè 500
8. Cell 38½
9. Lennons
10. Pimento

ENTERTAINMENT
11. George Bernard Shaw Theatre

SHOPPING
12. Made in Carlow

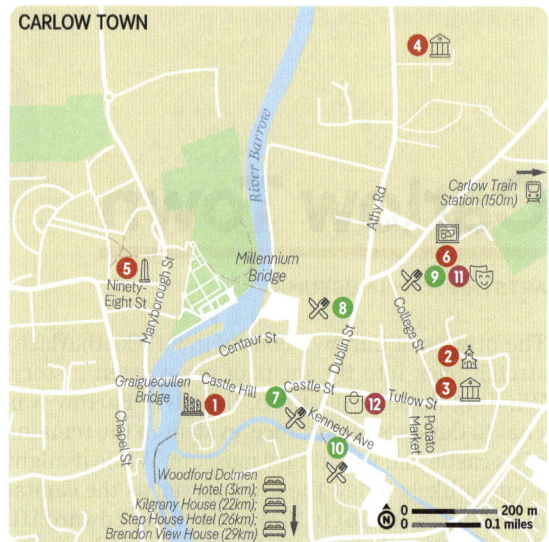

CARLOW TOWN

Check Out Local Landmarks

Castle, cathedral and county museum

Above the River Barrow, the early 13th-century **Carlow Castle** *(heritageireland.ie; free)* was once one of Ireland's most strategically important, but only the keep and two towers have survived, after a disastrous renovation attempt in 1814 to turn it into a psychiatric facility saw most of the structure destroyed.

The spire of **Carlow Cathedral**, aka the Cathedral of the Assumption *(carlowcathedral.ie)*, rises 46m above the town's rooftops. Built in 1828 from blue-grey limestone and white granite, it's the second-oldest Catholic cathedral in Ireland. Just south in a former convent with stained-glass windows, a carved cathedral pulpit is among the exhibits at the **Carlow County Museum** *(carlowmuseum.com; free)*. Some of its most intriguing displays are archaeological finds dating from 6700 BCE to the Middle Ages, including arrowheads, axes, granite hammers, pottery and an Iron Age glass bead, which were unearthed during the construction of the Carlow M9 bypass.

EATING IN CARLOW TOWN: OUR PICKS

Lennons: Visual Centre for Contemporary Art's day-cafe/night-bistro. Sustainable Irish produce. *11am-3.30pm Sun, Wed & Thu, to 3.30pm & 5.30-9.30pm Fri & Sat* €€

Caffè 500: Handmade pastas, wood-fired pizzas and antipasti platters, surrounded by Fiat parts, flags and canned tomatoes. *1-9.30pm Tue-Sun* €€

Pimento: Tapas with an Irish spin (cider-sautéed prawns; pickled fennel and black pudding). Riverside terrace, inventive cocktails. *5-10pm Sun-Thu, to 11.30pm Fri & Sat* €€

Cell 38½: All-day brunches and classic pub favourites (Irish whiskey-glazed ribs or smoked fish pie), plus a cocktail bar, in Clink boutique hotel. *8am-11pm* €€

Discover the Arts Scene
Galleries, performances and festivals
Adjacent to 1782-founded Carlow College, St Patrick's, the **Visual Centre for Contemporary Art** *(visualcarlow.ie; exhibitions free)* displays local and international works in five gallery spaces. It's also home to the **George Bernard Shaw Theatre**, presenting dance, film, music, plays and comedy.

On Tullow St, Carlow's main shopping street, gallery and design shop **Made in Carlow** *(madeincarlow.shop)* represents more than 100 Carlow artists, and the jewellery, prints, paintings, textiles, clothing, woodwork, ceramics, sculpture and photography make unique souvenirs.

Cultural festivities include June's five-day **Carlow Arts Festival** *(carlowartsfestival.ie)* and August's four-day **Carlow Fringe Festival** *(facebook.com/CarlowFringeArtsFestival)*.

Learn about Carlow's Military History
Resistance and rebellion
Given its strategic location on the Barrow and Slighe Cualann (one of the main roads to Tara, p476), control of Carlow was crucial for prospective rulers of Leinster, and Carlow has seen plenty of military action over the centuries. At the **County Carlow Military Museum** *(carlowmilitarymuseum.eu; €4/3.50)* you can see replica medieval suits of armour and swords, original 1798 Rebellion artefacts, including a Brown Bess musket, a display on WWII armoured vehicle production in Carlow and uniforms dating from the foundation of the Irish state to those currently in use. On the Barrow's western bank, in Governey Park, **Croppies Grave** is a monument to the 600 Carlow men massacred by British troops during the 1798 Rebellion.

> ☑ **TOP TIP**
> Many of the most appealing places to stay are on Carlow's town fringes and in the surrounding countryside, including over the border in neighbouring counties Laois and Kildare.

Beyond Carlow Town

Megalithic remains and majestic landscaped gardens lie in the fertile countryside fanning out into the county beyond Carlow town.

Places

Strawhall to Clonegal
p168

River Barrow to St Mullins
p169

GETTING AROUND

Buses serve main destinations in County Carlow, and trains south from Carlow town stop at Muine Bheag (Bagenalstown) en route to Kilkenny, Thomastown and Waterford city (from where trains run via County Tipperary to Limerick Junction). To reach out-of-the-way sights (including the majority of its gardens), you'll need your own wheels. Many hotels and B&Bs in the county rent bikes.

County Carlow covers just 897 sq km in its entirety (only County Louth is smaller), making it easy to cover in a day. It's worth planning to spend longer here though, especially to appreciate its famed gardens with vivid displays of colourful flowers to the east and south of Carlow town, with numerous walking opportunities. Outdoors enthusiasts will want to spend time exploring the River Barrow. Its towpath offers gentle walking and cycling between Carlow town and St Mullins (either the full distance or a shorter section). Paddling on the river in a kayak or canoe is a wonderful alternative to take in the scenery of this pretty part of the country.

Strawhall to Clonegal

TIME FROM CARLOW TOWN: **45MIN**

Follow Carlow's garden trail

Along the **Carlow Garden Trail** (*carlowgardentrail.com*), many of the county's renowned gardens are a legacy of its 'Big Houses' that are now spectacular horticultural works of art.

A trail highlight, just 2km north of Carlow town, is the not-for-profit **Delta Sensory Gardens** (*adult/child €6/5*) containing 20 interlocking, wheelchair-accessible gardens, including a 'five senses' garden, a musical fountain garden and a sculpture garden. Proceeds benefit the adjacent centre for adults with learning disabilities.

Duckett's Grove (*free*), 11km northeast of Carlow town, makes a dramatic impression. Alongside the ruins of a grand 18th-century mansion destroyed by fire in 1933, two interconnected walled gardens shelter historic varieties of roses and peonies, and a fruit orchard with heirloom Irish apple varieties such as Kerry Pippin and Irish Peach. A great kids' playground here has slides and an obstacle course.

One of Ireland's largest Spanish chestnut trees and a monumental beech tree guard the entrance to the 1-hectare **Hardymount Gardens** (*adult/child €5/free*), 15km southeast of Carlow town. Espaliered apple trees, trailing wisteria, sunflowers, foxgloves and agapanthus shelter inside the granite-walled garden.

Altamont Gardens (*free*), 24km southeast of Carlow town (5km east of Ballon) combine formal and informal gardens, and expansive lawns bordered by yews and hedges. An ice-age glen with mossy granite outcrops leads to riverside walks, with Sessile oaks dating from the 1750s towering above snowdrops and bluebells. Its herbaceous walled garden is home to a cafe.

At **Huntington Castle & Gardens** (*castle tour & gardens adult/child €13.95/6.50, gardens only €6.95/3*), 30km south-east of Carlow town in **Clonegal** (the southern terminus of the long-distance walking route the Wicklow Way), French lime trees line the avenue leading to the castle entrance and Italianate parterre gardens that were laid out in the 17th century. Gravel paths flanked by topiary and fountains pass fishponds, rose gardens and manicured lawns. Beyond the 500-year-old yew walk lies woodland and farmland on the 65-hectare estate. Tours of the castle itself, parts of which date from 1625, take place in summer.

In late July and early August, the eight-day **Carlow Garden Festival** has open gardens, talks, workshops, tours and picnics all across the county.

River Barrow to St Mullins

TIME FROM CARLOW TOWN: **50MIN**

Navigate the River Barrow

Extending for 192km in all, Ireland's second-longest river, the River Barrow (thought to be named after Borvo, the ancient Celtic god of spring water and minerals), travels through County Carlow on its way to Waterford Harbour. The original towpath, the **Barrow Way**, runs 48km from Carlow town to St Mullins and can be walked or cycled. You'll pass small villages; tower-house, mill and church ruins; and cascading weirs. Wildlife includes kingfishers, herons, dragonflies, damselflies, otters, hedgehogs and badgers.

With its wide, grid-like streets, Muine Bheag (Bagenalstown), 16km south of Carlow town, was said to have been modelled on France's Versailles in the 18th century by Walter Bagenal, whose plans were foiled by the diverted coach road. Its 1846 neoclassical railway station, designed by William Deane Butler, is one of Ireland's most beautiful.

A further 12km south is Borris (An Bhuiríos). Check seasonal tour dates and book ahead for **Borris House** (*borrishouse.ie; guided tours €10*), a rare estate dating back to ancient Ireland's royal families as the ancestral home of the MacMurrough-Kavanaghs, kings of Leinster.

To get out on the water, **Go With the Flow** (*gowiththeflow.ie; self-guided/guided tours from €25/29*) runs kayak and canoe tours, and has rentals to paddle yourself. Boats can be picked up and dropped off at various points on the river, such as **Clashganny** (Clais Ghainimh; 'sandy river trench'), a beautiful recreational area 5km south of Borris (9km north of St Mullins) with swimming, picnic facilities and looped forest trails.

Roam St Mullins' monastic ruins

Beyond Graiguenamanagh (p180), between the Blackstairs Mountains and Brandon Hill, the Barrow Way's southern terminus **St Mullins** (Tigh Moling) is today a serene little

IRELAND'S BIG HOUSES

Grand estate manors surrounded by demesne and parkland were built during the Protestant Ascendancy from the 17th century that saw an Anglican minority dominate socio-politically and economically; the term 'Big Houses' highlighted the stark differences between estate landlords and their tenants' living conditions, and imperial influence.

The 1903 Land Act encouraging sale to tenant farmers saw many landlords migrate and abandon the properties. During the Irish revolutionary period many Big Houses were attacked or destroyed. Very few were rebuilt; after the 1923 Land Act, the Irish Land Commission compulsorily acquired and redistributed untenanted estates, with demesnes divided into small farms.

River Barrow (p169)

COUNTY CARLOW'S MEGALITHIC SITES

Dubbed 'dolmen county', County Carlow is home to numerous megalithic sites, including its most famous portal tomb **Brownshill Dolmen**, topped by Europe's largest capstone, weighing 103 tonnes. Believed to date back 4900 to 5500 years, it's visible from the R726 in a field 4km east of Carlow town. **Haroldstown Dolmen**, 20km east of Carlow town, stands at over 2m, with two overlapping capstones and a large doorstone. On the eastern slopes of Knockroe Mountain, 12km east of Borris, **Knockroe Dolmen** has a tilted capstone with a horseshoe-like engraving and a spiral motif on one of its portal walls. Carlow County Museum has details of other sites throughout the county.

spot but was once one of Ireland's most important ecclesiastical sites and kings of Leinster burial place. Founded by St Moling (St Mullin) in the 7th century, near the holy waters of St Moling's Well are the ruins of **St Mullins Monastery** *(heritageireland.ie; free)*. Remains include church buildings, part of a round tower and a 9th-century high cross. Nearby is the grave of General Thomas Cloney, a hero of the 1798 Rebellion, and a monument marking the tomb of Art, King of Leinster (1357–1416). Although in the 12th and 13th centuries St Mullins became a major Anglo-Norman settlement (the hummocks on its village green are the remains of a motte-and-bailey castle), it never grew into a town. It's a beautiful and peaceful place for exploring the river.

 EATING BEYOND CARLOW TOWN: OUR PICKS

Mullicháin Café: Restored 18th-century storehouse. Soups, pizzas, open sandwiches and salads by the River Barrow in St Mullins. *11am-5pm Mar-Oct* €

Birdcage Cafe: All-day brunches in Muine Bheag (Bagenalstown). Local eggs, free-range meats, artisan breads, sausage rolls, pastries, sweets. *9am-2pm Mon-Sat* €

Clashganny House: An 1830s millhouse 5km south of Borris. Try black truffle-stuffed wood pigeon with redcurrant jus. *6-11pm Thu-Sat, 12.30-3.30pm Sun* €€

Sha-Roe Bistro: Enjoy Blackstairs Mountain lamb or pheasant with wild raspberries and nettles in a charming Clonegal cottage. *7-9.30pm Thu-Sat, 12.30-2.30pm Sun* €€€

Kilkenny City

HISTORY | ARCHITECTURE | CULTURE

With its turreted castle and the knot of narrow streets, Kilkenny is a medieval treasure. Known as the Marble City for its dark, fossil-speckled limestone, the city has played an outsize role throughout Ireland's history.

Kilkenny's Irish name, Cill Chainnigh, comes from the 6th-century monastery founded by St Canice. At the northern end of the medieval mile, which links the major sights, monumental St Canice's Cathedral dates from the 13th century. While Kilkenny's Anglo-Norman parliament instituted the 1366 Statutes of Kilkenny, intended to prevent the Anglo-Norman aristocracy's adoption of Irish culture and language, the 1641 Confederation of Kilkenny alliance of Irish and Anglo-Normans aimed to return Catholics' land and power, and Kilkenny was the capital of Ireland until Cromwell's invasion.

Today home to 27,184 people, legacies of Kilkenny's heritage resonate in its architecture, atmospheric pubs, sporting events (including Ireland's national game of hurling) and its many festivals.

Sightsee along Kilkenny's Medieval Mile
Castle, cathedral and intriguing museums

Starting from the landmark castle, Kilkenny's medieval mile connects its major sites in the city's historic heart.

Northwest of the castle, St Mary's Church was built by William Marshal in the early 13th century. It now houses the **Medieval Mile Museum** *(medievalmilemuseum.ie; audio museum tour adult/child €7/3, guided museum tour €10/5)*; its interactive map and timeline put 800 years of city history into context. Artefacts include maces, sceptres, keys, coins, civic records and skeletons, along with tombs in the Rothe Chapel and graves in the former churchyard, where upwards of 40,000 Kilkenny citizens (more than the current population) lie buried.

Works are underway to combine it with the adjacent **Tholsel** – the 1761 City Hall, with architectural features including a

Continues on p174

GETTING AROUND

Located 1.2km northeast of Kilkenny Castle, **MacDonagh Station** has trains north via Muine Bheag (Bagenalstown) and Carlow town to Dublin Heuston, and south via Thomastown to Waterford city. Stopping at the station and through the centre, buses serve outlying suburbs.

The centre is easily walkable. **Kilkenny Cycling Tours** *(kilkennycyclingtours.com)* rents wheels. **Bolt** *(bolt.eu)* has app-based e-bikes. You'll find car parks in and around the centre, with the largest off Parliament St.

☑ TOP TIP

Given its proximity to Dublin, 130km north, Kilkenny is hugely popular year-round, especially on weekends and during festivals/events. Book central accommodation well ahead at peak times or consider visiting midweek or staying in its surrounds.

TOP EXPERIENCE

Kilkenny Castle

Marking the southern end of the Medieval Mile, beside the River Nore in 21-hectare gardens, Kilkenny Castle fulfils every storybook fantasy of what a castle should look like. Dating back to the early days of the Anglo-Norman conquest, over the centuries it has undergone successive rebuilding, extensions and adaptations. Strolling its magnificent rooms, gardens and parkland evokes its rich past.

PANASPICS/SHUTTERSTOCK

TOP TIPS

- Guided tours last 50 minutes and access otherwise off-limits areas, including the castle's west wing and medieval foundations.

- Book tickets up to a week ahead to guarantee entry and minimise queuing for limited first-come, first-served same-day tickets.

PRACTICALITIES

- kilkennycastle.ie
- self-guided tours adult/child €8/4, guided tours €12/6
- 9.15am-5.30pm Apr-Sep, 9.30am-5pm Oct-Mar

History

Kilkenny Castle occupies the site of a wooden defensive tower built by Strongbow. His son-in-law, William Marshal, replaced it in 1192 with a stone castle; three of its four round towers still survive. Acquired in 1391 by the powerful Butler family, who lived here for almost six centuries, it was sold to the city for a token £50 in 1967 and has been open to the public since 1976.

Interior

In the chequered-floored entrance hall, the copper-green walls are hung with Butler family portraits, swords, daggers and (since extinct) Irish elk antlers. Also on the ground floor are the state dining room and beautifully wallpapered 'Chinese withdrawing room'.

The 19th-century Jamaican mahogany grand staircase leads to the 1st-floor tapestry room, adorned with 17th-century tapestries, as well as the anteroom, library and drawing room.

The 2nd floor is home to the children's nursery, 'blue bedroom', 'Chinese bedroom' and the Moorish staircase to the east wing's superb picture gallery.

Grounds

The castle's formal gardens featuring a terraced rose garden, central fountain, statues and 19th-century lake are surrounded by woodlands and open parkland teeming with wildlife.

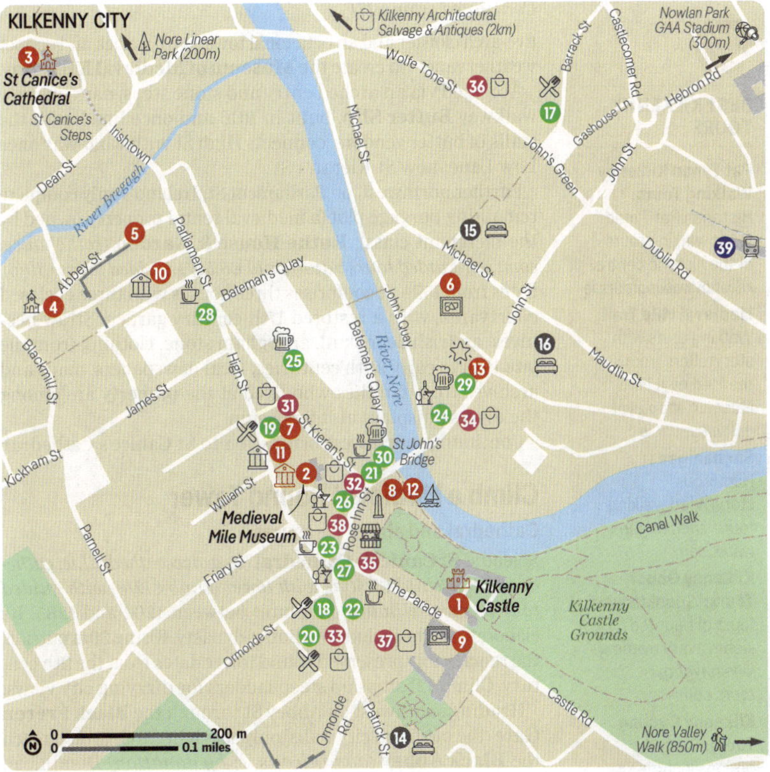

KILKENNY CITY

HIGHLIGHTS
1. Kilkenny Castle
2. Medieval Mile Museum
3. St Canice's Cathedral

SIGHTS
4. Black Abbey
5. Black Freren Gate
6. Butler Gallery
7. Butter Slip
8. Kilkenny Hurlers Statue
9. National Design & Craft Gallery
10. Rothe House & Garden
11. Tholsel

ACTIVITIES
12. Boat Trips Kilkenny
13. Kilkenny Cycling Tours

SLEEPING
14. Butler House
15. Celtic House
16. Langton's Hotel Kilkenny

EATING
17. Campagne
18. Ember
19. Petronella
20. Zuni

DRINKING & NIGHTLIFE
21. Brewtaly
22. Cafe La Coco
23. Chocolate Garden Cafe
24. Dylan Whisky Bar
25. Kyteler's Inn
26. Lanigan's Legends Bar
27. Left Bank
28. Little Green Grocer
29. Sullivan's Taproom
30. Tynans Bridge House Bar

SHOPPING
31. 38co
32. Butterslip Gift Shop
33. Folkster
34. Hurley Depot
see 9 Kilkenny Design Centre
35. Kilkenny Farmers Market
36. Padmore & Barnes
37. Rudolf Heltzel
38. Yvonne Ross

TRANSPORT
39. MacDonagh Train Station

EATING IN KILKENNY CITY: BEST RESTAURANTS

Ember: Irish meats/seafood flame-grilled over sustainable charcoal on a South African braai (barbeque) in the stylish dining room. *12.30-3pm & 5-9pm* €€

Campagne: By the old railway arches, regional French cuisine from seasonal Irish produce. *5.30-9pm Wed-Sat, 12.30-2.30pm Sun* €€€

Petronella: Modern Irish cuisine in a stone-walled, oak-beamed building in a narrow medieval alleyway. *noon-2.30pm & 4-9.30pm Tue-Sat, noon-5pm Sun* €€€

Zuni: Sophisticated yet informal; try glazed pork belly with a black pudding croquette, parsnip purée and beetroot and red-onion marmalade. *12.30-2.30pm & 5-9pm* €€€

BEST KILKENNY TOURS

Pat Tynan Kilkenny Walking Tours: Historian Pat Tynan leads walking tours of the historic centre. *kilkennywalkingtours.ie*

Medieval Mile Trail: Walking tours with storytellers from the Medieval Mile Museum. *medievalmilemuseum.ie*

Shenanigans: Humorous, story-filled walking tours. *shenanigans walks.com*

Kilkenny Ghost Tours: 'Spooktacular' tours of haunted sights every evening. *kilkennyghosttours.com*

Kilkenny Cycling Tours: Guided options include sunset tours. *kilkennycyclingtours.com*

Boat Trips Kilkenny: River cruises along the Nore take you below the castle. *boattrips.ie*

Kilkenny Road Train Tours: Commentary and singalongs aboard a miniature 'train' (on wheels). *kilkennyroadtraintours.com*

Continued from p171

five-arch cloister and an octagonal tower with a clock and copper weathervane – to create the **Museum of Medieval Kilkenny**.

Accessed via an arched entry and stone steps, dark, narrow walkway **Butter Slip**, built in 1616 and once lined with the stalls of butter vendors, connects High St with what was once Low Lane, now St Kieran's St.

Further northwest, on Parliament St, Ireland's only complete remaining burgage plot (a medieval rental property owned by the merchant class), **Rothe House & Garden** *(rothehouse. com; self-guided tours adult/child €8.50/4, guided tours €10/6)*, dates from 1594. It comprises three houses with three enclosed courtyards, with a restored 17th-century garden. Straw beehives, an Irish deer skull, an Ogham stone, clothing from the late 19th to early 20th centuries, local newspapers, maps and archives from families who lived at the property are among the diverse displays at its museum.

Continuing northwest brings you to St Canice's Cathedral.

Climb a Medieval Round Tower
Cathedral and abbey treasures

Splendid **St Canice's Cathedral** *(stcanicescathedral.ie; cathedral adult/child €7.50/5, with tower climb €12/8, with guided tour & tower climb €16/9)*, built between 1202 and 1285. Its elaborate tombs include the Butler dynasty. Rising 30m outside, the remarkably preserved round tower dates from the 9th century. Climb 121 steps up steep ladders for dizzying city views.

Heading southwest on Abbey St through the **Black Freren Gate** (the medieval city walls' only surviving arch), you'll reach the **Black Abbey** *(dominicans.ie; by donation)* Dominican priory, built in 1225 by William Marshal. Measuring almost 45 sq metres, Ireland's largest stained-glass window, which depicts the 15 mysteries of the rosary, was created in 1892. Among the abbey's other treasures are a pre-Reformation statue of St Dominic carved from Irish oak and an alabaster sculpture of the Holy Trinity, which has a rare depiction of God holding Jesus on the crucifix and was hidden behind a wall until its 19th-century discovery.

Hear Tales of Kilkenny's Witchcraft Trials
Intriguing inn

Several sights along the medieval mile have connections to the infamous witchcraft trial of Dame Alice Kyteler in medieval Kilkenny.

Dame Alice established **Kytelers Inn** *(kytelersinn.com)* on St Kieran's St in the early 14th century. Fantastically atmospheric spaces including its oak-beamed, Liscannor-stone main bar, vaulted Kilkenny-marble tavern bar and baronial hall-style top bar make it a must-visit for a pint, a meal and live music.

After Dame Alice's four wealthy husbands died in mysterious circumstances, she fled Ireland to avoid conviction for witchcraft; in her absence, her maid, Petronella de Meath, was burned at the stake in 1324 on the spot immediately north of St Mary's Church where Kilkenny's Tholsel was built in 1761. St Canice's Cathedral's central tower collapsed in 1332 after Dame Alice's son, William, was made to carry out roof repairs as penance.

Browse Irish Crafts & Design

Galleries and artisan shops

Opposite Kilkenny Castle, its former stables and coach houses, **Castle Yard**, is now Ireland's showcase for contemporary craft and design, the **National Design & Craft Gallery** *(dcci.ie; free)*. Textiles, ceramics and jewellery are the focus of its exhibitions. It also hosts events and workshops. Irish-made homewares, clothing, stationery, art and other artisan wares are for sale at the adjacent **Kilkenny Design Centre** *(kilkennydesign.com)*.

The **Butler Gallery** *(butlergallery.ie; free)*, in a former almshouse on the River Nore's eastern bank, mounts mainly modern and contemporary art exhibitions, and sculptures stud its walled garden. Its on-site shop sells arts and crafts made in Kilkenny and its surrounds, such as Jerpoint glass, Moth to a Flame candles, Caroline Dolan ceramics and Tinnakeenly leather bags and wallets.

Jewellers worth seeking out in the city centre include **Yvonne Ross** *(yvonneross.com)*, creating contemporary custom pieces; and **Rudolf Heltzel** *(rudolfheltzel.com)*, using traditional gold- and silversmithing techniques.

Feel Kilkenny's Hurling Pride

Catch a game or tour

The oldest and fastest field sport in the world, Ireland's ancient game of hurling dates back almost 3000 years. Hurling and the women's game camogie (pronounced 'kuh-mow-gee', with a hard 'g') were inscribed on UNESCO's representative list for Intangible Cultural Heritage in 2018. Founded in 1887, Kilkenny's hurling team, the Cats, are the most successful in Irish history, winning the Provincial Leinster Championships 77 times and the All-Ireland Championship 36 times to date. The Cats' home ground is GAA stadium **Nowlan Park** *(kilkennygaa.ie)*, with a capacity of around 27,000. The hurling season runs from January to July.

You can take a two-hour 'ultimate hurling experience' with **The Kilkenny Way** *(thekilkennyway.com; adult/child €30/25)*. It includes a stadium tour, with the chance to try the

---

BEST SHOPPING IN KILKENNY CITY

Kilkenny Farmers Market: In Market Yard on Thursdays: farmhouse cheeses, artisan breads, farm produce, preserves. *@kilkennyfarmersmarket*

Butterslip Gift Shop: Colourful shop with toys, games, babywear, cards, jewellery. *butterslip.com*

Kilkenny Architectural Salvage & Antiques: Vintage treasures like signs, furniture, art, industrial equipment, lighting. *eurosalve.com*

Folkster: Founded by Blanaid Hennessy: own-design dresses. Clothing and accessories from small, independent labels. *folkster.com*

38co: Lifestyle boutique with fashion, leather bags, ceramic jewellery. *facebook.com/thirtyeightco38*

Padmore & Barnes: All-weather clothing, footwear, tents, fishing gear, mountaineering equipment. *padmore-barnes.com*

 DRINKING IN KILKENNY: OUR PICKS

Sullivan's Taproom: Reviving brewing with its Black Marble Stout, Maltings Red Ale and Irish Gold. Huge beer garden. *noon-11pm Sun-Thu, to 12.30pm Fri & Sat*

Tynans Bridge House Bar: Charming former grocery-pub with original timber cabinetry opposite St John's Bridge. *10.30am-11.30pm Sun-Thu, to 12.30pm Fri & Sat*

Dylan Whisky Bar: Cosy snugs, open turf fire and tasting flights from 200-strong whiskey collection. *5pm-midnight Mon-Fri, from 3pm Sat & Sun*

Left Bank: Magnificent 1870s Bank of Ireland building, with nine bars, regular live music, a heated courtyard and 1st-floor nightclub. *noon-11pm Sun-Thu, to 2am Fri & Sat*

BEST KILKENNY FESTIVALS

St Patrick's Festival Kilkenny: Celebrations over four days in March. *stpatricksfestival kilkenny.com*

Kilkenny Tradfest: Four-day mid-March event: gigs, sessions, workshops, trad-music trail. *kilkennytradfest.com*

Kilkenny Roots Festival: Bluegrass, swing, folk, rockabilly, Cajun music during May's four-day fest. *kilkennyroots.com*

Cat Laughs Comedy Festival: Irish and international comedians over four days in June. *thecatlaughs.com*

Kilkenny Arts Festival: Over 250 artists, more than 150 events at historic venues during August's 11-day extravaganza. *kilkennyarts.ie*

Savour Kilkenny: Harvest celebrations: four days in October. *savourkilkenny.com*

Yulefest: Winter cheer: late November to late December. *yulefestkilkenny.ie*

Kilkenny camogie player (p175)

game yourself, before watching classic games at **Lanigan's Legends Bar**, surrounded by sporting memorabilia.

Across the road from Lanigan's is the 4.2m-high, striped limestone **Kilkenny Hurlers statue**, featuring three players reaching for a sliotar (ball).

At the **Hurley Depot** (*facebook.com/TheHurleyDepot*), you can buy equipment, including Kilkenny-made hurleys (sticks) and black-and-amber Cats clothing.

Explore the River Nore

River strolling and summer swimming

Tracing the banks of the River Nore, the **Nore Linear Park** (*trailkilkenny.ie*) is a series of signposted walking trails covering 6.5km. You can take on a short section or allow around two hours for the complete stretch, which starts on the eastern bank just south of the city centre on Maudlin St. From here, follow it downstream via a boardwalk to the city's ring road and then cross the pedestrian bridge to the western bank and head upstream past the castle and its gardens through the city centre and the Bishop Meadows parkland. Finish by cooling off at the weir swimming area, which is patrolled by lifeguards in summer.

Leading east from the ring road, the **Nore Valley Walk** shadows the river for 10km from Kilkenny to the pretty village of Bennettsbridge; look out for wildlife, including kingfishers and otters en route.

DRINKING IN KILKENNY: BEST COFFEE

Little Green Grocer: Sustainable deli serving Cork's Badger & Dodo coffee in compostable cups: organic dairy or plant-based milk. *9am-6pm Mon-Sat*

Cafe La Coco: Cute striped-awning cafe specialising in unusual lattes (pumpkin, rose and lavender). *8am-3pm Mon, Tue, Thu & Fri, to 4pm Sat, 9am-4pm Sun*

Chocolate Garden Cafe: Complimentary handcrafted chocolates with coffee, hot/iced chocolates, matcha lattes. *9.30am-4.30pm Mon-Fri, 10am-5.30pm Sat & Sun*

Brewtaly: Italian cafe brewing espressos, cappuccinos, iced lattes and frappuccinos with fresh-baked focaccia and tiramisu. *9am-5pm Mon-Fri, 10am-5pm Sat & Sun*

Beyond Kilkenny City

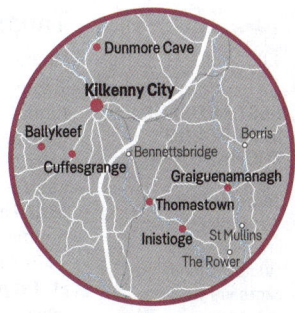

Leaving the lively city's limits, County Kilkenny's countryside is home to charming towns, villages, gardens, artisans and evocative monastic ruins.

The rural corners of County Kilkenny are some of the loveliest in Ireland. Thomastown's colourful streetscapes are the jumping-off point for the superbly preserved ruins of Jerpoint Abbey, fascinating medieval remains unexpectedly discovered at working farm Jerpoint Park, as well as a trove of artisan producers and craftspeople, the prestigious golf course at magnificent estate Mount Juliet and rescued Romantic-era gardens. Grand Victorian gardens have been regenerated on the edge of Inistioge, a photogenic gem of a village above the River Nore. On the River Barrow, Graiguenamanagh's ancient abbey endures as a Catholic Parish church. Walking trails lead along the river and high up on Brandon Hill, from where you can survey the surrounding landscapes.

Places
Dunmore Cave p177
Thomastown p178
Inistioge p178
Cuffesgrange to Ballykeef p179
Graiguenamanagh p180

Dunmore Cave

TIME FROM KILKENNY CITY: **14MIN**

Descend into the 'darkest place in Ireland'

As famous for its history as for its otherworldly calcite formations, **Dunmore Cave** *(heritageireland.ie; adult/child €5/3)*, 11km north of Kilkenny city, has yielded many archaeological treasures. Guided tours lead you down a steep descent to caverns full of dazzling stalactites, stalagmites and columns. There are 700 steps in all. Although the show cave is well lit and spacious, it's damp and chilly, so dress warmly.

According to the *Annals of the Four Masters* chronicles of medieval Irish history, in 928 marauding Vikings slaughtered 1000 people at two ringforts near the cave. When survivors hid in the caverns, the Vikings tried to smoke them out by lighting fires at the entrance. Excavations in 1973 uncovered the skeletons of at least 44 people, mostly women and children (the men being dragged off and enslaved). They also found coins dating from the 10th century, potentially dropped by the marauding Vikings (who often carried them under the arms, secured with wax); though few marks of violence on the skeletons mean suffocation was more likely the cause of death.

GETTING AROUND

Thomastown is on the trainline linking Dublin Heuston, via Kilkenny city, Muine Bheag (Bagenalstown) and Carlow town, with Waterford city; Thomastown Station is 1km west of town on Station Rd. Buses serve other main towns and villages, but you'll need your own wheels to reach sights further afield. Some accommodation providers have bike hire, or rent them in Kilkenny city. Find walking-trail routes at *trailkilkenny.ie*.

BEST ARTISANS IN & AROUND THOMASTOWN

Jerpoint Glass: Watch glassblowing in action at this studio in Stoneyford, 6km southwest of Thomastown. *jerpointglass.com*

Eoghan Leadbetter: In Stoneyford, woodturner Eoghan Leadbetter transforms timbers from local wind-felled trees into beautiful, practical items. *eoghanleadbetter.com*

Brid Lyons: Ceramicist Brid Lyons has a gallery in Thomastown. Also runs pottery courses. *bridlyonsceramics.com*

Nicholas Mosse: Shop (and cafe) of renowned potter–ceramicist Nicholas Mosse. In charming stone mill on River Nore in Bennettsbridge, 9km north of Thomastown. *nicholasmosse.com*

Moth to a Flame: Exquisite handcrafted candles at this Bennettsbridge workshop. *mothtoaflame.ie*

Thomastown

TIME FROM KILKENNY CITY: **17MIN**

Unearth Thomastown's architectural treasures

Thomastown (Baile Mhic Andáin; historically known as Grennan), 17km southeast of Kilkenny city, centres on a quadrant of streets lined by colourfully painted buildings and enticing cafes. Few fragments of its medieval town walls remain today; among them are the ruins of circa 1350 former tollhouse, **Mullin's Castle**, by the bridge spanning the River Nore; a popular spot for trout fishing.

More spectacular ruins are located 2.5km southwest of town at **Jerpoint Abbey** (*heritageireland.ie; adult/child €5/3*), one the most complete Cistercian abbey ruins in Ireland. The abbey dates from the 12th century, and the tower and cloister were constructed in the 15th century. From March to October, 45-minute tours depart from the visitor centre, which has an exhibition on the abbey's history as well as details of children's 'treasure hunts' to find saints, knights, mythological beasts and exotic animals carved into the abbey's stonework.

Sprawling across a hectare of pastoral landscapes 10.5km west of Jerpoint Abbey (16km south of Kilkenny), **Kells Priory** (*heritageireland.ie; free*) was founded in 1193 by Geoffrey FitzRobert, brother-in-law of Strongbow. Extensive ruins of this fortified Augustinian monastery remain, including a nave, chancel, chapel, bread oven and mill – much of what you see today dates from the 15th century, before King Henry VIII's suppression of Catholic monasteries. Tours run from mid-June to August. At dusk, the silhouetted ruins have an ethereal enchantment. Rising 2km south of the priory is the 29m-high **Kilree round tower**, dating from 1100, alongside the remains of a church. Outside, the Celtic high cross thought to date from the 9th century is believed to mark the non-Christian burial place of Irish high king Niall Caille.

Inistioge

TIME FROM KILKENNY CITY: **30MIN**

Fall for Inistioge's charms

With its 18th-century, 10-arch stone bridge and central green ringed by quaint houses, churches, cafes and pubs, Inistioge (Inis Tíog), on the River Nore 26km southeast of Kilkenny, is one of Ireland's prettiest villages. Parallel to the river, the **Nore Valley Walk** (*trailkilkenny.ie*) links Inistioge with Thomastown on a beautiful 11km route through pastoral and wooded landscapes and passing the ruins of Dysart and Grennan castles.

EATING IN & AROUND THOMASTOWN: OUR PICKS

Truffle Fairy: Handmade chocolates, muffins, slices, cookies at this aqua-painted cafe/shop. *10am-4.30pm Wed & Thu, to 5pm Fri & Sat* €

Tābú: Serving local tapas twists like Irish stew empanadas and calamari *frittura* with wild garlic aioli. *5-9pm Thu & Fri, 1-3pm & 5-9pm Sat & Sun* €€

Kings Mill: Classic Italian cuisine in 16th-century stone mill overlooking a weir 13km west of Thomastown. *10am-8pm Tue-Thu & Sun, to 9pm Fri & Sat* €€

Dizzy Goat: All ingredients come from this working goat/wild boar farm, and surrounding suppliers. *5.30-8pm Wed & Thu, to 9pm Fri & Sat, noon-4.30pm Sun* €€

Bridge, Inistioge

Inistioge's greatest attraction lies just outside the village 1.5km to the south. At **Woodstock Gardens & Arboretum** *(woodstock.ie; per car €5)*, 20 hectares of formal and informal gardens have been restored to the Victorian era of 1840 to 1890, when they were originally developed. Its long avenues are lined with noble fir and monkey puzzle trees. Foxgloves, lavender and cornflowers on the terraced flower garden are linked to the rose garden by the yew walk. Adjoining the walled kitchen garden, the enchanting cast-iron conservatory containing tearooms opens to a sunny outdoor terrace. In the arboretum is Ireland's tallest silver fir and a coast redwood, as well as Bentham cypress, beech and oak trees. Numerous walking paths include a waterfall trail past cascading streams. Allow at least a couple of hours to explore.

Plans are underway for a **greenway** *(woodstocktosegreenway.ie)* linking Woodstock with the South East Greenway at New Ross, County Wexford (p152).

Cuffesgrange to Ballykeef

TIME FROM KILKENNY CITY: **21MIN**

Taste Kilkenny's tipples

Kilkenny's lush landscapes and limestone soils are ripe for farms and producers. With distinctive red-painted iron gates, **Highbank Orchards** *(highbankorchards.com; self-guided orchard walk €15)*, 13km southwest of Kilkenny city, is an organic apple orchard making apple cider, rum, brandies, gin, schnapps and wine, along with apple juice, syrups and vinegars. Book ahead to take a self-guided tour of the orchards, stopping at a dozen QR-code checkpoints, and stock up at its farm shop (part of the tour admission is refundable when you buy).

Head 6km to the west to find **Ballykeefe Distillery** *(ballykeefedistillery.ie; customised tours on request)*, which produces whiskey, poitín, vodka and gin from grain grown on

MOUNT JULIET ESTATE

Ranging over 200 hectares 6km southwest of Thomastown, **Mount Juliet** *(mountjuliet.ie)* was originally two properties, Walton's Grove and Ballylinch, both held by Anglo-Norman families before their 1653 seizure by Cromwell. In 1654, Cromwell granted Ballylinch to a supporter, whose daughter's marriage brought it into the Butler family. Somerset Hamilton Butler, the 1st Earl of Carrick, purchased Walton's Grove (owned by the Duke of York), building the Georgian manor in 1757 and naming it for his wife, Lady Juliana Boyle, daughter of the 1st Earl of Shannon. Mount Juliet was home to seven earls before its last private owners, the McCalmonts, bought it in 1914. It's now a five-star hotel and championship golf course.

Graiguenamanagh

BEST OUTDOORS ACTIVITIES IN & AROUND GRAIGUENAMANAGH

Graiguenamanagh Bike Hire: By the River Barrow at Waterside Guesthouse. Rents bikes to traverse the 8km towpath to St Mullins, County Carlow. *watersideguesthouse.com*

Pure Adventure: On the quay. Runs white-water kayaking trips, scenic canoe tours and SUP trips. *pureadventure.ie*

Kilkenny Hydrobikes: From Graiguenamanagh's quayside rowing club, you can hire 'hydrobikes' (pedal-powered canoes). *kilkennycyclingtours.com*

Barrow Valley Activities Hub: On the Barrow's banks, this 1.6-hectare park is a central hub for walking, cycling, swimming. *barrowvalleyactivitieshub.ie*

Brandon Hill Loop: This 19km (five- to six-hour) loop walk up Brandon Hill (Cnoc Bhréanail) yields a 360-degree panorama of the Barrow Valley, Mt Leinster and Blackstairs Mountains. *trailkilkenny.ie*

its farm and water from its 80m-deep aquifer. Tours take in its millhouse, brewhouse, copper pot stills, barrel-aging room and bottling plant, finishing with tastings.

Graiguenamanagh TIME FROM KILKENNY CITY: 30MIN

Discover Duiske Abbey

A hub for river activities, engaging Graiguenamanagh (pronounced 'greg-nuh-mah-na' and locally dubbed Graig, ie 'greg') sits 28km southeast of Kilkenny, where the Barrow marks the border with County Carlow, with Tinnahinch on the Carlow side; the greater township is often referred to as 'Graiguenamanagh-Tinnahinch'. Its Irish name, Graig na Manach, means grange (valley or village) of the monks.

Monumental **Duiske Abbey** *(villageofthemonks.com/duiskeabbey; by donation)* was built in 1204 by William Marshal, making it one of the first and largest Cistercian abbeys in Ireland. Constructed mainly of imported yellow limestone, its remarkable carvings include a Norman knight with a sword and still leaf foliage. After 1536, when it was suppressed by Henry VIII, it fell into ruin; and in 1744, the tower collapsed into the nave, before a full restoration in the 1980s that retained its medieval floor tiles and processional door. Outside are two high crosses from the 8th and 9th centuries.

Soak up Graiguenamanagh's spirit

An equally noteworthy sight is Graiguenamanagh's unchanged-in-generations traditional Irish pub, grocery and hardware store **Mick Doyle's** *(facebook.com/mickdoylesgraig)* for live trad sessions and pints.

For three days in August, this 'village of the monks' transforms into a **Town of Books** *(graiguenamanaghtownofbooks.ie)*, with independent and antiquarian sellers setting up throughout town.

Places We Love to Stay

€ Budget €€ Midrange €€€ Top End

Wexford Town

Blue Door €€ Central yet peacefully situated B&B in a restored Georgian townhouse run by a welcoming owner/chef.

Talbot Hotel €€ Harbourside landmark with stylish rooms, dining and leisure facilities (including a pool) and free parking.

Killiane Castle Country House €€ A 17th-century manor with eight rooms and four self-catering apartments adjoining a 15th-century castle, 5km south of town.

Beyond Wexford Town

Riverside Park €€ Modern hotel on the banks of the River Slaney less than 10 minutes' walk from Enniscorthy's centre.

Dunbrody Country House Hotel €€€ Celebrity chef Kevin Dundon's Georgian property incorporates restaurants, a cookery school and beautifully wallpapered guest rooms.

Waterford City

Granville Hotel €€ Early 1700s quayside showpiece with antique-furnished rooms, spectacular stained glass and outstanding dining, including breakfasts.

Fitzwilton Hotel €€ Contemporary street-art-painted hotel with modern rooms (four wheelchair accessible), welcoming staff and limited free parking.

Waterford Castle €€€ Turreted castle on its own island in the River Suir 5km east of the city (reached round-the-clock by private car ferry).

Faithlegg €€€ Elegant 18th-century manor 9km east of the city, with exceptional dining and a golf course.

Beyond Waterford City

Hanora's Cottage €€ Charming guesthouse beside the river in the Nire Valley, with a gourmet restaurant and Jacuzzi-equipped rooms.

Beach Haven House €€ Spotless Tramore property a short stroll from the beach with B&B and self-catering accommodation, and super-friendly hosts.

Round Tower Hotel €€ Family-run 1920s Ardmore hotel beneath St Declan's monastery ruins, with an on-site bar and restaurant.

Park Hotel €€ Dungarvan resort-style complex in landscaped grounds with 84 rooms, 15 self-catering lodges, a 20m swimming pool and gym.

Cliff House Hotel €€€ Cliff-perched small luxury property in Ardmore with sea-view rooms, a swimming pool, spa and Michelin-starred restaurant.

Beyond Carlow Town

Step House Hotel €€ Boutique gem on Borris' main street, with a brasserie and cellar restaurant.

Brandon View House €€ B&B 3km northeast of St Mullins with organically grown farm produce (including packed lunches) and views of the heather-clad mountains.

Woodford Dolmen Hotel €€ Riverside hotel in 4-hectare grounds with an on-site restaurant and bar, 3km south of Carlow town.

Kilgraney House €€€ Georgian country house 7km north of Borris with guest suites, cottages and extensive gardens.

Kilkenny City

Langton's Hotel Kilkenny €€ Kilkenny empire with historic and modern rooms, gardens, multiple restaurants and bars and nightly live music.

Celtic House €€ Superbly located B&B with full Irish breakfasts and four rooms decorated with its artist-owner's landscapes.

Butler House €€€ In private gardens with an entrance to Castle Yard, this 1786 mansion has 17 sumptuous period-furnished rooms.

Beyond Kilkenny City

Tower House €€ One of the three stylishly renovated rooms in this medieval Thomastown tower house has an arrow-slit 'murder hole'.

Lawcus Farm €€ On the King's River 10km northwest of Thomastown with B&B rooms in an old stone farmhouse, and a self-contained treehouse.

Waterside €€ A Graiguenamanagh landmark, this converted grain store has comfy guesthouse accommodation and a great restaurant.

Grove Farmhouse €€ Countryside views extend from this 200-year-old house's four rooms on a working farm 5km southwest of Inistioge.

Left: musician, Cork Jazz Festival (p191); right: Mizen Head (p214)

For places to stay in Cork, see p219

Researched by
Catherine Le Nevez

Cork

URBAN BUZZ, ARTISAN PRODUCERS, WILD COASTLINE

From Cork, the rebel city, and the culinary hot-spots of Kinsale and Ballymaloe to the wild scenery of the far west peninsulas, Ireland's biggest county has it all.

Everything good about Ireland can be found in County Cork. Surrounding the country's second city – a thriving metropolis made glorious by location and its almost Rabelaisian devotion to the finer things of life – is a lush, undulating landscape dotted with charming villages. The city's understated confidence is grounded in its plethora of food markets and ever-evolving cast of creative dining venues; and in its selection of pubs, entertainment and cultural pursuits.

Ireland's largest county can fairly lay claim to being the nation's food and drink capital, with 60% of the country's artisan producers located here. Lush pastures provide prime meat and dairy products, while superb seafood is landed around the coast. It seems as if you can't move here without bumping into a traditional cheesemaker, artisan baker or boutique coffee roaster. The gateway to the Wild Atlantic Way, Kinsale, is famous for its seafood; Clonakilty for its black pudding; and Ballymaloe as the birthplace of Ireland's dedication to local produce.

Further west, you'll follow narrow roads around rugged, rock-girt coastlines and pass through a dozen or more old fishing villages where boats bob at their moorings and harbourside bars entice you in. The scenery is especially enchanting along the Mizen Head, Sheep's Head and Beara peninsulas, where you can wander the wild hills and get in touch with Ireland's ancient past.

THE MAIN AREAS

CORK CITY
Ireland's second city. **p188**

CLONAKILTY
Market towns and harbour villages. **p202**

BANTRY
Coast and mountain scenery. **p210**

Find Your Way

Cork is Ireland's largest county, and it takes a fair bit of travelling to cover it all. Its highlights capture its fascinating diversity, from city to coast, offshore islands, fertile farmland and wild mountain scenery.

Bantry, p210
A lively market town with a grand stately home, Bantry is a gateway to the rugged mountain scenery of the far west peninsulas.

CAR
A car is pretty much essential for exploring County Cork's remote corners away from the main towns, especially along the coast and around the Mizen Head, Sheep's Head and Beara peninsulas. Major car-rental companies are located at Cork airport, 8km south of the city.

TRAIN
Trains link Dublin Heuston and Tralee, County Kerry, with Cork city's Kent Station, which has frequent services to Midleton, Fota and Cobh, useful for day trips in either direction. No trains serve the west of the county; you have to go by car or bus.

BUS
Regular buses run from Cork city to Youghal, Kinsale, Clonakilty, Skibbereen and Bantry; and from Skibbereen to Baltimore. Skibbereen and Bantry also have services to Glengarriff and on to Kenmare and Killarney. Many smaller Cork villages are connected by a local network of minibuses.

Cork City, p188
Set on an island amid a maze of river channels, Ireland's second-largest city is cosmopolitan and cultured, with a reputation for fine food and drink.

Clonakilty, p202
The birthplace of black pudding is a foodie town par excellence, with a produce-filled farmers market, a choice of great dining options and its own distillery.

Plan Your Time

Cork city is well worth a visit, but make sure to check out Cobh and Kinsale and put aside at least a few days for touring the coast and the West Cork peninsulas.

Kinsale (p195)

Pressed for Time

● If your schedule is tight, with only a day or two, plan to spend your time between **Cork city** (p188) and/or **Kinsale** (p195); at a push you could visit both, as they're only 30 minutes apart by car or bus.

● The best sight in Cork is the city itself – soak it up as you wander the streets, but don't miss the world-renowned **English Market** (p192), established in 1788, with colourful stalls filled with the produce for which Cork is famed, followed by visiting the **Cork City Gaol** (p190) or wandering the historic, hilly streets of **Shandon** (p194).

● In Kinsale, a wander around **Charles Fort** (p196) is a highlight, as is a **harbour cruise** (p195). Both Cork and Kinsale are awash with great places for dinner.

Seasonal Highlights

Summer is peak season for watching marine life, including whales, and for island excursions and sea-kayaking trips. Autumn has food festivals.

APRIL
Most of County Cork's seasonal sights are open in April, which increasingly brings warm, sunny weather. Irish and international writers pour into Cork city for the vibrant literary festival, the **Cork World Book Fest** (p191).

MAY
Enjoy bountiful seafood banquets, live music in the square and traditional sailboats racing round the harbour during the twin festivities of the **Baltimore Seafood & Wooden Boat Festival** (p208) in this classic maritime village.

JUNE
Long daylight hours stretch late into the evening in June, making it a great month to visit. In Cork city, the **Cork Midsummer Festival** (p191) celebrates music, theatre, dance, literature and visual arts over 10 days.

Three Days to Travel Around

● Visit **Blarney Castle** (p200) first thing and then explore Cork city, joining a culinary or food tour of the city, or a distillery or **brewery** tour (p191).

● On day two, depending on your interests, you could tour Midleton's **Old Jameson Whiskey Distillery** (p197), or visit **Fota Wildlife Park** (p197) or **Fota House, Arboretum & Gardens** (p198). At nearby **Cobh** (p198) learn stories of the RMS *Titanic* at its final port, now the **Titanic Experience Cobh** (p199), and book a boat trip to fascinating **Spike Island** (p199), followed by an hour's drive to Kinsale.

● Finally, head west along the coast, stopping for lunch at **Clonakilty** (p202) or **Skibbereen** (p205), and ending up with a visit to spectacular **Mizen Head** (p214).

More Than a Week

● After a few days of enjoying the sights and cuisine of Cork city, Kinsale, history- and music-filled Clonakilty and ends-of-the-earth Mizen Head, take a deep dive into the wilds of West Cork. Go midnight kayaking on Marine Nature Reserve **Lough Hyne** (p205) and devote two days to a leisurely cycle around the **Sheep's Head Peninsula** (p218) and walk to the **lighthouse** (p218) at its windswept tip.

● Allow another two days for the Beara Peninsula – take Ireland's only **cable car across the sea to Dursey Island** (p216) and hike from the fascinating **Allihies Copper Mine Museum along the Copper Mine Trail** (p216). Tour grand **Bantry House & Garden** (p210), and don't miss a boat trip from Glengarriff to the extraordinary subtropical oasis on **Ilnacullin – Garinish Island** (p217).

JULY
Cork is at its busiest in summer, so be sure to book activities and accommodation ahead. Music, drama and drag events during **Cork Pride** (p191) culminate in a colourful parade through the city centre.

AUGUST
Seafaring activities are in full swing all along the county's coast. The yachting hub of Schull hosts yacht and dinghy races during early August's **Calves Week** (p217), finishing with a weekend regatta, festivities and fireworks.

SEPTEMBER
Seasonal sights and activities are still open, making the most of the often still-temperate weather. People flock to **Cape Clear International Storytelling Festival** (p209) for three days of traditional storytelling, workshops and walks.

OCTOBER
Chillier weather and shorter days don't dampen Cork's spirits. The **Cork Jazz Festival** (p191) has an all-star lineup of jazz, rock and pop performances in venues across the city, plus a fringe offshoot in Kinsale.

Cork City

FOOD & DRINK | HISTORY | ARCHITECTURE

☑ TOP TIP

Avoid city centre parking problems by using **Black Ash Park & Ride** on the South City Link Rd, on the way to the airport. Parking costs €5 a day, which includes the bus fare for the 10-minute journey into the city; buses depart at least every 15 minutes.

Known as the Rebel City, Ireland's second city is first in every important respect – at least according to its inhabitants, who cheerfully refer to it as the 'real capital of Ireland'. Liberal, youthful and cosmopolitan, Cork is the country's fastest-growing city (it's planned for the current population of 224,004 to reach 335,000 by 2040), with transformation gathering pace in its spruced-up streets, revitalised stretches of waterfront that include the massive redevelopment of its port and docklands, and a wave of startups.

At heart, Cork is still happily traditional: set on an island in the River Lee, the compact city centre is packed with grand Georgian avenues, cramped 17th-century alleys alongside modern masterpieces like its opera house. Narrow streets are crammed with snug pubs hosting live-music sessions; alongside shops, and restaurants and cafes fed by arguably the best food scene in the country – and a genuinely proud welcome from the locals.

 GETTING AROUND

Cork Airport *(corkairport.com)*, 8km south, is linked to the centre by buses, stopping at **Parnell Place Bus Station** and **Kent Train Station**. Trains run to Dublin Heuston, Tralee in County Kerry, and nearby Cobh and Midleton.

Most sights are within 20 minutes' walk of Emmet Place, the pedestrianised main shopping square. To get further afield, the city bus network is comprehensive; in the coming years, the proposed Luas Cork project will bring light-rail services.

Cork's bike-sharing scheme is run by **TFI Bikes** *(bikeshare.ie)*, though city-centre cycling is hampered by fragmented bike lanes often shared with motorised traffic.

The central area has several signposted car parks. On-street parking requires the Park by Phone app or scratch-card parking discs available from many city centre shops.

CORK CITY

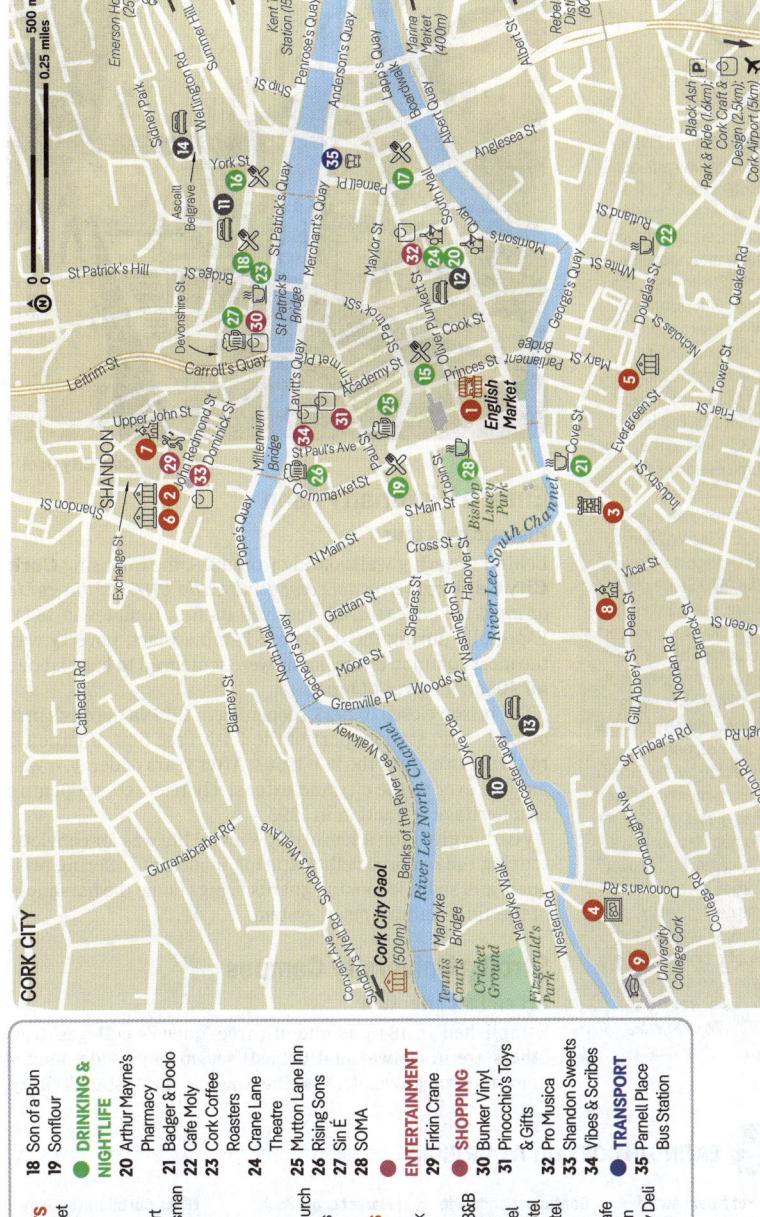

HIGHLIGHTS
1 English Market

SIGHTS
2 Cork Butter Museum
3 Elizabeth Fort
4 Lewis Glucksman Gallery
5 Nano Nagle Place
6 Old Butter Market
7 St Anne's Church
8 St Fin Barre's Cathedral

ACTIVITIES
9 University College Cork

SLEEPING
10 Anam Cara B&B
11 Hotel Isaacs
12 Imperial Hotel
13 River Lee Hotel
14 Sheila's Hostel

EATING
15 Farmgate Cafe
16 Glass Curtain
see 5 Good Day Deli
17 Market Lane
18 Son of a Bun
19 Sonflour

DRINKING & NIGHTLIFE
20 Arthur Mayne's Pharmacy
21 Badger & Dodo
22 Café Moly
23 Cork Coffee Roasters
24 Crane Lane Theatre
25 Mutton Lane Inn
26 Rising Sons
27 Sin É
28 SOMA

ENTERTAINMENT
29 Firkin Crane

SHOPPING
30 Bunker Vinyl
31 Pinocchio's Toys & Gifts
32 Pro Musica
33 Shandon Sweets
34 Vibes & Scribes

TRANSPORT
35 Parnell Place Bus Station

REBEL CITY HISTORY

With its long history of rebellion against British rule, Cork is inextricably linked with Ireland's struggle for nationhood. By the 12th century, the monastic-founded, Viking-expanded settlement had become the Kingdom of South Munster's chief city, but by 1185 it was in the possession of the English. It survived Cromwellian assault but fell to William of Orange during the 1690 Siege of Cork. During the 18th century the city's port exported butter, beef, beer and whiskey but a century later was devastated by famine.

In 1920, police directed by the British government murdered Sinn Fein Lord Mayor Tomás MacCurtain at his home, and Crown forces burnt down the centre, including Cork's City Hall and Public Library. Cork was also a regional focus of Ireland's 1922–23 Civil War.

Cork City Gaol

Enter a Victorian Prison

Historic gaol tour

Behind towering walls dating from 1818, the imposing **Cork City Gaol** (*corkcitygaol.com; adult/child €11/7, audio guide or guided tour extra €2*) received its first inmates in 1824. Especially during the desperate Famine years, poverty was the most common crime; many were sentenced to hard labour for stealing loaves of bread.

The prison closed in 1923, reopening in 1927 as the city's first official radio station, part of the Irish Free State's national radio service, until the late 1950s. After years of decay, it was handed over to the city and extensively restored, reopening as a heritage attraction in 1993.

Visiting gives you a sense of how awful life was for convicts: touring the restored cells featuring models of suffering prisoners and sadistic-looking guards brings home the harshness of the 19th-century penal system.

Stroll a University Campus

Art and architecture

Established in 1845 as one of three 'queen's colleges' (the others are in Galway and Belfast) set up to provide nondenominational alternatives to the Anglican Protestant Trinity

EATING IN CORK CITY: OUR PICKS

Son of a Bun: Award-winning burgers using Irish produce on locally baked brioche buns. *noon-9pm Sun & Mon, to 9.30pm Tue-Thu, to 10pm Fri & Sat* €

Sonflour: Handmade pastas, focaccia, Roman-style pizzas are vegetarian (many are vegan), made with local ingredients. *5-10.30pm Tue-Fri, 1-10.30pm Sat* €€

Market Lane: Bright corner bistro with broad, hearty menu reflecting what's fresh at the English Market. *noon-9.30pm Sun-Wed, to 10pm Thu & Fri, to 10.30pm Sat* €€

Glass Curtain: In an early 19th-century bakery, creating contemporary Irish cuisine like lamb belly with black garlic and whey. *5.30-10.30pm Tue-Thu, from 5pm Fri & Sat* €€€

College in Dublin, the campus of **University College Cork** *(ucc.ie; free, guided tours adult/child €5/3)* spreads around an attractive collection of Victorian Gothic buildings, gardens and historical attractions, including a 19th-century astronomical observatory.

Guided tours lasting 70 minutes depart from the visitor centre. It's located along the covered walkway on the north side of the main quad, known as the Stone Corridor, which houses Ireland's biggest collection of Ogham stones, carved with runic inscriptions dating from the 4th to the 6th century CE.

In the campus' northeast corner is the award-winning **Lewis Glucksman Gallery** *(glucksman.org; by donation)*, a startling construction of limestone, steel and timber built in 2004 by Dublin architects O'Donnell and Tuomey. Three floors of galleries display national and international contemporary art and installation.

(Note that Cork's city-centre Crawford Gallery is closed for refurbishment until 2027; check updates at *crawfordart gallery.ie*.)

Savour Cork's Food Scene
Markets, tours and more

Cork's food and drink scene is renowned. Restaurants and cafes citywide make the most of the county's famed local produce, showcased at the 1788-established English Market (p192).

In the regenerating southern docklands 2km to the city's southeast, the 2020-opened **Marina Market** *(marinamarket. ie)* is one of the city's favourite hangouts. The hangar-like space is lined with artisan food and drink stands (don't miss Prátaí for loaded Irish fries) around a central dining area. Open daily, the venue really comes to life at weekends and during events (anything from concerts to DJs, film screenings and Zumba).

Guided food tours visiting producers throughout the city include Fab Food Trails' 2.5 to three-hour **Cork Tasting Trails** *(fabfoodtrails.ie; €80)* and Bonner Travel's three-hour **Cork Culinary Tour** *(bonner-travel.com/the-culinary-tours; €130)*.

Raise a Glass
Breweries, distilleries and coffee roasteries

In Cork pubs, locally brewed Murphy's and Beamish stouts, not Guinness, are the preferred pints.

You can also go behind the scenes of some fantastic independent breweries offering guided tours of the

BEST EVENTS IN CORK CITY

Cork World Book Fest: Six-day literary festival in April featuring Irish and international writers. *corkworldbook fest.com*

Cork Harbour Festival: Ten-day late May/early June extravaganza includes a mass rowing race (An Rás Mór). *corkharbourfes tival.com*

Cork Midsummer Festival: Ten-day mid-June arts fest. *corkmidsummer.com*

Cork Pride: Weeklong, citywide July/August LGBTIQ+ festival. *corkpride.com*

Cork on a Fork Fest: Five-day, late-August food festival. *corkcity.ie*

Cork Jazz Festival: For five days in October, jazz fills venues citywide. *guinnesscorkjazz.com*

Cork International Film Festival: Ireland's oldest and largest film festival over 11 days in November. *corkfilmfest.org*

 DRINKING IN CORK CITY: OUR PICKS

Crane Lane Theatre: Three bars, a covered laneway beer garden, roaring 1920s decor, live bands (from jazz and bluegrass to rock) as well as DJ sets. *4pm-2.30am*

Arthur Mayne's Pharmacy: Former apothecary with a ground-floor wine bar and upstairs speakeasy with cocktails. *10am-2am Sun-Thu, to 2.30am Fri & Sat*

Mutton Lane Inn: Tiny, inviting trad pub lit by candles and fairy lights. *9am-11.30pm Mon-Thu, to 12.30am Fri & Sat, 12.30pm-11pm Sun*

Sin É: Everything a craic-filled pub should be: long on atmosphere and short on pretension, with live music almost every night. *12.30pm-11.30pm Sun-Thu, to 12.30am Fri & Sat*

TOP EXPERIENCE

The English Market

Cork's English Market opens from the Grand Parade and Princes St (with smaller entrances off Oliver Plunkett and Patrick streets) in the city's beating heart. Dating from 1788, the covered market is one of Europe's oldest and most beautiful, with ornate vaulted ceilings, columns and a polished marble fountain, where colourful stalls showcase the region's exceptional local produce.

History

Once a stark reminder of Cork's political and economic divide, the 18th-century market was set up by the Protestant ('English') municipal corporation that controlled the city, attracting a wealthy clientele. When the city's Catholic ('Irish') majority took power after local government was reformed in 1840, they established their own market, St Peter's (now an events and exhibitions space) nearby on North Main St: it was known as the Irish Market, differentiating it from the English Market.

Today, it's beloved by locals, and visitors that have included Barack Obama and Queen Elizabeth II, Rick Stein and Gordon Ramsay.

Market Stalls

Scores of independent traders sell everything from meat, poultry and game, fish and seafood, to fruit and vegetables, herbs and spices, oils, condiments, cheeses, breads, pastries, cakes and sweets (plus nonedibles like cookware).

Highlights include **Hederman**'s sublime smoked salmon; **On the Pig's Back**'s patés, terrines, charcuterie and farmhouse cheeses; **Toons Bridge Dairy**'s handcrafted mozzarella from its West Cork water-buffalo herd; **Cork Rooftop Farm**'s urban organic produce; the **Alternative Bread Company**'s handmade sourdoughs and soda bread; and third-generation-run the **Roughty Foodie**'s local honeys and homemade jams.

TOP TIPS

● Standout ready-to-eat snacks include fourth-generation **O'Flynn's**, serving 'proper' gourmet sausages here since 1921.

● Climb the stairs to find the **Farmgate Cafe**, perched on a balcony overlooking the stalls below that are the source of its dishes, from cooked breakfasts to lunches.

PRACTICALITIES

● englishmarket.ie
● free ● 8am-6pm Mon-Sat

Rising Sons

operations, lasting around one to 1½ hours and including tastings (book ahead). **Rising Sons** *(risingsonsbrewery.com; tour €15)* occupies a huge red-brick former printing works; try its trademark dry stout, Mi Daza. Southern docklands-set **Rebel City Distillery** *(rebelcitydistillery.com; tour €28, with cocktail masterclass €50)* repurposed a century-old Ford factory in 2020 to distil small-batch spirits, including absinthe, vodka and gin.

Cork also has well-known coffee roasteries with on-site cafes, including **Badger & Dodo**, **SOMA**, **Cafe Moly** and **Cork Coffee Roasters**.

Explore South of the Centre

City landmarks

South of the River Lee from the island-set city centre – urban kayaking tours around it were paused at the time of writing, due to port construction; check Atlantic Sea Kayaking *(atlanticseakayaking.com)* for updates – are some of Cork's landmark sights.

On the site where St Fin Barre founded a monastery (and ultimately the city) in 606 CE, **St Fin Barre's Cathedral** *(stfinbarres.ie; adult/child €9/free)* was designed by William Burges in Gothic Revival style with spiky spires, gargoyles and sculptures, and consecrated in 1870. Allow around 45 minutes for a self-guided tour, with interior highlights including marble floor mosaics, a colourful chancel ceiling and huge pulpit and bishop's throne.

To its east on a rocky outcrop, Cork's superbly preserved star-shaped artillery **Elizabeth Fort** *(corkcity.ie; free, guided tour/audio guide €5/3)* was built in the 1620s (replacing an earlier fort), and served as a *garda* (police) station from 1929 to 2013. Stroll the ramparts for great city views.

The area east again is changing fast, as restoration and gentrification take hold. Seek out the renovated red-brick former

BEST SHOPPING IN CORK CITY

Cork Craft & Design: Traditional and contemporary pieces from local artisans. *corkcraftanddesign.com*

Vibes & Scribes: Cork's largest independent bookshop. *vibesandscribes.ie*

Shandon Sweets: Handmade liquorice, fudge, clove rocks and bullseyes use the owner's grandfather's recipes at this 1929-established shop. *shandonsweets.com*

Pro Musica: Traditional, classical and modern instruments, and sheet music and books. *promusica.ie*

Bunker Vinyl: Vintage, preloved, new releases and reissues handpicked by the owner. *bunkervinyl.ie*

Pinocchio's Toys & Gifts: Traditional, often one-of-a-kind items include baby rattles, wooden toys, music boxes, cuddly toys, puzzles and boardgames. *pinocchios.ie*

Nano Nagle Place

convent **Nano Nagle Place** *(nanonagleplace.ie; site free, museum guided/self-guided tour €11/8.50)*, housing a museum dedicated to **Honora Nagle**, a remarkable 18th-century woman who devoted herself to providing education for poor children in Cork. Beyond the museum is an oasis of peaceful terraced gardens, home to the sustainable **Good Day Deli** *(gooddaydeli.ie)*.

Wander Through Shandon
Butter museum and bell-ringing

Overlooking the city centre, hillside Shandon (from the Irish Sean Dún, meaning 'old fort') is an atmospheric spot to wander, with galleries, antique shops and cafes along its lanes. Generations of workers raised huge families in basic conditions in its tiny old row houses, now sought-after pieds-à-terre.

Built in 1855, the large, circular **Firkin Crane** (a firkin is a wooden barrel, and a crane is a weighing device) is where Cork's butter was weighed and packed for export; it now houses a dance centre. Neoclassical columns adorn the facade of the **Old Butter Market** (look for the cow's head above the arched entrance). During the 1860s, Cork had the largest butter market in the world; the trade's history is told through the displays and dioramas of the adjacent **Cork Butter Museum** *(thebuttermuseum.com; adult/child €5/1.50)*.

Shandon is dominated by the 1722 **St Anne's Church** *(stanneshandon.ie; church €3, with tower climb adult/child €9/5)*, aka the 'Four-Faced Liar' as each of the Italianate tower's four clocks told a slightly different time. On the tower's 1st floor, aspiring campanologists can ring the Shandon Bells (once the repair works have finished), then continue up the 132 steps to the top for 360-degree views of the city.

Beyond Cork City

Nature lovers, history buffs and fine-food connoisseurs will all find something beyond Cork's city limits.

Cork city's hinterland is a hub of food towns par excellence. The picturesque yachting harbour of Kinsale is famed for its seafood, while aficionados of a particularly fine Irish whiskey will recognise the name Midleton – the main reason to linger in this busy market town is to visit the old Jameson whiskey distillery, along with a meal at one of the town's famously good restaurants. The surrounding region of East Cork is full of pretty villages and is also home to Ballymaloe House, the fountainhead of Irish gastronomy.

Cobh, on the other hand, is more famous for history than cuisine – this was *Titanic*'s last port of call before its doomed maiden voyage.

Places
Kinsale p195
Midleton p197
Fota p197
Cobh p198
Blarney Castle p200

GETTING AROUND

A car is helpful for out-of-the-way destinations but you can cover much of this area without one. Midleton, Fota and Cobh are served by rail, with trains travelling to and from Cork city every 30 minutes, making it possible to combine destinations in a single day trip. Regular buses link Cork with Kinsale's town carpark, some running via Cork Airport. **TFI Local Link Cork** *(locallinkcork.ie)* also runs a network of minibus routes covering smaller villages.

Kinsale

TIME FROM CORK CITY: **45MIN**

Stroll picturesque Kinsale

The yachting harbour of Kinsale (Cionn tSáile), 25km south of Cork city, is one of many colourful gems strung along the County Cork coastline. Beside a handsome natural harbour guarded by a huge 17th-century fortress, the town's narrow, winding streets are lined with galleries, along with lively bars and superb dining venues (especially seafood).

Discover the history of the town by joining Dermot Ryan of **Kinsale Heritage Town Walks** *(kinsaleheritage.com; adult/child €5/free)* for a one-hour walking tour. For a food focus, **Kinsale Food Tours** *(kinsalefoodtours.com; town/coast tour €85/75)* has options including a two to 2 ½-hour Walking Town Food Tour and a 2½-hour Foraging and Coastal Tour.

Tour the harbour

Boating is the ultimate way to experience Kinsale's maritime air. To get out on the water, take a one-hour boat trip of the harbour with **Kinsale Harbour Cruises** *(kinsaleharbourcruises.com; adult/child €15/7)* or a two-hour open-topped adventure boat trip with **Kinsale Sea Safari** *(kinsaleseasafari.ie; €53)*.

Browse Kinsale's galleries

Kinsale's charms continue to artists. In the town's streets and lanes, look out for impressionist artist Philip French and sculptor Kate French at **Gallery 23** *(artistsfrench.com)*, B&W

Kinsale harbour cruise (p195) passing Charles Fort

BEST THINGS TO DO IN KINSALE

Giles and **Catherine Norman** run the Giles Norman Gallery and Townhouse in Kinsale. Giles is one of Ireland's leading landscape photographers. @gilesnorman

A perfect day in Kinsale starts with breakfast at **OHK Cafe**, followed by a relaxing stroll along **Scilly Walk**, which brings you to the spectacular **Charles Fort**. After you've experienced the fort's panoramic views, enjoy lunch by the sea at the **Bulman Bar** and then head back towards the town along the High Rd for more incredible views. Spend a couple of hours exploring Kinsale's many independent shops and galleries. End the day at the **Black Pig**, which has a delicious tapas-style menu and an incredible wine list.

landscape and seascape photographer **Giles Norman** *(giles norman.com)*, and architectural and abstract photographer **Rohan Reilly** *(rohanreilly.com)*.

Walk along the waterfront to a 17th-century fortress

The **Scilly Walk** (6km round trip) is a lovely coastal trail that leads to **Charles Fort** *(heritageireland.ie; adult/child €5/3)*. One of Europe's best-preserved star-shaped artillery forts, this vast 17th-century fortification has spectacular views; inside the walls, 18th- and 19th-century ruins make for fascinating wandering. Built in the 1670s to guard Kinsale Harbour, the fort was in use until the early 1920s Civil War, when much of it was destroyed as the British withdrew. Displays explain the typically tough lives led by the soldiers who served here and the comparatively comfortable lives of the officers.

Return along High Rd – Kinsale's 'Golden Mile', with millionaires' holiday homes overlooking the harbour.

Learn about the Lusitania

On a prominent headland 13km south of Kinsale via the R604, the **Old Head Signal Tower** *(oldheadofkinsale.com; adult/child €6/free)* was built between 1804 and 1806 during the Napoleonic Wars as part of a network of 81 signal towers around the Irish coast; an early warning system in case of a French invasion. The tower houses a museum dedicated to the

EATING IN KINSALE: OUR PICKS

Seeds: Artisan bakery with sourdoughs, sausage rolls, croissants, Danish pastries and gluten-free options. *8.30am-3.30pm Mon-Sat, 9am-3pm Sun* €

Bia: West Cork seafood, grass-fed meats and vegetables form the basis for top-notch bistro cooking at Bia (the Irish word for 'food'). *6-10pm Mon, 5-10pm Tue-Sat* €€

Fishy Fishy: One of the most famous seafood restaurants in the country, with a sophisticated nautical interior; all the fish is caught locally. *noon-9pm Wed-Mon* €€€

Bastion: Michelin-starred but a relaxed and informal foray into the world of *haute cuisine*, celebrating seafood in innovative tasting menus. *5.30-10pm Thu-Sun* €€€

RMS *Lusitania*, which was torpedoed by a German U-boat in 1915 with the loss of 1200 lives.

You can walk to the nearby clifftops for impressive views south towards the Old Head, the nearest point of land to the disaster. Bird colonies on the western cliffs include puffins, guillemots, kittiwakes, peregrines and choughs. At the tip of the headland, part of the prestigious **Old Head Golf Links** *(oldhead.com)*, the lighthouse has occasional open days; check kinsale.ie for dates.

Midleton

TIME FROM CORK CITY: **35MIN**

Sip whiskey at the source

The charming market town of Midleton, 20km east of Cork, is best known as the home of the **Jameson Midleton Distillery Experience** *(jamesonwhiskey.com; afternoon tour adult/child €31/12)*, where the art of creating world-famous Jameson Irish whiskey is brought vividly to life.

The beautiful old distillery buildings were revamped for its 200-year anniversary in 2025 (Jameson is today made in a nearby modern distillery). Immersive 75-minute tours explain the process of converting barley into whiskey, leading past the old grain stores, malting floors and copper stills – including the world's largest pot still, built in 1825 – ending with a tasting session, comparing Jameson with Scotch and bourbon (tours are cheaper before noon).

You can also book extended behind-the-scenes tours, premium whiskey tastings, cask openings and cocktail-making classes, or just drop by to browse its distillery shop and whiskey vault, or dine at its cafe, the Malthouse.

Fota

TIME FROM CORK CITY: **15MIN**

Meet endangered creatures at Fota Wildlife Park

Giraffes, Asian lions, Sumatran tigers, Indian rhinos, gibbons and red pandas roam at **Fota Wildlife Park** *(fotawildlife.ie; adult/child €21.70/15, tour train per trip extra €1, VIP experiences adult/family €140/195)*, a huge 40-hectare outdoor zoo on the Cork harbour island of Fota, which helps restore endangered species' populations through its conservation breeding programs. A tour train (on wheels) runs a circuit round the park daily from April to October and weekends November to March, but walking its 4.5km of paths offers a more close-up experience. Behind-the-scenes VIP experiences include

BEST SHOPPING IN KINSALE

Mamukko: Salvaged nautical materials and rubber life rafts are used to create unique satchels, handbags and wallets. *mamukko.ie*

Zirkulu: Independent sustainable outdoor-clothing shop; equipment includes lunchboxes and water bottles. *zirkulu.com*

Granny's Bottom Drawer: Top-quality Irish linen, woollens and more. *grannys-bottomdrawer.com*

Sister Vintage: High-calibre 1960s to 1990s threads. *sistervintage.com*

Prim's Bookshop: Rare books, first editions, classical literature and poetry. Hosts intimate gigs and wine nights in summer. *@primsbookshop*

Don Meaney: Make an appointment to visit this artist's studio, 3.5km south of Kinsale's centre. *donmeaney.com*

 EATING IN EAST CORK: OUR PICKS

Ferrit & Lee: Next to Midleton's old Jameson distillery. Whiskey in dishes from beef to ice cream and crumble. *noon-8.30pm Tue-Thu, to 9pm Fri & Sat* €€

Arch: Cafe just back from Cobh's waterfront. Morphs into an evening wine bar with sharing platters and small bites. *8am-10pm Mon-Sat, 9am-9pm Sun* €€

CUSH: Smart Midleton restaurant for modern Irish dishes (John Dory with mussels, seaweed butter). *5-9pm Thu, noon-3pm & 5-9pm Fri & Sat, noon-3pm Sun* €€

Ballymaloe House: Three-course lunch and four-course dinner menus exemplify farm-to-fork dining from its walled garden and fields. *12.30-2pm & 6.30-9pm* €€€

BEST FARMERS MARKETS & FARM SHOPS

Midleton Farmers Market: Held on Saturdays on the Green, this is one of Ireland's oldest and best. *@midletonfarmersmarket*

Cobh Farmers Market: On Saturdays, Cobh's waterfront is lined with stalls. *@cobhfarmersmarket*

Kinsale Farmers Market: Wednesdays on the square. *@kinsalefarmersmarket*

Rostellan Farm: Dairy farm 10km south of Midleton selling milk, cream, cheese and ice cream. *rostellanfarm.ie*

Joe's Farm Crisps: Vegetable farm 18km northeast of Midleton, making beetroot, carrot and potato crisps; and selling preserves, jams and chutneys. *joesfarmcrisps.ie*

Ballymaloe Shop: Farm/craft shop and cafe at Ballymaloe House. *ballymaloe.ie*

a two-hour ranger-guided tour. There are cafes and picnic areas. The park has its own entrance at Fota railway station.

Visit magnificent Fota House, Arboretum & Gardens

The grand estate encompassing **Fota House, Arboretum & Gardens** (fotahouse.com; house guided tour adult/child €13/6.50, garden tour €10/5) has been superbly restored since 2007 by the Irish Heritage Trust. Guided tours of Regency-style Fota House, redesigned by John 'the Magnificent' Smith Barry in the 1820s, focus on the original kitchen and ornate plasterwork ceilings. Equally beautiful are the Victorian gardens, with a fernery set amid blocks of fluted limestone, a magnolia walk, a walled garden and a host of attractive trees, including huge Japanese cedars overlooking the lily pond.

A 10-minute walk from Fota train station, it shares a car park with Fota Wildlife park (which was once the estate's pheasant run).

Admire restored Barryscourt Castle

Painstakingly restored by skilled craftspeople using traditional techniques and reopened in 2025, one of Ireland's finest surviving medieval tower houses, **Barryscourt Castle** (heritageireland.ie; free), 6km east of Fota, was built between 1392 and 1420 during the reign of the 7th Lord Barry, John Ciotach Barry. It remained the family's seat throughout conflict, including the 16th-century Irish rebellions (when they partially destroyed it to avoid capture by Sir Walter Raleigh), and 17th-century Irish Confederate War (cannonballs are still lodged in its walls). Interior highlights include the main and great halls, bedroom, kitchen, dungeon and chapel (complete with 16th-century graffiti); outside, its herb and knot gardens and orchard are protected by outer defensive walls.

Discover the secrets of smoking salmon

No trip to Cork is complete without a visit to an artisan food producer, and **Hederman Smoke House** (frankhederman.com; tasting tour & talk €85), previously known as Belvelly, where it's located 2.5 km south of Fota on the R624 towards Cobh, is a treat.

Hederman's speciality is fish, particularly salmon. In a traditional process that takes 24 hours, the fish is filleted and cured before being hung to smoke over beech woodchips. Taste the delectable result during a lunchtime tasting tour and talk (mid-March to October, minimum two people, book online) or drop by on weekdays to buy produce. Alternatively, stop by the Hederman stall at Cork's English Market (p192) or at the Cobh or Midleton farmers markets.

Cobh

TIME FROM CORK CITY: **26MIN**

See Cobh's landmark cathedral

An appealing waterfront town 23km east of Cork city – if you're driving, five-minute Passage West/Glenbrook **Cross River Ferries** (crossriverferries.ie; pedestrian/cyclist/car one-way €3/3/9) are a handy shortcut – Cobh (pronounced 'cove') is dotted with brightly coloured houses and overlooked

St Colman's Cathedral

by the single-spire, Gothic Revival-style **St Colman's Cathedral** (cobhcathedralparish.ie; by donation). In 1849 Cobh was renamed Queenstown after Queen Victoria paid a visit. The name lasted until Irish independence in 1921 when the local council reverted to the Irish original.

Contemplate Cobh's Titanic heritage

Cobh was the RMS *Titanic*'s final port of call: the original White Star Line offices on Cobh waterfront, where 123 *Titanic* passengers embarked (and one lucky soul absconded), now house the poignant **Titanic Experience Cobh** (titanicexperiencecobh.ie; adult/child €13/9), where guided tours provide a powerful insight into the ill-fated liner's first and final voyage in 1912.

You can find more *Titanic* exhibits at the nearby **Cobh Heritage Centre: The Queenstown Story** (cobhheritage.com; adult/child €15/9.50), an interactive museum that also chronicles Irish emigration across the Atlantic in the wake of the Great Famine – from 1848 to 1950, no fewer than 2.5 million emigrants passed through Cobh's port.

Sail to an island fortress

Clearly visible from Cobh, **Spike Island** (spikeislandcork.ie; adult/child including ferry & guided tour €27.95/14.95) lies low and green in Cork Harbour. It was once an important part of the port's defences, topped by a huge 18th-century artillery fort that commanded the harbour entrance. In the second half of the 19th century, during the Irish War of Independence and from 1984 to 2004, it served as a prison, gaining the nickname 'Ireland's Alcatraz'.

A trip to Spike Island begins with a 12-minute boat trip across the harbour, departing from Cobh's central Kennedy Pier. On arrival, you get a 45-minute guided walking tour of the former prison buildings, the old punishment block, the shell

COBH'S MARITIME HISTORY

Cork's one-time port, Cobh has a long-held connection with Atlantic crossings. In 1838 the *Sirius*, the first steamship to cross the Atlantic, sailed from Cobh. During the harrowing Famine, Cobh was the last glimpse of Ireland for many emigrants. The *Titanic* made its last stop here on its doomed voyage in 1912, and, when the *Lusitania* was torpedoed off the coast of Kinsale in 1915, it was here that many of the survivors were brought and the dead buried.

The world's first yacht club, the Royal Cork Yacht Club, was founded in 1720 on Haulbowline Island (now home to the Irish Naval Service); its 1850s location, Cobh's beautiful Italianate Old Yacht Club, now houses the Sirius Arts Centre. It currently operates from Crosshaven across Cork Harbour.

BALLYMALOE'S REVOLUTION OF IRISH CUISINE

Credited with virtually single-handedly transforming Ireland's culinary landscape, Cork farmer, cookery writer and teacher, hotelier and chef **Myrtle Allen** (1924–2018) has been described as the person who engineered the 'Big Bang of Irish food' when she opened her house to diners in 1964 (and later overnight guests), trailblazing a sustainable, farm-to-table ethos with daily menus using local suppliers and seasonal produce she and husband Ivan grew on their property.

Today, **Ballymaloe House** remains an exceptional place to dine (p197), stay (p219) and shop (p198), with the prestigious **Ballymaloe Cookery School** *(ballymaloecookeryschool.ie)*, 3km east.

Spike Island (p199)

store (once used as a children's prison) and No 2 Bastion with its massive 6in gun. You're then free to explore on your own.

Highlights include the Gun Park, with a good display of mostly 20th-century artillery; the Mitchell Hall, with an exhibit on the SS *Aud*, a German ship loaded with arms for the 1916 Easter Rising that was sunk in the entrance to Cork Harbour; and the Glacis Walk, a 1.5km trail that leads around the walls of the fortress, with great views of Cobh town and the harbour entrance. There's a cafe and toilets on the island; allow around four hours in all.

Blarney Castle

TIME FROM CORK CITY: **40MIN**

Kiss the Blarney Stone

One of Ireland's most popular tourist attractions, **Blarney Castle** *(blarneycastle.ie; adult/child €23/11)* is just 8km northwest of Cork. The castle itself is an impressive tower house built on the site of two earlier castles in 1446 by Dermot McCarthy, King of Munster, and set in 24 hectares of gorgeous grounds. Perched at the top of claustrophobic spiral steps is the famous Blarney Stone, which supposedly gives one the gift of the gab (legend has it Queen Elizabeth I coined the term 'blarney' from the attempts by Cormac MacCarthy, the then Lord of Blarney, for his charming yet misleading responses to her demands for control of the castle and land). On the panoramic battlements, you bend backwards over a long, long drop (with a safety grill and attendant to prevent tragedy) to kiss the stone (sprayed with disinfectant between visitors). Escape the crowds in the Fern Garden and Arboretum, investigate toxic plants in the Poison Garden or explore the nooks and crannies of the Rock Close.

STROLL THROUGH HISTORY IN YOUGHAL

A seaside resort on the Blackwater estuary, the ancient seaport of Youghal's rich history reveals itself on a town stroll.

START	END	LENGTH
Market Square	College Gardens	1.7km; 1–2hrs

From ❶ **Market Square**, head inland along Quay Lane to reach the ❷ **Clock Gate Tower** astride Main St. It was built in 1777 and served as a town gate, clock tower and jail. Several prisoners taken in the 1798 Rising were hanged from its windows. Continue north on Main St to the beautifully proportioned ❸ **Red House**, designed in 1706 by Dutch architect Leuventhen. Across the road is the 15th-century tower house ❹ **Tynte's Castle**, which originally had a defensive riverfront position.

A few doors further along are six ❺ **almshouses** built by the first Earl of Cork in 1610. Turn left on Church St; at the end 13th-century ❻ **St Mary's Collegiate Church** incorporates elements of an earlier Danish church dating from the 11th century.

Hidden behind high walls to the north of the church, 15th- to 18th-century ❼ **Myrtle Grove** (not open to the public) is the former home of Sir Walter Raleigh and a rare Irish example of a late-medieval Tudor-style house.

The churchyard is bounded to the west by a stretch of the ❽ **old town wall**. Follow the parapet until you can go down a set of stairs to the outer side, then enter the next gate along to descend back to Main St through the 17th-century ❾ **College Gardens**, now a public park.

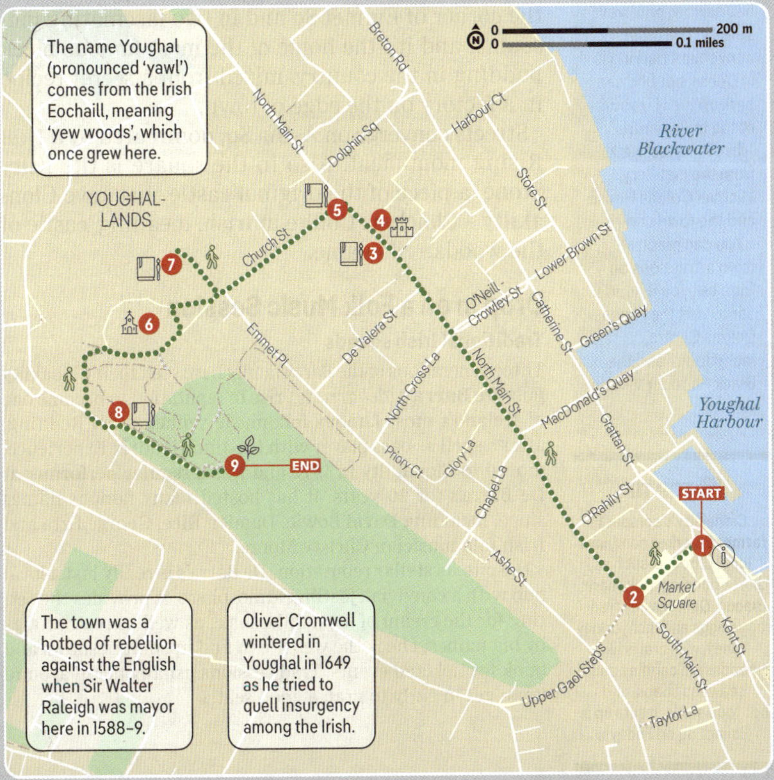

The name Youghal (pronounced 'yawl') comes from the Irish Eochaill, meaning 'yew woods', which once grew here.

The town was a hotbed of rebellion against the English when Sir Walter Raleigh was mayor here in 1588–9.

Oliver Cromwell wintered in Youghal in 1649 as he tried to quell insurgency among the Irish.

Clonakilty

HISTORY | MUSIC | FOOD & DRINK

GETTING AROUND

Clonakilty is on the bus route from Cork city to Skibbereen; some services continue west to Goleen.

The centre of town has narrow, one-way streets. The most convenient parking is in Deasy's public car park on the N71 south of the town centre – five minutes' walk from the distillery, Michael Collins House and the town centre.

You can reach all town attractions on foot, but you'll need a car to visit the Michael Collins Centre, Inchydoney and the Black Pudding Visitor Centre.

☑ TOP TIP

Clonakilty's compact **farmers market** combines local produce, such as black pudding, Baltimore bacon, Dunmanway free-range eggs and Inchydoney honey, with crafts like handmade candles and seaweed soaps, and hot-food stalls. It sets up in Emmet Sq on Fridays.

Cheerful, brightly painted Clonakilty is a buzzy market town of 5112 inhabitants that serves as a hub for the scores of beguiling villages strung out along the West Cork coast. You'll find smart B&Bs, good restaurants and cosy pubs alive with music. Little waterways coursing through town add to the charm.

Clonakilty is famous for two things: it's the birthplace of Irish Free State commander-in-chief Michael Collins (1890–1922), embodied in a large statue on the corner of Emmet Sq and in two fascinating museums; and it's the home of the most famous black pudding in the country, mixed from a secret recipe in a factory on the edge of town.

Streets converge on Astna Sq, dominated by a 1798 Rising monument. Also in the square is the Kilty Stone, a piece of the original castle that gave Clonakilty – Cloich na Coillte in Irish, meaning 'castle of the woods' – its name.

Drop in on a Folk Music Session
Traditional Irish sounds

Three generations of the Barry family have seen their Clonakilty pub, **De Barra's** *(debarra.ie)*, rise in reputation to become one of Ireland's most famous folk-music venues. Noel Redding, after a spell as bass player with the Jimi Hendrix Experience, moved to Clonakilty in 1972 and was a regular performer at De Barra's for 20 years. It has hosted many famous names since, including David Bowie, Damien Rice, George Ezra and Irish folk musician Christy Moore.

Despite its stellar reputation, De Barra's is really just a local pub with a convivial, jostling atmosphere. It provides the setting for the cream of local folk music, as well as regular gigs by big names; check the website to find upcoming shows and book for ticketed events. Trad sessions usually begin around 8pm; get in early to grab a good seat.

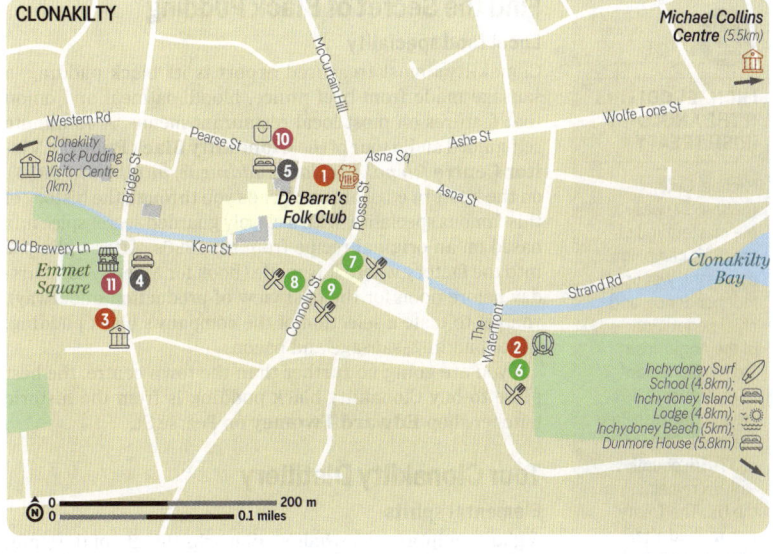

- **HIGHLIGHTS**
1 De Barra's Folk Club
- **SIGHTS**
2 Clonakilty Distillery
3 Michael Collins House
- **SLEEPING**
4 Emmet Hotel
5 O'Donovan's Hotel
- **EATING**
6 Kirby's @ the Whale's Tail
7 Lil's
8 Pike Deli
9 Scannells
- **SHOPPING**
10 Edward Twomey
11 Farmers Market

Immerse Yourself in Irish History
Museums and storytelling

Born on a farm just outside Clonakilty, Michael Collins is one of County Cork's most famous sons, playing a central role in the War of Independence with Britain, and in 1922 becoming commander-in-chief of the army of the newly founded Irish Free State. He lived for a time on Emmet Sq in Clonakilty town centre, where the excellent history museum and interpretive centre **Michael Collins House** (michaelcollinshouse.ie; adult/child €6/2) now sits. Videos, artefacts and interactive displays, along with passionate and knowledgeable staff, lead you through Collins' life and his importance in modern Irish history.

A visit to the evocative **Michael Collins Centre** (michaelcollinscentre.com; adult/child €8/5), signposted off the R600 to Timoleague 7km east of Clonakilty, is a powerful way to make sense of his life and the times in which he lived. A 1½-hour session with a storytelling guide reveals personal items including photos and letters, a recreation of a firing squad execution yard, and a reconstruction of the 1920s country lane where Collins was killed, complete with an armoured vehicle. Presentations take place between mid-June and mid-September, and must be booked in advance.

CLONAKILTY FESTIVALS

The **Irish Yogurts Clonakilty Street Carnival** (clonakilty.ie, June) turns Pearse St into an outdoor dining room serving food from local restaurants and artisan suppliers; entertainment is provided.

The **Clonakilty Old Time Fair** (facebook.com/ClonakiltyOldTimeFair, July) has traditional crafts, vintage cars, music, markets and a parade.

The **Clonakilty International Guitar Festival** (clonguitarfest.com, September) has five music-filled days.

MICHAEL COLLINS & THE ANGLO-IRISH TREATY

Michael Collins (1890-1922) was the mastermind of the IRA's campaign during the War of Independence, and chief negotiator of the Anglo-Irish Treaty. Signed on 6 December 1921, it created the Irish Free State, made up of 26 of 32 Irish counties, with six remaining in the UK. The Treaty was ratified after bitter debate, and the June 1922 elections resulted in a victory for the pro-Treaty side.

Within two weeks of the elections, civil war broke out between comrades who, a year previously, had fought alongside each other, and Collins was assassinated on 22 August.

Collins himself had foreshadowed the hostility that would result from the Treaty: on signing it, he is said to have declared he was signing his own death warrant.

Find the Secret of Black Pudding
Local food speciality

Clonakilty's most treasured export is its black pudding, a sausage made from beef mince, blood, oatmeal and onion that features on most local restaurant menus. A 45-minute self-guided audio tour of the **Clonakilty Black Pudding Visitor Centre** *(clonakiltyblackpudding.ie; adult/child €10/5)*, on the western edge of town, leads you through the history of this famous speciality, with a closely guarded secret spice mix based on an original recipe from the 1880s. After a glimpse into the factory where it is made (book for Monday to Thursday before noon for the best view of production underway), you get to taste a selection of the company's black pudding, white pudding, sausage and bacon.

If you are going no further than the town centre, the best place to buy Clonakilty black pudding is from the historic butcher shop **Edward Twomey** on Pearse St.

Tour Clonakilty Distillery
Elemental spirits

A giant sculpture of a whale's tail marks the site of the state-of-the-art **Clonakilty Distillery** *(clonakiltydistillery.ie; tour & tasting €20-35)*, established in 2016 by the Scully family, who have farmed here for nine generations. It produces triple-distilled single-pot-still Irish whiskey made with grain grown on the owners' family farm nearby, diluted with artesian well-drawn spring water and matured in oak casks exposed to the Atlantic. The 75-minute guided tour leads you through the various stages of production, ending with a tasting session. There are up to three tours per day; book in advance via the website.

Ride the Waves at Inchydoney
Blue Flag beach

Signposted 5km south of Clonakilty, **Inchydoney** has two gorgeous golden strands either side of a rocky peninsula set on a scenic inlet. You can take lessons and rent surfboards from **Inchydoney Surf School** *(inchydoneysurfschool.com; 90-minute lesson adult/child €44/33, 90-minute board & wetsuit rental €30)*.

 EATING IN CLONAKILTY: OUR PICKS

Pike Deli: Busy artisan bakery/deli: fresh breads, savoury tarts, pastries and pies (eg beef and Clonakilty black pudding) to take away. *8.30am-3.30pm Mon-Sat* €

Kirby's @ the Whale's Tail: Buzzy space serving the likes of Courtmacsherry crab and Union Hall smoked salmon. *3.30-9pm Wed-Sat, 1-7.30pm Sun* €€

Scannells: Cosy pub with regular live music and a flower-filled beer garden at the back serving superb steak sandwiches and seafood chowder. *kitchen noon-4pm Tue-Sat* €€

Lil's: Chef Sam Cronin's fine-dining cuisine includes his signature beef fillet with bone marrow tarragon custard. *5-9pm Thu & Fri, noon-9pm Sat, noon-4pm Sun* €€€

Beyond Clonakilty

Dive into west Cork: take a boat trip to watch marine life and spectacular sunsets, and kayak beneath the stars.

The West Cork coast begins the slow build-up of scenic wild Atlantic beauty that culminates in County Kerry to the west, but what you find here is already enough to have you reaching for the camera. Picturesque villages, ancient stone circles and sandy beaches mark the meandering coastal route from Kinsale to Clonakilty and on to Skibbereen and Baltimore. Rather than follow the main N71 road, take the R600 and explore the maze of minor roads along the coast, perfect for aimless wandering.

West Cork's superb food is celebrated in farmers markets and food festivals throughout the region. Seafood is a speciality here – don't miss the opportunity to sample whatever is fresh from the quayside.

Places
Skibbereen p205
Baltimore p206
Drombeg Stone Circle p209

Skibbereen
TIME FROM CLONAKILTY: **30MIN**

Learn about the Great Famine
The town of Skibbereen (Sciobairín), 30km west of Clonakilty, is a pleasant, workaday market town, with an attractive, upmarket centre on the banks of the River Ilen. But during the Famine, Skibb was hit perhaps harder than any other town in Ireland, with huge numbers of the local population emigrating or dying of starvation or disease.

Skibbereen Heritage Centre (*skibbheritage.com; adult/family €6/14*) houses a haunting exhibition about the Famine, with audio of actors reading heartbreaking accounts from the time. A visit here puts Irish history into harrowing perspective. A kilometre west of town, beside the N71 road towards Schull, is **Abbeystrowry Famine Cemetery**, which contains the mass grave of 8000 to 10,000 local people who died during the Famine, marked by a memorial of polished black stone.

Go midnight kayaking on Lough Hyne
Lough Hyne, 8km southwest of Skibbereen, is one of Ireland's natural wonders and became the country's first marine nature reserve in 1981. Its glacier-gouged depths were originally filled with fresh water until rising sea levels breached one end around 4000 years ago. It is now linked to the sea by a narrow tidal channel known as the Rapids, where the tide pours in and out twice a day in a rush of white water.

GETTING AROUND

Cork city is as close as you'll get by train, but the West Cork coast is served by frequent bus services, which go along the N71 via Clonakilty to Skibbereen (some continuing further west to Goleen), and from Skibbereen via Bantry to Killarney, County Kerry. **TFI Local Link Cork** (*locallinkcork.ie*) also runs a network of minibus routes. However, your own transport is helpful for exploring further inland and along the minor coastal roads.

THE GREAT FAMINE

The Great Famine of 1845–51 remains Ireland's greatest national tragedy. With farmers already crippled by repressive Penal Laws, when a blight hit potato crops, prices soared. Inevitably most tenants fell into arrears and were evicted or sent to the dire conditions of the workhouses. Yet Ireland was forced to export its food to Britain. Lord Dufferin and GF Boyle, who journeyed from Oxford to Skibbereen in 1847 to see if reports of the Famine were true, reported that accounts were not exaggerated and it was impossible to conceive of anything more frightful. The Poor Law deemed landlords responsible for the maintenance of their poor and encouraged many to 'remove' tenants from their estates by paying their way to America aboard the scourged 'coffin ships'.

Atlantic Sea Kayaking *(atlanticseakayaking.com; tours €75)* offers guided sea-kayak tours of the lough, including superbly atmospheric 2½-hour 'starlight paddles' after dark. On these trips, you are almost guaranteed to experience marine phosphorescence – bioluminescent plankton in the seawater emit sparkles of greenish light when disturbed by your kayak paddle, a truly magical experience. Tours last from around 9.30pm to midnight and are suitable for beginners (over 16s only). Daytime tours begin around 12.30pm and run for 3½ hours, and are suitable for over 12s. Both day and night tours are popular, so be sure to book in advance.

There are also lovely walks along the lough-side road and in the neighbouring **Knockomagh Wood Nature Reserve** *(npws.ie)*, a beautiful 12.5-hectare patch of mixed woodland, which adjoins the lough. A waymarked 2km-long nature trail leads through the forest up a steep hill (197m). At the top, you're rewarded with stunning views of the coastline, including Roaringwater Bay's Sherkin and Cape Clear islands.

Camp on a hilltop farm

For a wonderfully rural West Cork experience, **Top of the Rock Pod Pairc** *(topoftherock.ie)* is a gorgeous campsite set on a remote working cattle farm near Drimoleague, 14km north of Skibbereen. Its hilltop location is a haven of peace, offering grand views of the Mullaghmesha hills. Goats, lambs, ducks and chickens wander freely, and the friendly owners give free tours of the third-generation family farm where kids can feed and pet the animals. As well as tent sites and a couple of campervan pitches, there are eight comfortable timber camping pods. A sociable communal campfire is lit at 7pm most nights.

The area to the north is laced with hiking trails, some of which you can begin right from the campsite. One of the more intriguing hikes is the **Glounaclohy Walk** (9.5km; three to four hours), a loop from the impressive ruined tower of Castledonovan into the hills, where you will find the House of George the Sky, the ruins of a farmhouse built way above the valley floor.

Baltimore

TIME FROM CLONAKILTY: **45MIN**

Be a salty seadog

Dominated by the stone tower of its 13th-century castle, Baltimore (Dún na Séad, meaning Fort of the Jewels; its English name is an anglicised version of Baile an Tí Mhóir meaning 'town of the big house') is a classic maritime village, its

---

EATING BEYOND CLONAKILTY: OUR PICKS

| **Antiquity Café & Bookshop**: All-vegan Skibbereen cafe/bookshop serving salads, sandwiches and cakes, plus hot stews and soups. *10am-4pm Mon-Sat* € | **Field Kitchen**: Situated 8km southwest of Clonakilty. Organic farm-to-table produce; zero-waste philosophy. Music and camping in summer. *6-11pm Thu-Sat* €€ | **Glandore Inn**: Harbour views from outdoor tables, whitewashed nautical interior and seafood from Union Hall across the water. *12.30-8.30pm Thu-Tue* €€ | **Dede at the Customs House Baltimore**: Two-Michelin-starred tasting menus by chef Ahmet Dede. *5.30-9pm Thu & Fri, noon-2pm & 5.30-9pm Sat, 12.30-2.30pm Sun* €€€ |

Baltimore Beacon

sheltered anchorage filled with pleasure yachts in summer. The focus of life here is the central terrace overlooking the harbour, the ideal spot to sup a pint or slurp an ice cream while watching the boats go by. All around spreads a multitude of holiday cottages, catering to the summer swell of sailing folk, sea anglers, divers, and visitors to nearby Sherkin and Cape Clear Islands.

The harbour has long been a favourite of mariners and was the haunt of pirates in the 17th century. The most infamous date in its history is 20 June 1631, when the village was sacked by a fleet of Barbary pirates who carried off more than 100 prisoners to a life of slavery. The remaining villagers fled to Skibbereen, and Baltimore lay abandoned for many decades afterwards.

Inside 1215-built **Dún na Séad Castle** (*baltimorecastle.ie; castle adult/child €6/free, walking tours €10/free*), the great hall houses seasonal art displays and exhibits on the town's piratical history, but the main attraction is the view from the battlements. Heritage walking tours of the village lasting 90 minutes also depart from here.

The white-painted conical **Baltimore Beacon**, dubbed Lot's Wife, stands on the headland 2km southwest of town, marking the entrance to Baltimore Harbour and making a good objective for a pleasant walk, especially at sunset.

PROTECTING WEST CORK'S MARINE LIFE

The waters off the coast of West Cork have traditionally offered some of Ireland's best marine-life watching. The most frequently spotted species include common dolphins, grey seals and harbour seals, but the big draws are whales. But, in recent years, overfishing of sprat by large trawlers, and warming waters believed to be pushing sprat west and north, have disrupted the marine food chain and diverted humpback, minke and fin whales as well as dolphins. In 2025, long-running Union Hall-based Cork Whale Watch closed, due to reduced sightings. In response, the Irish government has promised increased protection of fish stocks and marine biodiversity, and many companies still run engaging and rewarding nature-based boat trips.

 EATING BEYOND CLONAKILTY: PUB DINING

Jacob's Bar: Overlooking Baltimore's docks. Try Galley Head prawns, Cape Clear lobster, Sherkin Island oysters, Roaring Bay mussels. *12.30-9.30pm* €€

Mary Ann's: Castletownshend pub since 1846, serving seafood like pan-seared tiger prawns with wild garlic, scallop mornay or seafood pie. *noon-9pm* €€

Bushe's Bar: Famed for its crab sandwiches and outdoor tables on Baltimore's main square (perfect for a sundowner). *11.30am-5pm Mon-Thu, 12.30-5pm Sat & Sun* €€

Dock Wall: Union Hall pub with an outdoor, harbour-view terrace with great seafood chowder and beer-battered fish and chips. *5-9.30pm Wed-Sat, 1-8.30pm Sun* €€

BEST BOAT TOURS BEYOND CLONAKILTY

Atlantic Whale & Wildlife Tours: Marine-life-spotting tours departing from Courtmacsherry Harbour. *atlanticwhaleandwildlifetours.com*

West Cork Ocean Life Tours: Sustainable tours from Reen Pier near Union Hall. *westcorkoceantours.ie*

Baltimore Sea Safari: Trips span 20-minute seal-watching harbour jaunts to two-hour sea safaris. *baltimoreseasafari.ie*

Aquaventures: Options include sunset tours past Sherkin Island and circumnavigating Fastnet Rock. *aquaventures.ie*

Cape Clear Ferries Fastnet Rock Tours: Day tours to Fastnet Rock (no landing) from Baltimore and Schull (p214), some with time ashore on Cape Clear Island, plus twilight tours. *capeclearferries.com*

On the last weekend in May, the two-in-one **Baltimore Seafood & Wooden Boat Festival** *(baltimorewoodenboatfestival.com)* provides a showcase for local seafood while traditional wooden sailboats race around the harbour.

Escape to Cape Clear Island

Lying some 12km offshore from Baltimore, Cape Clear Island (Oileán Chléire), with its lonely inlets, pebble beaches and gorse- and heather-clad cliffs, is an escapist's heaven. Only 5km long and just over 1.5km wide at its broadest point, this small, rugged Gaeltacht (Irish-speaking) area is the southernmost inhabited island in the country.

Information boards near the harbour highlight a couple of marked walking trails, the 6km Red Loop (Lúb an Ghleanna) and 4km Green Loop (Lúb na Cnoiciní), while unmarked roads wander all over the island – bring your bike on the boat to make exploring them easier. The remains of a 12th-century church and holy well are near the pier, while on the coast to the west, the ruins of 14th-century Dunamore Castle, the stronghold of the O'Driscoll clan, can be seen perched on a rock.

Cape Clear is one of the top bird-watching spots in Ireland, known for its seabirds including Manx shearwater, guillemot, gannet, fulmar and kittiwake. Tens of thousands of migrating birds can pass hourly, especially in the early morning and at dusk. The best time of year for twitching here is October. Bring rain gear at any time of year.

Cape Clear Island

In early September, the island forms the backdrop for the rich Irish tradition of storytelling when it hosts the three-day **Cape Clear International Storytelling Festival** *(cape clearstorytelling.com)*.

Passenger ferries *(capeclearferries.com; Baltimore return adult/child €20/9, Schull return €25/10, bicycle extra €4)* makes the 45-minute crossing from Baltimore to Cape Clear Island three or four times a day in summer and twice a day in winter. There are also seasonal services from Schull (p214).

Drombeg Stone Circle

TIME FROM CLONAKILTY: **20MIN**

Ponder Drombeg's standing stones

On an exposed hillside, with fields falling away towards the coast, the **Drombeg Stone Circle** *(heritageireland.ie; free)* is superbly atmospheric. Its 17 stones, oriented towards the winter solstice sunset, once guarded the cremated bones of an adolescent. The 9m diameter circle probably dates from the 5th century CE and is a sophisticated Iron Age update of an earlier Bronze Age monument. Just beyond the stones are the remains of a hut and an Iron Age cooking pit, known as a *fulachta fiadh*. Experiments have shown that its heated rocks could boil water and keep it hot for nearly three hours, long enough to cook meat. Take the signposted turn off the R597, approximately 4km west of Rosscarbery.

FASTNET ROCK

Known as 'Ireland's Teardrop' because it was the last sight of home for emigrants sailing to America, including those aboard disaster-bound RMS *Titanic*, Fastnet Rock is Ireland's most southerly point. Its Irish name, An Charraig Aonair translates as 'the lonely rock', while 'Fastnet' is thought to come from the Old Norse Hvasstein-ey, meaning 'sharp-tooth isle'.

This isolated rocky outcrop rises some 7km southwest of Cape Clear Island (19km from Baltimore), topped by a mighty 54m-high lighthouse built in 1904; the last of its lightkeepers left after its automation in 1989. In good weather, it's visible from many places on the coastline from Baltimore to Mizen Head. Its image graces countless postcards, coffee-table books and framed art photographs.

Bantry

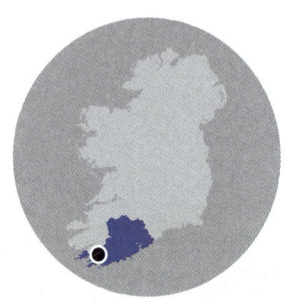

HISTORY | SCENERY | OUTDOORS

GETTING AROUND

No trains serve Bantry, but it's possible to travel by public transport from both the east and west. A bus line runs between Cork city and Bantry (some services continue to Glengarriff and Castletownbere), and another runs between Skibbereen via Bantry and Kenmare to Killarney in Kerry.

Bantry is a small town, so you'll have no trouble getting around on foot. Bantry House has a large car park but you can easily walk from the town centre in 15 minutes using the arched pedestrian entrance on the Quay. Rent bikes from **O'Donovan Cycles** *(odonovancycles.ie)* on Market St.

Framed by the Sheep's Head hills and the craggy Caha Mountains, magnificent and sprawling Bantry Bay is one of the country's most attractive seascapes. Sheltered by islands at the head of the bay, Bantry town, with a population of 2858 residents, is neat and orderly, with narrow streets of old-fashioned independent shops, lively traditional pubs, a choice of excellent seafood restaurants and a picturesque waterfront.

Pride of place goes to the splendid Georgian mansion of Bantry House, the former home of Richard White, who earned his place in history when, in 1798, he warned authorities of the imminent landing of Irish patriot Wolfe Tone and his French fleet, in support of the United Irishmen's rebellion. In the end, storms prevented the fleet from landing, and the course of Irish history was definitively altered. All Wolfe Tone got for his troubles was a square and a statue bearing his name.

Spend a Night in a Stately Home

Tour or stay in a country house

With its air of faded gentility, the 18th-century **Bantry House & Garden** *(bantryhouse.com; adult/child €14/5, afternoon tea incl estate entry €50)* makes for an intriguing guided/self-guided tour. From the Gobelin tapestries in the drawing room to the columned splendour of the library, the house conjures up a lost world of aristocratic excess. But the gardens are its greatest glory, with lawns sweeping down towards the sea; and the magnificent Italian garden at the back, with its staircase of 100 steps offering spectacular views. (Check ahead for seasonal opening times, as it often hosts private events.)

Owned by the same family since the mid-18th century, the estate was bought in 1765 by Whiddy Island–born Richard White, father of the First Earl of Bantry, and rooms brim with treasures brought back from successive generations' travels. The entrance hall is paved with mosaics from Pompeii, there

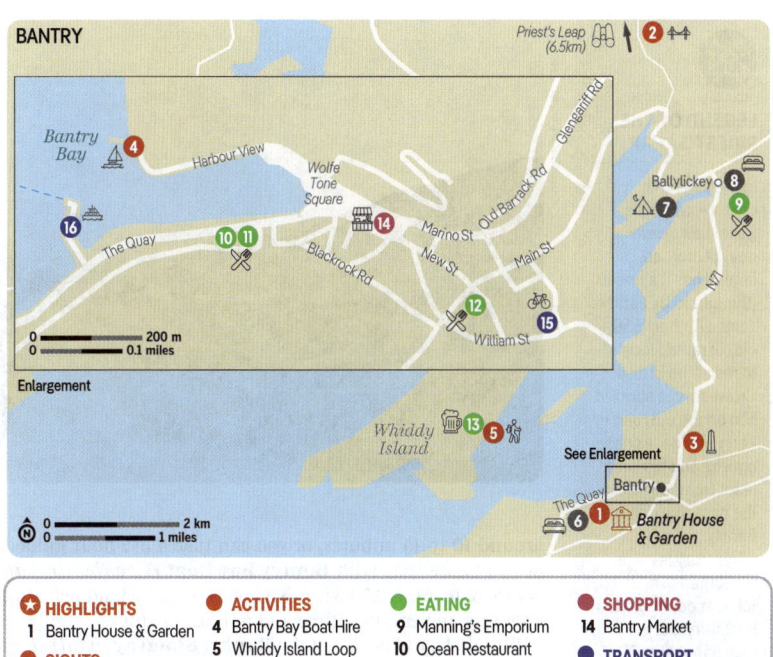

BANTRY

HIGHLIGHTS
1 Bantry House & Garden

SIGHTS
2 Coomhola Bridge
3 Priest's Leap Memorial Plaque

ACTIVITIES
4 Bantry Bay Boat Hire
5 Whiddy Island Loop Walk

SLEEPING
6 Bantry House
7 Eagle Point Camping
8 Seaview House Hotel

EATING
9 Manning's Emporium
10 Ocean Restaurant
11 Sam's Cara
12 Stuffed Olive

DRINKING & NIGHTLIFE
13 Bank House Bar

SHOPPING
14 Bantry Market

TRANSPORT
15 O'Donovan Cycles
16 Whiddy Island Ferries

---

are French and Flemish tapestries adorning the walls, and Japanese chests sit next to Russian shrines. There's a lovely tearoom in the west wing; book ahead for afternoon tea served on fine china.

It's possible to **stay** (p219); overnight B&B guests can book a private house tour.

Venture to Whiddy Island

Bantry Blueway explorations

Views of Bantry House unfold on the short boat ride from Bantry to Whiddy Island, which measures 5km long and 3km wide, with a sheltered position between the Beara and Sheep's Head peninsulas. Its microclimate sees fuchsia bloom through summer and autumn. Bring your hiking boots for the 5km **Whiddy Island Loop Walk** *(thesheepsheadway.com)*, or 7.7km with spur trails, winding past fields and two lakes with spectacular vantage points over the bay. The island is home to a single pub, the **Bank House Bar**, where local musicians often perform live music on summer Sundays.

Whiddy Island Ferries *(whiddy.ie; adult/child return €8/4)* carry passengers year-round from Bantry Pier to the island in

☑ TOP TIP

Much of Bantry's income and employment derives from seafood. Bantry Bay mussels are on menus in the town's many seafood restaurants and throughout County Cork. Bantry's weekly **market** sets up in Wolfe Tone Sq every Friday, with the largest on the first Friday of the month.

LEGEND OF THE PRIEST'S LEAP

In the early 17th century, when the Penal Laws were being enforced, legend has it a priest (thought to be Father James Archer, 1550–c1620) rallied locals to resist the British; Crown forces spotted him on the old road to Kerry and gave chase until he and his horse leapt from the top of the pass to escape to Bantry.

The story is recounted in a 1612-set poem written by Bantry-born Irish nationalist TD Sullivan (1824–1914), a journalist, politician, poet and songwriter who was Lord Mayor of Dublin from 1886 to 1888.

A **memorial plaque** at the side of the main road (N71) just south of Lidl supermarket on Bantry's northern edge marks the spot where the priest and his horse are said to have landed safely.

around 10 to 15 minutes, or you can take a 3½-hour guided Sea to Shore tour with **Bantry Bay Boat Hire** (bantrybay boathire.ie; tour €75) with two hours on the island learning about its ancient, maritime and military history.

Whiddy Island is part of the **Bantry Blueway** (bantrybay port.com), Ireland's first water-based trail network. It has three trails graded for beginners, intermediate and advanced kayakers around the bay, which spans 35 km from northeast to southwest into the Atlantic and is up to 4km wide at the head and 10km at the entrance. Bantry Bay Boat Hire rents kayaks (per hr from €16) and runs 1½-hour kayak to Whiddy Island trips (€28.95), after which you return by ferry, as well as sunset kayaking trips (€50) with the chance of seeing dolphins and bioluminescence.

Hike, Bike or Drive the Priest's Leap

Spectacular mountain road

If you're a faint-hearted driver, don't even think about heading up the vertiginous, single-track road to the **Priest's Leap** (Léim an tSagairt), 15km north of Bantry. If you're feeling brave, this original 400-year-old route between Bantry and Kenmare rewards intrepid travellers with monumental views across the mountains to Bantry Bay.

 EATING IN BANTRY: OUR PICKS

Stuffed Olive: Bakery/cafe with gourmet sandwiches, wraps/bagels, quiches, soups, and sweets such as Maltese cheesecake. 8am-3.30pm Tue-Sat €

Sam's Cara: Gallery/cafe on the Quay with an ivy-clad walled garden where coffee, biscuits and cakes are served on artist Sam's glazed pottery. 8am-5pm Thu-Mon €

Manning's Emporium: Deli/cafe supporting local suppliers. Toasties, sausage rolls, pizzas. 10am-3pm Wed, Thu & Sun, 10-3pm & 5-9pm Fri & Sat €€

Ocean Restaurant: Elegant setting. Dishes like smoked salmon and seaweed terrine, mussel-stuffed plaice, chicken with West Cork whiskey sauce. 6-8.30pm Mon-Sat €€

Priest's Leap

From Bantry, take the N71 north for 8km and turn right after the bridge at the head of the bay. Keep the river on your right for 1.7km to **Coomhola Bridge**, but don't cross the bridge – turn left and then take the first right. A long straight gets increasingly steep before relenting a bit. There are big drops on the left and few passing places on the final climb to the small parking area at the top. (It's not suitable for motorhomes or caravans.) You can complete a circular route by descending the far side to Bonane, on the main N71 road 11km south of Kenmare, and returning to Bantry.

The road has long been a classic challenge for cyclists, climbing almost 400m in 4.5km, and it's exceptionally steep (15%) in parts. Any fit rider will make it to the top, but you'll likely be off and pushing the bike at three or four places. A mountain bike is recommended as you'll need that bottom gear, and the road surface is uneven in places with a grass strip in the middle. Make sure your brakes are in good order for the descent!

It's also possible to hike up the road. If you park at Coomhola Bridge, it's a straightforward, if steep, 6km walk to the top. Allow 1½ hours each way. The summit of the pass is marked by a memorial stone and a wind-buffeted crucifix.

Beyond Bantry

Get your hiking boots on – Cork's far west peninsulas and islands are laced with walking trails.

Places
Schull p214
Mizen Head p214
Castletownbere p215
Glengarriff p217

Bantry is the jumping-off point for exploring County Cork's 'far west peninsulas' – Mizen Head and Sheep's Head to the southwest and Beara to the northwest. Each has a distinct identity and atmosphere. The Mizen is mostly green and lush, with heathery hills backing the yachting harbour of Schull. The long, narrow finger of the Sheep's Head is more barren and rocky, with steep hills and narrow roads, but has a rugged charm all of its own. The Beara is the biggest of all. Its intricate coast and sharp-featured mountains are a geologist's paradise of exposed and contorted rock strata, making for dramatic scenery at almost every turn.

GETTING AROUND

Regular bus services ply the main N71 road from Cork city, Clonakilty and Skibbereen through Bantry and Glengarriff with services on to Kenmare and Killarney. **TFI Local Link Cork** *(locallinkcork.ie)* runs a network of minibus routes connecting Bantry to Castletownbere, Allihies, Kilcrohane and other villages on the peninsulas, but services can be limited; check timetables online. To properly explore the Mizen Head, Sheep's Head and Beara peninsulas, it's far better to have your own wheels.

Schull
TIME FROM BANTRY: **25MIN**

Stroll Schull's yachting harbour

The N71 rolls south from Bantry through Ballydehob, from where the R592 leads southwest to the pretty yachting harbour of Schull (pronounced 'skull'). Attracted by the sailing crowd, local creatives have turned this former fishing village into a buzzing little place with art and craft shops and galleries. On the main street, don't miss the wonderful cherry-red-painted **Hackett's Bar** *(facebook.com/hackettsbarschull)* for a pint of stout and a crab sandwich, and exuberant live-music sessions.

Mizen Head
TIME FROM BANTRY: **50MIN**

Brave the bridge at Mizen Head

On a clear day, the road west from Schull enjoys great views out to Cape Clear Island and the Fastnet lighthouse. The landscape becomes wilder around Goleen, where narrowing roads run out to a dead end at the impressive cliffs of Mizen Head (Carn Uí Néid; its English name rhymes with 'wizen').

Completed in 1909 to help warn ships off the rocks, **Mizen Head Signal Station** *(mizenhead.ie; adult/child €7.50/4.50)* is perched high above crashing waves and contorted sea cliffs on a small island connected to the mainland by a dizzying 45m-high footbridge. From the visitor centre, it's a 10-minute walk via 99 steps to reach the station, which houses exhibits on the station's history and on marine wildlife. Keep your eyes open for whales and dolphins. Various ramps and steps lead to different viewpoints and photo opportunities. Plan to spend at least 1½ hours here. If you're pushed for time, the best cliff scenery is from Dunlough Bay View (across the bridge and up the steps to the right; 20 minutes).

Beyond the Mizen Head turnoff, at the end of the minor road you'll find a car park from where a pleasant 30-minute walk across sheep pastures leads to the ruins of **Dunlough Castle** at Three Castle Head. The path crosses private land (no dogs allowed) and is closed from mid-January to April.

Castletownbere

TIME FROM BANTRY: **55MIN**

Check out the 'capital' of the Beara Peninsula

One of Ireland's biggest fishing ports, buzzing Castletownbere (Baile Chais Bhéara) has great appeal for those looking for the 'real' Ireland, and is home to the world-famous pub **MacCarthy's Bar** *(maccarthysbar.com)*, featured in the late Pete McCarthy's bestseller, *McCarthy's Bar* (2000), where he thought it might be the best pub in the world. The town has a thriving food scene, with delis, cafes and a number of good restaurants. Castletownbere's **market** *(castletownbere.ie)* sets up on the Square on the first Thursday of the month (every Thursday during the summer months).

Enjoy a picnic overlooking the sea

Stock up in Castletownbere for a fantastic summer picnic on a promontory overlooking the southern entrance to the sheltered harbour of Berehaven, home to the ruins of 15th-century **Dunboy Castle**. A former stronghold of the O'Sullivan Beare clan, it was destroyed by English forces during the Siege of Dunboy in 1602.

On the way to the castle, you pass the fenced-off shell of Puxley Manor, a grand Victorian mansion that was once home to a copper-mining magnate and provided the inspiration for Clonmere in Daphne du Maurier's 1943 novel *Hungry Hill*. The manor was burnt out by the IRA in 1921 after it had been rumoured that the castle was to be occupied by British military from nearby Fort Berehaven. It has lain abandoned since the 2008 property crash shelved plans to turn it into a luxury hotel, but since its 2022 purchase by an Irish businessperson they're back on the agenda.

Dunboy is at the end of the narrow L8935, which leaves the main road 2.5km southwest of Castletownbere.

THREE CASTLE HEAD

On the isolated cape immediately north of Mizen Head, the evocative ruins of Dunlough Castle reveal one of Ireland's most unusual medieval structures: a dry-stone curtain wall that combines with a lake and sea cliffs to fortify an entire headland. Its three towers give the headland its name; the castle, from the Irish Dún Loch, means Fort of the Lake.

A castle was built here in 1207 by the chieftain of the O'Mahony clan, Donagh 'the Migrator', who resisted Anglo-Norman invaders by settling in remote West Cork, and it once commanded the sea route along the coast. It's thought what remains today was built on top of the 13th-century fortifications in the 15th century. It was occupied by the O'Mahony family until 1627.

EATING BEYOND BANTRY: OUR PICKS

Sugarloaf Cafe: Cute Glengarriff spot for all-day breakfasts (full and mini Irish fry-ups, omelettes, BLTs) and homemade cakes. *10am-4pm* €

Townhouse O D's: On Schull's main street. Gastro-pub menu with steak sandwiches, burgers, mussel fritters. *4-9.30pm Thu-Sat & Mon, from 12.30pm Sun* €€

Blairscove House: Near Durrus. Fire-roasted dishes in chandeliered stone barn, with views across Dunmanus Bay. *6-9.30pm Tue-Sat mid-Mar–early Nov* €€€

Nottage: Fine dining at Crookhaven, Mizen Head, with inventive twists like crab lasagne, whiskey-marinated mussels and oyster *crème brûlée*. *5.30-10.30pm Tue-Sat* €€€

BEST TOURS BEYOND BANTRY

Outdoors Ireland: Sunrise, sunset and half-day sea kayaking plus bioluminescence night kayaking. *outdoorsireland.com*

Dursey Boat Trips: Bull Rock Trips pass Dursey Island; **Castletownbere Harbour Trips** from Castletownbere pass Bere Island's Martello towers. *durseyboattrips.com*

Bantry Bay Charters: Wildlife tours, angling and scuba diving. *bantrybaycharters.ie*

West Cork Sailing: Seal-spotting kayaking tours, sailing lessons and skippered sailing tours. *westcorksailing.com*

Cape Clear Ferries: From Schull, 25-minute crossings to Cape Clear Island (p208) run three times weekly June, six times weekly July and August; it also offers tours around Fastnet Rock (p208). *capeclearferries.com*

Catch a cable car to Dursey Island

At the end of the Beara peninsula, tiny Dursey Island (Oileán Baoi), is reached not by ferry but Ireland's only **cable car** *(durseyisland.ie; adult/child return €10/5)*. A quaint 1960s contraption that sways precariously 30m above Dursey Sound (it was thoroughly renovated in 2023), it travels 374m, taking 7½ minutes each way. In a perfect photo op, livestock take precedence over humans in the queue.

The island, just 6.6km long by 1.5km wide, is a wildlife sanctuary, and dolphins and whales can sometimes be seen in the surrounding waters. The **Dursey Island Loop** winds around the island for 14km; allow four hours for the complete circuit. The **signal tower** is an obvious destination for a shorter walk (8km round trip).

Walk the Copper Mine Trail

The isolated village of Allihies (Na hAilichí), 20km west of Castletownbere, with its colourfully painted houses, has a fascinating history of copper mining. Your first stop should be the community-run **Allihies Copper Mine Museum** *(acmm.ie; adult/child €7/3)*, where you can get historical context and pick a map of the **Copper Mine Trail**, an 11km waymarked hike among the remains of the old workings.

From the museum, the trail leads downhill and then goes left along a classic Irish *boreen* (small lane) that winds up to another minor road near the ruined engine house of Kealoge Mine. Follow the road for 1.5km and turn right on a gravel track past the scant remains of Caminches Mine. Follow the signposted trail to your ultimate objective: the Mountain Mine, the biggest and highest of the old copper mines. The impressive engine house dates from 1862 and once contained

Cable car, Dursey Island

the Man Engine, a primitive steam-powered elevator that transported miners to and from the bottom of the mine, as well as hoisting ore to the surface (the mine reached a depth of 421m below the surface, around 280m below sea level).

The open pits and tunnels are safely fenced off, but you can explore the rest of the site and soak up the expansive views across the village to the beautiful white sand of **Ballydonegan Beach**, largely made of crushed quartz washed out from the old mine workings.

Glengarriff

TIME FROM BANTRY: **20MIN**

Sail to a subtropical island garden

From mid-March to October, a scenic 15-minute boat trip from Glengarriff ferries you to the horticultural miracle of **Ilnacullin – Garinish Island** (heritageireland.ie; adult/child €5/3). It was created in the early 20th century when the island's owner commissioned architect Harold Peto to design a garden on the then-barren outcrop. Topsoil was shipped in, and subtropical species were planted: camellias, magnolias and rhododendrons now provide a seasonal blaze of colour.

The centrepiece of the island is a enchanting Italianate garden. Nearby, a cypress avenue leads to a faux-Grecian temple with a stunning view of Great Sugarloaf. There are more views from the island's highest point, a 19th-century Martello tower. Plan to spend at least 1½ hours here.

Harbour Queen (harbourqueenferry.com; adult/child return €16/8) and **Blue Pool** (bluepoolferry.ie; adult/child €12.50/7.50) take you to the island past colonies of basking seals and a nesting site for white-tailed eagles.

BEST FESTIVALS IN & BEYOND BANTRY

Fastnet Film Festival: Schull's five-day festival (late May), over 500 short films from more than 40 countries. fastnetfilmfestival.com

Jim Dowling Uilleann Pipe & Trad Festival: Glengarriff's traditional Irish music festival over three days in mid-June. jimdowlingfestival.ie

West Cork Chamber Music Festival: Ten-day late June/early July festival. Concerts at venues in Bantry and all over West Cork. westcorkmusic.ie

West Cork Literary Festival: Talks, readings, writing workshops, book launches over eight days in mid-July. westcorkmusic.ie/literary-festival

Calves Week: Schull's early August yacht and dinghy racing culminates in weekend regatta that includes a fireworks display. shsc.ie

SPIN AROUND THE SHEEP'S HEAD PENINSULA

Hire a bike in Bantry for an invigorating ride along this windblown peninsula to its remote lighthouse.

START	END	LENGTH
Bantry	Bantry	70km; 1–2 days

Head west from ❶ **Bantry** on the N71 and turn right on the minor road past the Westlodge Hotel. At a fork 10km further on, bear right (signposted Kilcrohane). ❷ **Goat's Path Farm & Pod Park** is a good overnight spot if you've made a late afternoon start. Past Gortnakilla Pier, keep left at a fork to begin the long climb up the Goat's Path road to the narrow spine of the peninsula 195m above sea level at ❸ **Seefin**.

Descend the hairpins on the far side to ❹ **Kilcrohane**, where you can get coffee and cake at the Old Creamery, and then continue southwest, following signs for the Sheep's Head Cafe to reach the end of the road at ❺ **Bernie's Cupán Tae**, a tiny tearoom famous for its scones and salmon sandwiches. A superb waymarked walk leads for 2km to the ❻ **Sheep's Head lighthouse** at the tip of the peninsula.

Return to Kilcrohane and continue along the coast road to ❼ **Ahakista**, where you have a choice of watering holes: the Ahakista Bar, a charming, tin-roofed stone cottage known locally as the Tin Pub; the Heron Gallery Cafe & Gardens for lunches, coffee and cake; or Arundels By The Pier for a waterfront beer garden. From here, it's a straightforward 19km via the pretty village of ❽ **Durrus** back to Bantry.

The views are spectacular from Seefin, aka Sui Finn, or Finn's Seat, as in legendary giant Finn MacCool.

Allow 1½ to two hours round-trip for the walk to Sheep's Head lighthouse amid astounding sea-cliff scenery.

Fit riders can complete the circuit in a day, but take two if you want to dawdle and take in a walk.

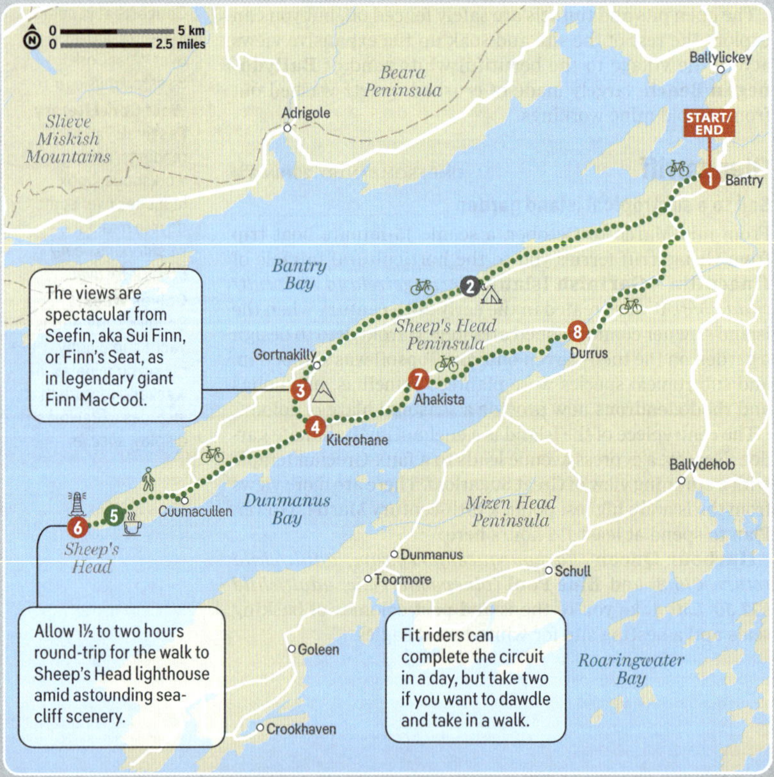

Places We Love to Stay

€ Budget €€ Midrange €€€ Top End

Cork City MAP p189

Sheila's Hostel € Popular backpacker's hostel in a handy location for exploring the city, with great facilities, including a cinema room and sauna.

Anam Cara B&B €€ Cute little Georgian-style cottage with a homely, country-house feel.

Hotel Isaacs €€ Housed in a Victorian furniture warehouse in a buzzing central location. Spacious, well-decorated rooms.

Imperial Hotel €€€ History-filled, two-century-old landmark in the heart of Cork, with lavish rooms and contemporary amenities and spa.

River Lee Hotel €€€ Modern city-centre riverside hotel with a glass-walled atrium, state-of-the-art gym facilities and on-site parking.

Kinsale

Giles Norman Townhouse €€ Stylish guest rooms with elegant bathrooms, espresso machines and a discount at the downstairs gallery.

Old Presbytery €€€ Luxury self-catering apartments set in a gorgeously refurbished 18th-century Georgian property.

Pier House €€€ Pristine contemporary rooms, some opening to balconies with garden and harbour views. No breakfast.

East Cork

An Stór Townhouse € Midleton accommodation straddling the boundary between upmarket hostel and budget guesthouse, with self-catering facilities.

WatersEdge Hotel €€ Spacious rooms, in-house dining and a great waterfront location for Cobh's attractions.

Commodore Hotel €€ Classic seaside hotel in Cobh with soaring hallways and well-appointed rooms (it's worth paying extra for a sea view).

Ballymaloe House €€€ Exquisitely decorated rooms and facilities including free e-bikes; breakfast includes bread from its own bakery and eggs from the farm.

Clonakilty MAP p203

Emmet Hotel €€ Lovely Georgian hotel on the elegant main square mixes period charm with the perks of a contemporary boutique hotel, and indoor and outdoor dining.

O'Donovan's Hotel €€ Behind a vintage exterior in Clonakilty's heart, this classic old-fashioned hotel has comfortable en-suite rooms and free parking.

Dunmore House €€€ In the same family since 1934, this genteel seaside hotel has handmade furniture, beautiful cashmere rugs, and top-notch West Cork cuisine.

Inchydoney Island Lodge €€€ A seawater spa, stylish rooms overlooking the ocean from private balconies, and family-friendly facilities; 5km south of Clonakilty.

Beyond Clonakilty

Bridge House €€ Behind its vivid teal facade, Mona Best's Skibbereen B&B is a work of art, filled with Victorian tableaux and period memorabilia.

Rolf's Country House €€ Upmarket B&B in a restored and extended farmhouse, and self-catering courtyard cottages in restful gardens on Baltimore's upper fringes.

Casey's of Baltimore €€€ Most rooms in this super-comfortable hotel have sea views, as does its seafood restaurant; there are also cheaper cottage studio apartments.

Bantry MAP p211

Eagle Point Camping € Superb campground with an enviable waterside location on a pine-fringed promontory 6km north of Bantry.

Bantry House €€€ From April to October, this stately home's owners offer B&B accommodation in six period-furnished rooms in the east wing.

Seaview House Hotel €€€ Country house hotel with large, antique-furnished rooms and spa with seawater bath suites and cedar steam barrels, 5km north of Bantry.

Beyond Bantry

Dzogchen Beara € Buddhist meditation centre with hostel accommodation, self-catering cottages and a vegetarian cafe, 9km southwest of Castletownbere.

Gallán Mór €€ Gorgeous boutique B&B midway between Durrus and Ahakista. Minimum two-night stay; closed October to February.

Eccles Hotel €€€ At the east end of Glengarriff, this historic hotel and spa has counted George Bernard Shaw and WB Yeats as former guests.

Researched by
Catherine Le Nevez

Kerry

THE JEWEL IN IRELAND'S SCENIC CROWN

Home to Ireland's highest mountain range, both its oldest and newest national parks, and its most remote islands, Kerry is crammed with superlatives.

County Kerry (Ciarraí) contains some of Ireland's most iconic scenery: surf-pounded sea cliffs, soft golden strands, emerald-green farmland crisscrossed by tumble-down stone walls, mist-shrouded bogs and mountain peaks that tear the clouds. Off the coast, the jagged, improbable outpost of Skellig Michael is one of the Republic's two UNESCO World Heritage sites.

With one of the country's finest national parks as its backyard, the lively hub of Killarney spills over with colourful shops, restaurants and pubs with spirited trad music. The town is the jumping-off point for Kerry's famed circular driving route, the Ring of Kerry, which skirts the mountainous, island-fringed Iveragh Peninsula, with photo-worthy views unfolding at every turn.

The more compact Dingle Peninsula is like a condensed version of its southern neighbour, with the Slea Head Drive linking ancient prehistoric ringforts, beehive huts, Christian sites, sandy beaches and glimpses of a hard, unforgiving land. The lively fishing port of Dingle is known for its seafood restaurants. For a taste of traditional culture, the nearby Gaeltacht (Irish-speaking) region of West Kerry provides a unique opportunity to experience the Irish language and customs firsthand.

Kerry's exquisite beauty makes it one of Ireland's most popular tourist destinations, but if you need to escape from the crowds, there's always a mountain pass, an isolated cove or an untrodden trail to discover.

THE MAIN AREAS

KILLARNEY NATIONAL PARK
Lakes and mountains. **p226**

DINGLE
Charming harbour town. **p244**

TRALEE
Historic market town. **p253**

For places to stay in Kerry, see p259

THE GUIDE

KERRY

Left: Faha Ridge, Mt Brandon (p249); right: Upper Lake, Killarney National Park (p226)

Find Your Way

County Kerry covers a large area, much of it mountainous and remote with narrow winding roads. Regular public transport is confined to the main towns and villages, so a car helps to maximise your time.

Tralee, p253
The enchanting capital of North Kerry offers a delightful blend of historical charm, elegant Georgian streets and friendly locals.

Dingle, p244
Charming harbour town packed with colourful streets, lively pubs and warm-hearted locals, where the spirit of the Gaeltacht is alive on every corner.

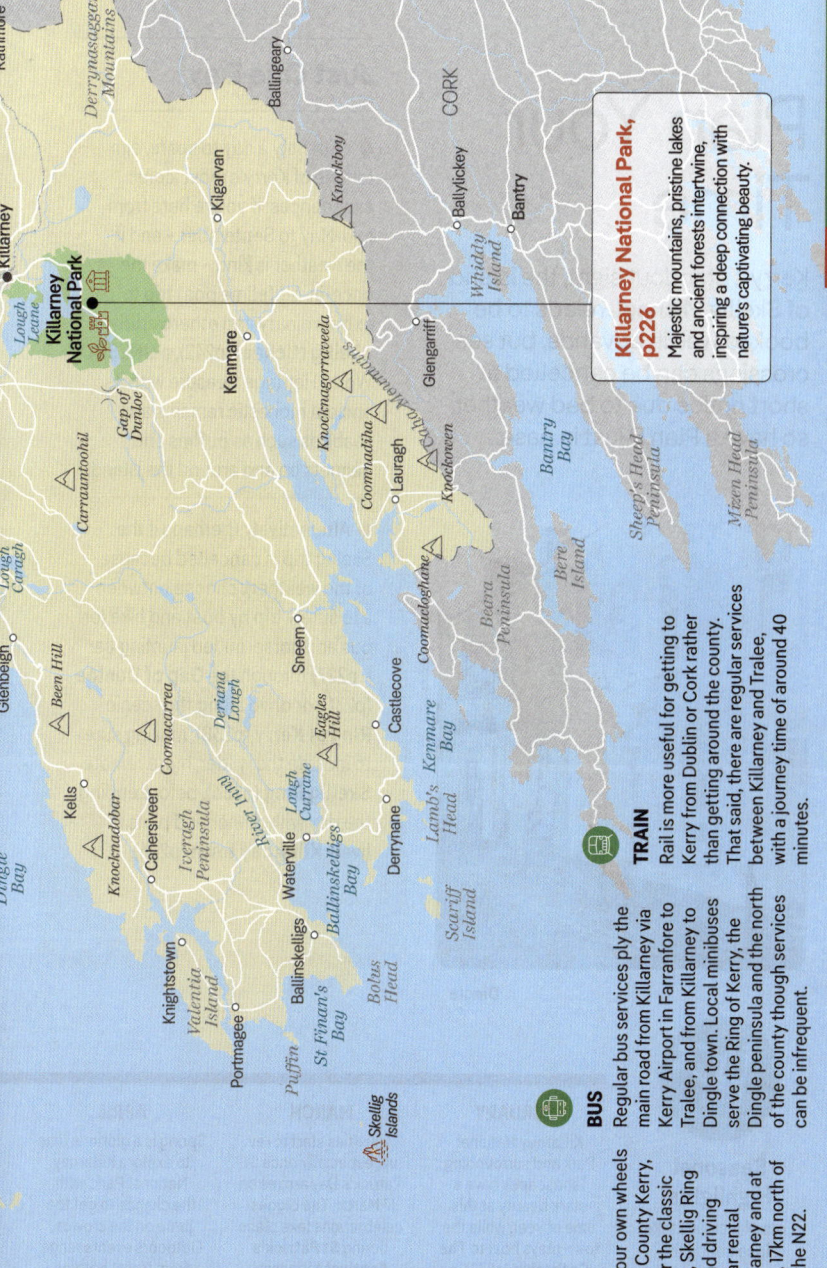

Killarney National Park, p226
Majestic mountains, pristine lakes and ancient forests intertwine, inspiring a deep connection with nature's captivating beauty.

THE GUIDE

KERRY

CAR
You'll want your own wheels for exploring County Kerry, especially for the classic Ring of Kerry, Skellig Ring and Slea Head driving tours. Find car rental outlets in Killarney and at Kerry airport, 17km north of Killarney on the N22.

BUS
Regular bus services ply the main road from Killarney via Kerry Airport in Farranfore to Tralee, and from Killarney to Dingle town. Local minibuses serve the Ring of Kerry, the Dingle peninsula and the north of the county though services can be infrequent.

TRAIN
Rail is more useful for getting to Kerry from Dublin or Cork rather than getting around the county. That said, there are regular services between Killarney and Tralee, with a journey time of around 40 minutes.

Plan Your Time

Kerry's standout sight, the island of Skellig Michael, needs to be booked well in advance, but sea crossings can be cancelled at short notice due to bad weather, so have a Plan B just in case.

Dingle

Just One Day

● With only a day to spare, aim for one of Kerry's most iconic experiences. If you're here from mid-May to September – and if the weather is kind – make the once-in-a-lifetime boat trip to extraordinary and otherworldly **Skellig Michael** (p242), a UNESCO World Heritage treasure with its ancient monastic remains and seabirds such as puffins and gannets on and around the island.

● Alternatively (perhaps if the Skellig trip is cancelled because of the weather), choose between a leisurely trip by boat and bike (or bus and horse-pulled jaunting car – p227) through the **Gap of Dunloe** (p230) or drive along the scenic **Ring of Kerry** (p238), making sure to include the wilder, more remote **Skellig Ring** (p236), before ending the day with dinner and pints in lively **Killarney town** (p226).

Seasonal Highlights

Lots of festivals take place during the warmer months; book accommodation well ahead. Check ahead for seasonal closures in winter.

FEBRUARY

Killarney National Park and surrounding landscapes have a stark beauty at this time of year, while the town plays host to **The Gathering** (p233), a convivial five days filled with traditional Irish music and dance.

MARCH

Activities start to rev up, especially once St Patrick's Day arrives on 17 March. The biggest celebrations take place during **St Patrick's Festival Killarney** (p233), with green illuminations, and a parade, concerts and funfair.

APRIL

Spring is a glorious time to explore Killarney National Park, with the chance to get the jump on the crowds. Outdoors events range from forest bathing to mountain ascents during the **Wander Wild Festival** (p233).

Three Days to Explore

- Allocate a day to one of the iconic trips in the one-day itinerary and split the other two days between Killarney and Dingle.

- Begin day two at **Killarney House & Gardens** (p226), then devote the day to exploring **Killarney National Park**: take a jaunting car ride out to **Muckross House** (p227), followed by a boat trip on **Lough Leane** (p229).

- On day three, head to the charming fishing port of **Dingle town** (p244) for a boat cruise of Dingle Bay, searching for dolphins, whales and seals, and wander its artisan shops and galleries. Enjoy a seafood lunch (and Dingle-made Murphy's ice cream). In the afternoon, set out on a tour of the scenic **Slea Head Drive** (p252), at the western tip of the Dingle Peninsula.

More Than a Week

- Start off exploring Killarney National Park and its stunning surrounds, allowing time along the Ring of Kerry for under-the-radar highlights like the rainforest and skywalk at magnificent **Kells Bay House & Gardens** (p241).

- From Portmagee, where boats depart for Skellig Michael, cross the bridge to **Valentia Island** (p237) with its fascinating transatlantic cable history. Stop by **Inch Strand** (p251) en route to Dingle town and build in an overnight of traditional music in its atmospheric pubs. Follow that by discovering the ancient sites and spectacular coastlines along the Slea Head Drive, stopping at **Dunquin's Blasket Centre** (p249), and (weather permitting) taking a boat trip to abandoned **Great Blasket** (p249).

- Finish at the museums and wetlands in **Tralee** (p253), or continue north to clifftop **Ballybunion** (p257).

THE GUIDE

KERRY

JUNE
Summer kicks off and festivities abound. An impressive international list of authors, including Booker Prize winners, make their way to the elegant town of Listowel in northern County Kerry for the **Listowel Literary Festival** (p258).

JULY
Long summer days are great for watersports on Kerry's lakes, rivers and beaches, and festivals are in full swing. On the Dingle Peninsula's northern side, **Féile Lúghnasa** (p251) celebrates the ancient Celtic harvest festival.

AUGUST
Everywhere is busy in August, so build extra time into your schedule. Festivities abound; in Killorglin, a horse fair, street theatre, concerts and fireworks are part of the **Puck Fair**, first recorded in 1603.

OCTOBER
Falling temperatures and shortening days. Some sights and activities wind down but there's still plenty to enjoy. The **Dingle Food Festival** (p247) celebrates Dingle town's local produce, artisans and sustainability.

Killarney National Park

HIKING | BOATING | NATURE

GETTING AROUND

Killarney is well served by buses and trains; the adjacent **bus** and **train stations** are on the town centre's eastern edge. **Kerry Airport** *(kerryairport.ie)* is 17km north of Killarney at Farranfore, linked by bus and taxi (trains stop 1.4 km southwest); major car companies have desks here, and some have offices in town.

Bicycles are ideal for exploring the scattered sights of the Killarney region, many of which are best reached by two wheels or on foot. Many hostels, campsites and hotels offer bike hire. Alternatively, try Killarney Rent A Bike at **O'Sullivan Cycles** *(killarneyrentabike. com)*, which has locations on **Muckross Rd** and **College St**.

Sprawling over 10,236 wild hectares, the sublime Killarney National Park is an idyllic place to explore. Ross Castle and Muckross House draw the biggest crowds, but it's always possible to escape to the hills where native red deer roam the country's largest area of ancient oak woods and glassy lakes reflect panoramic views of Ireland's highest mountains.

The core of the national park is the Muckross Estate, donated to the state by Arthur Bourn Vincent in 1932. The park was designated a UNESCO Biosphere Reserve in 1982. The Killarney Lakes – Lough Leane (the Lower Lake, or 'Lake of Learning'), Muckross (or Middle) Lake and the Upper Lake – make up about a quarter of the park and are surrounded by natural oak and yew woodland. The high crags and moors of Purple Mountain (832m) to the west and Knockrower (552m) to the south overlook the lakes.

Discover the Gateway to Killarney National Park

Ornamental gardens with mountain views

Right in Killarney town, just inside the park boundary, **Killarney House**'s glory is its vast ornamental gardens, sweeping majestically towards a gorgeous view of the Kerry mountains, with a cherry blossom walk and Ireland's longest herbaceous border. Pack a picnic, stroll across the huge lawns past colourful flower beds and choose a peaceful spot where you can soak up the view.

Originally the stable block of a much larger French-chateau-style mansion built for the landowning Browne family in the 1720s, the 18th-century house was demolished in the 1870s when the family moved to nearby Knockreer House, and when that was destroyed by fire in 1913, the stables were remodelled as a family residence and then abandoned in the 1950s. Restored in 2016, it's now home to the **Killarney National Park Visitor Centre** *(nationalparks.ie/killarney; free)*, where an interactive exhibition presents a stunning overview of the park's flora, fauna and history across 15 rooms, and staff offer a wealth of information on exploring the park.

Clip-Clop in a Jaunting Car
Horse-drawn buggies

The tradition of touring Killarney's sights in a horse-drawn buggy took off in the 1860s following Queen Victoria's widely reported visit to the area in 1861 (many family businesses today can trace their lineage back to that time). These traditional horse-drawn jaunting cars provide tours from Killarney town to Ross Castle and Muckross Estate, complete with amusing commentary from the 'jarvey' (driver). Jaunting cars also travel through the Gap of Dunloe between Lord Brandon's Cottage and Kate Kearney's Cottage.

In Killarney, the main **pickup point**, nicknamed 'the Ha Ha' or 'the Block', is on Kenmare Pl. Cars typically fit up to four people; the cost varies depending on the distance. Expect to pay around €20 per person for a one-hour tour from Killarney to Ross Castle and back, or around €35 per person for a two-hour tour to Muckross Estate and back. It's also possible to prebook tours online with companies such as fifth-generation-run **Killarney Jaunting Cars** *(killarneyjauntingcars.com)*. Horses (many Irish Draught or Irish Cob) are well cared for and have close bonds with their jarveys.

Explore Muckross Estate
Historic house and farming museum

The impressive Victorian mansion of **Muckross House** *(muckross-house.ie; adult/child house & farms €16/10; house or farms only €9/6)*, some 6km south of Killarney, was built as a hunting and fishing lodge for the Herbert family in 1843. Self-guided tours reveal a house crammed with fascinating objects (70% of the contents are original); portraits by John Singer Sargent adorn the walls alongside trophy stag heads and giant stuffed trout, while antique Killarney furniture, with its distinctive inlaid scenes of local beauty spots, graces the grand apartments along with tapestries, Persian rugs, silverware and china commissioned for Queen Victoria's visit in 1861. Sloping down to the Middle Lake, the beautiful Muckross Gardens are free to explore.

On the far side of the visitor centre and car park from the house are three farms (small to large) making up the **Muckross Traditional Farms** *(closed November to February)*. These

BEST SHOPPING IN KILLARNEY

Killarney Art Gallery: Paintings, prints, sculptures and photography by local artists. *killarneyartgallery.com*

Portwest: Killarney's largest outdoor shop with clothing, hiking boots, tents, backpacks and accessories including first-aid kits and water bottles. *theoutdoorshop.ie*

Variety Sounds: Stocks a large range of traditional Irish instruments, and sheet music and recordings; you might also catch impromptu performances in store. *instagram.com/variety_sounds*

Mr McGuires Olde Sweet Shop: Handmade Irish chocolates, fudge, boiled sweets, jellies and ice cream, including sugar-free, gluten-free and vegetarian candies. *@mcguires.sweetshop*

Hazel's Nuts About Vintage: Tiny shop with quality men's and women's vintage clothing, jewellery and bags. *@hazelsnutsaboutvintage*

EATING IN KILLARNEY TOWN: BEST CAFES

Curious Cat Café: Quirky little cafe serving breakfast burritos, sweet and savoury pancakes, and tapas on weekend evenings. *9am-5pm Sun-Thu, to 9pm Fri & Sat* €

Lir Café: Some of Killarney's best coffee. Food spans toasties, pastries, cakes and handmade chocolates like Guinness caramels. *7am-7pm* €

LUNA: Modern industrial décor and dishes such as spicy sausage rolls, wild garlic and cheese scones, chia pudding and filled baguettes, with natural wines. *8am-6pm* €

Mug & Bean: Vegan, vegetarian and traditional Irish breakfasts or whiskey-drizzled porridge, with coffee or fresh mint tea. *7.30am-4pm Mon-Sat, 9am-4pm Sun* €

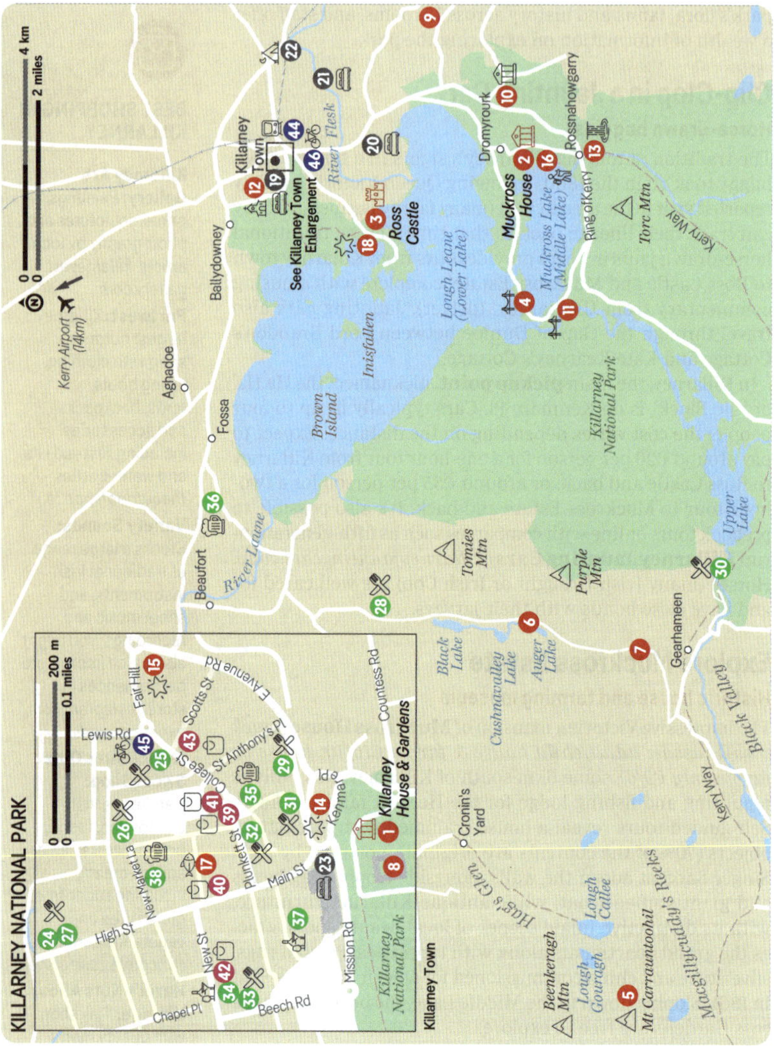

EATING IN KILLARNEY TOWN: BEST RESTAURANTS

Mad Monk: Freshly landed southwest Ireland seafood from its own fishing fleet with hand-cut chips in a bright, bare-brick space. *12.30-8.30pm Sun-Thu, to 9pm Fri & Sat* €€

Cronin's Restaurant: Kerry produce includes Skellig prawns, Kenmare oak-smoked salmon and MacGillycuddy Reeks venison. *4-9.30pm Mon-Fri, 3-9.30pm Sat & Sun* €€

Brícín: Charmer with antique lamps, stained glass and vintage art; try the apricot-and-sage-stuffed pork and house-speciality boxty (potato pancake). *6-9.30pm Tue-Sat* €€

Foley's Townhouse Restaurant: A 1795 townhouse is the setting for à la carte modern Irish cuisine using French techniques and a 300-strong wine list. *5-10pm* €€€

HIGHLIGHTS
1. Killarney House & Gardens
2. Muckross House
3. Ross Castle

SIGHTS
4. Brickeen Bridge
5. Carrauntoohil
6. Gap of Dunloe
7. Head of the Gap
8. Killarney National Park Visitor Centre at Killarney House & Gardens
see 11 Meeting of the Waters
9. Muckross Creamery
10. Muckross Traditional Farms
11. Old Weir Bridge
12. St Mary's Cathedral
13. Torc Waterfall

ACTIVITIES
14. Jaunting Car Tours Main Pickup Point
15. Killarney Jaunting Cars
see 18 Killarney Lake Tours
16. Old Boathouse Nature Trail
17. O'Neill's
see 18 Outdoors Ireland
18. Reen Pier

SLEEPING
19. Black Sheep Hostel
20. Cahernane House Hotel
21. Crystal Springs
22. Fleming's White Bridge Caravan & Camping Park
23. Killarney Plaza Hotel

EATING
24. Brícín
25. Cronin's Restaurant
26. Curious Cat Café
see 11 Dinis Cottage
27. Foley's Townhouse Restaurant
28. Kate Kearney's Cottage
29. Lir Café
30. Lord Brandon's Cottage
31. LUNA
32. Mad Monk
33. Mug & Bean

DRINKING & NIGHTLIFE
34. Celtic Whiskey Bar & Larder
35. Courtney's
36. Killarney Brewing & Distilling Co
37. Killarney Grand
38. O'Connor's
see 46 Taproom at Killarney Brewing & Distilling Co

SHOPPING
39. Hazel's Nuts About Vintage
40. Killarney Art Gallery
41. Mr McGuires Olde Sweet Shop
42. Portwest
43. Variety Sounds

TRANSPORT
see 44 Bus Station
44. Killarney Train Station
45. O'Sullivan's Bike Hire College St
46. O'Sullivan's Bike Hire Muckross Rd

---

recreations of 1930s to 1940s farms evoke authentic sights, sounds and smells: cow dung, hay, wet earth and peat smoke, and a cacophony of chickens, ducks, pigs and donkeys. Costumed staff bring the traditional farm buildings to life, and the petting area lets kids get close to piglets, lambs, ducklings and chicks. Allow at least a couple of hours to do the estate justice.

Visit Ross Castle
Medieval history

A lovely 2.6km walk or bike ride southwest of Killarney town's St Mary's Cathedral pedestrian entrance to the park (you may well spot deer along the way), **Ross Castle** *(heritageireland. ie; adult/child €5/3)*, a traditional tower house and keep, dates to the 15th century, when it's thought to have been built by Irish chieftain O'Donoghue Mór, and was restored in 1970. The entertaining 45-minute guided tour (no prebookings; arrive early to minimise wait times) combines an easily digested history lesson with real insight into life in medieval Ireland.

The castle is picturesquely set on Ross Island, an inlet of Lough Leane, with several loop trails. When Cromwell's forces finally attacked Munster's last stronghold, they did so by boat. Today, tour operators depart for lake excursions here.

Ply the Waters of Lough Leane
Boating adventures

Kayaking is a serene way to experience the beauty of the lower lake, Lough Leane – Killarney's largest lake. Three-hour morning, afternoon or sunset guided kayak tours with **Outdoors Ireland** *(outdoorsireland.com; per person €60)* take in limestone caves and wooded inlets as well as landing on Inisfallen.

Continues on p232

KILLARNEY TOWN'S TOURISM EVOLUTION

Killarney is the natural base camp for excursions into the neighbouring national park. The town is a well-oiled tourism machine, welcoming visitors since 1747, when Thomas Browne, 4th Viscount Kenmare, tapped into its tourism potential. This was followed by the railway's arrival in 1853, and, more recently, the 2014 launch of the Wild Atlantic Way.

Green initiatives, such as the 2023 ban on single-use coffee cups (BYO or pay a €2 deposit for a reusable 2GoCup), and the Killarney Hotels Sustainability Charter are paving the way for its sustainable future.

BOAT & BIKE TRIP

Gap of Dunloe

A boat trip across the lakes followed by a bike ride through the mountain scenery of the Gap of Dunloe is the classic Killarney experience. Your hostel, hotel or campsite can arrange it for you, including boat tickets and bike hire, or you can book online at gapofdunloetours.com. The total biking distance is 23km. Allowing time for stops and lunch, you should be back in Killarney by 3.30pm.

1 Reen Pier

Boats depart from Reen Pier (p232) near Ross Castle (p229) at 11am, with bikes propped in the bow. The 1½-hour cruise alone justifies the price. Ask your boater about the highest and lowest water levels seen in the lakes and sit back to enjoy the stories.

The Cruise: You glide past Inisfallen island with its ruined monastery and then turn south to sail under pretty **Brickeen Bridge** and reach the most beautiful part of Killarney's lakes, the **Meeting of the Waters**, the point where they converge.

2 Old Weir Bridge

The boat then surges up a rocky channel beneath the **Old Weir Bridge**. After prolonged dry weather, when lake levels are low, passengers may have to get out and walk a short distance while the boat gets hauled up this shallow, fast-flowing section.

The Cruise: The Long Range is next, a winding channel that is half-lake, half-river. It uncoils

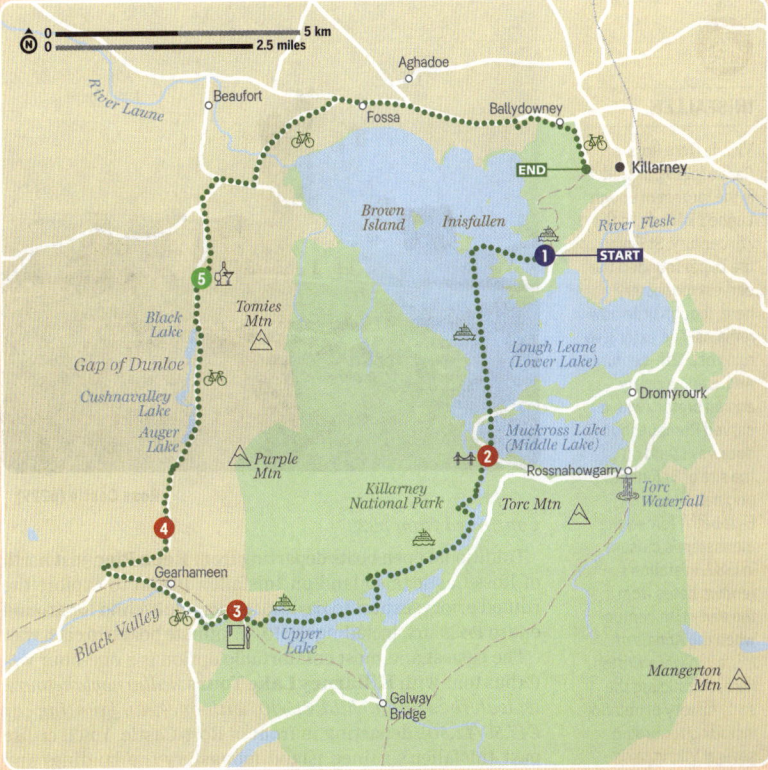

beneath the crags of **Eagle's Nest mountain** (golden eagles once nested here) before entering the long, narrow Upper Lake.

3 Lord Brandon's Cottage

Disembark at **Lord Brandon's Cottage**, a 19th-century hunting lodge surrounded by lush, green water meadows. It has a simple open-air cafe (cash only) as well as public toilets. The cycling section begins here.

The Ride: The bike section begins with a 4.5km climb to the head of the Gap. It's a steady uphill, but not too steep, and there's no shame in getting off and pushing for a bit.

4 Head of the Gap

At the summit, known as the **Head of the Gap**, you're rewarded with stunning views in both directions. Head back down to the Upper Lake and forward into the narrow pass of the Gap itself, a wild and scenic glaciated valley formed some 25,000 years ago.

The Ride: Enjoy a 6.5km downhill run to Kate Kearney's Cottage, passing through the Turnpike Boulders and crossing the Wishing Bridge, both good photo opportunities.

5 Kate Kearney's Cottage

History-filled 19th-century pub **Kate Kearney's Cottage** (*katekearneyscottage.com*) at the northern end of the Gap of Dunloe is a welcoming spot for cold beers and tasty pub food (check ahead; kitchen hours can be reduced at short notice). The bar hosts live Irish music every night in summer.

The Ride: Follow signs for Killarney along minor roads to the N71 and then a cycle path that hugs the side of the road before veering off through the golf course to end near the town centre opposite **St Mary's Cathedral**.

INISFALLEN

Visible from Ross Castle (p229), Inisfallen is the largest of Lough Leane's islands. In the 7th century, St Finian the Leper founded the earliest monastery here, though little now remains. The extensive ruins of a 12th-century Augustinian priory and an oratory with a carved Romanesque doorway stand on the site of St Finian's original; Queen Elizabeth I forced the monastery's closure in 1582. Inisfallen's renown dates from the early 13th century when the *Annals of Inisfallen* were written here, chronicling the early history of Ireland, including recording several Viking raids and an attack by the O'Donoghue clan in 1180. Now in the Bodleian Library at Oxford, England, they remain a vital source of information and gave the lake its Irish name, Lough Léin (Lake of Learning).

☑ TOP TIP

Killarney is at its most idyllic in spring and autumn, with manageable crowds and mild weather. During some events, such as May's Rally of the Lakes and June's Ireland BikeFest (see right), local roads (including the N71 Killarney–Kenmare route) may be temporarily closed.

Ross Castle (p229)

Continued from p229

Traditional open boats departing from **Reen Pier**, just north of Ross Castle, also land on Inisfallen Island to explore the ruined priory; expect to pay €15/10 per adult/child for around one to 1½ hours, including the 10-15-minute boat trip each way.

The easiest and most comfortable option is a one-hour waterbus tour with **Killarney Lake Tours** (*killarneylaketours. ie; waterbus adult/child €15/10, with one-way jaunting car €47.50/42.50*), departing in front of Ross Castle. You'll cruise past Inisfallen's ruined island monastery (no landing) and then on to the roadless west shore to view O'Sullivan's Cascade and Purple Mountain, returning via Brickeen Bridge. Combination tours include travel by jaunting car from Killarney to the castle.

Cast a Line
Gone fishing

Killarney's lakes and rivers are also popular for salmon and trout fishing. In town, 1947-opened **O'Neill's** has reams of advice, rents rods and tackle, and sells permits and licences; alternatively buy them online at Inland Fisheries Ireland (*fisheriesireland.ie*).

Climb Ireland's Highest Peak
Challenging hillwalk

Macgillycuddy's Reeks is Ireland's highest mountain range, and towering **Carrauntoohil** (Corrán Tuathail), at 1039m, is the country's highest summit.

The traditional route is via the **Devil's Ladder**, a gruelling trudge over unpleasantly loose stony ground southwest of the loughs (lakes) in Hag's Glen. An alternative route ascends via **Brother O'Shea's Gully** (rock scrambling and good route-finding ability required), a steep and challenging route through spectacular mountain scenery. The easiest descent is via the **Zig-Zags** to the east of the Devil's Ladder.

Climbing Carrauntoohil should never be attempted without a map and compass (and the skills to use them), proper hillwalking boots, waterproofs and spare food and water. **Kerry Mountain Rescue** *(kerrymountainrescue.ie)* has route descriptions and details of required maps. If you're the slightest bit unsure, go with experts like **Kerry Climbing** *(kerry climbing.ie; €65–85)*, which leads guided ascents year-round, weather permitting (booking is essential).

Sample Killarney's Flavours
Behind-the-scenes tours at the source

At the family-run working dairy farm **Muckross Creamery** *(muckrosscreamery.ie; tour €28)*, 5km southeast of town, 90-minute tours include meeting the cows, seeing the milking room and learning about its ice cream production, before tasting skyr (yoghurt) and ice creams, and savouring a scoop in the two-century-old cottage.

Independently owned **Killarney Brewing & Distilling Co** *(killarneybrewingdistilling.com; brewery tour €24.50, distillery tour €31, gin school €140)*, 7km northwest of Killarney in Fossa, runs hour-long brewery tours and 75-minute distillery tours of its gleaming 2022-opened facilities (both including tastings), and also runs a 2.5-hour gin school (minimum four people) where you can blend your own botanicals. Enjoy a pint or craft cocktail and dine on dishes incorporating its wares overlooking the lakes and MacGillycuddy's Reeks at its bar/restaurant, or head to its in-town **taproom**.

BEST FESTIVALS IN KILLARNEY

The Gathering: Rousing traditional Irish music, from fireside sessions to foot-stomping concerts in February. *thegathering.ie*

St Patrick's Festival Killarney: Killarney lights up in green for 17 days in March. There's a parade on 17 March. *stpatricks festivalkillarney.ie*

Wander Wild Festival: Dive into Killarney's great outdoors during three adventure-packed days in April. *wander wildfestival.com*

Rally of the Lakes: On-road rally drivers twist and turn around the lakes and mountains over the May bank holiday. *rallyofthelakes.com*

Ireland BikeFest Killarney: Motorcycle festival with tours, a bike show, parade and rock concerts during the June bank holiday. *irelandbikefest.com*

Quest Killarney: Running, cycling and kayaking races (32km to 82km) in October. *questadventure series.com*

DRINKING IN KILLARNEY TOWN: OUR PICKS

O'Connor's: Live music plays every night at this tiny traditional pub. In warmer weather, crowds spill out into the adjacent lane. *noon-11.30pm Sun-Thu, to 12.30am Fri & Sat*

Celtic Whiskey Bar & Larder: Stunning bar stocking over 1600 whiskeys and 60-plus gins (tasting flights available). *1pm-midnight Mon-Sat, to 11.30pm Sun*

Courtney's: Cavernous 19th-century pub that bursts at the seams with regular Irish music sessions. *2-11.30pm Mon-Thu, 12.30pm-12.30am Fri & Sat, to 11.30pm Sun*

Killarney Grand: The various bars and clubs at this local institution host traditional live music, rock bands and a nightclub from 11pm. *6pm-2am Mon-Fri, 3pm-2am Sat & Sun*

LOOP AROUND MUCKROSS LAKE

Take in some of the most photogenic parts of Killarney National Park on this waymarked walking (or cycling) loop trail.

START	END	LENGTH
Muckross House	Muckross House	9.5km; 3–4hrs

Starting from 1 **Muckross House** (p227), head west through lovely lakeshore woods, which have lots of side trails to explore, to reach postcard-pretty 2 **Brickeen Bridge** (p230), spanning the channel linking Lough Leane and Muckross Lake, also known as Middle Lake. Continue to the quaint 200-year-old 3 **Dinis Cottage**, built by the Herbert family of Muckross House for the use of visitors to their estate. It is now a tearoom (closed from October to March), a popular stop for walkers and cyclists for fantastic soups and made-to-order sandwiches.

Beyond the cottage, you enter the sylvan glades that surround the 4 **Meeting of the Waters** (p230), where channels from Killarney's three lakes merge. Don't miss the 10-minute side trail (no bikes) to 5 **Old Weir Bridge** (p230), where you can watch tour boats powering through the narrow, rocky channel beneath its twin arches. A swiftly flowing current links the Upper and Middle Lakes.

On the return leg along the south shore of Middle Lake, the trail passes through woods before reaching the N71 Killarney–Kenmare road. Walkers have the option of climbing uphill on the other side of the road to visit the picturesque, 20m-high 6 **Torc Waterfall** cascading over mossy boulders amid mystical woodland. Detour along the 7 **Old Boathouse Nature Trail**, which leads around a scenic peninsula, on your return to Muckross House.

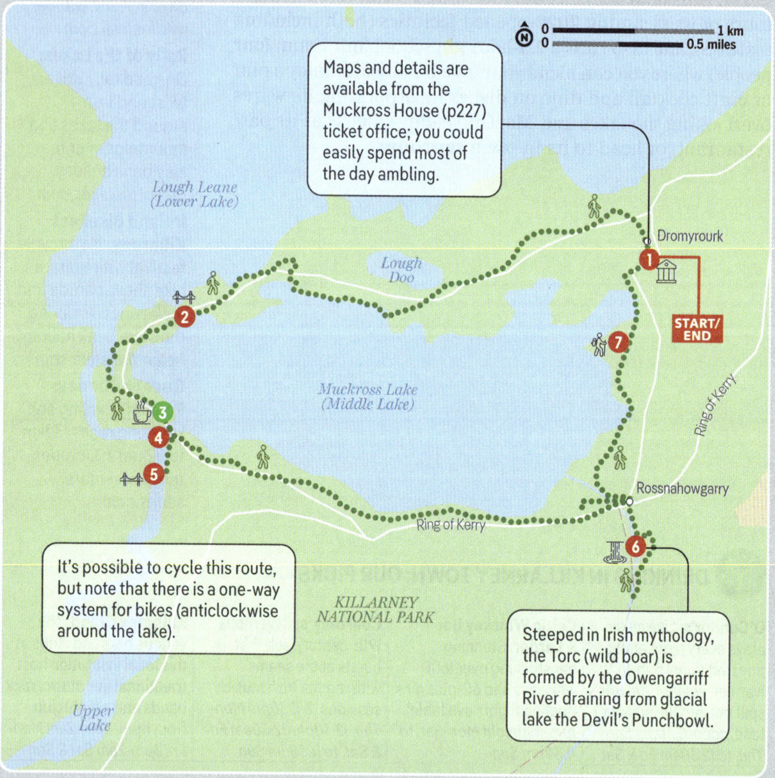
0 1 km
0 0.5 miles
Maps and details are available from the Muckross House (p227) ticket office; you could easily spend most of the day ambling.
Lough Leane (Lower Lake)
Lough Doo
Dromyrourk
START/ END
Muckross Lake (Middle Lake)
Ring of Kerry
Rossnahowgarry
Ring of Kerry
It's possible to cycle this route, but note that there is a one-way system for bikes (anticlockwise around the lake).
KILLARNEY NATIONAL PARK
Steeped in Irish mythology, the Torc (wild boar) is formed by the Owengarriff River draining from glacial lake the Devil's Punchbowl.
Upper Lake

Beyond Killarney National Park

Magnificent sights on and offshore include UNESCO World Heritage Skellig Michael, reached by an unforgettable boat ride.

Places
Kenmare p235
Caherdaniel p235
Waterville p236
Valentia Island p237
Cahersiveen p240

The Iveragh (pronounced *eev*-raa) Peninsula to the southwest of Killarney National Park is one of the most scenic parts of Ireland, circumnavigated by the famous Ring of Kerry driving route. The smaller but equally scenic Skellig Ring, which spins off the loop at Waterville, is less travelled but every bit as spectacular. Out in the Atlantic, jagged Skellig Michael keeps its lonely vigil.

If you want to get further off the beaten track, explore the interior of the peninsula – on foot along the eastern section of the Kerry Way from Killarney to Glenbeigh, or by car or bike on the minor roads that cut through the hills, notably the Ballaghisheen Pass between Killorglin and Waterville.

Kenmare
TIME FROM KILLARNEY: **40MIN**
Discover Kenmare Bay on horseback
Whether you're an experienced equestrian or a complete beginner, you can saddle up at **Dromquinna Stables** *(dromquinna-stables.com; lesson/trek from €25/75)*, 4.5km west of Kenmare on the N70. The trek leaders will pair you with a suitable mount before setting off for a 90-minute or longer trot along the shores of Kenmare Bay or up into the hills with grand views over the Beara and Iveragh peninsulas. You can also take lessons, starting from 30 minutes. Book ahead, but bring cash as cards aren't accepted.

Caherdaniel
TIME FROM KILLARNEY: **1HR 15MIN**
Learn about Caherdaniel's Heritage
History abounds in Caherdaniel. Located 2.5km west of the main N70 road, **Daniel O'Connell House – Derrynane House** *(heritageireland.ie; adult/child €5/3)*, open mid-March to October, was the home of Maurice 'Hunting Cap' O'Connell, a notorious local smuggler who grew rich on trade with France and Spain. His nephew Daniel O'Connell, the 19th-century campaigner for Catholic emancipation, grew up here in his uncle's care and inherited the property in 1825 when it became

GETTING AROUND

Numerous tour companies and hostels in Killarney offer daily coach tours of the Ring of Kerry, lasting from around 9.30am to 5pm. Operators include **Killarney Executive Tour** *(killarneytour.com)*, **Deros Tours** *(derostours.com)* and **Wild Kerry Day Tours** *(wildkerrydaytours.com)*. Different tours have different stops.

Year-round, **Local Link Kerry** *(locallinkkerry.ie)* runs daily services between Killarney and Waterville via Killorglin and Cahersiveen, and between Kenmare and Waterville via Sneem and Caherdaniel.

BEST BEACHES BEYOND KILLARNEY

Derrynane Beach: Wave-worn rock outcrops nestle amid scalloped coves of golden sand fringed by grassy dunes near Caherdaniel.

Ballinskelligs Beach: This Blue Flag Beach 'where the stars meet the sea' is at the centre of the Kerry Dark-Sky Reserve, hosting the four-day Skellig Coast Dark Sky Festival in March.

St Finian's Bay: Framed by Puffin Island to the north and Duchalla Head to the south, St Finian's Bay is a favourite with surfers for its consistent exposed beach break.

White Strand: Close to Cahersiveen, White Strand's Blue Flag rating and sheltered position make it popular for swimming.

Dooks Beach: Near Cromane, 9km west of Killorglin, this little-visited gem is at the mouth of the River Caragh, with gorgeous views of the Kerry and Dingle mountains.

his private retreat. The house is furnished with O'Connell memorabilia, including the impressive triumphal chariot in which he lapped Dublin after his release from prison.

The surrounding gardens, warmed by the Gulf Stream, nurture subtropical species including 4m-high tree ferns, gunnera (giant rhubarb). A network of walking trails leads through the woods; kids will love tracking down 'fairy houses' hidden among the trees on the fairy trail.

Just south of the house is beautiful Derrynane Beach; from the car park, you can walk 1km along the beach to explore **Abbey Island** and its picturesque cemetery. Look inside the ruined chapel to find the tomb of Daniel O'Connell's wife, Mary.

Forage for seaweed

Seaweed has been an important resource throughout Irish history for agricultural fertiliser, medicinal compounds and food. From March to October, John Fitzgerald of **Atlantic Irish Seaweed** *(atlanticirishseaweed.com; workshop €70)* leads 2½-hour 'seaweed discovery workshops' involving a guided walk along the Derrynane foreshore at low tide, foraging for edible seaweed (with instruction on identification and sustainable harvesting), followed by a tasting session of seaweed-based dishes and drinks. Workshops are tide and weather dependent; booking is essential.

Waterville
TIME FROM KILLARNEY: 1HR 30MIN

Explore the waters around waterville

Famed for its **Waterville Golf Links** *(watervillegolflinks.ie; green fees €350–375)*, a par 72 championship course on windswept dunes bordered by the Atlantic, the River Inny and estuary, and native bogland, Waterville has a stunning coastal setting with sweeping views.

Sea Synergy *(seasynergy.org; walks/activities from €20/55)* raises awareness of the marine environment and the challenges faced by wildlife through marine biologist-led 'seashore safari' beach walks popular with kids, and a range of water-based activities that include snorkelling, guided kayaking and stand-up paddleboarding trips along the coast and on nearby Lough Currane.

Get off the beaten track on the Skellig Ring

If you're driving the Ring of Kerry (p238), the Skellig Ring, an 18km spinoff loop, offers an escape from the crowds (the road is too narrow for tour buses, lorries and motorhomes)

EATING ON THE RING OF KERRY: BEST CAFES

Mill: Stop in for sweet and savoury crêpes, cakes, pastries and coffee at this cute spot with a handful of tables in Killorglin. *8.30am-4.30pm Mon-Fri, 9am-3pm Sat €*

Bari Café & Deli: Cahersiveen favourite for breakfast tacos, bacon-and-egg brioche, granola and flatbreads with beetroot hummus. *9am-5pm Mon-Sat €€*

Bridge Cafe: All-day brunches (American-style pancake stacks, nachos, club sandwiches and burgers) in a Sneem stone cottage. *9am-6pm Mon-Sat, to 5pm Sun €€*

Driftwood Surf Cafe: Big windows frame the Atlantic and Skelligs at this wood-fire-warmed St Finian's Bay cafe. *5.30-9.30pm Wed & Thu, 12.30-9.30pm Fri-Sun €€*

St Finian's Bay

and beautiful beaches. The wild, scenic drive links Waterville to Portmagee via a Gaeltacht (Irish-speaking area) centred on Ballinskelligs (Baile an Sceilg), with its ruined **castle**, **priory** and beach. Over the hill is St Finian's Bay (Bá Fhíonáin); another steep hill leads to the viewpoint at **Coomanaspig**, where you can look over Valentia Island to the hills of the Dingle Peninsula.

On the way down to Portmagee, the gateway to Valentia Island, pull in at the **Kerry Cliffs** *(kerry-cliffs.com; €5)*, a pay-to-enter walking trail along the top of precipitous 300m-high sea cliffs; take the left path for stupendous views of Skellig Michael (p242) and Irish Wildbird Conservancy reserve Puffin Island, along with the dramatic cliffs. Hours fluctuate seasonally and according to weather conditions.

Valentia Island

TIME FROM KILLARNEY: 2HR

Explore an island at the edge of the Atlantic

A beautiful and under-visited corner of Kerry, Valentia Island has a rich and fascinating history. Its Latin-sounding name is actually an anglicised version of the Irish Béal Inse, meaning 'the mouth of the island', a reference to the natural harbour entrance. Laced with narrow roads, it lends itself to leisurely exploration by bike. You can reach the island via the bridge

Continues on p240

DANIEL O'CONNELL

Cahersiveen-born Daniel O'Connell (1775–1847), known as 'the Liberator', devoted himself to the cause of Catholic emancipation. In 1828 he was elected to the British Parliament but, being a Catholic, he couldn't actually take his seat. To avoid an uprising, the government was forced to pass the 1829 Catholic Emancipation Act, allowing some well-off Catholics voting rights and the right to be elected as MPs. O'Connell continued to fight for Irish self-determination and spoke up against wide-ranging injustice, including slavery. When the government banned one of his rallies, O'Connell stood down to avoid potential violence and bloodshed. Given the Great Famine, however, his failure to defy the British was seen as capitulation. He was imprisoned for a time in 1844 and died three years later.

 EATING ON THE RING OF KERRY: BEST RESTAURANTS

No 35: In Kenmare, timber beams and an open fire set the stage for creative cuisine with Irish produce, including saddleback sausages and trout. *5.30-9.30pm Fri-Tue* €€

O'Neills The Point: Overlooking Valentia Harbour at Reenard Point, serving seafood landed metres away. *noon-3pm & 5.30-9.30pm Wed-Sat & Mon, 5.30-9.30pm Sun* €€

Jacks' Coastguard Restaurant: Shellfish specialist in a coastguard station looking across Castlemaine harbour, 8km west of Killorglan. *6-9pm Thu-Sat, 1-8pm Sun* €€€

Smugglers Inn: Henry Hunt's gourmet creations incorporate fresh seafood and are served in a seaview conservatory just outside Waterville. *1-3pm & 6-8.30pm* €€€

ROAD TRIP

Ring of Kerry

This famous circuit of the Iveragh Peninsula winds past pretty villages, pristine beaches, craggy mountains and sparkling loughs, with ever-changing views of the Atlantic. The 170km route starts and finishes in Killarney. There are some narrow sections, notably between Killarney and Moll's Gap. Tour buses travel the Ring anticlockwise; the route here is described clockwise to avoid getting stuck behind a bus.

❶ Moll's Gap
South of Killarney, the summit of the pass known as Moll's Gap is worth a stop for the great views towards the Gap of Dunloe and for breakfast at **Avoca Cafe**.

The Drive: The N71 road descends through a series of swooping bends to Kenmare.

❷ Kenmare
Picturesque small town Kenmare (pronounced ken-*mair*) has a neat triangle of streets lined with craft shops, art galleries, cafes and good-quality restaurants.

The Drive: From Kenmare's town centre, retrace your route north, but turn left on the N70 towards Cahersiveen.

❸ Sneem
The pretty village of Sneem is split by a river, with separate village squares on either side and a picturesque waterfall tumbling below the old stone bridge between the two.

The Drive: Beyond Sneem, the coastal scenery ramps into overdrive as the road winds over the hill to Caherdaniel.

❹ Caherdaniel
Caherdaniel, a tiny hamlet hidden among the trees at the head of Derrynane Bay, is stunning day and night, in the Gold Tiered **Kerry International Dark Sky Reserve** (*kerrydarkskytourism.com; tours on*

Moll's Gap

request). A short detour from the main road at Caherdaniel leads to Derrynane Beach, one of the most beautiful in Kerry.

The Drive: The N70 now climbs high above the sea, passing Beenarourke viewpoint, with grandstand views over scattered islands, before descending to Waterville.

5 Waterville

Strung along the N70 at the head of Ballinskelligs Bay, Waterville is an old-fashioned seaside resort famous for its golf and as the place silent-movie star Charlie Chaplin holidayed in the 1960s.

The Drive: Stay on the N70 to Cahersiveen, or detour via the Skellig Ring (p236) before continuing north.

6 Cahersiveen

Cahersiveen (pronounced caar-suh-*veen*) is the main town on the Ring, home to the highly worthwhile Old Barracks Heritage Centre (p240), early August's vibrant **Cahersiveen Festival of Music & the Arts**, and some excellent places to eat.

The Drive: Follow the N70 for 30km to Kerry Bog Village.

7 Kerry Bog Village

Family-favourite museum **Kerry Bog Village** recreates a 19th-century bog village, typical of the small communities that carved out a precarious living in the harsh environment of Ireland's ubiquitous peat bogs. You'll see the thatched homes of the turfcutter, blacksmith, thatcher and labourer, as well as a dairy, and Kerry bog ponies.

The Drive: Continue on the N70 to Killorglin – a statue of King Puck, a goat, stands on the north side of the river, commemorating mid-August's centuries-old Puck Fair (p225), which centres on the custom of installing a billy goat (a poc, or puck), the symbol of mountainous Kerry, on a pedestal in the town. Turn right on the N72 to return to Killarney.

STAR WARS SIGHTS

The dizzyingly steep, starkly beautiful monastic island of Skellig Michael (p242) made its dramatic big-screen debut in 2015's *Star Wars: The Force Awakens* and reprised its role as Luke Skywalker's Jedi temple on the planet Ahch-To in 2017's *Star Wars: The Last Jedi*. Fans of the franchise will instantly recognise sights like Skellig Michael's ancient stone steps and beehive-shaped huts.

Due to the logistics of filming on the protected World Heritage island, locations such as Kerry's Sybil Head (Ceann Sibeal) on the Dingle Peninsula, 4.5km northwest of Ballyferriter, were used as stand-in locations. Elsewhere in Ireland, other *Star Wars* shooting locations include Loop Head Lighthouse in County Clare, Brow Head and Crookhaven in County Cork, and Hell's Hole near Malin Head in County Donegal.

Continued from p237

at Portmagee or, from April to October, the five-minute **Valentia Island Car Ferry** *(valentiaferry.com; one-way car & passengers/pedestrian or cyclist €12/2)* at Knightstown, the island's only village.

Just across the bridge from Portmagee's rainbow of colourful houses on its single photogenic street and harbour filled with boats making the choppy crossing to the Skellig Islands (p242) is Valentia's southern end. This is home to the visitor centre **Skellig Experience** *(skelligexperience.com; adult/child €6/3.50)*, closed from December to February, with exhibits on local history, wildlife and the life of the Skellig Michael (p242) monks.

The local landowner has transformed Valentia Island's highest point, 266m-high **Geokaun** *(geokaun.com; car & passengers €8, walkers/cyclists €4)*, into a network of easy walking trails and viewpoints, with a breathtaking outlook over the Fogher Cliffs. It's possible to drive all the way to the top, so visitors with limited mobility don't miss out on the views.

Learn about Valentia Island's history

Valentia changed the course of human history as the eastern terminus of the first transatlantic telegraph cable (the other end was at Heart's Content in Newfoundland, Canada), established in 1866 and known as the 'eighth wonder of the world'. The **Valentia Transatlantic Cable Station** *(valentiaisland.ie; adult/child €7.50/4)* in Knightstown has an immersive exhibition about the birth of global telecommunications, and is currently campaigning for UNESCO World Heritage status *(valentiacable.com)*. Take note that it's closed Mondays and Tuesdays and from November to March.

Also in Knightstown, **Valentia Island Heritage Centre** *(valentiaisland.ie; free)*, closed October to March, is an intriguing local museum with a treasure trove of artefacts that tell the tale of the island's history.

Valentia Island Lighthouse *(valentiaisland.ie; adult/child €9.50/6)* is set in a 17th-century military fort at the island's northern tip. You can visit the lightkeeper's house and climb to the top of the lighthouse tower.

To view the island's earliest history – dating back 385 million years – visit the **Tetrapod Trackway**, where small depressions in an exposed sandstone bedding surface next to the sea. These fossil tracks left behind by a metre-long amphibious creature are among the world's oldest physical evidence of a vertebrate creature moving on land. It's 4.3km northwest of Knightstown.

Cahersiveen

TIME FROM KILLARNEY: **1HR 45MIN**

Discover the back roads by bike

The peaceful roads to the northwest of Cahersiveen (Cathair Saidhbhín) are ideal for exploring by bike. **Casey Cycles** *(bikehirekerry.com; 1 day touring bike/e-bike hire €20/25)* rents wheels.

Start down towards the river at the **Old Barracks Heritage Centre**. This eccentric Bavarian-castle-style building was built

Cahergal ringfort, Cahersiveen

as a Royal Irish Constabulary barracks in response to the Fenian Rising of 1867 and now houses fascinating exhibitions *(theoldbarracks.net; adult/child €6.50/4)* on the Rising and the life and works of local hero Daniel O'Connell. Its escape room *(two to six players; from €30)* is an entertaining way to learn about the building's history.

Cross the bridge and follow the signs for 'Stone Forts'. After 2km, you'll come to two extraordinary stone **ringforts** situated 600m apart, reached from a shared parking area. **Cahergal**, the larger and more impressive, dates from the 10th century and has stairways on the inside walls, a *clochán* (a circular, beehive-shaped stone building) and the remains of a roundhouse. The smaller, 9th-century Leacanabuaile contains the outlines of four houses. Both have a commanding position overlooking the ivy-strangled remains of 16th-century **Ballycarbery Castle** and Valentia Harbour, with superb views of the Kerry mountains.

Wander through a rainforest

Built in 1837 as a hunting lodge and estate, **Kells Bay House and Gardens** *(kellsbay.ie; day ticket adult/child €9.50/7.50)*, 13km northeast of Cahersiveen, is now home to the largest collection of tree ferns in the northern hemisphere, a miniature primeval rainforest that thrives in the mild, humid microclimate of coastal Kerry. The exotic gardens sprawl over 17 hectares and incorporate a waterfall, a beach and varied walking trails decorated with dinosaurs carved from fallen trees. Ireland's longest rope bridge, the 33.5m Skywalk, sways 11m above the swirling River Delligeenagh.

Walled kitchen gardens provide ingredients for the gardens' unexpectedly authentic **Sala Thai** restaurant and cafe. There's also luxury B&B accommodation in **Kells Bay House**.

BEST FOOD & DRINK SHOPS ON THE RING OF KERRY

Skelligs Chocolate: At St Finian's Bay, from April to October, get an overview of this factory's chocolate production, stock up at its shop and taste its wares at its cafe. *skelligschocolate.com*

Portmagee Whiskey: Small-batch, triple-distilled whiskeys, with tours, tastings and a shop on Portmagee's southern edge. *portmagee whiskey.com*

Skellig Six 18 Distillery: Named for Skellig Michael's 618 steps, this south Cahersiveen gin distillery with a shop and tours incorporates local botanicals. *skelligsix 18distillery.ie*

Wilma's Cheese & Farm Shop: Cheeses from Wilma's own Holstein cow herd are sold at her south Killorglin farm. *tastekerry.ie*

KRD Fisheries: Buy organic smoked salmon direct from this 1782-founded smokery, which smokes salmon caught in the River Laune estuary. *krdfisheries.com*

Monastery, Skellig Michael

TOP EXPERIENCE

Skellig Islands

Within the Páirc Náisiúnta na Mara, Ciarraí, Ireland's first marine national park, the larger of the two Skellig Islands, the jagged, 217m-high rock of Skellig Michael (Sceilg Mhichíl), rises dramatically out of the sea, topped with the remains of an improbable 1400-year-old early Christian monastery. The remote island 11.5km off the coast famously featured as Luke Skywalker's Jedi temple in two *Star Wars* movies, attracting a whole new audience to the Skelligs' dramatic beauty.

DON'T MISS

Little Skellig

Skellig Michael

The Steps

Beehive Cells

Oratories

The Hermitage

Skellig Michael

Skellig Michael (Michael's Rock; like St Michael's Mount in Cornwall and Mont St Michel in Normandy) is the larger of the two Skellig Islands and a UNESCO World Heritage site. Influenced by the Coptic Church (founded by St Anthony in the deserts of Egypt and Libya), the monks' determined quest for ultimate solitude led them to this remote, windblown edge of Europe. Not much is known about the life of the monastery, but there are records of Viking raids in 812 and 823 CE.

PRACTICALITIES

● heritageireland.ie ● landing tour/non-landing eco tour per person from €130/50 ● landing tour mid-May–Sep, non-landing tour mid-Mar–Oct, weather permitting

Although the site was expanded in the 12th century, the monks abandoned the rock soon afterwards. In the 1820s, two lighthouses were built on the island, along with the road that runs around the base.

The Landing
The landing point for visitors is at a tiny jetty on the northeast side of the island, from where you make your way along the lighthouse road, past a helipad to the cluster of sheds where the Office of Public Works (OPW) guides are based. You will get a safety briefing before you are allowed to climb up to the monastery.

The Steps
Three ancient staircases lead to the top of Skellig Michael, but only the one on the southeast side is currently in use. There are 618 steps cut into the steep face of the rock, with no handrails, save for a short length of chain low down. The steps ascend to the dip between the twin summits, known as Christ's Saddle, where you can catch your breath before the final climb to the monastery gate, 180m above sea level.

The Monastery
The 6th-century monastery is a miracle of masonry, set on platforms built on the vertiginous slope using nothing more than drystone walls and earth. Within the perimeter wall are six beehive cells, where the monks once lived, two domed oratories where they prayed and chanted, a cemetery and a small 10th-century church. You can also see the monks' south-facing vegetable garden and their cistern for collecting rainwater.

The Hermitage
The Hermitage is a small structure near the summit of Skellig Michael's south peak, opposite the monastery; it is not open to visitors. Probably dating from the 9th century, the tiny oratory (just 2.3m by 1.2m) was possibly used as a retreat by individual monks for solitary prayer.

Getting There
Landing tours usually run from mid-May to September, weather permitting; dates are announced each year by the OPW, which looks after the site and grants tour-boat permits. Boats depart from Portmagee, Valentia, Ballinskelligs and Derrynane Harbour. The number of daily visitors is limited to 180, with boats licensed to carry no more than 12 passengers each, so it's wise to book well ahead (landings are still subject to conditions on the day). Children must be aged over 12.

Morning departure times depend on tide and weather. The trip lasts around five hours in total with 2½ hours on the island, which is the bare minimum to visit the monastery, look at the birds (puffins arrive in April, leaving around the first week in August) and have a picnic.

LITTLE SKELLIG
The bird sanctuary of Little Skellig is a long, low and jagged rock 2km northeast of Skellig Michael. From a distance, it can look as if it's shrouded in a swirling snowstorm; close up, you realise you're looking at a colony of over 27,000 breeding pairs of gannets, the second-largest breeding colony in the world. Tour boats circle the island on the way to Skellig Michael so you can see the birds, and you may spot seals as well.

TOP TIPS
- Sea crossings can be rough; consider taking anti-seasickness pills or bringing travel wristbands.
- Bring all the food and water you will need for the day.
- Wear good walking shoes or boots, and warm, waterproof clothing, with a hood or hat to guard against bird droppings. Sea crossings are always colder and breezier than you expect.
- Toilets were finally installed on the island (at the base) in 2021.
- If you just want to see the islands up close without having to clamber out of the boat, take a non-landing eco cruise with operators such as Skellig Experience (p240) on Valentia Island.

Dingle

BOAT TRIPS | FOOD & DRINK | FESTIVALS

Framed by its fishing port, the Dingle Peninsula's charming little 'capital' manages to be quaint without even trying. Some pubs double as shops, so you can enjoy Guinness and a singalong among hats, hardware, horseshoes and wellies. It has long drawn runaways from across the world, making it a cosmopolitan and creative place. In summer, its hilly streets can be clogged with visitors, but in other seasons, its authentic charms are yours for the savouring.

Dingle is one of those towns whose very fabric is its main attraction. Wander up and down the streets and back alleys, stroll along the waterfront, and pop into shops, pubs, and art and craft galleries to see what you find.

Although Dingle is one of Ireland's largest Gaeltacht towns, its residents have voted to retain the name Dingle rather than go by the officially sanctioned – and signposted – Irish name of An Daingean.

Board a Harbour Cruise
Sea cliffs and wildlife

Ecotourism and awareness of the marine environment are a legacy of Fungie, Dingle's much-missed dolphin, resident from 1983 to 2020, with several companies now running wildlife-spotting boat tours. The standard 45-minute to one-hour harbour cruise operated by **Dingle Dolphin Tours** (*dingle dolphin.com; adult/child €17/12*) offers the chance to spot marine life, including wild dolphins, but it is worth doing for the sea cliff scenery alone. The highlight comes when the skipper (sea conditions permitting) backs the boat gingerly into Thunder Cove, a yawning cleft in the cliffs. Longer tours are also available, including to the Blasket Islands (p249).

Options with **Dingle Boat Tours** (*dingleboattours.com; two-hour tour adult/child €38/18*) include a two-hour Dolphin Discovery Eco Tour searching for pods of dolphins.

Dingle Sea Safari (*dingleseasafari.com; per person €75*) runs exhilarating 2½ to three-hour excursions aboard open

---

GETTING AROUND

Regular buses link Killarney with Dingle. The town is easily walkable. To venture further afield, hire a bike at **Dingle Electric Bike Experience** (*dinglebikes.com*) or **Paddy's Bike Shop** (*paddysbikesdingle. com*).

On-street parking is free, but hard to find, especially in summer. There are large, inexpensive car parks on Green St and at the harbour.

Taxis such as **Dingle Cabs** (*dinglecabs. com*) can arrange airport transfers, as well as private guided tours of Dingle Peninsula.

☑ TOP TIP

Dingle is famed for its independent shops. Along with its shop-pubs, you'll find local artists' galleries jostling for space with craft shops, fashion boutiques, jewellery makers, textile weavers, milliners, candlemakers and ceramicists.

DINGLE

HIGHLIGHTS
1. Dingle Distillery
2. Dingle Dolphin Tours
3. Dingle Oceanworld

ACTIVITIES
4. Dingle Boat Tours
5. Dingle Sea Safari
6. Dingle Traditional Rowing
7. Irish Adventures
8. Wild SUP Tours

SLEEPING
9. Base Dingle
10. Castlewood House
11. Dingle Harbour Lodge
12. Grapevine Hostel

EATING
13. Fish Box
14. Fish Factory
15. Murphy's Ice Cream Strand St
16. Murphy's Ice Cream The Pier
17. Out of the Blue
18. Solas Tapas & Wine

DRINKING & NIGHTLIFE
19. Curran's
20. Dick Mack's
21. Foxy John's
22. John Benny's

SHOPPING
23. Brian de Staic
24. Dingle Bookshop
25. Dingle Crystal
    see 19 Dingle Surf Shop
26. Kerry Woollen Mills
27. Little Cheese Shop
28. O Cathain Iasc Teo - Dingle Seafood

TRANSPORT
see 19 Dingle Electric Bike Experience
29. Paddy's Bike Shop

245

Dingle Distillery

FUNGIE THE DOLPHIN

For almost four decades, the classic Dingle experience was a boat trip to see Fungie, a solitary bottlenose dolphin with an unusual affinity for human company, who took up residence in Dingle harbour in 1983. First spotted by the Dingle lighthouse keeper, Fungie was a daily fixture in the life of the village, waiting to greet boat trips every morning and entertaining visitors with his playful repertoire of acrobatic antics until October 2020 when, sadly, he appeared no more.

But Fungie's huge influence on Dingle's tourism trade means that his memory lingers on in many ways. He's commemorated with a bronze statue in his image on the harbourfront and a mural on the gable of the lighthouse keeper's cottage overlooking the harbour entrance.

RIBs (rigid-hulled inflatable boats), spotting marine life such as basking sharks, seals and puffins.

Splash in Dingle Harbour

Sample a range of watersports

The sheltered waters of Dingle Harbour make it an ideal location for beginners to dip into watersports. **Irish Adventures** *(irishadventures.ie; adult/child €65/50)* runs three-hour sea-kayaking trips, where you learn basic skills and explore the caves and arches in the sea cliffs at the harbour mouth.

Alternatively, you could try stand-up paddleboarding with **Wild SUP Tours** *(wildsuptours.com; 3hr day/night tour €60/80),* which operates daytime stand-up paddleboarding safaris around the harbour, as well as a nighttime SUP adventure on a freshwater lake beneath the stars in the heart of the Kerry Dark Sky Reserve.

Dingle Traditional Rowing *(dinglerowing.com; tour €35)* offers the chance to wield an oar aboard a naomhòg (pronounced nuh-vogue), the Kerry name for a *currach*, a traditional Irish boat made from a wooden frame covered with tarred canvas (originally animal hides). They were used by the Blasket islanders for fishing and are now maintained and raced by local enthusiasts. Book a one-hour session in Dingle Harbour (minimum of two people) to learn how to row one.

 EATING IN DINGLE TOWN: OUR PICKS

Fish Box: Fast, friendly service and an inventive seafood menu from its own trawler at this informal, no-reservations, hugely popular eatery. *12.30-9pm €€*

Fish Factory: Pan-Asian street food dishes include Dingle prawn dumplings and Korean fried chicken with foraged seaweed aïoli. *5-9pm Tue & Wed, 12.30-9pm Thu-Sun €€*

Solas Tapas & Wine: Uses its own organic produce in tapas dishes like Dingle goat cheese and black pudding croquettes. *12.30-9pm €€*

Out of the Blue: Bright-blue-and-yellow fishing shack serving seafood and only seafood (resolutely no chips): if staff don't like the day's catch, they don't open. *4-9.30pm €€€*

Go Face to Face with a Shark
Discover Ireland's biggest aquarium

Dingle Oceanworld (*dingle-oceanworld.ie; adult/child €21/15*) makes a good rainy-day alternative to a wildlife cruise. Psychedelic fish glide through tanks that recreate such environments as Lake Malawi, the River Congo and the piranha-filled Amazon. Get up close to huge reef sharks and stingrays at the shark tank and stroke a thornback ray at the touch pool. Water pumped from the harbour fills the Ocean Tunnel tank, where you can spot native Irish species, such as dogfish, mullet, plaice, conger eels and the spectacularly ugly wreckfish. Tickets are cheaper if you book in advance online.

Savour Dingle's Flavours
Artisan food and festivities

A highlight on Dingle's calendar is the **Dingle Food Festival** (*dinglefood.com*). Held over three days around early October, this sustainably-minded foodie fest with a zero-waste ethos features a 'taste trail', street markets, cooking demonstrations, street entertainment, children's events and workshops (past workshops have included an introduction to beekeeping, a druid's guide to medicinal plants, cheese and wine pairing, cocktail mixing, cake decorating and how to grow herbs in your own kitchen).

Year-round, don't miss Dingle's fabulous artisan producers. Dingle-made **Murphy's Ice Cream** (*murphysicecream.ie*), with two branches in town, on **Strand St** and at the **Pier**, (plus a handful around Ireland), has daily changing spring water sorbets and ice cream in flavours like caramelised Irish brown bread, hand-harvested sea salt, local honey and Dingle gin.

You can visit Dingle gin's source, the **Dingle Distillery** (*tour/whiskey experience €23/45*), which runs 75-minute tours of its operation and guided tastings of five whiskeys.

Irish cheeses fill the shelves of the aromatic **Little Cheese Shop** (*thelittlecheeseshop.ie*).

Freshly landed seafood stars on restaurant menus throughout town, or you can buy it from **O Cathain Iasc Teo - Dingle Seafood** (*facebook.com/ocathaindinglefishshop*) right on the harbourside quay.

BEST SHOPPING IN DINGLE

Brian de Staic: Renowned local designer Brian de Staic's exquisite modern Celtic jewellery is individually handcrafted in Dingle. *briandestaic.com*

Dingle Bookshop: Independent bookshop with 4000+ titles, including local imprints and Irish language textbooks. *dinglebookshop.com*

Dingle Crystal: Master cutter Sean Daly's pieces are inspired by the Dingle Peninsula's mountains and coastline; you can also take 45-minute factory tours (*€11*). *dinglecrystal.ie*

Kerry Woollen Mills: Irish fleece, merino lambswool and tweed items include clothing, blankets, lanolin products and teddy bears. *kerrywoollenmills.ie*

Dingle Surf Shop: Surfboards, wetsuits and men's, women's and kids' surfwear (including its own prints); also runs surf lessons and SUP tours. *dinglesurf.com*

 DRINKING IN DINGLE TOWN: OUR PICKS

Foxy John's: Classic shop-pub, with hardware and outdoor clothing alongside stout and whiskey. *10.30am-11.30pm Mon-Thu, to 12.30am Fri & Sat, noon-11.30pm Sun*

Dick Mack's: Ancient wood and snugs inside, a warren of tables in the courtyard, plus the pub's very own craft beers from its restored 19th-century brewhouse. *noon-11pm*

Curran's: Shop-pub with original stained-glass snugs; regular spontaneous trad sessions. *noon-11.30pm Sun-Thu, to 12.30am Fri & Sat*

John Benny's: Local musos pour in most nights for rockin' trad sessions at this stone-floored traditional pub. *11.30am-11.30pm Tue-Thu & Sun, to 12.30am Fri & Sat*

Beyond Dingle

Keep your camera at the ready – beyond Dingle town, the peninsula's scenery goes into overdrive.

Places
Ventry p248
Mt Brandon p249
Dunquin p249
Connor Pass p250
Cloghane p251
Castlegregory p251

GETTING AROUND
Your own wheels are best for exploring this wild and remote area, giving you the freedom to set your own pace. If you're not pushed for time, it's possible to explore the peninsula west of Dingle town by bike. Several places in Dingle town rent them out.

Local Link Kerry (*locallinkkerry.ie*) operates regular bus services from Dingle town to Ventry, Ballyferriter and Dunquin, and from Tralee to Castlegregory, Clochane and Brandon Point; check schedules online.

A highlight of the Wild Atlantic Way (Slí an Atlantaigh Fhiáin), at the heart of the Páirc Náisiúnta na Mara (p250), Ireland's first marine national park, the Dingle Peninsula (Corca Dhuibhne) culminates in the Irish mainland's westernmost point at Dunmore Head. In the shadow of sacred Mt Brandon, a maze of fuchsia-fringed *boreens* (country lanes) weaves together an ancient landscape of prehistoric ringforts and beehive huts; early Christian chapels, crosses and holy wells; picturesque hamlets; and abandoned villages.

But it's along the narrow, twisting roads where the land meets the ocean around Slea Head – whether in a welter of surf-pounded rocks or where the waves lap quietly in secluded, sandy coves – that the Dingle Peninsula's beauty truly reveals itself.

Ventry
TIME FROM DINGLE TOWN: **10MIN**

Walk in the footsteps of saints
From the beach at Ventry (Ceann Tra), a waymarked 17.7km walking trail, the **Saints Road** (Cosàn na Naomh) follows the route of an ancient pilgrim path to Ballybrack (An Baile Breac) at the foot of Mt Brandon (Cnoc Bréanainn). The mountain is named for St Brendan the Navigator, who is said to have climbed it to seek divine guidance before setting sail to find the fabled 'Isle of the Blessed'.

A shorter variation is to walk the 3km between the Dingle Peninsula's two main early Christian sites. **Gallarus Oratory** (*heritageireland.ie; site free, visitor centre adult/family €5/12*), 8km northwest of Dingle town, is one of Ireland's most beautiful ancient buildings, with smoothly constructed dry-stone walls in the shape of an upturned boat. It has withstood the elements in this lonely spot beneath the brown hills since at least the 12th, or even possibly the 8th, century.

Kilmalkedar Church (*heritageireland.ie*), 3km northeast of Gallarus, has a beautiful setting with sweeping views over Smerwick Harbour. Built in the early 12th century on the site of a 7th-century monastery founded by St Maolcethair, it's a superb example of Irish Romanesque architecture. Its round-arched west door is decorated with chevron patterns and a carved human head. In the graveyard, you'll find an Ogham stone and a carved stone sundial.

Mt Brandon

TIME FROM DINGLE TOWN: 20MIN

Ascend Mt Brandon

Mt Brandon rises 952m in splendid isolation to the north of Dingle, bounded by spectacular cliffs and glacial lakes to the northeast and falling steeply into the sea to the northwest. The uplands are among the coastal mainland sites that form part of Páirc Náisiúnta na Mara (p250).

The easiest way to the summit is via the old pilgrim path from the car park at Ballybrack on the mountain's south side. From here, the path leads arrow-straight towards the top, passing numbered wooden crucifixes marking the 14 Stations of the Cross, before deviating to the right for a single zigzag before the summit, which is marked by a huge cairn and a 15th cross. Allow three hours for the 8.5km descent along the same route.

There are more challenging routes by the glacial paternoster lakes, and by the Faha Ridge. Guiding companies such as **Kerry Climbing** (kerryclimbing.ie; €65–85) lead guided ascents.

Dunquin

TIME FROM DINGLE TOWN: 20MIN

Journey to the Edge of Europe

The **Blasket Islands** (Na Blascaodaí) off the tip of the Dingle Peninsula are the most westerly part of Ireland and one of the westernmost points in Europe (after Iceland, the Azores and Rockall). All of the islands were lived on at one time or another; there is evidence of the largest, **Great Blasket** (An Blascaod Mór), being inhabited during the Iron Age and early Christian times. But no more – the last islanders abandoned their homes in 1953, moving to the mainland or North America after they and the government agreed that it was no longer viable to live in such harsh and isolated conditions.

At Dunquin (Dún Chaoin), the rich history and cultural life of the islands are celebrated at **Ionad an Bhlascaoid – The Blasket Centre** (heritageireland.ie; adult/child €5/3) from mid-March to early November. The interactive interpretative centre is housed in a striking modern building with a long white hall ending in a picture window looking directly at the islands. Great Blasket's rich community of storytellers and musicians is profiled along with its literary visitors, such as playwright JM Synge, author of *The Playboy of the Western World*. The more prosaic practicalities of island life are covered by exhibits on boatbuilding and fishing.

STAYING ON GREAT BLASKET

A rare break from the modern world, **Great Blasket** (greatblasketisland.net) has rustic accommodation from April to September, sea crossings permitting, in three restored cottages. Without electricity, hot running water, wi-fi or TV, there's instead a cold-water supply, gas cooker, wood-burning stove, candles and the chance to watch wildlife, including seals, dolphins and whales, along with kaleidoscopic sunsets and star-filled night skies. Cottages sleep up to six or seven people, with a two-night minimum stay; rates start from €440 for two people.

The island's annual search for a live-in caretaker duo to run the cottages and cafe for the six-month season is highly competitive – attracting 80,000 applicants internationally in 2020, numbers are now capped at 300 (see details online if you're keen).

EATING BEYOND DINGLE TOWN: OUR PICKS

Caifé na Trá: Enjoy homemade cakes, scones and crab sandwiches overlooking the Blaskets in Coumeenoole, 3km south of Dunquin. *11am-5pm Apr-Sep* €

Báinín: This cafe in Annascaul, 7km west of Inch Strand, serves homemade cakes and cookies, and toasties using local black pudding and goat cheese. *8am-4pm* €

Spillane's: Outside tables look across Brandon Bay to the mountains, with spectacular sunsets, at this laid-back pub; seafood (eg scampi) is a speciality. *5-9pm Wed-Mon* €€

Sammy's: At Inch Strand, this beach-facing bar-restaurant serves a vast range of sandwiches, burgers, fish and chips, chowder and steak. *9am-6pm Wed-Sun* €€

PÁIRC NÁISIÚNTA NA MARA, CIARRAÍ

Known by its Irish name **Páirc Náisiúnta na Mara, Ciarraí** *(nationalparks.ie/mara-ciarrai)*, the Kerry Seas National Park became Ireland's seventh national park, and its first marine national park, in April 2024. Centred around the Dingle Peninsula, its 29,000 hectares take in islands off the Kerry coast (including World Heritage Skellig Michael, p242), offshore marine reefs (notably the deep limestone Kerry Head Shoal), and coastal mainland sites such as the fore dunes and fixed dunes at Inch (both a Special Area of Conservation and a Special Protection Area), Mt Brandon's uplands and the peninsula's spectacular Connor Pass. The coast is home to seabirds including puffins, storm petrels and Manx shearwaters, with other bird species including gannets, fulmars, kittiwakes, guillemots and razorbills.

Great Blasket (p249)

From around April to September, weather permitting, several operators run **boat trips to Great Blasket** from Dunquin *(adult/child from €50/30)*, Dingle town *(per person from €70)* and Ventry *(per person from €97.50)*. These excursions allow you to explore the sea cliffs and coves around the islands and look for whales and dolphins; you can also go ashore on Great Blasket to visit the abandoned settlements, watch the seabirds, picnic on the gorgeous white-sand beach Trá Bán, and hike the island's many trails. During the season, the Office of Public Works (OPW) runs free 45-minute guided walks most days. There are public toilets, along with a basic lunchtime cafe; it's also possible to stay on the island.

Connor Pass   TIME FROM DINGLE TOWN: 15MIN

Brave the heights of the Connor Pass

Topping out at 456m, the R560 road across the Connor Pass (An Chonair; sometimes spelt 'Conor') from Dingle town to Cloghane is Ireland's highest public road. On a foggy day, you'll see nothing but the tarmac in front of you, but in fine weather, it offers phenomenal views of Dingle Harbour to the south and Mt Brandon to the north. The road is in good shape despite being narrow, steep and twisting on the north side. Large signs portend doom for buses and trucks, and caravans are forbidden.

🍸 DRINKING BEYOND DINGLE TOWN: OUR PICKS

Tig Bhric & West Kerry Brewery: Charming 19th-century Ballyferriter pub with accommodation and a brewery using its own well water. *2-8pm Mon-Thu, to 11pm Fri & Sat*

South Pole Inn: Antarctic explorer Tom Crean ran this Annascaul pub in his retirement and it's packed with memorabilia. *1-5pm Mon & Tue, to 11pm Wed-Sun*

Murphy's Bar: At Brandon pier near Cloghane, this cosy pub has smooth pints, a stone fireplace and outdoor tables facing the bay. *noon-11pm Mon-Thu, to 1am Fri-Sun*

Kruger's Bar: In Dunquin, Ireland's most westerly bar has regular trad sessions, West Kerry brews and Dingle whiskey. *noon-midnight Mon-Sat, to 11pm Sun*

One of the coastal mainland sites of the Páirc Náisiúnta na Mara, the pass is a classic challenge for cyclists. It's best to start in Dingle town, from where the road climbs 400m over 7km. The climb from the north is more brutal and has the added problem of being single track at the final, steepest section, so you'll be holding up traffic.

Cloghane

TIME FROM DINGLE TOWN: 30MIN

Celebrate the Celtic harvest

During the last weekend in July, Mt Brandon is the backdrop for the parish of Cloghane and Brandon's **Féile Lúghnasa** *(cloghanebrandon.ie)*, a revival of the ancient Celtic festival for the upcoming harvest. Alongside music, theatre, poetry, art exhibitions, children's activities and parades, there's a blessing of the boats and pilgrimage up Mt Brandon.

Castlegregory

TIME FROM DINGLE TOWN: 40MIN

Discover the world above an beneath the waves

Castlegregory (Caislean an Ghriare), on the north side of the Dingle Peninsula, is a quiet village with lovely views of the hills to the south. However, things change when you drive up the sand-blown road along the broad spit of land between Tralee Bay and Brandon Bay. Up here, it's a watersports playground offering adrenaline-inducing surfing, windsurfing, wing foiling and SUP; **Jamie Knox Watersports** *(jamieknox.com; watersports from €40)* runs sessions and rents gear.

Scuba divers can swim among shoals of pollack amid the kelp forests and anemone-encrusted rocks of the Maharees Islands. Overlooking them from its Fahamore base, **Waterworld** *(waterworld.ie; boat dive/gear hire from €55/25)* runs daily boat trips to the best dive sites for qualified divers, as well as half-day Try-a-Dive packages for beginners *(from €150)*.

INCH STRAND

A 5km-long sand spit and dune system extending into Dingle Bay, **Inch Strand** (Trá Inse) is one of Ireland's most picturesque beaches. Its sweeping sands, rolling surf and due westerly aspect with dramatic sunsets have long attracted film directors, featuring in iconic movies like *The Playboy of the Western World* (1962), *Ryan's Daughter* (1970), *Excalibur* (1981) and *Far and Away* (1992).

With a Blue Flag rating and lifeguards in summer, it's also popular with surfers, with waves averaging 1m to 3m, while its dune habitats have seen it included within Ireland's Páirc Náisiúnta na Mara, Ciarraí (Kerry Seas National Park). Cars are, controversially, allowed on the beach, although they frequently become stuck and submerged by the incoming tide (watching them being dug out by a tractor is common).

TWIST ALONG THE SLEA HEAD DRIVE

Tracing the tip of the Dingle Peninsula, this history-infused loop drive passes through the villages of Ventry, Dunquin and Ballyferriter.

START	END	LENGTH
Dingle town	Dingle town	42km; 4hr

Heading west from Dingle town, the Slea Head Drive takes in a host of superbly preserved structures from the ancient past, including beehive huts, ringforts, inscribed stones and early Christian sites.

Situated 5.5km beyond Ventry, ❶ **Dunbeg Fort** is a dramatic example of an Iron Age promontory fortification perched atop a sheer sea cliff. Inside the fort's four outer stone walls are the remains of a house and a beehive hut, as well as an underground passage. Another 800m further on is ❷ **Fahan Beehive Huts**, a gathering of five stone structures dating from 500 CE, including two that are fully intact. The road is at its narrowest, just a ledge blasted out of the steep rock face, as it rounds ❸ **Slea Head** itself, with views of Dunmore Head and Great Blasket Island. A car park on the left gives access to the picturesque cove of ❹ **Coumeenoole Beach** with golden sand and translucent water framed by rugged cliffs.

It's an easier drive through Dunquin, home to the Blasket Centre, with stunning views in both directions from the ❺ **Clogher Head viewpoint** before reaching ❻ **Músaem Chorca Dhuibhne – West Kerry Museum**, with displays on the peninsula's history, geology, archaeology and ecology. The route then passes the beautiful 1200-year-old ❼ **Gallarus Oratory** (p248) before returning over the hill to Dingle town.

Although it's short in distance, doing this drive justice requires a full day. Driving clockwise offers the best views.

From Coumeenoole Beach, you can easily hike out (2km round trip) to Dunmore Head, the Irish mainland's westernmost point.

Tralee

HISTORY | NATURE | ARTS

Although it's the biggest town in County Kerry, with a population of 26,079, Tralee is down-to-earth and more engaged with the business of everyday life than the tourist trade. Nonetheless, a fascinating museum, historic working windmill and wetlands wildlife haven make it well worth a stop.

Founded by the Normans in 1216, Tralee has a long history of rebellion. In the 16th century, the last ruling earl of the Desmonds was captured and executed here. His head was sent to Elizabeth I, who spiked it on London Bridge. The Desmonds' castle once stood at the junction of Denny St and the Mall, but any trace of medieval Tralee that survived the Desmond Wars was razed during the Cromwellian period.

Elegant Denny St and Day Pl are the oldest parts of town, with 18th-century Georgian buildings, while the Square, just south of the Mall, is a contemporary open space.

Meet Tralee's Local Heroes
History brought to life

Over 1750 sq m of exhibition space, the **Kerry County Museum** *(kerrymuseum.ie; adult/child €5/3)* does an admirable job of interpreting the lives and achievements of local heroes Sir Roger Casement and Tom Crean. In doomed preparations for the 1916 Easter Rising, Casement (1864–1916) was famously landed from a German submarine on Banna Strand north of Tralee. Crean (1877–1938) was an explorer who accompanied both Robert Falcon Scott and Ernest Shackleton on epic Antarctic expeditions.

Fragments from a knight's tomb and a medieval mason's mark unearthed during the excavation of the site of Tralee's Dominican Priory are among the Archaeology Hall's highlights. In the basement, the Medieval Experience recreates life (smells and all) in Tralee in 1450.

The museum is housed in the splendid Ashe Memorial Hall, built between 1924 and 1928 and dedicated to Kerry-born

GETTING AROUND

Tralee's **bus station** is next to its railway station, **Casement Station**, on John Joe Sheehy Rd in the town centre. Trains run via Farranfore (near Kerry Airport) and Killarney en route to destinations including Cork and Dublin Heuston.

The compact town centre is easily covered on foot. You can walk to Blennerville in 45 minutes via the Canal Walk, which begins at the south end of Basin Rd, or cycle in 15 minutes. The Tralee to Fenit Greenway is another popular cycle route. Hire bicycles at **Tralee Bike Renal** *(traleebikerental.ie).*

If you're travelling by car, use the main pay-and-display car park on Prince's St.

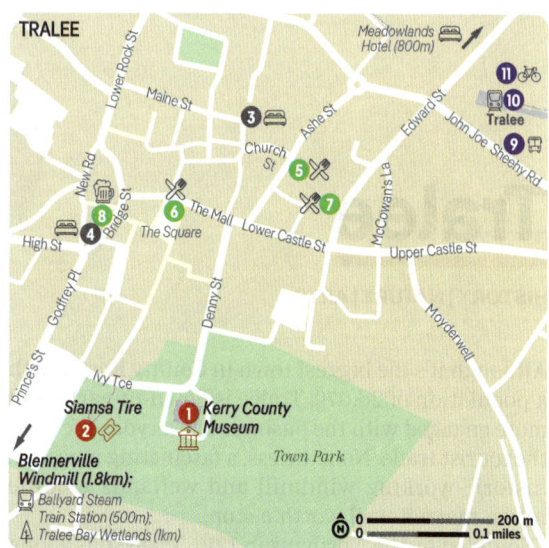

- ⭐ **HIGHLIGHTS**
  1. Kerry County Museum
  2. Siamsa Tíre
- ⚫ **SLEEPING**
  3. Ashe Hotel
  4. James Hotel
- 🟢 **EATING**
  5. Forge Wood Fired Pizza
  6. Quinlan's
  7. Ugly Mug
- 🟢 **DRINKING & NIGHTLIFE**
  8. Seán Óg's Bar
- 🔵 **TRANSPORT**
  9. Bus Station
  10. Casement Station
  11. Tralee Bike Renal

☑ TOP TIP

Check to see what's on at Ireland's National Folk Theatre, **Siamsa Tíre** *(siamsatire.com)*. The name (pronounced shee-*am*-sa tee-ruh) is Irish for 'mirth and music of the land', and the 350-seat venue specialises in traditional and contemporary aspects of Irish culture, presenting theatre, music and dance performances, workshops, festivals and exhibitions in its galleries.

Thomas Ashe (1885–1917), who played a pivotal role in the 1916 Rising and died while on hunger strike in September 1917.

Cruise Tralee's Wetlands

Nature safari

A 30-minute nature-safari boat ride is the highlight of a visit to the **Tralee Bay Wetlands** *(traleebaywetlands.org; guided electric boat tour adult/child €10/5, guided nature tour €5/3; self-guided tours €3/free)*, an eco and activity park with pedalo boats *(per four-person boat €20)* and a climbing wall *(per person €19)*, located on the town's southwestern edge. You can also get a good overview of the reserve's 3247 hectares, encompassing saltwater and freshwater habitats, from the 20m-high viewing tower (accessible by lift), and spot wildlife from bird hides. Adjacent to the state-of-the-art, solar-powered visitor centre, its light-filled cafe overlooks the main lake.

🍴 EATING & DRINKING IN TRALEE: OUR PICKS

Ugly Mug: Stylish contemporary space with sweet and savoury treats, including cupcakes. *8.30am-4pm Mon-Fri, 9am-3.30pm Sat, 10.30am-2.30pm Sun* €

Quinlan's: Great for fish and chips, Dingle Bay sweet chilli squid and Portmagee garlic butter crab claws. *noon-8pm Wed, Thu & Sun, to 9pm Fri & Sat* €€

Forge Wood Fired Pizza: Sourdough pizzas named after local surf spots, eg Stradbally (prosciutto, rocket and pine nuts). *5-9pm Wed-Fri, 4-9pm Sat & Sun* €€

Seán Óg's Bar: Live music plays most nights at this traditional pub fronted by an impossible-to-miss bright-purple facade in the heart of Tralee. *noon-11pm*

Blennerville Windmill

Tour a Working Windmill
History and engineering

Blennerville, 3.4km southwest of Tralee's centre on the N86 to Dingle, used to be the city's chief port, though the harbour has long since silted up. A relic of that time, **Blennerville Windmill** *(blennerville-windmill.ie; guided tour adult/child €8/7; self-guided tour €6/5)* dates from around 1800. Now restored, it's the largest working windmill in Ireland. Its visitor centre houses exhibitions on flour milling, as well as on the thousands of emigrants who boarded 'coffin ships' from what was then Kerry's largest embarkation point. Between 1889 and 1891, the building was used for storage during the construction of the Tralee & Dingle Light Railway and there's a charming model of the narrow-gauge railway on display.

ROSE OF TRALEE

Founded in 1959, the **Rose of Tralee International Festival** *(roseoftralee.ie)*, held over five days in August, sees beauty pageant contestants from across Ireland and Irish communities throughout the world compete for the coveted crown. Events include concerts, a funfair, circus acts, dance, a televised live show and a parade followed by a fireworks display.

Originally named the Festival of Kerry, the event was initially open to women from Tralee, then Kerry, and, from 1967, those of Irish birth or ancestry. Since the 1970s, its current name stems from a 19th-century ballad about local Catholic maid Mary O'Connor; she and her star-crossed lover, wealthy Protestant poet William Pembroke Mulchinock, are buried together on Tralee's outskirts in Clogherbrien. Cultivated for early festivals, Rose of Tralee roses bloom in Tralee's town park.

Beyond Tralee

Explore endless beaches with mountain views, a world-class golf course and a bucolic book-lover's town.

Places
Ardfert p256
Ballybunion p257
Listowel p257
Crag Cave p258

GETTING AROUND

Buses from Tralee serve Listowel, Ardfert and Ballybunion, but to explore properly, including Banna Strand and Crag Cave, you'll need a car.

If you are continuing north from Kerry to visit County Clare, a car ferry operated by **Shannon Ferries** *(shannonferries.com; car & passengers €25, foot passenger/cyclist €6)* makes the scenic, 20-minute trip from Tarbert in Kerry across the broad Shannon Estuary to Killimer in Clare that saves a 134km detour via Limerick. Check seasonal schedules online.

Consisting mainly of flat farmland – all those cows grazing the lush green pastures provide the milk that goes to make Ireland's famous Kerrygold butter – northern Kerry's landscapes can't compare to the spectacular Ring of Kerry or the Dingle Peninsula, but there are some interesting places that merit a stop.

Banna Strand is one of Ireland's finest beaches, and the little village of Ardfert boasts an impressive ruined cathedral. The seaside resort of Ballybunion is home to a world-class golf club and scenic clifftop walk. The elegant town of Listowel has more literary connections than most Irish towns outside Dublin, and is at its liveliest when it hosts the country's oldest literary and arts festival.

Ardfert
TIME FROM TRALEE: **15MIN**

Admire Romanesque ruins

The impressive remains of 13th-century **Ardfert Cathedral** *(heritageireland.ie; adult/child €5/3)*, open mid-March to September, are notable for the beautiful and delicate stone carvings on its Romanesque door and window arches.

Set into one of the interior walls is an effigy, said to be of St Brendan the Navigator, who was born nearby and founded a monastery here. Other elaborate medieval grave slabs can be seen in the visitor centre. Ardfert is 9km northwest of Tralee on the Ballyheigue road.

Sunbathe and swim with a view

A favourite weekend getaway for Tralee residents, **Banna Strand** is one of the biggest and best Blue Flag beaches in Ireland; a 10km stretch of fine golden sand backed by 10m-high dunes, with fantastic views southwest to Mt Brandon and the Dingle hills.

A monument 500m south of the main car park marks the spot where the Irish revolutionary leader Roger Casement was dropped off by a German U-boat shortly before the 1916 Easter Rising.

The beach is 13km northwest of Tralee (5km west of Ardfert). Signs lead to the main car park, which is often crowded, but there's another, more secluded (unsurfaced) parking area in the dunes 300m southwest of the **Roger Casement Monument**, which gives access to the much quieter south end of the beach.

Ballybunion
TIME FROM TRALEE: **30MIN**

Tee off at Ballybunion Golf Club
The beach town of Ballybunion is best known for its eponymous golf club. A statue of a club-swinging **Bill Clinton** in the middle of town commemorates his visit to the course in 1998 – he played here again in 2001. **Ballybunion Golf Club** (*ballybuniongolfclub.com; green fees Old Course €400, Old Course & Cashen Course €500*) is renowned as one of the finest links courses in the world. Weekends and bank holidays are reserved for members, but visitors can book tee times to play the par-71, 1893-established Old Course on weekday mornings or the par-72 Cashen Course on weekday mornings and afternoons.

Watch the sunset from the clifftops
Ballybunion faces west into the Atlantic and is famed for its glorious sunsets. The best place to soak up the view is from the **Cliff Walk**, a 1.5km signposted trail that follows the clifftop to the north of the town, starting opposite the Cliff House Hotel and finishing at the beautiful cliff-bound cove of **Nuns Beach**, named for the convent above it.

Overlooking the town's main beach are the restored remains of **Ballybunion Castle** (aka Fitzmaurice Castle), the 16th-century seat of the Fitzmaurices, with views to the Dingle Peninsula and Loop Head, County Clare.

Listowel
TIME FROM TRALEE: **25MIN**

Read up on Kerry's writers
The tidy Georgian streets of Listowel (Lios Tuathail) are arranged around an attractive main square. The two surviving towers of its 12th-century Anglo-Norman **Listowel Castle** (*heritageireland.ie; free*), open weekdays from late May to late September, rise 15m high overlooking the River Feale.

The town has more literary credentials than your average provincial town, with connections to half a dozen of Ireland's best-known writers. Next to the castle, the wonderful **Kerry Writers' Museum** (*kerrywritersmuseum.com; adult/child €10/5*), next to the castle, celebrates Listowel's observers of Irish life with rooms devoted to local greats, such as John B Keane and Bryan MacMahon, with simple, haunting tableaux

---

ST BRENDAN THE NAVIGATOR

Born in Fenit in 484 CE, Kerry's intrepid saint was baptised and mentored by Bishop Erc, and educated by St Ita of Killeedy. Ordained by Erc c512, Brendan (Bréanainn) established monastic communities around Ardfert's port, which inspired his explorations; his adventures were recounted in the c800 tale *Navigatio Sancti Brendani Abbatis* (*Voyage of Saint Brendan the Abbot*). Whether Brendan reached America's shores in a tiny *currach* (rowing boat) is debated, but there are old Irish Ogham carvings in West Virginia dating from as early as the 6th century, long before Christopher Columbus' arrival in 1492. Brendan died in Annaghdown, Galway in 577; his grave is outside Galway's Clonfert Cathedral on the site of his best-known monastery. He's the patron saint of travellers, seafarers and the US Navy.

EATING & DRINKING BEYOND TRALEE: OUR PICKS

Lizzy's Little Kitchen: This busy Listowel cafe is a top lunch spot, whether vegetarian dishes like chickpea stroganoff, or crab sandwiches. *9am-3pm Tue-Sat* €

Oyster Tavern: Tralee Bay oysters, pan-fried Kerry Head crab claws and lobster star at this restaurant in Spa, 7km west of Tralee. *5-9pm Mon-Sat, 12.30-8pm Sun* €€

West End Bar & Bistro: 'Fresh or nothing' is the motto of this fifth-generation-run restaurant in Fenit, 13km west of Tralee. *4.30-9.30pm Mon-Fri, 3-9.30pm Sat & Sun* €€

McMunn's Bar: Overlooking Ballybunion's castle ruins and coastline, with craft beers, ciders and 60-plus whiskeys, including its own 12-year-old spirit. *5-11pm Wed-Sun*

KERRY GREENWAYS

Kerry has two **greenways** *(greenwaysireland.org)*, with a third in the works.

The **Tralee to Fenit Greenway** runs from **Tralee**'s station along a former branch of the 1880s to 1970s Limerick to Tralee railway line. Covering 13.6km, it crosses the River Lee, taking in views of the Dingle Peninsula's coastline, hills and cliffs before reaching the working fishing port of **Fenit**.

The **Listowel to Limerick Greenway** traverses 16km of the Limerick to Tralee railway line along the River Feale's northern slopes to Abbeyfeale, County Limerick, where you can connect to the Limerick Greenway, which continues another 39km to Rathkeale.

Work is underway on the 32km-long **South Kerry Greenway**, following the 1892–1960 Great Southern and Western Railway rail line from Glenbeigh to Reenard, south west of Cahersiveen.

Listowel Castle (p257)

narrating their lives and recordings of them reading their work. Absorbing audio tours narrated by *seanchaí* (traditional Irish storyteller and historian) Bryan Murphy take 90 minutes.

During the **Listowel Literary Festival** in late May/early June, bibliophiles flock to Listowel for five days of readings, poetry, music, drama, seminars, storytelling and other events.

Crag Cave

TIME FROM TRALEE: **25MIN**

Explore an ancient fossil cave system

Crag Cave *(cragcave.com; adult/child €17/7)* was discovered in 1983 when problems with water pollution led to a search for the source of the local river. In 1989, 300m of the 4km-long cave were opened to the public; admission is by 30-minute guided tour involving 72 steps. The remarkable rock formations include a calcite straw-filled 'Crystal Gallery', a domed 'Cathedral' with stalagmites shaped like candlesticks, and a stalagmite shaped (to some) like a statue of the Madonna. Dress warmly for the cave's chilly 10°C temperature. There are play areas for kids, a cafe and a gift shop. The cave is signposted 18km east of Tralee.

Places We Love to Stay

€ Budget €€ Midrange €€€ Top End

Killarney   MAP p228

Black Sheep Hostel € Eco-focused traveller-designed hostel with custom-made bunks and built-in lockers, free breakfast and attached coffee shack.

Fleming's White Bridge Caravan & Camping Park € Lovely, sheltered family-run campsite on the banks of the River Flesk 2.5km southeast of town.

Crystal Springs €€ Wonderfully relaxing B&B just outside the centre with a glass-enclosed breakfast room overlooking the river. Two-night minimum.

Cahernane House Hotel €€€ Grand manor dating from 1877, with antique-furnished rooms (some with a claw-foot bath or Jacuzzi).

Killarney Plaza Hotel €€€ Epicentral 198-room modern hotel channelling art-deco-era style, with a lavishly tiled pool, sauna, steam room and spa.

Beyond Killarney National Park

Mannix Point Camping & Caravan Park € One of Ireland's finest campsites, with a sociable turf-fire-warmed lounge and stunning sunsets over Valentia Island.

Kells Bay House (p241) **€€** Beautiful 19th-century hunting lodge containing nine uniquely decorated rooms overlooking magnificent Kells Bay Gardens.

Kingstons Townhouse €€ Stylish B&B accommodation in Killorglin featuring smart rooms named after the local Kerry mountains.

Quinlan & Cooke Boutique Townhouse €€ Family-run Cahersiveen guesthouse with smart rooms set above a superb restaurant with seafood from the owner's own fleet.

Parknasilla Resort & Spa €€€ Majestic hotel 3km southeast of Sneem, wowing guests (including George Bernard Shaw) since 1895.

Dingle   MAP p245

Grapevine Hostel € Small, welcoming spot in a handy town-centre location with two- to eight-bed rooms, a kitchen and cosy, fire-lit lounge.

Rainbow Hostel & Camping € Set in large gardens 1.5km northwest of town, this bright, fresh bungalow is also the nearest place to Dingle you can pitch a tent.

Base Dingle €€ Contemporary lodgings in Dingle's heart, offering 30 sleek rooms sleeping from two to five people (no breakfast).

Dingle Harbour Lodge €€ This purpose-built, pared-down guesthouse's position above the harbour means no street noise and views from upper-level rooms.

Pax House €€€ Luxury B&B with outstanding sea views from the glass-framed terrace and balconies opening from some rooms. Minimum two nights; over 12s only.

Castlewood House €€€ A haven of country-house quiet and sophistication 10 minutes' stroll from town.

Beyond Dingle

Campaíl Teach An Aragail € Situated 450m west of Gallarus Oratory, this campground is just a 1km stroll from beautiful Wine Strand beach.

Inch Beach House €€ Splendidly located, this bright, cheerful B&B's higher-priced rooms directly face Inch Strand.

Cé Hideout €€ Stunning views of Brandon Bay extend from this elegant, newly built property on the Dingle Peninsula's northern side.

Tralee   MAP p254

Ashe Hotel €€ Boutique town-centre hotel offering great-value rooms decorated in stylish wallpapers, prints and furnishings.

James Hotel €€ Opened in 2024, this central townhouse hotel has 26 well-designed rooms, an exposed-brick bar hosting live music and a cellar restaurant.

Meadowlands Hotel €€ Strolling distance from town but far enough away to be quiet, with plush rooms and excellent dining (the family own their own seafood company).

Beyond Tralee

Listowel Arms Hotel €€ Listowel's principal hotel is a Georgian building that balances grandeur with country charm.

Cliff House Hotel €€€ Lovely family-run hotel in Ballybunion, with great sea views from the conservatory-style breakfast room.

Teach de Broc €€€ Framed by flowers, this low-rise boutique B&B next to Ballybunion's golf club has thoughtfully appointed, spacious rooms.

Left: Limerick City (p264); right: cottage, Adare (p268)

Researched by
Neil Wilson

Limerick & Tipperary

HEARTLANDS, HISTORY AND CULTURE

From marching songs to rhyming verse, the names Tipperary and Limerick are part of the Western lexicon, but both counties remain relatively unexplored by visitors.

Culture and history abound in this region, with castles and abbeys aplenty, mountain valleys and quaint, seldom-visited towns. Limerick is bordered to the north by the mighty Shannon, Ireland's longest river, and its estuary. Swelling uplands and mountains separate Limerick from Cork to the south and Tipperary to the east.

County Limerick is closely tied to its namesake city, which has a history as dramatic as Ireland's. In a nation of hard knocks, it has had more than its fair share. The city's streets have tangible links to the past and a gritty, honest vibrancy, while treasures abound in its lush, green countryside.

In contrast, Tipperary town is missable. But amid the county's rolling hills, rich farmland and deep valleys bordered by soaring mountains, it's a peaceful place that's perfect for following a river to its source or climbing a stile to reach a lonely ruin. The Gaelic Athletic Association (GAA) was founded in the town of Thurles, and the county is known as the home of hurling, though both counties have a strong devotion to traditional Irish sports and rugby. Drinking in a pub full of supporters on match day is an experience to remember.

In both counties, ancient Celtic sites, medieval abbeys and other relics endure in solitude, awaiting discovery. And even Limerick and Tipperary's best-known sights retain a rough, inspiring dignity.

LUKASZ PAJOR/SHUTTERSTOCK

THE MAIN AREAS

LIMERICK CITY
A buzzing city rich in history.
p264

CASHEL
A pretty town, a majestic monastery and lush countryside.
p272

THE GALTEES & THE GLEN OF AHERLOW
Stunning scenery, road trips and hillwalking. **p281**

Find Your Way

Limerick and Tipperary straddle the middle of the lower Midlands, spanning west to the mouth of the Shannon and east to the valley of the River Suir. It takes about two hours to drive between the furthermost edges of these counties.

Cashel, p272
This charming town is home to one of the most famous historical sites in Ireland, the Rock of Cashel.

The Galtees & the Glen of Aherlow, p281
Nestled between the hills and forests, the Glen of Aherlow offers scenic drives and hillwalks.

Limerick City, p264
The Republic's third-largest city has an impressive castle at the mouth of the country's longest river.

BUS & TRAIN
Limerick city is well connected to surrounding towns by bus, but in Tipperary, bus services can be limited in places. The train connects both counties. **Bus Éireann** (buseireann.ie) and **Iarnród Éireann** (irishrail.ie) serve both regions.

CAR
As in most places in Ireland, having your own car is the most convenient way to explore, especially if you want to get off the beaten path and into the heartlands of these counties.

Glen of Aherlow (p281)

Plan Your Time

Cities, towns and castles abound from the green hills of the Galtees to the Shannon Estuary, and the heartlands of Ireland give a real insight into the country's culture.

One Day Only

● Get to **Cashel** (p272) early to check out the impressive **Rock of Cashel** (p274) looming over the town below. After a morning at the Rock, enjoy a luxurious lunch at **Mikey Ryan's** (p273). Hit the road for **Cahir** (p277) to check out **Cahir Castle** and the **Swiss Cottage** (p277). Take the scenic drive through the **Glen of Aherlow** (p281) on your way towards Limerick.

Five Days to Explore

● Spend one day in **Limerick city** (p264) before heading to **Foynes Flying Boat Museum** (p270) and the charming village of **Adare** (p268). Spend your third day in the **Glen of Aherlow** (p281) and **Cahir** (p277), and dedicate another day to **Cashel** (p272). Visit **Thurles** (p278) and go on to **Upperchurch** (p280) to hit the trails. If it's a Thursday, grab a pint at **Jim O' the Mills** (p280).

SEASONAL HIGHLIGHTS

SPRING
Flowers are blooming (daffodils in March), and walking trails in the **Galtees** (p281) are starting to thaw out.

SUMMER
Expect longer days and better weather for exploring, as well as lots of local festivals and GAA matches.

AUTUMN
The weather is pleasant as the evenings darken and the trees turn wonderful shades of russet and gold.

WINTER
Enjoy roaring fires and live music in local pubs. Some attractions may be closed. Christmas lights twinkle.

Limerick City

MEDIEVAL HISTORY | WEEKEND MARKET | URBAN KAYAKING

GETTING AROUND
Limerick city is compact enough to get around on foot or by bike. There's a **bike-share scheme** *(bikeshare.ie)*, with 23 stations around town and costing €3 for three days with a €150 deposit for visitors. The first 30 minutes of each hire is free, then it costs €1.50 for up to two hours. Buses are frequent and reliable with many stops around the city centre.

'There once was a city called Limerick...' Umm, no, can't think of anything that rhymes with Limerick. And no one is quite sure why those humorous five-line verses are named after this Irish city, though the term dates from the late 19th century.

Founded by Vikings in 922 CE, Limerick was crowned Ireland's first City of Culture in 2014, and the subsequent investment saw a rejuvenated waterfront complete with a stylish boardwalk. It feels far removed from Frank McCourt's bleak portrayal in his autobiographical novel *Angela's Ashes*, for which he won the Pulitzer Prize. The city has a mighty castle, a spectacular arched stone bridge across the River Shannon and a burgeoning arts scene, and is often buzzing with hurling and rugby fans watching matches in the lively local pubs. Limerick has a decent range of quality accommodation and many excellent restaurants that focus on fresh Irish produce.

Besiege a Norman Fortress
See Limerick's showpiece castle

A brooding Norman mass looming over the River Shannon, **King John's Castle** *(kingjohnscastle.ie; adult/child €15/11)*, with its vast curtain walls and towers, was built on the orders of King John of England between 1200 and 1212. The massive twin gate towers still stand to their full height. A multimedia experience that provides an excellent potted history of Ireland in general, and Limerick in particular, is followed by exposed archaeology in the undercroft and a tour of the courtyard and fortifications.

Upstairs from the cafe, don't miss the exhibitions on the castle's archaeology and the development of Georgian Limerick, or the view from the top of the gate towers, though the best views of the castle itself are from the riverside walk on the far side of the Shannon. Book online for discounts.

☑ TOP TIP
The best approach (on foot) from the city centre to King John's Castle is to cross Sarsfield Bridge and follow the riverside walk north to Thomond Bridge – there are great views across the river to the city and castle.

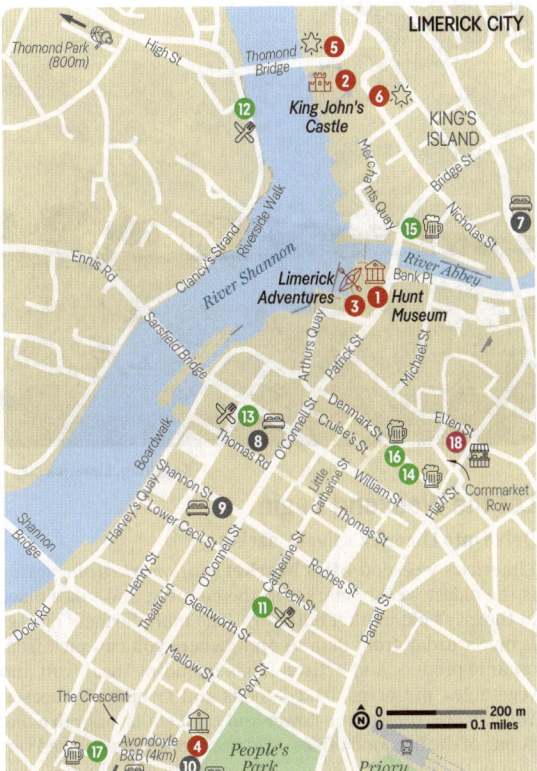

LIMERICK CITY

- **HIGHLIGHTS**
  1. Hunt Museum
  2. King John's Castle
  3. Limerick Adventures
- **SIGHTS**
  4. People's Museum of Limerick
- **ACTIVITIES**
  5. Limerick Civic Trust
  6. Treaty City Brewery
- **SLEEPING**
  7. Absolute Hotel
  8. Bedford Townhouse
  9. George Hotel
  10. No 1 Pery Square
- **EATING**
  11. Canteen
  12. Curragower Bar
  13. Hook & Ladder
- **DRINKING & NIGHTLIFE**
  14. Flannery's Bar
  15. Locke Bar
  16. Nancy Blake's
  17. South's
- **SHOPPING**
  18. Milk Market

Hunt for Historic Treasures

Visit the city's top museum

Named after its benefactors, the **Hunt Museum** (huntmuseum.com; adult/child €12.50/free) is also a treasure hunt. Visitors are encouraged to open drawers and poke around the finest collection of Bronze Age, Iron Age, medieval and modern art treasures outside Dublin. Highlights include a Syracusan coin that is claimed to be one of the 30 pieces of silver paid to Judas for his betrayal of Christ, a Renoir study, a Gauguin painting, a Giacometti drawing, and paintings by Picasso and Jack B Yeats.

There's also a tiny but exquisite bronze horse once attributed to Leonardo da Vinci (but now considered a much later copy), Cycladic sculptures, an alabaster vase from Ancient Egypt dated to the 3rd century BCE and a smattering of pieces from East Asia. The 2000-plus items are from the private collection of the late John and Gertrude Hunt, antique dealers and consultants, who championed historical preservation throughout the region. One-hour guided tours with dedicated volunteer guides are available.

THE TREATY CITY

From 1690 to 1691, Limerick acquired heroic status in the long saga of Ireland's struggle against occupation by the English.

After their defeat at the Battle of the Boyne in 1690, Jacobite forces withdrew to the west behind the famously strong walls of Limerick town. Months of bombardment followed and eventually the Irish Jacobite leader Patrick Sarsfield sued for peace.

The terms of the 1691 Treaty of Limerick were agreed, and Sarsfield and 14,000 soldiers were allowed to leave the city for France. The treaty guaranteed religious freedom for Catholics, but the English later reneged on it, an act of betrayal that came to symbolise the injustice of British rule.

Kayaking, Limerick city

Let the Weekend Begin
Delve into Limerick's lively market

Limerick's weekend **Milk Market** *(milkmarketlimerick.ie)* is the oldest weekly market in the country, and takes place in the city's old market buildings. The main farmers market is on Saturday from 8am to 4pm, where you can pick from organic produce and artisan foods including local fruit and vegetables, preserves, baked goods and farmhouse cheeses. You can also browse the flower and craft stalls, or grab a bite at one of the hot-food tables. Friday offers a more relaxed version with outdoor cafes and live music, while Sunday plays host to a range of art, antiques and garden fairs.

Join a Guided Kayak Tour
See Limerick from the river

Experience the city from a watery perspective with **Limerick Adventures** *(limerickadventures.com; per person €25-35)*, which offers tours by kayak, stand-up paddleboard or sailboat on the River Shannon. Tours start behind the Hunt Museum and take you past King John's Castle, Thomond Bridge and the Treaty Stone. For those who prefer to keep their feet dry but not necessarily on the ground, the company also offers an abseiling experience at King John's Castle, in which the brave can descend the walls of the fortress by rope.

 EATING IN LIMERICK CITY: OUR PICKS

Hook & Ladder: A haven of style and a champion of local produce, this cafe is set in a converted bank building. *8am-5pm Mon-Fri, to 7pm Sat, 9am-5pm Sun* €€

Curragower Bar: An appealing pub with superb outdoor terrace with views across the river, and a menu that leans towards seafood. *noon-9pm* €€

No 1 Pery Square (p285): Elegant hotel restaurant in the Georgian quarter is the spot for a sophisticated lunch or romantic dinner. *noon-2.30pm Mon-Sat, 5-9pm Thu-Sat* €€€

Canteen: Imaginative breakfast, brunch and lunch dishes from green eggs and ham to confit duck toasties. *9am-4pm Mon-Fri, from 9.30am Sat, from 10am Sun* €€

Try a Local Craft Beer
Hops and history
Housed in two renovated 18th-century buildings in the heart of Limerick's medieval quarter, **Treaty City Brewery** *(treaty citybrewery.ie; tours per person €23)* produces some of the finest craft beers in the country. On Fridays and Saturdays you can join an hour-long tour to learn about the city's rich brewing tradition and discover how the brewers use locally sourced hops and malts to develop unique beers, such as the signature Harris Pale Ale with its citrus and floral flavours.

Explore the City Streets
Join a guided walking tour
Walking the streets of Limerick's town centre is the best way to get to grips with this fascinating city. **Limerick Civic Trust** *(limerickcivictrust.ie; adult/child €10/6)* runs 90-minute guided walking tours of the medieval quarter around the castle, as well as bespoke private tours; book by phone or email.

The Civic Trust also operates the **People's Museum of Limerick** *(peoplesmuseum.ie; adult/child €5/3)*, a restored Georgian townhouse; it offers a walking tour of the city's attractive Georgian quarter, which includes the former school attended by Frank McCourt. For more detail, **Limerick City Walking Tours** *(limerickcitywalkingtours.com; €160 for up to 8 people)* can arrange entertaining tours covering the locations featured in *Angela's Ashes* (book and movie) on request.

Take a Tour of Thomond Park
Limerick's legendary stadium
Munster has a reputation as one of the strongest and most competitive rugby teams in Europe. For 12 seasons, from 1995 to 2007, they clocked up 25 consecutive Heineken Cup victories at legendary **Thomond Park Stadium** *(thomondpark.ie; adult/child €10/8)*. This was also the venue for their famous victory over New Zealand's All Blacks in 1978, a match that became the subject of a book, play and documentary film. Join a guided tour of the hallowed ground and visit the dressing rooms, dugouts and pitch, as well as its memorabilia-filled museum. The stadium is an easy 1km walk northwest of the centre along High St.

FRANK MCCOURT'S LIMERICK

Since the 1990s, no name has been so closely intertwined with Limerick as Frank McCourt (1930–2009). Born in Brooklyn, New York, he moved with his family to Limerick, and a life of grinding poverty, at the age of four. His autobiographical novel *Angela's Ashes* was a surprise sensation in 1996, winning him the Pulitzer Prize. The book was later made into a film.

When the book was published, the reaction in Limerick was mixed, with some claiming it portrayed the city in a negative light. Today, however, McCourt's legacy is celebrated. The city's tourist office has information about sights related to the book, and you can join an *Angela's Ashes* walking tour and drink in South's, one of the pubs McCourt mentions in the book.

 DRINKING IN LIMERICK CITY: OUR PICKS

Nancy Blake's: A cosy pub with sawdust on the floor and a covered beer garden with live music. *11am–midnight Mon–Wed, to 2am Thu & Fri, 10am–2am Sat, 12.30pm–2am Sun*

Flannery's Bar: Lively pub in a former soap factory, with more than 100 varieties of Irish whiskey and a roof terrace. *10.30am–11.30pm Mon–Thu, to 12.30am Fri & Sat, 12.30–11pm Sun*

South's: Author Frank McCourt had his first pint here. Check out the fantastically reproduced neoclassical interior. *9am–11pm Mon–Thu, to 12.30am Fri, 12.30pm–12.30am Sat, 12.30–11pm Sun*

Locke Bar: Attractive riverside setting, a menu that runs from breakfast to dinner, and live music sessions nightly. *9am–11.30pm Mon–Thu, to 12.30am Fri, 10am–12.30am Sat, to 11.30pm Sun*

Beyond Limerick City

Postcard-perfect villages, mountain-bike trails and a unique aviation museum await beyond the city boundaries.

Places
Adare p268
Lough Gur p269
Foynes p270
Ballyhoura p271

GETTING AROUND

Bus Éireann bus 13 links Limerick city with Adare every two hours; journey time is 20 minutes. Bus 314 runs from Limerick to Foynes every two hours or so; journey time is 70 minutes. You'll need your own wheels to get to Ballyhoura and Lough Gur.

County Limerick's low-lying farmland is framed on its southern and eastern boundaries by swelling uplands. Travellers often overlook this part of Ireland because it falls between the honeypots of Clare and Kerry, home to more famous Irish landmarks, but it's worth lingering here.

Slow down and meander along the shores of the Shannon Estuary to discover the fascinating history on display at Foynes Flying Boat Museum, or get the adrenaline pumping on the mountain-biking trails of the Ballyhoura Mountains. And in Adare you can stroll the charming streets of Ireland's prettiest village, renowned for its thatched cottages, play golf with a medieval castle as backdrop, and dine at its many fine eateries.

Adare

TIME FROM LIMERICK CITY: **25MIN**

Take a stroll around the village

Touted as 'Ireland's prettiest village', Adare takes its name from a crossing place on the River Maigue – the Gaelic Áth Dara means 'Ford of the Oak Tree'. Its current fame centres on its string of thatched cottages built by 19th-century English landlord, the Earl of Dunraven, for workers at his country seat, Adare Manor. Today the pretty cottages house craft shops and fine restaurants, while prestigious golf courses nearby cater to golf enthusiasts.

After visiting **Adare Heritage Centre** and taking a stroll through the pretty town park across the street, walk eastwards along the main street past the thatched cottages and continue past the Dunraven Arms Hotel for 350m to reach the **Augustinian Priory**, founded in 1316 and also known as the Black Abbey. The interior of the church is agreeable enough, but the real joy is the atmospheric little cloister (accessed through the large open doorway opposite the gates). A pleasant, signposted riverside path, with wayside seats, starts from just north of the priory gates. Look for a narrow access gap and head off alongside the river. After about 900m you reach a road; turn left to return to the centre of Adare (2.5km, allow one hour).

Play a round of golf

Keen golfers are spoiled for choice at Adare, with two superb courses on the edge of the village. Rather confusingly, Adare Manor Golf Club, north of the river, is quite separate from the

Golf Course at Adare Manor *(adaremanor.com)*, south of the river. The latter is a championship course redesigned in 2017 by Tom Fazio, and is open only to residents of the five-star Adare Manor luxury resort; it is hosting the Ryder Cup in September 2027.

The parkland course at **Adare Manor Golf Club** *(adare manorgolfclub.com; green fees €120)* is much more accessible. Narrow fairways wind among the trees, with picturesque medieval ruins as backdrop to several holes. Visitors can book tee times online, and clubs, trolleys and buggies can be hired at the clubhouse.

Lough Gur

TIME FROM LIMERICK CITY: **30MIN**

Heritage trails

The area surrounding picturesque, horseshoe-shaped Lough Gur is rich in Neolithic, Bronze Age and medieval archaeological sites. Short trails along the lake's edge lead to burial mounds, standing stones, ancient enclosures and other points of interest, and the whole area is ideal for easy walks and picnics.

A thatched replica of a Neolithic hut houses the **Lough Gur Visitor Centre** *(loughgur.com; adult/child €5/3)*, with a helpful information desk and good exhibits on the prehistoric monuments in the surrounding area, plus a small museum displaying Neolithic artefacts and a replica of the bronze Lough Gur shield dating from around 1000 BCE (the original is in the National Museum in Dublin). It's a good idea to come here first to get some context before exploring the surrounding sites.

The most rewarding trail leads steeply up steps north of the visitor centre to a grassy plateau where there are superb views over the lake as far as Mangerton Mountain and the twin peaks of the Paps in County Kerry, 80km away.

Grange stone circle

This stone circle, known as the Lios, is a superb 4000-year-old circular enclosure made up of 113 embanked upright stones, the largest prehistoric circle of its kind in Ireland. It's on the far side of the lake from the visitor centre, a 3km walk or drive; there's roadside parking and access to the site is free (there's a donation box).

ADARE MANOR

Built in the mid-19th century for Windham Henry Quin, the second Earl of Dunraven, the magnificent Tudor Revival Adare Manor replaced an earlier Georgian mansion. In 1987 it was acquired by US businessman Thomas F Kane, who converted it into a luxury hotel and golf resort.

It is a so-called 'calendar house', with 365 windows and 52 chimneys. Some interior parts, including the Great Hall (now the hotel lobby), were designed by Augustus Pugin, architect of London's Houses of Parliament, and his son Edward.

You can get a glimpse of the sumptuous interior by taking **afternoon tea** *(adult/child €75/35)* in the gallery, decorated with 15th-century carved wood panelling and remarkable stained-glass windows.

EATING IN ADARE: OUR PICKS

Good Room: Homely but busy place with inventive breakfasts, soups, salads, hot sandwiches and wraps in a thatched cottage. *8.30am-4.30pm Mon-Thu, to 5pm Fri, to 5.30pm Sat & Sun* €€

Restaurant 1826 Adare: One of Ireland's most highly regarded chefs, Wade Murphy, continues to wow diners at this art-lined thatched cottage. *5-9pm Thu-Sat, from 4pm Sun* €€€

Blue Door: Expect salads and sandwiches at lunch and more sophisticated dining in the evening at this upmarket restaurant. *noon-5pm & 6-9pm Wed-Sat, to 8pm Sun* €€€

Oak Room: Dine like a lord at Adare Manor's atmospheric restaurant where dinner service is lit only by candles. Dress code: smart casual. *6-9.30pm Wed-Sun* €€€

MAUREEN O'HARA MEMORIALS

Born in Ranelagh, Dublin, Maureen O'Hara (1920–2015) was one of the most famous Irish Hollywood actors from the 1940s to the 1970s. After the death of her third husband Charles Blair in 1978, she started spending holidays in Glengarriff in West Cork, and lived there full time from 2005 to 2012; she established the Maureen O'Hara Blair Memorial Golf Classic there. There's a statue of her in Cong (p328), and a bronze bust stands in Bective Sq in Kells, County Meath, her father's birthplace. Another bronze statue was erected in Glengarriff in 2022 but soon removed after criticism of its poor resemblance. In 2024 a commemorative plaque was unveiled at her childhood home at 32 Beechwood Ave Upper in Dublin.

Foynes

TIME FROM LIMERICK CITY: **45MIN**

Aviation history meets Hollywood

From 1937 to 1945, the Shannon Estuary off the village of Foynes was the landing place for the flying boats that linked North America with Europe. The one-of-a-kind **Foynes Flying Boat Museum** *(flyingboatmuseum.com; adult/child €17/10)* celebrates this brief but glamorous period of pioneering transatlantic aviation, and houses the world's only full-size replica of a Boeing B314 flying boat. Experience how these transatlantic seaplanes were the height of luxury at the time.

In 1968 Irish-born Hollywood actor **Maureen O'Hara** (1920–2015) married Charles Blair, who had piloted flying boats between the USA and Foynes during WWII. She cut the ribbon at the museum's opening in 1989 and remained a patron, visiting annually until her death. Her grandson donated a huge collection of her gowns and other personal possessions to create the museum's newest exhibition.

The museum is also home to the **Irish Coffee Centre**, where you can book an Irish coffee masterclass and learn about the history of the world-famous beverage (for groups of at least 10).

 DRINKING BEYOND LIMERICK CITY: OUR PICKS

Pat Collins Bar: A favourite of Adare locals, with good craic, good food (noon to 9pm), and live music on Wednesday nights. *11.45am–11.30pm Mon–Thu, to 12.30am Fri & Sat, noon–11.30pm Sun*

Bill Chawke's Lounge Bar: Covered in hurling memorabilia, this Adare pub hosts regular trad sessions and singalongs. *10.30am–11.30pm Mon–Thu, to 1.30am Fri & Sat, noon–11pm Sun*

Lakeshore Park Kiosk: A converted shipping container in the car park at Lough Gur houses this kiosk serving decent coffee and a small selection of cakes. *10am–8pm Jun–Aug*

Chill the Beans: This Kilmallock coffee shop is a good place to get properly caffeinated before hitting the MTB trails at Ballyhoura. *8am–6pm Mon–Fri, 9am–6pm Sat & Sun*

Foynes Flying Boat Museum

Ballyhoura

TIME FROM LIMERICK CITY: 1HR

Get on yer bike

The most extensive, purpose-built mountain-bike centre in the Republic, **Ballyhoura Mountain Bike Trail Network** (*trailriders.ie; car park €5*) has a choice of six purpose-built trails ranging from an easy 7km to a thigh-burning 51km in length. Grades range from blue through red to black; at 17km the Mountrussell Blue Loop makes a good introduction with easy climbing on forest roads and some superb flowing singletrack with great views. There are showers, toilets, bike hire and a bike shop at the car park.

THE BIRTHPLACE OF THE IRISH COFFEE

The creation of Irish coffee is attributed to Joe Sheridan, a chef at Foynes Port, which in the 1940s was one of the biggest civilian airports in Europe. One winter's evening in 1943, a flight had to turn back to Foynes Airbase midway through its journey. Feeling sorry for the cold and weary passengers, Sheridan whipped up something warm for them to drink.

The story goes that a silence descended as everyone tasted his invention. According to Sheridan, the perfect Irish coffee should include 'cream as rich as an Irish brogue, coffee as strong as a friendly hand, sugar as sweet as the tongue of a rogue, and whiskey as smooth as the wit of the land'.

 EATING BEYOND LIMERICK CITY: OUR PICKS

East Room: Elegant dining in the Palladian mansion of Plassey House on the University of Limerick campus just outside the city. *12.30-2.30pm & 6-11.30pm Wed-Fri, 5-11.30pm Sat* €€€

Copper & Spice: Savour the flavours of India and Thailand in a lovely setting overlooking the River Mulcair in Annacotty. *5-9.30pm Wed-Sat, 4-9pm Sun* €€

Mustard Seed at Echo Lodge: Its own fresh produce is incorporated into seasonal dishes at this 19th-century former convent in Ballygrant. *7-9.30pm* €€€

Silver Room: Traditional steak, lamb and chicken dishes are on the dinner menu at this Newcastle West restaurant, more casual menu at lunch. *12.30-8pm Wed-Sun* €€

Cashel

MEDIEVAL MONUMENTS | CHARMING STREETS | EATING OUT

GETTING AROUND

Cashel town is easily explored on foot. It takes about 10 minutes to reach the Rock of Cashel from the town centre. Good alternatives to the crowded and expensive car park below the Rock include Bishop's Walk car park in the town centre and the small, free car park at the foot of Rock Lane, north of the Rock.

'Cashel of the Kings' was once the seat of the high kings of the province of Munster, which includes counties Limerick and Tipperary. Cashel town has a long history entwined with folklore, and the main draw is the iconic Rock of Cashel, which stands on a limestone bluff overlooking the Golden Vale below. The imposing religious buildings that crown its blustery summit seem to emerge from the craggy landscape. The bustling and pretty little town itself rewards rambles around its charming streets, and dairy farming is still a way of life in the surrounding communities.

Set against a backdrop of lush countryside, this heritage-filled town has a lot to offer visitors. Fascinating historical sights, local artisanal producers, delightful shops, cute cafes and luxurious accommodation options await. Apart from the Rock, Cashel is best-known in Ireland and beyond for award-winning Cashel Blue farmhouse cheese, Ireland's first-ever blue cheese, still handmade locally.

Cashel Beyond the Rock
Check out this charming town

Despite the huge popularity of the dramatic Rock of Cashel, the neighbouring settlement manages to maintain a certain charm as a smallish market town that can be easily explored in a couple of hours. On Main St, the **Cashel Heritage Centre** *(cashel.ie; free)* is also the tourist information office, so it makes a great first port of call. Displays inside include a scale model of Cashel in the 1640s with audio commentary. It also houses a large craft shop stocking locally produced items, including **Rossa pottery** and Fearney Castle ceramics.

Across the street from the Heritage Centre is the 15th-century tower house known as **Kearney's Castle**. Once the home of the Kearney family, it's a historical landmark and the oldest surviving domestic building in Cashel. Check out the gargoyle water spouts on the wall above the arched window. Along Moor

☑ TOP TIP

The Rock of Cashel is open year-round, but it gets busy in summer. Big tour buses usually arrive around 10am so if you want a quieter visit, be there when the site opens at 9am or wait until after 4pm.

CASHEL

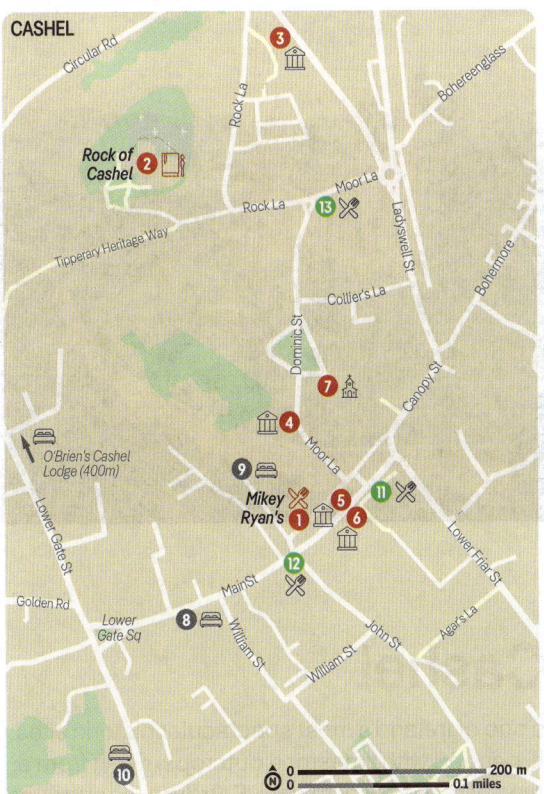

★ HIGHLIGHTS
1. Mikey Ryan's
2. Rock of Cashel

● SIGHTS
3. Brú Ború Heritage Centre
4. Cashel Folk Village
5. Cashel Heritage Centre
6. Kearney's Castle
7. St Dominick's Priory

● SLEEPING
8. Baileys Hotel
9. Cashel Palace Hotel
10. Copperfield House B&B

● EATING
11. Bake House
12. Bowes & Co
13. Chez Hans

Lane, behind the Heritage Centre, lies the hulking Gothic ruin of 13th-century **St Dominick's Priory**; the tower and tracery windows were added in the 15th century. Although you can't get inside, it's hoped that the priory will be open to the public in the future.

Back on Main St is the **Cashel Palace Hotel** (p285), originally a red-brick Palladian mansion built in 1732 for the use of Church of Ireland archbishops; it was restored and reopened as a five-star hotel in 2022. It's a great spot for a luxurious afternoon tea, or just strolling the manicured gardens and enjoying the views of the Rock.

Continues on p276

🍴 EATING IN CASHEL: OUR PICKS

Chez Hans: Since 1968 this former church has been a place of worship for foodies from all over. Book well in advance. *5.30-10pm Fri & Sat, 12.30-3pm & 5.30-8pm Sun* €€€

Mikey Ryan's: Gastropub serving up fresh seasonal dishes with quality ingredients. Check out the secret garden. *10am-11.30pm Mon-Sat, from noon Sun* €€

Bowes & Co: Great breakfast and lunch options, from pancakes to soups. Friendly service and good coffee. *8.30am-5pm Mon-Fri, from 9am Sat & Sun* €

Bake House: A longstanding local favourite that's great for baked goods and a full Irish breakfast. *8am-4.30pm Mon-Sat* €

TOP EXPERIENCE
Rock of Cashel

The Rock of Cashel is one of Ireland's most spectacular historic sites: a prominent green hill, banded with limestone outcrops, rising from a grassy plain and bristling with medieval towers. Sturdy walls surround an enclosure containing a 13th-century Gothic cathedral, a 28m-tall round tower and the finest 12th-century Romanesque chapel in Ireland, home to some of the land's oldest frescoes.

DON'T MISS

Frescoes in Cormac's Chapel

Cathedral

St Patrick's Cross

Round Tower

Hall of the Vicars Choral

View from the Rock

Hore Abbey

Cormac's Chapel

The undoubted highlight of the Rock is the early-12th-century Cormac's Chapel – an exquisite gem of Romanesque architecture with beautifully carved doorways and the only surviving Romanesque frescoes in Ireland. Gold-headed saints, lapis-lazuli blue ceilings and robes of blood-red are faint, but visibly there. The wall paintings in the chancel (dated to 1134) form the earliest known decoration of their kind; the ceiling is thought to depict the Adoration of the Magi; other paintings

PRACTICALITIES
● heritageireland.ie/visit/places-to-visit/the-rock-of-cashel/ ● adult/child €8/6 ● 9am-5.30pm 17 Mar-early Oct, to 4.30pm early Oct-16 Mar

record scenes from the early life of Christ. Inside the main door on the left is the sarcophagus said to house King Cormac, dating from between 1125 and 1150.

Cathedral

Constructed between 1235 and 1270, the cathedral was built in the shape of a cross with a huge square tower on the southwestern corner soaring above. Scattered throughout are various monuments, a 16th-century altar tomb, coats of arms, and stone heads on capitals and corbels, but the main impression is of its vast size.

Round Tower

The Round Tower is the tallest of the site's buildings and dates from the early 12th century. It was built using a drystone technique, though some spots have now been filled in with mortar for safety reasons. Standing 28m tall, the doorway to this ancient edifice is 3.5m above the ground.

Hall of the Vicars Choral

The 15th-century choristers' kitchen and dining hall was the last building to be completed on the Rock. It was restored in the 1980s complete with period furniture, tapestries and paintings beneath a fine carved oak roof and gallery.

St Patrick's Cross

Standing in the courtyard outside the Hall of the Vicars Choral, this cross is a replica of the eroded original, an impressive 12th-century crutched cross depicting a crucifixion scene on one face and animals on the other. The grounds of the complex also include an extensive graveyard with numerous Celtic high crosses marking some of the graves.

Enclosing Walls & Corner Tower

Constructed using lime mortar around the 15th century, and originally incorporating five gates, stone walls enclose the entire site. It's thought the surviving corner tower was used as a watchtower. Amble around to enjoy the views of the surrounding countryside and the Devil's Bit to the north.

Hore Abbey

Looking west from the Rock of Cashel you can see Hore Abbey down in the fields. Founded in the 1270s by a Benedictine order, the hauntingly beautiful abbey now lies in ruins, its nooks and crannies and weather-ravaged gravestones making for a peaceful visit. Watch where you step because the field is used for grazing cattle.

There's no entry fee. You can reach the abbey by walking 10 minutes downhill to the west from the Rock of Cashel or parking next to the abbey on the small access road.

LEGENDS OF THE ROCK

About 30km north of Cashel is Devil's Bit Mountain. Local folklore says that the Rock came to be when the devil came down from the sky and bit off a chunk of the mountain and spat it out towards Cashel, where it landed, forming the hill on which the complex sits. According to mythology, St Patrick came here to convert King Óengus to Christianity.

TOP TIPS

● Access to Cormac's Chapel is by guided tour only. The last tour is at 3.45pm daily. Tickets are limited and can be purchased on-site only.

● Allow an hour and a half to visit, including the Cormac's Chapel tour.

● It's a short but steep walk from the car park up to the entrance.

● Good vantage points to view the Rock are on the road into Cashel from the Dublin Rd roundabout or from the R660 to Holycross.

● The best photo opportunities are from the nearby ruins of Hore Abbey, 1km west.

KINGS OF MUNSTER

The word 'cashel' is an Anglicised version of the Irish word *caiseal*, meaning 'stone-walled circular fort'. In the 5th century, Cashel was chosen as a royal seat by the Eóghanachta dynasty, whose founder Conall Corc and his descendants ruled the ancient province of Munster. For some 400 years it rivalled Tara as a centre of power in Ireland. Óengus (430-489), the first Christian king of Munster, was baptised at Cashel by St Patrick himself. In the 10th century the Eóghanachta lost possession of the Rock to the Dál gCais (O'Brien) dynasty, culminating with Muircheartach O'Brien who was not only king of Munster but HIgh King of all Ireland. In 1101 he presented the Rock of Cashel to the church.

Rossa Pottery (p272)

Continued from p273

A Hotch-Potch of History
Fascinating folk museum

An engaging exhibition of old shopfronts, museum displays and memorabilia, **Cashel Folk Village** *(cashelfolkvillage.ie; adult/child €8/5)* is a charming hotch-potch of thatched cottages and old buildings with exhibits arranged around different themes including the Penal Laws, the Great Famine, the 1916 Easter Rising and the War of Independence. Keep an eye out for a 19th-century Travellers' caravan that once housed a family of 14. There's also a blacksmith's forge and 10,000-year-old antlers from a now-extinct giant Irish elk.

Explore Ireland's Musical Heritage
Cultural centre

Located at the base of the Rock, the **Brú Ború Heritage Centre** offers an absorbing insight into Irish traditional music, dance and song. The main daytime attraction is the **Sounds of History** *(bruboru.ie; adult/child €5/3)* cultural exhibition, where the story of Ireland and its music is told through imaginative audio displays. In July and August the centre stages performances of traditional Irish music and dance on Wednesday and Thursday evenings; book online.

Beyond Cashel

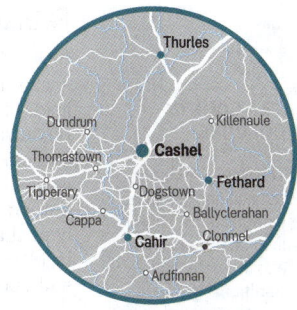

South Tipperary's rolling green pastures, walking trails, lush woodlands, ancient abbeys and castles spread beyond Cashel.

Because it's much less explored than other parts of the country, the area around Cashel is an experience of authentic Ireland where friendly locals welcome you with a smile. The town of Cahir has an imposing castle and an ornate Regency cottage, and has been a filming location for several movies. Don't miss the farmers market on Saturdays, where you can browse some of the county's finest produce. To the north, learn about traditional Irish sports in Thurles, where the GAA (Gaelic Athletic Association) was founded. Some of the most authentic Irish pubs await, and their traditional music sessions are put on more for locals than tourists. Welcome to the heart of Tipperary.

Cahir

TIME FROM CASHEL: **20MIN**

Imposing riverside castle
At the eastern tip of the Galtee Mountains, 15km south of Cashel, Cahir (An Cathair; pronounced 'care') is a compact and attractive town that encircles sublime **Cahir Castle** *(heritageireland.ie; adult/child €5/3)*. The building enjoys a river-island site with massive walls, towers and a keep, mullioned windows, original fireplaces and a dungeon. It's been used as a filming location multiple times, including in Ridley Scott's 2021 film *The Last Duel*.

A cute historic cottage
A 30-minute walk along a riverside path from Cahir Castle car park leads to Cahir's other major attraction, the **Swiss Cottage** *(heritageireland.ie; adult/child €5/3)*. This thatched cottage, surrounded by roses, lavender and honeysuckle, is a lavish example of Regency Picturesque. It was built in 1810 as a retreat for Richard Butler, 12th Baron Caher, and his wife, and was designed by London architect John Nash, creator of the Royal Pavilion at Brighton. The 30-minute (compulsory) guided tours are thoroughly enjoyable.

Places
Cahir p277
Fethard p278
Thurles & Around p278

GETTING AROUND

Thurles is easily reached by train from Cork and Dublin, but to really experience this part of Tipperary, it's best to have your own car. There's a large car park (paying) beside Cahir Castle, and another smaller one (free) across the river from Swiss Cottage.

GAA COUNTY COLOURS

The Gaelic Athletic Association (GAA), established in Thurles in 1844, protects and promotes the traditional Irish sports of hurling and Gaelic football. All 32 counties of Ireland, including the six counties of Northern Ireland, take part in inter-county competitions throughout the year, culminating in the annual All-Ireland Senior Football Championship and the All-Ireland Senior Hurling Championship. You can't travel around Ireland without noticing flags in the various county colours flying from lamp posts, telephone poles, houses and even cars. The flags reflect the colours of the players' kit – Tipperary plays in blue and yellow, Limerick in green and white, Kerry in green and yellow, Armagh in orange and white, and so on.

Fethard

TIME FROM CASHEL: **25MIN**

An undertaker's pub

A classic multifunctional Irish country pub with bucketloads of character, **McCarthy's** proclaims itself as 'publican, restaurant, undertaker'; motto: 'we'll wine you, dine you and bury you'. Closely spaced wooden booths and tables are wedged among a thicket of 19th-century bric-a-brac under a wood-panelled ceiling. In fact, the interior remains largely unchanged since Richard McCarthy opened for business in 1850. There's a shop at the front, a pub at the back and a still-operational undertaker's at the side.

Horse country experience

Housed in Fethard's 17th-century Tholsel (town hall), the **Horse Country Experience** *(fhcexperience.ie; adult/child €10/5)* traces the role of the horse in Irish history and culture, from military steeds and plough horses to horse racing and stud farms. In summer, twice-weekly 2½-hour guided tours go to nearby **Coolmore Stud** *(per person €75)*, the headquarters of the world's largest breeding operation of thoroughbred racehorses.

Thurles & Around

TIME FROM CASHEL: **20MIN**

Birthplace of the GAA

The Gaelic Athletic Association was founded in Thurles in 1844. Here the seven founding members established the 'Gaelic Association for the Cultivation and Preservation of National Pastimes', which later became the GAA. Thanks to this heritage, **Semple Stadium** in Thurles is Ireland's largest sporting arena outside Dublin.

Thurles' tourist office also houses the **Lár na Páirce Museum** *(facebook.com/LarNaPairceMuseum; adult/child €5/3)*, an interpretative centre explaining the history of the GAA and Gaelic games. It has an impressive collection of hurleys (flat ashen hurling sticks), *slíothar* (small leather hurling balls), signed jerseys, trophies and medals. The museum can also arrange tours of Semple Stadium.

A challenging heartlands hike

The **Devil's Bit** is a distinctively shaped hill that lies west of Templemore, 17km north of Thurles. Seen from the south, the summit ridge has a deep notch with vertical sides.

There is a hiking trail to the summit that starts from a car park at the end of a narrow country road (the L3229, signposted

 EATING IN COUNTY TIPPERARY: OUR PICKS

Sadler's: This Fethard restaurant impresses with its cosmopolitan lunch and dinner menu. *8am-5pm Mon-Wed, to 8pm Thu & Sun, to 11pm Sat & Sun* €€

The Cottage: A tour-de-force of traditional cooking, the full Irish breakfast at this Loughmore tearoom will set you up for the day, if not the week. *10am-4pm* €

Lava Rock: Award-winning Cahir restaurant with great coffee and cakes as well as lunches – simple food done well. *9am-4.30pm Wed-Sat, from 10am Sun* €€

Wytchway Inn: (CJ Skehan's) Old country pub 8km southwest of Thurles with a crowd-pleasing menu of pub grub classics. *noon-8pm Thu, to 9pm Fri & Sat, to 7.30pm Sun* €€

DISCOVERING MEDIEVAL FETHARD

An appealingly quaint little village, Fethard (pronounced 'feathered') has one of Ireland's most complete medieval town walls.

START	END	LENGTH
Fethard Horse Country Experience	North Gate	1km; 30min

Begin at the Horse Country Experience (p278), which is housed in the ❶ **Tholsel**, a beautifully restored 17th-century town hall and almshouse; you can get information and advice on exploring the town from the reception desk here. A gate beside the Tholsel leads to the 13th-century ❷ **Church of the Holy Trinity**; at the far side of the churchyard you can walk the parapet of the best-preserved section of the 13th-century ❸ **old town wall**.

Return to the street and turn right and right again down Watergate St, passing partly ruined ❹ **Court Castle**, one of the largest fortified townhouses in Ireland, dating from around 1400.

At the foot of the hill there's a rather grotesque ❺ **sheila-na-gig** (carved female figure with exaggerated genitalia) embedded in the wall to your left.

Turn right along the path between the old town wall and the little River Clashawley; cross the footbridge and continue on the other side of the river to emerge beside the restored 1940s ❻ **Fethard Ballroom**. Turn right and head along Main St, passing ❼ **McCarthy's Bar**; across the street from the pub, bear left along Chapel Lane and left again on Rocklow Rd to reach the ❽ **North Gate**, dating from the 1290s, the only survivor of the five gates that originally pierced the town walls.

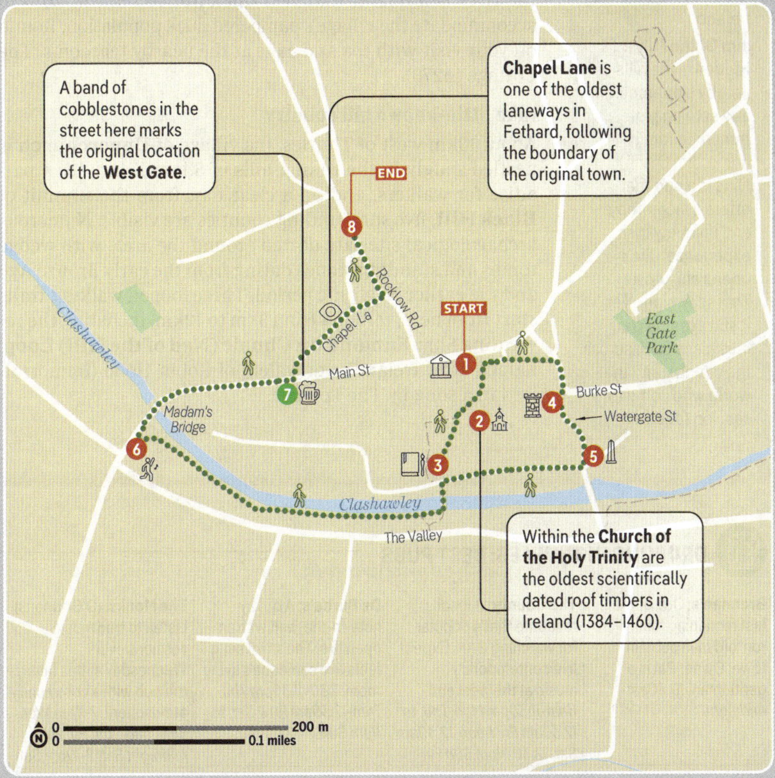

A band of cobblestones in the street here marks the original location of the **West Gate**.

Chapel Lane is one of the oldest laneways in Fethard, following the boundary of the original town.

Within the **Church of the Holy Trinity** are the oldest scientifically dated roof timbers in Ireland (1384–1460).

WHERE TO VISIT IN MID TIPPERARY

Jane Ryan, manager of the Thurles Tourist Office, shares her favourite spots in Mid Tipperary. @thurlestouristoffice

Thurles: If you dropped a pin halfway between Dublin and Cork, you would land in Thurles. Famous as the birthplace of the GAA, the area makes a perfect base for anyone wanting to experience authentic Ireland.

Jim O' the Mills: Hidden in the hills of nearby Upperchurch and serving pints from their family home, Jim O' the Mills is a pub that offers a memorable and uniquely Irish experience. Jim's opens only on a Thursday night, yet it still attracts trad musicians from across the country and the world who come to session together.

Devil's Bit from the R501, 3km west of Templemore). The trail climbs steeply up a rough track to reach a 19th-century stone tower known as Carden's Folly and continues past an altar with a statue of the Virgin Mary – an outdoor Mass is celebrated here each year on Rock Sunday (the nearest Sunday to 25 July, the feast of St James).

From here the trail becomes steep, narrow and muddy before arriving at a band of rock beneath the summit; traverse left along its foot then back up right to reach the top, which is crowned with a huge concrete cross. The views are panoramic. You can return the same way, or follow the waymarked loop trail around the back of the hill (5km total, allow two hours).

Visit a village with olde-worlde atmosphere

The village of **Loughmore** lies just east of the N62, 8km north of Thurles. This quiet, picturesque spot grew up around **Loughmore Castle**, also known as the Purcell Fortress. Although abandoned since 1762, the ruins still stand to full height. The castle is on private land, reached via a gate opposite the Cottage Tearooms. Ask permission at the big house to the left of the gate (or in the tearoom if no one is around).

At the east end of the village, at the bridge over the River Suir, is a pretty picnic area beside **Loughmore Mill**, a huge, five-storey corn and timber mill dating from 1842. Next to the river is a quaint thatched **duck house** built in 2016 to accommodate the village's pampered duck population. Round off your visit with tea and cake at the nearby tearooms, The Cottage (p278).

Hike little-known hill country

About 13km west of Thurles, the village of **Upperchurch** is nestled snugly in the rolling hills of Slieve Felim. It's a paradise for walkers, and on a clear day, from the summit of **Black Hill**, five surrounding counties are visible. Numerous archaeological sites are dotted around the area, with wedge tombs and standing stones dating from the early Bronze Age and the earlier Neolithic period. Three looped walking trails start from here, ranging from 3km to 12km, including the rewarding 8km **Eamonn an Chnoic (Ned of the Hill) Loop**, named after Ireland's equivalent of Robin Hood (immortalised in a song by The Pogues).

 DRINKING IN THURLES: BEST PUBS

Brennan's: One of the last remaining family-run 'old man pubs' in town. Owner Pat is a gentleman. *10.30am-midnight*

The County: A local favourite that's popular for watching GAA. Expect live contemporary music at the weekend. *11am-11.30pm Mon-Thu, to 12.30am Fri, noon-12.30am Sat, 12.30-11pm Sun*

De Búrca's: A quirky hole-in-the-wall with an open fire. The small snug feels like someone's living room. *7.30-11.30pm Thu, 7pm-12.30am Fri & Sat, to 11pm Sun*

The Monks: (O'Gormans) Listen to trad music sessions every Wednesday at this family-run pub with a community atmosphere. *7-11pm Wed, 5pm-midnight Fri, 2pm-midnight Sat, 2-10pm Sun*

The Galtees & the Glen of Aherlow

HILLWALKING | ROAD CYCLING | HISTORIC SITES

The Galtees are Ireland's highest inland mountain range, stretching over 20km east to west and marking a dramatic natural border between counties Limerick and Tipperary. Proudly towering over the surrounding countryside with sheep dotting their slopes, the Galtees offer a range of challenging hillwalking routes with fantastic views – when the weather plays ball.

On the north side of the mountains lies one of Ireland's hidden delights. The Glen of Aherlow is a lush valley floored with a patchwork of fields and hedgerows, slung like a hammock between the Galtees and the wooded ridge of Slievenamuck. Historically, it was an important pass between Limerick and Tipperary. Nowadays, the valley is popular with walkers, offering a variety of low-level loop trails, forest walks and more strenuous hikes along Slievenamuck. If hiking isn't your thing, the glen is also fantastic for cycling and car touring.

GETTING AROUND

A car is your best bet for getting around the wider region, but a bike is ideal for the Glen of Aherlow; you can rent bikes from the Glen of Aherlow campsite, and e-bikes from **BBikes** (bbikes.com) from €30 a day including delivery to and pick-up from your accommodation. The closest you can get by public transport is Bansha – **Local Link Tipperary** (locallinktipperary.ie) bus 855 from Cahir to Tipperary town and Cashel stops here three times a day, excluding Sundays.

The Galtees

PIERRE LECLERC/SHUTTERSTOCK

☑ TOP TIP

As with most mountain areas the weather in the Galtees can change quickly, so check the forecast before you go hiking to make sure you get the best views and don't get caught out by rain or poor visibility on the hill.

THE GALTEE MOUNTAINS & THE GLEN OF AHERLOW

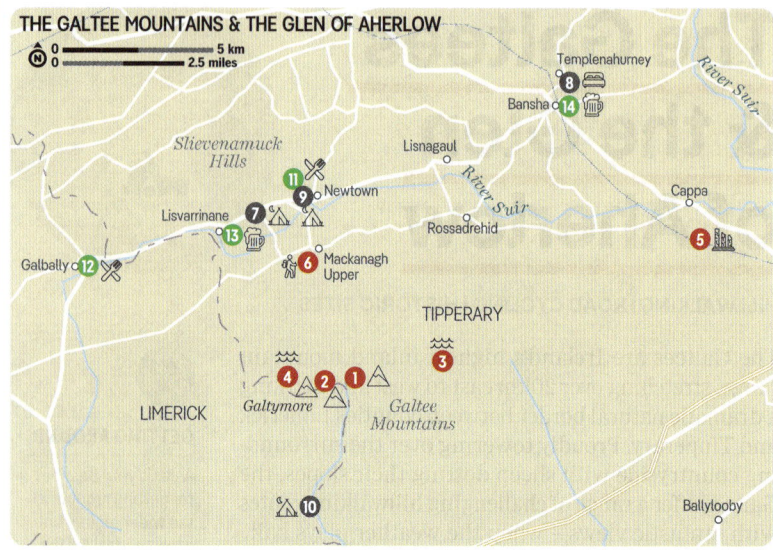

● **SIGHTS**
1 Galtybeg
2 Galtymore
3 Lake Muskry
4 Lough Curra
5 Toureen Peakaun

● **ACTIVITIES**
6 Glencush Boreen Trailhead

● **SLEEPING**
7 Ballinacourty House Caravan & Camping Park
8 Bansha House
9 Glen of Aherlow Caravan & Camping Park
10 King's Yard

● **EATING**
11 Aherlow House Hotel
12 Mulveys Coffee Shop

● **DRINKING & NIGHTLIFE**
13 Moroney's
14 Nellie's Bar

Magical Lake Muskry

Hike to a hidden lough

Lake Muskry is a small but gloriously scenic lough in a glacier-carved hollow high in the Galtees at around 490m, and the destination for one of Aherlow's most popular hikes. From the tiny hamlet of Rossadrehid, on the southern edge of the glen, a narrow road leads uphill to a parking area with an information board. The walk begins here, and it follows a rough but easily followed path with green waymarks (11km round trip; allow three to four hours).

 EATING & DRINKING IN THE GLEN OF AHERLOW

Aherlow House Hotel: The bistro bar at this converted hunting lodge in the hills serves excellent pub grub. *12.30-8.30pm* €€

Mulveys Coffee Shop: The only cafe in the Glen of Aherlow, this Galbally institution is famous for its home-baked cakes and scones. *9am-2.30pm Mon-Sat* €

Moroney's: Historic Lisvarrinane pub has been around for 200 years; many original 18th-century features survive. *7-11pm Mon-Thu, noon-midnight Fri & Sat, 12.30-11pm Sun*

Nellie's Bar: Authentic rural hostelry in Bansha frequented by a loyal band of locals, with hurling on the TV and a fire in the grate. *5-11.30pm Mon-Thu, to 12.30am Fri & Sat, 12.30-11pm Sun*

🚲 CYCLE THE GLEN OF AHERLOW

The network of quiet country roads that crisscross the Glen of Aherlow could have been made for cycling.

START	END	LENGTH
Bansha	Bansha	45km; 3hr

From the little park in the village of Bansha, head west on the R663. The road meanders gently up and down, with the lush valley of the River Aherlow to your right and the wooded ridge of Carrigeenina rising on your right. At the hamlet of ❶ **Newtown**, turn right on the R664 and climb steeply for 1.5km to reach a hairpin bend with a statue of ❷ **Christ the King**, a stunning viewpoint across the verdant valley to the peak of Galtymore. Freewheel back downhill and continue west on the R663 through the village of ❸ **Lisvarrinane** – Moroney's pub has a grocery where you can buy cold drinks (the bar doesn't open till evening).

Next up are the substantial ruins of ❹ **Moor Abbey**, a 15th-century Franciscan friary – nip inside to see the double piscina (a basin for washing communion vessels) – and the village of ❺ **Galbally**, near the halfway mark, where Mulveys cafe provides a welcome coffee stop. Turn left and head south on the R662, then left again at the Ballylanders crossroads (signposted LP1520 Lisvarrinane). This quiet road leads back along the south side of the valley, passing the ❻ **Glencush Boreen Trailhead** (for hiking to Lough Curra and Galtymore), before arriving at the crossroads in ❼ **Rossadrehid**. Turn right here for the Lake Muskry trailhead, or left to return to Bansha.

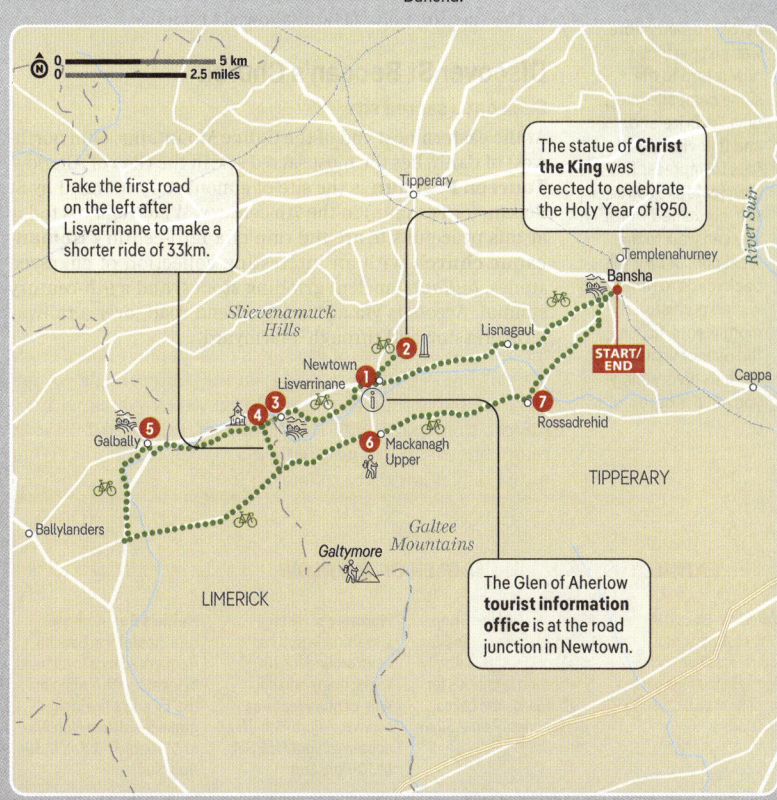

WHY I LOVE THE GLEN OF AHERLOW

Neil Wilson, writer

It's more than 15 years now since I first set eyes on the Glen of Aherlow. I came to climb Galtymore, as I was making my way through Ireland's list of 900m-plus peaks, but wasn't prepared for just how beautiful the glen is. I stayed at a campsite on the north side of the valley, and the view across to Galtymore was just perfect. I now return to the same campsite every time I'm in Ireland, and that view never fails to impress. The glen feels like a little self-contained world; you can walk to the local pub, or bike the back roads to rarely visited prehistoric monuments, fish in the river or wander the hills. Everything you need is here.

On Top of the Galtees
Summiting Galtymore

Standing on the border between counties Tipperary and Limerick, **Galtymore** (918m) is the highest peak in the Galtee Mountains. The easiest way to the top is via a well-worn trail (9km round trip; allow four hours) from **King's Yard** farm on the south side. There is a car park (€3) with toilets, showers and a small tents-only camping site here.

A more scenic and challenging route ascends from the Glen of Aherlow to the north. Start at the **Glencush Boreen Trailhead**, 2km south of Newtown. The walk begins along a forest road before emerging onto the hillside and following a line of marker posts up to a knoll where it joins the **Old Ice Road**, a trail constructed in the 19th century to retrieve blocks of ice from **Lough Curra** in winter to cool the cold stores of the local estates.

Leave the Ice Road and head up the broad grassy ridge to Slievecushnabinnia. Turn left and follow the summit ridge easily to the pointed peak of Galtymore, marked by a white-painted Celtic cross. Take care in poor visibility as there are steep drops on the north side of the summit ridge. You can return via the same route, but keen hillwalkers will continue on the ridge over the summits of **Galtybeg** and Cush before descending to the starting point (14km; allow six hours).

Discover St Beccan's Church
Seek out a sacred site

At the easternmost end of the Galtee Mountains, 6km northwest of Cahir, lies the most sacred site in the Glen of Aherlow. **Toureen Peakaun** is the site of a monastery founded by St Beccan (or Peakaun) in the 7th century. What remains today at this peaceful site are the ruin of a 12th-century **Romanesque church** with an interesting collection of engraved stones, *bullaun* (ancient grinding stones) and a 9th-century sundial. Access is via a short dead-end road, over a railway level crossing and through a farmyard.

Places We Love to Stay

€ Budget €€ Midrange €€€ Top End

Limerick City   MAP p265

Avondoyle B&B € Fantastic-value B&B in the Limerick suburbs, just 10 minutes' drive from the city centre and less than 15 minutes from Adare.

George Hotel €€ This brisk, buzzing and centrally located hotel is stylish and comfortable. It's frequently booked solid, so reserve well in advance.

Absolute Hotel €€ Exposed brick walls, polished limestone bathrooms and contemporary art give this gleaming hotel a smart, modern edge.

Bedford Townhouse €€ You can't get any more central than this smart, stylish and modern hotel just a few minutes' walk from all of Limerick's main sights.

No 1 Pery Square (p266) **€€€** Treat yourself to a night in Georgian Limerick at this elegant hotel, a feast of huge sash windows, high ceilings and capacious bathrooms.

Adare

Dunraven Arms €€ A family-run place built in 1792 with old-fashioned charm, four-poster beds, open fires and a great restaurant.

Adare Country House €€ Relaxed B&B with stylishly decorated rooms a short walk from town. Parking provided.

Adare Manor €€€ This magnificent 19th-century manor house is now a luxury hotel, dripping in antique furniture and class.

Cashel   MAP p273

O'Brien's Cashel Lodge €€ This converted 200-year-old coach house is a friendly and superb-value B&B just 10 minutes' walk from the Rock; there's also a small campground.

Baileys Hotel €€ Clean, contemporary lines give this restored, centrally located Georgian townhouse an elegant ambience.

Copperfield House B&B €€ This spacious suburban villa is just a five-minute walk from the town centre. Delicious breakfasts include home-baked bread.

Cashel Palace Hotel €€€ Beautifully restored Palladian mansion built for an archbishop provides a haven of luxury in the centre of town.

Cahir

Apple Caravan & Camping Park € New arrivals at this peaceful and picturesque site, set amid orchards 6km east of Cahir, are welcomed with a bottle of the farm's own fresh apple juice.

Cahir House Hotel €€ Set in an imposing Georgian building on a prominent corner of the town square, this landmark hotel has elegant rooms, a spa, and helpful and efficient staff.

Annaswood B&B €€ Spacious modern house set in idyllic countryside 5km south of Cahir, with views of the Galtee Mountains from the breakfast room.

Fethard

Cozie B&B €€ An attractive home on the edge of town with bright, modern bedrooms, welcoming owners and a large garden for guests to enjoy.

Clonacody House €€€ Fantastic Georgian guesthouse 4km south of Fethard; popular for weddings and events so be sure to book ahead.

Glen of Aherlow   MAP p282

Glen of Aherlow Caravan & Camping Park € A tidy, well-equipped and well-groomed campsite with helpful owners and a stunning setting.

Ballinacourty House Caravan & Camping Park € Set against the spectacular backdrop of the Galtee Mountains, this tranquil family-friendly site has excellent facilities.

Bansha House €€ Expect hearty breakfasts and good old-fashioned hospitality at this lovely Georgian country house, surrounded by fields full of horses.

Researched by
Neil Wilson

Clare

CAVES, CLIFFS, COAST AND CRAIC

Walk the weird limestone landscapes of the Burren, cruise beneath the world-famous Cliffs of Moher, and immerse yourself in Doolin's lively trad music scene.

County Clare combines spectacular windswept landscapes and vibrant Irish culture. The ocean relentlessly pounds the coast year-round, eroding rock into fantastic formations, sea stacks and sheer precipices, including those at the ends-of-the-earth Loop Head Peninsula and the iconic Cliffs of Moher. These world-famous cliffs attract tens of thousands of visitors from all over the world to County Clare each year.

Stretching down to the shore – and out as far as the Aran Islands, which are linked to the town of Doolin by ferry – is the moonscape-like bare limestone expanse of the Burren. This karst limestone landscape has ancient megalithic tombs and more than 160km of mapped caves. Hikers have a selection of trails to choose from, with options for every fitness level.

Along the coast, the waves are a magnet for surfers, and surf schools set up on many of Clare's beaches in summer. The jagged coast is also a birdwatcher's paradise, and dolphins leap around in the dark blue waters. Stand in awe of towering sea stacks and natural arches to feel the full power of the Atlantic Ocean.

If the land is hard, Clare's soul certainly isn't. Traditional Irish culture and music flourish here, and it's not just a show for tourists. In larger towns and even the tiniest of villages, you'll find pubs with trad music sessions year-round.

THE MAIN AREAS

THE BURREN
Lunar landscape of limestone.
p290

ENNIS
Charming historic town. **p301**

LOOP HEAD PENINSULA
Spectacular scenery and walks.
p307

For places to stay in Clare, see p313

THE GUIDE

CLARE

Left: Lahinch (p297); right: the Burren (p290)

Find Your Way

Ennis is the county's transport hub, with bus and train services to Galway and Limerick cities, where you can connect to the rest of the country. Clare has tens of kilometres of walking trails to explore.

The Burren, p290

This starkly beautiful landscape has plentiful trails, caves and ancient tombs that are best explored on foot.

Ennis, p301

The county town's medieval origins are recalled by its irregular, narrow streets, and the intriguing stone carvings of Ennis Friary.

Loop Head Peninsula, p307

Stay in a former lighthouse-keeper's cottage and soak up the dramatic views at the edge of Ireland.

CAR

You need a car to reach many of the trailheads, spectacular beaches and small villages. With your own wheels, you can cover a fair amount of ground and explore the many unnamed back roads.

BUS

Bus Éireann (buseireann.ie) passes through the region at least once each day, and a summer-only shuttle bus links the main attractions. However, public transport doesn't reach some smaller villages, and some services are reduced on Sundays.

Ennis Friary (p301)

Plan Your Time

Outdoorsy types will love the jaw-dropping views on epic coastal hikes. Come evening, visit a pub for a pint and some of the best trad music in the country.

One Day Only

● Head to the **Cliffs of Moher** (p298) early to beat the crowds. Continue to **Poulnabrone Dolmen** (p296) and stop at **An Feár Gorta** (p293) in Ballyvaughan for lunch. Your next stop is the **Aillwee Cave** (p290) for an afternoon tour, squeezing in a stop at **Hazel Mountain Chocolate** (p294). Drive to **Doolin** (p294) for a toe-tapping evening of trad in the pub.

Five Days to Explore

● From Doolin, dig into the stark beauty of the **Burren** (p290) on one of the many marked **walking trails** (p293). Lunch at the **Burren Perfumery** (p294), then head to **Lahinch** (p297) for sunset pints. The next day, head south to **Kilkee** (p307) and walk along the cliffs. Explore the landscapes and villages on the **Loop Head Peninsula** (p307) by car or e-bike.

SEASONAL HIGHLIGHTS

SPRING
Enjoy spots of post-winter colour in the **Burren** (p290), which bursts with wildflowers, particularly in May.

SUMMER
Clare is busy with visitors, but summer is the ideal time for boat trips and beach time.

AUTUMN
Catch sunsets along the Clare coast, especially from the **Cliffs of Moher** (p298) and the **Loop Head Peninsula** (p307).

WINTER
Winter swells bring the best waves for surfers. Warm up from outdoor explorations by a pub fire.

The Burren

LIMESTONE LANDSCAPES | FAMOUS CAVES | TRADITIONAL MUSIC

GETTING AROUND

It's easiest to explore all the nooks and crannies of the Burren with your own car. Cycling is an excellent way of getting off the beaten track and exploring the minor roads; contact **Burren e-Bike Adventures** *(burrenebike adventures.ie)* in **Kinvara** or **Doolin Rent-a-Bike** *(doolinrentabike.ie)* in Doolin for rentals.

Bus Éireann bus 350 between Galway and Limerick stops at Doolin, Lisdoonvarna and Ballyvaughan. From May to August, the **Burren and Cliffs Explorer** *(cliffsofmoher.ie)* shuttle bus links the Burren National Park visitor centre with Ballyvaughan, Doolin, Aillwee Burren Experience and Poulnabrone Dolmen.

Stretching across northern County Clare, the Burren (from the Irish *boireann*, meaning 'rocky country') is one of Europe's largest areas of karst landscape (ie formed from limestone that has been dissolved and eroded by rainwater), protected in part by the **Burren National Park**. Its striking scenery is dominated by vast areas of naked, pale grey rock interspersed with areas of hazel scrub and vivid green pasture, sprinkled with rare wildflowers that lend splashes of brilliant, if ephemeral, colour.

Atmospheric show caves draped with flowstone penetrate deep beneath the land's surface, and picturesque villages dot the region, including the traditional music hub of **Doolin** on the west coast, charming **Ballyvaughan** in the north, and the matchmaking town of Lisdoonvarna in the south. Narrow, twisting roads crisscross the limestone plateaus; even the main N67 south of Ballyvaughan negotiates a series of severe bends as it climbs up Corkscrew Hill.

Going Underground

Depths of Aillwee Cave

When local farmer Jack McGann followed his rabbit-chasing dog into a small cave entrance in 1940, little did he know he would uncover one of the Burren's top tourist attractions. Jack went back many times to explore the cave by candlelight, crawling on his hands and knees as far as a flowstone-covered waterfall, before sharing his discovery in 1973. Once word was out, the entire cave was mapped by experienced cavers, boulder-choked passages were cleared and an access tunnel blasted, and the cave was opened to the public in 1976.

The 45-minute guided tour of **Aillwee Cave** *(aillweeburren experience.ie; adult/child €27/17)* leads along the passage originally explored by Jack McGann (now cleared of debris), past hibernation pits last used by cave bears 10,000 years ago, some lovely flowstone formations and a collection of stalactites and stalagmites before reaching a huge boulder-strewn

THE BURREN

★ HIGHLIGHTS
1. Aillwee Cave
2. Burren National Park
3. Mount Vernon

● SIGHTS
4. Burren Perfumery & Floral Centre
5. Hazel Mountain Chocolate
6. Martello Tower
7. Mullaghmore
8. Poulnabrone Dolmen
9. Slieve Roe

● ACTIVITIES
10. Doolin Cave

● SLEEPING
11. Atlantic Hotel
12. Atlantic View B&B
13. Burren Glamping
14. Cliffs of Moher Hotel
15. Falls Hotel & Spa
16. Hylands Burren Hotel
17. Nagles Camping & Caravan Park
see 21 O'Connor's Guesthouse
see 18 Wild Burren Cottages

● EATING
18. An Fear Gorta
19. Burren Perfumery Tea Rooms
20. Cafe Linnalla
21. Ivy Cottage
22. Linnane's Lobster Bar
23. Russell's

● DRINKING & NIGHTLIFE
see 23 Fitzpatrick's Bar
24. Gus O'Connor's
see 23 McDermott's
see 23 McGann's

● ENTERTAINMENT
25. Doolin Music House

● SHOPPING
26. Burren Smokehouse
see 22 Russell Gallery

● INFORMATION
27. National Park Information Point

● TRANSPORT
28. Doolin Pier

BURREN BEAR BONES

Hundreds of animal bones were found in Aillwee Cave in 1976 as it was being developed into a tourist site.

More than 20 bones belonging to the cave bear *(Ursus spelaeus)* were identified, and the bear became a symbol of Aillwee. Radiocarbon dating revealed that a cave bear skull found at Aillwee was 10,400 years old, dating back to the Early Mesolithic period. The bear remains indicate that the Burren would have been heavily forested during this period, as bears could not have survived on the Burren landscape of today.

Cave bears became extinct in mainland Europe 24,000 years ago, but appear to have survived in Ireland until the 11th century CE.

☑ TOP TIP

The bare limestone pavement of the Burren is often riven with deep cracks known as grykes, which are often hidden by grass – wear boots with good ankle support and take great care when walking over limestone areas.

Matchmaker Bar, a sit for the Lisdoonvarna Matchmaking Festival

chamber – only cave-divers can penetrate the water-filled sump beyond. The return journey is via a 250m-long tunnel, passing the entrance to a hibernation roost of endangered horseshoe bats. Wear sturdy shoes and bring a jacket, even if it's warm outside – the cave floor can be wet and muddy and the temperature inside is a constant 10°C.

Walk along the Flaggy Shore

The footsteps of poets

The **Flaggy Shore Loop** is a 9km walking and cycling route on quiet back roads that starts and finishes at the harbour village of New Quay on the north coast of the Burren. Set off west from **Linnane's Lobster Bar**, and fork right at the **Russell Gallery**. You will soon pass **Mount Vernon**, an 18th-century country house once owned by Lady Augusta Gregory, a playwright and mentor of WB Yeats. She hosted many famous literary figures here, including Seán O'Casey, JM Synge and George Bernard Shaw; her son Robert was a WWI pilot whose demise in 1918 inspired Yeats' famous poem 'An Irish Airman Foresees His Death'.

The road clings to the coast past slabby outcrops of thin-bedded limestone that give the place its name, immortalised in Seamus Heaney's poem 'Postscript' – 'make the time to drive out west, into County Clare, along the Flaggy Shore…' Further west, you pass **Lough Murree**, which Heaney described as 'lit by the earthed lightning of a flock of swans', before reaching a T-junction; turn right to enjoy an ice cream at **Cafe Linnalla**, then continue west to see the early-19th-century **Martello Tower** at Finavarra Point. Return along the southern side of the loop via Finavarra village (keep left at the junction here).

Finding Love in Lisdoonvarna
Pubs over apps

The little town of Lisdoonvarna was once a centre for *basadóiri* (matchmakers) who, for a fee, would fix up a single person with a spouse. Most of the – mainly male – hopefuls would hit the town in September, feet shuffling, cap in hand, after the hay was in. Today, the tradition is maintained by the month-long **Lisdoonvarna Matchmaking Festival** *(matchmakerireland.com)*, which takes place each September. Billed as Europe's largest singles' festival, drawing in around 60,000 people aged from 18 to 80, there's music and dancing every day from noon until the small hours, with crowds peaking at the weekends. Book accommodation well in advance.

Sssssssmokin'...
Making smoked salmon

Peter Curtin and his Swedish wife Birgitta set up their Lisdoonvarna smokehouse in 1989 to preserve the ancient Irish art of smoking salmon. They use only sustainable, organically farmed Irish salmon, Irish sea salt and natural oak shavings from carpenters' workshops to create both cold- and hot-smoked salmon.

The 45-minute Atlantic Salmon Experience at the **Burren Smokehouse** *(burrensmokehouse.com; adult/child €12.50/7)* begins with a short video presentation, followed by a demonstration of the smoking process and a tasting of the end product, before browsing the interactive displays in the neighbouring visitor centre.

Hike the Burren National Park
Climb Mullaghmore

Burren National Park protects 1500 hectares of limestone landscapes to the north of Corofin. It is centred on the small hills of **Mullaghmore** (191m) and **Slieve Roe**, whose dramatic scenery and rare flora are emblematic of the greater Burren region, which covers some 360 sq km. A red-waymarked trail traverses Mullaghmore from a trailhead at Gortnalecka crossroads in the southwest to the minor road at Cooloorta in the northeast (10km round trip; allow five hours), offering panoramic views across vast areas of exposed limestone, ephemeral lakes and the gently folded rock strata of Slieve Roe, which have created distinctive curved terraces on the hillsides.

BURREN & CLIFFS OF MOHER GEOPARK

The geology that underlies the rugged scenery of the Burren and the Cliffs of Moher is protected as a **UNESCO Geopark** *(burrengeopark.ie)*. During the Carboniferous period 350 million years ago, this whole area lay at the bottom of a warm, shallow sea. The remains of coral and shells fell to the sea bed, then coastal river deltas dumped sand, silt and mud on top. Time and pressure turned the sediments to stone, with fossil-rich limestone below and stratified shale and sandstone above, while continental collisions tilted and folded the rock layers. As you travel south, you move from the limestone landscapes of the Burren into the overlying shale and siltstones exposed in the Cliffs of Moher.

EATING IN THE BURREN: OUR PICKS

Ivy Cottage: Thatched cottage and courtyard in Doolin, serving classic dishes such as seafood chowder and bacon with cabbage. *12.30-4pm & 5.30-8pm* €€€

Russell's: Doolin coffee shop by day turns into a seafood restaurant in the evening, both sit-in and takeaway. Nice outdoor seating round the back. *8am-9pm* €€

Burren Perfumery Tea Rooms: Cottage tearooms with freshly baked bread, cakes, scones and pies along with salads from the kitchen gardens. *10.30am-5pm* €€

An Feár Gorta: A Burren institution, this Ballyvaughan cafe, housed in an 18th-century garden cottage, serves the best cakes in the county. *11am-5pm Thu-Mon* €€

BURREN BOTANY

No matter when you visit the Burren, wildflowers are in bloom. The region supports an incredibly diverse range of flora, with more than 70% of Ireland's 900 native species, as well as many of the country's native orchids. A bizarre mix of Arctic, alpine, subtropical and Mediterranean plants grow side by side, made possible by the varied microclimates created by the limestone landscapes, from rocky hilltops to moist, sheltered grykes (deep cracks in the limestone pavement). The characteristic natural vegetation of the Burren is hazel scrub, which produces a golden haze of catkins in spring, while more exposed areas are dotted with the blue of gentian and the hot purple-pink of bloody cranesbill.

A free shuttle bus runs from the **National Park Information Point** in Corofin to the trailhead at Gortnalecka crossroads daily (every 30 minutes between 9.30am and 4.30pm, May to August). If you have your own transport, the shortest route to the summit is from Cooloorta (limited parking; 5.5km round trip; allow two hours).

Scents of the Burren
Master perfumiers at work

The road to the **Burren Perfumery** *(burrenperfumery. com; free)* leads deep into the heart of the Burren, a narrow ribbon of tarmac unrolling amid a patchwork of pale grey limestone and green hazel scrub bejewelled with the blooms of bloody cranesbill, blue gentian and a rainbow of orchids. Established in 1972 by visionary poet and ex-priest Brian Mooney, and taken over by French-trained perfumer Sadie Chowen in 2001, the business was inspired by the subtle scents of the local wildflowers. It's the very definition of a cottage industry, set in a cluster of stone cottages surrounded by gorgeous gardens.

The shop and gardens are open daily year-round (tearooms closed November to March) but the perfume and blending rooms operate on weekdays only. Here you can see (and smell!) the various scents, soaps, candles and cosmetics being crafted and bottled by hand before browsing the shop, wandering through the gardens or enjoying lunch in the tearooms (p293). And don't miss the 10-minute audiovisual presentation that details the area's diverse flora – a visual feast of luscious landscape photography created by Sadie's husband Ralph Doyle.

Sweet Treats
Indulge in artisan chocolate

Set on the northern edge of the Burren, halfway between Ballyvaughan and Kinvarra, **Hazel Mountain Chocolate** *(hazelmountainchocolate.com)* is an artisan chocolate factory housed in a red-roofed cottage on a quiet back road. From Tuesday to Sunday you can watch chocolate bars, chocolate-coated marshmallows and Irish whiskey truffles being made in small batches using sustainable cacao beans, raw sugar and milk from local dairy farms; many of the flavours are also sourced locally, including Irish sea salt, elderberries, honey, juniper and wildflower petals.

Toe-Tapping in Doolin
Ireland's best trad-music scene

Doolin, famous as the heartland of Irish traditional music, is barely a village at all, but rather a scatter of houses strung out along a mile of minor road. Among them, its four pubs host trad music sessions 365 days of the year, peaking in mid-June with the **Doolin FolkFest** *(doolinarts.ie)* when all the local accommodation gets booked out.

There is **Fitzpatrick's Bar** *(Fitz's Pub; hoteldoolin.ie)* in the Hotel Doolin at the central crossroads; 10 minutes' walk to the

Gus O'Connor's

southwest in the direction of Doolin Pier is **Gus O'Connor's** (*gusoconnorsdoolin.com*), amid the row of colourful cottages known as Fisherstreet. The same distance to the northeast, either side of the bridge over the River Aille, are **McGann's** (*mcgannsdoolin.com*) and **McDermott's** (*mcdermott-s-pub.com*). Of the four, O'Connor's is the most 'touristy' while McDermott's is most favoured by the locals, but in all of them the craic is mighty and the conversation, like the stout, is always flowing.

To find out who's playing where, check the pub websites and Facebook pages, or just ask at any bar. Local names to look out for include **Blackie O'Connell**, one of the best uilleann pipe (Irish bagpipe) musicians in the country, fiddler **Eogan Neff**, bouzouki player **Vincent Fogarty** and concertina virtuoso **Aoíbheann Murphy**.

Treat Yourself to a Trad Experience

Irish music at home

If you're looking for a more intimate music experience than a night in one of Doolin's pubs, consider booking a session at **Doolin Music House** (*doolinmusichouse.com; per person €20*). On Mondays, Tuesdays and Fridays at 7pm, local musician Christy Barry welcomes guests into his home for a 90-minute session of Irish music along with drinks, snacks and craic. Book in advance – audiences are limited to 12–25 people.

Slip into a Seaweed Bath

Outdoor tub with views

Just to the north of Doolin Pier, you will see a row of large whiskey barrels perched on a stone terrace above the sea. Filled with heated seawater and fronds of locally harvested kelp, these **seaweed baths** (*wildatlanticseaweedbaths.com;*

BEST PHOTO SPOTS IN THE BURREN

Photographer and tour guide **Sean Nee** shares his favourite locations in the Burren for photography.

Black Head: This area of limestone slabs and hand-stacked stone walls stretches down to the coast of Galway Bay. The rock formations and windswept plants are striking in black and white.

Poulnabrone Dolmen: This ancient portal tomb is a must-visit. With low light pollution, it's a great place to practise long exposures.

Corcomroe Abbey: This 13th-century abbey is hauntingly beautiful, and it has some of the finest decorative stone carvings of any Irish monument. Climb the hill behind the abbey in spring to take macro photos of the wild orchids and gentians.

KARST SCENERY

Karst, named after the Karst Plateau in Slovenia where it was first described, defines a type of scenery where limestone bedrock has been dissolved by rainwater to create a range of distinctive landscape features including caves, sinkholes and dry valleys. The Burren is one of the largest karst areas in Europe. The karst features include **limestone pavement** (flat areas of exposed limestone where natural rainwater erosion has created blocks – known as 'clints' – separated by deep cracks – known as 'grykes'); **doline** (also known as a sinkhole – a depression in the land surface caused by the collapse of an underground cavern); and **turlough** (an intermittent lake that fills with water during wet weather, then drains away via underground passages).

per person €60) allow you to slip into a tub of warm water and relax while enjoying a view of the Aran Islands. You can liven up the hour-long experience by taking the occasional cold plunge, or just ask for a top-up with more hot water. It's available Wednesday to Sunday from June to August (more limited hours September and October) and there's also a small **sauna** *(per person €20)*; book online.

Descend into Darkness
Longest stalactite in Europe

About 4km north of Doolin village lies the entrance to **Doolin Cave** *(doolincave.ie; adult/child €18.50/8.50)*, the Burren's other underground attraction (along with Aillwee Cave). The 50-minute guided tour descends a 24m-deep vertical shaft via 125 metal steps before following a natural tunnel to a pitch-black chamber where dramatic lighting reveals the main attraction – the 7.3m-long Great Stalactite, looking weirdly like a giant squid dangling from the roof. After the tour, you can visit the muddy hole in the hillside that was the original entrance used by the Yorkshire potholers who discovered the cave in 1952.

Potter Caireann Browne uses glacial clay hand-dug from deep within the cave to create a unique range of ceramics that are on sale in the cave visitor centre's shop.

Prehistory at Poulnabrone
Iconic archaeological monument

Standing amid a patchwork of lush grass and limestone pavement 9km south of Ballyvaughan, **Poulnabrone Dolmen** *(free)* is one of Ireland's most photographed ancient monuments. Built more than 5000 years ago, this otherworldly portal tomb (a large slab perched on stone uprights) was in continuous use for more than 600 years. There's a car park nearby, and guides are on hand to explain the site to you.

TO THE ARAN ISLANDS

From **Doolin Pier** (p299), ferries run to the **Aran Islands** (p348). You'll reach **Inisheer** in 15 minutes, **Inishmaan** in 25 minutes and **Inishmore** in 35 minutes. Return via the Cliffs of Moher to take in the views on your way back to the mainland.

Beyond the Burren

The majesty of the Cliffs of Moher gives way to the gentle beaches of Lahinch and the waterfalls of Ennistimon.

To the south of the Burren, the limestone bedrock dips beneath the overlying shales and siltstones that are exposed in the dramatic Cliffs of Moher, one of Ireland's top sights. Nearby are the attractive villages of **Ennistimon** and **Miltown Malbay**, where trad music is on tap and creamy pints are waiting to be downed.

South of the cliffs the land flattens, with vistas that sweep across pastures and dunes to the horizon. Some of Ireland's finest surf rolls into shore near the low-key beach towns of Liscannor and Lahinch, where many visitors spend their days chilling out. Beautiful stretches of sand, stunning coastal scenery and amazing food are all on offer.

Lahinch

TIME FROM BALLYVAUGHAN: **40MIN**

Golf Lahinch's famous greens

Lahinch Golf Club *(lahinchgolf.com)* dates from the 19th century and remains one of the country's finest – it calls itself the St Andrews of Ireland. First marked out through the dunes

Continues on p300

Lahinch

Places
Lahinch p297
Cliffs of Moher p298

GETTING AROUND

From 1 May to 31 August, the **Burren and Cliffs Explorer** *(cliffsofmoher.ie)* shuttle bus links Liscannor, Lahinch and Milton Malbay to the Cliffs of Moher visitor centre. Bus Éireann bus 350 between Galway and Limerick stops at the cliffs, and there are several operators offering day trips to the cliffs from as far away as Galway city and Dublin. The back roads between Miltown Malbay, Ennistimon and the Cliffs of Moher are ideal for exploring by bike.

TOP EXPERIENCE

Cliffs of Moher

Stars of a million tourist brochures, the Cliffs of Moher are the most popular sight in Ireland outside of Dublin – at peak times the site can pull in more than 10,000 visitors per day. The views are certainly spectacular – the vertical cliffs rise to a height of 203m in a series of receding headlands – but the crowds can be overwhelming.

DON'T MISS

Cliffs of Moher Visitor Centre

O'Brien's Tower

Birdwatching

Coastal walk

Boat tours

Visitor Centre

Covered in turf and cut into the hillside, the state-of-the-art **Cliffs of Moher Visitor Centre** has engaging exhibitions that span two floors and cover the fauna, flora, geology and climate of the cliffs. Hear stories from the guides about the formation of the cliffs, the traditions of busking and local characters. At the back of the circular exhibition area is the 'Ledge Experience', a virtual-reality film that takes you flying over the cliffs and diving into the ocean below before returning to the clifftop for a bird's-eye view.

PRACTICALITIES
- cliffsofmoher.ie • parking €15 at gate, €8 booked online • cyclists and pedestrians free • 8am-9pm May-Aug, shorter hours Sep-Apr

O'Brien's Tower

A 10-minute walk leads from the visitor centre to O'Brien's Tower at the highest point of the cliffs. It was built by the local landowner in 1835 as an observation point for visitors – you can clatter up the spiral iron staircase to the rooftop viewing platform for the best photo op. On a clear day, you can see the Aran Islands just off the coast, and in the distance, you can often spot the Twelve Pins in Connemara on the far side of Galway Bay.

Spotting Wildlife

The Cliffs of Moher are one of the most important seabird-nesting sites in Ireland and a huge draw for birdwatchers. More than 35 species of birds call the cliffs home, including razorbills, fulmars, kittiwakes, guillemots, choughs and peregrine falcons. The largest colony of puffins in mainland Ireland is on Goat Island, the long, narrow, grass-topped promontory below O'Brien's Tower. Early May to late August is the best time to see nesting birds here.

Cliffs of Moher Coastal Walk

An 11km hiking trail (part of the Burren Way) runs along the top of the Cliffs of Moher, linking Liscannor in the south to Doolin in the north via the visitor centre. However, erosion of the cliff edge has created a serious safety hazard – two people died after falling from the clifftop in separate incidents in 2024 – and the trail is currently closed except for a 2km section either side of the visitor centre where a wall separates walkers from the cliff edge.

Although you can follow the trail for 5km south from Doolin to a point on the road 1km north of the visitor centre, there is currently no pedestrian access all the way to the centre. At the south end, you can walk five minutes to Hag's Head from a privately run **car park** (*€5 per car*) for a view of the cliffs, but no further. There are plans to rebuild the path further inland with new viewing platforms, but as yet there is no timescale for reopening.

Cliffs of Moher Cruises

A great alternative to battling the crowds on the clifftop is to experience the cliffs from the sea. Boat trips with **Doolin Ferry** (*doolinferry.com*) depart from **Doolin Pier** up to four times daily and last 45 minutes – the last trip of the day is the best for photography. Boats get up close to the rocks, and you can peer into the sea cave used as a location in the movie *Harry Potter and the Half-Blood Prince*.

BUSKING AT THE CLIFFS

Dennis 'Dinny' McMahon became the Cliffs of Moher's first (unofficial) tourist guide in the 1950s, spinning tall tales, selling souvenirs and playing the tin whistle for visitors in exchange for tips. He began the tradition of busking at the cliffs, a tradition that continues today with up to a dozen busking pitches along the clifftop occupied by itinerant musicians.

TOP TIPS

- If you arrive on foot, bike or public transport, admission to the cliffs and visitor centre is free.

- Visitor numbers peak between 11am and 4pm; visit early or late to avoid the worst of the crowds.

- The classic photo op at the cliffs, with serried headlands receding in the distance, is the view south from O'Brien's Tower.

- The best time for photography is towards sunset, when the west-facing cliffs are bathed in warm, orange light.

- Late April to early July is the best time to see puffins at the Cliffs of Moher; bring binoculars for a closer look.

Aileen's

BIG-WAVE SURFING AT AILEEN'S

Discovered in 2004 by surf photographer Mickey Smith and a group of local bodyboarders, and first ridden by Irish surfing champion John McCarthy in October 2005, Aileen's is one of the best-known big-wave surfing spots in the world. This intimidating and exposed reef break lies beneath the Cliffs of Moher, just north of the visitor centre, accessed via a scary 30-minute hike down a goat track. In the right conditions this monster wave can reach heights of more than 15m, attracting some of the most notable names in big-wave surfing. If you're visiting when a big swell hits, you can watch the action unfold from the top of the cliffs, which form a natural amphitheatre.

Continued from p297

in 1892 by British Army officers of the Black Watch Regiment, Lahinch's renowned par-72 **Old Course** *(green fees €375)* was designed by Old Tom Morris in 1894 and reworked by Alister MacKenzie in the 1920s and again by Martin Hawtree in 1999. The flatter par-70 **Castle Course** *(green fees €60)* overlooks ruined Dough Castle.

Goats have roamed the fairways since the early 20th century, when their ancestors belonged to a local caddie. They act as a barometer of sorts: when they're out in the dunes, conditions are favourable, but if you see them around the clubhouse, adverse weather is likely on its way.

Clare's surfing scene

Like swells after a storm, Clare's surfing scene keeps getting bigger and better. On weekends in Lahinch, the exposed beach break, with both left-hand and right-hand waves, attracts hundreds of surfers. Conditions are excellent for much of the year, with the bay's cliffs funnelling regular and reliable sets. Beginners will find the northern end gentler. Watch out for rocks and rips. Surf schools and stores, such as **Ben's Surf Clinic** and **Green Room**, cluster near the seafront, offering lessons and board rental.

 DRINKING BEYOND THE BURREN: OUR PICKS

Vaughan's Anchor Inn: Liscannor pub noted for its gourmet seafood menu. Settle in by a peat fire, or take the air at a picnic table. *noon-11pm*

Hillery's: Opened in 1891, Miltown Malbay's oldest pub has stained-glass windows and framed photos on the walls. Live trad sessions every weekend. *3pm-12.30am Mon-Sat, to midnight Sun*

Friel's Pub: This old-style charmer in Milton Malbay has an open fire and walls crammed with photos and books, plus regular trad sessions. *4-11.30pm Mon-Thu, to 12.30am Fri & Sat, 3-11pm Sun*

Byrne's: Enjoy a pint on the deck out back, overlooking the Ennistymon Cascades, or check out the seafood specials on the menu. *noon-11pm Mon-Sat*

Ennis

MEDIEVAL HISTORY | ATMOSPHERIC STREETS | TRAD MUSIC

County Clare's charming commercial hub Ennis (from the Gaelic *inis*, meaning 'water meadow') lies on the banks of the River Fergus, which flows east and then south into the Shannon Estuary. The town's medieval origins are recalled by its irregular, narrow streets, but the most important surviving historical site is Ennis Friary with its magnificent stone carvings, founded in the 13th century by the O'Briens, kings of Thomond. The friary became a major centre of religious learning, and by 1375 had more than 350 friars and 600 students. This set the scene for Ennis to become the county's administrative centre and a bustling market town.

Today formal sights are few, but the town centre, with its narrow, pedestrian-friendly streets, is enjoyable to wander. Ennis is also well known for its low-key traditional music scene, less crowded and less 'touristy' than the more famous venues in Doolin.

Marvel at Medieval Masons' Art

Historic friary with beautiful stone carvings

Founded by the Franciscans in the 13th century, **Ennis Friary** *(heritageireland.ie; adult/child €5/3)* is the burial place of the kings of Thomond and the reason Ennis town exists. It has survived impressively intact and is an atmospheric place to explore.

The medieval kingdom of Thomond (which covered what is now counties Clare and Limerick) was ruled by the O'Brien dynasty – King Turlough O'Brien oversaw the completion of the church in 1282 and was the first to be buried here; the centrepiece of the friary is the reconstructed **Royal or McMahon tomb** of 1470, decorated with exquisitely detailed limestone carvings depicting scenes from the Passion.

The most impressive of these shows the risen Christ stepping out of his tomb, surrounded by sleeping soldiers and flanked by angels with censers and a banner marked with a swastika (used as an early Christian symbol long before it was

GETTING AROUND

The narrow streets of Ennis town centre are best navigated on foot – it only takes 15 minutes to get from one end to the other. If you're arriving by car, it's best to leave it in one of the car parks just outside the town centre – the GAA Cloister car park is free (convenient for Ennis Friary), while the Friars Walk car park near the tourist office is pay-and-display.

☑ TOP TIP

Ennis' tourist office provides a handy map of the town, complete with a heritage trail to follow. While you're there, ask about any trad music gigs taking place in town.

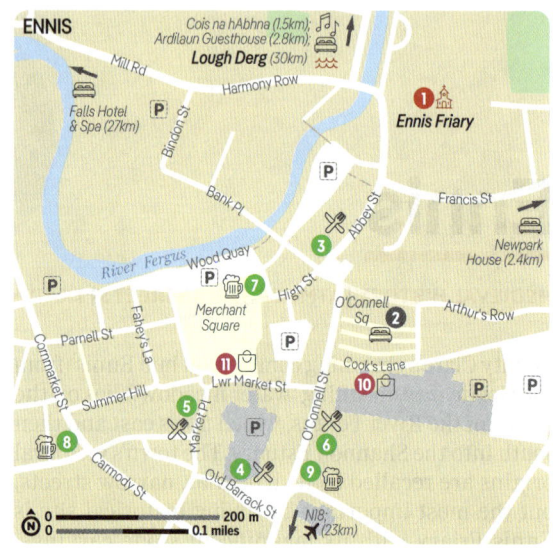

HIGHLIGHTS
1 Ennis Friary

SLEEPING
see 9 Old Ground Hotel
2 Temple Gate Hotel

EATING
3 Cafe Aroma
4 Ennis Gourmet Store
5 Ryan's Traditional Fish & Chips
6 Town Hall Bistro

DRINKING & NIGHTLIFE
7 Considine's
8 Kelly's
9 Poet's Corner Bar

SHOPPING
10 Custy's Music Shop
11 Scéal Eile Books

appropriated by the Nazis). There are other carvings to look for throughout the friary buildings, including a small **Ecce Homo** (a figure of Christ bound at the wrists) that is rich in symbolism, and a figure of **St Francis** displaying his stigmata (wounds on his right hand and his chest). Don't forget to take a stroll around the cloister and the peaceful graveyard.

Trad Tunes
Discover Clare's capital music scene

As the capital of a renowned music county, Ennis is not short of pubs hosting trad sessions – favourites include **Poet's Corner** in the Old Ground Hotel, **Kelly's** on Carmody St and **Considine's** on Parnell St. Custy's Music Shop is a great place to find out about live gigs; the tourist office also collates weekly listings.

Cois na hAbhna (*coisnahabhna.ie*), 1.5km north of the town centre along the N18, is a focal point for traditional music and culture, hosting regular concerts and *céilidh* dances; the Teach Cheoil bar here holds lively weekly music and singing sessions.

Annual events include the lively eight-day **Fleadh Nua** (*fleadhnua.com*) traditional music festival in May, and

 EATING IN ENNIS: OUR PICKS

| **Ennis Gourmet Store**: Deli-cafe serving simple but delicious dishes that change daily. *11am-9.30pm Mon-Sat* € | **Town Hall Bistro**: Local ingredients take centre stage at this smart bistro attached to the neighbouring Old Ground Hotel. *10am-4pm & 6-9.45pm* €€ | **Cafe Aroma**: Popular spot always bustling with locals grabbing a freshly made sandwich or hot lunch. *8.30am-6pm Mon-Sat, from 9am Sun* € | **Ryan's Traditional Fish & Chips**: The town's top takeaway spot, with calamari and scampi joining cod and haddock on the menu. *3-9pm Wed-Sun, to 10pm Sat* € |

Trad music, Ennis

November's five-day **Ennis Trad Festival** *(ennistradfest.com)*, when venues across town keep the tunes flowing.

Seek Out a Souvenir
Browse Ennis' independent shops

Browsing Ennis' newly renovated and pedestrianised town centre, watched over by a towering monument to Daniel O'Connell, is a real pleasure. The best shopping in the county includes a range of independent shops. Two of the best are **Custy's Music Shop** *(custysmusic.com)*, with a terrific stock of Irish music, instruments and general info about the scene; and **Scéal Eile Books** *(scealeilebooks.ie)*, a delight to explore, which overflows with new and secondhand literature including rare titles across all genres. Get chatting to the staff and you'll be there all day!

THE WEST CLARE RAILWAY

Running from Ennis to Kilrush and Kilkee, the West Clare Railway was in operation from 1892 until 1961. The narrow-gauge line was notorious for its poor timekeeping and was parodied in the 1902 song 'Are Ye Right There Michael' by popular entertainer Percy French, after a late train caused him to miss a paying gig. Having taken his revenge via song, French was sued for libel, but was late for his court appearance. When the judge asked for an explanation, French replied: 'I took the West Clare Railway, your honour,' and the case was immediately thrown out. The song can still occasionally be heard in County Clare pubs.

Beyond Ennis

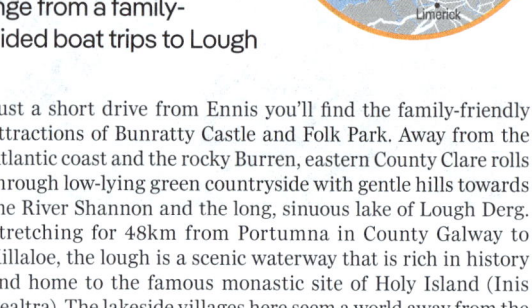

East Clare delights range from a family-friendly folk park to guided boat trips to Lough Derg's Holy Island.

Places

Dysert O'Dea p304
Bunratty p304
Mountshannon p305

Just a short drive from Ennis you'll find the family-friendly attractions of Bunratty Castle and Folk Park. Away from the Atlantic coast and the rocky Burren, eastern County Clare rolls through low-lying green countryside with gentle hills towards the River Shannon and the long, sinuous lake of Lough Derg. Stretching for 48km from Portumna in County Galway to Killaloe, the lough is a scenic waterway that is rich in history and home to the famous monastic site of Holy Island (Inis Cealtra). The lakeside villages here seem a world away from the rugged, evocative west of Clare, set in a picturesque landscape of water, woods and panoramic views.

GETTING AROUND

There are frequent bus services between Ennis and Limerick that stop at Bunratty, and up to four buses a day from Limerick to Killaloe and Ballina. But for exploring Dysert O'Dea and Lough Derg, you will need your own transport.

Dysert O'Dea

TIME FROM ENNIS: **15MIN**

A meadow full of medieval ruins

You can feel the past encroaching as you navigate the narrow, grassy tracks to **Dysert O'Dea Church**, where St Tola founded a monastery in the 8th century. Most of what remains of this fascinating site dates from the 12th century, including the church, round tower and high cross. The church has a remarkable **Romanesque doorway** decorated with intricate carvings of chevrons and Celtic knots, while the arch above is lined with 19 carved heads, both human and animal. Beside the church is the 12m stump of a ruined **round tower**.

The **White Cross of St Tola**, standing in a field 100m east of the church (check for bulls before entering!), depicts the crucified Christ above a bishop (possibly St Tola himself) carved in deep relief on the east face, and Celtic interlacing on the west. On the south side of the cross's base is a carving of Daniel in the lion's den above a Victorian inscription.

There's a car park beside 15th-century **Dysert O'Dea Castle** *(dysertcastle.ie; adult/child €6/4)*, 300m north of the church, which houses a museum; from here a 5km archaeology trail takes in the church and some two dozen ancient monuments, from ringforts and high crosses to a holy well and a graveyard.

Bunratty

TIME FROM ENNIS: **20MIN**

Family fun at castle and village

Dating from 1425, hulking **Bunratty Castle** *(bunrattycastle.ie; adult/child €18/12.60)* is the latest of several fortresses to occupy this strategic location beside a bridge over the River Ratty.

Fully restored in 1954 and loaded with 14th- to 17th-century furniture, paintings, wall tapestries and antlers, the castle is home to a dungeon, a main hall and the magnificent and colossal Great Hall.

Admission includes entry to **Bunratty Folk Park**, a reconstructed traditional Irish village with smoke coiling from thatched-cottage chimneys, a forge complete with working blacksmith, weavers, post office, grocery-pub, small cafe and more. In peak season, guides in period garb explain the more family-friendly and rose-tinted aspects of the late 19th century. Medieval banquets in the castle and traditional Irish evenings in the folk park's corn barn are other crowd pleasers.

Mountshannon

TIME FROM ENNIS: 45MIN

Discover the 'Island of Burials'

Opened in 2025, the **Inis Cealtra Visitor Experience** *(inis cealtra.ie)* chronicles the history and culture of Holy Island (also known as Inis Cealtra, 'Island of Burials' in Gaelic) and the Lough Derg region through colourful displays, videos and audio booths. It's right beside Mountshannon Harbour, and it's the place to check in for boat trips to the island.

Boat trip to an island monastery

Lying 2km offshore from Mountshannon, **Holy Island** (Inis Cealtra) is the site of a monastic settlement thought to have been founded by St Cáimín in the 7th century. The island has a round tower over 27m tall, along with the ruins of several churches, a hermit's cell and some early Christian gravestones dating from the 8th to 12th centuries. Irish novelist **Edna O'Brien** (1930–2024) is buried in the island's graveyard.

Visits to the island in the company of a **local guide** *(adult/child €20/10)* depart from Mountshannon Harbour four times daily in summer and last about 90 minutes, including a 20-minute boat trip each way; book tickets online.

Make your own chocolate bar

At the heady open-plan factory of **Wilde Irish Chocolates** *(wildeirishchocolates.com)* in Tuamgraney you can watch chocolates being made and packed (free), or book a hands-on, make-your-own-chocolate-bar experience (per person €12).

EDNA O'BRIEN

A farmer's daughter from County Clare, Edna O'Brien (1930–2024) rebelled against her strict Catholic upbringing and moved to London, where she became a literary phenomenon.

Her first novel, *The Country Girls* (1960), created a scandal in Ireland through its frank depiction of female sexuality. At a time when Irish life and literature were dominated by men, O'Brien's writing exposed a patriarchal society in thrall to a Catholic Church that was cruel and oppressive to women. Her character Cait in *Girls in Their Married Bliss* (1964) famously said: 'The vote, I thought, means nothing to women, we should be armed.'

O'Brien was born in Tuamgraney, where a memorial plaque marks the gateway to her childhood home, and is buried in her mother's family grave on Holy Island in Lough Derg.

EATING BEYOND ENNIS: OUR PICKS

Derg Inn: Stylish modern bar in Terryglass; everything from breakfast boxty to falafel burger to pulled pork bao buns. *10am-11pm* €€

Wooden Spoon: Bustling cafe-bakery near the bridge in Ballina, serving fresh salads, sandwiches, cakes and pastries. Plenty of vegetarian options. *9am-4pm* €

Nuala's Bar & Restaurant: Top spot in Tuamgraney for breakfast, lunch or dinner, from full Irish fry-up to Sunday roast. *9.30am-10pm* €€

Durty Nelly's: Dating from 1620, this cottage pub beside Bunratty Castle is a warren of snugs, timber beams and peat fires. *12.30-11.30pm* €€

EXPLORING LOUGH DERG

Discover lovely Lough Derg on a circuit that leads you through three counties – Clare, Galway and Tipperary.

START	END	LENGTH
Killaloe	Ballina	118km; 2½hr driving

If you plan to visit Holy Island during the drive, book a boat trip departing at noon and leave Killaloe by 9.30am. Head north from Killaloe on the R463 through rolling wooded countryside with views over the lough. Pause at Tuamgraney to visit ❶ **Wilde Irish Chocolates** (p305) and pay homage to Edna O'Brien, who was born here. Continue east on the R352 to Mountshannon to visit the ❷ **Inis Cealtra Visitor Experience** (p305) before joining a boat trip to ❸ **Holy Island**.

There's little to see on the next 30km until you arrive at Portumna in County Galway, where ❹ **Portumna Castle and Gardens** is worth a stop; the marina, just on the other side of the castle, has good views of the lough. Cross the Shannon at Portumna Bridge to enter County Tipperary and turn right on the R493. Stop for refreshments at the ❺ **Derg Inn** in Terryglass before continuing south along the lough's eastern shore.

Stretch your legs at the little beach in the pretty lakeside village of ❻ **Dromineer**, then head west on the R494 through Newtown and Portroe. Stop at ❼ **the Lookout**, a large parking area on the right of the road 3.5km west of Portroe; there's a fantastic view across the lough to Holy Island and Mountshannon. Another 9km on the R494 leads to Ballina, just across the bridge from your starting point.

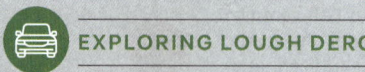

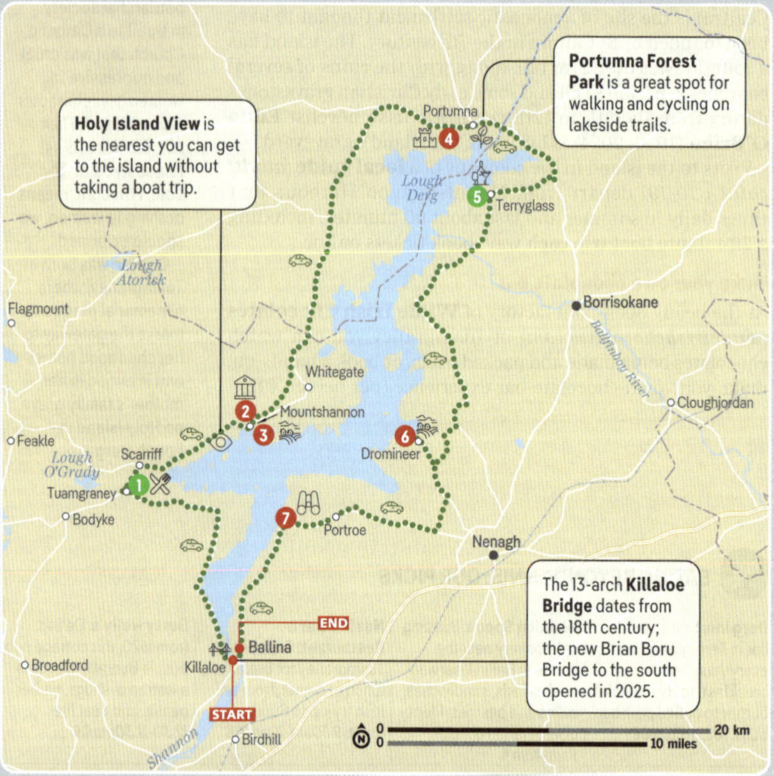

Portumna Forest Park is a great spot for walking and cycling on lakeside trails.

Holy Island View is the nearest you can get to the island without taking a boat trip.

The 13-arch **Killaloe Bridge** dates from the 18th century; the new Brian Boru Bridge to the south opened in 2025.

Loop Head Peninsula

CLIFFTOP WALKS | WILD SWIMMING | BACK-ROAD CYCLING

A sliver of land between the Shannon Estuary and the pounding Atlantic, the windswept Loop Head Peninsula has an ends-of-the-earth feel. As you approach along the R487, the sea begins to appear on both flanks as the land tapers to a narrow point. On a clear day, the lighthouse-capped headland at Loop Head (Ceann Léime), Clare's westernmost point, has staggering views north and south to the hills of Galway and Kerry.

The peninsula's lively main town, Kilkee (Cill Chaoi), sits on a sweeping semicircular bay with high cliffs at the northern end and tidal rocks to the south, its broad golden beach thronged with holidaymakers in the warmer months. It's a perfect base for swimming, hiking and cycling, with natural rock pools, a scenic cliff walk to the south, and quiet back roads leading to Loop Head itself, where the cliffs form a breeding ground for seabird colonies.

Do the Cliff Walk

Kilkee's sea cliff views

West of the bay, the **Kilkee Cliff Walk** offers magnificent views of the cliffs, sea stacks and caves, battered by the full force of the Atlantic Ocean below. Begin at the Diamond Rocks Cafe (p308; named for the sparkling white quartz veins in the rocks nearby) beside a statue of actor **Richard Harris**; the path is accessible to buggies and wheelchairs for 1.2km, where the climb to the highest point of the cliffs proves too steep for most.

About 150m from the cafe, there's a **natural amphitheatre** in the rocks to the right of the path. This was used for open-air performances from the 19th century on; Harris himself honed his acting skills here in the 1940s and '50s. Further along, at a white-painted shelter, steps lead down to a natural **blowhole** where seawater spouts skywards during a heavy swell. As you round the corner at Knockroe Point, there's a grand view of the sea stacks across **Intrinsic Bay**, named after a ship that was wrecked here in 1836. A stiff climb now leads to the highest

GETTING AROUND

Regular buses serve Kilkee from Limerick and Ennis via Kilrush, while **TFI Local Link** (transportforireland.ie/tfi-local-link) bus 339 (demand-responsive, so book in advance) runs twice-daily from Kilrush to Loop Head Lighthouse via Kilkee. There is a large car park at the north end of Kilkee beach.

The Loop Head Peninsula is small enough to explore comfortably by bike (26km from Kilkee to the lighthouse, around two hours each way); **Loop Head E-Bikes** (loopheadbikes.ie) in Carrigaholt can set you up with everything you need for a day of pedal-powered adventure.

CHE GUEVARA IN KILKEE

In the summer of 1961, student **Jim Fitzpatrick** was working as a barman in the Marine Hotel in Kilkee when Che Guevara walked into the bar. The Cuban revolutionary was returning to Havana from Moscow when his flight was fogbound at Shannon Airport, and he was put up in a Kilkee hotel.

The two had a brief conversation about Che's Irish roots and, after Guevara's death in 1967, Jim created 'Viva Che!', the famous poster image that graced many a student's bedroom wall, and is reproduced in a mural on Kilkee's sea wall.

Jim went on to design album covers for Thin Lizzy and Sinead O'Connor, and is still a working artist to this day.

point of the cliffs; either retrace your steps or descend to the road and turn left to return to Kilkee (5km round trip).

Enjoy a Dip at Pollock Holes
Kilkee's wild swimming scene

Kilkee's sandy Blue Flag beach is a safe and sheltered spot for sea bathing (lifeguards on duty from June to August), but if you fancy something a bit wilder head for the Pollock Holes on the headland west of the bay, opposite the Diamond Rocks Cafe. These natural rock pools are home to small fish, colourful seaweeds and sea anemones, but are only safe to swim in for two hours either side of low water – be sure to check tide times. And wear swimming shoes – the rocks are covered in barnacles.

About 300m east of the Diamond Rocks Cafe, a gap in a white-painted section of wall beside the road leads down to two diving boards set in the cliffs above the sea. Known as **New Found Out**, or just Newfie, this has been a public diving spot for more than a century. Dive here if you're brave enough – the upper board is 10m above the water – but only when the tide is in.

Ride the Loop Head Trail
A road less travelled

Following 65km of dramatic coastline, the **Loop Head Heritage Trail** can be cycled in a day or two. The route is mostly flat with no major climbs, and largely follows quiet country roads (follow signs for Euro cycle route 1). You can download a free **audio guide** *(abartaheritage.ie/loop-head-audio-guide)* to accompany the route.

From Kilkee, a minor road hugs the north coast of the peninsula. The scenery along this stretch is spectacular and includes Bishop's Island, St Kee's Well and the Candle Stick before reaching a scenic Wild Atlantic Way (Slí an Atlantaigh Fhiáin) discovery point at **Kilkee Cliffs** after 7.5km. The road then turns south to join the R487. Fork right on the L2000 (signed Ross 3km) to find the **Bridges of Ross**; once upon a time there were three sea arches here but nowadays just one remains. This spot is a haven for birdwatchers, and thousands of seabirds pass through in late summer and early autumn as they migrate south.

Continue on the coast road to the Loop Head Lighthouse and take a tour before returning through rolling farmland to the village of **Kilbaha** and on along the southern shore of the

EATING IN KILKEE: OUR PICKS

Pantry: Popular bakery and cafe, where locals drop by in the mornings for top-notch coffee and freshly baked pastries. *8.30am-5pm Fri-Mon, to 4pm Tue* €

Holly's Cafe: Grab a terrace table and order Caesar salad for lunch, or just a cappuccino with melt-in-the-mouth tiramisu. *9.30am-4pm Wed-Sun* €

Naughton's Yard: This hidden courtyard with Airstream caravan food truck is a great place to tuck into a beefy burger or lobster roll. *5-10pm Fri & Sat, 2-6pm Sun* €€

Diamond Rocks Cafe: Have a full Irish breakfast before setting off on the cliff walk, or savour a crab sandwich on the terrace for lunch. *10am-4.30pm Mon, to 5pm Thu, Sat & Sun* €€

LOOP HEAD PENINSULA

★ HIGHLIGHTS
1. Kilkee Cliff Walk
2. Loop Head Heritage Trail
3. Loop Head Lighthouse

● SIGHTS
4. Bridges of Ross
5. Carrigaholt Castle
see 2 Diarmuid and Gráinne's Rock
see 2 EIRE Sign
6. Kilkee Cliffs

● SLEEPING
7. An Sean Teach
see 10 Bay View Hotel
8. Glencarrig B&B

● EATING
9. Diamond Rocks Cafe
see 10 Holly's Cafe
10. Naughton's Yard
see 10 Pantry

● DRINKING & NIGHTLIFE
see 10 Greyhound Bar
see 13 Keane's Bar & Grocery
11. Keane's Oyster Bar
12. Keating's
13. Long Dock
see 13 Morrissey's Village Pub
see 10 Murphy's
see 10 O'Mara's

peninsula. Stop to visit **Carrigaholt Castle**, wander around town and sample the local pubs, then continue on minor roads through the small villages of Doonaha and Querrin. At the junction with the N67, you can turn left to return to Kilkee, or right to continue to Kilrush.

Lighthouse Lookout
Climb the tower for magnificent views

The 23m-tall **Loop Head Lighthouse** (loopheadlighthouse.ie; adult/child €8/5) sits on top of a dramatic headland fringed by 50m-high sea cliffs. There's been a lighthouse here since 1670;

☑ TOP TIP

Kilkee Community Market is held every Saturday (except January and February), from noon to 2pm, outside the Greyhound Bar. Browse a fantastic selection of local foodstuffs including fresh fish, eggs, honey, organic vegetables, artisan cheeses, jams and chutneys.

DRINKING IN KILKEE: OUR PICKS

Keane's Oyster Bar: Old-school pub, shop and restaurant 3km east of Kilkee; peat fires and murals in the bar, fresh oysters in the dining room. *6.30-11.30pm Thu-Tue*

O'Mara's: Snug but lively local on Kilkee's main drag with good Guinness, friendly staff and live music Thursday to Sunday. No food. *11am-11pm*

Murphy's: Classic Irish grocery-pub vibes with flagstone floors, ancient wooden counter and vintage advertising signs. *noon-11.30pm*

Greyhound Bar: Kilkee's top live music venue. Outdoor tables streetside at the front, and a sheltered beer garden at the back. *4-11pm Thu, to midnight Fri-Sun*

WWII 'ÉIRE' SIGNS

During WWII, neutral Ireland constructed a series of of lookout posts around its coast to keep an eye on shipping movements. But with the entry of the US into the war in 1941, increasing numbers of aircraft encountered Ireland as their first landfall after crossing the Atlantic, causing diplomatic problems due to crash landings and refuelling requests. At the request of the US, large, white **ÉIRE signs** (eiremarkings.org) were laid out on the ground beside each of the 82 lookout posts, to act as air navigation marks.

The signs are numbered clockwise around the coast from Ballagan Point in Louth to Inishowen Head in Donegal; the Loop Head sign is number 45.

Local enthusiasts have uncovered and restored many of these signs.

Loop Head Lighthouse (p309) and the ÉIRE sign

the present structure dates from 1854. Guided tours take you up the tower and onto the balcony for panoramic views; in fine weather, you can see as far as Mt Brandon on the Dingle Peninsula to the south and the Connemara hills to the north.

Loop Head Walks

Hike around the headland

You can explore the clifftops around Loop Head Lighthouse by following a grassy trail around the north side of the lighthouse enclosure. You'll soon catch the stink of guano wafting up from the seabird colony that inhabits the crags around **Diarmuid and Gráinne's Rock**, a sea stack separated from the mainland by a narrow, atmospheric slot. Continue to the point of Loop Head to a relic of WWII, piles of white stones that spell out **ÉIRE**, and return on the south side of the headland with views of spectacularly folded rock strata (2km; allow 45 minutes).

Loop Head is scheduled for a new development that will include a cafe, visitor centre and expanded car park, as well as four looped walks.

 DRINKING IN LOOP HEAD PENINSULA

| **Keane's Bar & Grocery**: Nearly 200 years old, Keane's is an authentic Carrigaholt pub with a grocery store attached. *10.30am-12.30am Mon-Sat, from 1pm Sun* | **Morrissey's Village Pub**: Fresh, creamy pints and a warm welcome await at this Carrigaholt favourite, with music and dancing throughout the year. *11am-midnight* | **Long Dock**: Atmospheric Carrigaholt pub-restaurant with stone floors, a welcoming fire and regular live music. *12.30-11pm Mon-Fri, 10.30am-midnight Sat & Sun* | **Keating's**: Overlooking Kilbaha Bay, Keating's has outdoor tables by the sea wall. Freshly caught local fish as well as creamy Guinness. *11am-9pm Jun-Aug, shorter hrs Sep-May* |

Beyond the Loop Head Peninsula

Around the harbour town of Kilrush, County Clare turns a gentler face south towards the narrowing Shannon Estuary.

To the east of the Loop Head Peninsula, southwest Clare rolls through gentle farmland alongside the Shannon all the way to Ennis and Shannon Airport. The only town of any size is Kilrush (Cill Rois), an interesting place that looks south across the Shannon Estuary to the hills of Kerry. The main street, Frances St, runs directly uphill from the harbour and is more than 30m wide, reflecting Kilrush's origins as a port and market town in the 19th century, when there was much coming and going between land and sea. Offshore, amid dolphin-haunted waters, lies fascinating Scattery Island, home to a medieval Christian monastery.

Kilrush

TIME FROM KILKEE: **15MIN**

Explore an early Christian settlement

The uninhabited, windswept and treeless **Scattery Island** *(heritageireland.ie)*, lying 3km southwest of Kilrush, was the site of an early Christian settlement founded by St Senan in the 6th century. Here you can explore the evocative remains of six medieval churches dating from the 9th to the 14th centuries; the largest is the **Cathedral of Sts Mary and Senan**, which has a carving of a bishop's head atop the eastern window, flanked by two serpent-like monsters. Nearby is a 36m-high, 11th-century **round tower**, the best preserved in Ireland.

From late May to September, **Scattery Island Tours** *(scatteryislandtours.com; adult/child return €20/10)* ferries visitors from Kilrush Marina to the island; the crossing takes 15 to 20 minutes. You'll be met at the island by Office of Public Works (OPW) guides who offer a free guided tour. Look out for the birdlife – the island is home to a nesting colony of rare hen harriers.

Discovering a Victorian garden

Set at the edge of a 170-hectare forest just east of Kilrush, the **Vandeleur Walled Garden** *(vandeleurwalledgarden.ie; adult/child €7/5)* was once the private domain of the Vandeleur family, wealthy merchants and landowners who engaged

GETTING AROUND

Bus Éireann bus 336 runs up to eight times a day from Ennis to Kilrush and on to Kilkee. Kilrush itself, Vandeleur Garden and Scattery Island are all easily explored on foot. If you want to venture further afield, Gleeson's Hardware store just off Market Sq rents bikes and e-bikes.

At Killimer, 9km east of Kilrush, a regular car ferry service runs across the Shannon to Tarbert in County Kerry.

KILRUSH & THE VANDELEUR FAMILY

The Vandeleur family is descended from Maximilian van der Leur, a wealthy Dutch merchant who arrived in Ireland in the 17th century. His grandson became rector of Kilrush in the 1680s and by the mid-19th century his descendants were prominent politicians and owners of some 80 sq km of County Clare.

The family played a major role in the development of Kilrush town in the early 19th century and built the Catholic church, a convent, a fever hospital and the workhouse; many streets (eg Frances, Moore, Grace, Hector, Toler and Burton streets) are named after Vandeleur family members. But today they are primarily remembered as absentee landlords who treated their tenants harshly during and after the Great Famine.

---

in harsh evictions and the forced emigration of local people in the 19th century. Abandoned for many years, the garden has been beautifully renovated with immaculate lawns, colourful flowerbeds, magnolias, acacias, a beech-hedge maze and a courtyard with garden shop and cafe. Woodland trails lead into the surrounding forest.

You can walk to the garden from Kilrush town centre in 10–15 minutes.

Shannon dolphins

The Shannon Estuary is home to a 140-strong resident population of bottlenose dolphins. They are genetically distinct from other Irish populations and are one of the most intensively studied groups of dolphins in Europe. Sadly, the Shannon Dolphin Centre research facility in Kilrush is closed to the public for the foreseeable future, but from June to September **Dolphin Discovery** *(discoverdolphins.ie; adult/child €40/20)*, based at Kilrush Marina, runs two-hour boat trips offering plenty of dolphin-spotting opportunities.

West Coast RIB Adventures *(westcoastribadventures.com; per person €60)*, also at Kilrush Marina, offers the chance to venture further afield, with two-hour cruises in a fast RIB. Trips pause at Scattery Island to look for seals, then head across the estuary to explore the cliffs and sea caves around Ballybunion in County Kerry.

EATING IN & AROUND KILRUSH: OUR PICKS

Potter's Hand: Shelves stacked with books sit beside counters showcasing crumbly fruit scones and homemade treats. *10am-4pm Tue-Sat* €

Harbour Restaurant: Modern bistro with a long and appealing menu – everything from sandwiches to local seafood. Tables outside in summer. *noon-9pm* €€

Brambles Woodland Cafe: Housed in the restored stable block at Vandeleur Walled Garden, serving tempting breakfast and lunch dishes. *10am-4pm* €

Oileán: Best to book a table at this stylish modern eatery where the focus is on top-quality seasonal produce. *5-9pm Thu, from 1pm Fri-Sun* €€€

Places We Love to Stay

€ Budget €€ Midrange €€€ Top End

Doolin
MAP p291

Nagles Camping & Caravan Park € Just 100m from Doolin Pier, with 85 serviced hard stands and green camping on 1.6 hectares.

O'Connor's Guesthouse €€ Working farm with an L-shaped barn-style guesthouse sporting 10 spick-and-span rooms, two of which are equipped for visitors with limited mobility.

Fiddle & Bow Hotel €€€ Doolin's most luxurious option – choose from 16 boutique hotel rooms or the extensive collection of cute self-catering cottages and lodges.

Ballyvaughan
MAP p291

Wild Burren Cottages €€ These whitewashed cottages with thatched roofs overlooking the bay are available to rent by the week.

Hylands Burren Hotel €€ A family-owned hotel with comfortable rooms, superb food from its Brazilian chef, and often live music in the bar.

Kilfenora
MAP p291

Burren Glamping €€ This stylishly converted horse truck with a wood-burning stove set on a sustainable farm sleeps up to six people.

Ennistimon
MAP p291

Falls Hotel & Spa €€€ Vast Georgian hotel with large indoor pool, a spa and modern rooms overlooking the River Inagh, with walking trails through 20 hectares of wooded grounds.

Lahinch & Liscannor
MAP p291

Atlantic View B&B €€ Rooms have a country-cottage feel at this primrose-yellow B&B set amid farmland 4km north of Liscannor, and minutes from the Cliffs of Moher.

Cliffs of Moher Hotel €€ A lovely combination of traditional and modern design, including bedroom balconies with cracking views and original Irish art on the walls of the library.

Atlantic Hotel €€ Grand old hotel with a golfing theme and pleasantly old-fashioned atmosphere, but spotless modernised bedrooms and bathrooms.

Ennis
MAP p302

Ardilaun Guesthouse € You could drop a fishing line into the River Fergus, or just watch the sunset, from the rear deck of this modern B&B around 3km north of town.

Newpark House €€ An elegant, vine-covered country mansion dating from 1750, 3km northeast of Ennis, with six rooms featuring plush furnishings, antiques and lots of polished wood. Incredible value.

Temple Gate Hotel €€ The soaring cathedral-ceilinged lobby at this central hotel was once part of the 19th-century Sisters of Mercy convent.

Old Ground Hotel €€€ Entered through a lobby of polished floorboards, cornice work, antiques and open fires, this prestigious landmark hotel dates from the 1800s.

Lough Derg

Clareville House €€ A large and comfortable B&B in Tuamgraney; try to get a room at the back of the house overlooking the garden.

Lakeside Hotel €€ Prices work in direct ratio to the sweeping views across the water to Ballina's 16-arch bridge; family fun with 40m-long water slide and large indoor swimming pool.

Kilkee
MAP p309

Bay View Hotel €€ Family-run since the 1880s, this hotel is often touted as one of the best in Clare with spacious modern rooms and cracking central location.

Stella Maris Hotel €€ Charming old-school family-run hotel dating from 1880; enjoy your morning coffee on the verandah with a view across the beach.

Loop Head Peninsula
MAP p309

An Sean Teach €€ Modern, minimalist and well-appointed self-catering cottage with ocean views in a quiet, peaceful location west of Kilbaha.

Glencarrig B&B €€ You can watch grazing cattle from your bedroom window and enjoy home baking at the breakfast table at this warm and welcoming farmhouse B&B.

Left: Roundstone (p346) and the Twelve Bens (p333); right: Crane Bar (p320), Galway city

Researched by
Neil Wilson

Galway

FESTIVALS, RUGGED LANDSCAPES AND WINDSWEPT ISLANDS

Contrasting lively Galway city with the rugged wilderness of Connemara – think remote islands, beautiful beaches and postcard-perfect villages – this county showcases the essence of Ireland.

County Galway's exuberant namesake city, called 'Dublin of the west', is the halfway point of the weaving 2500km Wild Atlantic Way and a swirl of colourful shop-lined streets filled with buskers and performance artists, enticing old pubs that hum with trad music sessions throughout the year, and a sophisticated food scene that celebrates local produce. Known as the festival capital of Ireland, bohemian Galway city hosts some 120 festivals a year.

ROBERT ORMEROD/LONELY PLANET

Some of Ireland's most picturesque scenery fans out from Galway's city limits, particularly along the breathtaking Connemara Peninsula. Tiny roads wander along a coastline studded with islands, dazzling white sandy beaches and intriguing villages; the interior shelters heath-strewn boglands, glassy lakes, looming mountains and isolated valleys. Stone walls and sheep are always on the horizon, and trips along the winding roads are an unforgettable experience. A few places have featured on the silver screen, such as in *The Quiet Man* and *Marley and Me*. In the county's east, towns with medieval remains give way to rolling farmland.

Galway doesn't stop giving at its western coastline. Offshore lie the beautiful Aran Islands. Desolate, windswept yet entrancing, the trio of rugged islands offer a glimpse into Irish life of centuries past.

The county, Ireland's second-largest, gets its nickname of 'Hooker County' from a traditional fishing boat called a Galway hooker.

THE MAIN AREAS

GALWAY CITY
Artsy and music-loving foodie city. **p320**

CONNEMARA NATIONAL PARK
Ruggedly beautiful landscapes, mountains and road trips. **p330**

CLIFDEN
Picturesque, lively and pub-filled town. **p337**

ARAN ISLANDS
Deserted beaches, coastal cliffs and ancient forts. **p348**

FERRY
Ferries to the Aran Islands sail year-round from Rossaveal, 38km west of Galway city, linked by shuttle bus. Ferries to the islands also depart from Galway Harbour from April to September, and from Doolin in County Clare from March to October. Crossings are subject to favourable weather conditions.

BUS
Bus Éireann (buseireann.ie) operates most bus services in the region, linking Galway city to other major cities in Ireland and to Barna and Clifden in Connemara. **Local Link Galway** (locallinkgalway.ie) serves more rural areas including Roundstone, Letterfrack and southern County Galway. Minibuses operate on the Aran Islands from May to September.

CAR
Driving is the best way to explore all that Galway has to offer, getting you to remote spots that are difficult to access by public transport. Fuel up in larger towns when you can.

Find Your Way

Stretching from the eastern hidden heartlands to the Atlantic Ocean, County Galway is sprawling. It takes about two hours to drive from the easternmost town of Ballinasloe to Roundstone on the Connemara coast.

Plan Your Time

Galway's attractions are many and varied. Spend some time soaking up the buzz of the city but don't miss out on the mountain scenery of Connemara and the rugged Aran Islands.

Inishmore, Aran Islands (p348)

One Day in Galway

● Check out the landmarks of **Galway city** (p320) on a DIY **walking tour** (p322) along the banks of the River Corrib, and then experience the vibrant food scene in the company of **Galway Food Tours** (p323), or check out the exhibits at **Galway City Museum** (p323).

● Take a seaside stroll to **Salthill** (p325) and enjoy a late lunch at **Gourmet Food Parlour** (p326). Pack your swimmers and do as the locals do by taking a dive off the **Blackrock Diving Tower** (p325).

● For a dinner of top-notch local seafood, book a table at **Oscars**. In the evening go on a pub crawl of trad music sessions in the lively **Latin Quarter** (p320), ending the night in **Taaffe's Bar**.

Seasonal Highlights

Galway city is buzzing year-round. April to October offers the best weather, and places in rural parts are open. July and August are the busiest.

MARCH

Most towns have **St Patrick's Day** parades. Galway city's St Patrick's Day Festival has live music and traditional dance workshops.

APRIL

The **Cúirt International Festival of Literature** (p324) in Galway city features a week of poetry, theatre, talks and author interviews.

JULY

The **Galway International Arts Festival** (p324) features theatre, music, comedy, visual arts, dance and literary events from global and homegrown artists.

Three Days to Travel Around

- After a day in **Galway City** (p320), hit the road west via Oughterard for an epic trip through **Connemara National Park** (p330), pausing to visit **Connemara Heritage & History Centre** (p339).

- Spend the night in **Clifden** (p337), and the next day visit the site of Marconi's telegraph station at **Derrigimlagh** (p343) before continuing to **Roundstone** (p346) for your second night via **Ballyconneely** (p345).

- Drive east to Rossaveal to catch a ferry to the **Aran Islands** (p348). If you only have time for one island, make it **Inishmore** (p348), where you can visit **Dún Aonghasa** (p350), Ireland's oldest prehistoric fort. Back on the mainland, stop off at **Spiddal** (p329) to admire the crafts made by local artists.

If You Have a Week

- Spend a few nights in **Galway city** (p320) and enjoy exploring the streets and the nightlife.

- Catch a ferry to the **Aran Islands** (p348), staying a night on **Inishmore** (p348), where coastal walks and clifftop fortresses await. Make your way around the coast via **Roundstone** (p346) to **Clifden** (p337), a great base for exploring **Connemara National Park** (p330) by car, bike or on foot.

- To the east, take a cruise on Ireland's only fjord, **Killary Harbour** (p335), and visit the photogenic **Kylemore Abbey** (p334). Stop by historic monuments, ruined castles and secluded beaches on a **drive around Lough Corrib** (p327) and finish your trip through Galway at **Kinvara** (p328) with a sunset over the Atlantic Ocean.

AUGUST
The **Galway Race Week** (p324) is Ireland's longest and liveliest horse-racing meet. There's good food, music and fashion, and the craic is mighty.

SEPTEMBER
Wash down oysters with pints of Guinness to the sounds of live music at the **Clarenbridge Oyster Festival** (p329).

OCTOBER
October marks the red deer rutting season in **Connemara National Park** (p330), an ideal time to see and hear the roaring of the stags.

DECEMBER
The enchanting **Galway Christmas Market** (p324) runs from 14 December to Christmas Eve in the city.

Galway City

BRILLIANT PUBS | GREAT FOOD | LIVE MUSIC

GETTING AROUND

Galway city is easily explored on foot, but Quay St is cobbled, so wear comfy shoes. Buses are reliable and run to the main attractions. Buy a **Visitor Leap Card** *(about.leapcard.ie/leap-visitor-card)* online or at a corner shop to save up to 30% on fares.

Use the **bike-share scheme** to get around the city on two wheels. A bus connects Shannon Airport to Galway city.

☑ TOP TIP

Accommodation can get booked up fast at weekends and during the Galway Races and the various festivals the city hosts, so it's wise to book ahead. Eyre Sq is a great base as it's close to the Latin Quarter and it offers a range of options to suit all budgets.

Galway (Gaillimh) is one of Ireland's most engaging cities. Brightly painted pubs heave with live music, and the faint hum of fiddles, banjos and bodhráns (hand-held goatskin drums) drifts out of its numerous pubs, particularly in the cobbled streets of the Latin Quarter. Restaurants and cafes offer front-row seats for observing buskers and street theatre. The large student population brings out a lively contemporary music scene.

Remnants of the medieval town walls lie between shops selling handcrafted Claddagh rings, books and musical instruments, bridges arch over the salmon-haunted River Corrib, and a long promenade leads to the seaside suburb of Salthill, on Galway Bay, the source of the area's famous oysters. Cosmopolitan culinary options abound that make use of the best local and Irish produce. The city hosts a vast array of festivals and cultural events throughout the year, making it a great spot to visit at any time.

Traditional Music Pub Crawl

Pints, jigs and reels

No visit to Galway city is complete without catching some traditional Irish music. For the best of the toe-tapping tunes, head to the **Latin Quarter**. Named for the city's historic trading links with Spain and Portugal, this lively district is clustered around pedestrianised Quay St, High St and Shop St.

Where Shop St and High St merge you'll find the fire-engine-red **Tig Cóilí**, a favourite among local musicians. This atmospheric gem of a pub hosts two evening trad sessions, usually around 6pm and 9.30pm. **Taaffe's Bar** across the road is popular with locals and GAA sports fans. Heading down to Quay St you'll find the heart of the Galway music scene, family-run **Tigh Neachtain** (pronounced 'tee-g knocktin'), founded in 1894.

Cross the Wolfe Tone Bridge to the West End, where the **Crane Bar** holds Irish music sessions nightly in the downstairs pub.

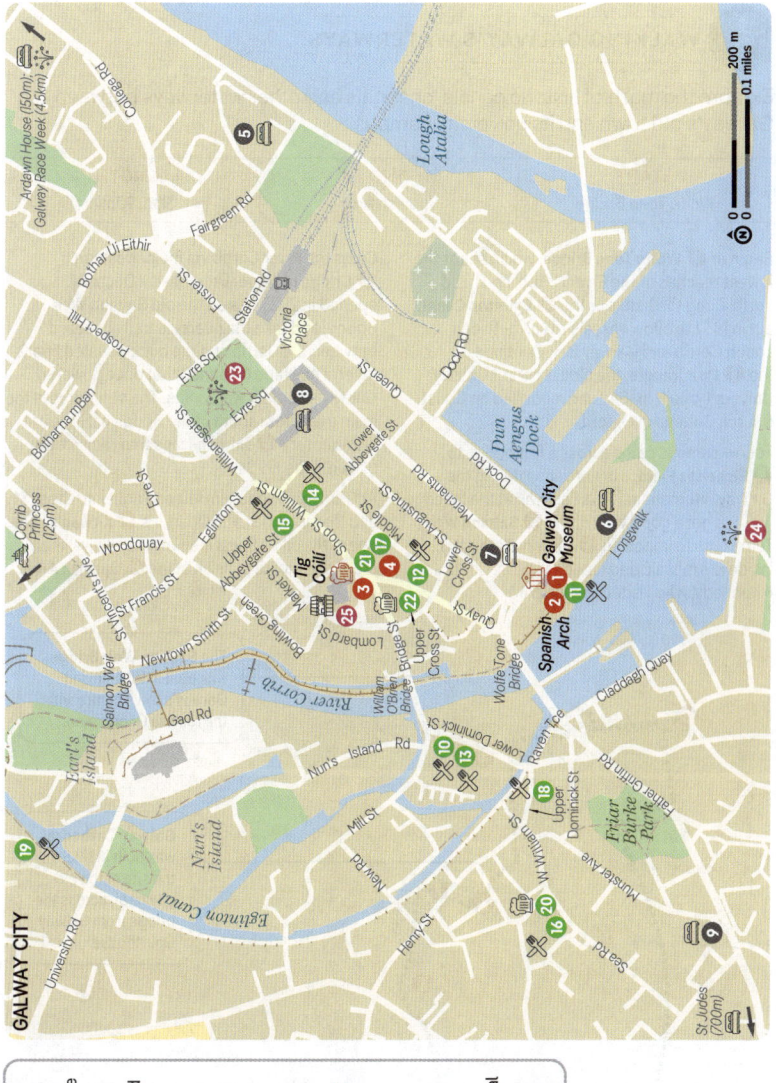

GALWAY CITY

★ HIGHLIGHTS
1. Galway City Museum
2. Spanish Arch
3. Tig Cóilí
   see 2 Latin Quarter

● SIGHTS

● ACTIVITIES
4. Galway Food Tours

● SLEEPING
5. Galmont Hotel & Spa
6. Heron's Rest
7. House Hotel
8. Kinlay Hostel
9. The Stop

● EATING
10. Aniar
11. Ard Bia at Nimmo's
12. Cava Bodega
13. Dela
14. Food for Thought
15. Jemi Lighthouse
16. Kai
17. King's Head
18. Oscars Seafood Bistro
19. Suit

● DRINKING & NIGHTLIFE
20. Crane Bar
21. Taaffe's Bar
22. Tigh Neachtain

● ENTERTAINMENT
23. Galway Christmas Market
24. Galway International Oyster & Seafood Festival

● SHOPPING
25. Galway Market

WALKING GALWAY'S WATERWAYS

Explore the maze of historic canals, channels and other waterways between Galway's old town and its university campus.

START	END	LENGTH
Wolfe Tone Bridge	Spanish Arch	3km; 90min

Begin at ❶ **Wolfe Tone Bridge**, which spans the lowest reaches of the River Corrib, and head north along the banks of the ❷ **Eglinton Canal**, cut in 1852 to allow vessels to sail between Lough Corrib and Galway Bay. Continue to the ❸ **Quadrangle**, the oldest part of Galway University, built in 1849 and modelled on Christ Church College in Oxford.

Follow campus paths across a footbridge to ❹ **Fisheries Field**, a major venue during the Galway International Arts Festival; at the far edge, you can get a good view of the ❺ **Salmon Weir**. Turn south to imposing ❻ **Galway Cathedral**; inside is a mosaic dedicated to US president John F Kennedy, who visited in June 1963.

Cross the River Corrib via the pedestrian ❼ **Bridge of Hope** (Droichead a Dóchais), opened in 2023 beside the old Salmon Weir Bridge, and take the riverside trail squeezed between the Corrib and the duck-haunted Friar's River, a mill lade (channel) that once powered Galway's earliest watermills. The structures in the main river 150m south of the Bridge of Hope are 19th-century ❽ **salmon traps** that remained in use until the 1990s.

At O'Brien's Bridge turn left and right into Cross St and then into the Latin Quarter's ❾ **Kirwan's Lane**, one of the city's finest medieval laneways, then cross the square to finish at the ❿ **Spanish Arch**.

The **Salmon Weir Bridge** was built in 1818, linking Galway's town centre with the road to Connemara.

Galway Cathedral was built in 1965 on the site of the old city gaol, across the bridge from Galway Courthouse.

When tides and river levels allow, white-water kayakers can be seen playing on the standing wave below **Wolfe Tone Bridge**.

Galway's Gastronomic Delights
Sublime seafood and Michelin-star cooking

From Michelin-star dining to the freshest fish and chips, Galway's food scene runs the gamut. Book an outing with **Galway Food Tours** *(galwayfoodtours.com; per person €90)* to sample everything from local oysters and craft beers to artisan cheese and chocolate.

If indulging in a Michelin-starred meal has been on your bucket list, you can tick it off at Galway's **Aniar**. Here, chefs use seasonal, wild and foraged food sourced locally from land and sea, so expect an immersive dining experience of Irish food through the ages with a contemporary twist. **Kai** joined the club in 2024 with a prestigious Michelin Green Star in recognition of chef Jess Murphy's commitment to local, sustainable and organic produce.

Stroll Through the Spanish Arch
Famed historic landmark

The Spanish Arch, one of Galway's best-known landmarks, is thought to be an extension of the medieval city walls, designed to protect ships moored at the nearby quay while they unloaded goods from Spain. It was partially destroyed by the tsunami that followed the 1755 Lisbon earthquake; today it reverberates with buskers and drummers, and the lawns and riverside form a gathering place for locals and visitors snapping selfies.

Board a Boat for Lough Corrib
Cruise to the Republic's largest lake

Join a 90-minute cruise aboard the open-top **Corrib Princess** *(corribprincess.ie; adult/child €20/10)*, passing ruined castles and other historic landmarks along the River Corrib en route to the Republic's largest lake, Lough Corrib, the haunt of herons, swans and, if you're lucky, leaping salmon. From May to September there are two or three departures daily from Woodquay, just north of the Salmon Weir on the east side of the river.

Dip into Galway's Colourful Past
A fascinating history museum

Exhibits at the modern **Galway City Museum** *(galwaycitymuseum.ie; free)* engagingly convey the city's archaeological, political, cultural and social history. Look out for the iconic

THE SALMON WEIR

Upstream from the old Salmon Weir Bridge, which crosses the River Corrib just east of Galway Cathedral, the river cascades down the Salmon Weir, one of its final descents before flowing into Galway Bay. When the salmon (known in Irish as bradán) are running you can often see shoals of them waiting in the waters above the bridge before heading upriver to spawn; most fish pass through during May and June.

The salmon fishing rights were originally held by the Franciscan friary that once stood on the east side of the river here, and later to the Lynch family and finally the Irish state, before commercial fishing was suspended in the 1990s for conservation reasons.

EATING IN GALWAY CITY: OUR PICKS

Ard Bia at Nimmo's: Long-established cafe-restaurant right beside the Spanish Arch, working hand-in-hand with local producers. *10am-3pm daily, 6-9pm Tue-Sun* €€

Food for Thought: Good-value organic, vegetarian and vegan sandwiches, savoury scones and wholesome lunch dishes. *8am-5pm Mon-Sat, noon-3.30pm Sun* €

Oscars Seafood Bistro: Outstanding seafood restaurant in the West End helmed by cookbook author Michael O'Meara. *6-9pm Tue-Thu, to 9.30pm Fri & Sat* €€€

Sult: Riverside cafe-bar-restaurant on Galway University campus with prices half of those in the city centre. *8.30am-8pm Mon-Fri* €

GALWAY CITY'S BEST EVENTS

Cúirt International Festival of Literature: April sees one of Ireland's premier literary festivals, featuring talks, interviews, poetry sessions, theatrical performances and readings.

Blas na Bealtaine: 'A Taste of May' is a month-long celebration of Galway's buzzing culinary scene, including farm tours, foraging and cooking demonstrations.

Galway International Arts Festival: The biggest event on the calendar is held in late July, a two-week fiesta of theatre, comedy, music and art.

Galway Race Week: A week of horse racing in late July, drawing tens of thousands of punters for a week of partying.

Galway International Oyster & Seafood Festival: Going strong since 1954, the world's oldest oyster festival draws thousands of visitors over the last weekend in September.

Musician, Latin Quarter (p320)

Galway hooker (fishing boat) suspended from the ceiling, a gold Claddagh ring dating from around 1700 (the oldest in existence), examples of Tim Robinson's minutely detailed, hand-drawn maps of the Aran Islands, and sections covering Galway's role in the revolutionary events that shaped the Republic of Ireland. Ask at reception about free guided tours, talks and workshops, and rotating displays of works by local artists.

Go to Market

Unmissable weekend event

The city's bohemian spirit comes alive at **Galway Market**, which has been set up in this spot (around St Nicholas Church on Lombard St and Churchyard Lane) for centuries. Saturdays and Sundays from 8am to 6pm are the standout for food, when farmers and fisherfolk sell fresh produce alongside stalls selling flowers, arts, crafts and street food; buskers add to the festive atmosphere. Additional markets take place from noon to 6pm daily in July and August, and there's an atmospheric **Christmas Market** from 14 to 24 December.

EATING IN GALWAY CITY: OUR PICKS

Cava Bodega: Tapas are given a gourmet twist by star chef JP McMahon of Michelin-starred Aniar (p323). *5-10pm Mon-Fri, noon-10.30pm Sat, 3-9.30pm Sun* €€

Dela: Brunch seven days a week – the buttermilk pancakes are outstanding – and imaginative vegan dishes at dinner. *9.30am-3pm daily, 6-10pm Thu-Sat* €€

Jemi Lighthouse: Cute and cosy cafe with varied and interesting plant-based menu. *10am-5pm Mon-Sat* €€

King's Head: Old-fashioned pub with plenty of seafood on the menu, including freshly shucked oysters, crab claws and chowder. *noon-9pm* €€

Beyond Galway City

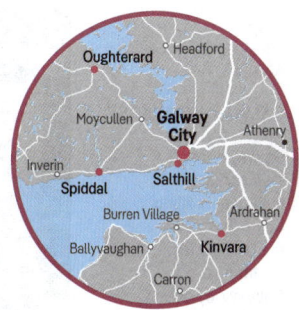

West of Galway city, quaint seaside towns and villages await. Find glassy lakes and ancient castles to the north and east.

Sleepy seaside suburbs and villages spread west of Galway. Within walking distance of Galway city is Salthill, and not much further on to the west, you'll find yourself in the Galway Gaeltacht (Irish-speaking area), regarded as the cultural heartland of Gaeilge, where the old traditions and heritage of the Irish are at their strongest.

The dramatic island-strewn coastline of Galway Bay is a stark contrast to the county's interior of bog and stone walls. To the south is oyster country in the fishing villages of Clarinbridge and Kilcolgan. To the north, there's superb angling at Oughterard on Lough Corrib's shores as well as scenic road trips. Castles populate towns steeped in historical and literary connections to the east.

Places

Salthill p325
Oughterard p326
Kinvara p328
Spiddal p329

GETTING AROUND

The best way to explore at your leisure is with your own wheels. Main roads are well marked, but be careful of narrow bends and wandering sheep on smaller roads.

Frequent bus services operate from the suburbs of Salthill, Spiddal and Oranmore to Galway. A train line connects Athenry and Gort to each other and to Galway city.

Salthill

TIME FROM GALWAY: 1HR

Swimming at Salthill

Within an hour's walk of Galway city, or more easily reached by bus, Salthill offers a quintessential Irish seaside town experience. The sandy Blue Flag beach stretches for 800m along the prom, with lifeguards on duty daily in July and August, ending at **Blackrock Diving Tower**, a popular swimming and diving spot – the tower dates from the 1950s, with springboards at 1m, 3m and 10m heights, and also changing rooms, showers, toilets and lockers.

A proper Irish pub

Round off a day at Salthill beach with a visit to **O'Connor's Famous Pub**, where the video for Ed Sheeran's hit song 'Galway Girl' was filmed. Antiques fill every nook, cranny, wall

EATING BEYOND GALWAY CITY: BEST SEAFOOD

Moran's Oyster Cottage: An atmospheric thatched pub overlooking Dunbulcaun Bay, where oysters are reared before they arrive on your plate. *1-9.30pm Tue-Sun €€*

O'Grady's on the Pier: Simply prepared fresh seafood with great service at this nautical-themed seafront restaurant in Barna. *12.30-2.30pm Sat & Sun, 5-9pm Tue-Sun €€*

Paddy Burkes Bar & Restaurant: A traditional pub in Clarinbridge that serves oysters, seafood platters, and fish and chips. *noon-8.30pm Wed-Sun €€*

Pier Head Bar & Restaurant: Fish chowder, steamed mussels, seafood platters and fresh fish of the day; all the classics are on offer at this Kinvara pub. *noon-9pm €€*

Teampall na Naoimh

GALWAY HOOKERS

Galway hookers (*húiceár*) are traditional sailing boats that were the basis of local seafaring around Galway Bay during the 19th and early 20th centuries. Small, tough and highly manoeuvrable, they were used for fishing – their name comes from 'hook-and-line' fishing, where a string of baited hooks was trailed behind the boat – and for cargo transport, shipping turf (peat) for fuel from the bogs of Connemara to the villages of County Clare, and bringing back lime (for building mortar and whitewash) on the return journeys.

Easily recognised by their black hulls, long bowsprits and gaff-rigged red-brown sails, they are popular today with weekend sailors and hobbyists, with an annual festival at Kinvara (p328).

and ceiling space: clocks, crockery, farming implements, gas lights, sewing machines, fishing equipment, a stag's head and an almost life-size statue of John Wayne from *The Quiet Man*. With no food or TVs, and nightly trad music singalongs, it's a proper Irish pub experience.

Oughterard

TIME FROM GALWAY: **30MIN**

Sail to a sacred island

The largest of Lough Corrib's 360-plus islands, **Inchagoill** lies bang in the middle of the lake, halfway between Oughterard and Cong. A lonely place dotted with ancient remains, the island is home to a burial ground and two ancient churches. The pretty **Teampall na Naoimh** (Saints' Church) was probably built in the 9th or 10th century, with carvings around its elaborate Romanesque arched doorway. **Teampall Phádraig** (St Patrick's Church) is a small, rectangular oratory of a very early design, with some later additions.

The island's most fascinating sight is a 6th-century obelisk called **Lia Luguaedon Macci Menueh** (Stone of Lugnad, Son of Menueh), standing about 75cm tall near the Saints' Church. It's claimed that the Latin writing on the stone is the second-oldest Christian inscription in Europe, after those in the catacombs in Rome.

EATING BEYOND GALWAY CITY: TOP CAFES

Pear Tree Cafe & Wine Bar: Salthill spot serving brilliant brunches by day and biodynamic wines by night. *8am-4pm Sun-Wed, to 10pm Thu & Fri, 9am-10pm Sat* €

Gourmet Food Parlour: Salthill branch of Dublin favourite serves delicious tapas and cocktails. *9am-4pm Mon-Thu, to 9pm Fri & Sat, to 6pm Sun* €€

My Little Flower: Coffee is king at this Oughterard barista haven, where eating options are limited to cakes and pastries. *8am-4pm Mon-Sat, from 9am Sun* €

POTA: Popular community cafe in Inverin serving hot lunches including seafood chowder and filled focaccia sandwiches. *9am-4pm Tue-Sat, 10am-4pm Sun* €€

LOUGH CORRIB LOOP

Explore some Hollywood history on one of Galway's lesser-known scenic drives, a loop around Lough Corrib.

START	END	LENGTH
Galway city	Galway city	115km; 4hr

Leave Galway on the N59 for ❶ **Oughterard**, a busy market town and one of Ireland's principal angling centres – Lough Corrib offers some of the best trout fishing in Ireland. Just before town, take a quick detour to visit the mighty ❷ **Aughnanure Castle**, renowned for its six-storey tower house and unusual double bawn (walled area outside the main castle).

Continuing into Connemara, the landscape changes dramatically, with lush green fields giving way to barren mountains and bog. About 7.5km west of Oughterard off the N59 (signposted Leam) is the ❸ **Quiet Man Bridge**, a picturesque stone bridge featured in the homonymous 1950s film. Continue to Maam Cross and turn north onto the R336, enjoying stunning mountain views in all directions. A kilometre before remote Maam Bridge lies the ruin of ❹ **White O'Morn Cottage** – also in *The Quiet Man*. Turn east onto the R345, hugging the shores of Lough Corrib, where you'll see several parking places with picnic tables.

Cross the border into County Mayo to reach the picturesque village of ❺ **Cong**, the main setting for *The Quiet Man*. Superfans can check out the **Quiet Man Museum** or explore the beautiful grounds of ❻ **Ashford Castle**. On the way back to Galway on the N84, pause to explore the peaceful ❼ **Ross Errilly Friary**, the most complete Franciscan monastery ruins in Ireland.

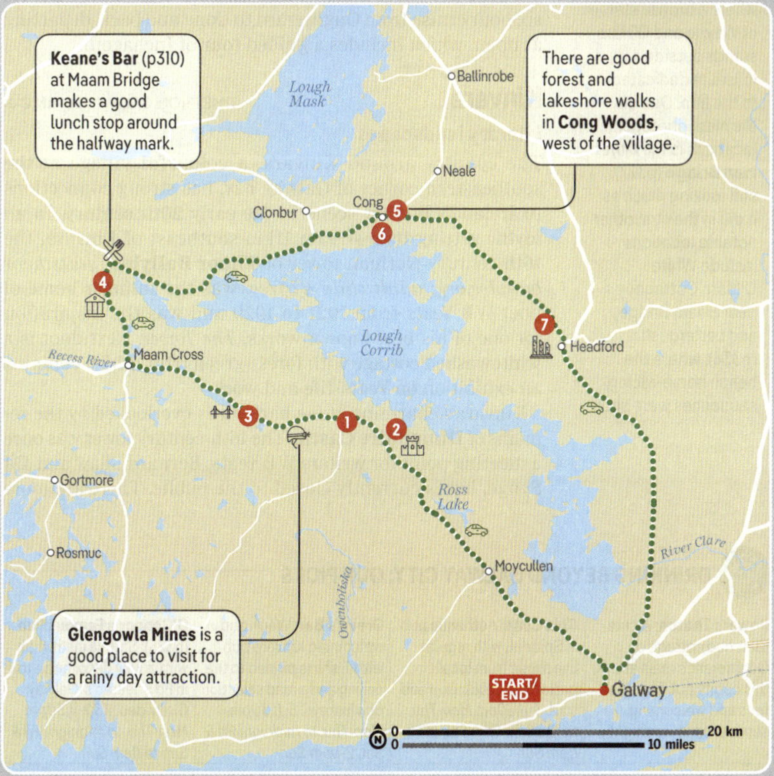

Keane's Bar (p310) at Maam Bridge makes a good lunch stop around the halfway mark.

There are good forest and lakeshore walks in **Cong Woods**, west of the village.

Glengowla Mines is a good place to visit for a rainy day attraction.

THE QUIET MAN

The 1952 movie *The Quiet Man* is a romantic comedy that tells the story of a retired American boxer who returns to his birthplace in Ireland to purchase the old family farm. Mayhem ensues. It starred John Wayne and Irish-born Maureen O'Hara, and won an Oscar for director John Ford.

The outdoor scenes were shot on location in counties Galway and Mayo, notably in the village of Cong, where a bronze statue of Wayne and O'Hara stands outside a museum dedicated to the film. One of the most photogenic locations is the **Quiet Man Bridge** (p327), still looking much as it did in the film; other notable locations include White O'Morn Cottage near Maam Bridge, and Lettergesh (p336), where the beach horse-racing sequences were shot.

Spiddal

From June to September **Corrib Cruises** *(corribcruises.com; adult/child €30/15)* runs a daily two-hour cruise departing from Lisloughrey pier near Cong at 3pm, which allows a 40-minute visit on the island. On Saturdays only, there's a six-hour cruise from Oughterard to Cong and back, departing at noon, which includes a guided tour of Inchagoill.

Kinvara

TIME FROM GALWAY: **40MIN**

Literary landscapes

The country around Kinvara, a colourful village at the southeastern corner of Galway Bay, has strong connections to Ireland's literary scene in the early 20th century. In an idyllic setting by a stream 11km southeast of Kinvara, the 16th-century Norman tower of **Thoor Ballylee** *(yeatsthoorballylee.org; adult/child €7/free)* was the summer home of poet WB Yeats from 1921 to 1929 and was the inspiration for one of his best-known works, *The Tower*. Next door is a whitewashed cottage with forest-green trim, which contains an exhibition on Yeats' life and work.

Kinvara's charming stone harbour is overlooked by the remains of **Dunguaire Castle**. The 16th-century tower was once a meeting point for writers WB Yeats, Bernard Shaw and JM Synge, but is currently closed to the public. There are more

DRINKING BEYOND GALWAY CITY: OUR PICKS

Powers Thatch: A cute thatched cottage on Oughterard's main street, this comfy pub has open fires and welcoming service. *noon-midnight*

Cois Cuan: Authentic pub in Spiddal, with regular live music from local performers, rock, pop and trad. *3-11.30pm Mon-Thu, to 12.30am Fri & Sat, to 11pm Sun*

Green's Bar: Warm and welcoming Kinvara pub with T-shirts pinned to the ceiling and a mad selection of whiskeys. *5-11.30pm Mon-Thu, to midnight Fri & Sat, 2-11pm Sun*

O'Connor's Famous Pub (p325): Salthill institution with quirky decor and a role in Ed Sheeran's 'Galway Girl' video. *7.30-11.30pm Mon-Thu, to midnight Fri & Sat, to 11pm Sun*

literary connections along the Flaggy Shore (p292), west of Kinvara in County Clare.

Sailboats and shellfish

This normally peaceful corner of County Galway bursts into life on the second weekend of August when it hosts **Cruinniú na mBáid** *(cruinniu.ie)*, the 'Gathering of the Boats'. This annual regatta sees around a hundred Galway hookers. As well as boat races, there are trad music sessions, a farmers market, kids' events and the Green Island Swim, a 400m open water swimming race.

September marks the beginning of oyster season, marked on the first weekend of the month by the **Clarenbridge Oyster Festival** *(galwaytourism.ie)*. Established in 1954, this is a quieter alternative to the Galway Oyster Festival, with great food, creamy Guinness, music and entertainment on the banks of the River Clarenbridge. The oysters come from nearby Dunbulcaun Bay, and more than 100,000 of them are eaten during the weekend-long celebration.

Spiddal

TIME FROM GALWAY: **25MIN**

The Galway Gaeltacht

West of Galway city is the Galway Gaeltacht, the country's largest Irish-speaking area. It's a region rich with heritage and folklore, where Irish culture and traditions are still very much alive. Though it's only 18km away from Galway city, Spiddal (An Spidéal), one of the most vibrant Gaeltacht towns in the country, feels vastly removed from the buzz of urban life. **Coláiste Naomh Éanna** *(St Enda's College; colaistenaomheanna.ie)* runs one- and two-week Irish language courses based in Spiddal, offering total immersion in Gaeltacht life, culture and tradition.

Watch artists at work

Spiddal Craft Village *(spiddalcrafts.com)* is an Irish handicrafts haven where in-house artisans such as painter Andrea Rossi, jeweller Eric Byrne and potter Rob D'Eath design, create and sell their unique wares. You can visit the artists' studios and see basket weaving, acrylic painting, stained glass, ceramics, screen printing and Celtic jewellery in the process of creation.

CLADDAGH RINGS

Proudly adorning fingers around the world, the Claddagh ring is traditionally a symbol of love. The two open hands represent friendship and hold a heart that signifies love. They're topped by a crown of loyalty. Traditionally, your relationship status would indicate how the ring is worn.

Single: On your right hand, with the point of the heart facing your fingers and away from your heart.

In a relationship: On your right hand, with the point of the heart pointing at your wrist and heart.

Engaged: On your left hand, with the point of the heart facing your fingers.

Married: On your left hand, with the point of the heart facing your wrist.

Connemara National Park

RUGGED MOUNTAINS | FAMILY-FRIENDLY HIKES | NATIVE WILDLIFE

GETTING AROUND

Driving is the easiest way to get to the national park; there's free parking at the visitor centre. Walking is the only option for getting around within the national park.

Connemara National Park, once part of the privately owned Kylemore Estate, was opened to the public in 1980. Set in the northern part of County Galway, near the village of **Letterfrack**, it encompasses 20 sq km of mountain, bog, heath and woodland, showing off the region's wild, rugged and raw landscape at its best, and is home to rare plant species, wild red deer and Connemara ponies.

The park encloses several of the Twelve Bens (or Pins), Connemara's signature mountain range, including County Galway's highest point, Benbaun (729m). The heart of the park is An Gleann Mór (the Big Valley), through which flows the River Polladirk. There's adventurous walking to be had up the glen and over the surrounding mountains, but there are also short, self-guided walks on easy trails near the national park visitor centre and, if the Bens look too daunting, you can hike the waymarked trails on nearby Diamond Hill.

Take a Walk in the Park
Easy trails for laid-back days

Short family-friendly walks offer a great introduction to Connemara National Park. The **Ellis Wood Nature Trail** offers a relaxing 1km (30 minutes) stroll through the woods near the visitor centre, past a stream, a little waterfall and wood carvings of local wildlife. For a slightly more challenging walk, the **Sruffaunboy Trail** (yellow waymarks) climbs gently on broad gravel paths and provides great views over Ballynakill Harbour (1.8km; allow one hour); it's wheelchair- and buggy-accessible.

Park rangers lead free guided walks from the **Connemara National Park Visitor Centre** *(nationalparks.ie/connemara; free)*, housed in a historical building that dates from 1890 and once belonged to Letterfrack Industrial School. Pick up free trail maps here and check out the exhibits describing the peatland landscape and conservation projects. There's a

TOP TIP

If visiting the park by car, try to get there before midmorning as the visitor centre car park is often full up by midday, especially at weekends and during school holidays.

HIGHLIGHTS
1 Connemara National Park Visitor Centre
2 Diamond Hill
3 Pony Paddock

SIGHTS
4 Connemara National Park

SLEEPING
5 Cloverfox Hostel
6 Oyster Cottage
7 Rosleague Manor

EATING
8 Connemara Woodfire
see 1 Hungry Hiker Cafe
9 Kabo Coffee
10 Veldon's Seafarer

good cafe, as well as a playground and indoor and outdoor picnic facilities.

Hike Up Diamond Hill
Take to the park's tougher trails

Rising steeply to a prominent conical summit, Diamond Hill (442m) takes its name both from its shape and from the rocks on its upper slopes – when the sun shines, the white quartzite sparkles and shimmers like precious stones. The hike to the top is well worth the effort; you'll be rewarded with panoramic mountain and coastal views.

Hikers have two trail options on Diamond Hill. Both trails start at the Connemara National Park Visitor Centre and are well made and well marked. The easier of the two is the 3km **Lower Diamond Hill Walk** (allow 1½ hours for the return

EATING IN LETTERFRACK: OUR PICKS

Veldon's Seafarer: Classic Irish pub with rustic restaurant open all day; plenty of seafood on the menu, including the local oysters. *10am-9pm* €€

Hungry Hiker Cafe: The national park visitor centre's courtyard cafe serves decent cakes, salads and sandwiches. *10am-5pm* €

Connemara Woodfire: Authentic Italian wood-fired pizza, along with burgers, brisket, and fish and chips. Best to book ahead. *1-8.30pm* €€

Kabo Coffee: Coffee so good you might have to queue, and a tempting brunch menu served 10am to 2pm. *8am-6pm Fri-Wed, 8.30am-5.30pm Thu* €

LETTERFRACK'S HIDDEN HISTORY

Ellis Wood in Connemara National Park is named after James and Mary Ellis, a wealthy Quaker couple from Bradford in Yorkshire who moved to Connemara in 1849 to bring aid to the region during and after the Great Famine. They leased a huge tract of land and built houses for local people, a shop, a school and a temperance hotel, which formed the nucleus of what became the village of Letterfrack.

Much later, in 1887, St Joseph's Industrial School was established here. It became notorious for revelations about the extreme cruelty and abuse suffered by its pupils until its closure in 1974. It is thought that more than 100 boys died while attending the school. They are commemorated in the school graveyard next to the park visitor centre.

trip), which turns back at the Halfway Stone, returning to the visitor centre via a boardwalk over a bog road. You don't get the same amazing panorama as you would from the summit, but you're still rewarded with breathtaking views of the surrounding Connemara coastline and islands.

The 7km **Upper Diamond Hill Trail** takes about three hours. While you don't need to be a seasoned hillwalker to reach the summit, the trail is somewhat challenging and involves a steep haul up a narrow, zigzag path with stone steps, which can be slippery after rain. The trail continues down the far side of the hill and loops back via a valley on the south side; boardwalks and stepping stones help keep your feet dry on the boggy sections. Check the weather before you set off and be prepared for all seasons with adequate layers and proper footwear.

Watch Out for Wildlife

Learn about the environment

Connemara National Park is home to a range of wildlife, from hares, foxes and otters to sparrowhawks and peregrine falcons. There's also a small population of red deer, descended from a group that was translocated from Killarney National Park in the 1980s, but the most famous and well-loved inhabitants of the park are Connemara ponies. Although they are domesticated animals, they roam wild in the park, but can often be seen up close in the **Pony Paddock** beside the Sruffaunboy Trail. In July and August, the park visitor centre

The Twelve Bens

runs information sessions where you can learn about the breed and visit the Pony Stables.

Connemara Wild Escapes *(connemarawildescapes.ie; tour €500 for up to four persons)* runs an early-morning (5.30am start) guided 4x4 safari to view red deer in their natural environment; rutting season in October is the best time to go. They can also organise tours departing from Galway city that include a guided walk in the national park.

Tackle the Twelve Bens
Climb to County Galway's highest point

At the heart of the Connemara hills rises the Twelve Pins (or Twelve Bens) mountain range. Though small in stature, these craggy hills are characterised by acres of naked, pewter-tinged quartzite rock that creates some of Ireland's roughest hiking terrain.

The most popular objective in the Twelve Bens is **Benbaun**, at 729m the highest peak in Connemara and in all of County Galway. It's a long and strenuous hike (11km; seven hours) starting in Glencorbet to the north of the summit and, once again, is for experienced and well-equipped hillwalkers only, involving a river crossing and no clear trail for much of the ascent. If you're unsure of your abilities, **Mountain Trails** *(mountaintrails.ie; per person €40)* offers a seven-hour guided hike up Benbaun on one Sunday a month from May to September, meeting at Leenane, then car-sharing to the start point.

WHY I LOVE CONNEMARA

Noelle Kelly, Lonely Planet writer

As Oscar Wilde put it, Connemara is home to a 'savage beauty'. For me, the region's dramatic scenery truly encompasses what rural Ireland is all about. With bleak bogs, mountain peaks, grand castles, thatched cottages, and stone bridges and walls, the area is varied in physical beauty while maintaining a deep connection with traditional Irish culture.

I first visited as a teenager, and it was my first experience of such a rugged Irish landscape. Dotted with lost sheep, beautiful beaches and stunning scenery around every turn, Connemara never fails to take my breath away whenever I return.

Beyond Connemara National Park

Connemara National Park's gateway town of Letterfrack is a great base for exploring Kylemore Abbey, Leenane and Killary Harbour.

Places
Kylemore p334
Leenane p335
Renvyle p336

North Connemara extends north of Letterfrack and the N59, stretching from Renvyle in the west to Killary Harbour – Ireland's only fjord – in the east. The coast is awash with gorgeous beaches with mountain vistas and sunset views over Inishturk and Clare Island. Forsake the N59 for the network of minor roads that follow the twists and turns along the coast, promising off-the-beaten-path experiences and adventures on both land and sea.

To the east of Letterfrack lies Kylemore's 19th-century abbey, whose stunning neogothic architecture and ornate Victorian walled garden make it one of the most popular places to visit in the county.

GETTING AROUND

Driving is the most convenient option to get around at your leisure. **Bus Éireann** *(buseireann.ie)* bus 419 runs from Ceannt Train Station in Galway city and goes along the N59 to Clifden and on to Letterfrack and Leenane once a day. **City Link** *(citylink.ie)* operates four buses a day from Galway Bus Station to Letterfrack via Oughterard, Clifden and Cleggan.

Kylemore
TIME FROM LETTERFRACK: **5MIN**

Tour postcard-perfect Kylemore Abbey

Perched photogenically on the shores of Pollacapall Lough, 4km east of Letterfrack, the crenellated neogothic **Kylemore Abbey** *(kylemoreabbey.com; adult/child €18/free)* looks like a scene from a fairy tale. Mitchell Henry, the son of a wealthy Manchester cotton merchant of Irish origin, originally built this 19th-century structure as a country house – then called Kylemore Castle. In 1920 the castle was purchased by a community of Benedictine nuns, becoming the first Benedictine abbey in Ireland.

Allow at least two hours to explore the abbey and its gardens. The admission fee includes a self-guided tour of restored period rooms from when the castle was used as a hunting lodge, including the drawing room with an Italian marble fireplace and the impressive wood-panelled entrance hall. A 10-minute stroll east of the abbey lies a **neogothic church** and a mausoleum where Mitchell Henry and his wife, Margaret, are interred. In 1874 Margaret contracted dysentery on holiday in Egypt and died 16 days later. Distraught, Mitchell had his wife's body embalmed and brought back to Connemara, and built this cathedral-in-miniature in her memory. A pleasant 20-minute walk or a free shuttle bus ride west from the abbey, past little Maladrolaun Lake, is an extravagant **Victorian walled garden**.

The abbey can get very busy – get there soon after 10am opening to avoid the worst of the crowds.

Leenane

TIME FROM LETTERFRACK: **20MIN**

Take to the water in Killary Harbour

Slicing 16km inland and more than 45m deep in the centre, **Killary Harbour** is strikingly scenic and often referred to as Ireland's only fjord. The small village of Leenane sits on its southern shore, nestled among the Mweelrea, Devilsmother and Maamturk Mountains, and the approach is spectacular from all directions. *The Field* (1990), a famous Irish film directed by Jim Sheridan and starring Richard Harris, Tom Berenger and Sean Bean, was filmed mainly in Leenane and around Killary Harbour.

Hop aboard the super-comfortable catamaran operated by **Killary Fjord Boat Tours** *(killaryfjord.ie; adult/child €27/ free)* for a 90-minute cruise along the harbour to Barna island and back; keep your eyes peeled for dolphins. You also pass a mussel farm and pause at a salmon farm.

Experience life on a sheep farm

At **Killary Sheep Farm** *(killarysheepfarm.com; per person €12)* you can experience life on a traditional Connemara farm with Tom Nee, who puts on impressive displays of sheep herding with his dogs, as well as demonstrations of sheepshearing by hand (June to mid-August). You might even get the opportunity to feed baby lambs (mid-March to mid-August). The farm is on the shores of Killary Harbour, 9km west of Leenane, and is open year-round; booking is essential.

Joyce Country Sheepdogs *(joycecountrysheepdogs.ie; adult/child €15/5)* occupies a working hill farm on the slopes above lovely Lough Na Fooey, 14km east of Leenane. From March to September, they run demonstrations of the amazing herding feats performed by their beautiful border collies working with the local Connemara blackface sheep; you'll get to see cute collie pups too. There's no need to book ahead – just turn up shortly before the scheduled demonstration times at 11am, 1pm and 3.30pm from Monday to Saturday.

NUNS ON THE RUN

In 1914 a group of Benedictine nuns fled Ypres in Belgium after their abbey was destroyed during the early days of WWI. The Irish Dames of Ypres, as they were known, had a long history dating back to 1598, but now found themselves refugees first in England, then in Ireland. They arrived in Connemara in 1920 and set up in **Kylemore Castle**, establishing Ireland's first Benedictine abbey.

In 1923 the nuns founded an exclusive convent boarding school here, attracting students from Ireland, Europe, Asia and the USA, until it closed down in 2010. With the opening of the new Monastery of the Immaculate Conception in the abbey grounds in 2024, Kylemore continues to be a working convent as well as a flourishing tourist attraction.

 EATING AROUND LEENANE: OUR PICKS

Leenane Hotel: The bar serves regional specialities such as fresh Killary Bay salmon, seafood chowder and rack of Connemara lamb. *noon-9pm* €€

Purple Door Cafe: Great breakfast and lunch stop that dishes out soup, sandwiches, delicious coffee and cakes. *9am-5pm* €

Gaynor's Bar: Famous Leenane pub serving simple homemade food – soup with soda bread, toasted sandwiches, apple pie. *noon-9pm* €€

TIA Food Truck: Sleek aluminium trailer on the shores of Doo Lough, 14km north of Leenane; excellent coffee, sausage rolls and panini. *11am-4pm* €

THE CONNEMARA RAILWAY

Opened in 1895, the Galway to Clifden railway line had a short life, closing down in 1935 as road travel became increasingly important. The line ran through Moycullen, Oughterard, Maam Cros, Recess and Ballynahinch, and was popular with tourists during its lifetime. Parts of the line have been converted into cycle trails as part of the **Connemara Greenway**, which will eventually provide an off-road link between Galway and Clifden.

A short section of rails and associated buildings has been restored at Maam Cross Station, 35km east of Clifden, as part of the **Connemara Railway** (connemararailway.ie) heritage project. It opened to the public in July 2025, when trains ran on the track here for the first time in 90 years.

Glassillaun

Renvyle

TIME FROM LETTERFRACK: **10MIN**

Feel sand between your toes

Connemara's north coast is home to three superb beaches. All three have car parks but none have public toilets or showers and all are at their best at low tide, when the expanse of sand is at its largest. **Renvyle Beach** in the west is usually the busiest of the three, with a sizeable caravan park at its back and a Wild Atlantic Way discovery point (Islands View). **Glassillaun**, in the east, is quieter, with a perfect semicircle of pale gold sand slung between two rocky headlands.

Arguably the best of the three is **Lettergesh Beach**, where the famous horse-racing scene from the 1952 movie *The Quiet Man* (p328) was shot. From the car park, you can walk 800m to the north end, where Connemara Camping's campsite overlooks the sands. Check the tide times – for two hours either side of low water you can wade across the mouth of the Culfin River here (just over knee deep) to reach the northern part of the beach, a 500m stretch of silver sand with no other access that you'll likely have all to yourself.

Clifden

ARTS FESTIVALS | INDEPENDENT SHOPS | CONNEMARA PONIES

A definitive stop on any tour of Connemara, the region's 'capital', Clifden (An Clochán, meaning 'stepping stone'), is an appealingly picturesque Victorian-era market town and tourist centre presiding over the head of the narrow bay where the River Owenglin tumbles into the sea. Founded by local landowner John D'Arcy in 1812, the town grew from almost nothing to a population of 1200 by 1831, not far short of its current population of around 1600.

Despite its small size, Clifden's triangle of central streets is home to a colourful collection of craft shops, galleries, designer boutiques and lively pubs, plus a weekly farmers market. The town has a strong cultural and artistic scene, hosting several annual festivals, and is ideally situated for exploring Connemara by bike with the wildly indented Atlantic coast to the west, the Twelve Bens mountain range to the east and the level, lake-splattered expanse of Roundstone Bog to the south.

Take a Stroll around the Square
Monuments and market stalls

Clifden is unusual in Ireland in being a planned town, created in 1812 by the local landowner John D'Arcy. The town centre is a rough triangle formed by Bridge St, Market St and Main St, the latter two of which converge on **Market Square**, the bustling heart of Clifden, marked by a tall, triangular obelisk made of perforated stainless steel. Known as **The Beacon**, and created by Wexford artist Declan Breen, the pillar is lit from within and was installed in 2000 to mark the advent of the new millennium. In front of it stands a bronze statue commemorating the transatlantic flight of Alcock and Brown.

Outdoor pub and restaurant tables throng the east side of the square and, if it's a Friday, the weekly **farmers market** will be in full swing, where you can savour a delicious crêpe from **Le Crepe Wagon** before looking over the stalls filled

GETTING AROUND

Clifden is easily explored on foot, and cycling is the best option for reaching places outside town as parking is often difficult to find on the narrow country roads. You can hire a **bike** from Mannion's (Clifden Bike Hire) on Bridge St.

☑ TOP TIP

The roads leading in and out of Clifden are all narrow and twisting with no footpath or sidewalk. Don't be tempted to walk along them – travelling by bicycle or car is safer.

CLIFDEN

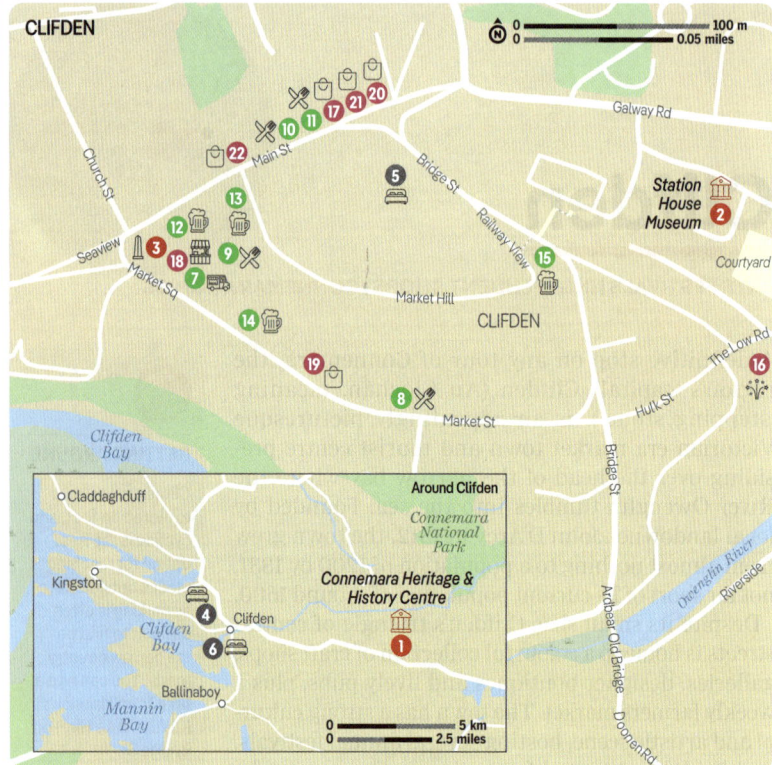

HIGHLIGHTS
1. Connemara Heritage & History Centre
2. Station House Museum

SIGHTS
3. The Beacon

SLEEPING
4. Abbeyglen Castle Hotel
5. Ben View House
6. Quay House

EATING
7. Le Crepe Wagon
8. Mannions Seafood Bar & Restaurant
9. Mitchell's
10. Off the Square
11. Upstairs Downstairs Cafe

DRINKING & NIGHTLIFE
12. EJ Kings
13. Guys Bar
14. Lowry's Bar
15. MC McGraths

ENTERTAINMENT
16. Connemara Pony Show

SHOPPING
17. Clifden Bookshop
18. Clifden Farmers Market
19. Conn O'Mara
20. Connemara Blue
21. Lavelle Art Gallery
22. Millars

with local produce from Connemara, from organic vegetables, herbs, bread and pies to preserves, cheese and honey.

Browse the Town Museum

Local history and heritage

A peaceful hidden square to the east of Clifden town centre marks the site of the town's former railway station. Here the **Station House Museum** *(connemara.net/the-station-house-museum; adult/child €3/2)*, located in a red-brick former train shed, offers the chance to learn about pivotal aspects of Clifden's history including the Connemara Railway (in service from 1895 to 1935), Guglielmo Marconi's transatlantic wireless station at Derrigimlagh, and the transatlantic flight of Alcock and Brown in 1919. There's also a wealth of information on Connemara ponies.

Soak Up Connemara's Heritage
History, tradition and farm animals

For an immersion in traditional Connemara culture, the award-winning, family-run **Connemara Heritage & History Centre** (connemaraheritage.net; adult/child €9/4.50), 6km from Clifden, is open from April to November. The restored pre-Famine cottage of Dan O'Hara is the main draw and illustrates the life of a typical 19th-century Connemara tenant farmer. There's a multilingual audiovisual history presentation that tells O'Hara's life story, from his eviction from the farm to his emigration to New York. The centre also shows the history of Connemara from the prehistoric to the present.

Trot along to the Pony Show
Connemara ponies galore

Clifden stages the four-day **Connemara Pony Show** (connemaraponyshow.ie) every August, and has done so since 1925, attracting visitors from near and far. The highlight of the festival is the biggest showcase of Connemara ponies in the world, which stand out for their versatility, resilience and gentle nature. There's also a dog show, a domestic arts show and Irish dancing.

Check Out Clifden's Arts Festival
A cultural cornucopia

Ireland's longest-running community arts festival, the **Clifden Arts Festival** (clifdenartsfestival.ie) started out in 1977 and has now become a major event on County Galway's cultural calendar. For 11 days in September, the town is given over to a celebration of all things creative, with shops and cafes doubling as exhibition venues for paintings and photography. There are film society screenings, plays, *sean-nós* (traditional storytelling), books and music, plus workshops on everything from Irish dance to Indian cookery and poetry to astrophotography. Book accommodation well in advance if you plan to stay in Clifden during the festival.

CLIFDEN'S ALCOCK & BROWN CONNECTION

Clifden's Market Sq is overlooked by the Alcock and Brown Hotel, and dominated by a bronze statue of the two airmen, complete with sheepskin jackets, leather flying helmets and goggles. The commemorative plaque reads: 'To mark the centenary of the first nonstop transatlantic flight from North America to Europe by Alcock and Brown, June 1919'.

The pioneering flight of John Alcock and Arthur Brown, in a twin-engine Vickers Vimy biplane, took off from St John's in Newfoundland, Canada, and – 16 hours and 1890 miles later – crash landed in a bog at Derrigimlagh, 4.5km south of Clifden. News of their successful crossing was transmitted to London from Marconi's telegraph station nearby. The aircraft was recovered and is on display in London's Science Museum.

 EATING IN CLIFDEN: OUR PICKS

Off the Square: Surf meets turf on the menu of this busy town-centre bistro serving full Irish breakfasts, casual lunches and hearty dinners. *10am-9pm* €€

Mitchell's: Seafood from the surrounding waters takes centre stage at this elegant spot, from velvety chowder to seafood platters. *noon-10pm* €€

Mannions Seafood Bar & Restaurant: This family-run restaurant serves mouthwatering local produce from burgers to vegetarian dishes. *noon-9pm* €€

Upstairs Downstairs Cafe: Great coffee and cakes. The breakfast menu includes bagels, pastries and American-style pancakes. *9am-5.30pm Mon-Sat, 10am-5pm Sun* €

CYCLING TOUR

The Sky Road Loop

Starting and ending in Clifden, this 20km route traces a dizzying loop to the township of Kingston and back, taking in rugged, stunningly beautiful coastal scenery. Without stopping, the bike ride would take only two hours, but it's best to allow half a day to soak up the spectacular scenery and stop along the way. The Sky Rd separates into the lower and upper road routes. For the best views, take the upper road.

1 Clifden

The Sky Rd route begins in the lively town of Clifden, where you can hire a bike and get caffeinated in one of several excellent cafes.

The Ride: A stiff uphill of little more than 1km from Clifden leads to a brown signpost that points you in the direction of the John D'Arcy Monument. Leave your bike at the gate and climb to the monument on foot.

2 John D'Arcy Monument

Founded in the 19th century, Clifden is a relatively new town by Irish standards and was founded by John D'Arcy. Following D'Arcy's death in 1839, this monument was erected in his memory at the peak of the hill that overlooks the western end of town. There are expansive views of the Connemara landscape of mountains, bogs and coast. It's one of the best spots to snap photographs of Clifden.

Sky Road Viewpoint

The Ride: Continue northwest on Sky Rd for about 2km to reach Clifden Castle. You'll see a wide opening on your left that includes a turn to the south along another road to a small car park. An arched gateway leads to the castle.

❸ Clifden Castle

The D'Arcy family built this manor house, now derelict and roofless, as their family home. It looks older than it actually is, and it was constructed in Gothic Revival style in 1818. It faces Clifden Bay, which makes for a picturesque photo.

The Ride: Back on Sky Rd, continue climbing steadily northwest for 2.7km.

❹ Sky Road Viewpoint

This viewpoint, marked by one of the wrought-iron Wild Atlantic Way signs, is the pinnacle of the road trip and the best spot to take photos. There's a car park with some picnic tables, making it a perfect place for a snack with a view.

The Ride: Freewheel downhill and through the township of Kingston, reaching the coast after 3km.

❺ Eyrephort Beach

Visitors to quiet and secluded Eyrephort Beach are rewarded with far-reaching views of the nearby offshore islands of Inishturk and Turbot, as well as the Connemara countryside and the Atlantic Ocean. This beautiful beach is a little off the beaten track, providing a welcome seaside reprieve. Remnants of Viking history, including a grave, sword and shield, have been discovered here. Make your way back to Clifden via the rest of the signposted Sky Rd loop. The northern side of the peninsula is less dramatic.

CLIFDEN'S BEST SHOPS

Lavelle Art Gallery: Art gallery established in 1988 that represents a broad range of local artists; strong on Connemara landscapes, wildlife and ponies.

Connemara Blue: Glassware shop with a glinting array of plates, bowls, vases and sculptures in traditional and contemporary designs.

Clifden Bookshop: Local history, memoirs, Irish literature and plant and wildlife guides are among the titles at this well-stocked bookshop.

Conn O'Mara: Cracking gift shop with a wide choice of Irish crafts, the ideal place to browse for souvenirs.

Millars: Established in 1890, this is the place to shop for Connemara tweeds, designer clothes and accessories.

Salt Lake outflow and bridge

Take a Dip in the Salt Lake
Wild swimming and snorkelling

The coast near Clifden is indented with countless coves and inlets that are ideal for swimming and snorkelling. The most unusual is the Salt Lake, a tidal lagoon whose inflow and outflow surges beneath a road bridge 3km south of the town. The lake's deepest point is over 40m, but there is lots of marine wildlife to spot in the shallows, including jewel anemones, sea slugs and thornback rays.

Most of the lake is surrounded by private property; the only public access is across the road from Clifden Community School, and on the south side of the bridge. It's a six-minute bike ride from Clifden; there is limited parking for cars on the verge opposite the school.

DRINKING IN CLIFDEN: OUR PICKS

Lowry's Bar: Voted the best pub in Ireland at the National Hospitality Awards. Traditional music nightly in summer. *12.30-11.30pm Sun-Thu, to 12.30am Fri & Sat*

EJ Kings: A good spot for live music, regularly hosts local musicians and locals. *10am-11.30pm Mon-Thu, to 12.30am Fri & Sat, to 11pm Sun*

MC McGraths: Enjoy a creamy pint in one of the oldest family-owned bars in Clifden. *noon-11.30pm Mon-Thu, to 12.30am Fri & Sat, to 11pm Sun*

Guys Bar: Expect turf fires, excellent pub grub, small intimate snugs and corners, and live trad music. *noon-11pm Mon-Fri, to 11.30pm Sat, 12.30-11pm Sun*

Beyond Clifden

Epic bike rides, coastal drives, beautiful boglands, golden beaches and tidal island hikes reward visitors exploring beyond Clifden.

The Irish name for Clifden is An Clochán, which means stepping stone, and it's a fitting description because the town is often used as a stepping stone for exploring the wider region. Beyond Clifden, some of Ireland's most breathtaking and secluded beaches await. The area is also home to some of the region's best cycle trails as well as epic scenic road trips, such as the aptly named Sky Rd. The walking trails of Connemara National Park are easily accessible, or you can walk across the sand to Omey Island at low tide. Stay a while in this lesser-explored part of Galway and you'll be rewarded with sleepy seaside villages and stunning views around every turn.

Places
Cleggan p343
Derrigimlagh p343
Ballyconneely p345
Roundstone p346
Gortmore p346

Cleggan

TIME FROM CLIFDEN: **15MIN**

Connemara on two wheels

The Cleggan Loop is a 33km cycling route north from Clifden to the rocky coastline around the charming fishing village of Cleggan, following the fringes of Streamstown Bay. The route passes Omey Island (p344) – you can visit this beautiful island on foot when the tide is out.

Derrigimlagh

TIME FROM CLIFDEN: **15MIN**

GETTING AROUND

The area around Clifden is best explored by car or bike. Bikes can be rented in Clifden from **Clifden Bike Shop** (clifdenbikeshop.ie) and **Mannion's Bikes** (facebook.com/mannionbikehire).

Top transatlantic history

The Wild Atlantic Way signature discovery point at Derrigimlagh has a twofold historical significance. Not only was it the site of the world's **first wireless telegraph station**, established here in 1907 by Guglielmo Marconi, but also the landing site of the **first nonstop transatlantic flight**. A 5km scenic trail runs from the car park to **Marconi's Station** *(free)*, where a wealth of interactive exhibits dot the windswept bogland: crystal radio sets play original recordings – these messages were the earliest transatlantic wireless communications. The station operated until 1922, when it was attacked by Republican forces.

Artistic information panels also mark the area's other claim to fame: in 1919 British aviators **John Alcock and Arthur Brown** completed the first nonstop transatlantic flight when they crash-landed into the bog barely 500m away. Both aviators

HIKING TO OMEY ISLAND

Omey is a small, uninhabited island that you can reach by walking across the sands of Omey Strand near Claddaghduff.

START	END	LENGTH
Omey Strand parking	Omey Strand parking	8km; 3hr

Omey is accessible for three hours either side of low tide, so time your walk to begin about three hours before low water (check tide times online or at Clifden tourist office). Aim straight across the strand towards the obvious cemetery. 1 **Omey Strand** is a vast expanse of firm sand; horse races have been held here on the first Saturday in August for more than 60 years.

Take a look around 2 **Omey Island Cemetery**, which is filled with interesting gravestones, then continue along the north side of the island. St Fechin established a monastery here in the 6th century – its name comes from the Gaelic Iomaidh Feichín, 'Fechin's Bed'. All that remains is 3 **Teampaill Feichin**, a ruined medieval church that was uncovered in 1981 after being buried in the sand dunes for centuries.

4 **Illaunakeegher** at the northwest corner provides a fine viewpoint; rabbit burrows on the headland often reveal shells and bones from ancient middens. On the north side of the bay on Omey's west shore, you'll find 5 **St Fechin's Holy Well**, marked by a wooden cross and a circle of stones. A sandy track leads to a cluster of 6 **holiday cottages** and a tarred road that leads to the strand; follow the marker poles back to the mainland.

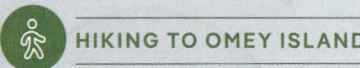

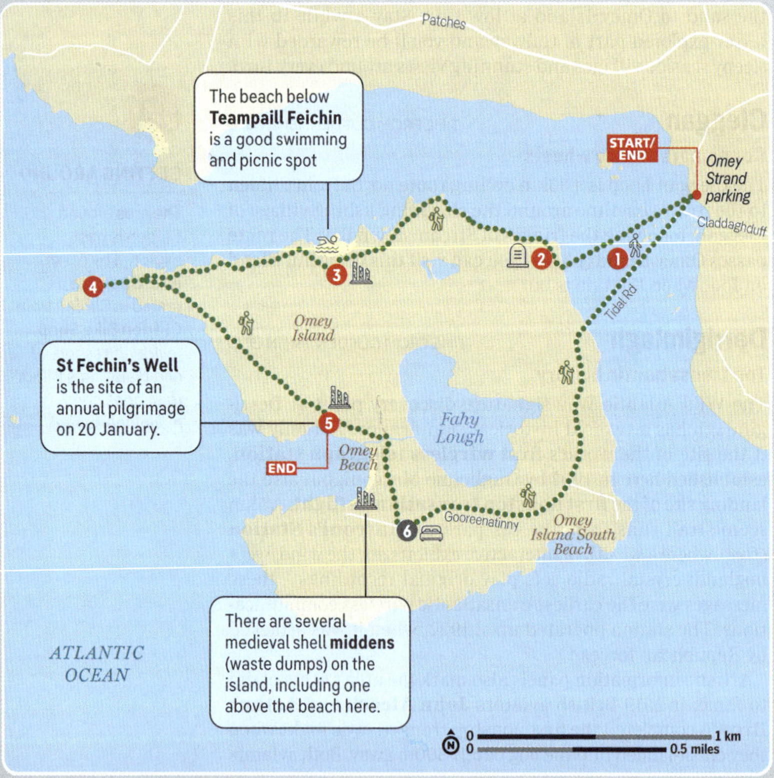

Patches
The beach below **Teampaill Feichin** is a good swimming and picnic spot
START/ END
Omey Strand parking
Claddaghduff
Tidal Rd
Omey Island
St Fechin's Well is the site of an annual pilgrimage on 20 January.
END
Omey Beach
Fahy Lough
Gooreenatinny
Omey Island South Beach
There are several medieval shell **middens** (waste dumps) on the island, including one above the beach here.
ATLANTIC OCEAN
0 1 km
0 0.5 miles

Omey Island

survived and were awarded the honour of Knight Commander of the British Empire (KBE) a week later by King George V.

Ballyconneely

TIME FROM CLIFDEN: 15MIN

Sample local smoked salmon

If you're curious to discover how the area's famous salmon is smoked, you can tour the family-run **Connemara Smokehouse** *(smokehouse.ie; per person €55)*. On Wednesdays from June to August guided tours show you the hand filleting, traditional preparation, slicing and packing of the wild and organic salmon, and shed light on various smoking methods before finishing up with a tasting session. Advance reservations are essential. Outside high season it's usually possible to stop by the smokehouse and stock up if you call ahead.

Ride a horse along a beach

If you have ever imagined yourself cantering on horseback along a sandy beach, with the Atlantic waves foaming on one side and the hills of Connemara rising on the other, it's a dream that can come true at **Point Pony Trekking** *(thepointpony trekkingcentre.com; per person from €60)*, near Ballyconneely. From April to August, the company runs daily (except Sunday) one- or two-hour beach treks for riders of all abilities along

TIM ROBINSON

Tim Robinson (1935–2020) was an English writer, artist and cartographer who moved to the west of Ireland in 1972 and became famous for his intimate studies of Irish landscapes, language and history.

Living first in the Aran Islands, he produced detailed, hand-drawn maps of the islands and two groundbreaking books: *Stones of Aran: Pilgrimage* (1986) and *Stones of Aran: Labyrinth* (1995). In 1984 he and his wife Máiréad moved to Roundstone, where he produced a similarly detailed map of South Connemara and a trilogy of award-winning books: *Listening to the Wind* (2006), *The Last Pool of Darkness* (2008) and *A Little Gaelic Kingdom* (2011).

The original, self-published maps are collectors' items; reproductions can be seen in Galway City Museum (p323).

EATING BEYOND CLIFDEN: OUR PICKS

O'Dowd's: Local lobster, crab and mackerel smoked in-house are sourced off the old stone dock directly opposite this authentic Roundstone pub. *10am-9pm €€*

Coffee Cottage: Quayside cafe in Roundstone famed for its excellent coffee and delicious ice cream. Serves breakfast and lunch too. *9am-4pm €*

POTA: Popular community cafe in Ballynahown serving hot lunches from noon to 3pm, including seafood chowder and filled focaccia sandwiches. *9am-4pm Tue-Sat, 10am-4pm Sun €€*

Oliver's Seafood Bar: Cleggan pub serving breakfast, lunch and dinner including locally landed lobster, scallops and crab. *9.30am-9pm €€*

THE BODHRÁN

The bodhrán is an Irish frame drum, traditionally made of goatskin stretched over a circular wooden frame, typically 45cm in diameter. Although the earliest known mention of the word bodhrán is to be found in a 15th-century manuscript, it is possible that the instrument dates back to the time of the ancient Celts.

It is played by holding the drum with one hand and beating it with the other, either with the back of the fingers or with a wooden beater known as a *cipín*.

The **Craiceann International Bodhrán Summer School** *(craiceann. com)* is a five-day event held each June on the Aran island of Inisheer (p348), where you can sign up for classes, including some for absolute beginners.

the gorgeous silver-sand strands of southwest Connemara. From September to October, rides are limited to Thursday to Sunday. Book in advance via phone or email.

Roundstone

TIME FROM CLIFDEN: **25MIN**

A creative Connemara village

Clustered around a boat-filled harbour, Roundstone (Cloch na Rón) is one of Connemara's gems, whose idyllic surroundings have lured film-makers, artists, writers and musicians to make their home here. Wander along its seafront of colourful terrace houses and inviting pubs, and pause to take in the view across Roundstone Bay, home to fishing boats and traditional *currachs* (rowing boats) with hulls of tarred canvas stretched over wooden frames.

At the south end of the village, bear left along Monastery Rd, where you'll find the workshop of **Malachy Kearns** *(bodhran. com)*. Here you can watch Ireland's only full-time maker of bodhráns handcrafting these traditional goatskin drums. Other traditional Irish instruments are also for sale here, along with sheet music and recordings. Next door is **Roundstone Ceramics**, where you can admire (and buy) the decorative cups, bowls and tiles produced on-site by Rosemarie O'Toole and Seamus Laffan.

On Sundays from 11am to 4pm you can browse the stalls at the village's **Country Market**, which sets up in the car park opposite the Roundstone Hotel.

Gortmore

TIME FROM CLIFDEN: **40MIN**

Patrick Pearse's cottage

Pádraig Pearse (Patrick Pearse; 1879-1916) was a teacher, writer, poet and political activist who established the influential Irish-language school St Enda's in Dublin, and was one of the leaders of the Easter Rising of 1916; after the revolt he was executed by the British at Kilmainham Gaol along with his fellow rebels. In 1909 he had a cottage built at Ros Muc in Connemara as a summer home where he wrote many of his poems and short stories. To mark the centenary of the uprising in 2016 his cottage, **Teach an Phiarsaigh** (Pearse's House) was restored and a cultural centre, **Ionad Cultúrtha an Phiarsaigh** *(heritageireland.ie; adult/child €5/3)* built nearby. Exhibits here celebrate Pearse's life and writings, from where you can make the five-minute walk to the cottage, which occupies a breathtakingly beautiful spot overlooking the shore of Lough Aroolagh.

🚲 BIKING THE BOG ROAD

This route combines a recently opened cycle track with a return across Connemara's famous Bog Rd.

START	END	LENGTH
Clifden	Clifden	32km; 3hr

Leave Clifden via Bridge St. Where the main road bends right, keep straight on across the bridge above ❶ **Owenglin Falls**, where salmon can be seen leaping in June and July. Follow this minor road for 3.2km and turn right on the ❷ **Connemara Greenway**, a planned 76km cycle route from Galway to Clifden. After only 850m turn left to reach a cycle track that runs parallel to the N59 road and follow it to the ❸ **Connemara Heritage & History Centre** (p319).

Ride along the N59 for 3km and turn right to ❹ **Ballynahinch Castle Hotel** (p353), where the Garden Cafe provides a coffee stop (closed Monday and Tuesday). A little further on is the ❺ **Connemara Greenway car park**, where another section of greenway leads east. Ignore this and continue on the road to ❻ **Toombeola Bridge**, built in 1831, a popular salmon fishing spot; 1.6km past the bridge, where the R341 swings a sharp left, continue straight.

You are now on the ❼ **Bog Road**, which runs for 10km across Roundstone Bog with grand views of the Twelve Bens; water-filled ditches on either side of the road show where peat has been cut in decades past. At the far end, turn right past the ❽ **Salt Lake**, a tidal lagoon, to return to Clifden.

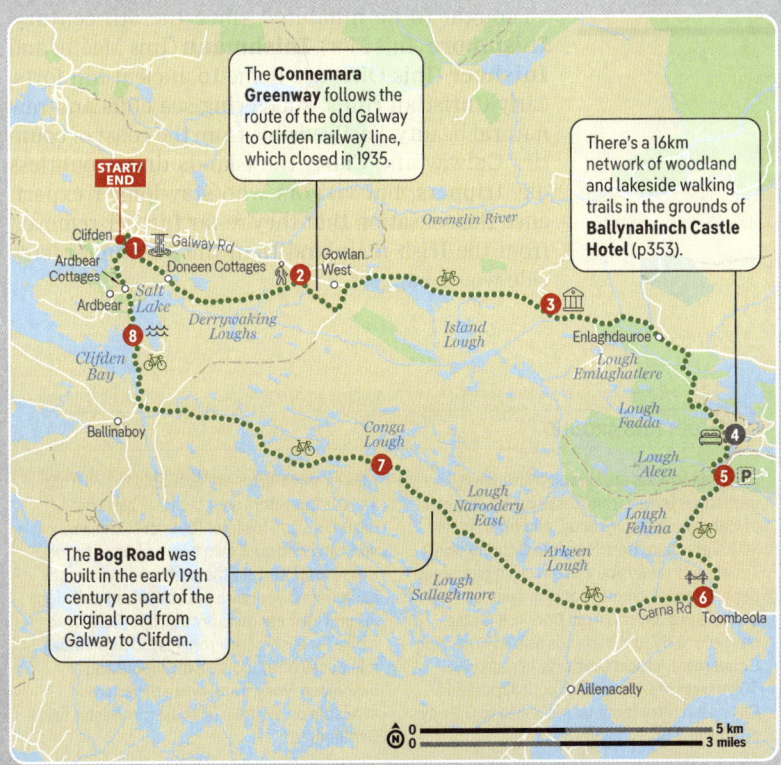

The **Connemara Greenway** follows the route of the old Galway to Clifden railway line, which closed in 1935.

There's a 16km network of woodland and lakeside walking trails in the grounds of **Ballynahinch Castle Hotel** (p353).

The **Bog Road** was built in the early 19th century as part of the original road from Galway to Clifden.

Aran Islands

ANCIENT FORTS | SPECTACULAR CLIFFS | IRISH CULTURE

☑ TOP TIP

The best way to see Dún Aonghasa is to get the 9am ferry from Doolin, pick up a prebooked e-bike at Kilronan, and head straight to Dún Aonghasa – you'll be there by 10.15am and have the site almost to yourself. By noon the place is mobbed.

Blasted by the wind and washed by Atlantic waves, the eroded slivers of rock known as the Aran Islands hold an eternal fascination for travellers. Their exposed landscapes are home to descendants of unimaginably hardy folk who forged their own culture of survival. Left to nature, these three islands would be bare rocks, but generations of islanders have gathered and spread seaweed and sand by hand over the centuries, creating fertile fields.

Thought to be inhabited since the 5th century, **Inishmore** (Inis Mór), **Inishmaan** (Inis Meáin) and **Inisheer** (Inis Oírr) are home to ancient hill forts, early Christian ruins, staggering sea cliffs and raw natural beauty. Easily visible from the coast of counties Galway and Clare, the islands draw countless day trippers, but visitors who stay longer experience the sensation that they're far further removed from the Irish mainland than the 40-minute ferry ride would suggest.

GETTING AROUND

The Aran Islands are served by frequent passenger ferries from Rossaveal (38km west of Galway city) year-round, and from Doolin in County Clare from March to October only. Timetables mean you can only visit one island per day; only Inishmore and Inisheer can be done in a day trip from Doolin. It is also possible to fly to the islands as a day trip from Connemara Airport (Aerfort Chonamara), 30km west of Galway city; both airport and Rossaveal ferry terminal are linked to Galway by shuttle bus.

Bikes and e-bikes are available to hire from various operators near the ferry piers on Inishmore and Inisheer (but not Inishmaan; you can bring your own bike on ferries from Rossaveal), and are the preferred option for exploring at your own pace. You can walk right around Inisheer on a day trip, but you'll need a bike for Inishmore. From May to September, minibuses offer tours on Inishmore and Inishmaan. Pony traps with a driver are available on all three islands from Easter to September.

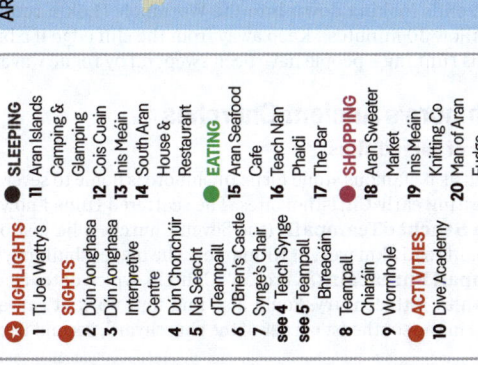

Ireland's most Spectacular Hill Fort
Clifftop prehistoric site

Inishmore's **Dún Aonghasa** *(heritageireland.ie; adult/child €5/3)*, 7km west of the ferry pier at Kilronan, is one of the most iconic stone forts in Ireland, perched on the very edge of an 87m-high cliff overlooking the Atlantic. Its three massive, semicircular drystone walls run right up to a sheer drop to the ocean below. Built around 1100 BCE, it was refortified around 700 CE and is protected by remarkable chevaux-de-frise: a fearsome defensive feature composed of densely packed limestone spikes. A complete lack of railings or other modern additions that would spoil this incredible site means that you can not only go right up to the cliff's edge, but also potentially fall to your doom below – take care, especially with children.

At Kilmurvey, the **Dún Aonghasa Interpretive Centre** provides information on the site's history, along with bike parking, shops and food trucks. From here it's a 900m walk on a stony path to the fort.

Witness the Wormhole
Hike to Inishmore's weirdest rock formation

One of the Aran Islands' strangest and most impressive natural features lies hidden on the coast around 1km southeast of Dún Aonghasa. The Wormhole (also known as the Serpent's Lair, or Poll na bPéist in Gaelic) is a huge rectangular basin in a wave-cut limestone platform, connected to the open sea by flooded subterranean tunnels. Although it looks artificial, it is entirely natural, the result of a cavern collapse. This spectacular feature was a venue for the Red Bull Cliff Diving World Series in 2014 and 2017, but don't be tempted to go swimming here – there are dangerous currents, and while jumping in might be easy, getting out again is problematic.

The hiking trail to the Wormhole begins in the hamlet of **Gort Na gCapall** (signposted off the main road 400m east of Kilmurvey Beach). A vague path, marked by the occasional red-painted arrow, leads over limestone slabs and along a broad rock shelf beneath small crags; just when you start thinking 'how much further?' you arrive at an amphitheatre in the cliffs looking down into the Wormhole (1.6km round trip; allow 30 minutes). Keep away from the cliff edge if a big swell is running – people have been swept off by rogue waves.

Inishmore's Ancient Churches
A tour of sacred sites

As well as its famous stone forts, Inishmore is home to several interesting early Christian sites. The scattered ruins known as **Na Seacht dTeampaill** (the Seven Churches) lie just off the main road 3km west of Kilmurvey. The biggest building is **Teampall Bhreacáin** (St Brecan's Church), which dates from the 8th to 13th century. You'll also find four upright carved stones in the southeast corner of the churchyard; second from

---

SOUVENIRS FROM THE ARAN ISLANDS

Pick up an Aran knit as a keepsake from your trip. At the pier on Inishmore, the **Aran Sweater Market** is famous for its handmade jumpers, created by talented craftspeople who live on the island. All Aran knit garments must pass the highest quality standards and are examined by hand before being issued a signed and stamped certificate of authenticity.

On Inisheer, visit **Man of Aran Fudge**. Even though these sweet treats are available at farmers markets across the country, here you can savour them in their home setting. You'll also meet Tomás, who has been making award-winning fudge for more than 20 years and continues a longstanding family tradition.

WALKING AROUND INISHEER, THE SMALLEST ARAN ISLAND

Inisheer (Inis Oírr), the smallest of the Aran Islands, has wildflower-strewn landscapes and enduring traditional culture.

START	END	LENGTH
Inisheer ferry pier	Cnoc Rathnaí	11km; 4–5hr

From ❶ **Inisheer ferry pier**, walk west along the narrow road parallel to the shore and go straight on to the small fishing pier at the northwest corner of the island. Continue along the road with the shingle shore on one side and a dense patchwork of fields enclosed by stone walls on the other.

About 1km beyond a sharp junction, turn left at a painted sign – about 100m along the paved lane is the ❷ **Sacred Well** (Well of Enda). Continue southwest as the path becomes a rough track. After about 600m, head roughly south across limestone pavement and strips of grass to the shore.

Follow the gently sloping rock platform around the southwestern headland and continue east to ❸ **Inisheer Lighthouse**. Follow the road, then the coastal path and the road again to reach the ❹ **wreck of the Plassy**. Follow the track, which becomes a sealed road at ❺ **Lough More**, and on along the northern shore of the island, past the ❻ **airstrip**. Detour to ❼ **Teampall Chaoimháin**, the burial site of St Caomhán, patron saint of the Aran Islands; the ruins date from the 10th century. Soak in the incredible views from nearby ❽ **O'Brien's Castle** and check out ❾ **Cnoc Rathnaí**, a remarkably intact Bronze Age burial mound dating from 1500 BCE.

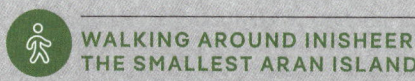

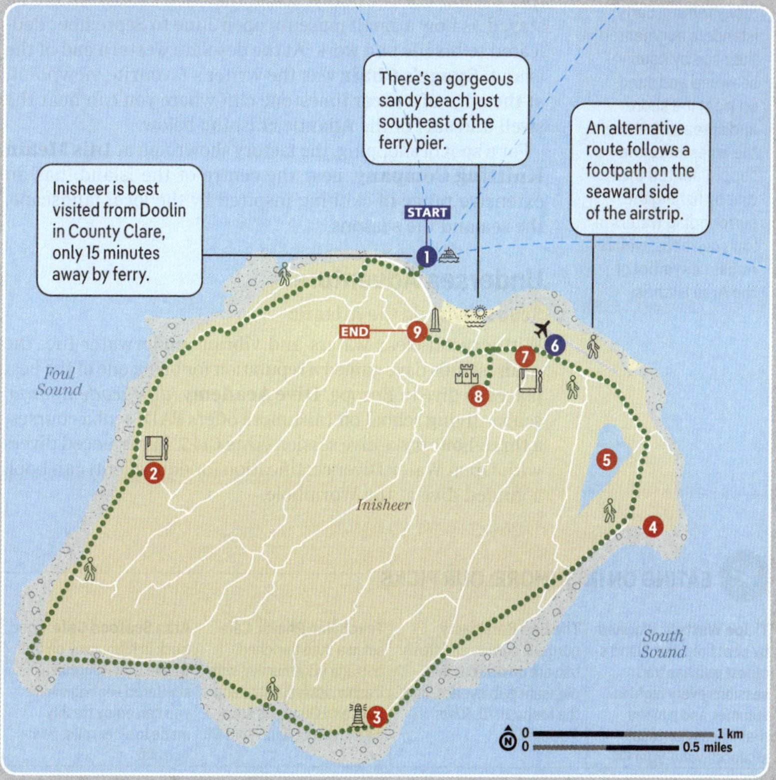
There's a gorgeous sandy beach just southeast of the ferry pier.
An alternative route follows a footpath on the seaward side of the airstrip.
Inisheer is best visited from Doolin in County Clare, only 15 minutes away by ferry.
START
END
Foul Sound
Inisheer
South Sound
0
1 km
0
0.5 miles

ARAN HISTORY

Little is known about the people who built the massive Iron Age stone structures on Inishmore and Inishmaan. Commonly referred to as 'forts', they are believed to have served as pagan religious centres.

Folklore holds that they were built by the Firbolgs, a people who invaded Ireland from Europe in prehistoric times. It's thought that people came to the islands to farm, a major challenge given the rocky terrain. Early islanders augmented their soil by hauling seaweed and sand up from the shore and spreading it over the limestone, and supplemented their diet by fishing the surrounding waters in long *currachs*, which remain a symbol of the Aran Islands.

the left bears the inscription 'VII ROMANI' (seven Romans), thought to commemorate medieval pilgrims from Rome.

Teampall Chiaráin (Church of St Kieran), 1.5km northwest of Kilronan, has a beautifully carved boundary cross with a circular hole at the top that was possibly used as a sundial. It's thought the church was founded in the 12th century by St Kieran (aka St Ciarán), who studied under St Enda and later established his own monastery at Clonmacnoise.

Seeking Solitude on Lonely Inishmaan
Off the beaten path

Inishmaan is the least visited and least populated of the three islands despite being the second largest. An information board at the ferry pier details the **Lúb Dún Chonchúr** waymarked walking trail, which takes in most of the main sights (8km; allow two to three hours). Built between the 1st and 7th centuries CE, **Dún Chonchúir** sits on the highest point of Inishmaan and is the largest stone fort on the Aran Islands. Drink in incredible views of the island's limestone valleys and mazes of stone walls.

John Millington Synge, the Irish playwright who wrote *The Playboy of the Western World*, spent five summers here between 1898 and 1902, and little has changed since. **Teach Synge** *(per person €3)*, the 300-year-old thatched cottage where he stayed, is now a small museum open June to September dedicated to his life and work. At the desolate western end of the island, **Synge's Chair** was the writer's favourite viewpoint, at the edge of a sheer limestone cliff where you can hear the swell and surf of the Atlantic crashing below.

For a spot of shopping, the factory showroom at **Inis Meáin Knitting Company**, near the centre of the island, has an extensive range of clothing inspired by the local landscape, the sea and the seasons.

Undersea Adventure
Scuba diving in the Atlantic

With crystal-clear waters and vibrant underwater life, the Aran Islands have gained a reputation for being one of the best places to dive in Europe. **Dive Academy** *(diveacademy.info)* scuba-diving school on Inishmore offers PADI scuba courses; a three-hour try-a-dive session costs €145. Experienced divers with Open Water Diver certification (or equivalent) can book a guided dive at the Wormhole.

EATING ON INISHMORE: OUR PICKS

Ti Joe Watty's: Warmed by peat fires, the island's oldest pub has trad sessions every night in summer, and a menu that's heavy on local seafood. *noon-9pm* €€

The Bar: Breakfasts, burgers, curries and fresh fish are on offer at this pleasant pub overlooking the harbour. *10.30am-9.30pm* €€

Teach Nan Phaidi: Cafe set in a cute thatched cottage in Kilmurvey, with fresh mackerel salad and beef and Guinness stew on the menu. *11am-4pm* €€

Aran Seafood Cafe: Food truck in Kilmurvey on the way to Dún Aonghasa; sheltered seating where you can enjoy freshly made lobster rolls. *11am-4pm* €€

Places We Love to Stay

€ Budget €€ Midrange €€€ Top End

Galway City MAP p321

Kinlay Hostel € Centrally located hostel just off Eyre Sq, a stroll away from Shop St's traditional pubs.

House Hotel €€ Boutique hotel in a converted warehouse with an amazing location in the Latin Quarter.

Ardawn House B&B €€ Attractive red-brick house towards the end of the B&B-lined College Rd. Inside, antique-style furniture sits in elegant, sparingly decorated bedrooms.

The Stop €€ Done up with contemporary artworks, stripped floorboards and bold colours, this design-conscious hotel delivers.

St Judes €€ A 1920s manor house in Salthill with bedrooms featuring antique-style chairs, polished floorboards and gleaming bathrooms.

Galmont Hotel & Spa €€€ With scenic Galway Bay views, this luxury city-centre hotel features a pool and underground parking.

Heron's Rest €€€ Boutique B&B in a lovely row of houses on the banks of the Corrib; sit outside and enjoy the views. Breakfast hampers include organic local produce.

Kinvara

Kinvara Guesthouse €€ Smart modern styling, bold colours and fresh flowers brighten this welcoming 22-room guesthouse right on the central square.

Kinvara Inn B&B €€ Lovely, spacious home in the countryside 2km east of Kinvara with an open fire in the lounge and views of the Burren hills.

Letterfrack MAP p331

Cloverfox Hostel € Affordable, charming and great value, with restaurant and craft shop; choose between six-bed dorms or private en-suite rooms.

Oyster Cottage €€ Luxurious cottage at DK Connemara Oysters with panoramic views of the Atlantic and Connemara's hills.

Rosleague Manor €€ Richly coloured rooms furnished with antiques and original art, overlooking Ballynakill Harbour and the Twelve Bens.

Leenane MAP p331

Otter Hostel € Very comfortable modern hostel set in a restored 19th-century house overlooking Killary Harbour 6km west of Leenane.

Leenane Hotel €€ Despite dating from the 19th century, there's a smart, modern feel to this stately hotel on the western fringes of Leenane where an open peat fire warms the bar.

Clifden MAP p338

Clifden Eco Beach Camping € Ireland's first climate-neutral campground has well-maintained facilities near the beach, 10km northwest of Clifden.

Ben View House €€ Great-value, welcoming, family-run B&B in a 19th-century townhouse in the heart of town.

Quay House €€ Small hotel set right beside the water in an 1820s property built for the harbour master, with elegant antique-filled rooms with proper bathtubs.

Abbeyglen Castle Hotel €€€ Complete with turrets and straight out of a fairy tale amid landscaped grounds on Sky Rd.

Ballynahinch Castle Hotel (p347) €€€ Luxury country house hotel with fishing on private lakes and the River Owenmore running through its vast, mountain-ringed property.

Roundstone

Gurteen Beach Caravan & Camping Park € Plenty of space for caravans and tents at this idyllic spot just 50m from Gurteen Beach.

Roundstone House Hotel €€ Views across the bay from the front rooms of this family-run hotel. All rooms have tea- and coffee-making facilities and service couldn't be friendlier.

Aran Islands MAP p349

Aran Islands Camping & Glamping €€ Smart, modern campground and beehive-shaped glamping huts on Inishmore with direct access to the beach.

South Aran House €€ Rustic Inisheer B&B with broad Atlantic views, underfloor heating, wrought-iron beds and scrumptious breakfasts.

Cois Cuain B&B €€ Spotless rooms, fine breakfasts and a wealth of tips on exploring Inishmaan at this traditional, whitewashed stone Aran house.

Inis Meáin €€€ Boutique suites sit among curving stone walls, wraparound windows and cinematic views of Inishmaan.

Researched by
Kathy Donaghy

Mayo & Sligo

IDYLLIC ISLANDS, BREATHTAKING BEACHES AND OUTDOOR ADVENTURES

Despite their natural wonders and languid charm, counties Mayo and Sligo remain well-kept secrets, offering all of Ireland's wild, romantic beauty without the crowds.

Punctuated with vibrant towns, magnificent mountain peaks, big surfing waves and terrific trails, Mayo and Sligo often slip under visitors' radars. Mayo is the more rugged of the two counties, with scraggy peaks, sheer cliffs, heather-covered moors and beautiful offshore islands, where life is dictated by the elements. Sligo is more pastoral, and its lush fields, fish-filled lakes and flat-topped mountains inspired William Butler Yeats to compose some of Ireland's most ardent verses.

Both counties boast grand stretches of golden sands and legendary breaks that lure the surfing cognoscenti from around the globe. Visit, and you'll find all this plus an improbable bounty of prehistoric sites, elegant Georgian towns, abandoned manor houses, charming fishing villages and old-fashioned, warm-hearted hospitality – without all the visitors you're likely to encounter elsewhere in Ireland. Mayo and Sligo may just be Ireland's best-kept secrets, with unlimited possibilities for adventure.

Both counties have some of Ireland's most outstanding accommodation options, from waterside castles to spotless B&Bs, remote island getaways and cheerfully run guesthouses, all set within some of the finest landscapes in the country. Glorious seafood is the staple here as you wind your way along the shore, but beyond seafood chowder, lobster and mussels, there's a host of inventive delights from locally sourced ingredients. You certainly won't go hungry.

DAMIENJKENNEDYPHOTOGRAPHY/SHUTTERSTOCK

THE MAIN AREAS

WESTPORT
Picturesque, pretty and plenty of craic. **p360**

ACHILL ISLAND
Remote, wild and untouched. **p367**

ENNISCRONE
Beaches, dunes and seaweed baths. **p377**

MULLAGHMORE
Raw, rugged Atlantic views. **p385**

> For places to stay in Mayo and Sligo, see p391

Left: Benbulben (p389); right: Great Western Greenway (p364)

Find Your Way

While some of the major towns are connected by public transport, driving is the best way to get out into the magic of this remote region. Cyclists and hikers will find plenty of paths to explore.

Achill Island, p367
Home to breathtaking cliffs, challenging hikes and jaw-dropping beaches, Achill Island is remote, unspoilt and a world unto itself.

Westport, p360
This picturesque spot is one of Ireland's few planned towns and has great restaurants and pubs, and brilliant live music.

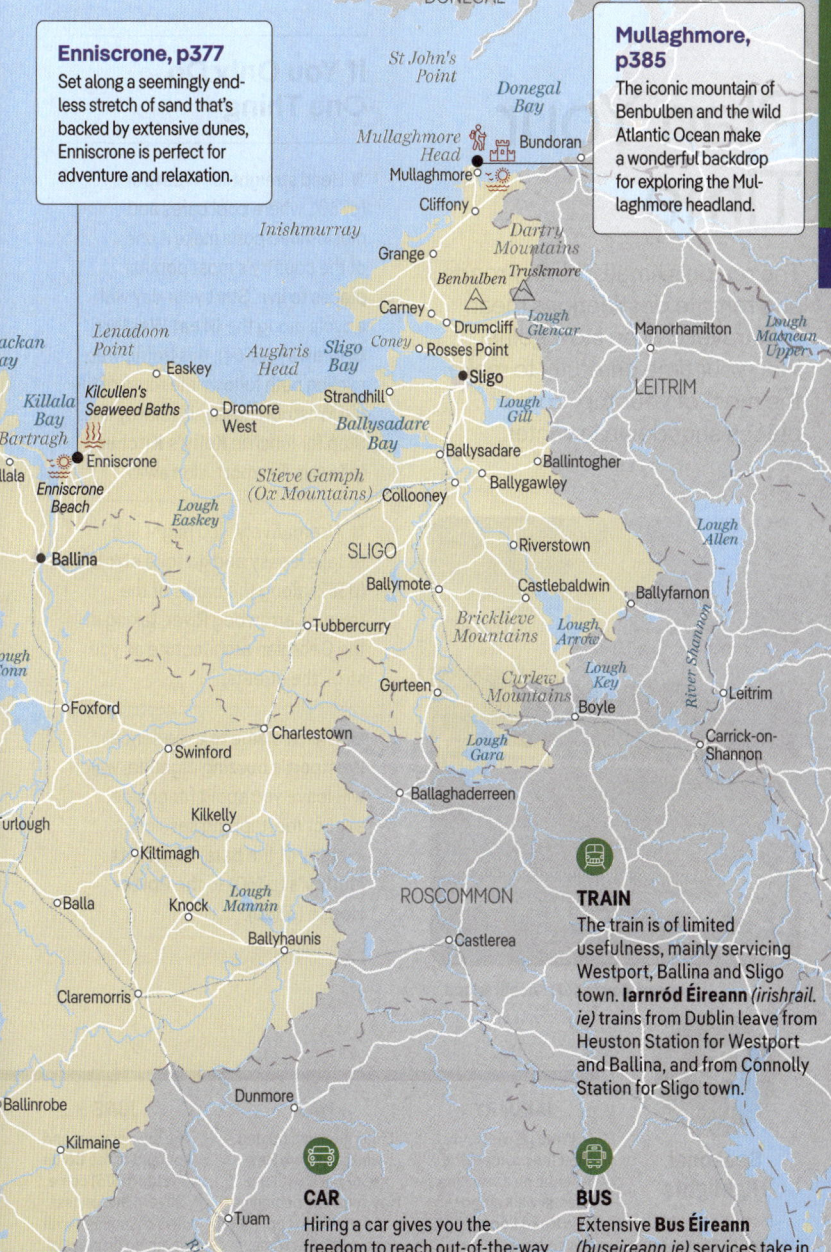

Enniscrone, p377
Set along a seemingly endless stretch of sand that's backed by extensive dunes, Enniscrone is perfect for adventure and relaxation.

Mullaghmore, p385
The iconic mountain of Benbulben and the wild Atlantic Ocean make a wonderful backdrop for exploring the Mullaghmore headland.

TRAIN
The train is of limited usefulness, mainly servicing Westport, Ballina and Sligo town. **Iarnród Éireann** (irishrail.ie) trains from Dublin leave from Heuston Station for Westport and Ballina, and from Connolly Station for Sligo town.

CAR
Hiring a car gives you the freedom to reach out-of-the-way places and set your own agenda. Petrol stations are easy to find, and parking is generally easy. Drive with care on the winding country roads.

BUS
Extensive **Bus Éireann** (buseireann.ie) services take in most destinations within Mayo and Sligo, and other counties in the region and beyond.

Plan Your Time

The region's small country roads and remote destinations mean that travel can be slow going. Plan your time carefully to make the most of your trip. Some places shut down in winter.

If You Only Do One Thing

● Head straight for **Westport** (p360), where cool cafes and music-filled pubs make it one of the country's most popular places to live. Start your day with a cycle along the **Great Western Greenway** (p364); this traffic-free cycling path follows the route of the old Westport-to-Achill railway line. Stop for lunch in **Kelly's Kitchen** (p364) in Newport, 11km away.

● Alternatively, you might like to take it easy and go for a **stroll** (p362) along the banks of the town's Carrowbeg River, taking in the Georgian architecture as you stroll the streets.

● Then it's time to experience Westport's buzzing nightlife, which will leave you spoilt for choice; expect toe-tapping sessions in many of the bars, from **Matt Molloy's** (p360) to the **Porter House** (p360).

Keem Bay (p367), Achill Island

Seasonal Highlights

It could be a toe-tapping music session, a surf festival or a food fair – there's always plenty to do in Mayo and Sligo no matter when you visit.

JANUARY
Wrap up well and feel the power of the Atlantic on a stunning coastal walk along the **Erris Head Loop** (p374). Watch the gannets and the gulls, and feel the deep belly of the Atlantic roar.

MAY
Enjoy stunning guided walks at **Keem Bay** (p367), and with the May sunshine beginning to warm things up, try your hand at some surfing at **Trawmore Beach** (p367).

JUNE
The long grasses and bogland of the **Céide Fields** (p375) come alive in the longest days of summer, with stunning displays of heath-spotted orchids and insect-eating sundews.

Five Days to Travel Around

- You could easily while away a few days on **Achill Island** (p367) with its jaw-dropping scenery and bucket-list swimming opportunities. Make sure to plan a trip to the island's deserted village of **Slievemore** (p370) before a swim at **Keem Bay Beach** (p367) and a pint at **Gielty's** (p370). The next day, book in for some surf lessons with **Soundwave Surf School** (p369).

- Back on the mainland, devote another day to the otherworldly beauty of **Wild Nephin National Park** (p372), then round things off with a visit to **Belmullet** (p374), staying overnight in the town. The next morning, walk the **Erris Head Loop** (p374) and marvel at the restless Atlantic Ocean lashing the coast below. End your trip with a visit to the **Erris lighthouses** (p375).

A Week in the West

- Take a week to indulge in the classic sights and the area's rich culture. Head to **Enniscrone** (p377) for two days for some beachside fun. Don't forget to make time for a soak in the famous **Kilcullen's Seaweed Baths** (p378).

- With a brand-new surf school, **Strandhill** (p382) is a must. After hitting the waves, stop for lunch at the town's popular **Shells** (p382) cafe and stay in one of the area's many B&Bs.

- Leave two days and nights for **Sligo town** (p387) to sample its buzzing cafe culture and cool pubs before exploring the area's connection to **William Butler Yeats** (p389).

- End your trip with two nights in the fishing village of **Mullaghmore** (p385), enjoying delicious seafood and watching the boats bobbing in the harbour.

JULY
The week-long **Ballina Salmon Festival** (p380) celebrates the town's deep connection to the River Moy, with highlights including the Crinniú na Mbád (Gathering of the Boats) and one of Ireland's oldest river swims.

AUGUST
Late summer brings with it with the most beautiful colours on the bog, making it the perfect time to witness the diverse flora and fauna of **Wild Nephin National Park** (p372).

SEPTEMBER
With the kids back at school, it's the perfect time to get on your bike and cycle the **Great Western Greenway** (p364), the longest off-road cycling experience in the county.

OCTOBER
From poetry writing for kids to big band acts, Westport's **Westival** (p361) is a creative melting pot. Theatre, visual art, film and workshops for all the family are festival staples.

Westport

TRAD SESSIONS | NIGHTLIFE | GEORGIAN ARCHITECTURE

GETTING AROUND

Westport is easy to get around on foot. To go further afield, rent a bike at Westport Bike Hire or Westport Bike Shop (p363).
Bus Éireann *(bus eireann.ie)* heads to nearby hubs such as Castlebar and Galway. Route 450 serves Dooagh on Achill Island to Louisburgh via Westport.
Local Link Mayo *(locallinkmayo.ie)* has regular bus services within the county. There are regular **trains** *(irishrail.ie)* to and from Dublin's Heuston Station to Westport Train Station on Altamount St.

☑ TOP TIP

The area is great for cycling, with gentle coastal routes and more challenging mountain trails. The Great Western Greenway (p364) begins 500m northwest of the town's centre, off the N59. Just follow the 'fingerpost' signs.

Bright and vibrant even in the depths of winter, Westport is a photogenic Georgian town with tree-lined streets, riverside walkways and great vibes. Sitting on the edge of spectacular Clew Bay, it has some beautiful beaches nearby and the impressive peak of Croagh Patrick on its doorstep. Westport Quay, the town's harbour, is a picturesque spot lined with shops and cafes.

With an excellent choice of accommodation and a central location that makes it a convenient and enjoyable base for exploring the county, Westport is a hugely popular place, yet it has never sold its soul to tourism. You'll find Mayo's nightlife hub here, with the town thronged with pubs that are renowned for their traditional music; many of them host regular live sessions. To sample its superb restaurants and cafes, just wander along Bridge St and the little alleyways off it to make some tasty discoveries.

Listen to Trad Music

Tap your toes

Westport has tons of pubs, and many put on live music regularly. **Matt Molloy's** *(mattmolloy.com)*, the fife player from traditional Irish folk band the Chieftains, runs an old-school pub that bears his name. This is where Mayo's musical heritage comes vividly to life seven nights a week; the intimate setting has plenty of little nooks and crannies, and Molloy himself makes an appearance from time to time. The atmosphere is electric when things get going – when the fire is roaring and the music is playing in the back bar, there's nowhere better to be.

Originally a shoe repair shop, the **Cobbler's Bar** *(@cob blersbar)* now attracts some of the best local musicians for regular trad sessions every Thursday and Sunday night. They also put on live music every other night, plus afternoon sessions on Fridays, Saturdays and Sundays.

The award-winning **Porter House** *(theporterhousewestport. ie)* is a great place for music and pints. There's live music seven

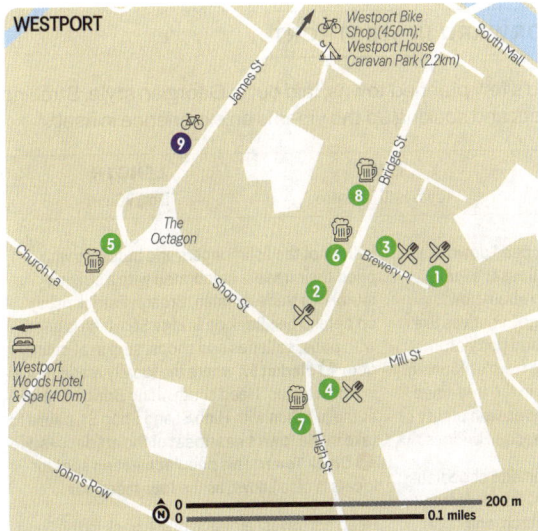

THE WEST IS AWAKE

Westival (westival.ie) is the oldest music and arts festival in the west of Ireland. It takes place each October and had its 50th anniversary in 2025. Originally founded by a team of volunteers keen to showcase the flourishing arts and music sector in the west of Ireland, the festival has grown from strength to strength. It showcases the northwest as a creative melting pot and explores the contemporary cultural identity that's unique to this part of the world.

With a diverse programme of offerings, from visual arts to theatre, live music to kids' workshops, there's something for everyone, including a number of free events. Tickets sell out early, particularly for headline shows, so book early to avoid disappointment.

- **EATING**
  1. Gallery Cafe
  2. Savoir Fare
  3. Sol Rio Restaurant
  4. This Must Be the Place

- **DRINKING & NIGHTLIFE**
  5. Cobbler's Bar
  6. Matt Molloy's
  7. McGing's Bar
  8. Porter House

- **TRANSPORT**
  9. Westport Bike Hire

nights a week, with afternoon sessions on Fridays, Saturdays and Sundays. It's not unusual for visiting musicians to show up and join in on an impromptu session.

Another firm favourite on the music scene is **McGing's** (@mcgingsbar) on High St. This pub brings the best of live folk, American and bluegrass to the town. Sunday evenings are devoted to jazz, and if you're lucky enough to be in town on the last Saturday of the month, you'll catch the much-loved local institution that is the Octagon Quartet.

One of the best things about an evening or night out in Westport is that all the town's popular night spots – from live music venues to gastro-pubs – are within walking distance of one another. Stroll easily from dinner to drinks, stopping in for a few toe-tapping sessions along the way.

EATING IN WESTPORT: OUR PICKS

This Must Be the Place: Grab a window seat and watch the world go by, with tasty food and good vegetarian options. *8am-4pm Tue-Sat* €

Savoir Fare: Irish-French bistro with a range of artisan dishes on the menu; expect simple, delicious food, including Keem Bay fish. *noon-5pm Tue-Fri, 11am- 5pm Sat* €€

Sol Rio Restaurant: Sol Rio offers Portuguese flair, a large selection of seafood, and extensive vegan and vegetarian options. *12.30-3pm & 5.30-9pm Wed-Mon* €€

Gallery Cafe: Wine bar and cosy vinyl/coffee house with sharing platters with an Irish flavour, and tasty treats from further afield. *6-10.30pm Tue-Sat May-Oct* €

BEST FOOT FORWARD IN WESTPORT

Westport is one of Ireland's few planned towns, laid out in Georgian style. Strolling around its gorgeous streets and soaking up the vibes is an experience in itself.

START	END	LENGTH
Town Hall Theatre	Town Hall Theatre	1km; 90min

From the ❶ **Town Hall Theatre**, head down the alleyway beside the iconic ❷ **Blouser's Pub** on James St. Here you can learn about how supporting biodiversity – through initiatives like the introduction of swift boxes and pollinator-friendly plants – is central to the town's planning. Heading back to James St, take in the tree-lined promenade of the Carrowbeg River, with plenty of time for photo stops at its picturesque bridges.

Next, stop in for a taste of homemade chocolate at ❸ **Marlene's**. From Marlene's, follow James St to the river, past St Mary's Church, and take the first right onto Bridge St. Following along Bridge St, dip into ❹ **Shambles Lane**, where the history of the fishmongers and butchers who plied their trade is celebrated with a striking mural of a tradeswoman, Croagh Patrick rising up behind her. Back on Bridge St, which is lined with pubs, galleries and shops, stop in at culinary gem ❺ **Market 57**, where the locally made fudge is worth a stop. Head south along Bridge St and at the junction with High St and Shop St, pause to take in the town's heartbeat at the art deco–style ❻ **Clock Tower**. This popular meeting spot for locals is also known as the four-faced liar.

Head northwest along Shop St, back to the Town Hall Theatre, where you can take in the Octagon Monument, which is dedicated to St Patrick.

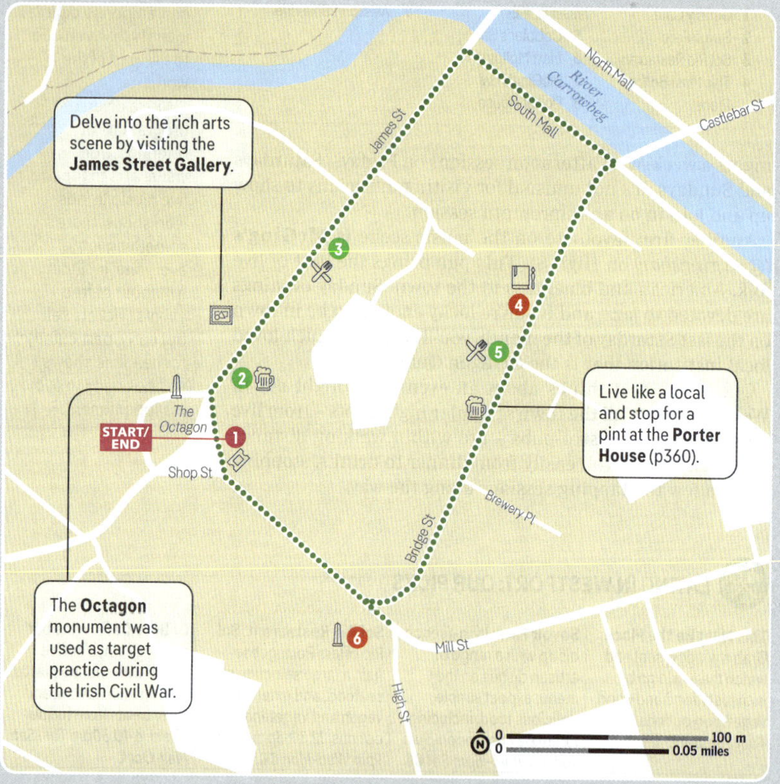

Delve into the rich arts scene by visiting the **James Street Gallery**.

Live like a local and stop for a pint at the **Porter House** (p360).

The **Octagon** monument was used as target practice during the Irish Civil War.

Beyond Westport

Ireland's holy mountain, the surrounding hills and the stunning Clew Bay offer plenty of opportunities for outdoor adventures.

Get stuck into country life outside of Westport. Learn about rural Ireland at a fascinating national museum, take on the scenic drive through Doolough Valley – one of the most beautiful routes in the country – or venture out to Clare Island to get away from it all.

The town of Louisburgh has fantastic cafes, and you can learn to surf from its beaches. The region is also home to one of Ireland's most iconic mountain peaks – and some grim reminders of Famine-related tragedies.

For many travellers, the great outdoors is the draw around Westport, with plenty of opportunities for hiking, cycling, swimming and just chilling at the beach.

Castlebar

TIME FROM WESTPORT: **17MIN**

Look at country life

Just 8km northeast of the town of Castlebar is the **National Museum of Ireland – Country Life** *(museum.ie; free)*, the only branch of Ireland's National Museums that's outside of Dublin. The extensive and engrossing displays at this riverside museum delve into Ireland's fascinating rural traditions.

The museum is set in a modern, photogenic facility overlooking a lake in the lush grounds of the 19th-century Turlough Manor. The museum explores everything from the role of the potato to boat building, herbal cures and traditional clothes. Before you visit, check the programme of events, which often includes activities and walks that further breathe life into the whole experience.

The lovely **Turlough Round Tower** is visible from the grounds. Stretching up to 23m and featuring a single lofty window, this 11th-century structure crowns a hilltop beside a ruined 18th-century church. The tower and church are state-owned national monuments, and while you can walk around the site, a level of care and caution should be maintained during your visit.

Places

Castlebar p363
Louisburgh p364
Clare Island p364
Newport p364
Croagh Patrick p365
Doolough Valley p366

GETTING AROUND

It's best to get around this area in your own car, although organised tours also run. **Car hire** *(enterprise.ie)* is available; if you don't fancy driving, many rural towns and villages are linked by scheduled bus services under **Local Link** *(locallinkmayo.ie)*.

For cycling adventures outside of town, bike hire is available in Westport with **Westport Bike Hire** *(westportbikehire.com)* or **Westport Bike Shop** *(westportbikeshop.ie)*. They have a range of bikes to suit all ages and abiliities; prices start from €25 for a standard bike to €50 for an e-bike.

THE PIRATE QUEEN

The life of **Grace O'Malley** (Gráinne ní Mháille or Granuaile, c 1530–1603) reads like fantasy adventure fiction. Twice widowed and twice imprisoned for acts of piracy, she was a fearsome presence in the troubled landscape of 16th-century Ireland.

Born into a powerful seafaring family who controlled most of the Mayo coastline and traded internationally, the independent Grace soon decided she should join the family business.

Legend has it that while still a child, she asked her father if she could join a trip to Spain but was refused on the grounds that seafaring was not for girls. She promptly shaved off her hair, dressed in boys' clothing, returned to the ship and announced that she was ready to sail.

Louisburgh

TIME FROM WESTPORT: 25MIN

Learn to surf

With 1168km of beaches, cliffs and inlets, Mayo has the longest coastline in Ireland and is a popular destination for surfers. The friendly vibe in Louisburgh makes the town a great place to learn to surf. Run by local surfers, **Surf Mayo** (surfmayo. com; two-hour surf lesson adult/child €30/25) was the first dedicated surf school in the county and offers lessons at Carrownisky Strand.

Afterwards, head to the **Wild Atlantic Sauna** (wildatlantic sauna.ie; 45-minute shared session €15) at **Old Head** beach to relax in the heat while enjoying stunning views of Clew Bay.

Clare Island

TIME FROM WESTPORT: 25MIN + 10MIN

Cruise to Clare Island

Clew Bay is dotted with some 365 islands, the largest of which is the mountainous Clare Island, located 5km offshore but feeling half a world away. Dominated by the rocky **Knockmore** (462m), the island's varied terrain is terrific for walking and climbing, and swimming can be enjoyed at its safe, sandy beaches.

Clare Island also boasts the windswept ruins of the 13th-century **Clare Island Abbey** and **Granuaile's Castle**, both associated with the pirate queen Grace O'Malley. The abbey's chancel roof is dotted with faded fragments of murals dating from around 1500. Also look out for the tomb reputed to be that of Grace O'Malley, where a stone inscribed with her family motto formidably declares: 'Invincible on land and sea'.

Stop in for a pint in the **Anchor Bar** and you might be rewarded with a traditional music session.

Clare Island Fast Ferries (clareislandfastferries.com) and **Clare Island Ferry** (clareislandferry.com) offer sailings from Roonagh Pier to the island all year-round. The journey takes roughly 10 minutes.

Newport

TIME FROM WESTPORT: 11MIN

Cycle the Great Western Greenway

Following the route of the old Westport–Achill Railway (which was in operation from 1895 to 1937), the **Great Western Greenway** (greenway.ie) is a terrific reason to cycle – or walk – through this part of Mayo. The 49km trail, which begins in Westport and travels via Newport and Mulranny to Achill

---

 EATING IN NEWPORT: OUR PICKS

Kelly's Kitchen: Enjoy award-winning Irish breakfasts, coffee and delicious baking at Kelly's. *9am-5pm Mon-Sat* €

Gráinne Uaile: Gastro-pub with an extensive menu and lively trad sessions. Enjoy a pint with bay views in the outdoor area. *noon-9pm May-Sep; hours vary Oct-Apr* €€

Port Chipper: Grab fish and chips from this local favourite. It's mainly takeaway, but there are a few seats outside. *5-9pm Wed-Sat, 4.30-9pm Sun* €

Hotel Newport: Chic bistro-style dining with fresh, local produce – the Keane's burger from the local butchers is always popular. *noon-9pm Jun-Aug, to 8pm Sep-May* €€

Sound, passes gorgeous countryside and waterfront scenery along the way. The best thing is that's it's car-free, making it perfect for family adventures.

The trail is divided into three main sections, none of which require more than moderate effort. Count on spending a full day cycling the route, factoring in photo stops along the way; it's also possible to cycle sections and arrange for a bike hire company to pick you up at a designated spot.

You can easily rent bicycles all along the Great Western Greenway. Westport Bike Hire (p363) on James St in Westport can set you up with everything you need for this epic adventure. You can follow the 'fingerpost' signs from Westport to the start of the Greenway, but it's not hard to find: it's 500m from the town centre in the direction of Newport.

Croagh Patrick

TIME FROM WESTPORT: **12MIN**

Climbing Croagh Patrick

St Patrick couldn't have picked a better spot for a pilgrimage than conical Croagh Patrick (also known as 'the Reek'). On a clear day, the tough two-hour climb up the mountain rewards with stunning views over Clew Bay and its sandy islets.

It was on Croagh Patrick that Ireland's patron saint fasted for 40 days and nights, and it was from here that he reputedly banished all of Ireland's venomous snakes. Climbing the 764m holy mountain is an act of penance for thousands of believers on the last Sunday of July (Reek Sunday). The truly contrite take the 35km **Tóchar Phádraig** (Patrick's Causeway), an ancient pilgrim route that starts from **Ballintubber Abbey**; they usually ascend the mountain barefoot.

The 7km trail taken by the less repentant begins from the signed car park in the west end of **Murrisk**, roughly 8km west of Westport. The steep trail is rocky in parts, and it gets crowded on sunny weekends. At the summit, you'll find a whitewashed church dating from 1905 and a 9th-century oratory fountain. The views are sublime and the average return trip takes three to four hours.

Sitting at the foot of Croagh Patrick is the **National Famine Memorial**, a spine-chilling sculpture by artist John Behan of a three-masted ghost ship wreathed in swirling skeletons, commemorating the lives lost on the so-called 'coffin ships', which emigrants fleeing Ireland sailed on in search of a better life abroad. They endured horrendous, cramped and unhygienic conditions as they crossed the Atlantic.

WHY I LOVE LIVING IN MAYO

Rachel Nolan, a Mayo-based tour guide, shares why she loves living in the rural landscape of County Mayo. @rachelsirish adventures

Growing up in my Mam's B&B in Ballina, it felt like I was destined to be an explorer. I started travelling around the world and soon realised my home – the north Mayo coast – is a very special place that has it all: the wild Atlantic crashing on the rugged cliffs at Downpatrick Head and the unspoiled vastness around Nephin. The grassy roads of the many peninsulas have a rich history dating back to the Stone Age, and there are the warmest welcomes by local communities. It's a unique place for outdoor lovers looking to get off the beaten path and experience Ireland's true nature and soul.

 DRINKING NEAR CROAGH PATRICK: OUR PICKS

| Cronin's Shebeen: This traditional pub overlooking Clew Bay champions local producers and ingredients. *5-11pm Wed & Thu, to 1am Fri & Sat, 3-11pm Sun* | Tavern Bar & Restaurant: Known for its extensive menu, the Tavern is located in Murrisk near the base of Croagh Patrick, making it the perfect post-hike pub. *12.30-8.30pm Wed-Sun* | Staunton's Pub: Serving pints for more than 100 years, this historic family-run pub in Lecanvey is worth a stop-off; also serves food. *11am-midnight Mon-Thu, to 1am Fri & Sat, noon-11pm Sun* | Campbell's Pub Quaint, old-fashioned Irish pub at the foot of Croagh Patrick that's the perfect stop after climbing the mountain. *3.30-11.30pm Mon-Thu, 12.30-11.30pm Fri-Sun* |

THE DOOLOUGH TRAGEDY

On 30 March 1849, in the midst of the Famine, hundreds of starving men, women and children set off from Louisburgh for Delphi Lodge, where they had heard they would be reassessed for Famine relief.

There was no food for them upon their arrival, so they walked back to Louisburgh. The weather was freezing and bitter, and the people so malnourished and weak that many died. Marked today by a grim memorial cross in the Doolough Valley that serves as its epitaph, the Doolough Tragedy still casts a black shadow across the sublime landscape. Every year, a Famine Walk to Louisburgh from Delphi commemorates the disaster.

Doolough Valley

Doolough Valley

TIME FROM WESTPORT: **37MIN**

Driving through the Doolough Valley

The R335 from Westport to Leenane in County Galway is one of Ireland's most beautiful scenic routes.

Largely untouched by housing, cut turf or even stone walls, the road through the desolate Doolough Valley is a sublime journey, with the steep sides of the surrounding mountains sliding into the steely grey waters of Doo Lough as sheep graze placidly on the hills – they occasionally park themselves in the middle of the road, too.

This is also one of Ireland's most poignant spots – the site of the Doolough Tragedy – a Famine catastrophe that occurred in 1849.

Choose a dry and clear day to tackle the road, as curtains of rain can greatly diminish the views. If you have time, wander down the side roads to the north and west of the valley to reach glorious, often-deserted beaches.

COFFEE STOPS BEYOND WESTPORT: OUR PICKS

Seven Wanders Cafe: Stylish cafe in Louisburgh with a friendly vibe. *8.30am-3.30pm Mon-Fri, 9am-4pm Sat & Sun* €

Brú: Serves doorstop sandwiches as well as homemade pastries and coffee in Castlebar. Grab a seat at the window and watch the world go by. *8am-5pm* €

Louisburgh 74: Award-winning cafe with a delicious selection of baking and local crafts. Also serves evening meals. *9am-8.30pm* €

Murrisk Cafe: Located in the local community centre, this cafe is a handy meeting point and coffee stop for those climbing Croagh Patrick. *9am-5pm Apr-Oct, hours vary Nov-Mar* €

Achill Island

BUCKET-LIST SWIMS | DESERTED VILLAGES | COASTAL VIEWS

Ireland's largest offshore island, Achill Island (Oileán Acaill) is linked to the mainland by a short bridge. Despite the accessibility, there's plenty of remote-island feel here: soaring cliffs, rocky headlands, sheltered sandy beaches, broad expanses of blanket bog and rolling mountains. Surfers hit the swells on the island's magnificent Blue Flag beaches, while kitesurfers and windsurfers harness the power of the wind. The island also has its share of history, having been a frequent refuge during Ireland's various rebellions.

Achill is at its most dramatic in winter, when high winds and lashing seas make it seem downright inhospitable. The year-round population, though, remains as welcoming as ever. In summer, heather, rhododendrons and wildflowers bloom, splashing the island with colour.

The village of Keel is the island's main centre of activity, which is a relative term. Shops and services also cluster at the end of the bridge leading onto the island, at Achill Sound.

GETTING AROUND

Dooagh-based **Achill Bikes** *(achillbikes.com; e-bike/hybrid €55/30)* can hook you up with everything you need to explore the island by pedal power. **Bus Éireann** *(buseireann.ie)* bus 450 runs a few times a day from Westport to the village of Dooagh. Achill is car friendly – you take the R139 – but be aware that sheep graze freely and can often be found leisurely crossing the island's main roads.

Achill Island's Best Beaches

Bay of beauty

Tucked away at the far west of the island, **Keem Bay Beach** is Achill's most remote Blue Flag beach. Grassy slopes lead down to the beach, and the crescent of golden sand sits at the foot of steep cliffs, hemmed in by rock on three sides. The perfectly clear turquoise water and the fine white sand make this a firm favourite with visitors, and spiralling down to this perfect cove feels like finding the pot of gold at the end of an Irish rainbow.

It's a stunning drive here from Keel, 8km to the east. The route takes in expansive views across the water as the road climbs beside steep cliffs. The 4km-long **Trawmore Beach** – also known as Keel Beach – is arguably the best-known stretch of sand on Achill, with great pubs, cafes and restaurants, plus a large car park and surf schools. It sits in the shadow of the

☑ TOP TIP

Instead of following the main road (R319) from Mulranny to Achill Island, take the signposted Ocean Rd, which curves clockwise around the Corraun Peninsula. The narrow road passes a fortified tower, and as it hugs the isolated southern edge, the views across Clew Bay and out to sea are stunning.

magnificent Minaun Cliffs, and this long, flat stretch of sand is a haven for watersports. Sunbathers have plenty of space to chill out in summer, and it's the perfect place for a ramble, with incredible views of the cliffs to soak in along the way.

On the northern side of the island, at the base of Mt Slievemore, small **Dugort Beach** offers excellent mountain views from its sheltered golden sands.

Colony Tour of Achill
Fascinating explorations

The **Colony Tour** (thecolonytour.com; per person €25), which begins at Dugort Beach, provides a fascinating glimpse into life on the island in the 1800s, when the charismatic Rev Edward Nangle (1800–83) founded a Protestant mission here.

The arrival of Protestant colonists on Achill Island in the 1830s was bitterly opposed by the local Catholic Archbishop, Dr John MacHale, who waged an unceasing struggle to destroy those he termed 'venomous fanatics'.

Led by BAFTA award-winning writer Kevin Toolis, the walking tour is an immersive experience that takes you to the heart of what was the old mission, with Toolis providing a lively account of the battle between the two men and how it shaped the history of the island and its people.

On the Water
Adventures and watersports

Achill has many scalloped bays that are tame enough for swimming, but more adrenaline-fuelled activities are also possible. Keel Lake has shallow, calm waters and great wind, all of which provide the ideal location for kitesurfing, windsurfing, wing foiling and paddleboarding. The **Achill Outdoor Education and Training Centre** (achilloutdoor.ie) has been open since 1971, offering a range of activities including kayaking, sailing, windsurfing and coasteering. Budding surfers have several schools to choose from.

Soundwave Surf School (soundwave.ie; surf lesson €35) has surf lessons, stand-up paddleboarding (SUP) and regular music events. After a day in the waves, relax in their Rust Box sauna or listen to some cool tunes at one of their music events.

Blackfield Watersports Surf School (blackfield.com; surf lessons adult/child €40/35) specialises in small, personal surf and SUP lessons at Keel Beach. **Achill Surf School and**

WHY I LOVE LIVING ON ACHILL

Kevin Toolis, writer and tour guide at the Colony Tour, shares why the ever-changing landscape of Achill inspires him.

Achill Island is still a unique part of Ireland – like stepping back in time to an older version of the things I love about being Irish. There are mountains and beaches, surfing and wild swimming. At gems like Keem Beach, you can often see basking sharks and dolphins from the shoreline. But there is a wildness to Achill you won't find anywhere else. Sheep roam freely on the roads, the weather can be wild, and the sky another ocean of change as red, yellow, and black and grey clouds fill up the eye to infinity. And a whole other landscape of history from Neolithic ruins [to] famine stories, and music and song.

 EATING ON ACHILL ISLAND: OUR PICKS

Beehive Craft & Coffee Shop: Sit out on the deck in fine weather for gourmet lunches and good coffee. *11am-4pm Feb-Nov* €€

Salt Dock: Cool, colourful cafe, with coffee beans from Sligo's Carrow Coffee Roasters, plus lots of homemade treats. Try the sea-salt caramel squares. *10am-4pm Thu-Sun Jun, daily Jul & Aug* €

Lili Bán Cafe: Little cafe with a big heart; plenty of coffee, cakes and drinks for sale. *11am-4.30pm Fri-Sun Jun & Sep, daily Jul & Aug* €

Amethyst Bar: Gastropub serving hearty meals and delicious daily specials, including oysters and mussels. *1-8.30pm Jul & Aug, hours vary Sep-Jun* €€

BANSHEES OF INISHERIN FILMING LOCATIONS

Cloughmore: The crew constructed JJ Devine's pub on the southeast corner of the island.

Purteen Harbour: Between the villages of Pollagh and Keel, the harbour was host to a specially built portside street scene that included O'Riordan's shop and a post office.

Keem Bay: The private building on Keem Bay was the home of Colm Doherty.

Corrymore Lake: Mrs McCormick's cottage was here, and it was also the setting for one of the film's major tragedies.

St Thomas' Church: The Mass scenes were filmed at this 19th-century church.

Slievemore

Adventure Centre *(achillsurf.com; surf lessons adult/child €45/40)* runs the activities gamut, from orienteering and climbing to surfing and sea kayaking, guaranteeing a great time in the outdoors.

An Island Ghost Town
Left to the elements

The bleak remains of more than 80 houses in the deserted village of **Slievemore** – at the foot of the mountain of the same name – are slowly being reduced to rock piles, a poignant reminder of a vanished way of life, and the island's past hardships. Research into why the village was abandoned is ongoing; some historians believe the Famine forced villagers to emigrate or move closer to the sea and its alternative food sources. The adjacent graveyard only compounds the desolation.

Hiking Achill Island
Ireland's highest sea cliffs

Achill Island is a wonderful place for hiking, and the views are terrific. Ramblers can climb **Mt Slievemore** (671m). The trail begins at the deserted village of Slievemore, where you'll

DRINKING ON ACHILL ISLAND: OUR PICKS

Gielty's: The most westerly pub in Europe is a third-generation-run spot that has great music and wonderful food. *noon-11.30pm*

Lynott's: With a thatch roof and stone walls, Lynott's is hailed as the smallest pub in Ireland, but it has a big atmosphere. *3-11.30pm Mon-Thu, to 12.30am Fri, from 2pm Sat, to 11pm Sun*

Lourdie's: This old-fashioned Irish pub is loved by both visitors and locals. *3-11.30pm Mon-Thu, to 12.30am Fri & Sat, 3-11.30pm Sun*

Ted's: Established in 1951 and still family-run, Ted's has regular music sessions, great food and outdoor seating. *11am-11.30pm Mon-Thu, to 12.30am Fri & Sat, from 11am Sun*

find the remains of some stone cottages. The views of Blacksod Bay are terrific. Or, you can take on the longer climb up **Mt Croaghaun** (664m). The route goes over the mighty, 687m-tall **Croaghaun Cliffs**, the highest sea cliffs in Ireland. The starting point for the trail up Croaghaun is from the car park at Keem Bay (p367); allow two hours.

Such Great Heights
The best views of Achill

In the centre of Achill Island is **Minaun Heights**, where you can soak up incredible views of the island. As you drive up the narrow, winding road to the small car park, the views get more impressive the higher you climb.

Hop out at the car park and take a short ramble to the summit at 466m to enjoy views of Achill Island, Clare Island and Blacksod Bay. On a clear day, the vistas are incredible, but even when there are clouds, the sun still manages to peek through.

Castle of the Pirate Queen
Grace O'Malley's stronghold

The 12m-high, 15th-century building that is **Grace O'Malley's Castle** *(free)* rises beside the shore at Kildownet. Associated with Ireland's famous pirate queen (p364), it's an eerie experience when you enter through a steel turnstile, revealing a tall, hollow shell with slits for windows and a square hole in the roof.

Pondering Achill-Henge
A mysterious structure

Built by property developer Joe McNamara in 2011 without planning permission, **Achill-Henge** is something of a controversial structure. Nobody knows why it was built, with some saying it was a political statement, and others maintaining it was intended as a tourist attraction.

Achill-Henge consists of 30 concrete columns topped by a ring of stone. Roscommon-based street artist Joe Caslin transformed the site into a temporary art installation with 30 3.5m-tall drawings as part of his *Our Nation's Sons* project.

JOHN LENNON & CLEW BAY

Clew Bay is said to have 365 islands, one for every day of the year. The views of the bay from the surrounding area are spectacular, and in fact, the location is stunning enough to have caught the eye of musician John Lennon, who bought the 38-hectare **Dorinish Island** in 1967 and planned to build a house there. The island widely became known afterwards as 'Beatle Island'.

The former Beatle visited Achill on 27 June 1967, and visited again with Yoko Ono in 1968, when they dined in the Amethyst Bar (p369).

In 1970 Dorinish Island was used by a hippie commune that built a summer camp there before it was later sold to a farmer in 1984, who still grazes sheep on the land.

Beyond Achill Island

Get stuck into Wild Nephin National Park, do some stargazing, and explore the rugged, wild and remote west Mayo coastline.

Places
Wild Nephin National Park p372
Mullet Peninsula p374
Céide Fields p375
Dún Briste p376

GETTING AROUND

A free **shuttle bus** (nationalparks.ie/wild-nephin/free-shuttle-bus-service) operates in June, July and August, connecting Bangor Erris and Westport with Wild Nephin National Park. The bus runs from Tuesday to Saturday with stop-off points at Newport, Letterkeen, Mulranny, Claggan Mountain Coastal Trail and the Ballycroy Visitor Centre. There is a year-round Local Link bus 978 running between Castlebar, Newport and Belmullet, which also serves the national park and Mulranny. Otherwise, the best way to explore the area is by car.

Home to some of the darkest and clearest skies in the world, Wild Nephin National Park is a paradise for stargazers, set far from any urban light pollution. By day, take in views of the expansive blanket bog and immerse yourself in the wild landscapes with spectacular views of Achill Island and the churning Atlantic Ocean.

To the northwest, the thinly populated Gaeltacht (Irish-speaking area) of the Mullet Peninsula dangles some 30km into the Atlantic and feels more cut off than many of Ireland's islands, with a similar sense of loneliness. However, you'll find pristine beaches along its sheltered eastern shore and lots of sheep – often fully blocking the road. The main settlement is the town of Belmullet (Béal an Mhuirthead).

Wild Nephin National Park

TIME FROM ACHILL ISLAND: **40MIN**

Exploring Wild Nephin National Park

The huge and scenic **Wild Nephin National Park** (nationalparks.ie) – comprising some of Europe's greatest areas of blanket bog – is home to magnificent natural diversity, including otters, mountain hares, native red deer, peregrine falcons, corncrakes and whooper swans. A short nature trail with interpretation panels leads from the **National Park Visitor Centre** in Ballycroy across the bog, revealing superbly sublime views of the surrounding mountains. Staff at the visitor centre are on hand to provide helpful information on visiting the park, and there are displays on whaling and the ubiquitous purple heather.

The views of Achill Island, the mountains and the shore do their best to upstage the food in the appealingly airy Ginger & Wild cafe in the visitor centre, but the quiches, soups, scones and cakes more than hold their own.

It's most convenient to visit the park by car, with the entrance signposted along the N59 between Mulranny and Bangor Erris.

Walk the Tóchar Daithí Bán

Named after the mythical giant Daithí Bán, who built a fortress on Wild Nephin's tallest mountain, **Corslieve** (721m), this 2km **loop walk** gives a good flavour of what the national park has to offer. It starts at the visitor centre on sections of boardwalk – some of which are wheelchair accessible. The star attraction of this walk is the panoramic view of Achill Island and the Nephin Beg Mountains.

Take on the Bangor Trail

If you're an experienced hillwalker and looking for a challenge, the waymarked 40km Bangor Trail is a great choice. The trail takes you along a range of terrain in Wild Nephin, including bog tracks, open countryside, country roads and across rivers.

Immerse yourself in solitude and enjoy the isolation of nature. The trail follows a path – originally designed to move livestock – that likely dates as far back as the Iron Age; pre-Famine ruins can be seen at certain points. Keep an eye out for deer, frogs, grouse and hares.

As you will be crossing bogland and rivers, waterproof boots and good rain gear are essential. Note that the Bangor Trail begins in Newport (p364).

Walking the Letterkeen loops

Accessible from a well-signposted road outside the town of Newport, the Letterkeen walking loops lead into Wild Nephin and are colour-coded with different options to choose from.

The shortest walk is the 6km **Bothy Loop**. The blue and purple loops follow the same trail for about 3km before branching out. All three of these trails require a reasonable level of fitness. The purple loop is the most challenging, as it's rough underfoot and includes a climb. The full 12km **Letterkeen Loop** is a strenuous path that takes about three hours to complete. The incredible mountain scenery is worth every step, and Newport has some great pubs where you can celebrate your completion of the circuit.

Stargaze at Wild Nephin

By night, Wild Nephin becomes **Mayo Dark Sky Park** *(mayo darkskypark.ie)*, Ireland's first International Dark Sky Park. It's a must-visit for stargazers, or indeed anyone who wants to appreciate the pristine night skies. Extending across more than 150 sq km, this area has almost zero light pollution, allowing the skies above to truly shine. The site is completely free to access anytime, and the website has a checklist for anyone new to stargazing. You can also download the seasonal star maps to guide you. Three night-sky viewing-points are located at easy-to-access locations throughout the park, with the Brogan Carroll Bothy one of the best sites.

FLORA & FAUNA IN WILD NEPHIN

Listen to nature speak by tapping into the diverse range of plants, animals and habitats of Wild Nephin National Park. The park protects a wealth of important habitats, including alpine heath, upland grassland, lakes and river catchments. Greenland white-fronted geese, golden plover, red grouse and otters are just some of the important fauna found within the park – begin your visit at the Wild Nephin National Park Visitor Centre in Ballycroy, where an interactive exhibition offers an an overview of the biodiversity of the park (as well as the cultural heritage of the region).

 EATING NEAR WILD NEPHIN NATIONAL PARK: OUR PICKS

Waterfront Bistro: This Mulranny hotel's bistro serves family-friendly food all day, with stunning views of Clew Bay. *1-9pm* €€

Number 9 Doherty's Bar: Established in Mulranny in 1920, this bar and eatery is open for breakfast, lunch and dinner. The roast of the day is worth working up an appetite for. *10am-8.30pm* €€

Ginger & Wild: Based at the National Park Visitor Centre, this cafe is airy and fresh; expect light lunches and salads with ingredients all grown in County Mayo. *10am-5pm Mar-Nov* €€

MAYO'S DARK SKIES

Mayo is now internationally recognised as one of the best places in the world to view the wonders of the night sky. Nestled between the remote Nephin Mountains and the unspoiled Atlantic coastline, the borders of the Dark Sky Park encompass the lands of Wild Nephin National Park.

Although the Ballycroy Visitor Centre closes during some of the winter months, the viewing points within the Dark Sky Park are still open to the public all year-round.

The darkest accessible site is the **Brogan Carroll Bothy**, located on the eastern side of the park (20km north of Newport town). The stone bothy is open 24 hours for shelter and is an excellent viewing point for all stargazers.

The park also hosts the annual three-day **Mayo Dark Sky Festival** *(mayodarkskyfestival.ie)*, which puts on family-friendly events to celebrate the nightscapes, allowing you to learn more about astronomy as well as the park's heritage and environment. With rocket-making displays, storytelling workshops, educational talks and plenty of activities that the whole family can enjoy, this festival is always a big hit.

Wild camping is permitted in the park, but campers and hikers are asked to register via the online registration system. If you're not camping in the park, your best accommodation option is overnighting in Newport (p364) or on Achill Island (p367).

Mullet Peninsula

TIME FROM ACHILL ISLAND: 1HR

Swim in the tidal pool in Belmullet

The 20m tidal pool located along the Shore Rd is beloved by visitors and locals. With magnificent views out over Blacksod Bay and the mountains of Achill Island in the distance, this is a swimmer's paradise with a friendly vibe.

There's a shallow end and a deep end, both accessible by ladder. It's free to use and can be accessed all year-round, and lifeguards are on duty in July and August.

Walk the Erris Head Loop

Designated as a special area of conservation, **Erris Head** is home to diverse flora and fauna, including nesting fulmars and guillemots, as well as gannets, seals, dolphins and porpoises.

The Erris Head Loop Walk is a 5km trail that follows a gradual incline along the headland; allow two hours. This straightforward walk treats you to mind-blowing Atlantic views, with Eagle Island and its famed lighthouse coming into view about halfway along the trail.

The ground can be boggy, so wear sturdy boots and pack your raincoat, as the weather can change quickly.

Watch the water at Dún na mBó

On the northwestern edge of the Mullet Peninsula is the impressive blowhole of Dún na mBó, a 15-minute drive from Erris Head. When wild Atlantic swells charge against the cliff, the water is quickly funnelled upwards, exploding through the blowhole in magnificent fashion. A sculpture that mimics old-style megaliths and fortresses surrounds the blowhole.

DRINKING ON THE MULLET PENINSULA: TOP SPOTS

Talbot's Bar	McDonnell's Bar	Corner House	O'D's Bar
Talbot's Bar: This lively bar is attached to the Talbot Hotel, one of the main hotels in the town of Belmullet. It's equally popular with locals and visitors. *10.30am-12.30pm Mon-Sat, to 11.30pm Sun*	**McDonnell's Bar**: Known to Belmullet locals as 'the Lobster Pot' (once you go in, you can't get out), McDonnell's has been an Erris institution for over 80 years. *noon-midnight Mon-Sat, to 11.30pm Sun*	**Corner House**: A traditional Irish pub in Belmullet with a warm welcome; it's popular for live country-music gigs. *10.30am-11.30pm Mon-Thu, to 12.30am Fri & Sat, to 11.30pm Sun*	**O'D's Bar**: A popular local hostelry with a pool table, live music and a big screen for viewing sports. *10.30am-11.30pm Mon-Thu, to 12.30am Fri & Sat, to 11pm Sun*

Céide Fields

Céide Fields

TIME FROM ACHILL ISLAND: 1HR 20MIN

Visit the oldest stone-walled fields in the world

Set on a clifftop high above the Atlantic Ocean, the **Céide Fields** *(ceidefields.com; adult/child €5/3)* contain some of the world's most extensive Stone Age monuments. So far, stone-walled fields, houses and megalithic tombs – equating to roughly half a million tonnes of stone – have been found, the legacy of a farming community dating back nearly 6000 years old. The **visitor centre**, in a glass pyramid overlooking the site, gives a fascinating glimpse into these times. Stop for lunch at the visitor centre or picnic outside with stunning views of the Mayo coastline and Downpatrick Head in the distance.

Take a guided tour of the site to fully appreciate the findings. As much of the tour is outside, be sure to wear appropriate footwear and clothing. The tours last an hour, are available throughout the day and are included as part of the admission price.

THE LIGHTHOUSES OF ERRIS

The Erris region is home to four lighthouses, at Blacksod, Eagle Island, Blackrock and Ballyglass. That might seem like an excessive number of lighthouses in a span of just 25km, but when you see the jagged, rocky shoreline, you might come to understand why these beacons are so important.

A tour of **Blacksod Lighthouse** *(visit blacksodlighthouse.ie; adult/child €12/6)* is a great way to spend an hour, and you'll learn the fascinating story of how a weather forecast from this remote outpost saved the D-Day invasion, changing the course of history.

Léim Siar (p391), a B&B in Belmullet, provides **bike hire** *(full/half-day €10/7)*, allowing you to head off on a two-wheeled adventure to take in the views of all four lighthouses.

EATING IN BELMULLET & BANGOR ERRIS: OUR PICKS

Talbot's Seafood Lodge: This popular, casual spot in Belmullet's Talbot Hotel is dedicated to using fresh, local produce. Open for breakfast, lunch and dinner. *9am-noon & 12.30-8.15pm* €€

Cois Cuain: This large, family-run diner in Belmullet serves tasty food – breakfasts, snacks, lunches and dinners – from morning 'til night. *10am-10pm Mon-Sat* €

An Builín Blasta: The name of this family-run bakery-cafe in Belmullet translates as 'The Tasty Bun'. It's a bustling meeting-spot for locals and visitors. *9am-6pm Mon-Sat* €

Sizzlers: Home-cooked food and delicious fast food to eat in or take away. *9am-10pm Mon-Wed, to 11pm Thu & Fri, to 10.30pm Sat & Sun* €

ARCHAEOLOGICAL SCIENCE AT CÉIDE FIELDS

The Céide Fields site was discovered in the 1930s by local schoolteacher Patrick Caulfield, who, as he was cutting away some peat (turf) for fuel, noticed linear piles of rocks in the soil. He deduced that the rocks must have been placed there by people, because their configuration appeared both unnatural and deliberate.

The ensuing excavation of the habitation sites and tombs revealed the way of life of people living 200 generations (or 6000 years) earlier. They were a community of farmers who cleared large areas of forest for use as farm land. Their main economy was cattle-rearing, but among them were also craftspeople and builders of both wood and stone.

Dún Bríste (p375)

Dún Bríste

TIME FROM ACHILL ISLAND: **1HR 30MIN**

Witness the power of the ocean

An astonishing sea stack lashed by foaming ocean water, Dún Bríste is Mayo's top natural sight, measuring 45m tall, 63m long and 23m wide. Legend has it that St Patrick drove all the vipers from Ireland onto this stack on Downpatrick Head, leaving the mainland snake-free. Try to choose a clear day for a visit to amplify the visuals.

The sea stack was shorn from the mainland in 1393 by a severe storm that left some poor unfortunates stranded upon it (who were, thankfully, later rescued). The remains of buildings survive on the stack to this day, and a viewing area has been constructed by the huge blowhole set back slightly from the cliff edge. It has numerous plaques detailing the history and folklore of the area. During storms, seawater is dramatically blasted through the blowhole.

You can drive most of the way up to the sea edge, but then you'll need to walk the last 400m or so.

Enniscrone

STUNNING BEACH | SEAWEED BATHS | COASTAL WALKS

In County Sligo, the low-key holiday town of Enniscrone, which faces Killala Bay, is all about ocean, glorious views and sunsets. Enniscrone Beach is the main reason to visit and is one of the best on Ireland's west coast, pulling in surfers, walkers, sunseekers and sandcastle builders.

The town is equipped with several excellent B&Bs and guesthouses, and seafood rightly features strongly on the menus of the cafes, bars and restaurants dotted along Main St.

In high summer, the town can be very busy, and parking can be an issue. But don't let that put you off. Enniscrone has a welcoming, family-friendly vibe with plenty of activities on offer, whether you've got little ones in tow or you're looking for a romantic getaway.

Wander along the windswept beach in November and chances are you'll have it all to yourself, allowing you to bask in the dramatic winter sunrises that turn the beach golden.

Enjoy Enniscrone's Coast

Sea-filled scenes

The beautiful **Enniscrone Beach** – which seemingly goes on forever – is 5km long and backed by expansive sand dunes that are rich with flora and fauna. Cars can drive straight onto the beach, and a lifeguard is normally on duty from June to September. To catch some waves, book a surf lesson with **7th Wave Surf School** *(surfsligo.com; surf lessons from €30)*. The school also offers rental equipment, prices start at €15 for a wetsuit and €35 for a hardboard and wetsuit.

Alternatively, head off on a coastal walk to take in the views. The 2km coastal loop walk starts from **Enniscrone Pier** and offers beautiful views. From the pier, head north, following the flat trail to take in stunning views of Killala Bay and the surrounding coastal scenery. At the end of the path, turn right and follow the road back to the pier where you started. You can also take the same coastal path back to the pier, allowing

GETTING AROUND

Enniscrone is a compact town, so getting around on foot is easy. **Bus Éireann** *(buseireann.ie)* bus 458 runs from Sligo town. The nearest train station is in Ballina, 15km away. There are also a number of taxi operators in Ballina.

Having a car is the best way to reach Enniscrone, but note that parking spaces fill up quickly in high summer.

☑ TOP TIP

Summer is the busiest time of the year in Enniscrone, so book your accommodation in advance if you're planning to visit at this time. After a day of activity on the beach or in the surrounding area, try a seaweed bath (p378) to unwind, relax and recharge.

HIGHLIGHTS
1 Enniscrone Beach
2 Kilcullen's Seaweed Baths

SIGHTS
see 2 Enniscrone Pier

ACTIVITIES
3 7th Wave Surf School
4 Enniscrone Pitch and Putt

SLEEPING
see 7 Ocean Sands Hotel & Spa
5 Waterfront House

EATING
6 Gilroy's Bar & Áit Eile
7 Ocean Bar
see 7 Pizzeria La Piazzetta
8 Surf's Up

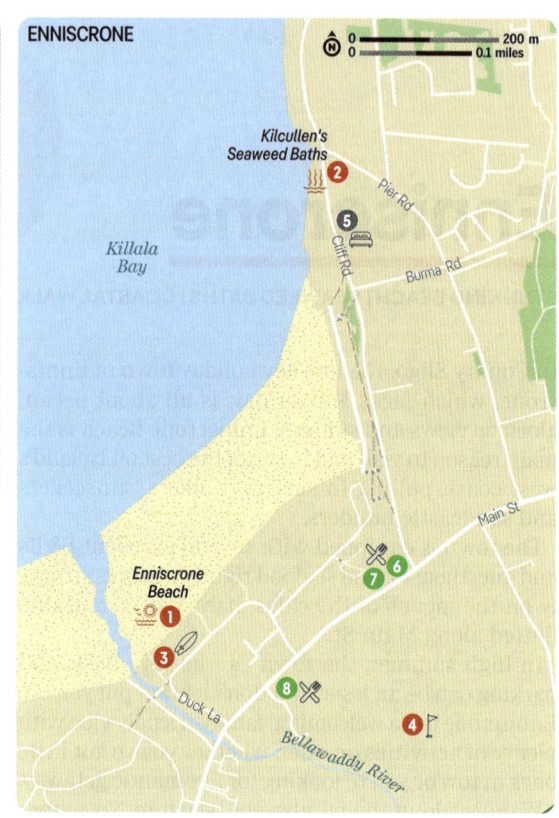

you to soak up vistas of the beach and Mayo's Nephin Mountains in the distance. It takes most walkers about 40 minutes to complete the coastal walk.

Soak in a Seaweed Bath
Take the plunge

Enniscrone is famous for its traditional seaweed baths, which are some of the most atmospheric in the country. **Kilcullen's Seaweed Baths** *(kilcullenseaweedbaths.net; hot seaweed and steam bath €30)* is an Edwardian bathhouse with buckets of

EATING IN ENNISCRONE: OUR PICKS

Pizzeria La Piazzetta: This fantastic Italian restaurant on Main St serves gourmet pizzas, pasta and tasty risotto alongside a great selection of wines. *5-9.30pm Sun-Wed, to 10pm Thu-Sat* €€

Gilroy's Bar & Áit Eile: Don't miss this award-winning restaurant. The menu uses locally sourced produce and fresh seafood; a guaranteed winner every time. *5-8.30pm Thu-Mon, from 1pm Sun* €€

Ocean Bar: Bistro-style dining inside the Ocean Sands Hotel. This restaurant has a variety of lunch and dinner options, with magnificent views of Enniscrone Beach. *12.30-8pm Oct-Apr, seasonal hours vary* €€

Surf's Up: A little cafe that packs a punch, with breakfast, lunch, brunch and a good-value kids' menu to boot. *9am-4pm Mon-Fri, to 5pm Sat & Sun* €

Kilcullen's Seaweed Baths

character; think vast porcelain baths, solid brass taps and panelled wood cabinets.

Settle into a large porcelain tub, soak in the hot seawater and let the nutrients in the seaweed do their work. Towels are provided, and private rooms are available. There's no better way to treat yourself after a day of adventuring, hiking or hanging out at the beach.

Play Pitch & Putt

Par for the course

Enniscrone is home to one of the oldest (and best) pitch and putt courses in the west of Ireland. The par-3 **Enniscrone Pitch and Putt course** *(@enniscronepitchandputt; adult/child €10/8)* is open seven days a week and is a fun family activity. The entrance to the course is off Main St, and there's no need to book in advance. Golf balls are available for €1 each.

WHY I LOVE LIVING IN ENNISCRONE

Kane Kilcullen of **Kilcullen's Seaweed Baths** on Enniscrone's surf culture.

We have such a vast amount of coastline, from Killala to Enniscrone and north to Easkey. There's a lot of different conditions for surfing, which I'm obsessed with. The surf culture keeps getting bigger, and people are moving to places like this, with a whole new generation pushing the standards of surfing.

My work life revolves around low tide and seaweed harvesting, but that also gives me time to check out the conditions for surfing. Visitors appreciate the magic of this place – it's not overly built up, and people are very friendly, and the culture is welcoming.

Beyond Enniscrone

From ancient stone-walled fields to jaw-dropping coastal vistas and spectacular beaches, the area around Enniscrone is simply breathtaking.

Places
Ballina p380
Foxford p381
Easkey p381
Strandhill p382
Carrowmore Megalithic Cemetery p383
Moyne Abbey p383
Caves of Keash p383
Carrowkeel Megalithic Complex p384

Following the wild shore from Enniscrone back into County Mayo rewards travellers with some of the finest views in Ireland, and a bunch of amazing beaches, too. But it's a scenic journey from Enniscrone, no matter which way you're headed. Travellers have opportunities to fish, surf, hike, and explore castles and other historic buildings.

Along the coast, you won't have much difficulty finding a place for the night, with many accommodation options set in a gorgeous landscape of unblemished rural beauty, offering sweeping views over the sea, and there are plenty of off-the-beaten-track beaches for a wild surfing experience, plus excellent food and accommodation options in Ballina, which is famous for its annual salmon festival.

GETTING AROUND

Driving is the best way to get around this rural part of Ireland, as many sights are not connected by public transport. **Bus Éireann** (buseireann.ie) offers daily services between nearly all of Mayo's towns and the rest of Ireland. **Local Link Mayo** (locallinkmayo.ie) provides local services on fixed routes between the area's towns and villages; check online for timetables. Bigger towns such as Ballina have taxi services in operation.

Ballina
TIME FROM ENNISCRONE: **16MIN**

Enjoy Ballina Salmon Festival

Ballina, County Mayo's third-largest town, is synonymous with salmon and is dubbed the 'salmon capital of Ireland'. If you find yourself here during fishing season, you'll be joined by droves of green-garbed waders, poles in hand, heading for the River Moy – which pumps right through the heart of town. The popular five-day **Ballina Salmon Festival** *(ballinasalmonfestival.ie)* is the longest-running community festival along the Wild Atlantic Way – it has been a summer fixture for more than 50 years and includes parades, dances, an art show and fishing competitions.

The festival takes place every July, with the ethos remaining the same since its inception in 1964: to celebrate all that is great about the community, and the jewel in its crown, the River Moy. There are dedicated walkways along the river where tourists can observe anglers at the world-renowned pools, beats and weirs. The teddy-bear's picnic is a highlight for little ones.

Rare collection of arms and armoury tour

Just over 2km north of town, **Belleek Castle** *(belleekcastle.com)* was built between 1825 and 1831 on the site of a medieval abbey. The castle, which is now a romantic hotel, was bought in the 1960s by fossil collector Marshall Doran, who gave it an eclectic and eccentric interior, some of it nautical (including the Spanish Armada bar).

Tours visit the Banquet Hall and Doran's collection of fossils, weaponry and armour. **Tours** *(from €14.50)* leave the hotel reception every day at midday and 2pm.

To fully get in the castle mood, check in for the night – this grand spot also serves as a hotel – and dine in the excellent restaurant.

The surrounding **Belleek Woods** are one of the largest urban forests in Europe, with several marked trails for walkers and cyclists.

Foxford

TIME FROM BALLINA: **20MIN**

Visit the famous Foxford Woollen Mill

Midway between Ballina and Castlebar, **Foxford Woollen Mill** *(foxford.com)* was founded in 1892. It was originally set up to ease post-Famine suffering and provide much-needed work. It remained open until 1987, during which time its woven goods achieved great acclaim. Now operated by locals, it employs a fraction of the hundreds who previously worked here. Free 20-minute **tours** *(tours@foxford.co)* detail the history, manufacturing and craft that these woollen mills are known for. The shop sells scarves, blankets, throws and other items that are all made in the mill.

Easkey

TIME FROM ENNISCRONE: **15MIN**

The charms of Easkey

Easkey Beach is one of Europe's best year-round surfing destinations, and the cool little town is a good addition to any itinerary, whether or not you brought your board. Head to the beach for a surf lesson, walk the 2km stretch of golden sand, go for a swim in the crystal-clear waters, or sit back and enjoy a spectacular west-coast sunset.

To take in stunning views of the rugged coastline, take a walk along the windswept cobbles of Easkey Pier, with Benbulben Mountain in the distance and, on a clear day, the spectacular Slieve League Cliffs further north. To the edge of the pier is **Easkey Castle** (also O'Dowd Castle or Roslee Castle), which was built in 1207. Perched on the edge of the Atlantic, the ruins make a great photo and a brilliant vantage point to watch local surfers in action. More advanced surfers are drawn to Easkey's two reef breaks, which make for epic barrels.

SPLIT ROCK OF EASKEY

Sitting in a field off the R297 near Easkey is Split Rock. This massive boulder – a huge chunk of gneiss measuring 6m long and 2.5m tall – was moved north from the Ox Mountains (on the west coast of Sligo) by retreating glaciers at the end of the last ice age.

It's known locally as Fionn's Stone; legend has it that Fionn MacCumhaill – aka Finn McCool, the famed warrior from Irish mythology – was involved in a giant's stone-throwing competition. Angry that his throw didn't reach the ocean, he leapt down and struck the rock with his sword. In actual fact, the split is a natural fracture in the stone.

Locals believe that if you walk through the crack in the rock three times, it will close on you.

EATING IN BALLINA: OUR PICKS

Crocket's Quay: This restaurant on the banks of the River Moy does well-executed pub grub. *4-9pm Mon-Fri, from 1pm Sat, 12.30-8.30pm Sun* €€

Poacher Restaurant: Cosy, intimate restaurant serving up imaginative, seasonally led menus with superb attention to detail. *5-9pm Wed-Fri, from 4pm Sat, 1-8pm Sun* €€

Ice House: This restaurant in the Ice House Hotel was once used to preserve fish. Groups will enjoy the extensive menu, which also has vegetarian and vegan options. *1-8.30pm Sun-Thu, to 9pm Fri & Sat* €€

Post House: This friendly spot serves an array of breakfasts, lunches and desserts. *9am-4pm Mon-Sat* €

SLIGO'S UNESCO BID

Sligo's megalithic heritage is the subject of a bid for UNESCO World Heritage status. The passage-tomb landscape of Sligo, with is interconnected megalithic passage-tomb sites and undisturbed cairns, is one of a number of cultural sites in seven Irish counties seeking the major accolade.

Sligo's unique landscape was placed on Ireland's 'tentative' list in July 2022, an essential first step towards heritage inscription. The World Heritage Committee must determine that the site or sites are of 'outstanding universal value' for humanity.

Currently two famous Irish spots managed by the Office of Public Works hold World Heritage status: Skellig Michael (p242) in County Kerry and Brú na Bóinne (p460) in County Meath.

MARK GUSEV/SHUTTERSTOCK

Strandhill

Strandhill

TIME FROM EASKEY: **40MIN**

Surf Strandhill

The great Atlantic rollers that sweep the shore of Strandhill make this long, red-gold beach a magnet for surfers. This northwest-facing beach picks up just about any type of swell from north to southwest, resulting in one of the most consistent beach breaks in the entire country. These conditions have produced some of the best surfers in Ireland.

Strandhill Surf School *(strandhillsurfschool.com; adult/child lessons €50/30)*, **Atlantic Surf School** *(atlanticsurfschool strandhill.ie; adult/child lessons €50/40)* and **Rebelle Surf** *(rebellesurf.co; adult/child lessons €45/40)* all offer lessons and rentals; all are based at the National Surf Centre in Strandhill.

Legend and history of Knocknarea Cairn

Sligo's ultimate rock pile sits atop a magical mountain hike. Knocknarea Cairn is popularly believed to be the grave of legendary Medbh (Queen Maeve; p444), who is said to be buried upright in the cairn, holding a spear and facing her adversaries in Ulster. The 40,000 tonnes of stone have never been excavated, despite speculation that a tomb on the scale of the one at Newgrange (p463) lies buried below. William Butler Yeats was enthralled by the myth and lore of Knocknarea, and

EATING IN STRANDHILL: OUR PICKS

Shells: From good coffee to fish and chips done in their signature batter, this cafe packs a punch. *9am-6pm* €€

Strand Bar: This long-established family-run pub and restaurant is popular for its wonderful food, including stonebaked pizzas. *12.30-4.15pm & 5-8pm Wed-Fri, to 8pm Sat & Sun* €€

The Venue: Serving great local food with spectacular views, this place also has live music at weekends. *12.30-8.30pm Sun-Thu, to 9.30pm Fri & Sat* €€

Stoked: This spot wows diners with its international cuisine and array of tapas that encourage sharing and tasting. *5-9pm Mon-Fri, from 4pm Sat & Sun* €€

its magic wormed its way into his verse. In 'Red Hanrahan's Song about Ireland' (1894), he writes: 'The wind has bundled up the clouds high over Knocknarea / And thrown the thunder on the stones for all that Maeve can say'.

The cairn is perched high atop a limestone plateau (328m), and a 1.2km trek up the mountain reveals spectacular views. From the top, you can gaze out over Benbulben, Rosses Point and the Atlantic Ocean beyond. Having got to the mountaintop, signs urge you not to climb the cairn itself. An estimated 100,000 walkers visit the site each year, and an increase in the number of people clambering over the stacked stones has caused erosion to this historic structure. Climbing is strictly forbidden.

The site is 2km northwest of Carrowmore, with Strandhill and Sligo town making good bases. The parking area is off the R292. The hike to and from the cairn is a 6km loop.

Carrowmore Megalithic Cemetery

TIME FROM ENNISCRONE: **45MIN**

A must-see attraction

One of the largest Stone Age cemeteries in Europe, **Carrowmore Megalithic Cemetery** (*heritageireland.ie; adult/child €5/3*) is a must-see attraction in Sligo. Some 30 monuments, including passage tombs, stone circles and dolmens, adorn the rolling hills of this haunting site, which is thought to predate Newgrange (p463) in County Meath by 700 years. Along with Carrowkeel, Loughcrew and Brú na Bóinne, Carrowmore is considered one of the 'big four' important megalithic sites in Ireland and dates back 6000 years.

To get here, follow the R292 southwest from Sligo town for 4km and follow the signs.

Moyne Abbey

TIME FROM ENNISCRONE: **28MIN**

Ruins of Moyne Abbey

Overlooking the mouth of the River Moy 3km east of Killala is Moyne Abbey, complete with a tower, church and cloisters. This Gothic-style abbey was built in 1462, and the Franciscan order thrived here for more than 130 years. In 1590 the English governor of Connacht set the friary alight in an effort to destroy the wealth of a local family. Cromwellian soldiers later desecrated the altar and killed the friars.

This site is off the beaten path, and there is no dedicated parking. Park with care on the roadside nearby and cross through the fields to access this stunning ruin.

Caves of Keash

TIME FROM ENNISCRONE: **1HR**

Dramatic and ancient caves

The Caves of Keash, also known as the Caves of Kesh or Caves of Keshcorran, are a series of limestone caves located near the village of Keash. These are some of Ireland's most visually striking caves, appearing as black mounts set in the white limestone rock face of Keshcorran Hill, with the magnificent caves towering over the little village.

COASTAL WALKS

With over 190km of coastline and some of the country's most unspoiled beaches, you'll be hard-pressed to find more impressive coastal walks in Ireland. At **Aughris Head**, an invigorating 5km walk traces the cliffs around this remote headland. Keep your eyes peeled for dolphins and seals swimming in the bay. Birdwatchers should look out for kittiwakes, fulmars, guillemots, shags, storm petrels and curlews.

With almost 360-degree views out over the Atlantic Ocean, the **Raghly Cliff Walk** is also not to be missed. The 3km route begins at Raghly Beach car park. Walk south, keeping the coast to your right, and continue to the blowhole. In stormy weather the sea shoots up through the blowhole vertically as the water gushes through holes created over millions of years through the porous limestone rock.

LIVING IN SLIGO

Archaeologist and tour guide **Auriel Robinson** on why the landscape of Sligo inspires her.

I chose to live in Sligo because of its notable scenery, archaeological sites, beautiful beaches, wild coastline and diverse landscapes.

Despite it being a small county, Sligo offers numerous opportunities for outdoor activities, including hiking, surfing, sailing, kayaking [and] climbing, plus it has stunning wilderness areas for nature lovers. Its coastline is stunning and wild, with an abundance of marine megafauna.

It has a lively city environment with artists, writers, musicians and creative individuals. Geographically, Sligo has an interesting post-glacial landscape and some of the oldest megalithic tombs in Europe.

All of this appealed to me and spurred me into setting up my tourism business in 2013.

Caves of Keash (p383)

The caves consist of 16 simple chambers, some interconnecting. Investigations in the caves during the early 20th century discovered bones from animals that stalked Ireland towards the end of the Ice Age – with evidence of hares, brown bear, red deer, Arctic lemming and wolves all dating to more than 12,000 years ago. The caves are said to be named after 'Corran', an Irish harpist who, thousands of years ago, lulled a sow to a sleepy state while it was being hunted by the Fianna, the ancient Irish warrior tribe.

Although the hike up to the caves is reasonably short, at around 20 minutes, it's tricky underfoot in places, especially on the descent. Park across from St Kevin's Church in the village of Keash; it's about a 20-minute walk along the road to where the trail begins. There is also space for cars at the trailhead.

Carrowkeel Megalithic Complex

TIME FROM ENNISCRONE: **1HR 10MIN**

An ancient site

Carrowkeel is a beautifully situated megalithic hilltop passage-tomb complex consisting of 14 passage cairns that were ancient burial sites of early Irish farmers. It's estimated they were built between 3200 and 2400 BCE. The passage cairns are spread across a number of hills that form part of the Bricklieve Mountain range – in Irish the name Breac Sliabh means 'Speckled Mountain'. Carrowkeel is one of a series of limestone plateaus aligned towards Knocknarea.

One of the tombs you can visit on the site is aligned with the setting sun on the summer solstice; when the light hits the back of the tomb, it's a magical place to be, while another tomb has a well-preserved corbelled roof, giving it a temple-like feel.

It's best to visit this important site with a guide to understand the full complexity of Carrowkeel. Archaeologist and Wild Atlantic Way ambassador **Auriel Robinson** *(seatrails.ie)* takes visitors to the site and explains their significance.

Mullaghmore

SEA VIEWS | HIKING | FISHING VILLAGE

The sweeping arc of sand and the safe, shallow waters make the pretty fishing village of Mullaghmore a popular family destination. It's a place of incredible natural beauty and world-class surf, which has helped put Ireland on the international big-wave surfing map. When large winter swells push in from the North Atlantic, they create waves that can tower to more than 18m, giving 'Mully' the reputation as one of the heaviest, coldest and most unpredictable big-wave spots in the world.

Even if you're not here to watch the Atlantic wave action, you can enjoy all that the area has to offer. The golden sands of horseshoe-shaped Mullaghmore Beach stretch out for 3km, and the sheltered bay, backed by expansive sand dunes, is ideal for walkers. Hikers can take on the scenic Mullaghmore Head Loop, or you can head into the pubs for live music.

GETTING AROUND

In summer, Local Link bus 982 links Sligo town and Mullaghmore. Getting around the village and Mullaghmore Head is possible on foot. If you want to venture further afield, you're best off with your own vehicle.

Explore Mullaghmore Head

Wander the wild headland

Starting in the village, the **Mullaghmore Head Loop** is a fantastic walk that follows the road that hugs the coast. Birdwatchers should keep an eye out for oystercatchers, gannets, fulmars and Manx shearwaters. Walkers are treated to stunning views of Classiebawn Castle, Donegal Bay, Slieve League and Sligo's iconic Benbulben Mountain. Allow an hour and a half to complete the loop.

Alternatively, you can drive the loop, taking in panoramic views of counties Sligo, Donegal and Leitrim along the way.

Get a Glimpse of Classiebawn Castle

A scenic setting

Built in 1874, photogenic Classiebawn Castle sits proudly on Mullaghmore Head and gained international acclaim after it was featured on the TV show *The Crown*. Set on 1215 hectares of land, the neoGothic turreted pile is privately owned and not open to the public, but the views of it against a dramatic backdrop of mountains and sea make for a terrific sight.

☑ TOP TIP

Abandoned in 1948, Inishmurray Island is 7km from the mainland and has early Christian remains and pagan relics, including three well-preserved churches, beehive cells and open-air altars. There's no regular boat service; organise a boat trip from the harbour. Landing on the island is weather dependent, so enquire early.

- **SIGHTS**
  1 Classiebawn Castle
- **SLEEPING**
  see 4 Pier Head Hotel
  2 Seacrest B&B
- **EATING**
  3 Boatman's Bistro Bar
  see 3 Harbour Cafe
  4 Quay Bar

TRAGEDY IN MULLAGHMORE

On 27 August 1979, an IRA bomb killed former Viceroy of India Lord Louis Mountbatten shortly after setting out on his boat from Mullaghmore harbour. Three other passengers also lost their lives.

The death of Lord Mountbatten, a second cousin once removed of Queen Elizabeth II, was so shocking that it attracted more global attention than a separate IRA ambush that killed 18 British soldiers a few hours later at Warrenpoint, 120 miles away.

With his royal connections, Lord Mountbatten was targeted in a scenic idyll that had seemed remote from the Troubles, a dark period in recent Irish history.

The castle was built for Lord Palmerston in 1856 and was later home to the ill-fated Lord Mountbatten, who was killed near the castle by an IRA bomb.

The castle has an atypical charm and is seen as an architectural marvel. While you can't visit it, it's one of Ireland's most iconic buildings, and you'll have no trouble photographing it and admiring it from a distance.

Court Tomb of Creevykeel

Ancient structure

The neatly stacked piles of rocks at Creevykeel Court Tomb stretch some 50m and sketch a shape similar to a lobster's claw. They outline what is one of Ireland's finest court tombs and enclose several burial chambers. The structure dates from around 4000 BCE to 2500 BCE, with chambers being added over time. Once in the unroofed oval court, smaller visitors can duck under the stone-shielded entrance to reach the site's core.

EATING IN MULLAGHMORE: OUR PICKS

Harrison's Bar & Restaurant: From posh scampi to gourmet burgers, you'll be spoilt for choice in this Cliffony gastro-pub. *4-9pm Tue-Sat, 1-8pm Sun* €€

Harbour Cafe: A new kid on the culinary block; you'll find delicious, fresh produce here. *10.30am-8.30pm Fri & Sat, to 5pm Sun & Mon* €€

Quay Bar: Casual bar food, from pizza to fish and chips, in the bar of the Pier Head Hotel. *12.30-5pm May-Oct* €€

Boatman's Bistro Bar: Serving chicken boxty and Wild Atlantic Way fishcakes in the lively bar of the Beach Hotel. *12.30-8pm Thu-Sun Apr-Oct* €€

Beyond Mullaghmore

Evocative coastal drives and lonely mountain paths highlight the heart of Yeats country, and the scenery is nothing short of sublime.

County Sligo's lush hills, ancient monuments and simple country life inspired Nobel Laureate, poet and dramatist William Butler Yeats from an early age. Despite living almost all of his life abroad, Yeats returned here frequently, enamoured of the lakes, the looming hulk of Benbulben and the idyllic pastoral setting.

Northern Sligo still captivates travellers today, and you can visit important places in Yeats' life and work. His memorial in the village church in Drumcliff rests in the shadow of forbidding and iconic Benbulben Mountain, which you can hike up and around.

Elsewhere, watch sheepdogs at work and explore some of the most important megalithic sites in Europe.

Places
Sligo Town p387
Benbulben & Around p389
Drumcliff p390
Lissadell p390

GETTING AROUND

Much of County Sligo is explorable by bus, but for more flexibility, hire a car. **Bus Éireann** *(buseireann.ie)* operates several routes from Sligo town that service the wider area. **Europcar** *(europcar.ie)*, **Enterprise** *(enterprise.ie)* and other car-hire companies have offices south of Sligo town on the Old Dublin Rd.

Sligo Town
TIME FROM MULLAGHMORE: **30MIN**

Visit Sligo Abbey
Founded in 1252, **Sligo Abbey** *(heritageireland.ie; adult/child €53)* is the town's most well-known landmark. This handsome Dominican friary burned down in the 15th century and was later rebuilt. Friends in high places saved the abbey from the worst ravages of the Elizabethan era and rescued the previously sold sculpted altar to ensure it survived the Reformation.

Despite the ravages of history, the abbey retains a great wealth of carvings, including Gothic and Renaissance sculptures. Visitors can also explore the remains of the dining hall and dormitories on the upper floor, as well as the historic graveyard, which surrounds the complex.

EATING IN SLIGO TOWN: OUR PICKS

Eala Bhan: This lively restaurant on the banks of the River Garavogue offers excellent seafood and steak dishes, and veg and vegan choices. *5-9pm Mon-Fri, noon-4pm & 5-9pm Sat & Sun* €€€

Hargadons: A superb 1868 inn, with old-world fittings and gastro pub style. The great-value food is renowned, transforming local ingredients with continental flair. *noon-midnight Tue-Sat* €€

Hooked: This restaurant is dedicated to serving local food; expect an array of all-day options, with the help of nearby producers. *noon-9pm Mon-Thu, 9.30am-9pm Fri-Sun* €€

Funké: This Afro-Caribbean-style restaurant is a great new addition to the local food scene. *12.30-8.30pm Tue-Thu, to 9.30pm Fri & Sat* €€

Sligo town

WILLIAM BUTLER YEATS

WB Yeats (1865–1939) is considered to be one of the greatest poets of the 20th century. While he was born in Dublin and lived in London for much of his childhood, his summers as a boy were spent in Sligo, and the county is widely regarded as his spiritual home. His visits planted the seeds that would last a lifetime, and the landscape became central to his writing.

As well as writing poetry and plays, together with Lady Gregory, he founded the Irish National Theatre, which would later become the Abbey Theatre. But it's his poetry, inspired by his youth, that make him a household name in Ireland to this day. Filled with a romantic longing for the past – both mythic and his own – his words conjured up a magical land.

Learn about Sligo town

Sligo town often flies under the radar, but it's teeming with history, culture and buzzing nightlife. Stroll along the banks of the River Garavogue and stop for a pint to find an impromptu trad session taking place in one of the many bars. Or wander down Tobergal Lane and dine in style in one of the eateries celebrating food culture from all over the world. The town is a great low-key and easily manageable base for exploring Yeats country and beyond.

But it also has lots of things for culture vultures to soak up, including arts festivals, museums and galleries. A visit to the **Model** *(model.ie)*, one of Ireland's most important contemporary arts centres, with an extensive and vibrant programme of visual and performing arts, is a must. The Model is home to the Niland Collection, which is significant for its focus on the northwest of Ireland, and contains some of the most important works of Jack B Yeats, brother of the famous poet WB Yeats.

The **Hawk's Well Theatre** *(hawkswell.com)* and the **Blue Raincoat Theatre Company** *(blueraincoat.com)* are both important venues for the performing arts and creativity in the northwest, with rich and varied programmes on offer.

GETTING A DRINK IN SLIGO TOWN: OUR PICKS

Snug Bar: This cosy little bar has great live music and is touted to have the best pint of Guinness in town. *hours vary*

Furey's: A lively spot with a great atmosphere and a good chance of a live music session breaking out. *5-11.30pm Mon-Thu, to 12.30am Fri & Sat, to 11pm Sun*

Thomas Connolly: Operating since 1780, Thomas Connolly offers more than 160 whiskeys and a large selection of gins. *noon-11.30pm Mon-Thu, to 12.30am Fri & Sat, to 11pm Sun*

Garavogue Bar: Situated along the riverbank, this is the perfect spot for a cocktail or a glass of wine outside on a fine evening. *4pm-2am Sun-Fri, noon-2am Sat*

Benbulben & Around

TIME FROM MULLAGHMORE: **16MIN**

Walk around Benbulben

A stolid greenish-grey eminence visible all along Sligo's northern coast, Benbulben (525m), often written Ben Bulben, resembles a table covered by a pleated cloth: its limestone plateau is uncommonly flat, and its near-vertical sides are scored by earthen ribs.

Walking the peaks is not for the uninitiated, but the relatively flat **Benbulben Loop**, also known as the Gortarowey Walk, is a more accessible trail. In the shadow of the iconic mountain, the 5.5km circular walk runs through protected lands home to spruce and fir trees.

This forest walk allows you to get up close to the country's most distinctive mountain, sometimes referred to as Ireland's Table Mountain. The trail begins in a secluded forest before opening out to provide stunning views of Benbulben Head. As the walk loops around you, take in the views of Slieve League and Donegal Bay, as well as Classiebawn Castle at Mullaghmore. The loop walk takes about an hour and a half. It's best to pack walking boots, as the trail can be boggy in places.

Watch sheepdogs at work

Ireland is home to countless sheep, and with so many to manage, farmers rely on the help of their intelligent and well-trained sheepdogs. In Streedagh, expert trainer Martin Feeney of **Atlantic Sheepdogs** *(atlanticsheepdogs.ie; adult/child €14/5)* showcases these dogs' incredible abilities in their working environment.

Feeney, who has represented Ireland for 20 years on the international stage with his dogs, puts on an hour-long show for visitors. You'll see the dogs seamlessly move sheep around the fields and learn about how the dogs are trained. If you visit in summer, you might also have the opportunity to see sheepshearing in action.

The majestic Streedagh

Blow away the cobwebs on the majestic stretch of coastline that is **Streedagh Strand**. The 3km beach links Streedagh Point to Connor's Island. The area is home to a rich array of flora and fauna, but it's the stunning coastal views that will take your breath away. Bring a picnic and watch the Atlantic rollers sweep in, or bring your board and experience a spot of surfing.

ON THE YEATS TRAIL

The signposted **Yeats Trail** *(yeatstrail.ie)* is a touring route that incorporates 14 significant locations in County Sligo that have close associations with the poet WB Yeats.

The traditions, stories and landscape of Sligo provided Yeats with the inspiration for some of his best-loved poems, and the Yeats Trail provides visitors with a space to enjoy and interpret the poet's work in their own way, at their own pace.

At number nine on the trail is **Innisfree**, an island close to the southeast shore of Lough Gill. The famous poem 'The Lake Isle of Innisfree' was composed by the poet in 1888. It begins with the famous words: 'I will arise and go now, and go to Innisfree'.

DRINKING AROUND DRUMCLIFF: OUR PICKS

Davis's Restaurant & Yeats' Tavern: This popular spot also serves great food. It's perfect for a pint after visiting Yeats country. *12.30-9pm Mon-Thu, to 11.30pm Fri & Sat, 12.30-9.30pm Sun* €

O'Donnell's Bar: This historic watering hole was built in 1802 by British Prime Minister Lord Palmerston. It's said his ghost still haunts the pub, but the locals are very welcoming. *5-11pm* €

Henry's Bar & Restaurant: Situated in Cashelgarren, this lively and welcoming spot is a great spot for a pint or a cocktail; also does lunch and dinner. *noon-8pm Wed-Sun* €

Lang's Bar: A traditional bar/grocery shop in Grange that has retained its original features; hooks still hang from the ceiling and the weighing scales are ready for use. *5-11.30pm Mon-Sat, 3-11pm Sun* €

FOODIE DESTINATION

The **Sligo Food Trail** *(sligofoodtrail.ie)* is a network of over 70 food-related businesses from County Sligo who have joined together to showcase and develop new food experiences, highlighting the finest, freshest food on the Wild Atlantic Way.

You can map your own route to choose the cuisine that you love best or see where you're travelling and find what's available in that area. Just download the map and nourish your body while basking in the incredible scenery and culture of the surrounding area.

You can also book a **tour** *(sligofoodtours.ie; per person €64)* to explore Sligo town's thriving culinary food scene, visiting up to eight different food businesses for tastings. From oysters to seaweed, fermented foods to sourdough bread, local tapas to craft beer, there's something to whet every appetite.

Streedagh's swaying marram grasses and windswept sands, with the Atlantic Ocean backdrop, gave it a starring role on the Hulu TV adaptation of Sally Rooney's *Normal People*.

Drumcliff

TIME FROM MULLAGHMORE: **17MIN**

The burial place of WB Yeats

Benbulben's beauty was not lost on WB Yeats (1865–1939), one of the greatest poets of the 20th century. Before he died near Menton, in France, in 1939, he had requested: 'If I die here, bury me up there on the mountain, and then after a year or so, dig me up and bring me privately to Sligo.' His wishes were apparently followed in 1948, when what was thought to be his body was interred in a grave in the churchyard at Drumcliff, where his great-grandfather had been rector, though doubts later emerged as to whether they were actually Yeats' bones that had been reburied.

The poet's epitaph is from Yeats' 1939 poem, 'Under Ben Bulben':

Cast a cold eye
On life, on death.
Horseman, pass by!

Lissadell

TIME FROM MULLAGHMORE: **20MIN**

Tour Lissadell House

Step back in time with a tour of the childhood home of Irish revolutionary Constance Markievicz (1868–1927) and her famous sister, Eva Gore Booth (1870–1926). WB Yeats was friendly with the Gore Booth sisters and stayed at Lissadell in 1892 and 1893, immortalising them in his poetry. Since it was purchased by couple Edward Walsh and Constance Cassidy in 2003, the house and gardens have undergone extensive restoration.

A tour of **Lissadell House** *(lissadellhouse.com; adult/child €14/8)* provides an interesting exploration of the Irish 'big house' as it takes visitors through the grand rooms, and into the kitchen and servant's quarters below. Both house and gardens are open to the public to visit from June to August. The tearooms at Lissadell also provide lovely home-baked food, including delicious golden pastries, tarts, cakes and cheesecakes.

BEST CAFES AROUND LISSADELL: OUR PICKS

Vintage Lane Cafe: Based in the Benbulben Craft Village, this little cafe serves breakfast, lunch and brunch in a sumptuous setting. *9.30am-4pm Wed-Sat* €

Pink Clover: The former site of the Drumcliff Cafe, this refurbished cafe does delicious home baking. *10am-4.30pm Mon-Sat* €

Anois Cafe: This is a lively cafe in Cliffoney that dishes up brunch and sweet treats. *10am-4pm Mon-Fri* €

Jam Pot Cafe: A sweet little place in the village of Grange where you'll find great coffee and cake. *10am-4pm* €

# Places We Love to Stay

€ Budget €€ Midrange €€€ Top End

Westport MAP p361

Westport House Caravan Park € Well-serviced camping and glamping on the edge of the magnificent Westport House. It's a popular option, so book ahead.

Westport Woods Hotel & Spa €€ An out-of-town gem nestled in the woods. Clean, comfortable rooms at great value, with an airy dining area.

Beyond Westport

Mayo Glamping € With a range of pods, this is a fun stay for families, with hobbit huts and a railway carriage available. There's also a woodfired oven, a BBQ and a kids play area on-site, close to the town of Castlebar.

Clare Island Lighthouse €€ With a mix of B&B and self-catering options, this spot offers the romance of a lighthouse stay with luxury on Clare Island. It's a popular option, so book ahead.

Achill Island MAP p368

Achill Cliff House Hotel & Restaurant €€ Quaint hotel with a rustic and lively restaurant. The sea-view rooms overlooking Keel Bay are always in demand.

Bervie €€ Irish B&B hospitality at its best, with wonderful dining and the most welcoming hosts. You won't want to leave.

Beyond Achill

Léim Siar €€ Léim Siar means 'Jump West' in Irish – a fitting name for a B&B just a short walk from the Blacksod lighthouse. A remote, end-of-the-earth feel combines with all the modern comforts: bright rooms, underfloor heating, fantastic breakfasts and cracking views.

Mulranny Park Hotel €€ With 39 rooms and 19 serviced apartments, this hotel has a range of accommodation options, plus a swimming pool and good dining options. A good family choice.

Talbot Hotel €€ Comfortable hotel in the middle of Belmullet with a lively bar and restaurant. A great base for exploring the wider Erris area.

Enniscrone MAP p378

Ocean Sands Hotel & Spa €€ Airy and modern hotel with great views of the ocean. Clean, comfy rooms and wonderful bistro-dining.

Waterfront House €€ This B&B has 16 rooms, amazing sea views and good mid-week deals.

Beyond Enniscrone

Nest Hostel € Pared-back, simple rooms with shared bathrooms in Strandhill. The star attraction is the ocean just a stone's throw away. Book early if you want to secure weekend accommodation.

Ice House Hotel €€€ One of Mayo's most popular places to stay, this is luxury with fine dining on the Ballina quayside.

Mullaghmore MAP p386

Seacrest B&B € With five rooms – three doubles and one single – this comfortable and welcoming B&B overlooking the sandy beach books out early.

Pier Head Hotel €€ A family favourite, with sumptuous views over the harbour. The swimming pool is great for rainy days, and the bar serves quality food. It closes from the end of October until April. Book early to avoid disappointment.

Beyond Mullaghmore

Glasshouse €€ With modern, sleek and spacious rooms, this property has a cool vibe, with a bar and dining area overlooking the River Garavogue in Sligo town.

Lissadell on the Sea €€€ Privacy and luxury are guaranteed in this heavenly, blow-the-budget option on the grounds of Lissadell House. It's set on its own private beach, with a dreamy outdoor dining area; you might never want to go home.

Left: Mt Errigal (p401) and Dunlewey Lough (p402); right: Slieve League Cliffs (p414)

Researched by
Kathy Donaghy

Donegal

IRELAND'S UNMISSABLE YET FORGOTTEN COUNTY

Towering cliffs, spectacular beaches, remote wilderness and wild coastal views await visitors to Donegal.

County Donegal is the wild child of Ireland, home to some of its most ravishingly sublime scenery, not to mention beautiful beaches. It's a county of extremes: at times desolate and battered by brutal weather, it's also a land of unspoilt splendour, where stark peaks and sweeping beaches bask in glorious sunshine, and port-side restaurants serve fine food. The local dining scene is flourishing, and Donegal's long coastline offers a veritable seafood feast that's matched by excellent restaurants specialising in modern Irish cuisine, gastro-pub fare and international flavours.

Donegal shares a small border with County Leitrim to the south, isolating it from the rest of the Republic of Ireland, while its rugged interior, with remote mountain passes and shimmering lakes, is only marginally outdone by the long, labyrinthine coastline of windswept peninsulas and isolated pubs. Proudly independent, one-third of Donegal is official Gaeltacht territory, with Gaeilge (Irish) being the lingua franca.

After its northern start in County Derry, the Wild Atlantic Way (Slí an Atlantaigh Fhiáin) really begins to strut its stuff here, as the county's untamed craggy coastline truly puts the 'Wild' into the 'Way'.

Donegal is also well-supplied with outstanding places to stay. The only problem is that you may not want to check out. You'll find everything from simple B&Bs and guesthouses to historic heritage hotels, grand country houses and well-equipped hostels, many immersed in glorious scenery.

NICOLAS D'HOEDT/LONELY PLANET

THE MAIN AREAS

GLENVEAGH NATIONAL PARK
Adventure awaits in the Derryveagh Mountains. **p396**

MALIN HEAD
Explore Ireland's most northerly point. **p405**

SLIEVE LEAGUE CLIFFS
Europe's highest walkable sea cliffs. **p414**

Find Your Way

Buses link all of Donegal's major towns, but by far the best approach is to hire a car and hit the county's roads and byroads. Alternatively, rent a bicycle and tackle the demanding terrain.

Malin Head, p405
Visit Ireland's most northerly point to see the magnificent northern lights and take in dramatic coastal scenery – in the company of alpacas.

Glenveagh National Park, p396
Experience the wild beauty of the Derryveagh Mountains, learn about the history of Glenveagh Castle and admire the surrounding spectacular gardens.

Slieve League Cliffs, p414
Enjoy the awe-inspiring vistas of Europe's tallest walkable sea cliffs from one of the many hiking trails, or view them from the ocean below.

FERRY
Ferry services – **Tory Island Ferry** (toryferry.com) and **Lough Foyle Ferry** (loughfoyleferry.com) – run to many of Donegal's islands and also link up some of the peninsulas. Check the weather ahead of time and book in advance to avoid disruptions to your plans.

CAR
Driving is the best way to get around Donegal. With your own wheels, you can move at your own pace, cover more ground and access those off-the-beaten-track destinations that public transport can't reach.

Wild Atlantic Way (p626)

Plan Your Time

Many of Donegal's most popular destinations take time to reach, travel between and explore. It's wise to have a plan of action to maximise your time.

Pressed For Time

- Base yourself in **Donegal town** (p420) and start your morning with a tour of **Donegal Castle** (p420). Head to the **Slieve League Cliffs** (p414) for a hike or a boat trip, and watch the sunset from **Malin Beg Beach** (p416). Leave early the next morning for **Glenveagh National Park** (p396) via the **Glengesh Pass** (p418), stopping in the town of **Ardara** (p417) on the way.

Six Days To Explore

- Follow the previous itinerary and then pay a visit **Arranmore Island** (p402). The next morning, head to **Tory Island** (p404) before driving the Wild Atlantic Way to Doe Castle. Overnight in Letterkenny, with the fort of **Grianán of Aileách** (p410) your first stop the next morning. Explore the **Inishowen Peninsula** (p411) before finally making your way north to **Malin Head** (p405).

SEASONAL HIGHLIGHTS

SPRING
March is one of the best times of the year to see the **northern lights** (p406) from Malin Head.

SUMMER
Festival-goers are spoilt for choice. Check out the **MacGill Summer School** (p419) in July.

AUTUMN
As the season winds down, you'll have the trails in the Derryveagh Mountains and the Bluestacks all to yourself.

WINTER
Surfers can experience the incredible power of the Atlantic off **Bundoran** (p421) and **Rossnowlagh** (p422).

Glenveagh National Park

PEACEFUL HIKING | FAIRYTALE CASTLE | AWE-INSPIRING SCENERY

☑ TOP TIP

With so much to do in Glenveagh National Park, it's wise to give yourself a full day to explore. Break up the day with lunch at the castle tearooms, or at the restaurant in the visitor centre. When hiking the trails, good footwear is essential, as is rain gear.

Ireland's second-largest national park, Glenveagh is a sublime panoply of lakes overlooked by brooding mountains, with valleys scooped from the land and scattered with forest and bog. It's both enticing and unspoilt, with plenty of wonderful options for hiking. Glenveagh is also home to a wealth of wildlife, including the golden eagle – which was hunted to extinction here in the 19th century but reintroduced in 2001 – and the country's largest herd of red deer.

Glenveagh Castle, with its chequered history of ruthless landowners, is at the heart of the national park. On a self-guided tour, you can understand why it was such a magnet for Hollywood stars, from Greta Garbo to Marilyn Monroe. But it's the landscape around the castle that really fires the imagination, with steep zigzagging paths rising to provide jaw-dropping views of the glaciated valley. Here, it's possible to find yourself alone on a mountain trail, watching the waterfalls cascade into Lough Beagh.

 GETTING AROUND

Driving is the best way to reach and explore Glenveagh National Park, situated 23km northwest of Letterkenny. If you're driving from Letterkenny, you'll soon find yourself in rolling hills, with the Derryveagh Mountains in the distance.

By public transport, take **Local Link** bus 971 from Letterkenny Bus Station *(35 minutes)*; it stops right at the entrance to the park visitor centre (p398), where you can access information on the park, its trails and its history. See **Local Link Donegal Sligo Leitrim** *(locallinkdsl.ie)* for timetables.

A shuttle bus goes from the visitor centre to the castle every 15 minutes from 10am. Both pedal and e-bike hire are available with **GrassRoutes Bike Hire** *(grassroutes. ie; e-bike/hybrid €22.50/16.50)*, located right beside the visitor centre. Hiring an e-bike takes the strain out of seeing the park and can be a good option if you're pushed for time; book in advance.

GLENVEAGH NATIONAL PARK

⭐ HIGHLIGHTS
1. Glenveagh Castle

● SLEEPING
2. Arranmore Lighthouse Accommodation
3. Rockhill House
4. Teac Jack
5. Wild Atlantic Camp

● EATING
6. Coffee Time
7. Lagoon Bar & Restaurant
8. Nellie's Restaurant
9. Synge & Byrne

● INFORMATION
10. Glenveagh National Park Visitor Centre

● TRANSPORT
see 10. GrassRoutes Bike Rental

The Dark Side of the Rooms

A tour of Glenveagh Castle

Modelled on Scotland's Balmoral Castle, **Glenveagh Castle** (*nationalparks.ie; adult/concession €7/5*) is a characterful building with a dark history. John George Adair was a Scottish-Irish businessman and landowner who made his fortune by acquiring estates that went bankrupt after the Famine. He began construction on Glenveagh in 1867, completing the building in 1873. He died suddenly in 1885, leaving the estate to his wife, Cornelia, who laid the stunning gardens.

After Cornelia passed away in 1921, Arthur Kingsley Porter, a professor at Harvard University, purchased the castle. However, he went missing on a trip to Inishbofin under mysterious circumstances and was never found (he was presumed drowned but later rumoured to have been spotted in Paris). In 1937, an Irish-American named Henry McIlhenny bought the castle. After restoring it and redeveloping the gardens, he sold the estate to the Irish government in 1975.

On a self-guided tour, you can learn about the history of the castle via the information points in each room. The most eye-catching of the flamboyantly decorated rooms are in the round tower, home to the tartan-and-antler-encrusted **Music Room** and **Blue Room**. You'll see some unique design touches as you stroll through the boudoirs and hallways, including the use of shells (mussels and periwinkles) from some local beaches in the entrance hall. The outdoor swimming pool on the edge of the lake wouldn't be out of place in a villa on Lake Como.

The castle is closed Mondays and Fridays, except for Bank Holiday Mondays. Seasonal opening hours differ, so it's best to check the website.

JOURNEYING THROUGH TIME IN GLENVEAGH

Clare Bromley, head of education at **Glenveagh National Park**

There is so much more to Glenveagh than you might realise. Many people come to see the obvious parts, but perhaps miss the bigger significance of this stunning protected landscape.

The head of the valley is my favourite spot. On guided walks, I ask visitors to use their imagination here, pointing out that thousands of years ago, this valley was filled with ancient forests. Then we journey down the trail, talking about why it looks so different today and what we're doing to restore our native Irish woodlands.

I love talking to people about the well-being and health aspects of spaces like this, too. A day in Glenveagh is good for the soul.

Through the Seasons in the Castle Gardens
Gardens of delight

Glenveagh Castle's exotic gardens are similarly spectacular, boasting terraces, an Italian garden, a walled kitchen garden and the **Belgian Walk**, built by Belgian soldiers who stayed here during WWI. The gardens' cultured charm is in marked contrast to the wildly beautiful landscape that enfolds the area.

The original **Victorian Garden** was laid out for Cornelia Adair, John George Adair's wife, in 1885. Later, Henry McIlhenny lavished money on the gardens, the fruits of which are enjoyed today.

The **Walled Garden** is in the *jardin potager* (kitchen garden) style, with flowers, fruit, vegetables and herbs grown for their ornamental effect. There are magnificent displays throughout the year, from snowdrops in early spring and old-fashioned narcissi in late spring, to rhododendrons and azaleas in April and unique red dahlias in July and August. The sight of the Eucryphia in bloom, its petals falling like snowflakes, is a sight to behold in late summer.

Hiking in Glenveagh National Park
Walks for every fitness level

One of the best ways to appreciate this vast and varied park is by wandering the majestic sweep of its forbidding golden landscape.

The park has numerous nature trails that weave past lakes, through woods and along blanket bog. Plan your route, get advice and study the trail maps at the park **visitor centre**. The park's six marked trails are well signposted. The walks vary in length and difficulty; experienced hikers will find more challenging routes beyond the marked trails.

Although the 1km **View Point Trail** is on the short side, it's one of the steepest routes. The trail begins outside the castle gardens and follows a stony path to a viewpoint high above the castle. From the top, the views of the surrounding mountains, the lake and the castle below are incredible.

The **Garden Trail** is a 1km looped walk that follows a well-marked route of the gardens and their main features. The garden is in stark contrast to the rugged nature of the park.

Beginning at the visitor centre, the 2km **Lakeside Walk** follows the shores of Lough Veagh to Glenveagh Castle. Native broadland trees are plentiful along the trail, and the terrain is mostly flat. It's a great alternative to taking the shuttle bus to the castle.

The 2km looped **Derrylahan Nature Trail** takes you through more remote areas of the park, where you are treated to bogland views while you meander through forests of Scots pine. The path is a gravel track that covers both flat and steep ground.

For a half-day hike, the 8km **Glen Walk** (Bridle Path) is worthwhile. This walk takes you a little further off the beaten path into the Derryveagh Mountains, rewarding hikers with spectacular views of the valley below. The route begins on a

Glenveagh Castle (p397)

flat gravel path before climbing upwards for the last 3km or so. You'll need to arrange a pick-up at the other end, or return the same way you came.

Your best chance of spotting **red deer** in their natural habitat is on the 7km **Lough Inshagh Trail**. Like the Glen Walk, this is not a looped walk, so you need to arrange for a pick-up or drop-off at Lackanoo Car Park, or return via the same trail. The terrain is a little more challenging, but the scenery is worth every step, and you can really appreciate just how vast the park actually is.

Cycle Glenveagh's Trails

Pedal the backcountry

If you're pressed for time, cycling the park offers visitors an efficient and eco-friendly way to get around. GrassRoutes Bike Hire (p396) rents both pedal and e-bikes from May to October.

From the visitor centre, the cycle to **Glenveagh Castle** (p397) is along a flat, mainly paved surface that skirts along the lakeshore, giving visitors their first inklings of the sheer vastness of the park. The 8km **Glen Walk** (Bridle Path) is the shortest and most easily negotiated route through the Derryveagh Mountains. Along the route, look out for old settlements

GLENVEAGH VISITOR CENTRE

Make the most of your visit to Glenveagh by stopping in at the **Glenveagh National Park Visitor Centre** (p398).

Here you can watch short videos on the ecology of the park and learn about the notorious estate owner, John George Adair, who incurred infamy throughout Donegal by ruthlessly evicting 244 tenants in the Derryveagh evictions of 1861. You can also learn about the reintroduction of the golden eagle and find out how to make your visit a meaningful one by being mindful of your impact on the pristine landscape. Information officers are on hand to chat about the park and its trails, and there is a large car park, toilets, baby-changing spaces and a restaurant.

 EATING IN & AROUND GLENVEAGH NATIONAL PARK: OUR PICKS

Synge & Byrne: The castle tearooms are a great place to fuel up after a hike. *10-5pm* €

Nellie's Restaurant: Delicious meals are served at the restaurant in the visitor centre; it's named after Glenveagh Castle's renowned cook, Nellie Gallagher. *9.30-5pm* €

Lagoon Bar & Restaurant Award-winning restaurant in Termon serving delicious daily specials and roast dinners; they also have a wood-fired pizza oven. *noon-9pm* €

Coffee Time This picturesque cottage-style eatery offers a unique take on comfort food, where everything is made from scratch; the coffee is perfection. *10am-5pm Wed-Sun* €

Cycling (p399), Glenveagh National Park

GLENVEAGH'S RED DEER

Glenveagh National Park is home to the largest herd of red deer in Ireland, and they are the park's largest and most famous animals. The park services protect the herd, but the deer are able to roam freely through the landscape.

Although red deer are native to Ireland, the herd was expanded with stock brought in from Scotland in the 17th century. Red deer are located in almost all areas of the national park, with higher concentrations in the uplands. As these are wild animals, they can be difficult to spot. During the rutting season from mid-September to mid-November, the male deer bugle to prospective mates and are more active overall, making sightings more common.

that are now derelict, as well as native oak woodland and wildlife. The terrain is a mostly flat gravel road that rises gently. It's suitable for cyclists of all ages, though little legs might find the last 3km challenging. The Glen Walk isn't a looped trail, so you return the way you came.

GrassRoutes Bike Hire are located right beside the visitor centre at the park entrance and are open seven days a week. Ability bikes are also available free of charge to help those with mobility issues explore; kids' bikes and buggies also available. Booking is not essential, but it's best to book ahead in the summer months when the park is at its busiest. (Note that bikes are not allowed on the park roads – there are designated cycling paths through the park for cyclists and walkers.)

Wild Camping

Sleep under the stars

There's no better way to experience the park than by sleeping under the stars for a night or two. Glenveagh has no serviced camping or caravan sites, but if you're planning a multi-day hiking trip and seeking a wilderness experience, you're welcome to pitch your tent as long as you follow the **Leave no Trace policy**.

Wilderness camping is the only sort permitted in the park. Camping within the exclusion zone – which extends from the visitor centre and car park to beyond the Stalker's Hut – is prohibited.

Beyond Glenveagh National Park

Surrounding Glenveagh National Park are stunning beaches, remote islands and historic sites that should not be overlooked.

Adventures await outside the boundaries of Glenveagh, including challenging hikes, wild islands and jaw-dropping beaches.

Few places in Ireland are more savagely beautiful than northwestern Donegal. The rocky Gaeltacht (Irish-speaking) area between Dungloe and Crolly is known as the Rosses (Na Rossa) and is scattered with shimmering lakes, grey-pink granite outcrops and golden-sand beaches pounded by Atlantic surf, while the islands of Arranmore and Tory are fascinating to those eager for a glimpse of a more traditional way of life.

It's also easy to see why the county's main airport is seen as one of the world's most beautiful in terms of runway approaches, while nearby, one of the county's most iconic buildings – the old church at Dunlewey – stands as a sentinel to time itself.

Places
Mt Errigal p401
Arranmore Island p402
Tory Island p404

Mt Errigal
TIME FROM GLENVEAGH NATIONAL PARK: **12MIN**

Reach new heights

The pinkish-grey quartzite peak of **Mt Errigal** (751m) dominates the landscape of northwestern Donegal, appearing conical from some angles, but like a ragged shark's fin ripping through the heather bog from others. The name comes from the Gaelic *earagail*, meaning 'oratory', as its shape brings to mind a preacher's pulpit.

Errigal is the highest point in County Donegal, and the steepest of the Seven Sisters range. Its looming presence immediately commands attention and dares walkers to attempt the strenuous but satisfying climb to its pyramid-shaped summit. If you're keen to take on the challenge, pay close attention to the weather: it can be a dangerous climb on windy or wet days, when the mountain is shrouded in cloud and visibility is minimal.

Nevertheless, hikers tackle the summit throughout the year, and the less steep route up the mountain's south face is the most popular approach. The 4.5km hike begins from the car park located along the R251. There's room for about a dozen cars here. Conservation work has taken place in recent years, and a 1.4km path from the car park now covers what used to

GETTING AROUND

The best way to get around northwestern Donegal is by car. Car hire is available from **Donegal Airport** as well as from **DMG Motors** *(dmgmotors. ie)* in Letterkenny and Donegal town.

Buses do connect some local towns and villages, with the **Local Link** bus service providing a network of affordable buses through the area. **Local Link Donegal Sligo Leitrim** *(locallinkdsl. ie)* has a detailed timetable of routes. A Local Link service also runs to and from Donegal Airport.

THE WORLD'S MOST SCENIC AIRPORT?

Donegal Airport might not be the biggest or the busiest airport in the world – it only has flights to Dublin and Glasgow – but it regularly tops lists of the world's most scenic airport landings.

The airport's 1.5km runway darts straight down the middle of a narrow headland, flanked on either side by white sand. In the air, the views over the surrounding coastline, with mountains on one side and countless islands below, is mind-blowing. Those views give Donegal Airport every chance of winning beauty contests, time and time again.

Photographs don't do the landing justice. On approach, sit on the left-hand side of the plane for views of Mullaghderg and Carrickfin beaches.

be a very boggy section. Rough hewn steps are in place for much of the way to the summit.

For experienced climbers, the approach via the north face follows two steep ridges. Expect grade 1 scrambling on the first ridge; the route then becomes steeper and more exposed on the second section, **Tower Ridge**, which involves grade 3 scrambling. Most climbers require a rope and climbing gear to ascend safely. Previous mountain and scrambling experience is advised.

The old church at Dunlewey

Nestled at the foot of Mt Errigal, at the entrance to the Poisoned Glen, is the stunning ruin of **Dunlewey Church**. This beautiful building, consecrated in 1853, is a lasting memorial to the great love affair between James Russell, the landlord of the Dunlewey Estate, and his wife Jane. Built of white marble and blue quartzite (which was quarried locally), the church is one of Donegal's most iconic buildings. It's a breathtaking and oft-photographed scene, with the glen and **Dunlewey Lough** in the background.

On a clear day, the reflections of Mt Errigal on Dunlewey Lough create a picture-perfect sight; if you're lucky enough to see the valley shrouded in snow, it's an ethereal sight.

Legend has it that the glen got its name from Balor, the King of Tory Island, who lost his eye here, with the poison flowing from his wound into the valley, thus the name 'Poisoned Glen'.

Arranmore Island

TIME FROM GLENVEAGH NATIONAL PARK: **44MIN** 🚗 **+ 20MIN** ⛴️

A walker's paradise

Ringed by dramatic cliffs, cavernous sea caves and clean, sandy beaches, Arranmore Island (Árainn Mhór) lies just 5km from the mainland. Measuring just 9km by 5km, this tiny island has been inhabited since the early Iron Age (800 BCE), and a prehistoric promontory fort can be seen near the southeastern corner.

Arranmore is a walker's paradise, with a wide selection of coastal and inland trails to choose from. The 14km **Arranmore Island Loop** treats hikers to jaw-dropping views of the coast as it winds into the rugged island interior and along its inhabited southern and eastern sides.

Don't forget to check out the famous **Arranmore Island Steps** that are carved directly into the stone. Originally

EATING NEAR MT ERRIGAL: OUR PICKS

Sean Óg's Bar & Restaurant: This welcoming spot serves great pub-grub and is renowned for its tasty seafood. *5-9pm Wed-Mon mid June-mid-Sep; 5-9pm Fri-Sun May-Oct* €

An Chúirt: Lunchtime specials, a junior menu and an extensive cocktail list make this eatery at An Chúirt Hotel a popular choice. *noon-8.45pm* €€

Dunlewey Centre: This amalgam of craft shop, museum, activity centre and concert venue also has a restaurant serving light bites and full meals. *10.30am-4.40pm Apr-Sep* €

Braai Restaurant: This cool Creeslough eatery is inspired by South African traditions. *5-9pm Thu-Mon May-Sep; 5-9pm Fri-Sun Oct-May* €€

Dunlewey Church

constructed to service the island's lighthouse – a 5km walk from the ferry pier – the 151 steps are a major draw for visitors. But be careful, they're slippery when wet.

To reach Arranmore, take a ferry from **Burtonport Ferry Terminal**. **Arranmore Ferry** (*arranmoreferry.com*) provides sailings from the mainland to Arranmore Island. The journey takes between 15 and 20 minutes.

Activities on Arranmore

Join a two-hour sea safari and maritime heritage tour with **Arranmore Charters** (*arranmorechartes.ie; adult/child €47.50/30*) to witness the extensive wildlife along Dungloe Bay. Tours leave from the island and go at a pace that is respectful to the local wildlife, including seals and dolphins, and their young. If you're time-poor, Arranmore Charters also offers one-hour seal and birdwatching tours departing from the island and Burtonport Harbour. There are ample opportunities to observe seals, cormorants, oystercatchers, terns and grey herons.

Cumann na mBád (*madeinarranmore.com/workshops*) also offer sailing, kayaking tours, stand-up paddleboarding, rowing, surfing and bike hire between April and September.

EATING ON TORY & ARRANMORE: OUR PICKS

Tory Island Hotel: The island's sole hotel serves delicious local fare in the bar and restaurant. *noon-8pm Mar-Sep; winter hours vary* €€

An Club: This cosy little pub on Tory, not far from the ferry port, serves traditional pub-grub, as well as toasties, soup and pizza. *noon-8pm July & Aug; winter hours vary* €

Early's Bar: Great food on Arranmore, with everything from haddock and chips to steak. The stonebaked pizzas in summer are always popular. *1-7.30pm; winter hours vary* €

Neily's Bar: With a deck for summer and a bar in winter, this little pub on Arranmore is always worth stopping into for a pint. There's live music in the bar on weekends in summer. *hours vary* €

THE KING OF TORY

Tory Island was the location of Ireland's last kingship. Between the 6th century (possibly even before that) and 2018, a king oversaw the island and was its spokesperson. Throughout the 1800s, the kings came from a particular lineage.

The King of Tory Island also acted as an ambassador to the island, greeting people as they arrived from the mainland.

Dublin-born Patsy Dan Rogers, who moved to Tory at the age of four, was Tory's last king. The title has remained vacant since his passing in 2018. A self-described primitive artist, musician and storyteller, Rogers would entertain all who arrived on the shores of Tory. He was an outspoken and passionate advocate for the island's way of life, and its people.

Arranmore Island Steps (p402)

Tory Island

TIME FROM GLENVEAGH NATIONAL PARK: **30MIN** 🚗 + **45MIN** ⛴

Explore Tory

Blasted by the sea and stung by salt spray, Tory Island has captured the imaginations of writers and artists for years. Stepping off the boat onto the island, there is a tangible sense of time slowing down. Here, you can immerse yourself in the rich Gaeltacht culture, the spectacular scenery and, if you're lucky, stay for a live music session.

The best way to see Tory is on foot, along the 6.6km **Tory Island Loop Trail**, where you'll experience that edge-of-the-world-feeling. You can also peruse the island's historical sites, including the ruins of the 6th-century **St Colmcille's Monastery** and the **Tau Cross**, which is believed to date from medieval times.

Off the Beaten Path *(offthebeatenpath.ie)* provides electric fat bikes for an alternative way to see Tory; when cycling around, keep your eyes peeled for puffins, who breed here between April and early August.

To reach Tory Island, take a ferry from **Magheraroarty Ferry Terminal**; see toryferry.com for more information on sailing times.

Malin Head

WILDLIFE | RUGGED SCENERY | STARGAZING

The rolling swells never stop coming across the sea at Malin Head, the northern extreme of Ireland. It's a name familiar to sailors and meteorological buffs – Malin Head is one of the weather stations mentioned in the daily shipping forecast on BBC Radio.

You can almost imagine you can see Iceland (you can't) as you peer at the (sometimes) perfectly crystal-blue but ever-blustery skies, which can change from sun to squall at the drop of a sou'wester; the rolling grasslands beneath are dotted with suitably thick-coated donkeys, cows and well-wrapped-up hikers.

Photographers and stargazers might get the chance to witness the northern lights, as the low light pollution and clear skies create the perfect theatre for this mind-blowing light show. But there are also dramatic beaches, some of Europe's largest dunes and walks along Ireland's most northerly point – with an alpaca in tow.

Donegal might be known as the forgotten county, but Malin Head is an unforgettable destination.

GETTING AROUND

You'll need a car to get to and around Malin Head. The nearest town is somewhat confusingly for visitors also called Malin or Malin Town, a plantation village that's a 19-minute drive away. Letterkenny, Donegal's biggest town, is roughly a 90-minute drive away. **Local Link** bus 954 serves Malin Head from the market town of Carndonagh.

Hiking the Malin Head Trail
Spectacular coastal views

Get a feel for the rugged, unspoilt beauty of the most northerly tip of mainland Ireland on the **Malin Head Trail**. This clifftop walk gives you unbeatable views of the cliffs and the wild coastline beyond.

The trail beings at **Banba's Crown** – on the northernmost tip of Malin Head – and runs to Hell's Hole. At Banba's Crown stands a cumbersome tower that was built by the British admiralty in 1805 and later used as a Lloyds signal station. Around it are concrete huts that were used by the Irish army in WWII as lookout posts. To the west from the fort-side car park, the trail path leads to **Hell's Hole**, a chasm where the incoming water crashes against the rock forms. Brown signs mark the way.

☑ TOP TIP

Basking sharks, the world's second-largest fish, live in the waters around Malin Head. Weighing more than 4 tonnes and growing up to 12m long, these magnificent creatures are commonly seen from April to August, with sightings peaking in May and June.

BANBA'S CROWN

The highest elevation in this wild part of the coast is **Banba's Crown**, named after the mythological matron goddess of Ireland. It was built by the British in 1805 as a Napoleonic lookout tower to help defend against a possible French invasion.

As well as being strategically important, its location was vital for daily shipping, as the waters off Malin Head are notoriously treacherous. From here, you'll also spot the **'ÉIRE 80'** sign etched into the ground in white stone. More than just a patriotic landmark, this sign played an important role during World War II, as it told pilots which country they were flying over. A number of other ÉIRE signs are dotted around the Irish coast (p310).

The view to the west takes in the Inishowen Hills, Dunaff Head, low-lying Fanad Head with its lighthouse, the two 'horns' of Horn Head, and the twin bumps of Tory Island. In the far distance, to the left of Fanad's lighthouse, are the Muckish and Errigal Mountains. To the east lie raised beach terraces, and offshore you can see the lighthouse on the remote island of Inishtrahull. On a few nights a year, you can even see the northern lights.

The Malin Head Trail is a linear walk of roughly 650/700m one way; it takes about 30 minutes.

Watching Wildlife
Rich biodiversity and natural landscapes

As well as being an area of scenic beauty, and historical and scientific importance, Malin Head is also a great place to watch **wildlife**, so be sure to pack your binoculars.

From Malin Head, you can observe the autumnal movements of seabirds such as gannets, shearwaters, skuas and auks on their southward migration flights. This is also a good vantage point for viewing basking sharks and the resident pod of bottlenose dolphins. Large gaggles of barnacle geese come to winter at Malin Head and are often seen feeding in the fields around **Banba's Crown** (p405).

On the Trail with Wild Alpaca Way
New hiking buddies

If you're in search of a new hiking companion, check out **Wild Alpaca Way** *(wildalpacaway.com; adult/family of four €23.69/47.38)*, a family-run business at Knockamany Bens that gives visitors the opportunity to walk through spectacular scenery with an alpaca for company.

You're partnered with your very own alpaca before heading off on a stroll that takes a little over an hour. Guided by your alpaca, you can take in jaw-dropping views of Malin Head, the Isle of Doagh and beyond.

There are now 50 alpacas on site, and with their friendly nature, they make perfect walking companions amid the jaw-dropping ocean views.

See the Northern Lights
Witness the phenomenal aurora borealis

With low light pollution and a northerly position, Malin Head is arguably the best place in Ireland to get a glimpse of the northern lights (aurora borealis). You'll need a clear, cloud-free sky without a bright moon to increase your chances of seeing this astronomical phenomenon, so check the forecast before you go.

The best times of year to see the northern lights are September, October, March and April, but sightings throughout winter are also possible. The best place to see the phenomenon is at Banba's Crown, which has very little artificial light. The raised beach at Ballyhillion nearby is also a great spot

THE STAR WARS CONNECTION

It's easy to see why the stunning coastal vistas of Malin Head appealed to scouts looking for filming locations for *Star Wars: The Last Jedi* (2017). A replica of the Millennium Falcon was constructed here for filming, and while the Falcon has since been taken down, fans can still visit the spot where it used to sit.

Filming mainly centred around **Hell's Hole** (p405), a subterranean cavern that's visible from the **Malin Head Trail** (p405), while the actors were also known to enjoy some local 'hospitality' while filming, which included nipping into Farren's Bar for a pint.

Diehard fans can even have their photo taken at one of the road signs for the **R2D2**, previously the R242, but renamed in honour of the film.

to watch the skies while listening to the roar of the Atlantic. A number of providers offer northern lights photography tours; **Photos from Ireland** *(photosfromireland.com)* come recommended.

Have a Drink at Farren's Bar

Family run for six generations

Fancy a pint in Ireland's most northerly pub? Established in 1825, the old-style **Farren's Bar** has been in the Farren family for six generations and is still a family-run business.

Enjoy a warm welcome and take a seat by the fire while you wait for your Guinness to settle. It's located just 2km from Malin Head. The bar has a 23-hour licence, and it's the perfect spot to relax in after a day's adventure. You can get your photo taken with the giant mural of a crab, and Yoda from *Star Wars*, outside.

 EATING AROUND MALIN HEAD: TOP SPOTS

Caffe Banba: A coffee truck serving coffee, cold drinks and delicious pastries at Banba's Crown. *11am-6pm May-Sep; hours vary Oct-Apr* €

Ten Arches: A newcomer on the local food scene, with breakfast, brunch and lunch served. *9am-4pm Thu-Sat; noon-4pm Sun Apr-Oct; hours vary Nov-Mar* €€

Farren's Bar (p407): A stalwart of the area, the open Malin Head crab sandwich is always popular. *noon-4pm* €€

Seaview Tavern: Rave-worthy seafood served in a dining room with great views over Inishtrahull Island. *12.30-8.30pm Mon-Fri; 9am-8.30pm Sat & Sun* €€

ROAD TRIP

Fanad Peninsula

From lush mountain pastures to Atlantic Ocean views, this one-way road trip is a feast for the senses, with picturesque villages, forest delights and epic swim spots along the way.

❶ Ramelton

The pretty heritage town of **Ramelton** is fast gaining a reputation as a foodie town. On the bank of the River Lennon, food emporium the Blue Goat brings a gastronomic offering with Irish raw-milk cheeses as well as Irish and Spanish charcuterie. Great coffee and wines, and delicious desserts make it a feast for the eyes as well as the stomach.

The Drive: Hugging Lough Swilly, pass through the stunning town of Rathmullan before arriving at one of Donegal's most epic beaches.

❷ Ballymastocker Bay

Ballymastocker Bay stretches from the little harbour town of Portsalon to the Knockalla Hills. The sheer golden expanse of it means it's often voted one of Ireland's – and indeed the world's – most beautiful beaches. The beach is so otherworldly that you simply have to pull over and take a walk along the golden sand, which stretches for over a mile. Better still, pack a picnic and eat alfresco with stunning views across the bay to the Inishowen Peninsula.

The Drive: Continuing to skirt Lough Swilly (moving inland in sections), it's a 15-minute drive to Fanad Lighthouse.

❸ Fanad Lighthouse

The romance of **Fanad Lighthouse** is something that has pulled on people's heartstrings for generations, and it will probably steal your heart altogether. Voted one of the most beautiful lighthouses in the world, you can take a tour of the lighthouse and learn about the lightkeepers and their families. You can also climb to the top of the tower for spectacular 360-degree views of north Donegal, the Atlantic and Lough Swilly. This epic spot is also a Wild Atlantic Way signature point.

The Drive: Cut through Fanad Peninsula and cross the Harry Blaney Bridge. Continue south in the direction of the scenic village of Carrigart.

❹ Doe Castle

Tucked in behind Sheephaven Bay sits 15th-century **Doe Castle**, the stronghold of the MacSweeneys. It's a truly picturesque spot, with the castle's moat hewn out of the rock. The best way to appreciate the castle's beauty is to wander the peaceful grounds. The castle and grounds are free to enter; guided tours can be accommodated with advance notice.

The Drive: Continue for 10 minutes through pretty countryside, passing through the village of Creeslough before reaching Ards Forest Park.

❺ Ards Forest Park

With trees growing right at the water's edge, **Ards Forest Park** is undoubtedly one of Ireland's most beautiful national parks.

Ballymastocker Bay

There are several trails in the park, including the wheelchair and buggy-friendly Sand Dune Trail. The park covers approximately 480 hectares and includes a variety of habitats, among them sand dunes, beaches, salt marshes, salt water lakes, rock face and, of course, coniferous and deciduous woodlands. Deep in the park, you'll also find the hidden gem of Lucky Shell Beach.

The Drive: Follow the N56 for six minutes until Sheephaven Bay again comes into view at Port na Blagh; continue on to Dunfanaghy.

6 Dunfanaghy

A little village with a big heart, **Dunfanaghy** packs a punch in terms of dining options and things to do, with everything from golf to surfing on offer. For history buffs, the Workhouse Famine and Heritage Centre is a must see. Construction of this beautiful building began in 1843 and it opened two years later, making it the last of the originally planned workhouses to open in Ireland. While it started life as a monument to tragedy, it's now a centre for learning and culture.

The Drive: The 6km drive to Horn Head is along a narrow road; you may have to pull in to allow for cars coming from the other direction.

7 Horn Head

Less visited than neighbouring Fanad Head, the drive to **Horn Head** is the kind of road trip you dream of: narrow winding roads, epic coastal scenery and mountain pastureland as far as the eye can see. From the car park at the head, there is a short trail to a signal tower built during the Napoleonic wars. On a clear day, you'll see the Rosguill Peninsula, Tory Island and the famous and unmistakable hulking shapes of Mt Errigal and Mt Muckish.

The Drive: Meander back to Letterkenny at your leisure, winding through what's commonly known as 'The Gap', the mountain road that links Dunfanaghy and Letterkenny. Stop to take a shot of Mt Muckish on your way back. The journey from Horn Head takes around 45 minutes.

Beyond Malin Head

Ancient sites, ruined castles and old-world thatched cottages abound beyond Malin Head.

Places

Grianán of Aileach p410
Fort Dunree p410
Ballyliffin p411
Gap of Mamore p412
Inishtrahull Island p412

Northeastern Donegal is the perfect territory for exploring coastal roads that lead to headland tips, sheltered bays and out-of-the-way coves. This is where the wildness of Donegal finds its true fullness – on scenic and windswept peninsulas where the views go on forever.

Surrounded by vast sea loughs and open ocean, Inishowen (meaning 'Island of Eoghain', named after the chieftain who also gave his name to County Tyrone) attracts a lot of birdlife. The peninsula is often referred to as 'Ireland in miniature' due to its range of geographical features and mountains that sweep down to the sea. It's easy to find yourself the only one on its windswept coves, with not a soul in sight.

GETTING AROUND

You'll want a car to reach the Inishowen Peninsula, though bus services have improved through **Local Link** services. The main towns of Buncrana and Carndonagh, as well as smaller towns such as Moville and Greencastle, are all served with regular buses. See *transportforireland.ie/tfi-local-link* for timetables.

Grianán of Aileach

TIME FROM MALIN HEAD: 1HR

Step back in time

The amphitheatre-like fort of **Grianán of Aileach** *(heritageireland.ie; free)*, sitting atop Grianán Hill, is probably Inishowen's most iconic monument.

As a sentry to time itself, it began life as an ancient burial site, dating from roughly 1700 BCE to the time of the Tuatha dé Danann – a supernatural race in Irish mythology. The present structure, with its 5m-high walls sitting 250m above sea level, dates from the 6th century CE.

From the fort, the views of Lough Foyle and Lough Swilly are breathtaking. You can also look westward to Donegal's highest peak, Mt Errigal. The nearby Burt Chapel was designed by one of the country's finest architects, Liam McCormick, who drew inspiration from the ancient fort.

Fort Dunree

TIME FROM MALIN HEAD: 50MIN

Military history

Fort Dunree *(fortdunree.com; adult/child €8/6)* is the best preserved and most dramatic of six forts built by the British on Lough Swilly following the 1798 uprising of the United Irishmen. The lough is one of Ireland's great natural harbours and has played its part in many historical dramas, from Viking invasions and the Flight of the Earls to the 1798 Rising.

Huge naval guns were added to Fort Dunree in the late 19th century, and during WWI, Lough Swilly was used as a marshalling area for Atlantic convoys, and as an anchorage for the

Royal Navy's Grand Fleet. Unusually, it remained in British hands following the partition of Ireland in 1922 and was only handed over to the Republic of Ireland in 1938.

The original fort, built in 1813, houses a military museum. The Saldanha Suite in the museum is currently home to the 'Rockhill Collection' – a portion of an extensive private collection of military memorabilia that's on loan to the museum.

There are several good waymarked walks around the fort.

Inishowen's bucket-list swims

Surrounded by water, the Inishowen Peninsula is a swimmer's paradise. Miles-long Atlantic beaches and secluded coves mean that wherever you travel, you should have your swimming togs at the ready.

Lenan Beach, at the foot of the Urris Hills, is perfect for a high-tide dip, with views of Mt Errigal (p401) on clear days.

On the opposite side of the peninsula, not far from the fishing village of Greencastle, sits **Stroove** – also known as **Shroove Beach**. Under the watchful eye of the lighthouse, the beach is idyllic for a stroll and a swim. If you're feeling energetic, you can hike the **Inishowen Head Loop** and follow it with a cooling dip. The 8.5km loop walk follows a stunning route through some of Inishowen's most impressive coastal scenery. Begin from the beach.

Following the slatted path to the beach from the carpark, you'll feel like you're in another world when you step onto the golden sand at **Culdaff Beach**. This Blue Flag beach has lifeguards on duty in summer and is perfect for swimming and leisurely strolls. In winter, it's not unusual for the waves to be big enough for surfers to bring their boards. There's also a cool little playpark tucked into the dunes on the path to the beach, meaning little ones can have fun on the swings and slides. While this beach is busy with day trippers in summer months, there's every chance you'll have it to yourself in late autumn and winter, when the full power of the Atlantic is unleashed.

Ballyliffin

TIME FROM MALIN HEAD: **30MIN**

Golf on the Inishowen Peninsula

With two championship courses, **Ballyliffin Golf Club** (ballyliffingolfclub.com; €25–330) is one of the best places to play a round of golf in Donegal. The scenery is so beautiful that it can distract even the most focused golfer. It hosted the 2018 Irish Open, and the nearby village of **Ballyliffin** has an upmarket atmosphere with some good hotels and restaurants.

WHY I LOVE INISHOWEN

Kathy Donaghy, writer @missoulakate_ kathydonaghy

In all seasons, Inishowen offers itself as a place of freedom and wildness. Lashed by enormous waves in winter and providing endless opportunities for budding photographers with its lush sunsets, there is a magnetism about this most northerly place on the island. The raw power of the ocean will take your breath away, and the views of the Inishowen hills all around will fill your soul.

If you love epic scenery and the power of the ocean, this is your place. There's also plenty options for stopping for some epic food, with seafood so fresh it probably just came in on that morning's boat.

 DRINKING COFFEE IN INISHOWEN: BEST SPOTS

Gap Coffee Co: Don't leave without trying the raspberry and white chocolate scone at this cafe in Bridgend. *9am-5pm Mon-Sat; 10-5pm Sun*

Spill the Beans: Sit out on the deck and take in the beautiful views of Inch Island. *9.30am-4pm*

Norries Coffee Shop: Friendly vibes, with great coffee and cake; in Moville. *9am- 4pm Mon-Sat*

Diamond Cafe: For fine views of Carndonagh's Diamond, enjoy your brew upstairs. *8.30am-5pm Mon-Sat*

SAMPLE THE WORLD'S BEST CHOWDER AT NANCY'S BARN

Fans of seafood chowder – a rich, creamy, hearty soup filled with chunks of fish and seafood – should stop at **Nancy's Barn** in Ballyliffin. Having won the title of All-Ireland Chowder Champion at the annual chowder cook-off in Kinsale, County Cork, chef Kieran 'Duey' Doherty stepped up to compete against bowls from across the pond at the New England Great Chowder Cook-Off in the US. The Cook-Off is the longest-running event of its kind and deemed the pinnacle of success in the world of chowder. Nancy's Barn was the first overseas contestant to take part. After making nearly 950 litres of chowder, the Irish team emerged victorious. The recipe is so secret that only two people know it: Kieran and his sister Edel.

The golf club boasts two championship links courses, as well as an excellent 9 hole par 3 course called the Pollan Links. It's necessary to book in advance.

A 30-minute drive from Ballyliffin, enjoy spectacular views of Lough Foyle as it opens out into the Atlantic Ocean on the well-maintained 18-hole course at **Greencastle Golf Club** *(greencastlegolfclub.com; from €80)*. Set among staggering natural beauty, it's one of the most challenging courses in Donegal. Booking in advance is recommended, as the club hosts competitions over the weekends.

Gap of Mamore

TIME FROM MALIN HEAD: **47MIN**

Mind the gap

Arguably one of the best driving routes in Donegal is along the **Gap of Mamore**, which rises 263m above sea level and provides mind-blowing views of Lough Swilly, the Fanad Peninsula and the northern end of the Inishowen Peninsula. Located on the road that twists between Buncrana and Clonmany, it's best to drive cautiously on the Gap's twisting, steep, narrow section, which is beloved by motorists, walkers and cyclists.

Start in **Buncrana**, a busy but appealing town on the shores of Lough Swilly. Near the summit of the Gap, about 13km from Buncrana, is a shrine of Our Lady and a statue of St Padre Pio. An annual mass is held here every August in commemoration of penal times, when Catholics had to practise their religion in secret to avoid persecution.

As you descend the windy road, the market town of Clonmany is a short drive away.

Inishtrahull Island

TIME FROM MALIN HEAD: **27MIN** + **45MIN**

Set sail to Inishtrahull

Some 11km out to sea from Malin Head is the tiny, uninhabited and little-known island of Inishtrahull.

There is a real sense of time standing still here. It's on Inishtrahull that the story of Ireland begins, as it's here that the oldest rocks in the country – dating 1.8 billion years – were found. Inishtrahull is also said to be the departure lounge for the spirits to leave for Tír na nÓg, the Gaelic name for the Celtic otherworld.

In 1928, the island's residents were subjected to a mandatory evacuation, meaning the island is now uninhabited. It's

EATING IN INISHOWEN: BEST PLACES

McGrory's of Culdaff: Opt for fine dining in the restaurant, or more casual pub-grub and a pint in the bar of this Inishowen institution. *8am-noon Mon-Sun & 12.30-9 pm Mon-Sat, to 8pm Sun €€*

Butterbean: Open for breakfast, lunch and dinner, the chicken stacker on creamed potatoes is the star on an extensive menu. *9am-8pm Tue-Sun €€*

Tank & Skinny's: With two locations on the Inishowen Peninsula, this is a cafe that packs a punch. Arrive hungry and grab the Hunger's Mother sandwich. *9am-4pm Mon-Sat; from 10am Sun €€*

Boathouse: With stunning views over Lough Foyle, this shabby-chic style bistro has a cool vibe and great local produce. *4-9pm Mon-Sat, from 12.30pm Sun €€*

Gap of Mamore

impossible *not* to imagine how difficult life must have been for the islanders eking out a living on this remote settlement. While only wallsteads of the islanders' homes and the old schoolhouse remain, you can picture a time of productivity: of seaweed being gathered in creels to spread on beds of crops, of children running to lessons, of hefty catches of fish being landed ashore.

Inishtrahull's two lighthouses (the first built in 1912; the second built in 1957), old buildings, graveyard and schoolhouse can all be visited. The island is designated as a Special Area of Conservation and a Special Protection Area by the National Parks and Wildlife Service, so expect to see an abundance of sea- and bird-life. Keep to the paths so as not to disturb the nesting birds.

Although no ferry runs to the island, it's possible to visit on a full-day boat trip with **Amazing Grace Yacht Charters** *(amazing-grace.ie; adult/child €100/50)*, which departs from Bunagee Pier near Culdaff. As you make your way to the island, keep an eye out for basking sharks, dolphins and grey seals in the water.

BIRD SANCTUARY

Inishtrahull is becoming increasingly well-known for its wildlife and boasts one of the largest shag colonies in Ireland. The Inishtrahull Bird Observatory was founded in 2020 with the approval of the island's owner, the Commissioners of Irish Lights.

For birdwatchers, the island is significant: the safe, predator-free and (relatively) human-free landscape is incredibly important to nesting birds. It's a Special Protection Area under the EU Birds Directive and is an important site for shag, barnacle geese and common gulls.

While there are no restrictions on people visiting the island – its location and weather naturally make it difficult to get to in the winter months – particular care is needed during the breeding period (May to July).

PUBS IN INISHOWEN: TOP SPOTS

McGowan's Bar: This pub in Redcastle is famous for its perfect pints of Guinness, with the outline of a shamrock on top. *5-11.30pm Mon-Thu, to 12.30am Fri, from 2pm Sat, to 11pm Sun*

McGuinness' Bar: This 1792, family-run pub in Culdaff is as authentic as it gets; it's popular with both locals and visitors. *2-11.30pm Mon-Fri, 11am-12.30am Sat, noon-11.30pm Sun*

Rodden's Bar: With its bright yellow and blue exterior, this bar in Buncrana exudes charm and has live music every weekend. *12.30-11.30pm Mon-Fri, to 12.30am Sat & Sun*

Drift Inn: Once an old railway station, the Drift Inn is an unmissable stop in Buncrana for rustic charm and good music. *noon-11.30pm Mon-Thu, to 1am Fri, to 12.30am Sat, to 11pm Sun*

Slieve League Cliffs

EPIC SCENERY | BOAT TRIPS | HIKING

GETTING AROUND

From the village of Teelin, a road through the stark landscape leads to Slieve League's lower car park, located beside a gate in the road. A new ranger station and public toilets have also been built here. In general, vehicle access to the cliffs is limited, but you can park at the **Sliabh Liag Visitor Centre** and take the shuttle bus to Bunglass Point. Purchase bus tickets *(adult/child €8/6)* at the visitor centre. If you're taking public transport, hop on **Local Link** bus 293 from Donegal town to Carrick, and then walk the 25 minutes to the visitor centre.

The Cliffs of Moher in County Clare may get more publicity, but the Slieve League Cliffs (Sliabh Liag) are higher – and free to visit. In fact, these spectacular sea cliffs are among the highest in Europe, plunging some 600m to the ceaselessly churning sea below. Feeling the energy of the ocean, watching the water crash up on the rocks and taking in the jaw-dropping panoramic views is simply incredible.

Standing on top of these cliffs is a true edge-of-the-world experience. You can admire the cliffs from dry land, and walkers have a range of trails to choose from. Or head out on the water as part of a boat trip for a different perspective on these immense cliffs – maybe even braving a dip.

To get a flavour of how people eked out a living in this remote spot through the ages, visit the Glencolmcille Folk Village, a living history museum that recreates traditional village life.

Hiking the Slieve League Cliffs

Lace up

Getting into the wilderness is the best way to experience the remote, rugged landscape of the Slieve League Cliffs. Hikers can take three main paths, which are steep in sections and require appropriate footwear and clothing. The scenery along the trails is mind-blowing, and although the hikes can be challenging, the rewards are worth every step. The cliffs are subject to high winds and fog – before attempting these hikes, check the weather to ensure the conditions are appropriate.

The **Bunglass Road** route is the busy but more accessible option that offers spectacular views. Beginning at the lower car park, the trail climbs steeply for about 45 minutes before reaching **Bunglass Point**, the most popular vantage point of the cliffs.

The **Pilgrim's Path**, with its name harking back to the time of the Penal Laws in Ireland, when Catholic worship was outlawed, is an ancient trail. The start of the 4km trail

is way-marked with stone steps before it gives way to a steep, narrow path that continues up the hillside. From here, the trail is well-defined and takes you to the summit of **Cnockrawer** (Cnoc Ramhar).

The **One Man's Pass** is a continuation of the Pilgrim's Path, but this trail follows a knife-edge ridge for a few hundred metres. The narrow, rocky path has a sheer drop of more than 550m on one side and is for experienced hikers only.

Witness the Cliffs from the Water

All aboard

Looking down from the staggeringly high clifftops is certainly an awe-inspiring experience, but seeing this magnificent sight from the water gives you an entirely different perspective. **Sliabh Liag Boat Trips** (sliabhliagboattrips.com; adult/child €25/10) are located at the harbour in the village of Teelin. They operate two 12-person boats on multiple sailings per day, with sailings lasting nearly two hours.

On board, you'll learn about the history and legends of the area. If you're on the *Nuala Star* – the company's flagship vessel – you can even jump in for a quick dip in the Atlantic, and if you're lucky, you might spot dolphins while you're at it.

☑ TOP TIP

The Sliabh Liag Visitor Centre is a great source of information on walks and activities in the area. It also has exhibits about the cliffs, their geology and some local history. If you don't want to walk to Bunglass Point, you can buy tickets at the centre for the shuttle bus to the viewpoint.

OIDEAS GAEL

Based in the village of **Glencolmcille**, **Oideas Gael** (*oideasgael.ie*) runs weekend and week-long Irish language courses. Founded in 1984, it's aim was to provide education for Irish language-learners and to promote the Irish language. While both Irish (Gaeilge) and English are the official languages of Ireland, Irish is the native tongue. It's taught in all schools, but only pockets of the country speak it fluently on a daily basis.

As a Gaelic speaking community, Glencolmcille provides what is known as the 'immersive' experience – people come to learn Irish at a local Irish school such as Oideas Gael, stay in guesthouses or B&Bs where Irish is spoken, go to bars where traditional music is played, and basically immerse themselves in all things Irish.

Head to Glencolmcille Folk Village

Where tradition and beauty collide

Step back in time by visiting the seven traditional cottages at **Glencolmcille Folk Village** (*glenfolkvillage.com; adult/child €8/3*), all set in a *clachan* (group of small dwellings belonging to farming or fishing people).

Each cottage – representing a different era of Irish history from the 1700s to the 1900s – is neatly whitewashed, with the traditional half-door designed to keep the animals out. The roofs are thatched in the distinctive rounded Donegal style and tied down securely with rope and pegs to protect the thatching from those fierce westerly winds coming in off the Atlantic.

Here, you can learn how generations of Irish people lived and worked, what they cooked, and how they heated and lit their homes. The schoolhouse from the 1900s has a big open fireplace – the schoolchildren of the day were expected to bring a sod of turf with them to keep the fire lit.

There's also an example of a pub-grocers, now rare but once a staple of rural Ireland. Stop in at the village tearooms for some hearty homemade soup, and don't leave without sampling the delicious Guinness cake. The tearooms are occasionally host to traditional music sessions during the summer months.

Malin Beg: Donegal's Finest White-Sand Beach

Dig your toes in

Surrounded by tall horseshoe-shaped cliffs, **Malin Beg Beach** is one of the most off-the-beaten-path stretches of sand in the country. To access the beach, you need to make the drive – it's about 12 minutes by car from the folk village – and then descend the 174 steps to reach its stunning white sand.

The crystal-clear waters are perfect for swimming, and the sunsets are divine. Malin Beg is also known as Silver Strand because of its impossibly white sand, and you would be forgiven for thinking you have landed in the Caribbean.

PUBS AROUND SLIEVE LEAGUE: OUR PICKS

Rusty Mackerel: Established in 1892, this well-known Teelin establishment has a warm fire in winter and a deck for drinks in summer. *noon-11.30pm*

Evelyn's Central Bar: A lively bar on Carrick's Main St, there's a traditional music session every Sunday at 6pm. *noon-11.30pm*

Slieve League Lodge: With accommodation upstairs, this warm and cosy Carrick pub has live music every Saturday night. *10am-1am Mon-Sat, to midnight Sun*

Roarty's Bar: Close to the Irish language college, Oideas Gael, this is a place where you'll hear Gaeilge in full flow over a few pints. *noon-12.30am*

Beyond the Slieve League Cliffs

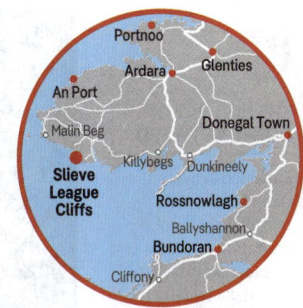

As you continue along the coast from the cliffs, County Donegal's scenery-o-meter is still set on high.

Donegal Bay and the surrounding areas are home to some true gems. In this part of the county, walkers will be blown away by the ethereal beauty of the Glengesh Pass, a drive that takes you into true isolation.

You can also experience the windswept beauty of An Port and imagine the people who lived in this remote place throughout the ages. This is where to truly get off the beaten track, escape the crowds and have the waterfalls and waves all to yourself, while the picturesque town of Ardara has some excellent pubs where a trad session is always on the cards.

Finding a good hotel or B&B in southwestern Donegal is not a problem, though some do close out of season.

Places
Ardara p417
An Port p419
Glenties p419
Portnoo p420
Donegal Town p420
Bundoran p421
Rossnowlagh p422

GETTING AROUND

Driving is the easiest way to get around this area, but there are also several **Local Link** bus routes. Donegal town is the hub for many of these services. See *transportforireland.ie/tfi-local-link* for timetables.

Some mountain roads can be slow going, so leave more than enough time for your journey.

Ardara
TIME FROM SLIVE LEAGUE CLIFFS: **30MIN**

Ardara's tweed heritage

The gateway to the switchbacks of the Glengesh Pass, the heritage town of Ardara (pronounced *arda-rah*; Ard an Rátha in Irish) means 'High Hill of the Fort' and is named for the earthen ringfort located to the northeast of the town. There are a lot of decent accommodation choices here, and the town makes for an excellent base for exploring the surrounding region. Walking down Ardara's streets, you'll hear Irish spoken as locals exchange greetings.

Ardara is also a great place to visit weavers at work, allowing visitors to see the region's most traditional crafts in action. Stop by **Eddie Doherty** *(handwoventweed.com)* to catch Doherty himself handweaving on a traditional loom. Now in his 80s, Eddie is a living bridge between the past and the present – he was just 14 years old when he sat at a loom for the first time. In recent years, an appreciation of this ancient craft of tweed manufacturing has grown, with people coming into the shop to watch him weave his magic at the loom. It's also possible to buy some of his creations, including fabric, cushion covers, coats, scarves and hats, at the shop.

Many of Ardara's other shops are dedicated to selling high-quality tweed and knitwear, and a stop in Campbell's

THE HISTORY OF DONEGAL TWEED

Entwined in every thread of Donegal tweed is a story of craft, tradition and connection to nature.

Donegal tweed is distinctive for its colourful flecks. What could be seen elsewhere as a flaw by having these 'neps' in the fabric has somehow come to embody the distinctive beauty, originality and authenticity of Donegal tweed. While the process of working with wool has changed since the early days – the origins of Donegal tweed go back as far as the 1800s – the essential components are still the same.

If southwest Donegal was once the tweed capital of Ireland, then Ardara was the Mecca. It was in the town's old mart that today's older handweavers first learned their craft.

Assaranca Waterfall

on Front St, with its dramatic window displays, is a must. It's just a few doors down from Eddie Doherty's.

Join a trad session

One of the area's most famous sons was John Doherty, a revered Irish fiddler, and traditional music is a big part of Ardara's draw. Many of the pubs here host regular traditional-music sessions – just stroll down the main drag until you hear the good cheer pouring out one of the doors.

Throughout the summer and at weekends, musicians from all over the world descend on this part of Donegal for trad sessions, with music in bars like the **Corner House** and **Nancy's Bar**. In the Corner House, live music can be heard seven nights a week, while there's entertainment in Nancy's every Saturday night from April to October.

Visit Assaranca Waterfall

Located 8km outside of Ardara is one of the most beautiful waterfalls in Donegal – and arguably one of the most picturesque in Ireland. The cascading water of **Assaranca Waterfall** flows down the side of the mountain right next to the roadside, making access a breeze.

There's plenty of parking available next to the waterfall, and the views over the coast behind you are magical. The idyllic and tranquil setting is the perfect place to sit back, relax and enjoy the sounds of nature.

Drive the Glengesh Pass

On a narrow road between Ardara and Glencolumbcille, the magnificent **Glengesh Pass** (Glean Géis; meaning 'Glen of the Swans') is one of Donegal's most scenic driving routes. It was scoured out aeons ago by implacably vast glacial forces and is approached down several switchbacks that lead towards thatched cottages and a swath of pastoral beauty. Pull over at the viewpoints to take in the whole epic scenario spilling out before you.

An Port

TIME FROM SLIVE LEAGUE CLIFFS: 38 MIN

See an abandoned village

Located right on the edge of the Atlantic Ocean, it can feel like you are driving to the edge of the world to reach the abandoned village of **An Port** (also Port). At the end of a single-lane road about 25km from Ardara, there sits a small pier and a stony shore with the most incredible sea stacks rising up out of the crashing Atlantic. While local stories say the village was abandoned during the Famine and in its immediate aftermath, the real story is that An Port's decline was slower and more gradual.

A small car park is available for visitors, and nearby lie the remains of an abandoned cluster of stone houses. It's hard *not* to pick your way among these cottages and imagine the life of the fisherfolk and their families who once lived in this wild place. We recommend bringing a picnic and taking a walk along the shoreline, or follow one of the trails up the hillside for a panoramic view of the surrounding landscape. Pick up supplies in Ardara and stay to watch the sun go down.

Glenties

TIME FROM SLIEVE LEAGUE CLIFFS: 30MIN

Festivals in Glenties

Nestled in the heart of the Bluestack Mountains, the heritage town of Glenties is the perfect base to explore the wider area; it's also a great festival hub.

The town is rightly proud of its connection to world-renowned playwright Brian Friel, with **Siopa Lughnasa** and the **Lughnasa Creative Arts Centre** sitting on opposite sides of the town's wide main street, named after one of Friel's most famous plays, *Dancing at Lughnasa* (1990). Fittingly enough, the town comes alive in August when the ancient Celtic festival of **Lughnasa** *(glenties.ie)* – named after the Celtic god of the harvest, Lugh – is celebrated over two days.

Every July, the town is transformed into one of the most important fora in Ireland for the discussion of national and international topics, with the annual **MacGill Summer School** *(macgillsummerschool.com)* taking place. The school has attracted many leaders of the day, as well as artists, poets and musicians. President Michael D Higgins and the late poet Seamus Heaney have given readings of their work here.

THE ROAD TO GLENLOUGH

The story of southwest Donegal unfolds over 600 pages, and more than 900 photographs and illustrations in Christy Gillespie's book, *The Road to Glenlough* (2023).

While it's called the 'road' to Glenlough, there is no road, or even a well worn path. This valley in the highlands of southwest Donegal is as remote and isolated as it is beautiful and windswept.

Gillespie draws on words, paintings and photographs to shed light on the valley and its people. He recounts the tales – if local stories are to be believed – of the numerous illustrious visitors that this area of Donegal has been host to, including Rockwell Kent, Dylan Thomas and Bonnie Prince Charlie.

EATING IN GLENTIES: OUR PICKS

Navvy Poet Bar and Grill: In the Highlands Hotel, this spot has good vegan and vegetarian options. Thursday night is the popular steak night. *5-8.30pm Sun-Wed; to 9pm Thu-Sat* €€

Thatch Bar & Restaurant: A creative menu, with all the starters also offered as main courses. *5-9pm Mon-Fri, from 3pm Sat, from 1pm Sun May-Sep* €€

Siopa Lúghnasa: A coffee shop combining arts and crafts. As well as good coffee, it serves delicious toasties, hearty soups and fine home baking. *10am-5pm Mon-Sat* €

Shellybean Bakery: Freshly baked bread, cupcakes, acai bowls and milkshakes to take away. *10am-4pm Thu-Sat* €

THE BRIAN FRIEL CONNECTION

Brian Friel, who died in October 2015 at the age of 86, was one of Ireland's most iconic playwrights. He spent his childhood summers in Glenties, in the home where his mother, Christina McCloone, grew up. Friel's play, *Dancing at Lughnasa*, is dedicated to the 'five brave Glenties women' who grew up there and who have been immortalised as the Mundy sisters in the play.

The Laurels – his mother's home – has been restored and will become a vibrant venue for the arts, while the old courthouse in Glenties is being transformed into a dynamic and creative attraction that will bring visitors through the playwright's life and work. A film version of the play, starring Meryl Streep, was released in 1998.

Portnoo
TIME FROM SLIEVE LEAGUE CLIFFS: **50MIN**

The endless Narin Strand

A short drive away from Glenties lies the village of Portnoo and the seemingly endless beach at **Narin**. One of County Donegal's most stunning strands – and a Blue Flag beach – Narin is home to impromptu yoga sessions and stand-up paddleboarding in summer.

It's possible to walk across the sandbar causeway to the uninhabited island of Inishkeel (also spellt Iniskeel), which lies approximately 600m from the shore and is accessible at low tide. The sandbar route out to the island has traditionally been a pilgrimage passage, and the remains of a graveyard and two churches – the earliest founded in the 6th century by Conal Caoill (Conal the Slender) – are visible on the island. Be sure to check the tide times before setting out to avoid getting cut off from the mainland.

Donegal Town
TIME FROM SLIEVE LEAGUE CLIFFS: **50MIN**

History in Donegal town

Pretty and compact, Donegal town occupies a photogenic spot at the mouth of Donegal Bay. With a backdrop of the Blue Stack Mountains, a handsome and well-preserved castle, and a good choice of places to eat and sleep, it makes an excellent base for exploring the popular coastline nearby.

On the banks of the River Eske, the town was the stomping ground of the O'Donnells, the great chieftains who ruled the northwest from the 15th to the 17th centuries. Today, despite being the county's namesake, it's neither its largest town (that's the much larger Letterkenny) nor its county town (that's the even smaller Lifford).

Guarding a picturesque bend of the river, the well-preserved **Donegal Castle** *(heritageIreland.ie; adult/child €5/3)*, which dates from the 15th century, is an imperious monument to Irish and English might. Built by the O'Donnells in 1474, it served as the seat of their formidable power until 1607, when the English decided to rid themselves of the pesky Irish chieftains once and for all. But Red Hugh O'Donnell was no pushover – he torched his own castle before fleeing to France in the infamous Flight of the Earls. The castle was rebuilt in 1623 by Sir Basil Brooke, along with the adjacent three-storey Jacobean house. Further restoration in the 1990s kicked things into shape.

EATING IN DONEGAL TOWN: OUR PICKS

Olde Castle Bar: This ever-busy pub off the Diamond serves some of the area's best food. *noon-8pm Mon-Fri & Sun; to 8.30pm Sat* €€

Simple Simon's: Fresh meals, including veggie and vegan options. The Donegal breakfast bap and the Killybegs seafood chowder are hits. *9.30am-5pm May-Sep; closed Sun Oct-Apr* €

Blueberry Tea Room: A perennial and cosy local favourite, this cafe serves simple, honest food in hearty portions. *9am-6pm Mon-Sat* €

Harbour Restaurant: This seafaring-themed restaurant is right on the quay and serves everything from steak to fish pie. *5-9pm Mon-Sat; 1-8pm Sun* €€

Olde Castle Bar

On your visit, don't miss the magnificent **Great Hall** upstairs, with its vast and ornate fireplace, French tapestries and Persian rugs. Afterwards, corkscrew down the spiral staircase to the storeroom. Guided tours run hourly.

Bundoran

TIME FROM DONEGAL TOWN: **20MIN**

Hit the waves in Bundoran

Blinking amusement arcades, fairground rides and fast-food diners give Bundoran the feel of a cheery beach town, but Donegal's best-known seaside resort also has solid waves and attracts a mixed crowd of young families, pensioners – and growing legions of surfers. The beach of **Tullan Strand** has riptides, so swimming can be risky, but the views are stunning, and the surfing is grade A.

Bundoran has several surf schools; they all rent out gear and have their own basic hostel-style accommodation. All offer deals on surf and accommodation packages. **Bundoran Surf Co** *(bundoransurfco.com)* has been providing surf experiences for 25 years and offers a range of lessons and surf rentals. **Murf's Surf School** *(murfssurfschool.com)* runs lessons and equipment hire from Tullan, while **We Surf** *(wesurf.ie)* has tailored packages, including hour-long classes and weekend courses.

If you'd rather stay on dry land, the scenic 2.5km **Roguey**

WHY I LOVE DONEGAL TOWN

Niamh Coughlan, tour guide *@donegal townwalkingtours*

A lot of the buildings in Donegal town date from the 1830s. I love looking around and imagining what life was like in the castle and in the Abbey back then. I'm passionate about telling the story of the Four Masters and explaining what the *Annals of the Four Masters* were all about – a chronological history of Ireland up to the 1600s. It's believed the book was written within a 30 mile radius of Donegal town. The best thing about living here is the sheer amount of visible history in this town, because so many of the old buildings still exist in one form or another; a visual daily reminder of our history.

 CAFES IN BUNDORAN: OUR PICKS

Buoys and Gulls: This vibrant cafe has amazing ocean views, tasty flat whites, and a range of treats and toasties. *8am-4pm* €

Foam: This minimalist coffee shop stands out. The menu includes seasonal dishes and vegan options, and it's the perfect place to start your day – or refuel between surf sessions. *9am-4pm* €

Salty Fox: Great coffee, freshly baked goodies and delicious breakfasts in a cool beach-style cafe. *9.30am-4pm Wed-Sun* €

Humble: There's lots to brag about in this cool eatery that serves harissa fried eggs and brioche French toast for brunch. *8am-4pm Tue-Sun* €€

WHY I LOVE LIVING IN BUNDORAN

Tom Losey, CEO of the surf charity Liquid Therapy
@liquid.therapy

I chose to raise my family in Bundoran for its blend of surf and community. The waves here are more than just a place to ride; they are where my family and I connect with the ocean. My morning coffee is a chance to catch up with friends old and new, and feel the town's welcoming vibe. With its powerful coastline, this place isn't just a backdrop – it's an integral part of our daily lives. It's the perfect mix of an inclusive community and a deep connection to the outdoors, allowing us to live our passion every single day.

Rossnowlagh Beach

Cliff Walk connects Bundoran's town centre with Tullan Strand. It passes a series of sea stacks known as the Fairy Bridges, once believed by locals to be haunted. The path begins at Promenade Rd, just east of the river.

Rossnowlagh

TIME FROM BUNDORAN: **20MIN**

Surfing Rossnowlagh Beach

Best surfed on mid to high tide, **Rossnowlagh Beach**, 16km north of Bundoran, is an excellent spot for beginners. The **Fin McCool Surf School** *(finmccoolsurfschool.com; adult/child €45/30)* offers beginner classes, group lessons and surf rentals. The waves are much more mellow than in Bundoran, and there's plenty of room to spread out. Wetsuits and surfboards provided.

Places We Love to Stay

€ Budget €€ Midrange €€€ Top End

Glenveagh National Park MAP p397

Wild Atlantic Camp €€ This award-winning glamping site in Greeslough provides a range of budget options, from wooden pods to luxury chalets; it's a 15-minute drive to the park.

Rockhill House €€€ A sumptuous 19-bedroom hotel at the end of a woodland driveway. It feels like a luxury family home brought back to life; a 25-minute drive of the park.

Beyond Glenveagh National Park

An Chúirt Hotel €€ You'll find a lively bar and restaurant at this comfortable family favourite at the foot of Mt Errigal.

Teac Jack €€ Perfect for groups, this boutique hotel in Glassagh is a home from home in the heart of the Donegal Gaeltacht. The views over the islands of Gola and Inis Meáin are stunning.

Muldowney's B&B €€ Located in the heart of Arranmore Island with stunning sea views, this comfortable property is cosy and comfortable and serves hearty breakfasts.

Arranmore Lighthouse Accommodation €€ Experience the romance of a lighthouse stay 5km from the village of Leabgarrow. Guests stay in the former lightkeeper's dwellings, perched high on a cliff. Three-night stay minimum.

Malin Head MAP p407

Seaview Tavern € Basic, comfortable rooms with a lively bar and restaurant downstairs, plus stunning sea views. If you eat in the restaurant, you can pitch a tent or park your caravan in the field next door.

Sandrock Holiday Hostel € This hostel has a rustic and comfortable communal area, and a self-catering kitchen overlooking Portronan Pier; dorm-style rooms.

Beyond Malin Head

McGrory's of Culdaff €€ Refurbished rooms above a bar and restaurant that serves delicious, locally-sourced food. It's within walking distance of the stunning Blue Flag Culdaff Beach.

Ballyliffin Lodge & Spa €€ A family-run hidden gem close to the Urris Hills. This spot offers comfort and charm for tired hikers, with a rooftop hot tub overlooking Pollan Strand.

Slieve League Cliffs MAP p415

Sliabh Liag Camping € Pet-friendly camping for motor homes and tents with good amenities; located at the beginning of the Slieve League hiking trail.

Rusty Mackerel €€ Simple, comfortable rooms attached to one of the county's most authentic bars, where delicious seafood is served; close to Teelin Pier.

Beyond the Slieve League Cliffs

Holyrood Hotel €€ A family favourite with both a swimming pool and leisure centre.

Harvey's Point €€ One of Donegal's most luxurious hotels, located on the shores of Lough Eske, where the welcome is warm. For a large hotel, it manages to feel both cosy and intimate.

Bee Pods Glamping €€ This Rossnowlagh hideaway offers luxury getaways for adults, with sea-view pods and a beach hut. Seaweed baths are also available for guests, but even the views alone are worth it.

Inver House €€€ Awe-inspiring Georgian property that is a feast for the senses and stocked with cool movie memorabilia – a blow-the-budget option that sleeps 10.

Lough Eske Castle €€€ Old-world luxury and charm meets modern dining in this charming hotel that has its own spa.

Researched by
Neil Wilson

The Midlands

THE IRISH HEARTLAND

Rolling countryside, archaeological treasures and stately homes: the Midlands offer a taste of Ireland off the main tourist beat – and it's all the better for it.

If you're in search of a genuine slice of rural Irish life, you'll find it here in the country's heart. Often bypassed by visitors moving from Dublin to the wildness of the west's coastlines, the Midlands region brims with verdant pastoral landscapes, stately homes, archaeological treasures, sacred monastic sites, lakeside vistas and sleepy towns where local people are genuinely glad to see you. And this is no exaggeration: that mythical Irish friendliness you've read about? You'll find it in abundance in the smaller cities and towns of Ireland's core.

Getting lost along the twisting back roads of counties Laois, Leitrim, Longford, Offaly, Roscommon and Westmeath is an unhurried pleasure, and you're virtually guaranteed to happen upon a local village shop, pub, garage or post office that's scarcely changed in decades. Mobile phone coverage can be patchy in parts, and internet connection is occasionally rudimentary, but there are fewer tour buses and souvenir stalls hawking tourist tat. Instead, you'll find an unvarnished version of Irish life and culture, albeit with some swanky hotels and wonderful country house restaurants.

The River Shannon dominates the Midlands, meandering through fields and forests, drawing boaters and anglers in shoals. Stylish hotels and gourmet restaurants continue to spring up along its banks, making it a wonderfully scenic and surprisingly cosmopolitan way to travel.

THE MAIN AREAS

ATHLONE
Formidable Norman fortress.
p428

STROKESTOWN
Noteworthy Famine museum.
p439

BELVEDERE HOUSE & GARDENS
Magnificent Georgian mansion.
p448

Left: Sean's Bar (p429); right: Rock of Dunamase (p438)

Find Your Way

The Midlands covers six counties – Laois, Leitrim, Longford, Offaly, Roscommon and Westmeath – that make up Ireland's belly. These places are often forsaken by mass tourism, and public transport can be patchy.

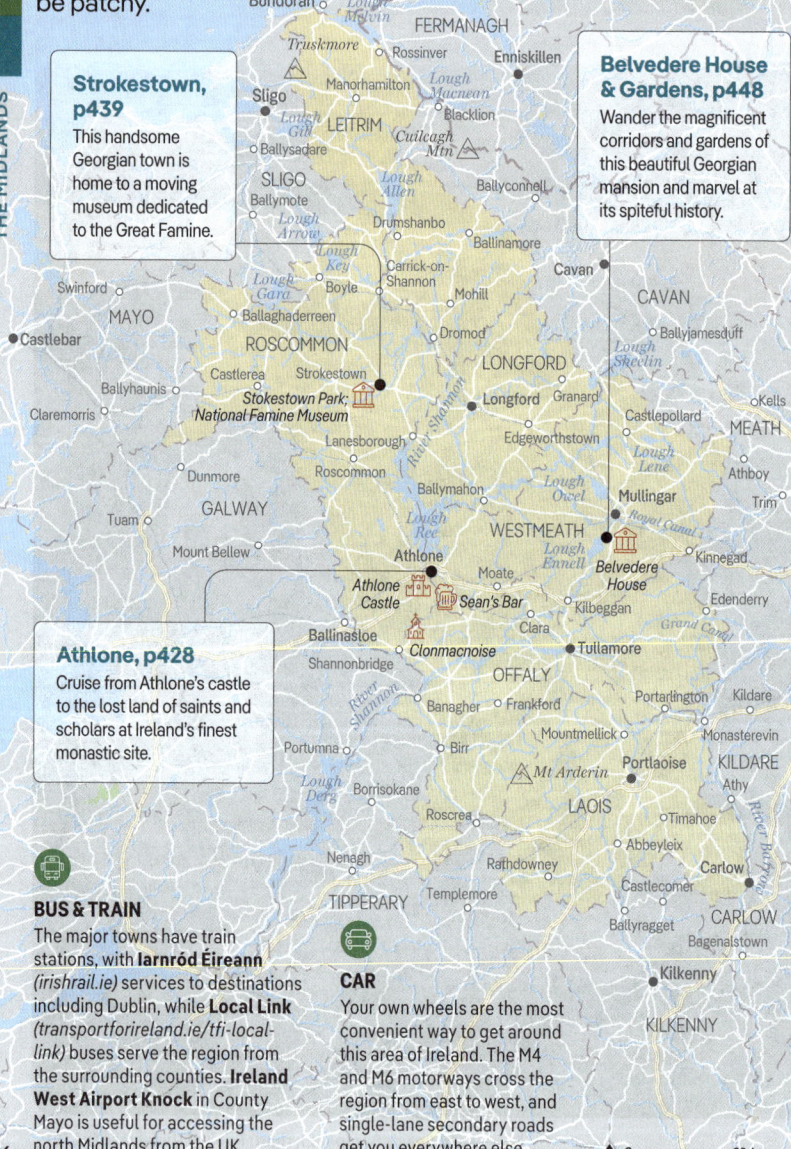

Strokestown, p439
This handsome Georgian town is home to a moving museum dedicated to the Great Famine.

Belvedere House & Gardens, p448
Wander the magnificent corridors and gardens of this beautiful Georgian mansion and marvel at its spiteful history.

Athlone, p428
Cruise from Athlone's castle to the lost land of saints and scholars at Ireland's finest monastic site.

BUS & TRAIN
The major towns have train stations, with **Iarnród Éireann** (irishrail.ie) services to destinations including Dublin, while **Local Link** (transportforireland.ie/tfi-local-link) buses serve the region from the surrounding counties. **Ireland West Airport Knock** in County Mayo is useful for accessing the north Midlands from the UK.

CAR
Your own wheels are the most convenient way to get around this area of Ireland. The M4 and M6 motorways cross the region from east to west, and single-lane secondary roads get you everywhere else.

Lough Ree (p433)

Plan Your Time

Journey through Irish history, from ancient days to more modern times, before exploring mountains and bogland, all fuelled by fine food and whiskey.

Pressed for Time

- Visit the monastic ruins of **Clonmacnoise** (p430) before heading west to Boyle to explore **Strokestown Park** (p440) and the **National Famine Museum** (p440). Take in the prehistoric site of the **Corlea Trackway** (p434), and then travel east towards Mullingar to discover **Belvedere House** (p448) and take a hike in the beautiful **Fore Valley**, home to the little-visited ruins of a 7th-century monastic site.

The Midlands in a Week

- Visit **Strokestown Park** (p440), then take a cruise along the **Shannon–Erne Waterway** (p445). Explore **Athlone Castle** (p428) and have a drink in **Sean's Bar** (p429) – Ireland's oldest pub – before engaging in some lakeland activities on **Lough Ree** (p433). Head south to County Laois and mountain bike in the **Slieve Bloom Mountains** (p435) before visiting **Birr Castle** (p434) and enjoying a drink in **Craughwell's** (p436).

SEASONAL HIGHLIGHTS

SPRING
Migratory birds, such as whooper swans and common terns, begin to arrive and breed on island-speckled **Lough Ree** (p433).

SUMMER
In early May, the Hill of Uisneach recreates the ancient fire festival of **Bealtaine** (p452) to celebrate the coming of summer.

AUTUMN
Samhain (p443), another ancient Gaelic festival, marks the end of the harvest season and the beginning of autumn.

WINTER
Winter in the Midlands brings cooler weather and shorter days, enlivened by festive markets and snug pubs with blazing log fires.

Athlone

NORMAN CASTLE | BOAT TRIPS | MEDIEVAL MONASTERY

GETTING AROUND

Athlone town centre is easily navigated on foot. There is on-street parking right next to Athlone Castle, and on the Quay between the castle and the river. If these are full, **O'Connell St Car Park** is 350m to the west.

Local Link (transportforireland.ie/tfi-local-link) bus 850 runs six times daily from Athlone to Birr and Roscrea, stopping at Clonmacnoise (p430), which is 25km south of Athlone on the N62 and R444.

There are plans to develop a 25km Pilgrim Greenway for walkers and cyclists that will link Athlone to Clonmacnoise.

The location of Athlone (Baile Átha Luain), smack-bang in the centre of the country, is both a blessing and a curse for Westmeath's county town. A curse because it's often bypassed by visitors on their way from Dublin to the honeypots of Galway; a blessing because it makes the perfect stopover between the two cities and is close to attractions such as Clonmacnoise and Lough Ree. Nevertheless, Athlone has been campaigning for city status; the opening of a new university in 2021, and the cohort of 14,000 students, has bolstered the claim.

The River Shannon splits this former garrison town in two, with most shops and businesses sitting on the river's eastern bank. The western bank, in the shadow of Athlone Castle, is an enchanting jumble of twisting streets, colourfully painted houses, historic pubs, antique shops and old bookbinders, as well as some outstanding restaurants.

A Mighty Fort

An 800-year-old Norman castle

From ancient times onwards, the river ford at Athlone was an important crossing point on the Shannon, hence the construction of **Athlone Castle** (athlonecastle.ie; adult/child €12/5.50), which asserted Norman dominance over the region. Within the curtain walls is an **octagonal keep** that retains part of the original 13th-century structure, but most of the castle was remodelled after major damage – a lightning strike in 1697 ignited 260 barrels of gunpowder, destroying much of the castle – and the town.

The keep and surrounding buildings now house a modern visitor centre where displays bring to life the castle's tumultuous history, notably the **Great Siege of Athlone** in 1691, when Jacobite defenders were defeated by a Williamite army after a 10-day onslaught involving 600 bombs and 12,000 cannonballs.

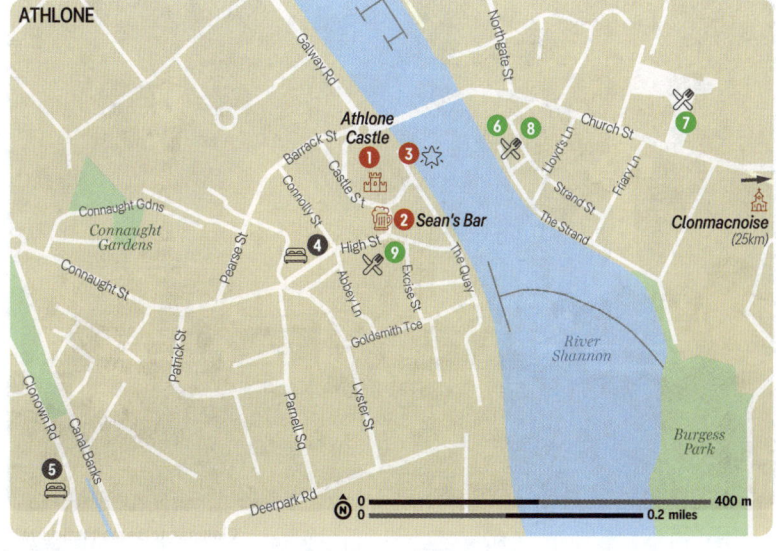

HIGHLIGHTS
1 Athlone Castle
2 Sean's Bar

ACTIVITIES
3 Viking Tours

SLEEPING
4 Bastion B&B
5 Riverdale House B&B

EATING
6 Dead Centre Brewing
7 Fatted Calf
8 Hatters Lane Bistro
9 Left Bank Bistro

Sip a Pint of History

Visit Ireland's oldest pub

There are plenty of places in Ireland that purport to be the country's oldest pub, but none have a PR campaign like **Sean's Bar** *(seansbar.ie)*, located round the back of Athlone Castle. Documentary evidence is said to support the claim that there has been an inn on this site since 900CE. Established by Luain Mac Luighdeach, the settlement that expanded here eventually became known as Áth Luain (the Ford of Luan), from which we get the name Athlone.

Head inside, buy yourself a pint of the black stuff and look for the framed **Guinness World Records Certificate**, issued in 2004, which certifies Sean's as 'the oldest public house in Ireland'. Nearby, a glass panel displays a portion of the pub's

Continues on p432

☑ **TOP TIP**

Athlone and Clonmacnoise are the ideal location for a midday break on the journey from Dublin to Galway; both lie just off the M6, about 90 minutes from Dublin and an hour or so from Galway.

 **EATING IN ATHLONE: OUR PICKS**

Left Bank Bistro: This sophisticated spot combines superior Irish ingredients with Mediterranean and Asian influences. *noon-9.30pm Tue-Sat* €€

Dead Centre Brewing: A working brewery (which you can tour) that also serves excellent gastropub-style grub. *5-9.30pm Mon & Wed-Fri, from 12.30pm Sat & Sun* €€

Fatted Calf: New York-style bistro that spotlights locally sourced meat; the daily steak special is superb. *5-9pm Tue, Wed & Fri, 4-9.30pm Sat, 2.30-6.30pm Sun* €€

Hatters Lane Bistro: Hollywood-themed bistro serving tasty meat and seafood dishes, including hake in a Dublin Bay prawn bisque. *5-9pm Thu-Sat, noon-8pm Sun* €€

Clonmacnoise monastic site

TOP EXPERIENCE

Clonmacnoise

St Ciarán couldn't have picked a finer setting for his monastery, overlooking a bend in the mighty Shannon. What he couldn't have known though, way back in 548 CE, was that in the centuries that followed, his get-away-from-it-all retreat would grow to become one of Ireland's holiest and most significant monastic sites, drawing scholars from all over Europe.

DON'T MISS

Cross of the Scriptures

South Cross

Grave Slabs

Whispering Arch

Temple Ciarán

O'Rourke's Tower

Temple Finghin

Nun's Church

Visitor Centre

The visitor centre's 20-minute audiovisual is a terrific primer on the importance of Clonmacnoise.

Among the artefacts in the adjacent museum are the original **high crosses** (replicas have been placed in their original location outside), and a fascinating collection of early Christian **grave slabs**.

There's a real sense of drama as you descend to the foot of the imposing **Cross of the Scriptures** (King Flann's Cross). This is one of Ireland's finest crosses and is very distinctive, with unique upward-tilting arms and richly decorated panels depicting the Crucifixion, the Last Judgment, the arrest

PRACTICALITIES
- heritageireland.ie ● adult/child €8/4 ● 9am-6.30pm Jun-Aug, 10am-6pm Mar-May, Sep & Oct, 10am-5pm Nov-Feb

of Jesus Christ, and Christ in the tomb. The equally ornate **South Cross** has mostly abstract carvings, with Celtic swirls and spirals on one side, and a Crucifixion scene on the other.

Cathedral

Opposite the visitor centre, a replica of the Cross of the Scriptures stands in front of the west door of the Cathedral, the largest building in Clonmacnoise, originally built in 909 CE but significantly altered and remodelled over the centuries. Its most interesting feature is the intricate 15th-century Gothic doorway in the north wall. Known as the **Whispering Arch**, the doorway was designed so a whisper could carry from one side of the door to the other, meaning that those suffering from leprosy could confess their sins without infecting the priest listening to them. Above the door are three effigies of St Dominic, St Patrick and St Francis.

Temple Ciarán

The smaller chapels in the grounds of Clonmacnoise are called temples, a derivation of the Irish word *teampall* (church). Tiny **Temple Ciarán** is reputed to be the burial place of St Ciarán, the site's founder. Its ground level is lower than the ground outside, as, for centuries, local farmers have been taking sacred clay from the temple to bless their crops and cattle. The floor has since been covered in slabs, but farmers still take handfuls of clay from outside the church in early spring.

O'Rourke's Tower

The round tower overlooking the River Shannon is known as **O'Rourke's Tower**. Lightning blasted the top off the tower in 1135, but the remaining structure was in use for another 400 years. Some say that the stones that came down after the lightning strike were used to help build Temple Finghin.

Temple Finghin & Tower

Temple Finghin and its round tower are on the northern boundary of the monastic site, overlooking the River Shannon. The building dates from around 1160 and has some fine Romanesque carvings. The herringbone-patterned tower roof is the only one in Ireland that has never been altered.

Nun's Church

From Temple Ciarán, a barely visible path leads northeast to a gateway and on through a modern cemetery (a raised grassy ridge) to join a minor road. Continue along the road for another 200m to reach the secluded ruin of the 12th-century **Nun's Church**. The west door and chancel arch are decorated with wonderful Romanesque carvings, including human heads and Ireland's earliest sheila-na-gig (carved female figure with exaggerated genitalia); the figure is halfway up the north side of the chancel arch.

> **A BRIEF HISTORY**
>
> St Ciarán founded Clonmacnoise at the most important crossroads in the country: the intersection of the north-south River Shannon and the east-west Eiscir Riada (Ridge of Riding). From the 12th century onwards, the monastery fell into decline, and by the 15th century, it was home to a sole impoverished bishop. In 1552, the English garrison from Athlone reduced the site to a ruin.

> **TOP TIPS**
>
> ● The site isn't large, but there's plenty to see, so put a couple of hours aside for your visit.
>
> ● Look around the visitor centre and then join the free guided tour of the site for interesting background info.
>
> ● If you want to avoid the crowds, try to visit early or late in the day.
>
> ● The tiny country lanes nearby can get clogged with coaches during peak periods.
>
> ● The Pilgrims's Path is a waymarked, 25km cycle route that leads from Ballycumber (28km southest of Athlone) to Clonmacnoise along the line of the Eiscir Riada (see above).

THE RIVER SHANNON

The Shannon is the longest river in Ireland, flowing for around 360km from its source at the Shannon Pot (p480) in County Cavan through loughs Allen, Boyle, Ree and Derg to its estuary west of Limerick, making it longer than the UK's longest river, the Severn. It has served as a major waterway since ancient times – even getting a mention in Ptolemy's *Geography* in 150CE – and as a strategically important barrier – Irish armies often retreated west of the Shannon in times of conflict, resulting in bloody sieges of Athlone and Limerick after the Battle of the Boyne. According to Irish mythology, the River Shannon's name comes from Princess Sionnan, granddaughter of Lír, the 'father god of the sea'.

River Shannon and Clonmacnoise (p430)

Continued from p429

wattle-and-daub (woven hazel branches plastered with clay) wall, which was discovered during renovations in 1970.

Records apart, peat fires warm the low-ceilinged interior, which has sawdust-sprinkled sloping floors (to help flood waters drain back down to the river). There is live music in the riverside beer garden most nights in summer.

Cruise to Clonmacnoise

Boat trip on the Shannon

Although the most popular method of visiting Clonmacnoise (p430) is by road, one of the nicest ways to approach is by boat. From May to September, **Viking Tours** *(vikingtoursireland.ie; adult/child €40/20)* run river trips in lookalike Viking longships. The 3½-hour expedition begins with a cruise along the Shannon, during which you'll get a quick history lesson, as well as the chance to spot wildlife. You'll then have 90 minutes to explore Clonmacnoise before returning to Athlone by bus (included in the price).

Beyond Athlone

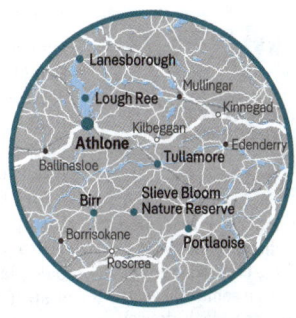

Bogland, battlements and archaeological remains sit cheek by jowl with busy towns and beautiful mansions.

To the north of Athlone, County Westmeath's attractions include Lough Ree, which cuts across the border into County Roscommon. North again is County Longford, where the big attraction is archaeological: the unique and impressive Iron Age Corlea Trackway.

To the south, green and watery County Offaly has vast swathes of bogland. Its main town, Tullamore, is famous for Tullamore D.E.W. Irish whiskey, while Birr has a fabulous castle with one of Europe's largest and most historic telescopes in its grounds. County Laois has some attractive historic villages, plus hiking and biking in the Slieve Bloom Mountains, as well as the beautiful Emo Court, one of Ireland's grandest buildings.

Places
Lanesborough & Lough Ree p433
Birr p434
Slieve Bloom Nature Reserve p435
Tullamore p436
Portlaoise p438

Lanesborough & Lough Ree

TIME FROM ATHLONE: 40MIN

Exploring Lough Ree

Monks once inhabited many of the 50-plus islands on Lough Ree, and their ecclesiastical treasures drew Vikings like bears to honey-laced beehives. These days, the lake lures visitors for boating, fishing and birdwatching. (The migratory birds that nest here include Bewick's swans, whooper swans and common terns; white-tailed eagles have been spotted hunting on the lake.) Most of Lough Ree's attractions can be accessed from the town of **Lanesborough**, located at the north end of the lake.

Inchcleraun, a large island in the middle of the lake, has a ruined monastery founded in the 6th century by St Diarmaid, who was a teacher to St Ciarán of Clonmacnoise; it contains the ruins of six churches and a fort that once guarded against Viking raids. **Lough Ree Access For All** *(loughreeboattrips. com; adult/child €25/12.50)*, based in Lanesborough, runs 90-minute cruises to Inchcleraun and other sites, departing three times daily in summer; the boat is wheelchair accessible. They can also arrange boat hire and fishing trips.

Paolo Roberto at **Gone Fishing Ireland** *(gonefishing ireland.ie; from €250)* is a friendly and knowledgeable guide who can take you and your kids fishing for pike and trout on Lough Ree and the River Suck, with a barbecue lunch included. If you know the ropes, he can also rent you a boat for the day or half-day.

GETTING AROUND

Tullamore and Portlaoise can be reached from Athlone by train with **Iarnród Éireann** *(irishrail.ie)*. For Lanesborough, take the train to Roscommon, then **Local Link** *(transportforireland. ie/tfi-local-link)* bus 426. It's possible to get from Athlone to Birr by bus, but it's a meandering country route that takes twice as long as driving.

For exploring around the shores of Lough Ree, you're better off using your own wheels.

THE CORLEA TRACKWAY

The Corlea Trackway was known locally as the Danes' road, even though it predated the first Vikings by at least some 800 years. For a wider historical context, the road was laid around the same time as the Siege of Carthage, which took place during the Punic Wars in North Africa.

The precise purpose of the track has not yet been fully established, but it is thought to have been constructed as a symbol of peace and cooperation between formerly warring regions. Objects that have been found beneath the track also point to similar tracks discovered in other parts of Europe, but the Corlea Trackway remains the largest of its kind to have been uncovered in Europe.

A 2000-year-old archaeological marvel

One of Ireland's archaeological highlights is the extraordinary **Corlea Trackway** *(heritageireland.ie; free)*, an Iron Age bog road built in 148 BCE that was discovered during industrial peat-harvesting works in 1984. Moving around the water-logged boglands of the Midlands was not an easy task, so Iron Age inhabitants often laid wooden paths across the terrain.

An 18m stretch of the timber road – the largest of its kind in Europe – has been preserved in a humidified hall at the site's visitor centre, where you can see the road's huge, roughly hewn oak planks. After watching a 15-minute background video, a staff member will show you around the hall and suggest theories about the trackway for you to conjecture; oddly, the timber planks show no signs of wear.

Following this, the shutters at the far end will be raised and you can see that the trackway continues – beneath the bog and a modern boardwalk – towards slightly higher ground; its total length is around 1km, with another 1km on the far side. You can stroll along the boardwalk and contemplate prehistory amid the bog's peace and quiet.

The centre is just off the N55 near Keenagh, 13km south of Lanesborough.

Birr

TIME FROM ATHLONE: **45MIN**

Battlements of Birr

It's easy to spend half a day exploring the attractions and gardens of **Birr Castle** *(birrcastle.com; adult/child €12/7)*. The castle dates from 1620, with alterations made in the early 19th century, and it is currently the private home of the 7th Earl of Rosse, Brendan Parsons, whose ancestors have lived here for 400 years.

Birr Castle gained fame as a centre for scientific research and innovation when William Parsons, the 3rd Earl of Rosse, built his **Great Telescope** here in 1845. Looking more like a medieval engine of war than a scientific instrument, the Leviathan of Parsonstown (as it was known) was the largest telescope in the world for 75 years and attracted a wide variety of scientists and astronomers. During its working lifetime, it helped to make innumerable astronomical discoveries, including the nature of spiral galaxies. Now restored, it sits in the middle of the castle grounds.

The story of William, his pioneering photographer wife Mary and their equally inventive descendants is well told in

---

EATING IN BIRR: OUR PICKS

Emma's Cafe & Deli: Join the locals and start the day with excellent coffee and a breakfast bagel or almond croissant at Emma's. *8am-5pm* €

Hackett's Eatery: This elegant Georgian dining-room at the County Arms Hotel is the ideal spot for a special dinner. *5.30-9pm Thu-Sat* €€€

Courtyard Cafe: A quirky courtyard with outdoor tables, located across the street from the castle entrance; serves cakes, sandwiches and wraps. *10am-4.30pm* €

The Thatch: A 200-year-old thatched cottage with a brick-and-stone interior warmed by open fires; serves upmarket pub-grub and Sunday roasts. *4-8.30pm Wed-Fri, from 12.30pm Sat & Sun* €€€

Birr Castle

a series of **museum galleries** in the castle courtyard. After browsing these, you can wander the 50-hectare castle grounds, famous for their magnificent gardens set around a large artificial lake and the roughly 1000 species of plants that come from all over the world. Look for the 500-year-old **Carroll Oak**, standing proud in the middle of a wildflower meadow that has not been ploughed since at least 1620.

Slieve Bloom Nature Reserve

TIME FROM ATHLONE: **50MIN**

Hiking and biking on Slieve Bloom

Rising out of the plains 15km to the east of Birr are the rounded Slieve Bloom Mountains, whose upper slopes are clad in heather and blanket bog, and protected by the 2300-hectare **Slieve Bloom Mountain Nature Reserve**. The area has some excellent **walking trails** *(slievebloom.ie/walking)*, from gentle ambles between Glenbarrow and Rosenallis to sections of the Slieve Bloom Way, an 84km signposted trail that does a complete circuit of the mountains, taking in most of the major points of interest. The high moors of the Slieve Blooms are home to a nesting population of rare and endangered hen harriers.

The Slieve Blooms straddle the border between counties Offaly and Laois, with an 80km network of **mountain biking trails** *(slievebloom.ie/biking)* on either side that are accessed from trailheads in the village Kinnitty (in the west) and Baunreagh car park (in the east). You can rent full-suspension mountain bikes *(three hours €60)* from the **Slieve Bloom MTB Centre** *(sbmbc.midirelandadventure.ie)* in Kinnitty. There are no rental outlets on the Laois side of the hills, and no facilities at the Baunreagh car park other than a composting toilet.

IRELAND'S MOST HAUNTED CASTLE

Around 12km southeast of Birr on the R421 is **Leap Castle** *(leapcastle.net)*, reputedly one of the most haunted castles in Europe. Originally the residence of the O'Carroll family, the 1514 castle was the scene of many dreadful deeds, including the murder of a priest in the onsite chapel.

During repair works in 1922, builders discovered the skeletal remains of around 150 people in a hidden dungeon, and visitors have reported many paranormal phenomena, including sightings of ghosts, unexplained noises and odd smells – its most renowned inhabitant is the 'elemental', a spirit that apparently leaves a lingering odour of putrefaction.

The castle is still lived in by its owner, Sean Ryan, who may show you around.

HISTORIC VILLAGES IN LAOIS

Little-visited County Laois ('leash') is home to many picturesque towns and villages.

Abbeyleix: A classic heritage town with a Georgian market house, graceful terraced housing and a wide, leafy main street.

Durrow: Neat rows of Georgian houses, pubs and cafes surround a manicured village green next to the imposing gateway of Castle Durrow.

Timahoe: A tiny, charming village straight out of a fairy tale; it's overlooked by a 12th-century round tower with a burbling stream nearby.

Mountmellick: A quiet Georgian town on the River Owenass that was renowned for its 19th-century linen production and its Quaker settlers.

Portarlington: Once known as the 'Paris of the Midlands', this town was influenced by French Huguenot settlers; see the 18th-century Huguenot house on French Church St.

Tullamore

TIME FROM ATHLONE: **40MIN**

Tasting Tullamore D.E.W.

The one big draw in Offaly's busy county town of Tullamore is the **Tullamore D.E.W. Visitor Centre** *(tullamoredew.com; tours per person €45)*, built on the outskirts of town in 2014 as a modern replacement for the original 1829 distillery.

The tour begins with a bit of theatre, with the making of **Irish coffee** to the original recipe (which used Tullamore D.E.W., named after 19th-century distillery manager Daniel Edmund Williams). You get to sip your alcoholic coffee while your guide explains the distilling process; then a curtain rises to reveal the gleaming stainless steel and polished copper of the mash tuns and pot stills.

After touring the factory floor, a minibus takes you to a warehouse containing 80,000 barrels of maturing whiskey, where you get to taste the hard stuff straight from the barrel while sitting in a secret snug. A tasting session back in the bar rounds off the 1¾-hour tour (over 18s only).

The beauty of the bogs

Clara Bog is one of the few expanses of raised bog in western Europe that has escaped being plundered for peat. Deceptively flat and seemingly lifeless, it offers a fascinating window into the natural world. At **Clara Bog Nature Reserve** *(clarabognaturereserve.ie; free)*, a 1km boardwalk loops into the middle of the bog, where the outside world melts away and all you'll hear is birds chirping and insects buzzing.

Look for the tiny insect-eating sundew plants growing amid the sphagnum moss and enjoy the sweeping views of distant green hills. There's a **visitor centre** that explains the history and ecology of the bog; it's located at the public library in Clara village.

There's limited parking at the boardwalk entrance, but you can walk there from the visitor centre (1.5km or 20 minutes each way).

Many of County Offaly's once extensive boglands were stripped of peat for electricity generation during the 20th century. Now Lough Boora, halfway between Tullamore and Birr and 17km from Clara Bog, is the focus of a scheme for bog restoration. More than 50km of walking and cycling trails cross the **Lough Boora Discovery Park** *(loughboora.com; free)*, with excellent birdwatching, fishing, rare flora and a Mesolithic site. Maps are available at the visitor centre, which has a cafe and bike hire.

 DRINKING IN BIRR: OUR PICKS

Chestnut: The Chestnut (from 1823) has snug stalls and a great beer garden with regular live-music sessions. *5-11.30pm Mon-Thu, to 12.30am Fri, from noon Sat, to midnight Sun*

Craughwell's: Deceptively big inside, Craughwell's is known for its rollicking trad-music sessions and impromptu singalongs. *5-11.30pm Mon-Fri, noon-1am Sat, 11am-11pm Sun*

Kennedy's Market House Tavern: Lovely old-fashioned pub with staff who pride themselves on pouring the perfect pint of Guinness. *4-11.30pm Mon-Fri, from 2pm Sat & Sun*

JJ Houghs Singing Pub: This 250-year-old vine-clad pub in Banagher, 12km north of Birr, is renowned for its nightly singing sessions. *noon-1am*

WALK THE SHANNONBRIDGE FORTIFICATIONS

This short walk takes in two quintessential features of the Irish midlands – the River Shannon and the bog.

START	END	LENGTH
Infantry Barracks	Infantry Barracks	5.2km; 2hr

Start off by taking a look at the free exhibition in the massive, foursquare ❶ **Infantry Barracks**, which details the history and military significance of the fortifications, built by the British in 1810 to defend against a feared French invasion. Then walk out onto ❷ **Shannon Bridge** itself. Here you can look back at the bridgehead defences, one of the finest examples of Napoleonic fortifications in Ireland.

Return to the car park and descend the steps in the corner to reach the riverbank, turning left under the bridge. At the corner of the ❸ **Fortress Walls**, you can turn left and make a circuit of the fortifications for a shorter walk (0.5km, allow 20 minutes). Otherwise, continue over the small metal footbridge and along the riverbank for almost 2km; the way is marked with small green arrows. (This section is grassy and can be wet; there may be cattle in one of the fields.)

At the ❹ **Field Boundary** where the river forks, turn left away from the river to reach an old bog road. This leads back south, past the desolate wasteland of ❺ **Cornaveagh Bog** (once harvested for peat), to join the R357; turn left for the final 700m back to the starting point.

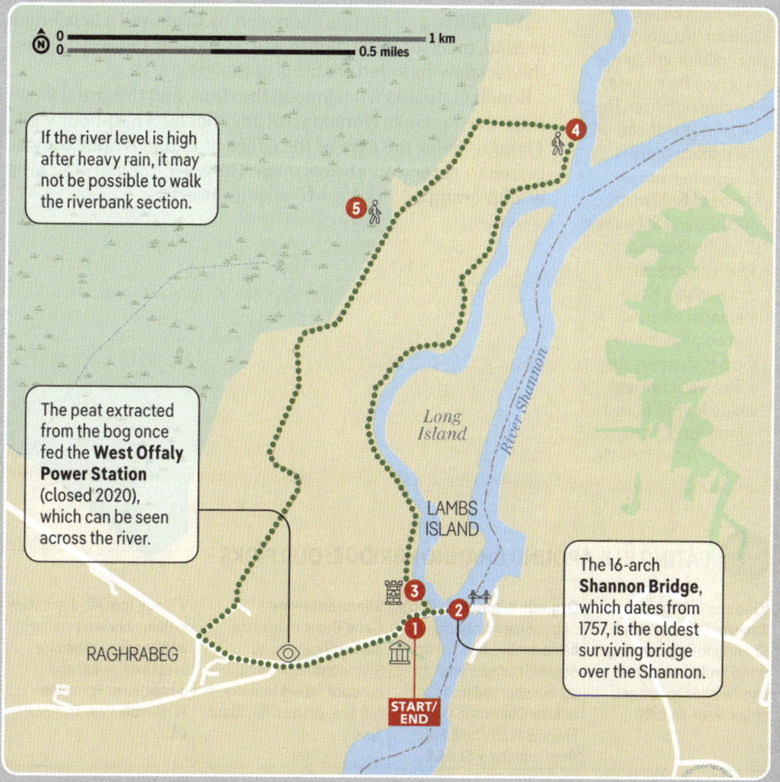
0
0
1 km
0.5 miles
If the river level is high after heavy rain, it may not be possible to walk the riverbank section.
5
4
Long Island
River Shannon
LAMBS ISLAND
The peat extracted from the bog once fed the **West Offaly Power Station** (closed 2020), which can be seen across the river.
3
2
1
RAGHRABEG
START/ END
The 16-arch **Shannon Bridge**, which dates from 1757, is the oldest surviving bridge over the Shannon.

Portlaoise

TIME FROM ATHLONE: 1HR

The estate at Emo Court

The neoclassical mansion house of **Emo Court** *(heritageire land.ie; adult/child €8/4)*, 13km northeast of Portlaoise, was designed in 1790 by James Gandon, architect of Dublin's **Custom House** and **Four Courts**. Originally the country seat of the first Earl of Portarlington, it later became a Jesuit novitiate.

From April to September, you can take part in a one-hour guided tour of the restored drawing room, library, kitchen and servants' quarters, and the house's crowning glory – the spectacular central rotunda.

The **grounds**, studded with Greek statues and once part of Ireland's largest country estate, are free to enjoy and open all year. Stroll around the lakeside trail or along the mile-long Wellingtonia Avenue, lined with giant Sequoia trees planted in 1853.

Dramatic ruins at the Rock of Dunamase

The **Rock of Dunamase** is a craggy limestone outcrop rising 45m above the flat plains to the east of Portlaoise and capped with the dramatic ruins of a medieval fortress. Archaeological excavations have shown that the rock was originally a 9th-century hill fort, but the castle that crowns its summit dates to the 12th and 13th centuries; despite being abandoned in the 1330s, and further damaged by Cromwell's henchmen in 1650, much of the structure still stands. At the very top rise the jackdaw-haunted remains of the great hall.

Rough footpaths wind among the ruins, and the grand views from the top make Dunamase a fine spot for a half-hour walk. Though under the care of the Office of Public Works, the site is free to enter and always open. However, the parking area is a bit cramped; it's best to visit midweek.

GOLDSMITH COUNTRY

Oliver Goldsmith (1728–74), author of *The Vicar of Wakefield* (1766) and *She Stoops To Conquer* (1773), was a hugely popular poet, playwright and novelist who influenced many later writers, including Jane Austen and Charles Dickens.

Born into an Anglo-Irish family near Ballymahon in County Longford, he is closely associated with the region on the eastern side of Lough Ree that's known as Goldsmith Country: his childhood home is at Lissoy Parsonage, the inspiration for *The Vicar of Wakefield*; the public library in Ballymahon has a statue of Goldsmith outside; and St Munis Church of Ireland, 4.5km southeast of Ballymahon, has a memorial window that commemorates the parish where the writer was born and where his father was curate for 12 years.

EATING IN & AROUND SHANNONBRIDGE: OUR PICKS

Killeens Village Tavern: Old-world pub in Shannonbridge serving good grub, from steak sandwiches to fish and chips. *9am-9pm* €€

Organic Kitchen: Fallon's pub in Shannonbridge has a concession serving organic burgers and steaks sourced from nearby Clanwood Organic Farm. *5-9pm Thu & Fri, from 1pm Sat & Sun* €€

Shannonbridge Cafe: Basic cafe in the old fortifications at Shannonbridge, with outdoor tables looking out across the river. *10am-5pm* €

Village Inn: All-day eatery in Ballynahown serving well-made classics for breakfast, lunch and dinner. *5am-9pm Mon-Wed, from 9am Thu-Sun* €€

Strokestown

PALLADIAN MANSION | FAMINE MUSEUM | WALKING TRAILS

As you arrive in Strokestown, you're left in little doubt as to the whole point of the place, which was to service the considerable needs of the local estate owners. The Mahon family received the land as a gift from King Charles II in 1666, and they eventually added the huge Palladian mansion of Strokestown Park. Around the same time, the town was built with the proviso that it included Europe's widest street (later surpassed by O'Connell St in Dublin), making it one of the few planned towns in Ireland.

While Strokestown is sleepy enough, it is notable for its historic estate (home of the Mahon family for 300 years) and the unmissable Famine Museum, which allows you to explore the contrasting yet parallel lives of the haves and have-nots in 18th- and 19th-century Ireland. There's so much to see that you could easily spend the best part of a day here.

A Grand Mansion...
Insights into the aristocracy

At the end of Strokestown's handsome main avenue, triple Gothic arches lead to **Strokestown Park** *(strokestownpark. ie; adult/child €19/10.50)*. Ireland has plenty of fine Palladian mansions, but this one, designed by Richard Cassels in 1730, is as much a time capsule of 18th-century privilege as it is an example of Georgian extravagance.

Full-price tickets include an hour-long guided tour of the house, plus admission to the Famine Museum, the Walled Garden and the Woodland Walk. A cheaper **combination ticket** *(adult/child €15/7.50)* excludes the house tour.

The informal guided tour is well worth doing; it covers the grand rooms of the main house, as well as a galleried kitchen with original ovens dating from 1740, a schoolroom with an exercise book of neatly written dictation from 1934 (which, according to her red pen, was deemed disgraceful by the governess), and a toy room complete with 19th-century toys and funhouse mirrors. Well-informed guides peel back the layers of the social structure of the time and reveal the tensions

GETTING AROUND

Although **Bus Éireann Expressway** *(expressway.ie)* operates a regular bus service to Strokestown from Dublin via Longford (2½ hours), you're better off with your own transport. The nearest bike hire spot is the **Midlands Cycle Hub** *(midlandscyclehub. ie)* in Cloondara on the Royal Canal, 16km east of Strokestown.

☑ TOP TIP

The guided tours of Strokestown Park, while advertised as lasting one hour, often overrun; make sure you leave enough time (at least one hour) before or after your tour to appreciate the Famine Museum.

THE MAHON FAMILY

The history of Strokestown is effectively the history of the Mahon family. The founder of the estate, Captain Nicholas Mahon, was gifted the land for services rendered during the Cromwellian invasion of 1649, but he and his successors were deemed to be pretty generous landlords. Thomas Mahon (1701–82) built the mansion you see today and oversaw the construction of the town for the workers on the estate. By the time Denis Mahon (1787–1847) took over, the estate was in huge debt, which resulted in the evictions that eventually led to his murder. The last Mahon to live in the house was Olive Pakenham-Mahon, who left in 1981.

among the landlords, mediators and tenants that exacerbated the effects of the potato blight which led to the Great Famine.

...and its Demesne

Walled gardens and woodland walks

A series of Victorian **walled gardens** (a good indicator of the family's wealth) extends to the south of the car park and contain a rose garden, a wildflower garden, glasshouses growing peaches and grapes, a fernery, a summer house and a restored croquet lawn and gazebo complete with stone tower, where the family used to take afternoon tea. You'll also find the longest herbaceous border in Ireland, which blooms in a rainbow of colours in summer. Beyond lies a deer park and a network of woodland walks, where kids can learn about local plants and animals, and make music on an outdoor xylophone.

In the estate's former granary are the **Woodland Cafe and Shop**, where you can buy replicas of some of the documents found in the exhibition, including the Cloonahee Petition.

The Spectre of Hunger

Examining Ireland's greatest disaster

'Our families are really and truly suffering in our presence and we cannot much longer withstand their cries for food. We have no food for them, our potatoes are rotten and we have no grain'. This haunting testimony is part of the **Cloonahee Petition**, dated 22 August 1846, and just one of the documents on display at the **National Famine Museum** *(included in entry fee)* in the Stable Yard of Strokestown Park. The story of those who died and those who were forced to leave during the Great Famine, which devastated Ireland from 1845 to 1852, is told in concise, harrowing detail at this extraordinary museum.

As well as some genuinely touching artefacts, the museum uses modern techniques to tell the story of the Famine, including projections, soundscapes and voiceovers, with the whole effort underpinned by thousands of documents from the time.

The role of Strokestown's owner and landlord, Denis Mahon, in the Famine was more than that of an observer. He evicted around 3000 of his tenants for nonpayment, 500 of whom died on the overcrowded 'coffin ships' he chartered to transport them away from Ireland. Two hundred perished in quarantine in Québec (the cheapest route). Perhaps unsurprisingly, Mahon was murdered by three of his tenants in 1847, two of whom were publicly hanged in Roscommon. The gun they used is on display, alongside details of the crime and its aftermath.

You'll emerge with an unblinking insight into the starvation of the poor, and the ignorance, callousness and cruelty of those who were in a position to help.

The National Famine Museum hosts an annual **Famine Summer School** (*irishfaminesummerschool.com*) to explore the legacy of the Famine. Held over a weekend in late June, the summer school features talks, films, exhibitions, live music and theatre.

Follow in the Footsteps of Emigrants
Walk from Strokestown to Dublin

Retracing the route walked by 1490 dispossessed tenants on their way to board emigrant ships to North America in 1847, the **National Famine Way** (*nationalfamineway.ie*) is a 165km walking and cycling trail that links Strokestown to Dublin.

From Strokestown, the trail takes back roads to cross the Shannon at Termonbarry, then follows the towpath of the Royal Canal all the way to the capital, finishing by the Famine Statues and the *Jeanie Johnston* famine ship on Dublin's Custom House Quay. Along the way, 30 bronze pairs of children's shoes mark significant points of interest.

Walking Ireland Tours (*walkingirelandtours.ie; per person €1450*) offer a nine-day self-guided hike along the trail, including B&B accommodation and luggage transfers.

JIM CALLERY

In 1979, local businessman Jim Callery bought Strokestown estate from Olive Pakenham-Mahon to provide space for his expanding trucking business. While raking through the contents of the house, he discovered a room full of papers relating to the estate during the Great Famine. Callery resolved to restore the house and use the archive of around 50,000 documents as the basis of the National Famine Museum.

Since 2015, the house, museum and estate have been managed by the Irish Heritage Trust; much restoration work has been undertaken, and many original items of furniture that had been sold off prior to 1979 were tracked down and bought back.

Jim Callery marked his 90th birthday in 2024 by walking the full length of the National Famine Way.

EATING AROUND STROKESTOWN: OUR PICKS

Keenans Hotel: Country pub and restaurant overlooking the Shannon at Termonbarry; it has been in the same family since 1838. *noon-8.30pm Mon-Sat, 12.30-7.30pm Sun* €€

Woodland Cafe: The coffee shop at Strokestown Park offers good cakes, sandwiches and hot dishes but can get very busy at lunchtime. *10am-5pm* €

Gleeson's Restaurant: Don't miss the sumptuous, slow-cooked Irish lamb stew at this iconic restaurant on the market square in Roscommon town. *9am-9pm* €€

Percy French Hotel: The best of a limited choice of eateries in Strokestown itself, with steaks, burgers, and fish and chips served. *noon-8pm* €€

Beyond Strokestown

Discover historic towns, an archaeological wonderland and an abandoned coal mine in rural County Roscommon.

Places
Tulsk p442
Roscommon Town p444
Boyle p445
Carrick-on-Shannon p445
Arigna p447

Studded with megalithic tombs, ringforts and mounds, Roscommon is shrouded in myth and history. To the west is Europe's most important Celtic site, while to the north is the historic town of Boyle. About 25km northwest of Boyle is Ireland's last coal mine – the underground tour here is way more interesting than it sounds.

A few kilometres east of Boyle is one of the great adventure playgrounds of the Midlands, home to a scenic lake surrounded by hiking paths and a treetop canopy trail. Over the border in County Leitrim is Carrick-on-Shannon, a hugely popular weekend destination and a centre for cruising holidays and dayboat trips on the Shannon, Ireland's longest river.

GETTING AROUND

You can travel between Boyle and Carrick-on-Shannon by train, while **Bus Éireann** *(buseireann.ie)* bus 468 runs from Strokestown to Carrick-on-Shannon. The frequent **Bus Éireann Expressway** *(expressway.ie)* buses from Dublin to Strokestown continue to Tulsk, from where it's an hour's walk to Rathcroghan Mound, but a car is the most convenient means of transport.

Tulsk
TIME FROM STROKESTOWN: 10MIN

Ireland's most important archaeological landscape

If you're interested in Irish prehistory, then **Rathcroghan** (Ráth Cruachan, meaning the 'Fort of Cruachan'; also called Cruachan Aí), near the village of Tulsk, is the archaeological

Ringfort, Rathcroghan

mother lode. Scattered across an area of just 6.5 sq km are some 240 archaeological sites spanning an impressive 5500 years of human history, including 37 Bronze and Iron Age burial mounds, numerous standing stones and ringforts, and a huge Iron Age ritual sanctuary. It was also one of the royal seats of the ancient Gaelic kings of Ireland, and the setting for some of the juiciest stories in Irish mythology.

Start at **Rathcroghan Visitor Centre** *(rath croghan.ie; adult/child €7/4)* in Tulsk, where an informative introduction to the sites is screened, plus an animated story about the great Irish epic of the Táin Bó Cúailnge (Cattle Raid of Cooley), which should appeal to all ages.

There are plenty of diagrams, photographs and maps that explain the significance of Rathcroghan; if you want to dig deeper, a very comprehensive guidebook is for sale that details all the latest research. As there's not all that much to see at the various sites other than mounds and ditches, and as many of the sites are on private property, it's well worth joining the 2½-hour guided tour *(weekdays only; adult/child €21/7)*; book online in advance.

Connacht's royal seat

If you opt not to take the guided tour, the easiest site to visit is **Rathcroghan Mound**; it's located right beside the N5, 4km northwest of Tulsk, with easy parking available. A grassy path leads to the circular, flat-topped mound, 80m in diameter, that sits on the highest point of a ridge commanding widespread views. Intensive surveys of the mound suggest it was topped by timber ramparts and approached via an avenue and ramp to the east. It was the focus of a major ritual centre and was the royal seat of the ancient kings of Connacht, on a par with – and possibly even more important than – the Hill of Tara to the east and Navan Fort to the north.

Entrance to the otherworld

Just 700m south of Rathcroghan Mound, but accessed via a minor road to the west, is **Oweynagat Cave** (Cave of the Cats); in Irish mythology, this place is known as a portal to the 'otherworld', the dwelling place of the Tuatha dé Danann – the semi-divine 'fairy folk' of Ireland. Later, 12th-century Christian scribes would refer to it as the 'Gates of Hell'.

As the cave is on private property, it can only be visited as part of the visitor centre's guided tour. Be aware that to enter you need to crawl on your hands and knees through a small, muddy hole (not for the claustrophobic!). Inside the entrance is a human-made chamber dating to the 1st century BCE that leads into a 37m-long natural limestone cave. A lintel stone bears an Ogham inscription, which has been translated as 'Fráoch, son of Medb'. According to legend, Queen Maeve (Medbh) – whose burial cairn is at the summit of Knocknarea (p382) in County Sligo – had her palace nearby at Rathcroghan.

IRELAND'S HIGH KINGS

Explore more sites associated with the high kings of Ireland at the **Hill of Uisneach** (p451), the **Hill of Tara** (p476) and **Navan Fort**.

SAMHAIN

The harvest festival of Samhain was a precarious time for the ancient Celts, who believed that the spirits of the underworld would wander through the gates of hell to walk among them. To ward off unwelcome visitors, they would disguise themselves as ghosts, carve ghoulish grins into turnips and go door to door collecting fuel for bonfires and loaves of bread to leave for the spirits. Fast-forward a few thousand years, and you've got Halloween, with pumpkins taking the place of turnips and sugary treats taking the place of bread. Curiously, Samhain has plenty of similarities to Day of the Dead celebrations, which came from Aztec and Toltec traditions.

QUEEN MAEVE & RATHCROGHAN

The figure of the Iron Age warrior Queen Maeve (Medbh) looms large in Irish myth and legend. Daughter of Eochu Feidlech, High King of Ireland, Maeve was made Queen of Connacht and ruled from Rathcroghan. The great Irish epic tale, the *Táin Bó Cúailnge* (Cattle Raid of Cooley), begins here when Maeve sends her army north to capture the legendary brown bull of Ulster, Donn Cúailnge. The bull is brought back to do battle with Finnbennach Ái, the equally impressive white bull of Maeve's husband. Legend states that the battle of the bulls took place at Ráth na dTarbh (Fort of the Bulls), a ringfort 600m west of Rathcroghan Mound.

Roscommon County Museum

Roscommon Town   TIME FROM STROKESTOWN: 20MIN

Discover local lore

Set in a former Presbyterian church (1863), the volunteer-run **Roscommon County Museum** (*roscommontownheritage.com; free*) features an idiosyncratic collection, including an inscribed 9th-century slab from St Coman's monastery and a superb medieval sheila-na-gig (carved female figure with exaggerated genitalia). The stained-glass Star of David window representing the Trinity is another unusual feature. Don't leave without hearing the story of Lady Betty, the 18th-century executioner. The museum is also the town's unofficial tourist office.

Explore historic ruins

The impressive ruins of the town's Norman **castle** stand alone in a field to the north of town, beautifully framed by the landscaped lawns and small lake of the town park. Built in 1269, the castle was almost immediately destroyed by Irish forces, and its turbulent history continued until the final surrender to Cromwell's forces in 1652, when the fortifications were then taken down. A conflagration in 1690 sealed the castle's fate.

EATING IN ROSCOMMON TOWN & BOYLE: OUR PICKS

Regan's Gastro Pub & Restaurant: Elegant gastro-pub in the middle of Roscommon town. *noon-9pm Mon-Thu, to 9.30pm Fri, from 12.30pm Sat, to 8.30pm Sun* €€

Rogue & Co Cafe: Gorgeous cafe in Roscommon town that serves tasty breakfasts, exquisite sandwiches and good wine. *9am-5pm Mon-Thu, to 6pm Fri & Sat, 10am-3pm Sun* €€

King House Tearooms: In Boyle's King House courtyard, this little cafe serves soups and sandwiches, and hot breakfasts till noon. *10am-4pm Mon, 9am-5pm Tue-Sat* €€

Bazaar: Cosmopolitan cafe in Boyle with a lunch menu ranging from sausage and mash to onion bhaji and falafel. *9am-6pm Mon-Sat* €€

Boyle

TIME FROM STROKESTOWN: 30MIN

Scenic town

A quiet town at the foot of the Curlew Mountains, Boyle makes a worthwhile stop on the road between Strokestown and Sligo. On the banks of the River Boyle is the finely preserved (and reputedly haunted) **Boyle Abbey** (*heritageireland.ie; adult/child €5/3*) founded in 1161 by the Cistercians and featuring a mix of architectural styles, including Romanesque and Gothic.

Sinister-looking mannequins at **King House** (*visitkinghouse.ie; adult/child €10/6*) tell the turbulent history of the Connacht kings, the town of Boyle and local landlords the King family, including a grim tale of tenant eviction during the Famine. Kids can try writing with a quill, build a vaulted ceiling from specially designed blocks, and try on replica Irish cloaks, breeches and leather shoes. One room is devoted to Hollywood star **Maureen O'Sullivan** (1911–98), who was born on nearby Main St.

The King House courtyard has a cafe and a large shop selling local crafts; it's also the location of Boyle's Saturday **farmers market**.

Adventures in the forest

Ireland's best-known adventure playground is **Lough Key Forest Park** (*loughkey.ie; free*) located just east of Boyle. It's a favourite with families for its adventure playground, rowing-boat hire and easy walking trails.

The park was once part of the **Rockingham Estate**, owned by the King family from the 17th century until 1957. **Rockingham Remembered** (*adult/child €10/5*) is a self-guided tour of the estate that leads visitors through eerie tunnels (built to hide servants from view), to a modern lakeside viewpoint tower and along a **treetop canopy walk** that rises 9m above the woodland floor.

Carrick-on-Shannon

TIME FROM STROKESTOWN: 30MIN

Cruising holidays

Carrick-on-Shannon has thrived as a boating centre since the completion of the **Shannon–Erne Waterway** in 1994, which linked Ireland's largest river with the two lakes that make up Lough Erne in Northern Ireland. A number of companies do a roaring trade for cruising holidays on the Shannon.

THE KINGS OF BOYLE

The history of Boyle is the history of the King family, former residents of King House.

In 1603, Staffordshire-born John King was granted land in Roscommon with the aim of 'reducing the Irish to obedience'. Over the next 150 years, through canny marriages and cold-blooded conquests, his descendants made their name and fortune, becoming one of the largest landowning families in Ireland.

Sir Henry King built the grand Georgian mansion of King House in Boyle in 1730, while the neoclassical palace of Rockingham House was built in 1810 for Robert King, 1st Viscount Lorton. When the latter burnt down in 1957, the estate was sold off and became Lough Key Forest Park.

EATING IN CARRICK-ON-SHANNON: OUR PICKS

Oarsman: This gastro-pub specialises in carefully prepped dishes such as pan-fried monkfish and slow-braised beef rib. *12.30-3pm Thu-Sat, 5-8.30pm Tue-Sat* €€€

Honestly Farm Kitchen: Ethical carnivore, vegetarian and plant-based cuisine in a glass space that once housed a KFC. *9am-7pm Sun-Thu, to 8pm Fri & Sat* €€

Red Bank: Artwork adorns the walls of this elegant eatery, but the real treat is in the tented dining space at the back. *5-9.30pm Thu & Fri, 1-9.30pm Sat, 1-8pm Sun* €€€

Olive Tree: Cosy nook in a hidden courtyard where hearty breakfasts, rustic toasties and homemade soups with homebaked bread are served. *9am-5pm Mon-Fri, 10am-3pm Sat & Sun* €

Cruising on the Shannon (p445)

HOW LEITRIM BEWITCHED A DUBLIN YOGA TEACHER

Noeleen Tyrrell is a yoga teacher living in Leitrim. Though the county gets relatively few visitors, she thinks it might just be the friendliest place in Ireland.
@noeleentyrrell_yoga

When I first moved to the county from Dublin, a friend from the US sent me a letter not knowing my address. But they knew the car I was driving, so the envelope read: 'Noeleen Tyrrell, the Red Mini, Dromahair'. And it arrived! From that moment, I was smitten. I'm still here more than 30 years later, and not a lot has changed. The wildness of the countryside, hedges unkempt and spilling with wild roses and columbine, a lake or mountain around every turn: this is Leitrim.

Emerald Star *(emeraldstar.ie)* has a huge range of boats, from budget options to luxury eight-berth cruisers. **Carrick Craft** *(cruise-ireland.com)* has 23 different boats to choose from, each with a range of berths (between two and 10). The minimum rental is three nights, and rates begin at around €500 for a two-berth boat. Previous experience is not required – you'll get a quick course in boat-handling before departure.

Boat trips

For day trips, **Moon River** *(moonriver.ie)* is your best bet. They rent out electric-powered day boats *(per full/half day €204/123)* that are ideal for a family picnic on the river. If you prefer to let someone else do the skippering, their **cruise boat** *(adult/child €21/11)* runs one-hour trips on the Shannon. Boats set off one to four times a day, depending on the season. Check online or at the information board on the quay for departure times.

EATING ALONG THE ROYAL CANAL: OUR PICKS

Bridge House: A lively pub on the eastern side of Mullingar that has an all-day menu, including breakfasts. *10.30am-8.30pm* €€

Rustic Inn: Head through to the back of this Abbeyshrule hotel and bar to find an elegant restaurant right on the canal bank. *5.45-9pm Mon-Sat, noon-8pm Sun* €€

Pewter Cafe: Part of Mullingar Pewter factory, located 8km east of Mullingar town; the outdoor terrace is popular with local cyclists. *9.30am-5pm Mon-Sat* €

Cunningham's: Country pub, general store and coffee shop near lock 22 of the Royal Canal; hungry cyclists feed on coffee, cake and toasties. *9am-5pm Mon-Sat, from 10am Sun* €

Arigna

TIME FROM STROKESTOWN: **45MIN**

Explore a genuine coal mine

Ireland's last working coal mine, operational from 1765 to 1990, is remembered at the **Arigna Mining Experience** *(arigna miningexperience.ie; adult/child €15/8)*, set in the hills with views over Lough Allen, 20km north of Carrick-on-Shannon. The coal extracted here was originally used for smelting iron ore mined in the nearby hills, then exported to Dublin via the River Shannon and the Royal Canal, before finally being used to fuel the Arigna Power Station.

Your visit begins with a short film, then you don a hard hat and enter the mine for a 45-minute guided underground tour. The coal seams here are near-horizontal, so the mine shafts extend into the mountain rather than downwards. It's an oppressive place, with a maze of dark, dripping caverns, the roofs supported by timber props. The coal seams were barely 50cm thick, so miners had to lay on their sides and hack out the coal with a pick and shovel – powered tools didn't arrive until the 1960s. The guides are ex-miners who really bring home the gruelling working conditions and dangers – at one point, the lights go out and there's simulated blast of explosives.

Walk the Miners Way

Wandering for 118km across north Roscommon, east Sligo and mid-Leitrim, the **Miners Way and Historical Trail** *(minerswayandhistoricaltrail.ie)* is a network of well-signposted tracks and hill passes that follow the routes taken by coal and iron miners on their way to work.

There are three looped trails of various lengths; the 62km Miners Way follows paths used by miners working in the Arigna coal mines and makes a circuit from Arigna to Keadue, Ballyfarnon and Corrie Mountain before returning to Arigna. The trail usually takes around three days to complete; a brochure with maps is available from local tourist offices.

THE GRAND & ROYAL CANALS

The Grand Canal threads its way from Dublin through Tullamore to join the River Shannon at Shannonbridge, a total of 132km through relatively unpopulated countryside.

The 145km-long Royal Canal passes over a massive aqueduct near Leixlip before it joins the Shannon at Cloondara in County Longford.

The two canals revolutionised transport in Ireland in the early 19th century, but their heyday was short-lived, as they were soon superseded by the railway.

Today, the canals are popular for cruising and fishing, while their banks are ideal for walking and cycling, and they pass through some truly picturesque villages. Adventurous cyclists can ride from Dublin to the Shannon along either the Royal or the Grand, and return along the other canal.

Belvedere House & Gardens

GEORGIAN MANSION | WOODLAND TRAILS | INTRIGUING STORIES

GETTING AROUND
Belvedere House is 7.5km south of Mullingar, served by **Local Link** *(transportforireland.ie/tfi-local-link)* bus 819 that runs between Athlone and Mullingar.

You can cycle from Mullingar town centre to Belvedere House in just over half an hour (10km); the most traffic-free route is to head west along the Royal Canal towpath for 4km to Kilpatrick Bridge, then turn left on the L1137, and right on the L1136; the entrance to Belvedere is on the right just before you reach the N52. There is bike parking at the visitor centre; cycling is not allowed within the parkland.

In a country stacked with gorgeous Georgian mansions, Belvedere House isn't just one of the most impressive examples of the style, it's also a pile that comes with its fair share of rattling skeletons. Even today, more than 250 years after the events that cemented its place in local lore, the house's potted history makes it one of the most compelling stops along Ireland's Georgian trail, as well as one of the Midlands' blockbuster attractions. Another huge aspect of Belvedere's appeal is its location on the shores of beautiful Lough Ennell – proof that the 18th-century landed gentry really did have their pick of the best places to build their homes.

Surrounding the house are 65 hectares of landscaped gardens, parkland and woodland trails, and there's a cafe and exhibition centre with regular events, plus a zipline and children's playground if the young ones get bored with Belvedere's rich history.

A Georgian Masterpiece
Splendour and sadness
In 1740, Robert Rochfort, the 1st Earl of Belvedere, engaged the services of noted architect Richard Cassels to build him a hunting lodge, or 'bolt hole', by the shores of Lough Ennell. The result was the immense **Belvedere House** *(belvedere-house.ie; adult/child €8/free)*, featuring semicircular bow ends and rococo ceilings with some of the finest stucco work in Ireland in the upper rooms (added around 1760 by French artist Barthelemij Cramilion). Downstairs is one of the most beautiful dining-rooms in the country, with plenty of Irish oak and a huge fireplace lined with Italian Carrara marble.

While the house has a stately grandeur, Robert's legacy is one of cruelty and horror – he was later known as 'The Wicked Earl'. As you exit the visitor centre into the grounds, look to your left and you will see chimney stacks poking above the trees. That is **Tudenham House**, which belonged to Robert's

Jealous Wall, Belvedere House

brother, George. Robert was so jealous of his brother's bigger mansion that he ordered Ireland's largest folly to be built so that it would block the view of Tudenham from his own house. This ready-made 'ruin' later became known as the **Jealous Wall**.

But Robert's wickedness went beyond envy of George. Suspecting that his wife Mary, whom he largely neglected after she bore him a daughter instead of the son he so desperately wanted, was having an affair with his other brother Arthur, he kept her locked up in Gaulstown House, with only servants for company. There she remained for 31 years, slowly going insane. When Robert died in 1774, Mary was finally released, whereupon she is said to have asked, 'Is the tyrant dead?'

At the time of research, the interior of the house remained closed to the public after flood damage; no date was given for reopening.

Belvedere's Victorian Gardens

Wander the beautifully landscaped grounds

Behind Belvedere House, you will find a statue of **Agu the bear** and an arched gateway leading into a little corner of paradise. The **walled garden** is a kaleidoscope of shape and colour, housing a Victorian glasshouse, a kitchen and herb garden, a rose garden and a garden of Himalayan plants collected by Belvedere's last private owner, Charles Kenneth Howard-Bury.

Exit at the far end through a fairy wood and continue on the **Inner Woodland Trail** (1.3km) to another 19th-century folly, the **Gothic Arch**. Then return along the shores of Lough Ennell, through beautifully landscaped parkland. Be sure to climb the steps to the **Terraces** in front of Belvedere to enjoy the lake views that its architect envisaged back in 1740.

Access to the walled garden and grounds is included in the admission fee for Belvedere House.

BELVEDERE'S ADVENTURER OWNER

Belvedere's last private owner, **Charles Kenneth Howard-Bury** (1881–1963), was a soldier, big-game hunter, explorer and mountaineer. He fought with distinction in WWI, but only after he hunted and killed a man-eating tiger in India that had devoured 21 men. He led the 1921 Everest reconnaissance expedition, where he found footprints that were declared to be those of the Abominable Snowman.

He bought Belvedere House and lived there with a younger actor, Rex Bart Beaumont, aka 'Sexy Rexy', and a pet bear called Agu that he wrestled daily in the gardens. Bury died aged 82, leaving Beaumont to eventually sell the house to the Irish state in 1980.

☑ TOP TIP

Check out Belvedere House's calendar of events, which span farmers markets to summertime concerts. Most events take place on Sundays; during National Heritage Week (p452) in August, free behind-the-scenes tours take place.

Beyond Belvedere House & Gardens

Rural Westmeath sits at the geographical centre of Ireland, home to miraculous ruins and mystical ancient sites.

Places
Fore p450
Castlepollard p451
Hill of Uisneach p451

Belvedere House is only a few kilometres south of the county town of Mullingar, which has few sights of its own but is a busy transport hub for the area and a good jumping-off point for exploring the wider region. The Royal Canal Way extends in either direction from the town, while the Old Rail Trail Greenway provides a cycle link to Athlone. East of the handsome town of Castlepollard lies a wonderful monastic site set in a peaceful valley, while to its west is an imposing castle with beautiful gardens. West of Mullingar is the magical Hill of Uisneach, an ancient site steeped in history and mythology.

GETTING AROUND

Local Link bus WR02 *(transportforireland.ie/tfi-local-link)* runs three times a day from Mullingar to Castlepollard, from where you can walk to Tullynally Castle (2.7km, 40 minutes) and Fore (5km, 70 minutes). **Local Link** bus 819 runs five times daily between Athlone and Mullingar, passing the Hill of Uisneach; just ask the driver to let you off at the entrance.

Fore
TIME FROM BELVEDERE HOUSE: **35MIN**

The seven wonders of Fore

Little explored but worth every effort to see, the emerald-green **Fore Valley**, 5km east of Castlepollard, is a stunning spot that is home to atmospheric monastic ruins. The valley sees few visitors, and is all the better for the peace and quiet.

In 630 CE, St Feichin founded a monastery just outside the village of Fore. There's nothing left of this early settlement, but three later buildings in the valley are closely associated with the 'Seven Wonders of Fore'. The oldest of the three buildings is **St Feichin's Church**, just above the car park. Above the Cyclopean entrance is a huge lintel stone carved with a Greek cross and thought to weigh about 2.5 tonnes. It's said to have been put into place by St Feichin's devotions – the wonder of 'the stone raised by prayer'.

A path runs steeply uphill from the church to a tiny Victorian gothic chapel that hides a 15th-century **Anchorite Cell** – the wonder of the 'anchorite in a stone' – which was lived in by a succession of hermits. The chapel is locked; to see inside, you need to ask for the key at the Seven Wonders pub in the village (which doesn't open until 3.30pm on weekdays, 2pm on Saturdays and 1pm on Sundays).

Visible across the fields are the extensive remains of a 13th-century **Benedictine Priory**, the wonder that is 'the monastery built on a bog'. An information board beside the car park explains the story of the Seven Wonders.

Walk St Fechin's Way
A 3km looped walk that is **St Fechin's Way** starts from the Priory car park, leading across the fields to the Benedictine Priory, whose walls still stand around its atmospheric cloister, capped with twin towers; at the back is a well-preserved medieval dovecote. The path then leads past several memorial benches, commemorative trees and chainsaw sculptures over a small hill and back through the village with its two pubs. Allow one hour.

Learn the secrets of poitín
If the weather is unkind, you can retreat to **Fore Distillery** *(foredistillery.ie; tours per person €20)*, just 1.5km west of Fore village. Established in 2021, the distillery produces Fore Valley Golden Irish Rum, White Irish Rum and Irish Poitín. The onsite **Barrel & Bean** cafe is a pleasant spot for lunch, with views over Lough Glore from the upstairs room (binoculars provided for birdwatchers).

Castlepollard
TIME FROM BELVEDERE HOUSE: **30MIN**
Gorgeous castle gardens
The imposing Gothic Revival **Tullynally Castle & Gardens** *(tullynallycastle.ie)*, seat of the Pakenham family, is 3km west of Castlepollard. Although the castle is still in use as a private home, a 45-minute guided tour *(adult/child €16.50/8.50)* runs on Thursdays, Fridays and Saturdays from May to September, allowing you to see the dining room, library and Victorian laundry, and hear stories about the illustrious Pakenhams. Tour tickets include admission to the 12 hectares of gorgeous gardens; on non-tour days, pay for garden tickets separately *(adult/child €8.50/4)*.

Hill of Uisneach
TIME FROM BELVEDERE HOUSE: **35MIN**
The mystical centre of Ireland
Despite being less visited than Newgrange and Tara, the **Hill of Uisneach** *(uisneach.ie; guided tour adult/child €15/free)* is perhaps even more important. Sitting in the middle of Ireland, only a few kilometres from the island's exact geographical centre, it was described by Giraldus Cambrensis, the 13th-century Welsh priest-historian, as *umbilicus Hiberniae*, the navel of Ireland. The hill is part of a privately owned working farm, so the only way to visit it is on a two-hour guided tour, which runs at 11am Saturdays and Sundays from April to September (Sundays only October to March). The hill is beside the R390, 16km west of Mullingar.

There's not a lot of physical evidence to see on the hill – apart from some mounds, earthworks, and the astonishing view over 20 counties in 40 shades of green – so it's the storytelling that makes the tour. And the stories are good. This is the sacred centre of Ireland, a place where myth and history intersect, where laws were made, and where the high kings

---

WHY I LOVE THE FORE VALLEY

Fionn Davenport, writer, on the charms of Fore.
@fionndavenport

My parents introduced me to the Fore Valley when I was a small boy, and I remember how beautiful and quiet it was, and how it all just seemed to exist without any kind of fanfare. As Irish tourism developed apace in the decades that followed, the Fore Valley stayed pretty much as it was when I was a kid. There's a trail now and a coffee shop, but otherwise, it's just as it was when my parents first brought me. Every time I go now, I find myself striking up random conversations with other walkers – about the weather, my camera, or how lovely my dog is. This kind of casual friendliness is everything I love about Ireland.

NATIONAL HERITAGE WEEK

From small beginnings in 2005, Ireland's **National Heritage Week** (heritageweek.ie) has grown into a nationwide celebration of history, culture, art and architecture, with around 2500 events taking place in recent years. Held around the third week of August, Heritage Week includes concerts, talks, guided tours, nature walks, sporting events, family activities and much more. There are free guided tours of historical buildings and archeological sites, and an Open Doors programme that allows people to explore the hidden heritage of many interesting buildings that are normally closed to the public. The website has a searchable database of events and locations so you can find out what's happening in whatever part of Ireland you happen to be in.

Statue of Ériu, on the Hill of Uisneach (p451)

of Ireland were ritually married to the land in the form of Ériu, the goddess of Irish sovereignty (who gives Éire – Ireland – its name).

After visiting the ritual sites on the summit, the tour finishes at the **Cat Stone**, a glacial limestone boulder that sits within an Iron Age ring barrow. In Gaelic it is called Ail na Míreann (Stone of the Divisions), as it's said to mark the meeting point of the four ancient provinces of Ireland, and the burial place of Ériu.

Ancient festival of fire

Bealtaine is one of the four key Celtic festivals that mark the passing of the seasons along with Imbolc (February; the first stirrings of spring), Lughnasadh (August; the harvest festival) and Samhain (November; the coming of winter, and the forerunner of Halloween). Traditionally held on 1 May, Bealtaine marked the coming of summer, and was celebrated with music, dancing and bonfires. Since 2009, the Hill of Uisneach has hosted its own **Bealtaine Fire Festival** (uisneach.ie/bealtaine), a huge family event usually held on a Saturday in early May.

# Places We Love to Stay

€ Budget €€ Midrange €€€ Top End

Athlone

MAP p429

Bastion B&B € Crisp, clean, white-on-white interiors are a canvas for eclectic artwork; ask for the split-level loft room. Rates are room-only; buy breakfast in the cafe across the street.

Riverdale House B&B €€ Lovely Edwardian house with period fireplaces, plasterwork and wainscoting; excellent breakfasts prepared by the owner, who trained as a chef under Neven Maguire.

Lough Ree

Hodson Bay Hotel €€ Huge resort hotel on the shores of Lough Ree, 7.5km north of Athlone. The Baysports activities centre is directly in front of the hotel.

Wineport Lodge €€€ Modern-rustic luxury lodge near Glasson, on the east side of the lough. Onsite amenities include hot tubs, boat trips, a spa and a fine-dining restaurant.

Glasson Lakehouse €€€ Spacious and stylish resort hotel with a spa, heated outdoor pool and 18-hole championship golf course.

Birr

Brendan House €€ Packed with knickknacks, books, rugs, art and antiques, this Georgian townhouse is a bohemian delight; the owners are artists who run the Tin Jug Studio.

Dooly's Hotel €€ Originally a coaching house in Birr's main square, Dooly's has an inviting, homey feel and old-world charm, with Georgian-style furnishings.

Kinnitty Castle Hotel €€€ Stunning neogothic castle 15km east of Birr, with 37 superbly atmospheric rooms, all with period furnishings; the State Rooms have ornate carved-wood beds and cast iron roll-top bathtubs.

Beyond Strokestown

Roundwood House €€€ An 18th-century Palladian mansion and 17th-century farmhouse with a private library set in secluded woods; convivial communal dinners provide the chance to mingle with other guests.

Castle Durrow €€€ Stately 18th-century country-house hotel offering activities including tennis, archery, clay pigeon shooting and fishing.

Ballyfin House €€€ This opulent Regency mansion on a vast private estate is one of Ireland's most luxurious hotels; some of the chandelier-lit, antique-furnished guest rooms have four-poster beds.

Clonalis House €€€ Come for a guided tour of this historic Georgian mansion in Castlerea, and stay in one of the four delightful self-catering cottages.

Kilronan Castle €€€ West of Arigna Mines, this luxury hotel is one of Ireland's finest, with neogothic halls, elegant rooms with four-poster beds, and antique furniture galore.

Carrick-on-Shannon

Bush Hotel € Charming heritage hotel dating from the 18th century, with bedrooms given a contemporary design makeover; Michael Collins stayed in Room 1 in 1917.

Drumhierney Woodland Hideaway €€ Eco-friendly alpine-style lodges, each sleeping six to eight people, spread around 40 hectares of dense woodland 7km north of Carrick.

Lough Rynn Castle €€€ Magnificent 19th-century castle with antique-filled bedrooms, including two sumptuous suites – one with a Jacuzzi and private crenellated roof terrace.

Beyond Belvedere House & Gardens

Railway House € Good-value, family-run B&B in a central location beside the Royal Canal. Rooms are basic but clean and tidy.

Annebrook House Hotel €€ Right in the town centre, the hub of this hotel is an elegant 17th-century manor house; there are family-friendly apartments, some with balconies overlooking the River Brosna.

Greville Arms Hotel €€ Dating from 1884, this grande-dame hotel in Mullingar has 40 spacious rooms; James Joyce was a frequent guest.

Left: Newgrange (p463); right: Cavan Way (p479)

Researched by
Neil Wilson

Meath, Louth, Monaghan & Cavan

THE STORY OF IRELAND

Visit the fertile fields that bear traces of Irish history from prehistoric times, and those that bore the bloody battles that defined modern Ireland.

Irish civilisation was born in the fields of Meath and Louth, where the earliest settlers made their homes. Although this area is now largely part of the ever-widening Dublin commuter belt, the earliest inhabitants' legacies endure at the mystical tombs of Brú na Bóinne and Loughcrew – both of which predate the Pyramids of Giza in Egypt – and on the Hill of Tara, the seat of Ireland's high kings and the gateway to the Celtic otherworld.

By the banks of the quiet River Boyne is a monument to the most decisive battle in Irish history. In 1690, the Protestant forces of William of Orange defeated the Catholic army of James II, defining the course of Irish history for the next 300 years and counting.

Following St Patrick's arrival, the faithful built abbeys, high crosses and round towers to protect their treasured manuscripts from Viking raids. Magnificent ruins at Mellifont and Monasterboice recall a time when Ireland was known as the 'land of saints and scholars'.

To the northwest, the undulating hills and fish-filled lakes of Counties Cavan and Monaghan are wild and remote, making them the ideal location for splendid walking trails amid rugged scenery and unspoilt landscapes, scenes that inspired one of Ireland's greatest modern poets, Patrick Kavanagh, and whose legacy is maintained at one of the best interpretative centres in the country.

THE MAIN AREAS

BRÚ NA BÓINNE
Stunning Neolithic complex. **p460**

TRIM
A classic medieval fortification. **p473**

COUNTY CAVAN
The lakeland county. **p478**

> **County Cavan, p478**
> An activity-filled playground on land and water, plus some of the best dining in the country.

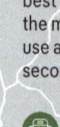

CAR
Driving is the best way of getting around, as many of the counties' best attractions are outside of the main towns. To get there, use a mix of motorways and secondary roads.

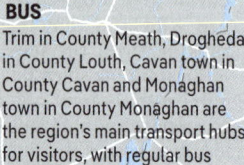

BUS
Trim in County Meath, Drogheda in County Louth, Cavan town in County Cavan and Monaghan town in County Monaghan are the region's main transport hubs for visitors, with regular bus services.

Find Your Way

These four counties stretch from the northeast right into the middle of the country, skirting the border with Northern Ireland. Transport links are excellent in Meath and into Louth, but get slightly thinner the more inland you go, making getting around by car a better bet.

Plan Your Time

Discover the wonders of prehistory at Brú na Bóinne and Hill of Tara, go medieval in Old Mellifont and Trim, and get outdoors in County Cavan.

St Patrick's Day parade, Drogheda (p466)

A Day Trip from Dublin

● Make sure you book at least a week in advance to get a place on the 9am tour at **Brú na Bóinne** visitor centre; choose the 'Brú na Bóinne Tour + Newgrange Chamber' option on the booking site. This will give you plenty of time to see the exhibition in the visitor centre, and get a guided tour of the Neolithic passage tombs of Knowth and **Newgrange** (p463). The tour will finish about 1pm; make the 10-minute drive west to Slane for lunch at **Inside Out** (p470) if it's the weekend, or at the **Conyngham Arms** (p485) if not.

● Spend an hour strolling around the summit of the **Hill of Slane** (p470) then drive to the **Hill of Tara** (p476) to experience Ireland's most sacred site, before returning to Dublin.

Seasonal Highlights

The summer and winter solstices are widely celebrated at the region's prehistoric passage tombs. St Patrick's Day in Drogheda is also a big deal.

MARCH
The **St Patrick's Day parade** on 17 March in Drogheda is one of the biggest in the country, with added events taking over the town centre for a couple of days.

APRIL
Huge crowds gather to watch the Paschal Fire being lit with great ceremony by the local priest on the summit of the **Hill of Slane** (p470) on Holy Saturday (the day before Easter Sunday).

JUNE
People flock to the **Hill of Tara** (p476) to watch the dawn of the longest day of the year, reenact ancient summer solstice rituals and participate in communal activities like bonfires, music and dancing.

Three Days in the Ancient East

● Heading north from Dublin, **Drogheda** (p466) is worth an hour or two before visiting the site of the pivotal **Battle of the Boyne** (p467) and the atmospheric monastic sites of **Monasterboice** (p468) and **Old Mellifont Abbey** (p468).

● If the ancient aura of **Brú na Bóinne** (p460) and **Hill of Slane** (p470) has whetted your appetite for things prehistoric, continue west to the scenic and mysterious **Loughcrew Cairns** (p471). Make sure to stop at **Trim Castle** (p474) and if time permits take a guided **kayaking tour** (p475) on the River Boyne.

● Round off this tour of Meath and Louth with a trip to the **Hill of Tara** (p476), the sacred seat of the high kings of Ireland.

A Week to Explore

● After spending three or four days in counties Meath and Louth, head northwest to the great outdoors of **County Cavan**. Explore the hiking trails and Neolithic tombs in **Cavan Burren Park** (p478), visit the source of Ireland's longest river at **Shannon Pot** (p480), and canoe to an island castle at **Killykeen Forest Park** (p480).

● Check opening times and book well in advance to enjoy a fine dining experience at either **MacNean House & Restaurant** (p480) or the **Olde Post Inn** (p480) before heading east to take in the highlights of County Monaghan – the **Patrick Kavanagh Centre** (p482) in Inniskeen, the **Monaghan County Museum** (p483) and the **Carrickmacross Lace Gallery** (p482).

AUGUST
History enthusiasts gather for battle reenactments and 'living history' events, where you can get an insight into the life of a 17th-century soldier at the site of the **Battle of the Boyne** (p467).

SEPTEMBER
Inniskeen sees crowds turn up for a weekend of music and poetry at the **Patrick Kavanagh Centre** (p482).

OCTOBER
Held over four nights at the end of October, the **Púca Festival** (p475) sees the streets of Trim come alive with music, processions and bonfires.

DECEMBER
Enter the lottery to view the **winter solstice sunrise** at **Newgrange** (p463), when a shaft of sunlight illuminates the passage grave, or watch remotely by livestream.

Brú na Bóinne

MEGALITHIC ART | DEEP HISTORY | ON THE FARM

Halfway between the busy town of Drogheda and the quieter village of Slane, the vast Neolithic necropolis known as Brú na Bóinne (Boyne Palace) is one of the most extraordinary sites in Europe. A thousand years older than Stonehenge, it's a powerful testament to the mind-boggling achievements of prehistoric humankind. The complex, a UNESCO World Heritage Site, was built to house the remains of those in the top social tier, and its tombs were the largest artificial structures in Ireland until the construction of the Anglo-Norman castles 4000 years later. The area consists of many different sites; the two principal ones are Newgrange and Knowth.

Over the centuries, the tombs decayed, were covered by grass and trees, and were plundered by everybody from Vikings to Victorian treasure hunters, whose carved initials can be seen on the great stones of Newgrange.

GETTING AROUND

Trains on the Dublin–Belfast line stop in Drogheda. County Meath has numerous **Bus Éireann** *(buseireann.ie)* services but to get off the beaten track, your own wheels are best. Tour companies hit the main sights, and most depart from Dublin. **Local Link** *(transportforireland.ie/tfi-local-link)* 163 bus goes from Drogheda to Brú na Bóinne (35 minutes, six times daily) via the Battle of the Boyne visitor centre, and departs from Drogheda train station and opposite the bus station.

☑ TOP TIP

Brú na Bóinne can get very crowded. As there are only a set number of tour slots, you may not be guaranteed a visit to either of the passage tombs. Tickets must be booked in advance online. It's best to visit early in the morning or visit midweek.

Take a Guided Tour of the Boyne Valley
One of Ireland's best guided tours

An alternative to visiting Newgrange on your own is to join a tour organised by **Mary Gibbons Tours** *(newgrangetours.com; per person €75)*. These daily tours depart from Dublin and take in both Newgrange and the Hill of Tara. Expert guides offer a fascinating insight into Celtic and pre-Celtic life in Ireland. But you don't have to just take our word for how good they are: Eamonn P Kelly, the former Keeper of Antiquities at the National Museum of Ireland, considered them the 'most detailed of all the tours' and 'an accurate account of Ireland's history'.

Ponder the Secrets of Dowth
The third and least famous passage tomb

On another hilltop 1.5km northeast of Newgrange sits yet another megalithic passage tomb. The circular mound at **Dowth** *(discoverireland.ie/meath/dowth)* is similar in size

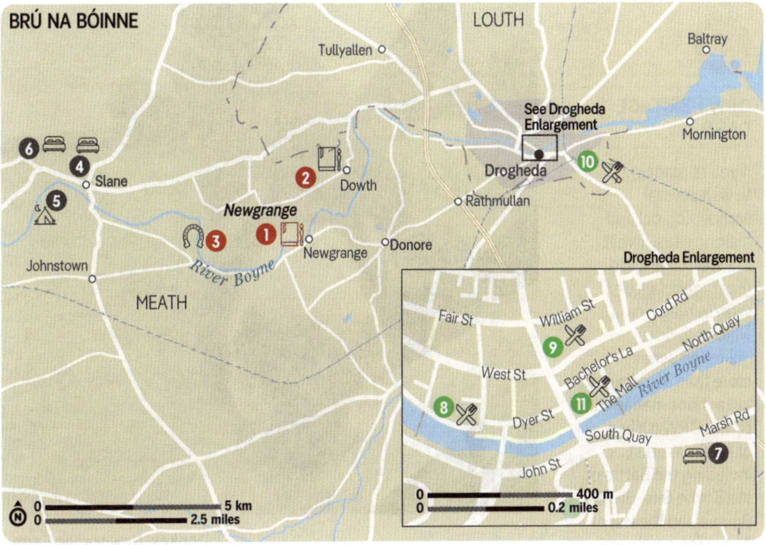

BRÚ NA BÓINNE

⭐ HIGHLIGHTS
1. Newgrange

● SIGHTS
2. Dowth
3. Newgrange Farm

● SLEEPING
4. Conyngham Arms
5. Rock Farm Slane
6. Slane Farm Hostel
7. Spoon & the Stars

● EATING
8. Aisha's Bistro
9. Ariosa
10. Black Bull
11. Salthouse Brasserie

to Newgrange – about 63m in diameter – but is slightly taller at 14m high. Due to safety issues, the interior passage is closed to visitors, but you can walk around the outside. There's a small parking area beside the L1607 road leading from the N51 west of Drogheda.

Dowth has two entrance passages leading to separate chambers (both sealed), and a 24m early Christian underground passage at either end, which connect with the western passage. This 8m-long passage leads into a small cruciform chamber, in which a recess acts as an entrance to an additional series of small compartments, a feature unique to Dowth. To the southwest is the entrance to a shorter passage and a smaller chamber.

The site has suffered badly at the hands of everyone from road builders and treasure hunters to amateur archaeologists, who scooped out the centre of the tumulus in the 19th century. For a time, Dowth even had a tearoom ignobly perched on its summit. Don't miss the view from the top.

MORE PASSAGE TOMBS
Ireland has at least 230 known passage tombs, with the best-known at **Loughcrew Cairns** (p471), and at **Carrowkeel** (p384) and **Carrowmore** (p383) in County Sligo.

OPW HERITAGE CARD

If you're planning to visit several archaeological and historic sites, invest in a **Heritage Card** *(heritageireland.ie/visit/heritage-card)*, which provides unlimited access to more than 45 different attractions managed by the OPW (Office of Public Works), including the Battle of the Boyne Site, Brú na Bóinne and the Hill of Tara. Free admission also covers guided tours.

The card is valid for one year and is available at all participating sites, as well as at tourist offices in major towns and cities. The card costs €40 for adults and €90 for a family of two adults and up to five children, so it's worth totting up how much you plan on visiting before investing in one.

Donkey, Newgrange Farm

Living the Farming Life

Family-friendly animal encounters

When you've reached your limit with Neolithic passage graves, the 135-hectare working **Newgrange Farm** *(newgrangefarm.com; adult/family of four €10.50/38)* is a great option, especially for kids who've had quite enough of prehistoric ruins. From mid-March to August this family-run operation allows visitors to feed the ducks, lambs and goats; milk a cow; pet a rabbit; and take a tractor ride. Children's play areas include a straw maze and toy tractors, and there are indoor and outdoor picnic areas, and a cafe. Sunday at 3pm is a very special time when the 'sheep derby' is run, with teddy bear 'jockeys' tied to the animals' backs. Visiting children are made 'owners' of individual sheep for the race. The farm is signposted from the N51.

EATING IN DROGHEDA: OUR PICKS

Black Bull: Cosy pub doing solidly good standards, such as chargrilled steaks, burgers and fish and chips. *11am-8.30pm Mon-Fri, to 9pm Sat, to 8pm Sun* €€

Salthouse Brasserie: Solid breakfasts and lunch options, freshly squeezed orange juice and good coffee. *8.30am-5pm Mon-Fri, from 9am Sat, from 10am Sun* €

Aisha's Bistro: Mediterranean dishes from falafel to pizza as well as a great kids' menu. BYOB. *6-9.30pm Sun-Thu, to 10pm Fri & Sat* €€

Ariosa: Excellent coffee to kickstart the day, plus pastries (awesome almond croissants!) and sourdough toasties. *8am-5pm Mon-Sat, 9am-4pm Sun* €

Newgrange

TOP EXPERIENCE

Newgrange & Knowth

A startling 80m in diameter and 13m high, Newgrange's circular stone ramparts, topped by a grassy dome and fronted by a wall of blazing white quartz, look eerily futuristic. Underneath lies the finest Stone Age passage tomb in Ireland, perched atop a hill that dominates a bend in the River Boyne. Dating from around 3200 BCE, it predates Egypt's Pyramids of Giza by some six centuries.

Visitor Centre

Built in a spiral design echoing Newgrange, the visitor centre houses interactive exhibits on prehistoric Ireland and its passage tombs. It's a terrific primer on the Neolithic culture, landscapes and monuments at Brú na Bóinne, and it preps you for your visit to Newgrange, Knowth or both; tours to the sites leave from here. The centre has regional tourism info, an excellent cafe, plus a bookshop and souvenir shop. Upstairs, a glassed-in observation mezzanine looks out over Newgrange.

DON'T MISS

Visitor Centre Exhibition

River Boyne Wildlife

Lunar Stone

Knowth viewpoint

Newgrange Spiral Kerbstone

Newgrange Tomb Chamber

Newgrange Quartz Wall

PRACTICALITIES

- heritageireland.ie
- adult/child from €5/3–€18/12
- 9am-4.15pm Oct-Feb, 9.30am-4.45pm Mar-Apr, 9am-5.45 May-Aug, 9am-5.15pm Sep

NEWGRANGE WINTER SOLSTICE

At 8.20am around the time of the winter solstice (between 18 and 23 December), the rays of the rising sun shine through the roof-box above the entrance to Newgrange creep slowly down the long passage and illuminate the tomb chamber for 17 minutes. There is little doubt that this is one of the country's most memorable, even mystical, experiences.

TOP TIPS

- All visits to Brú na Bóinne start at the Brú na Bóinne Visitor Centre, from where there's a shuttle bus to the tombs.

- Tickets must be booked in advance online for a defined time slot.

- If you turn up at either Newgrange or Knowth first, you'll be sent to the visitor centre, 4km from either site. Walking is discouraged, as the lanes are narrow and dangerous due to passing tour buses.

- Expect to spend an hour at the visitor centre, an hour at Knowth, and an hour at Newgrange.

- Most of the tour is outdoors with no shelter, so bring rain gear just in case.

River Boyne

You begin your tour with a 10-minute walk from the visitor centre over a footbridge that spans the River Boyne. The water meadows and riverbank willows here are alive with bird life while the Boyne itself is rich in brown trout and Atlantic salmon. The path leads gently up to a waiting area where you board a shuttle bus that will take you to the tombs.

Knowth

It might not have the same instant appeal as Newgrange, but the burial mound at Knowth is larger and more complex. It also has the greatest collection of passage-grave art ever uncovered in Western Europe – something like 60% of Europe's megalithic art is here in this one site.

A guide will meet you and show you the engraved kerbstones around the perimeter of the mound, including the **Lunar Stone** whose squiggly lines and circles have been interpreted as recording the phases of the moon and the rise and fall of the tide. Entry to the passage tomb is not allowed for safety reasons. Afterwards you can climb to the top of the mound – here you can grasp how this site commanded the surrounding landscape with the hills of Tara and Slane evident, and the Wicklow Mountains on the southern horizon.

The site was not excavated until the 1960s, when archaeologists cleared a passage leading to the central chamber, which at 34m is much longer than the one at Newgrange. In 1968, a 40m passage was unearthed on the opposite side of the mound. The site dates to around 3200 BCE, but human activity at Knowth continued for thousands of years after its construction, which accounts for the site's complexity.

Newgrange: The Passage Tomb

Another shuttle bus will take you from Knowth to Newgrange, where a guide will deliver a short briefing before entering the passage tomb. Expect to spend 15 minutes inside the tomb and 15 minutes looking around outside. A superbly carved **kerbstone with double and triple spirals** guards the tomb's main entrance; the area around it has been reconstructed with stairs so that visitors don't have to clamber over it to enter. Above the entrance is a slit, or **roof-box**, which lets light in at the winter solstice sunrise.

You walk down the narrow, claustrophobic **passage**, which is 19m long and lined with 43 stone uprights, some of them engraved, to reach the tomb chamber. There are three recesses here, and in these are large basin stones that are so big they must have been placed here before the rest of the tomb was built around them. They once held human remains and funeral offerings of beads and pendants, but these were stolen long before the archaeologists arrived. Above your head, more massive stones support a 6m-high **corbelled roof**. A clever and complex drainage system of sloping stone slabs means that not a drop of water has penetrated the interior in 40 centuries.

Your guide will switch the lights off for a **simulation of sunrise** on 21 December (winter solstice) when sunlight enters the roof-box and strikes the back wall of the chamber. The tomb's precise alignment with the sun at the time of the winter solstice suggests it was also designed to act as a calendar.

Newgrange: The Exterior

The spiral-engraved kerbstone at the entrance is matched by another beautifully decorated stone at the exact opposite side of the mound. Some experts say that a ring of standing stones encircled the mound, forming a great circle about 100m in diameter, but only 12 of these stones remain, with traces of others below ground level.

Holding the whole structure together are the 97 boulders of the **kerbstone ring**, designed to stop the 200,000 tonnes of earth and stone in the mound from collapsing outwards. Eleven of these are decorated with motifs similar to those on the main entrance stone, although only three have extensive carvings.

The most striking feature of the exterior is the massive **wall of white quartz** stones that flanks either side of the entrance – this structure was designed to be seen from afar. The quartz was originally obtained from Wicklow, 70km south; in an age before horse and wheel, it was transported by sea and then up the River Boyne.

When the mound was excavated, the quartz stones lay scattered on the ground. Experimental archaeologists 'reverse engineered' the wall by rebuilding short sections using different techniques and seeing how the stones fell. The wall you see is their best guess at how it looked originally.

SOLSTICE LOTTERY

To be in with a chance of witnessing the Newgrange sunrise on one of six mornings around the solstice, join 30,000 others in the free lottery, where 50 names are drawn in late September. Fill out the form at the Brú na Bóinne Visitor Centre or email brunaboinne@opw.ie. Alternatively, you can join a livestream of the event.

Kerbstone, Knowth

Beyond Brú na Bóinne

The region surrounding the Boyne Valley is a shallow bowl packed with history and heritage.

Places
Drogheda & Around p466
Slane & Around p470
Loughcrew p471
Carlingford p471

GETTING AROUND

Buses link Carlingford with Dundalk, which is the nearest major town. Otherwise, you'll need your own wheels. A car ferry travels between Carlingford and Greencastle, County Down, Northern Ireland.

The Neolithic ruins at Brú na Bóinne might grab all the headlines, but the surrounding region is dripping with history, including more passage graves ignored by most visitors. Other highlights include two beautiful monastic sites dating from the Middle Ages, an 18th-century castle that is still in use as a residence and as the setting for an annual mega-concert, and a site by the River Boyne that in 1690 bore witness to the most significant battle in recent Irish history.

At the northern end of County Louth is the pretty medieval town of Carlingford, while east of Brú na Bóinne is Drogheda, whose citizens bore the terrible brunt of Cromwell's invasion in 1649.

Drogheda & Around   TIME FROM BRÚ NA BÓINNE: 15MIN 🚗

A town with history

Straddling the River Boyne, **Drogheda** is a bustling town with a handful of interesting mementos of its tumultuous history. The 17th century was especially unkind, when Drogheda was the scene of Cromwell's most notorious Irish slaughter in 1649. Drogheda (from Gaelic *Droichead Átha*, which means 'bridge by the ford') was an important crossing point on the River Boyne, and has been around since at least the 12th century when a motte-and-bailey castle was built on the south bank. The site is now occupied by the **Millmount Museum** *(facebook .com/DroghedaMuseumMillmount; adult/child €8/4)*, which is the ideal place to begin exploring the town. It's a treasure trove of historical trivia, from Cromwell's brutal siege of the town and the Battle of the Boyne, to Drogheda's links to the Battle of Waterloo (there's a diorama of the battle).

Wander downhill and across the river to **St Peter's Roman Catholic Church**, whose main draw is the shrivelled head of St Oliver Plunkett, (1629–81), kept in a glittering brass and glass reliquary in the north transept. Further up the hill is **St Peter's Church of Ireland**, whose spire was burned by Cromwell's men, resulting in the death of 100 people seeking sanctuary inside.

Finally, walk along St Laurence St past **Highlanes Gallery** *(highlanes.ie; free)* which houses a collection of contemporary art set in a beautifully converted 19th-century monastery, to

St Laurence's Gate, Drogheda

St Laurence's Gate, the most impressive remnant of the medieval walled town.

Battle of the Boyne

Arguably the most consequential battle in Irish history took place at this site on the banks of the River Boyne, about 6km west of Drogheda. On 1 July 1690, more than 60,000 soldiers of the armies of King James II and his nephew and son-in-law King William of Orange clashed swords (and cannons and guns). Although the four-hour battle was not especially bloody (casualties topped out at 2250), it was the culmination of an almighty struggle for supremacy between the supporters of the Catholic James and the Protestant William, who had deposed his uncle as king of England two years earlier. By the battle's end, William had prevailed, and James eventually conceded defeat and slunk off to France.

The history is well told in the visitor centre, located in **Oldbridge House** *(battleoftheboyne.ie; adult/child €5/3)*, where you can watch a short film about the battle, see original and replica weaponry of the time, and explore a laser battlefield model. Take a self-guided walk through the parkland and battle site and ponder the events that saw Protestant interests prevail in Ireland until the 20th century.

DIARMUID & GRÁINNE

A widespread myth about the origin of the name **Newgrange** is that it comes from the Irish for 'Cave of Gráinne', a reference to a popular Celtic legend. *The Pursuit of Diarmuid and Gráinne* tells of the illicit love between the woman betrothed to Fionn Mac Cumhaill (or Finn McCool), leader of the Fianna, and Diarmuid, one of his most trusted lieutenants.

When Diarmuid was fatally wounded, his body was brought to Newgrange by the god Aengus in a vain attempt to save him, and the despairing Gráinne followed him into the chamber, where she remained long after he died.

This suspiciously Arthurian tale (substitute Lancelot and Guinevere for Diarmuid and Gráinne) was widely believed in medieval times.

EATING IN DROGHEDA: OUR PICKS

Five Good Things: The designer cafe in Highlanes Gallery is a great spot for brunch or lunch. *9am-3pm Mon-Thu, to 4pm Fri & Sat, 10am-3pm Sun* €€

D'vine: Convivial cellar bistro that does everything from Mediterranean tapas dishes to gourmet burgers. *5-11pm Wed-Fri, 1-11.30pm Sat, 1-11pm Sun* €€

Scholars Townhouse Hotel: The restaurant at this elegant hotel, set in a former monastery, is your best bet for fine dining. *noon-8.30pm Sun-Thu, to 9pm Fri & Sat* €€€

Duende: Gastro-pub serving classic crowd-pleasing menu of pizzas, burgers, chicken wings, fish and chips in relaxed bistro-style atmosphere. *noon-11.30pm* €€

Poetry and politics

Housed in a quaint cottage, the **Francis Ledwidge Museum** *(francisledwidge.com; adult/family €5/10)*, 1km east of Slane on the N51, was the birthplace of poet Francis Ledwidge (1887–1917). A keen political activist, Ledwidge was thwarted in his efforts to set up a local Gaelic League branch but found an outlet in verse. He died on the battlefield at Ypres in World War I, having survived Gallipoli and Serbia. The museum provides an insight into Ledwidge's works, and the cottage itself is a humbling example of how farm labourers lived in the 19th century.

Marvellous monastic ruins

In its Anglo-Norman prime, **Old Mellifont Abbey** *(heritageireland.ie)*, 1.5km off the main Drogheda–Collon road (R168), was the Cistercians' first and most magnificent centre in Ireland. Highly evocative and well worth exploring, the ruins still reflect the site's former splendour. The **visitor centre** *(heritageireland.ie; adult/child €5/3)* describes monastic life in detail. Admission to the abbey grounds and ruins is free, and you can wander at will. Take a turn around the ruined cloister and admire Mellifont's most recognisable building and one of the country's finest examples of Cistercian architecture – the 13th-century lavabo, which was the monks' octagonal washing room. Mellifont was eventually the mother house for 21 lesser monasteries, and at one point, as many as 400 monks lived here. In 1556, after the Dissolution of the Monasteries, a fortified Tudor manor house was built on the site.

A haven of Celtic art

Crowing ravens lend an eerie atmosphere to **Monasterboice** *(heritageireland.ie; free)*, an intriguing monastic site down a leafy lane amid sweeping farmland. The high crosses of Monasterboice are superb examples of Celtic art. The cross nearest the entrance is known as **Muiredach's Cross**, named after a 10th-century abbot. The western face relates to the New Testament, and from the bottom, it depicts the arrest of Christ, Doubting Thomas, Christ giving a key to St Peter, the Crucifixion, and Moses praying with Aaron and Hur.

The **West Cross** is near the round tower and stands 6.5m high, making it one of the tallest high crosses in Ireland. It's much more weathered than Muiredach's and only a dozen or so of its 50 panels are still legible. The more distinguishable ones on the eastern face include David killing a lion and a

---

CROMWELL'S INVASION OF DROGHEDA

Lauded as England's first democrat and protector of the people, Oliver Cromwell (1599–1658) was an Irish nightmare.

Cromwell hated the Irish for siding with Charles I during the Civil War. So when 'God's own Englishman' landed his 12,000 troops at Dublin in August 1649, he immediately set out to besiege Drogheda, a bastion of royalist support. When the town refused to surrender, Cromwell let fly with heavy artillery and after two days the walls were breached.

In order to set a terrifying example to any other town that might resist, around 3000 people were massacred, mostly royalist soldiers but also priests, women and children. Of the survivors, many were captured and sold into slavery in the Caribbean.

 EATING AROUND DROGHEDA: OUR PICKS

Fisherman's Catch: Freshly caught seafood served at a family-owned fish and chip shop at Clogherhead harbour. *noon-6pm Wed & Thu, to 7pm Fri-Sun* €€

Glyde Inn: This 18th-century pub in Annagassan dishes up locally caught seafood. Book for indoor tables; outdoor sea view terrace is walk-ins only. *noon-8pm Wed-Sun* €€

Delfino Bay: Busy Italian restaurant serving classic pizza and pasta dishes upstairs from popular Laytown pub, Gilna's Lounge. *4-10pm Thu-Sun* €€

Monasterboice Inn: (Donegan's) Wood-panelled country pub just east of the M1 north of Drogheda, serving classic breakfasts and pub grub. *9am-8pm Sun-Thu, to 8.30pm Fri & Sat* €€

WALK THE BOYNE VALLEY CAMINO

This waymarked trail follows part of the Boyne Valley Camino to an ancient monastic site; return to Drogheda by bus.

START	END	LENGTH
St Peter's Parish Church, Drogheda	Morning Star Pub, Tullyallen	16km; 5hr

From 1 **St Peter's Roman Catholic Church** in Drogheda, head west along West St, turn left down Dominic St and cross the river via 2 **St Dominic's Pedestrian Bridge.** Then head upstream on the riverside path through the green space of 3 **St Dominic's Park**. The Boyne Greenway continues along the riverbank on a boardwalk for 2.5km before passing under the impressive 4 **Mary MacAleese Boyne Valley Bridge**, which carries the M1 motorway across the River Boyne. The path now passes the lock gates on the 5 **Boyne Canal**, and follows the towpath to the gates of 6 **Oldbridge Estate**.

Cross the narrow 7 **Obelisk Bridge** beside the stump of a monument. From the Obelisk car park at the crossroads, where there is a map of the path network, follow the waymarked Camino trail through Townley Hall Woods, passing the Georgian mansion of 8 **Townley Hall** (not open the public), to emerge on a minor road. Go left for 900m then turn right to reach the highest point of the walk, with expansive views, at a right-angle bend in the road. Turn left at a T-junction for the final 1.5km to the 9 **Old Mellifont Abbey**. Follow the Camino signs for 3.7km back to Tullyallen village; the bus to Drogheda leaves from the 10 **Morning Star pub**.

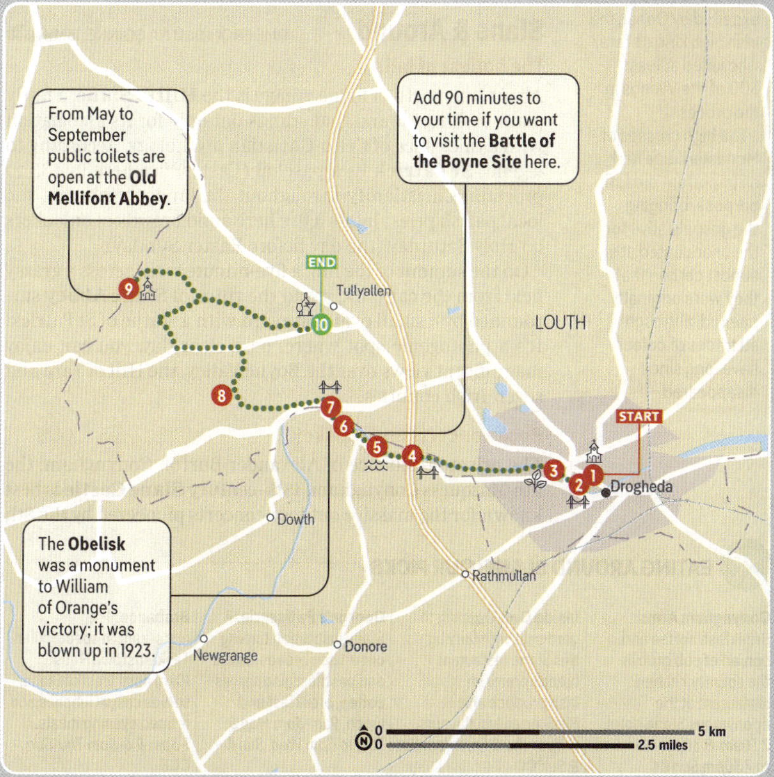

From May to September public toilets are open at the **Old Mellifont Abbey**.
Add 90 minutes to your time if you want to visit the **Battle of the Boyne Site** here.
END
Tullyallen
LOUTH
START
Drogheda
Dowth
Rathmullan
The **Obelisk** was a monument to William of Orange's victory; it was blown up in 1923.
Newgrange
Donore
0
5 km
0
2.5 miles

MONASTERBOICE HIGH CROSSES

The original monastic settlement here is said to have been founded in the 5th or 6th century by St Buithe, a follower of St Patrick, although the site probably had pre-Christian significance. St Buithe's name somehow got converted to Boyne, and the river is named after him. An invading Viking force took over the settlement in 968, only to be comprehensively expelled by Donal, the Irish high king of Tara, who killed at least 300 of the Vikings in the process.

The high crosses of Monasterboice had an important didactic purpose, bringing the gospels alive for the uneducated. It is almost certain that they were originally painted, although all traces of colour have long since disappeared.

Old Mellifont Abbey (p468)

bear. The **round tower**, minus its cap, is more than 30m tall. Records suggest the interior went up in flames in 1097, destroying many valuable manuscripts and other treasures.

Slane & Around

TIME FROM BRÚ NA BÓINNE: **15MIN**

The holiest of hills

About 1km north of Slane village is the **Hill of Slane**, a fairly plain-looking mound that stands out only for its association with a thick slice of Celto-Christian mythology. According to legend, **St Patrick** lit a paschal (Easter) fire here in 433 to proclaim Christianity throughout the land; to this day, the local parish priest lights a fire here amid crowds of onlookers on Holy Saturday (the day before Easter Sunday).

On the summit of the hill, a five-minute walk across a grassy field from the car park, stand the ruins of **Slane Abbey** surrounded by a small oval graveyard with a statue of St Patrick. It's a photogenic spot where, on a clear day, you can enjoy magnificent views over the Boyne Valley, the Hill of Tara and seven Irish counties.

Rock concerts and whiskey

The private residence of Alexander Burton Conyngham, the 9th Marquess Conyngham, 18th-century **Slane Castle** is best known for the massive outdoor concerts pioneered by the 8th

EATING AROUND SLANE: OUR PICKS

Conyngham Arms: Breakfast, coffee and upmarket pub grub in the country kitchen restaurant at the eponymous Slane hotel. *7.30am-8.30pm Mon-Sat, to 7.30pm Sun* €€

Inside Out: Opening to a garden lit with fairy lights, this Slane restaurant blends premium Irish produce and Mediterranean flavours. *5-11pm Thu & Fri, 1-11pm Sat & Sun* €€

George's Patisserie: A Slane institution turning out artisan breads, cakes and pastries; also serves coffee, breakfast and lunch. *9am-3pm Mon & Tue, to 5pm Wed-Sun* €

Brabazon: The restaurant at spectacular Tankardstown House, 10km northwest of Slane, serves casual lunches and refined evening meals. *1-3pm & 6-8pm Thu-Sun* €€€

marquess, Henry Conyngham (1951-2025) between 1981, when Thin Lizzy and U2 were headline acts, and Harry Styles' performance in 2023. Past performers include the Rolling Stones, Bruce Springsteen and Madonna; there are rumours that U2 might headline a concert in 2026 or 2027.

Built in Gothic Revival style by James Wyatt in 1785, the building was later altered by Francis Johnson for George IV's visits to Lady Conyngham, allegedly his mistress. Public **guided tours** *(slanecastle.ie; adult/child €14/8.40)* of the castle's neogothic ballroom, completed in 1821, and the King's Room are available on only a handful of days each summer; **private tours** *(€150 for up 6 people)* can be arranged at your convenience. Sunday **afternoon tea with a mini tour** *(per person €57.50)* is available all year round.

Tours and tastings of the castle's stable-housed whiskey distillery, **Slane Irish Whiskey** *(slaneirishwhiskey.com; per person €40)*, which produces triple-cask-matured whiskey, can also be arranged.

Loughcrew

TIME FROM BRÚ NA BÓINNE: **50MIN**

The tombs of Loughcrew

Brú na Bóinne gets most of the attention, but the Stone Age passage graves strewn about the **Loughcrew Hills**, along the R154 near Oldcastle, are just as old and equally as significant. They're well off the beaten track and attract relatively few visitors, which means you can enjoy this moody and evocative place in peace.

Although **Loughcrew Megalithic Cemetery** *(heritageire land.ie; free)* has 32 known tombs spread across four hills, most are on private land and inaccessible to the public. It is possible, however, to visit Cairn T at **Loughcrew Cairns**, a steep but scenic 15-minute climb from the car park (Office of Public Works guides are on hand for info and tours). The cairn is 35m in diameter, with an entrance passage on the east side where sunlight pierces the chamber on the spring and autumn equinoxes. Although you can't enter, you can see numerous stones carved with spirals and sun symbols through the gate. One of the kerbstones on the north side of the cairn, the Hag's Chair, is covered in gouged holes, circles and other markings including a cross, indicating that it may have been used as a mass rock.

There's a cafe and toilets 200m downhill from the car park at the privately run Loughcrew Megalithic Centre.

Carlingford

TIME FROM BRÚ NA BÓINNE: **50MIN**

The Cooley Peninsula

Forested slopes and multihued hills rise above the dark waters of **Carlingford Lough**, cleaving the picturesque Cooley Peninsula. Country lanes wind their scenic way down to deserted stony beaches, while sweeping views stretch north across the water (and the border) to the majestic Mourne Mountains in County Down.

THE PASCHAL FIRE AND THE SHAMROCK

The story goes that **St Patrick**'s fire on the Hill of Slane in 433 infuriated Laoghaire, the pagan high king of Ireland. He was warned by his far-sighted druids that the man who had kindled the flame would surpass kings and princes. When Laoghaire went to confront Patrick, all but one of the king's attendants, a man called Erc, greeted the saint with scorn. Undeterred, Patrick plucked a shamrock from the ground and used its three leaves to explain the paradox of the Holy Trinity, thus giving Ireland one of its enduring national symbols. Laoghaire agreed to let Patrick continue his missionary work; Erc was baptised and later became the first bishop of Slane.

TRACING YOUR ANCESTORS

With advance notice, genealogical centres in the region can help trace your ancestors.

Contact the **Meath Heritage Centre** *(meath.rootsireland. ie; Castle St; 9am-1pm & 1.30-5pm Mon-Thu, 9am-2pm Fri)* inside Trim's town hall.

The **Louth County Library** *(louthcoco.ie; Roden Pl; 10am-8pm Tue & Thu, to 5pm Wed, Fri & Sat)* in Dundalk has family history information.

Visit **Cavan Heritage and Genealogy Centre** *(cavan.rootsireland. ie; Farnham St; 10am-1pm & 2-5.15pm Mon, Wed, Fri & Sat, 10am-8.30pm Tue & Thu)* on the 1st floor of Johnston Central Library in Cavan town.

Contact **Monaghan Genealogy** *(monaghan genealogy.com; St Macartan's College, Mullaghmurphy)* to request information or book a visit.

BALLYGALLY VIEW IMAGES/SHUTTERSTOCK

Carlingford

Presiding over the peninsula is the medieval walled town of **Carlingford**, dominated by the massive waterside **King John's Castle**. Amid a cluster of medieval ruins, this colourful village buzzes with pubs, restaurants and boutiques. From April to October, **Carlingford Heritage Centre** *(carlingford heritagecentre.com; adult/child €3/free)* runs one-hour guided tours *(adult/child €10/4)* of the town and castle.

EATING IN CARLINGFORD: OUR PICKS

Fishy Dishy: Family-run restaurant on the main street serving fresh local seafood, from a half dozen oysters to lobster thermidor. *6-9pm Wed-Fri, 5-9.30pm Sat, 2-8pm Sun* €€

Bay Tree Restaurant & Guesthouse: Simple, stylishly presented dishes with seasonal, local ingredients (some grown in its own polytunnel). *5-8.30pm Thu, to 9pm Fri & Sat, 1-7.30pm Sun* €€

PJ O'Hares: Hearty main courses at this popular pub include pies, tapas-style dishes and platters of local oysters *au naturel*, baked or tempura. *noon-9pm Mon-Sat, to 8pm Sun* €€

Fitzpatrick's: A well patronised treasure with fantastic craic and excellent steak, seafood and chowder; book ahead for lunch or dinner. *noon-10.30pm* €€

Trim

MEDIEVAL FORTRESS | KAYAK TOURS | ABBEY RUINS

These days, Trim is a fairly ordinary dormitory town on the edge of the wider Dublin conurbation, but it was one of Ireland's most significant medieval settlements, and the primary evidence of that rises high above the town centre. It's hard to imagine nowadays, but a measure of Trim's importance was that Elizabeth I considered building Dublin's Trinity College here. One student who studied in Trim (at Talbot Castle and St Mary's Abbey) was Irish-born Arthur Wellesley (1769–1852), the first Duke of Wellington. Beyond the magnificent castle, Trim's history is everywhere, from atmospheric ruins to streets lined with tiny workers' cottages. There's a handful of good hotels and B&Bs, while Castle St has the best concentration of restaurants. If you're looking for a way to spend an evening, pubs are situated on both banks of the River Boyne.

GETTING AROUND

Bus Éireann *(buseireann.ie)* links Trim with Dublin (1¼ hours, hourly) and Drogheda (1¼ hours, hourly). If you're arriving by car, head for the Emmett St car park (€3 for all-day parking), a few minutes' walk west of the castle entrance.

Trim Castle (p474)

HIGHLIGHTS
1 Trim Castle

ACTIVITIES
2 Boyne Valley Activities

SLEEPING
3 Bellinter House Hotel & Spa
4 Caravogue House
5 Station House Hotel
6 Trim Castle Hotel

EATING
7 Harvest Home Bakery
8 StockHouse

DRINKING & NIGHTLIFE
9 James Griffin
10 Marcy Regan's

TOP TIP

The grounds of Trim Castle are free to enter, but it's well worth paying for the guided tour. Be aware that the tour involves climbing very narrow, claustrophobic spiral staircases.

The Ultimate Fortification
Ireland's mightiest Norman castle

If you need proof that medieval castles were built to last, the monumental three-storey keep of **Trim Castle** *(heritage ireland.ie; adult/child €5/3)* is it. It was Ireland's largest fortification, founded by Hugh de Lacy in 1173, destroyed within a year by Ruaidrí Ua Conchobair (Ireland's last high king), rebuilt around 1200 and hardly modified since.

Join a **guided tour** of the massive, cruciform central keep. Its 20 sides were protected by a ditch, curtain wall and water-filled moat that made it virtually impregnable. You'll clamber up cramped spiral stairs, cross walkways suspended above the interior spaces, and take in the view from the highest point. Your guide will point out features of interest, including the chapel and a garderobe (medieval toilet).

The castle is often referred to as King John's Castle, after a 1210 visit by King John (of Robin Hood fame). In 1399, Richard II stayed here just before he was deposed by Henry Bolingbroke, later Henry IV. Richard famously left Henry's two sons imprisoned at Trim Castle when he returned to negotiate with their father; one of those was Prince Hal, the future Henry V. The engaging tour takes you to the battlements at the top, from where you can imagine being a 17th-century defender fighting off Cromwell's attacks. (It didn't go well, as Cromwell took the castle in 1649.)

Folkloric characters from the Púca Festival

Besides playing a central role in a chunk of British and Irish history, Trim Castle starred in in the 1995 movie *Braveheart*, standing in for Edinburgh Castle, London, and the walled city of York.

Kayak Beneath Trim Castle

Paddle the Boyne blueway

The 8km stretch of the River Boyne from Trim downstream to Bective offers a gloriously serene paddle through verdant pastures and past an 18th-century mill. On summer weekends **Boyne Valley Activities** *(boynevalleyactivities.ie; per person/family €60/90)* run two-hour guided kayaking tours on the Boyne for complete beginners; look out for otters and plentiful birdlife.

Supernatural High Spirits

Dance the Halloween nights away

For four nights around 31 October the normally peaceful town of Trim comes alive with the spirit of Samhain, the ancient Celtic precursor of Halloween. The **Púca Festival** *(puca festival.com)*, named for the shapeshifting spirits of Irish folklore, celebrates with live gigs by big name bands and a colourful procession through the streets of Trim to the ceremonial lighting of the Samhain bonfire. Book tickets online and reserve accommodation well in advance.

THE WELLINGTON CONNECTION

Arthur Wellesley (1769–1852), the first Duke of Wellington, was born in Ireland. The family's country seat was at Dangan Castle, 6km south of Trim, and the young Wellesley attended the Diocesan School in Trim (now Talbot Castle, across the river from Trim Castle) before heading to Eton at the age of 12. Like his father before him, Arthur briefly served as MP for Trim in the Irish House of Commons.

The town's Wellington Memorial, on the corner of Emmet and Patrick streets, is a 23m-tall Corinthian column with the inscription 'This column was erected in the year 1817 in honour of the illustrious Duke of Wellington by the grateful contributions of the people of Meath.'

 EATING & DRINKING IN TRIM: OUR PICKS

Harvest Home Bakery: This little gem sells delicious breads, cakes, pies and biscuits as well as homemade soups and full-to-bursting sandwiches. *9am-5pm Tue-Sat* €

StockHouse: Cooked-to-order dry-aged steaks are the stock-in-trade of this always-packed restaurant. *5-9pm Mon, Wed & Thu, 4.30-10pm Fri & Sat, 2.30-8pm Sun* €€

James Griffin: This award-winning pub dates from 1904 and hosts trad-music sessions, live bands and DJs. *4-11pm Wed & Thu, 3pm-12.30am Fri, 1pm-12.30am Sat, 1-11.30pm Sun*

Marcy Regan's: Traditional, no-frills riverside pub at Norman-era St Peter's Bridge is steeped in olde-worlde atmosphere. *4-11.30pm Mon-Fri, noon-11.30pm Sat & Sun*

Beyond
Trim

Not far from Trim is a site of ancient significance and another rooted very much in modern entertainment.

GETTING AROUND

Tara's eastern edge pushes up against the M3 motorway. If you're visiting Tara by bus (there is an hourly service from Dublin and Drogheda to Trim), ask the driver to drop you off at Tara Cross. There's a small parking lot (free) next to the entrance to Hill of Tara, and a larger one (€2) opposite Maguire's Cafe.

The area around Trim is a mix of rolling fields and farmland between villages and townlands whose lifeblood are the ballooning residential estates built to house a growing population. A few kilometres east of Trim is one of Ireland's most sacred sites, Tara, home of druids and Celtic high kings. But it too has been threatened by the needs of expanding suburbs, with a motorway running alongside its eastern edges. To the south, in between the blossoming towns of Dunshaughlin and Ratoath, is Emerald Park, Ireland's version of the USA's Six Flags or the UK's Alton Towers amusement parks, albeit on a much smaller scale. Despite its size, it's immensely popular and fun.

Tara

TIME FROM TRIM: **25MIN**

Sacred Tara

Free to visit and always open, the **Hill of Tara** *(heritage ireland.ie)* is Ireland's most sacred stretch of turf, occupying a place at the heart of Irish history, legend and folklore. It is also one of the most important ancient sites in Europe, with a Stone Age passage tomb and prehistoric burial mounds that date back 5000 years.

A short walk from the car park leads to a visitor centre *(free)* which screens an introductory video every 30 minutes; get your bearings here before exploring the hilltop. Despite its historic significance, little remains other than humps and mounds in the grass, and you'll need a good imagination to visualise how it might have looked at its zenith – the satellite view on your phone is useful for orientation.

As you walk from the visitor centre, the first earthwork you cross is the **Rath of the Synods**, a triple-ringed enclosure where some of St Patrick's early synods (meetings) supposedly took place. Next you cross into the **Royal Enclosure**, a large oval Iron Age hill fort, 315m in diameter and surrounded by a bank and ditch cut through solid rock under the soil.

Just inside is the **Mound of the Hostages**, a Neolithic passage tomb that is the most ancient known part of Tara. A treasure trove of artefacts was unearthed here, including some ancient Mediterranean beads of amber and faience (glazed pottery). More than 35 Bronze Age burials were found here, as well as extensive cremated remains from the Stone Age.

Hill of Tara

You can peer through the bars at the entrance to see engraved stones lining the passage.

At the summit of the hill are two further enclosures, touching each other in a figure-of-eight, and the **Lia Fáil** (Stone of Destiny) which represents the joining of the gods of the earth and the heavens. It's said to be the inauguration stone of the high kings of Ireland. There are superb views of the surrounding Boyne and Blackwater Valleys.

Visit Emerald Park

Just off the M2 motorway, **Emerald Park** *(emeraldpark.ie; adult/child from €43/39)* is an incredibly popular amusement park that includes Europe's largest wooden inverted roller coaster (named after legendary hero Cúchulainn), a 5D cinema (yes, 5D), a high-speed spinning Rotator and the stomach-churning Air Race ride. Flight School and Dino Ride are family-friendly coasters, while the Viking Voyage is a water flume ride. There's also a zoo, rock climbing, a zip line and a fantastic playground.

The ancient Dunsany Castle

You can see how the other one percent lives at **Dunsany Castle** *(dunsany.com; adult/child €25/free;)*, 5km south of Tara. The residence of the lords of Dunsany, it's one of the oldest continually inhabited buildings in Ireland. Construction started in the 12th century, with major alterations taking place in the 18th and 19th centuries. Maintenance and restoration are ongoing.

From May to mid-September you can arrange a two-hour guided tour of the castle (must be booked in advance) for a fascinating insight into the family's history and their impressive private art collection. The castle houses many treasures related to important figures in Irish history, such as St Oliver Plunkett and Patrick Sarsfield, leader of the Irish Jacobite forces at the siege of Limerick in 1691.

TARA THROUGH HISTORY

Tara was once the home of the mystical druids, the priest-rulers of ancient Ireland who practised their particular form of Celtic paganism under the watchful gaze of the all-powerful goddess Maeve (in Gaelic, *Medbh*).

Later it was the ceremonial capital of the high kings, all 142 of them, who ruled until the arrival of Christianity in the 5th century marked the beginning of the end for pagan civilisation. The high kings began to desert Tara, though the kings of Leinster continued to be based here until the 11th century.

In August 1843, Tara saw one of the greatest crowds ever to gather in Ireland. Daniel O'Connell, leader of the opposition to union with Great Britain, held one of his galvanising rallies here, attended by 750,000 people.

County Cavan

WILD HIKING | NEOLITHIC SITES | CANOE TOURING

GETTING AROUND

TFI Local Link Cavan Monaghan *(locallinkcm.ie)* is the main provider of bus services around the county, including routes from Cavan town to Monaghan town and Ballyjamesduff.

County Cavan is a paradise for lovers of outdoor pursuits, especially of the watery variety. Boaters and anglers will find a slice of heaven in the 'Lake County' (Cavan's nickname) – supposedly there's a lake for every day of the year. Among the lakes is a gentle landscape of meandering streams, bogs and drumlins.

Cavan's county town is a solidly workaday place with some handsome Georgian houses; it's a handy stop for info and supplies but there are few sights. Head instead for the rural hinterland where Cavan's lakes create a tangle of narrow, twisting roads. Take your time and enjoy the views that appear unexpectedly around each bend, and pause to stretch your legs (or take to the water in a rented kayak) at one of the many forest parks. In the north, scenic walking trails wind through the wild Cuilcagh Mountains, which nurture the source of the 300km River Shannon.

Linger in a Local Museum

Historical relics

In a former convent in **Ballyjamesduff**, the wide-ranging collection at **Cavan County Museum** *(cavanmuseum.ie; adult/child €6/4)* includes a huge array of 18th-, 19th- and 20th-century costumes and relics from the Stone, Bronze, Iron and Middle Ages. Don't miss the Boat Room, which houses a 1000-year-old log boat excavated from Lough Errill in 1895; the Killycluggin Stone, an Iron Age monument decorated with Celtic engravings; and the spooky Corleck Head, a three-faced Celtic stone idol.

There's also a large exhibition on Gaelic sports and the outdoor, kid-friendly WWI Trench Experience has sound effects along its dug-out, sandbagged trenches.

Discovering Neolithic Tombs

Wander through a little-visited forest park

Just 3km south of Blacklion, the peaceful **Cavan Burren Park** *(cavanburrenpark.ie; free)* is a great place to stretch your legs. This megalithic site was identified in the 1870s but has been surrounded by forestry plantations since the 1950s

☑ TOP TIP

While Cavan town has places to stay, you'll find more charming options in the smaller villages and rural areas along with fantastic restaurants run by some of the best chefs in Ireland.

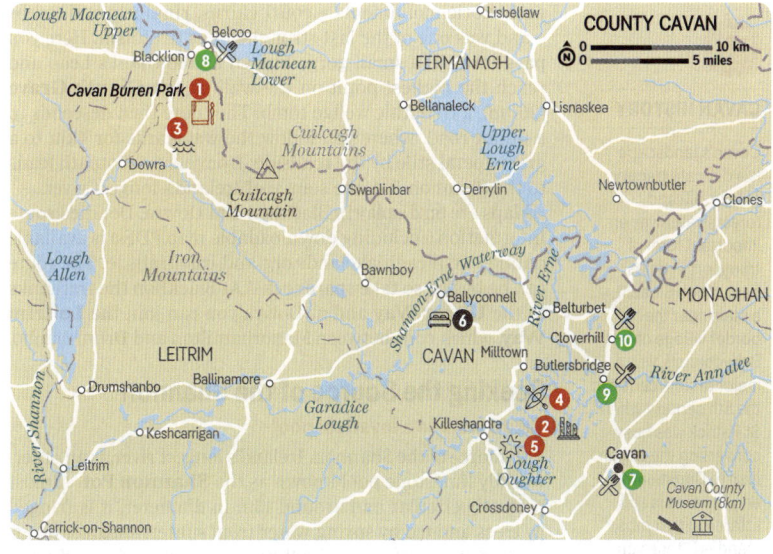

	HIGHLIGHTS	3 Shannon Pot	● SLEEPING	8 MacNean House & Restaurant
1	Cavan Burren Park	● ACTIVITIES	6 Slieve Russell Hotel	9 Murph's Gastro Pub
	SIGHTS	4 Cavan Adventure Centre	● EATING	10 Olde Post Inn
2	Clough Oughter Castle	5 Killykeen Forest Park	7 Chapter	

and only opened to the public in 2014. An unstaffed visitor centre (with toilets) beside the car park has interpretive panels explaining the history, archaeology and geology, and maps illustrating the 10km network of hiking trails.

The 1.3km, multi-access **Calf House Dolmen Trail** (green waymarks) is an ideal introduction, winding through the forest to emerge at **Tullygobban Viewpoint** where you get a grand view of table-topped Cuilcagh Mountain. You then pass the remains of **Tullygobban passage tomb** and descend back into the forest to reach the **Calf House Dolmen** itself, a remarkable Neolithic portal tomb made from a huge tilted slab of limestone; it was later converted for use as a livestock shelter. Allow 30 to 40 minutes to walk the trail.

Hiking the Cavan Way

Trek past prehistoric sites

The highlight for many walkers in the region is the **Cavan Way**, a 26km trail along the western flanks of the Cuilcagh Mountains between the hamlets of **Blacklion** and **Dowra**. The first 13km from Blacklion to Shannon Pot (p480) is by far the more interesting and is mostly on footpaths and forest tracks; the second half from Shannon Pot to Dowra is mainly on roads.

Heading south from Blacklion, the trail takes you along the eastern fringes of Cavan Burren Park, which is dotted with

BALLYWHO?

All over Ireland you'll see the town prefix 'Bally' (and variations thereof), from the Irish phrase 'Baile na'. Often mistranslated as 'town', a closer approximation is 'place of'. For example, Ballyjamesduff means 'Place of James Duff'. Dublin's Irish name is Baile Átha Cliath ('Place of the Hurdle Ford').

Other common place-name prefixes include Carrick (or Carrig), meaning 'rock' in Irish, and Dun, from the Irish dún (meaning 'fort').

CAVAN HISTORY

Cavan's landscape is a delicate tracery of lake, hill and forest; water was an important form of transport in times past. Magh Sleacht, a plain near the border village of Ballyconnell, was a major druidic centre in the 5th century when St Patrick was busy converting the pagan Irish to Christianity, and the area is still littered with tombs, standing stones and stone circles dating from this time. The Gaelic O'Reilly clan ruled until the 16th century, when they were defeated by the English. As part of the Ulster Plantation, Cavan was divided among English and Scottish settlers. After the War of Independence in 1922, the Ulster counties of Cavan, Monaghan and Donegal were incorporated into the Republic.

prehistoric monuments – court cairns, ringforts and tombs – and was one of the last strongholds of druidism. Here you pass through a small gorge known as the Giant's Leap and reach the highest point on the walk at the **Giant's Grave** (260m), a Neolithic wedge tomb. The route then descends to a minor road, where you follow the waymarks for 4km to a green metal stile by the roadside; from here a footpath leads to the Shannon Pot, the source of Ireland's longest river.

Maps are on display in Blacklion and Dowra. Detailed route information (including downloadable map PDFs) is available online at cuilcaghlakelands.org and irishtrails.ie. The route can be boggy, so take spare socks! At Blacklion the trail links to the **Ulster Way** and at Dowra you can join the **Leitrim Way**, which runs between Manorhamilton and Drumshanbo.

Seeking the Source of the Shannon
Take a walk to a mystical pool

The source of the Shannon, Ireland's longest river, is an otherworldly limestone pool known as the **Shannon Pot**. Almost perfectly circular and around 15m in diameter, it is fringed by trees and fed by spring water from subterranean caverns. The pot lies just east of the R206, 8km south of Blacklion. A new 'discovery centre' with an exhibition, interpretive panels, cafe and toilets, along with an improved car park and 500m walking trail, was under construction in 2025.

Paddle to an Island Castle
Explore Cavan's lakes

Sprawling over 240 hectares, **Killykeen Forest Park**, 12km northwest of Cavan, has various nature trails that lead through the woods and along the shore of **Lough Oughter**, which is popular with anglers.

Many of the low overgrown islands in the lake were *crannógs* (fortified, artificial islands). The most spectacular is home to **Clough Oughter Castle**, a 13th-century circular tower perched on a tiny speck of land. It was used as a lonely prison and then as a stronghold by rebel leader Owen Roe O'Neill before being destroyed by Cromwell's army in 1653. The castle lies out of reach over the water, but you can get there by canoe on a three-hour trip organised by **Cavan Adventure Centre** *(cavanadventure.ie; adult/child €39/20)*. If you don't want to paddle, there's the option of a boat trip to the castle (minimum of six people).

EATING IN COUNTY CAVAN: OUR PICKS

Chapter: This Cavan town favourite is crammed at lunchtime when locals dine on filled bagels, soups and hot and cold salads. *8.30am-6pm Mon-Sat, from 9.30am Sun* €€

Olde Post Inn: Chef Gearóid Lynch creates set menus of contemporary cuisine at this fine dining restaurant in Cloverhill. *5.30-9.30pm Thu-Sun, 12.30-2.30pm Sun* €€€

MacNean House & Restaurant: Book months ahead to sample the cuisine of celebrity chef Neven Maguire at his restaurant in Blacklion. *6-11pm Wed-Sat* €€€

Murph's Gastro Pub: A delightful riverside pub in Butlersbridge with a wood-and-brick decor and an outdoor terrace. *noon-9pm Wed-Fri, to 9.30pm Sat, 12.30-8pm Sun* €€

Beyond
County Cavan

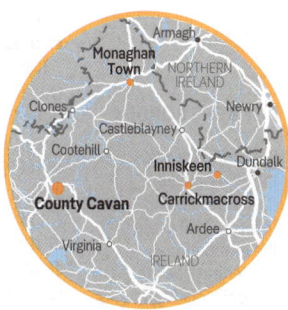

Celebrate the life and poetry of Patrick Kavanagh and admire the delicate lace of Carrickmacross.

County Cavan's neighbour to the east is Monaghan, whose undulating landscape is known for its tiny rounded hills that resemble bubbles in badly pasted wallpaper. Known as drumlins, these bumps are the result of debris left by retreating glaciers during the last Ice Age. But to many Irish, Monaghan is synonymous with the work of poet Patrick Kavanagh, whose work was influenced by the landscape and is celebrated in a wonderful centre in his birthplace of Inniskeen.

In the early 19th century, lacemaking became an important facet of the local economy. Carrickmacross was one of the key centres of the industry, and you can still see the fine needlework on display.

Places
Inniskeen p481
Carrickmacross p482
Monaghan Town p483

GETTING AROUND

Monaghan town and Carrickmacross are well served by bus, but elsewhere, you'll need your own wheels. No trains go to County Monaghan.

Inniskeen

TIME FROM CAVAN: **15MIN**

The life of a poet

About 12km northeast of Carrickmacross, the small village of Inniskeen is typical of so many rural settlements in this part of Ireland. However, this farming community is forever associated

Church in Inniskeen

BONKERS BORDER

If you drive along the N54 between Clones and Cavan town you will cross the international border between the Republic of Ireland and Northern Ireland no fewer than four times in 10 minutes. This geographical curiosity is known as the **Drummully Salient**, a chunk of County Monaghan that is almost surrounded by County Fermanagh.

It's a remnant of some ancient feud among landowners, preserved as a boundary when Ireland's counties were formalised in medieval times. After the partition of Ireland in 1921, activities such as taking goods to market, visiting family or travelling to church were complicated by customs restrictions or security policies.

Since the Good Friday Agreement of 1998 – and despite the complications of Brexit – the border today remains 'invisible', with no checkpoints or formalities.

with the life and work of its best-known son, the poet **Patrick Kavanagh** (1904-67), who was born and raised here.

Kavanagh's long work *The Great Hunger* (1942) blasted away the earlier clichés of Anglo-Irish verse and revealed Ireland's poor farming communities as half-starved, broken-backed and sexually repressed. One of his most famous poems, *Stony Grey Soil* (1943), sticks to the theme and expresses frustration and anger at the Monaghan landscape.

The village's old parish church where Kavanagh was baptised is now the **Patrick Kavanagh Centre** *(patrickkavanagh centre.com; adult/child €10/free)*, whose staff have a passion for his life and work that is contagious. The exhibition here really brings Kavanagh's poetry to life; **Kavanagh Weekend** in September celebrates the poet with words and music. The man himself is buried in the cemetery behind the centre, his grave marked by a simple wooden cross.

Pick up (or download) a map of the self-guided **Kavanagh Trail**, a literary tour of the village and the picturesque surrounding countryside (5.6km in all), taking in Kavanagh's birthplace, Billy Brennan's barn (immortalised in the poem *Inniskeen Road*) and many other sites identifiable from his poetry.

Carrickmacross

TIME FROM CAVAN: **15MIN**

The home of lacemaking

Carrickmacross was settled by English and Scottish Planters in the 17th century, and its broad main street, which hosts a busy market on Thursdays, is flanked by elegant Georgian houses with colourfully painted facades. It's most famous as the home of delicate Carrickmacross lace, an industry revived in 1871 by the local nuns, the Sisters of St Louis.

In the town's market courtyard at the north end of the main street, a local cooperative runs the thimble-sized **Carrickmacross Lace Gallery** *(carrickmacrosslace.ie; free)* where you can see lacemaking demonstrations and check out exquisite designs. Designs are appliquéd on organza using thick thread and close stitches and then embellished with a variety of point stitches, guipure, pops and the lace's distinctive loop edge. Lacemakers take commissions, and you can purchase delicate pieces made into fridge magnets, bookmarks and more.

From May to September you can join a free, 90-minute **guided walking tour** of the town, departing from the Courthouse (across the street from the market courtyard) at 11am every Saturday; no need to book, just turn up.

Carrickmacross workhouse

The town of Carrickmacross, like most of Ireland, suffered terribly during and after the Great Famine of 1845-49. The period of widespread destitution that followed saw many families driven to the workhouse, a 19th-century institution that provided relief to the poor on condition of them leaving their homes and living in the workhouse. Conditions were deliberately harsh, and inmates were forced to do hard and unpleasant labour such as breaking stones, picking oakum (separating old ropes for fibre) and operating treadmills.

Carrickmacross Workhouse

Following the Poor Law (Ireland) Act of 1838 more than 100 workhouses were built throughout Ireland, including the well-preserved **Carrickmacross Workhouse** *(carrickmacrossworkhouse.com; adult/child €8/free)* where you can join a guided tour of the building including a children's dormitory, fever hospital and famine graveyard.

Monaghan Town

TIME FROM CAVAN: **15MIN**

Monaghan County Museum

It may be the county town, but Monaghan's residents live their lives utterly unaffected by tourism. It's an enjoyable place to wander and admire the elegant 18th- and 19th-century limestone buildings. A number of colourful murals around the town are part of a project led by the excellent **Monaghan County Museum** *(monaghan.ie/museum; free)*. Housed over two floors in the attractively modern council building, the collection's crowning glory is the 14th-century **Cross of Clogher**, an oak altar cross encased in bronze panels richly decorated with Christian iconography.

Other galleries are devoted to Monaghan's history as a place defined by borders, notably the nearby border with Northern Ireland; a magnificent array of Bronze Age spears and axe

DRUMLIN LANDSCAPES

Drumlins are small, smoothly rounded hills, rarely more than 50m high, made of glacial debris that was moulded and streamlined by ice sheets moving across the land during the last Ice Age.

Ireland is home to the most extensive drumlin field in Europe (it was the Irish language that gave the drumlin its name, from *druimnín*, meaning 'little ridge'), with tens of thousands of these tightly-packed hillocks stretching from Clew Bay and Donegal Bay in the west through counties Sligo, Leitrim, Cavan and Monaghan to Fermanagh and Down in Northern Ireland.

Drumlins are responsible for the distinctive landscapes of the Cavan and Fermanagh lakelands, a mosaic of blue and green, little hills moated by little lakes.

 EATING IN COUNTY MONAGHAN: OUR PICKS

Matilda's Artisan Bakery: Ideal for picking up a quick breakfast or picnic ingredients in Carrickmacross; there's also a small cafe. *8am-5.30pm Mon-Fri, to 5pm Sat, 8.30am-4pm Sun* €

Riverbank County Pub: Idyllic stone-built country pub on the wooded banks of the tiny Longfield River, 6km southeast of Carrickmacross; booking recommended. *5-9pm Wed-Sat, 1-9pm Sun* €€€

Batch Loaf: Bright, contemporary two-level bistro in Monaghan town, where locally sourced ingredients are used in dishes like braised lamb shank with champ. *5-9pm Wed & Thu, to 10pm Fri & Sat, 3-8pm Sun* €€€

Wild Thyme & Saddle Bar: Sophisticated dining in elegant restaurant, and upmarket pub grub in neighbouring bar, 6km southwest of Monaghan town. *5-9pm Thu-Sat, 12.30-7pm Sun* €€€

Killykeen forest park

BEST FOREST PARKS IN CAVAN & MONAGHAN

Killykeen (p480): Hiking trails meander amid a watery maze of loughs, islands and wooded hills in the midst of the Cavan lakelands.

Cavan Burren (p478): Family-friendly hiking trails lead to scenic viewpoints amid archaeological sites like the unusual Calf House Dolmen.

Rossmore: Giant redwoods, a yew avenue, Iron Age tombs and the remains of the 19th-century castle. Rhododendrons and azaleas blaze with colour in early summer.

Dún an Rí: Colour-coded forest walks, all less than 4km long, with picnic places and a wishing well. Look out for mink and otters along the river.

Deerpark – Virginia: Lakeshore trails lead to an old boathouse along the banks of Lough Ramor amid broadleaved woodland planted over 100 years ago by Lord Headfort.

heads, and local celebrities including tea tycoon Sir Thomas Lipton, boxer Barry McGuigan and actor and comedian Ardal O'Hanlon (Father Dougal from the TV sitcom *Father Ted*).

Monaghan blues

For more than a quarter of a century, the annual **Harvest Time Blues Festival** *(harvestblues.ie)* has put Monaghan town on the musical map. The best festival of its genre is a four-day, three-night extravaganza that takes place in early September in venues throughout the town and on a variety of stages. The mix of local, national and international acts includes some of the top soul and blues artists around. Previous performers have included the perennially popular Derry-born Rob Strong, Mud Morganfield (Muddy Waters' son), Duke Robillard and Gerry McEvoy – a longtime member of Rory Gallagher's band. In 2025, star performers were Bronagh Gallagher (famous for the movie *The Commitments*) and Dublin band Hothouse Flowers.

Places We Love to Stay

€ Budget €€ Midrange €€€ Top End

Drogheda   MAP p461

Spoon & the Stars € Rory and Hannah's well-run budget accommodation blends vintage and contemporary furnishings and has a great, laid-back vibe.

Scholars Townhouse Hotel (p467) €€ Despite being on the small side, some of the bedrooms at this former monastery have four-poster beds, and there's nothing monastic about the facilities.

Slane   MAP p461

Rock Farm Slane € Glamping in yurts and huts on an organic farm on the banks of the River Boyne, shaded by oak, ash and chestnut trees. Pizza oven, outdoor hot tubs, bike and kayak rental on site.

Slane Farm Hostel € Former 18th-century stable courtyard has been converted into a wonderful hostel that's part of a working dairy farm, with free-range eggs and a vegetable plot for guests to use.

Conyngham Arms €€ Beautifully restored 18th-century coaching inn with airy rooms decorated with French country-style furnishings (some with canopied, four-poster beds) and a charming, rose-filled garden.

Carlingford

Carlingford House €€ This stately 1844 manor house achieves the perfect balance of olde-worlde character and contemporary comfort. Accommodation is room-only, breakfast at one of the cafes in town.

Bay Tree Guesthouse (p472) €€ An excellent deal, this lovely B&B has six cosy rooms with pine furniture and subtle lighting, themed around local Celtic history. Breakfast is served in the downstairs restaurant.

Ghan House €€€ Set in flower-filled gardens, this 18th-century Georgian house has 12 rooms, each exquisitely decorated with period antiques and original artworks.

Trim   MAP p474

Trim Castle Hotel €€ Expanses of glossy marble in the foyer set the scene at this contemporary hotel. Some of its stylish rooms come with balconies and the rooftop terrace overlooks Trim Castle.

Caravogue House €€ Looks like an ordinary red-brick suburban villa from the outside, but inside is a haven of peace and understated design with many thoughtful touches.

Station House Hotel €€ The 19th-century Kilmessan train station, 12km east of Trim, now houses this atmospheric hotel. Antique-filled rooms are spacious. The former signal box houses a separate two-storey bridal suite.

Bellinter House Hotel & Spa €€ This 18th century heritage hotel, 5km northwest of the Hill of Tara, is a haven of crackling open fires, rich artworks and antique-furnished rooms.

County Cavan   MAP p479

Slieve Russell Hotel €€ This resort hotel, built in 1990, is a vision of marble columns, fountains and Georgian-style features overlooking a championship golf courses (with pro lessons available).

Olde Post Inn (p480) €€€ The former postmaster's house in the lovely little village of Cloverhill has a superb restaurant and six luxurious guest rooms. Offers dinner, bed and breakfast packages.

MacNean House & Restaurant (p480) €€€ Celebrity chef Neven Maguire's restaurant provides dinner, bed and breakfast packages in this lovingly restored townhouse; take advantage of reduced rates midweek.

County Monaghan

Westenra Arms €€ A Monaghan town landmark, this huge red-brick hotel has comfortable rooms (some with four-poster beds) and grand public areas including a glass-roofed restaurant.

Shirley Arms €€ Right in the centre of town, the only hotel in Carrickmacross is a pleasant, family-run business where white linens, walnut floors and modern bathrooms give the rooms a contemporary flair.

Castle Leslie €€€ Magnificent Victorian pile 11km northeast of Monaghan town, where facilities include a Victorian spa and an equestrian centre. The Red Room here was once used by poet WB Yeats.

Researched by
Isabel Albiston

Belfast

CHARACTERFUL PORT CITY

A former industrial boomtown scarred by many years of sectarian conflict, Belfast has transformed into a modern city with a thriving cultural life and arts scene.

Belfast today is a different city from the Belfast of the Troubles, which lasted from the late 1960s until the signing of the Good Friday Agreement of 1998. Though political tensions remain, the years of paramilitary campaigns and sectarian violence have been left in the past.

Belfast's ethnic makeup is also changing. The 2021 census showed ethnic minorities make up 7% of Belfast's population, an increase from 3% in 2011. Nearly half of Belfast's population was raised Catholic, while those raised Protestant account for 36%. The nationalist party Sinn Féin is now the largest party in both the Belfast City Council and the Northern Ireland Assembly, and also holds the most UK parliamentary seats of any Northern Irish political party (although it does not occupy its seats in Westminster). However, there is a growing middle ground of voters who identify as neither unionist or nationalist.

Despite the trauma of the Troubles, an atmosphere of determined optimism has prevailed, allowing space for the arts to thrive. In 2021 Belfast was a UNESCO City of Music, pointing to a rich heritage. The most important event in the history of Irish music was perhaps the 1792 Belfast Harp Festival, which served to document traditional harp music that might otherwise have been lost. Years later, the violence and sectarianism in 1970s Belfast were fertile ground for a punk rock music scene, which provided an outlet for undercurrents of rage and disaffection. This story is told in the 2013 film *Good Vibrations*. The city also has a packed programme of arts festivals throughout the year, including the Belfast International Arts Festival in October.

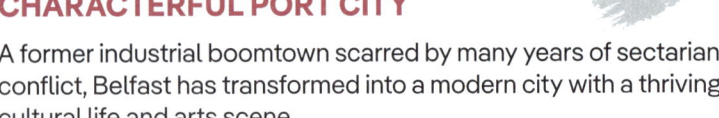

Over recent years, Belfast has also emerged as a major film and TV production destination. Titanic Studios was used to film HBO's blockbuster series *Game of Thrones*. Since then, the filming of further TV series and movies has helped rebrand Belfast, providing a boost to the local economy.

But history is rarely far from mind. The murals of West Belfast reflect issues of national identity at the root of the conflict. Meanwhile, no visitor leaves without learning something about the *Titanic*.

THE MAIN AREAS

CITY CENTRE
Shopping and architecture.
p492

CATHEDRAL QUARTER
Culture and nightlife. **p500**

TITANIC QUARTER & EAST BELFAST
Historic shipyards. **p506**

For places to stay in Belfast, see p529

THE GUIDE

BELFAST

Left: Pier, Holywood (p513); right: Commercial Court (p503)

HOLYWOOD
Restaurants, museums and a beach. **p513**

QUEEN'S QUARTER & SOUTH BELFAST
Leafy campus and riverside nature. **p516**

WEST & NORTH BELFAST
Community culture and hilltop walks. **p522**

487

BELFAST | THE GUIDE

Find Your Way

With the landmarks of the hills to the north and west and the iconic yellow gantry cranes to the east, Belfast is small and easy to navigate. The city centre, Cathedral Quarter and Titanic Quarter are best tackled on foot, while buses and trains link the centre with neighbourhoods further afield.

FROM THE AIRPORT

Belfast has two airports. Most flights arrive in **Belfast International**, 30km northwest of the city centre and a 40-minute journey by bus or car. **George Best Belfast City Airport** is a smaller airport 6km and around 10 minutes' drive east of the city centre.

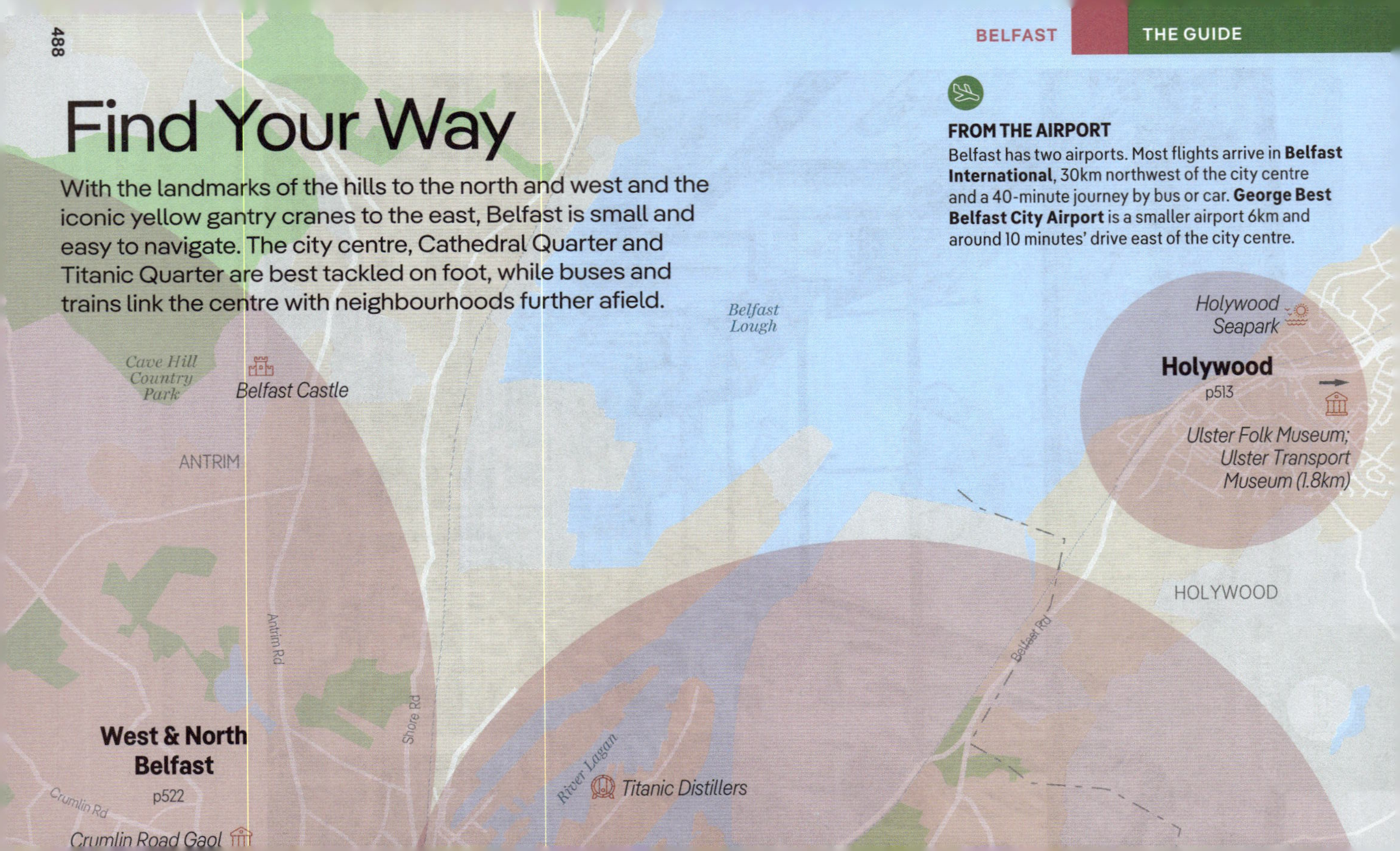

Holywood Seapark

Holywood
p513

Ulster Folk Museum; Ulster Transport Museum (1.8km)

HOLYWOOD

Belfast Lough

Titanic Distillers

River Lagan

Shore Rd

Belfast Castle

Cave Hill Country Park

ANTRIM

Antrim Rd

West & North Belfast
p522

Crumlin Rd

Crumlin Road Gaol

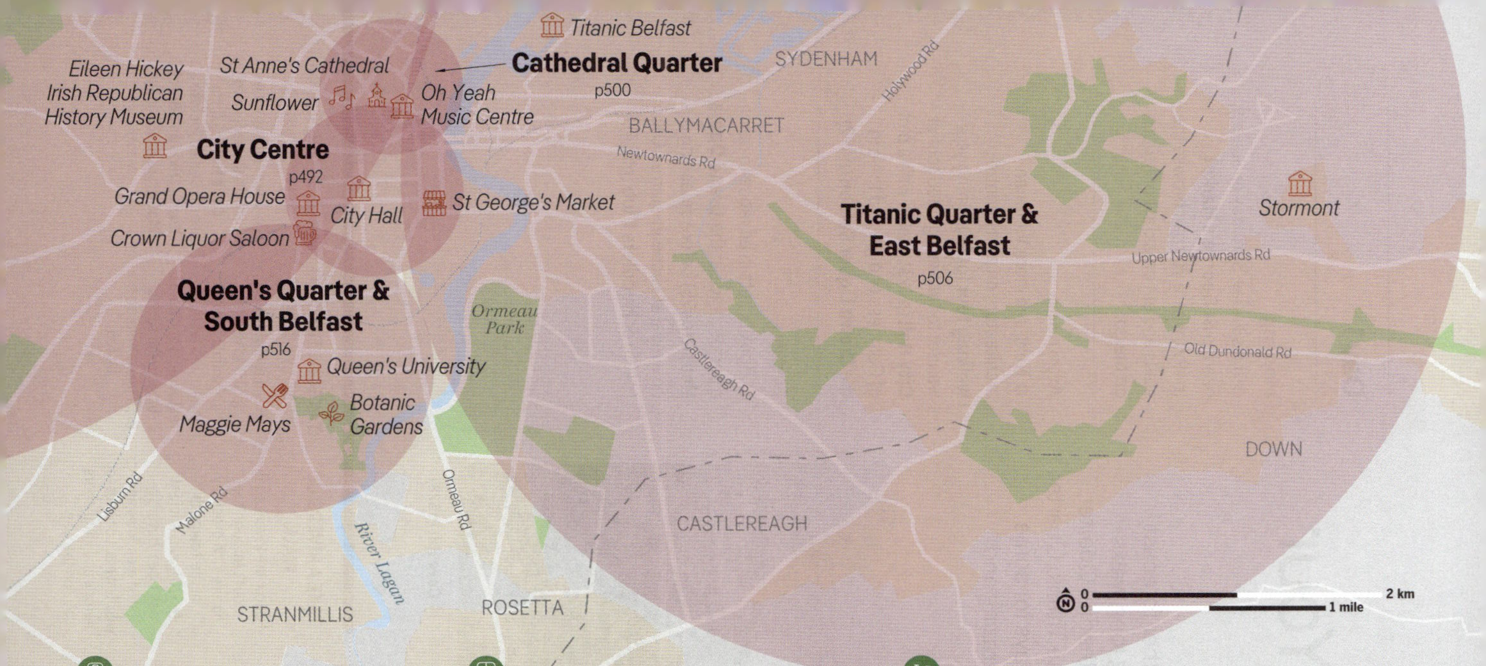

Map of Belfast

- Eileen Hickey Irish Republican History Museum
- St Anne's Cathedral
- Titanic Belfast
- **Cathedral Quarter** p500
- Sunflower
- Oh Yeah Music Centre
- **City Centre** p492
- Grand Opera House
- City Hall
- Crown Liquor Saloon
- St George's Market
- **Titanic Quarter & East Belfast** p506
- Stormont
- SYDENHAM
- BALLYMACARRET
- Holywood Rd
- Newtownards Rd
- Upper Newtownards Rd
- Old Dundonald Rd
- DOWN
- CASTLEREAGH
- Castlereagh Rd
- Ormeau Park
- Ormeau Rd
- **Queen's Quarter & South Belfast** p516
- Queen's University
- Botanic Gardens
- Maggie Mays
- River Lagan
- ROSETTA
- STRANMILLIS
- Malone Rd
- Lisburn Rd

0 — 1 mile
0 — 2 km

TRAIN

Trains are a useful way to reach certain suburbs to the north, south and east of the city centre, and for day trips to the coast. The beach at Holywood, County Down, is a 10-minute train ride east from Belfast city centre.

BUS
Metro and Glider buses fan out across the city from the central hub at Donegall Sq. During the day buses are a convenient way to get around, however most routes do not operate between around 11pm and 6am.

BICYCLE

The city's cycle network includes a number of traffic-free stretches. Cycling is quick and convenient, but frequent rain showers can put a dampener on things. Bikes can be rented through the city's bike-share scheme **Belfast Bikes** (*beryl.cc/scheme/belfast*).

Plan Your Days

Check the weather forecast before planning long walks through the Cathedral Quarter, city centre or the Titanic Quarter. Reserve rainy days for some indoor market grazing and museum visits.

Cave Hill (p528)

Day 1

Morning
- If it's Friday, Saturday or Sunday, head to **St George's Market** (p499), where you can browse the stalls and eat breakfast or brunch on the go.

Afternoon
- Next, see more Victorian architecture on a city centre **walking tour** (p496), timing your wander to take in a guided tour of **City Hall** (p493). Finish with a pint of Guinness or a gin and tonic in the **Crown Liquor Saloon** (p492).

Evening
- Book tickets in advance to catch a performance at the **Grand Opera House** (p495) before splashing out on a meal at Michelin-starred **OX** (p495) or **Muddlers Club** (p504).

You'll Also Want to...

Get out of the city centre and into the neighbourhoods to discover local beauty spots and learn more about Belfast's history.

TAKE A RIVERSIDE WALK
Follow the River Lagan south through the nature-rich greenery of the **towpath** (p520), with ancient oak trees, butterfly-filled meadows and wildflowers. Lookout for herons and kingfishers on the way.

TAKE THE TRAIN TO HOLYWOOD
Head to **Holywood** (p513) to visit the museums, eat at one of the fantastic restaurants and cafes, browse the shops, then take a walk on the beach.

EXPLORE THE BELFAST HILLS
For breathtaking views, tackle the ascent up **Cave Hill** (p528) in north Belfast, or take a hike at **Divis and Black Mountain** (p525) in the west.

Day 2

Morning
- Start the day at **Titanic Belfast** (p508) to learn all about the infamous ship. Allow several hours to view the multimedia exhibition and to explore SS *Nomadic*.

Afternoon
- Have lunch at **Drawing Office Two** (p512), then take a walk around the **Titanic Quarter** (p506), finishing with a tour and tasting at **Titanic Distillers** (p506).

Evening
- Head to Cathedral Quarter for a cocktail, followed by dinner at **Waterman** (p504) or a pizza in the beer garden of the **Sunflower** (p505). Check listings or ask around to find live music, comedy or storytelling events in the neighbourhood.

Day 3

Morning
- Have breakfast at **Established Coffee** (p502) or **Neighbourhood Cafe** (p502) before exploring the street art of the **Cathedral Quarter** (p500) and the **Entries** (p497). Spend the rest of the morning browsing **independent stores** (p515).

Afternoon
- Take the bus to Queen's Quarter and head straight to **Ulster Museum** (p519) to view the treasure-filled galleries. Then take a walk through the **Botanic Gardens** (p516), stopping to look inside the Palm House and Tropical Ravine greenhouses.

Evening
- Have dinner in Queen's Quarter at **Bo Tree Kitchen** (p518) or **Holohan's Pantry** (p518), then watch an arthouse film at the **Queen's Film Theatre** (p518).

VISIT A NOTORIOUS FORMER JAIL

Crumlin Road Gaol (p527) is a window into Belfast's dark history, from the Victorian era through to the Troubles. Hear stories of former inmates conveyed by holograms on a self-guided tour.

CYCLE THE TOWPATH OR GREENWAY

Hire a bike and explore the countryside via the off-road cycle paths at **Lagan Towpath** (p520) and **Comber Greenway** (p512).

SEE THE MURALS OF WEST BELFAST

Belfast's political and sectarian divisions are reflected in the murals painted to declare allegiances and stake-out territory; see them in **West Belfast** (p525).

EAT AN ULSTER FRY

Head to the **Pocket** (p497) in the city centre or **Maggie Mays** (p518) in Queen's Quarter to try the traditional breakfast of eggs, bacon, sausages, potato bread, soda bread, pancakes and more.

City Centre

SHOPPING AND ARCHITECTURE

GETTING AROUND

Belfast Grand Central Station is the central hub for Translink (Ulsterbus and NI Railways) bus and train services to and from Belfast, including the Enterprise train to Dublin. Aircoach buses to Dublin also leave from here. **Lanyon Place** train station is on the Belfast to Bangor line.

Metro bus and Glider services go to Donegall Sq (City Hall). **Belfast City Bike Tours** *(belfastcitybiketours.com)* has bikes for hire and offers tours.

There are several Belfast Bikes docking stations in the city centre. Most people get around the city centre on foot.

☑ TOP TIP

For views of the city centre and beyond, head to the free viewing platform in the dome in **Victoria Square** shopping mall.

Belfast's city centre is dominated by the green dome of City Hall. By day the neighbourhood bustles with shoppers and office workers. High-street chains and malls make up most of the shopping district here, but there are also independent stores selling quality arts and crafts and secondhand goods. At night the area's bars and restaurants fill with drinkers and diners; options range from market-stall snacks to Michelin-starred fine dining.

The neighbourhood's architecture tells the story of its past. Grand Victorian buildings are the legacy of the prosperous shipbuilding and linen-trading days: the Crown Liquor Saloon, Grand Opera House, St George's Market and City Hall were all built during that time. Blocks constructed in the 1970s and 1980s bear witness to the damage done by bombs during the Troubles, but the ambitious architecture of new buildings such as the Grand Central Hotel speaks of a new period of optimism in the city.

Flamboyantly Decorated Gin Palace

A pint in the Crown Liquor Saloon

Not only is the **Crown Liquor Saloon** *(nicholsonspubs.co.uk)* a historical monument and famous Belfast landmark, but it is also a pub in which you can admire the intricate interior as you drink. Located opposite the train station and Grand Opera House, the Crown was refurbished in the late 19th century to appeal to commuters and theatregoers.

Take a look at the exterior, decorated with ornate tiles, it also has a mosaic of a crown on the pavement at the bar's entrance. The interior is a maximalist expression of coloured glass, marble, ceramics, mirrors and mahogany.

Try to snag a table in one of the wooden snugs, complete with panelled doors that bolt closed for privacy. These cosy booths still have gunmetal plates, originally used for striking matches, and bells that once allowed drinkers to order without leaving their seats. Atmospheric gas-lamp lighting and a decorative carved ceiling add to the sense of history.

TOP EXPERIENCE

City Hall

Belfast's architectural centrepiece is the domed, classical Renaissance-style City Hall, where Belfast City Council meets. It was commissioned after Queen Victoria granted Belfast city status in 1888; she is represented by a bronze statue in the grounds, accompanied by figures representing education and Belfast's textile and shipbuilding industries. Much of the building's interior can be viewed on guided tours.

Guided Tours

The 45-minute visit begins at a grand staircase leading to **the rotunda**, with stained-glass windows, Greek columns and Italian marble. Look for the painting *The Founding of Belfast, 1613* (1951) by Irish artist John Luke.

In the **Lord Mayor's Corridor** are the idiosyncratic portraits of past lord mayors (each chooses their own artist and how they would like to be portrayed).

The tour continues through the robing room to the oak-panelled **council chamber**, where you can sit on the lord mayor's throne.

Stained-Glass Windows

Don't miss the themed stained-glass windows on the ground floor. The **Spanish Civil War window** recognises the role of the people of Belfast who fought with the International Brigade, while the **Dockers' Strike Centenary window** portrays Catholic and Protestant workers linked arm in arm during the strike of 1907. Most moving is the **Famine window**, which remembers the suffering of Belfast's citizens during the famine of the 1840s.

Grounds

In front of the main entrance is a bronze statue of Mary Ann McCracken (p526), unveiled in 2024. To the east is a memorial to *Titanic;* it lists the names of more than 1500 people who died in the tragedy.

TOP TIPS

● You can view the ground-floor stained-glass windows without taking a tour.

● A free ground-floor visitor exhibition has displays on Belfast's history and culture.

● In November and December a Christmas market is held in the grounds.

PRACTICALITIES

● belfastcity.gov.uk
● Tours: 11am, 2pm, 3pm & 4pm Mon-Fri, noon, 2pm, 3pm & 4pm Sat & Sun
● adult/child £6/free

DRINKING IN THE CITY CENTRE: COCKTAIL BARS

Muriel's: Has a fabulous Burlesque-style interior and an extensive array of gins and other spirits. *noon-midnight Sun & Mon, to 1am Tue-Thu, to 2am Fri & Sat*

Rattlebag: Dark and intimate with a changing menu of 12 cocktails designed to showcase 12 different spirits. *5pm-1am Wed-Fri, 3pm-1am Sat, 5pm-1am*

Margot: Has chic decor and a great vibe, with a cocktail list featuring some creative combinations. *noon-1am Mon-Thu, to 2am Fri, 11.30am-2am Sat, to 1am Sun*

Angel and Two Bibles: Buzz for entry to this speakeasy-style cocktail bar offering Old and New Testament–themed drinks lists. *5pm-1am Fri & Sat*

⭐ HIGHLIGHTS
1. City Hall
2. Grand Opera House
3. St George's Market

● SIGHTS
4. Crown Entry
5. Crown Liquor Saloon
6. Golden Thread Gallery
7. Jaffe Memorial Fountain
8. Joy's Entry
9. Pottinger's Entry
10. Robinson & Cleaver Building
11. Winecellar Entry

● ACTIVITIES
12. Belfast by the Glass
13. Belfast City Bike Tours
14. Belfast Food Tour
15. Belfast Free Walking Tour
16. Belfast Hidden Tours
17. Belfast Traditional Music Trail

see 41 Creative Tours Belfast
see 15 DC Tours
18. Linen Hall Library

● SLEEPING
see 38 Bullitt Hotel
19. Europa Hotel
20. Fitzwilliam Hotel
21. Flint
22. Grand Central
23. Hilton
24. Malmaison Hotel
25. Room2 Belfast Hometel
26. Ten Square

● EATING
27. EDO
28. James St
29. Jumon
30. OX
31. Pocket
32. Stock Kitchen
33. Yugo

● DRINKING & NIGHTLIFE
34. Angel and Two Bibles
see 7 Bittles Bar
35. Deer's Head
36. Garrick
37. Margot
38. Muriel's
39. Rattlebag
40. White's Tavern

● ENTERTAINMENT
41. Ulster Hall

● SHOPPING
42. Born and Bred
43. Daisies Belfast
see 40 Fresh Garbage
see 38 Miss Morans
44. Victoria Square
see 38 Young Savage

● INFORMATION
see 16 Visit Belfast Welcome Centre

BEST CITY CENTRE SHOPS

Born and Bred: Sells a range of items emblazoned with local sayings and artwork, including mugs, printed canvas bags, tea towels and prints.

Miss Morans: Dating from 1870, this historic, family-run tobacco store stocks fine cigars, tobacco and pipes from around the world.

Young Savage: Packed full with vintage clothing, shoes, records and books, with some fantastic items from the 1960s, '70s and '80s.

Fresh Garbage: Around since 1969, this alternative store sells tie-dye and hemp clothing and bags, incense and burners, and gothic gifts.

Daisies Belfast: Hand-crafted chocolates made with cocoa from Madagascar, including bars, chocolate liqueurs and hot chocolate to drink.

Elaborate Victorian Theatre
Visit the Grand Opera House

Built in 1895, the **Grand Opera House** (goh.co.uk) is one of Belfast's great Victorian landmarks. The best way to experience the building's grandeur is to attend a performance; the Opera House hosts visiting drama, ballet, opera, dance and musical companies, but you'll need to buy tickets in advance.

Otherwise, the theatre's interior can be seen on the one-hour-long, Saturday morning **guided tour** *(adult/child £12.50/9, book in advance)*. These take in the inner workings of the theatre and offer a glimpse backstage, as well as an opportunity to view the swirling wood and plasterwork, fancy gilt work, painted ceiling panels and carved elephant heads of the interior.

EATING IN THE CITY CENTRE: SPASH-OUT MEALS

OX: In a pared-back contemporary space by the River Lagan, Michelin-starred OX offers creative seasonal tasting menus. *6-9pm Wed, noon-2pm & 6-9.30pm Thu-Sat* £££

James St: Bistro known for its steaks, cooked on the Josper charcoal grill. Also serves fish, chicken and vegetarian dishes. *hours vary* £££

Stock Kitchen: Inside St George's Market, chef Danny Miller uses fresh local ingredients, including fish from the market vendors. *5-9pm Thu, 10am-9pm Fri-Sun* £££

Ginger Bistro: Ginger's flame-haired owner/chef sources top-quality Irish produce to create delicious plates. *5-9.15pm Wed, 4-9.15pm Thu, noon-9.30pm Fri & Sat* £££

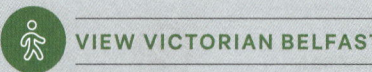

VIEW VICTORIAN BELFAST

Many of Belfast's grandest buildings date back to the Victorian era, when industry was booming and the town was bestowed with city status.

START	END	LENGTH
St George's Market	Grand Opera House	2km; 1½ hours

Start at the elegant, red-brick ① **St George's Market** (p499), completed in 1896. From here, walk west along May St and turn right onto Victoria St to reach ② **Bittles Bar** (p498), housed in an unusual 19th-century triangular building. Outside is the ③ **Jaffe Memorial Fountain**, a gilded, cast-iron drinking fountain (now dry). Retrace your steps south along Victoria St and turn right onto Chichester St to reach the ④ **Garrick** (p498), a pub that's been in operation since 1870. Stop to admire the wood panelling and Victorian tiles inside.

Continue west along Chichester St to pass more Victorian architecture, including the ⑤ **Robinson & Cleaver Building**, built in 1874 to house an upmarket department store (long-since closed). First established in 1788, the ⑥ **Linen Hall Library** is now housed in a former Victorian linen warehouse. Opposite is ⑦ **City Hall** (p493), fronted by a dour statue of Queen Victoria herself. Walk south through the grounds and continue south along Bedford St to reach the ⑧ **Ulster Hall**, a concert venue that opened in 1862. Walk west along Franklin St and Amelia St, then turn right on Great Victoria St. You are now outside the ⑨ **Crown Liquor Saloon** (p492), a magnificent Victorian gin palace decorated with ornate tiles. On the other side of Great Victoria St is the ⑩ **Grand Opera House** (p495), opened in 1895.

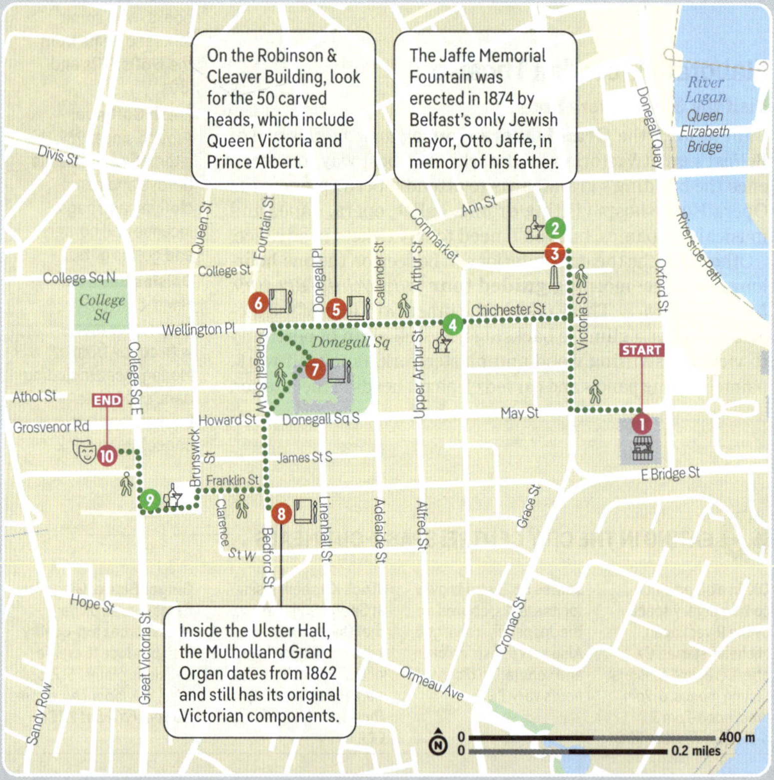

On the Robinson & Cleaver Building, look for the 50 carved heads, which include Queen Victoria and Prince Albert.

The Jaffe Memorial Fountain was erected in 1874 by Belfast's only Jewish mayor, Otto Jaffe, in memory of his father.

Inside the Ulster Hall, the Mulholland Grand Organ dates from 1862 and still has its original Victorian components.

Crown Liquor Saloon (p492)

Belfast's Oldest Library

Look inside Linen Hall Library

Take a look inside the historic **Linen Hall Library** *(linenhall. com; free),* which was established in 1788 by members of the United Irishmen and moved to its current location in a former linen warehouse a decade later. It houses an important Irish, local studies and political collection, including most of what has been written about Northern Irish politics since the 1960s.

Open Monday to Friday, don't miss the *Troubled Images* exhibition, a collection of iconic political posters that tells the story of Northern Ireland's sectarian conflict and peace process in the late 20th century. These visual representations show how the political landscape and attitudes towards armed conflict evolved in the 1970s, '80s and '90s.

Historic Alleyways with Contemporary Street Art

Explore the Entries

Amid the city centre bustle, don't miss these narrow alleyways. They were once commercial and residential thoroughfares connecting Ann St and Waring St with High St, where the River Farset flowed. Since 1848, the river has been contained

OLAUDAH EQUIANO & THE UNITED IRISHMEN

At the High St end of Joy's Entry (p498), a piece by street artist Dreph depicts Olaudah Equiano.

Born in Africa, Equiano was kidnapped and enslaved as a child. After purchasing his freedom, he became a writer and abolitionist.

In 1791 he travelled to Ireland to oversee the production and promotion of his book, *The Interesting Narrative,* in which he shared his experiences of slavery. While in Belfast, Equiano stayed with Samuel Neilson, one of the founders of the Society of United Irishmen and their newspaper, the *Northern Star,* which took an abolitionist stance. Influenced by ideas of the French Revolution, the United Irishmen sought religious equality and separation from England.

EATING IN THE CITY CENTRE: BRUNCH & SMALL PLATES

Yugo: Asian fusion dishes in a chic, industrial-style dining room. Sit at the counter to watch the chefs at work. *5-9pm Tue, noon-2.45pm & 5-9.30pm Wed-Sat* ££

The Pocket: Creative brunch dishes, including an excellent Ulster Fry, plus speciality coffee and booze. *8am-3pm Mon-Thu, to 4pm Fri & Sat, 8.30am-4pm Sun* ££

Jumon: Vegan and vegetarian Southeast Asian fusion (ramen, jackfruit curry, dumplings); has an upbeat atmosphere and wall murals. *hours vary* ££

EDO: Modern European tapas that are perfect for sharing. Dishes are cooked over apple and pear wood in a Bertha oven. *noon-9.30pm Tue-Sat* ££

BEST TOURS OF THE CITY CENTRE

DC Tours: Recommended daily 2½-hour History of Terror walking tours *(per person £22)*, focusing on the Troubles, plus other themed tours.

Belfast Free Walking Tour: Offers a good introduction to the city for first-time visitors; tours leave from City Hall at 11am and 2.30pm.

Belfast Hidden Tours: Entertaining 1½-hour walking tours led by local guides covering art, history, politics and culture.

Belfast Traditional Music Trail: Saturday afternoon trad music experience, taking in sessions and storytelling at different pubs. Begins in Maddens bar.

Creative Tours Belfast: Guided walking tours *(per person £27)* telling the story of Belfast's music and punk music scene; art tours also available.

by underground tunnels. As part of the **Belfast Entries Project**, a number of street artists were commissioned to brighten the alleyways with pieces reflecting the area's people, culture and history.

On **Pottinger's Entry** is the Morning Star, a family-run pub dating from 1810. Outside, look for street art by Nomad Clan depicting pelicans as seen on the Pottinger family crest. On **Winecellar Entry** is White's Tavern, Belfast's oldest tavern. Nearby is a piece by street artist Emic inspired by the poem *Belfast Confetti* by Ciaran Carson.

Joy's Entry is named after Francis Joy, who founded the *Belfast News Letter* in 1737; look for the statue of his grandson Henry Joy McCracken, the United Irishman who was jailed here in 1798. **Crown Entry** is where the Society of United Irishmen was founded in 1791 by Wolfe Tone; street art here depicts a salmon, a reference to the River Farset.

A Taste of Belfast
Sample local produce on a food tour

For an entertaining introduction to the local food scene, with plenty of samples, book the four-hour **Belfast Food Tour** with Taste & Tour *(tasteandtour.co.uk; per person £70)*.

Starting in St George's Market, these fun tours are a great way to learn about and taste the region's most traditional dishes, such as Irish stew, as well as innovative new produce. The company also runs other food and drink tours, including a gin jaunt and a wine wander.

Belfast's history is told through local drinks and animated films during the two-hour **Belfast by the Glass** at the **Spirit Circle** *(thespiritcircle.co.uk; £45)*. The experience includes six drinks relating to a different period in the city's history.

See Contemporary Art
Visit the Golden Thread Gallery

To see contemporary art, pop into **Golden Thread Gallery** *(goldenthreadgallery.co.uk; free)* to view the latest exhibition in the two large gallery spaces, inside the beautiful former Belfast Corporation Gas Showroom. It also offers free events, such as mindful colouring-in workshops. Bear in mind it's closed Sunday and Monday.

DRINKING IN THE CITY CENTRE: BEST PUBS

Deer's Head: Refurbished saloon bar and brewpub. Stouts, lagers and ales are brewed onsite at Bell's Brewery. Trad sessions Fridays. *11am-11pm Sun-Thu, to 1am Fri & Sat*

Garrick: Snug booths, friendly staff, regular live music and its own blended Irish whiskey. Serves a good pint of Guinness. *11.30am-1am Mon-Sat, noon-midnight Sun*

White's Tavern: Est. 1630, White's is Belfast's oldest tavern, with open fires and live music. Trad sessions on Mondays. *noon-midnight Sun-Thu, to 2am Fri & Sat*

Bittles Bar: Traditional bar with cramped interior covered in paintings of Ireland's literary heroes. Excellent whiskey selection. *11.30-11am Mon-Thu, to 1am Fri & Sat, noon-11pm Sun*

TOP EXPERIENCE

St George's Market

A morning spent browsing and snacking at St George's Market is the perfect way to sample local produce and shop for artisan crafts and souvenirs. The covered market is housed in a beautiful Victorian-era building with sandstone porticos and a glazed roof, with live music and different combinations of local food, drink, antiques and craft stalls each day.

Aunt Sandra's Candy Factory

Different Markets

Friday's variety market includes plenty of fresh fish and shellfish from Kilkeel and Portavogie in County Down, as well as locally grown fruit and vegetables, clothes, books and antiques. Saturday's food and craft market has more stalls selling prepared dishes like tapas, curries and vegan pastries, as well as artisan goods such as hand-poured candles and jewellery. Sunday's craft and antiques market has a mix of stalls from the Friday and Saturday markets. Many of the same stalls are open on all three days.

Vendors

The vendors are mostly the craftspeople, bakers, fishers and farmers who have grown, caught or created what they are selling, and they are happy to chat about their wares. Look out for mushrooms from **Sporeshore**, Irish cheeses from **Tom & Ally's**, and traditional sweets like rock, honeycomb and nougat from **Aunt Sandra's Candy Factory**. The egg, bacon and sausage-filled soda farls at the **Belfast Bap Co** are a popular hangover cure. Wash it all down with a flat white from **Drop Hopper Coffee**.

Market Building

The building's glass roof is supported by 70 cast iron pillars. Don't miss the **fish market clock**, which dates from the 1820s.

TOP TIPS

● Book a one-hour guided market tour *(adult/child £10/5)* through **Visit Belfast** *(visitbelfast.com)*.

● Live music adds to the market's buzz; quiet hours are 9am to 10am Friday and Saturday and 10am to 11am Sunday.

● Have a meal at Stock Kitchen (p495), overlooking the market.

Practicalities
● belfastcity.gov.uk
● 8am-2pm Fri, 9am-3pm Sat, 10am-3pm Sun
● Free

Cathedral Quarter

CULTURE AND NIGHTLIFE

GETTING AROUND

The Cathedral Quarter is small enough to explore on foot. At the centre of the neighbourhood is colourful Hill St; come evening, the chatter of local office workers gives way to the clacking of high heels over cobblestones, and the singing of musicians drifts out from nearby bars.

Buses G2 and G1 stop at Custom House Sq. Metro buses go to Donegall Sq in the city centre, less than 1km from the Cathedral Quarter.

☑ TOP TIP

The Cathedral Quarter is the area around St Anne's Cathedral that merges into the city centre. There is a more commercial feel to the city centre, while the Cathedral Quarter is more artsy and alternative, but it's easy to explore both neighbourhoods on foot on the same day.

At the heart of Belfast's nightlife are the pubs, bars and clubs of the Cathedral Quarter, a small artsy neighbourhood named for St Anne's Cathedral that is home to recording studios, media companies and dynamic arts venues. Cobbled Hill St comes alive at night; on long summer evenings, the party spills out onto the street, as revellers gather on Commercial Ct, surrounded by colourful street art and a canopy of hanging umbrellas. One of the most successful bands to emerge from Belfast in recent years is Snow Patrol, who played some of their first gigs at the Duke of York pub. On the surrounding blocks are several traditional pubs with regular live music, while the city's LGBTIQ+ bars are clustered around Union St in the north of the Cathedral Quarter.

In May the Cathedral Quarter Arts Festival brings music, drama, poetry, street theatre and art to the neighbourhood.

Anglican Cathedral with Striking Spire
Take a look inside St Anne's Cathedral

This area is named after Church of Ireland **St Anne's Cathedral** *(belfastcathedral.org; adult/child £5/free; with audioguide £8)*. Its most striking feature is its titanium-clad spire, which can also be seen from inside, where it extends from the nave to emerge through a glass platform in the roof, rising 80m high.

The highlight of the self-guided tour is the **baptistery,** notable for its Romanesque-style ceiling mosaic of the Creation, made with 150,000 pieces of glass. Don't miss the **Titanic Pall** (cloth draped over a coffin), embroidered with some 1500 crosses in memory of those who died in the tragedy. The piece was created in 2012 to mark the centenary of the disaster; the indigo blue colour evokes the night sky under which the ship went down. Allow around 30 minutes to look around.

BELFAST CATHEDRAL QUARTER

HIGHLIGHTS
1. Oh Yeah Music Centre
2. St Anne's Cathedral
3. Sunflower

SIGHTS
4. 2 Royal Avenue
5. Albert Memorial Clock
6. Big Fish
7. Commercial Court
8. Custom House
9. Duel of Belfast
10. Lagan Weir

ACTIVITIES
11. Bridges Urban Sports Park
- see 1 Circusful
- see 7 Sensorium
- see 7 Street Art Walking Tour
13. Studio 52
14. Waterman House

SLEEPING
15. Merchant Hotel
16. The Foundry

EATING
17. Coppi
18. Established Coffee
19. Great Room
20. HJEM
21. Muddlers Club
22. Neighbourhood Cafe
- see 12 TRAIT Coffee
- see 14 Waterman

DRINKING & NIGHTLIFE
23. Duke of York
24. John Hewitt
- see 12 National

ENTERTAINMENT
25. Berts Jazz Bar
- see 7 Black Box
26. Hit the North
27. MAC

SHOPPING
28. Art Shop
29. Craft NI
30. Mike's Fancy Cheese

BELFAST'S PUNK HISTORY

The violence and sectarianism of everyday life in 1970s Belfast were fertile ground for a punk rock music scene, which provided an outlet for the undercurrents of rage and disaffection in the city.

Belfast band Stiff Little Fingers formed in 1977, at the height of the Troubles. Their punk rock anthem 'Alternative Ulster' (1978) is an anti-establishment battle cry. After multiple personnel changes, the band's current line-up is still touring.

Derry band The Undertones were in Belfast when they got their break after meeting Terri Hooley of the Good Vibrations record shop and label. Their most successful hit was 'Teenage Kicks' in 1978. The story of Terri Hooley and Belfast's punk rock scene is told in the 2013 film *Good Vibrations*.

Contemporary Art & Performance Space
Visit the Metropolitan Arts Centre (MAC)

Check what's on at the **MAC** *(themaclive.com)*, a beautifully designed venue with an exposed brick and polished concrete interior. It has two theatres hosting drama, stand-up comedy, talks, and events for children. The MAC's three galleries stage a rolling programme of free exhibitions.

In the foyer look for Irish artist Mark Garry's sculpture *The Permanent Present,* a piece made with 400 metal wires that creates a spectrum of colours. It represents the futility of violence and the hopes of Belfast's young people.

Painted Walls
Discover neighbourhood street art

Belfast is known for sectarian murals, often painted on gable ends to stake out territory and declare political allegiances. But in the Cathedral Quarter, the culture has been reset with the emergence of a nonsectarian street art scene.

Much of the neighbourhood's street art was commissioned as part of **Hit the North** festival. Started in 2013 by a local arts organisation, it takes place each May.

Some of the world's leading street artists have left their mark. Walk along Hill St to see a number of pieces, including Irish artist Conor Harrington's ***Duel of Belfast***. A comment on colonialism, it depicts two historical figures fighting over a dead animal, while a third looks on.

Nearby, just off Talbot St, ***The Son of Protagoras*** by MTO shows a dove of peace killed by two arrows bearing the symbolism of the Catholic and Protestant churches.

Cross Royal Ave and walk along Kent St and Union St to see more than 50 different pieces. To find out more, check out the annotated map on the Seedhead Arts website (seedheadarts.com). On Sundays, Seedhead Arts offers a two-hour **Street Art Walking Tour** *(£12)*; some guides are street artists themselves.

From Folk Music to Snow Patrol
The history of Northern Irish music at Oh Yeah Music Centre

Housed in a converted whiskey warehouse, the **Oh Yeah Music Centre** *(ohyeahbelfast.com, closed Sunday)* is a social enterprise that provides rehearsal spaces for musicians

EATING IN THE CATHEDRAL QUARTER: COFFEE & BRUNCH

Established Coffee: Offers a range of drip brews, brunch until 3pm and cake; in a bright corner on Hill St. *7am-4.30pm Mon-Fri, 8am-4.30pm Sat & Sun* **£**

HJEM: Ulster University coffee shop with views of St Anne's, plus pastries from excellent local bakery Bakari. *7.30am-3.30pm Mon-Fri, 8.30am-3pm Sat, 9.30am-2.30pm Sun* **£**

TRAIT Coffee: Serves a range of sweet and savoury pastries (croissants, sausage rolls, cookies), plus matcha and coffee (of course). *7.30am-4.30pm* **£**

Neighbourhood Cafe: Head here for speciality coffee and dishes like mushroom toast, Turkish eggs and buttermilk pancakes. *7.30am-4pm Mon-Fri, 8.30am-5pm Sat & Sun* **££**

A WANDER AROUND THE CATHEDRAL QUARTER

This walking tour takes in the street art and architecture of the Cathedral Quarter.

START	END	LENGTH
Big Fish	St Anne's Cathedral	900m; 1 hr

Begin your walk on the banks of the Lagan at the 1 **Big Fish**, a 10m ceramic salmon sculpture symbolising the river's regeneration. It's next to 2 **Lagan Weir**, built to control the river's tidal levels. Cross the road to reach 3 **Custom House** (1857), one of several buildings in Belfast designed by architect Charles Lanyon. Continue west along Queen's Sq to reach the 4 **Albert Memorial Clock** (1865), a leaning, decorative clock tower made of Scrabo sandstone. Cross Victoria St via the pedestrian crossing, and look up to see the mural *The Chef & The Lobster* by Smug on the opposite side of High St.

Cross High St and walk up Skipper Street to reach Hill St. Look up to see the mural *Still Waters* by Nomad Clan, which features a wolf (a symbol of Belfast) and references the city's shipbuilding and linen trades. Further up Hill St, look for the mural 5 ***Duel of Belfast***. Next you'll reach 6 **Commercial Court**, where a canopy of colourful umbrellas covers the courtyard. Return to Hill St and continue up Exchange St to the red-brick exterior of the 7 **MAC**. From here there is a good view of the spire of 8 **St Anne's Cathedral** (p500). Turn left onto Academy St and left again onto Donegall St to reach the cathedral entrance.

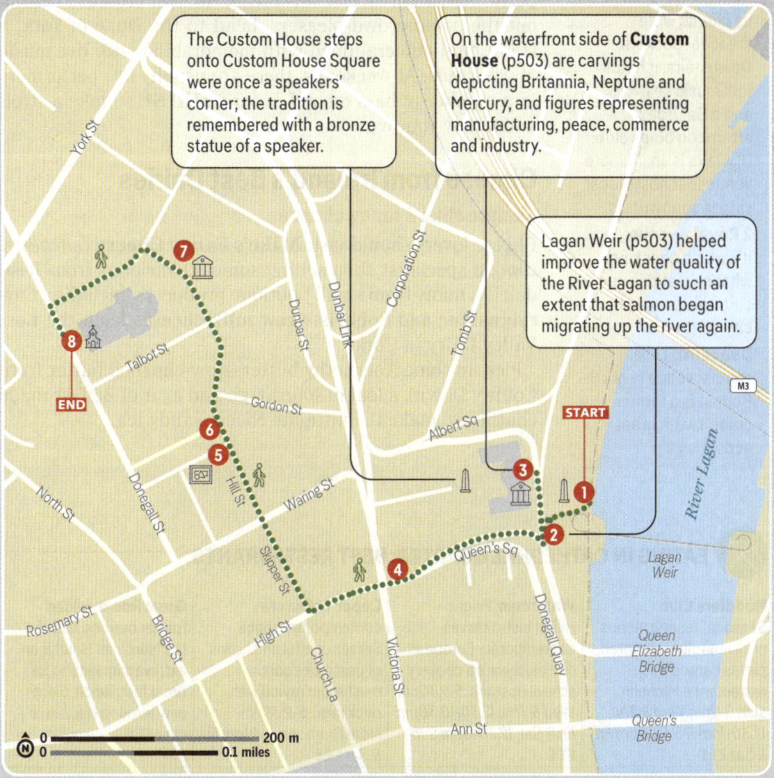
The Custom House steps onto Custom House Square were once a speakers' corner; the tradition is remembered with a bronze statue of a speaker.
On the waterfront side of **Custom House** (p503) are carvings depicting Britannia, Neptune and Mercury, and figures representing manufacturing, peace, commerce and industry.
Lagan Weir (p503) helped improve the water quality of the River Lagan to such an extent that salmon began migrating up the river again.
York St
Dunbar St
Dunbar Link
Corporation St
Tomb St
Talbot St
Gordon St
Albert Sq
Waring St
North St
Donegall St
Hill St
Skipper St
Queen's Sq
Rosemary St
Bridge St
High St
Church La
Victoria St
Donegall Quay
Ann St
River Lagan
Lagan Weir
Queen Elizabeth Bridge
Queen's Bridge
M3
START
END
1
2
3
4
5
6
7
8
0 200 m
0 0.1 miles

BELFAST'S LIVE MUSIC SCENE

Dolores of Creative Tours Belfast shares her favourite places to hear live music. *@creativetoursbelfast*

Cathedral Quarter: Some of Belfast's best gigs are held at the Black Box, the Oh Yeah Music Centre (p502) and the Sunflower.

American Bar: This old-style pub in Sailortown (north Belfast) with memorabilia on the walls is little changed from the days when its clients were the local dockers. Downstairs, it holds folk music sessions and a Saturday afternoon blues club. Upstairs is an intimate venue that hosts local singer-songwriters.

2 Royal Avenue: It's worth checking what's on at this new cultural space in the city centre.

Duncairn: This special venue in north Belfast is a former church, with great acoustics.

as well as being home to an exhibition on Northern Ireland's music history. The free *Northern Ireland Music Exhibition* takes around 20 minutes to view and includes memorabilia related to punk bands the Undertones and Stiff Little Fingers, and items from Terri Hooley's Good Vibrations record store.

Look out for a vintage sign from Cyprus Avenue, the east Belfast street made famous by Van Morrison. Another prized exhibit is the Fender guitar used by Snow Patrol's Gary Lightbody to write the hit 'Chasing Cars'. Conversations between Snow Patrol and members of the Belfast music industry were the impetus for the launch of the Oh Yeah Music Centre project in 2005.

Catch a Live Music Session

Trad, jazz, folk and rock

The Cathedral Quarter is Belfast's best neighbourhood for live music. For authentic trad sessions, head to the John Hewitt on Thursday nights, Saturday nights and Sunday afternoons, when local musicians gather around a table to play. Another safe bet for live music is the Sunflower, where there is something scheduled every day of the week, from open mic nights to jazz and blues, folk music, and Sunday evening trad sessions.

At the Merchant Hotel, **Berts Jazz Bar** has nightly jazz performances in an elegant setting. To hear crooners belting out the usual crowd-pleasers, head to the Duke of York, a traditional pub crammed with memorabilia with live music at weekends. At weekends, there are usually live performers in a number of bars on and around **Hill St**, so take a stroll and follow your ears.

Cheese from Ireland's Best Dairies

Sample Mike's fancy cheese

Cheese lovers should visit **Mike's Fancy Cheese** *(mfcheese.com)*, a specialist shop selling some 50 varieties from Irish dairies, many from small boutique producers, including Carraignamuc and Sobhriste raw milk cheeses from the Lost Valley Dairy in Cork.

Pick up some Abernethy butter (slow-churned butter from County Down), a loaf of sourdough and a jar of Belfast-made chutney to make the ultimate cheese sandwich.

EATING IN CATHEDRAL QUARTER: BEST RESTAURANTS

Muddlers Club: Seasonal tasting menus of beautifully presented plates earned this restaurant a Michelin star. *5-9pm Wed & Thu, 12.30-1pm & 5-9.30pm Fri & Sat* £££

Waterman: Bright Hill St bistro serves contemporary European dishes; there's a cookery school upstairs. *5-9.30pm Wed & Thu, 12.30-10.30pm Fri & Sat, 12.30-8pm Sun* £££

Coppi: Italian in a contemporary space. Serves comforting bowls of pasta, like porcini mushroom ravioli with duck ragu. *5-9.30pm Mon-Thu, noon-9.30pm Fri & Sat* £££

Great Room: Gilded former banking hall of the Merchant Hotel is an extravagant setting for breakfast, lunch, dinner or afternoon tea. *hours vary* £££

Musicians at the Sunflower

Local Art & Crafts
Buy paintings, prints, ceramics and textiles

The Cathedral Quarter is the perfect place to pick up an original piece by a local artist. At Ulster University, the Belfast School of Art (BSOA) **Art Shop** (closed Saturday and Sunday) sells pieces by students, alumni and other local designer makers; you might bag a piece by an up-and-coming star. It's open Monday to Friday.

Nearby, **Craft NI** *(craftni.org)* is a shop and gallery space displaying the work of more than 40 local designer makers in a range of media, from textiles and ceramics to wood and glass.

Innovative Arts Centre
Comedy nights, storytelling sessions and live music

If you've always wanted to learn circus skills or speak at a storytelling event, the Cathedral Quarter is for you. On Hill St, **Black Box** *(blackboxbelfast.com)* is an innovative arts centre with a dynamic programme of magic nights, comedy shows, art exhibitions and live music.

Submit a piece of themed writing for a chance to take the stage at the venue's monthly **Tenx9** storytelling night, or simply go along to hear that night's tales. Black Box also runs club nights for adults with learning disabilities, and has a gig buddies scheme to make its events more accessible.

BEST CATHEDRAL QUARTER ACTIVITIES

Circusful: Circus school teaching skills such as trapeze and aerial apparatus for children and adults. Also performs at festivals and events.

Studio 52: Vinyasa yoga and pilates studio overlooking Hill St. Offers a range of classes and workshops.

Sensorium: Guided taste, smell and sound cocktail experience, ending with a bespoke cocktail based on your preferences; held at the Spirit Circle at the National.

Waterman House: Cookery school with classes such as a fish and shellfish masterclass and how to cook the perfect steak.

Bridges Urban Sports Park: Skatepark underneath the motorway with skateboard, in-line skating, parkour and BMX facilities; friendly crowd. Bring your own gear.

 DRINKING IN THE CATHEDRAL QUARTER: BARS WITH LIVE MUSIC

Sunflower: Enter through the security cage (a relic of Belfast's social history); order wood-fired pizzas in the beer garden. *hours vary*

John Hewitt: Named after the Belfast poet, has an excellent selection of beers, including local brewery Boundary. *noon-midnight Sun & Tue-Thu, to 1am Fri & Sat*

Duke of York: The interior of this traditional pub feels like a living museum; one of Belfast's liveliest spots on Saturday nights. *11.30am-1am Mon-Sat, 1-9pm Sun*

National: Renovated former National Bank is a grand setting for cocktails and club nights on Friday and Saturday; large beer garden out back. *hours vary*

Titanic Quarter & East Belfast

HISTORIC SHIPYARDS

GETTING AROUND

A footbridge over Lagan Weir links the Cathedral Quarter (and the adjoining city centre) with the Titanic Quarter.

The G2, 26 and 26B buses link the Queen's Rd in the Titanic Quarter with the city centre.

A footbridge over the M3 motorway links the main sights with **Titanic Quarter** train station on the Belfast to Bangor line.

The city's bike-share programme, Belfast Bikes has docking stations at the Odyssey Complex, by SS *Nomadic*, and on Queen's Rd at Titanic Studios.

☑ TOP TIP

Consider exploring the Titanic Quarter by bike. Travelling on two wheels makes it quick and easy to cover ground in the flat, open spaces of the former dockyards, and cycling routes are largely traffic free.

These days the *Titanic* is so closely connected to Belfast's identity that there is even a neighbourhood named after it: the shipyards where the *Titanic* was constructed are now part of the redeveloped Titanic Quarter. At its centre is Titanic Belfast, a state-of-the-art multimedia museum that has become the city's number-one tourist draw. Around it are several other sites with links to the *Titanic;* this includes the centre of Belfast's burgeoning film industry, Titanic Studios.

The residential neighbourhoods of East Belfast, where the shipyard workers once lived, are now home to a growing creative community and a cooperative brewery. East Belfast is also a tangible presence in many of Van Morrison's songs, which have nostalgic references to the neighbourhood where he grew up; sites include the Hollow from 'Brown Eyed Girl' and Cyprus Avenue. Nearby is the landmark building known as Stormont, where the Northern Ireland Assembly meets.

Whiskey Distillery in a Former Pump House
Visit Titanic Distillers

Whiskey and *Titanic* history collide at **Titanic Distillers** *(titanicdistillers.com; distillery tours adult/child £25/12.50)*, housed in the pump house at Thompson Dock, where the ship was fitted out. The pump house has been beautifully restored, with much of the old machinery preserved in place next to new copper stills and mash tuns.

Walk around the building, learn about the distilling process and taste whiskeys on hour-long guided tours, which set the distillery in its historical context; the city was once a major whiskey producer, but until Titanic Distillers began production in 2023, there had been no working distillery in the city for 90 years. The distillers also offer 60-minute guided tours *(£10)* of the huge dry dock built to accommodate the *Titanic*.

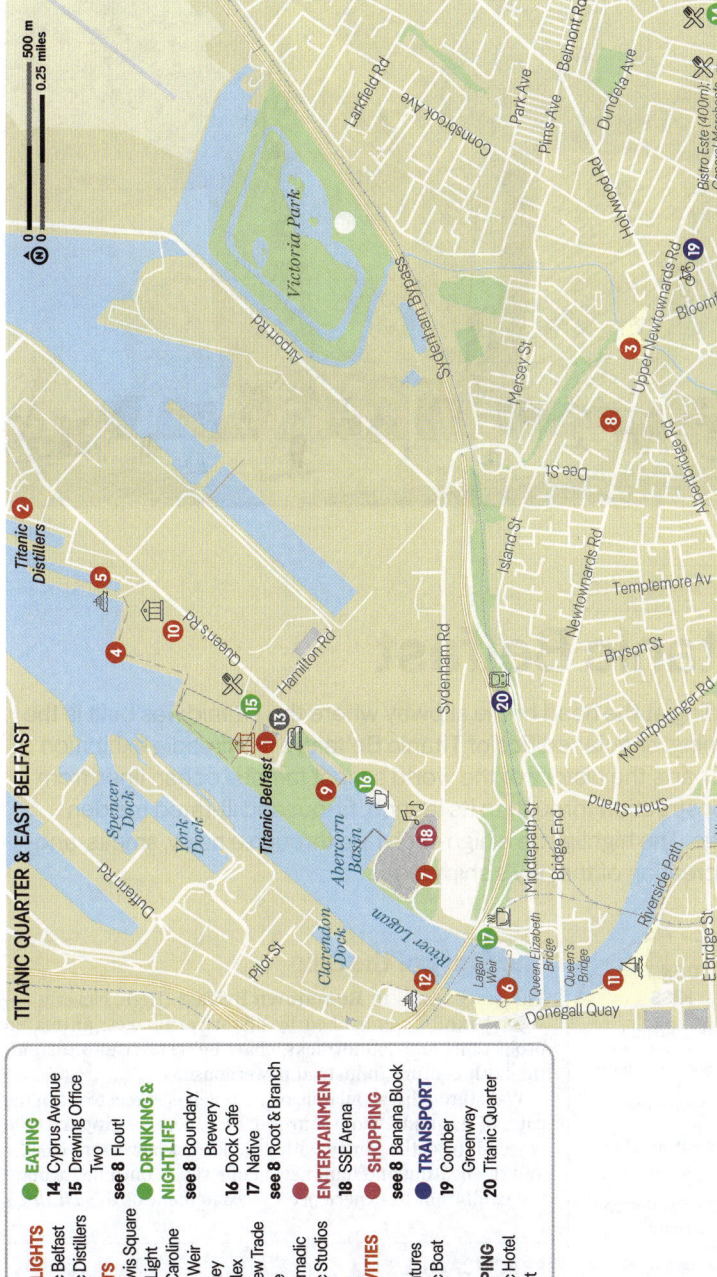

TITANIC QUARTER & EAST BELFAST

★ HIGHLIGHTS
1 Titanic Belfast
2 Titanic Distillers

● SIGHTS
3 CS Lewis Square
4 Great Light
5 HMS Caroline
6 Lagan Weir
7 Odyssey Complex
8 Portview Trade Centre
9 SS Nomadic
10 Titanic Studios
see 7 W5

● ACTIVITIES
11 Lagan Adventures
12 Titanic Boat Tours

● SLEEPING
13 Titanic Hotel Belfast

● EATING
14 Cyprus Avenue
15 Drawing Office Two
see 8 Flout!

● DRINKING & NIGHTLIFE
see 8 Boundary Brewery
16 Dock Cafe
17 Native
see 8 Root & Branch

● ENTERTAINMENT
18 SSE Arena

● SHOPPING
see 8 Banana Block

● TRANSPORT
19 Comber Greenway
20 Titanic Quarter

TOP EXPERIENCE

Titanic Belfast

Standing at the head of the slipway where the *Titanic* was built is the gleaming, angular edifice of Titanic Belfast, a multimedia exhibition that charts the history of the world's most famous ocean liner, from its construction through to its launch, fit-out and ill-fated maiden voyage. The highlight is a high-tech ride through a noisy, smells-and-all recreation of the city's shipyard.

DON'T MISS

- Shipyard ride
- Fit-out virtual tour
- SS *Nomadic*
- Recreation of the launch
- Letters written on board
- Original lifejacket
- Ship of Dreams gallery

The Story of the Ship

The story starts in **Boomtown Belfast**. Here, cleverly designed exhibits enlivened by historical images, animated projections and soundtracks, chart Belfast's rise to turn-of-the-20th-century industrial powerhouse.

Walk through a simulation of a 1911 Belfast street to reach the gates of Harland & Wolff shipyard. From here, a **shipyard ride** descends from the gantry, with a soundtrack of workers' chatter and the heating and hammering of rivets. Continue through the exhibition to experience the excitement of the *Titanic*'s

PRACTICALITIES

- titanicbelfast.com
- adult/child/family £26.95/13/68; tickets include admission to the SS *Nomadic*
- 8.30am-7.30pm Jul & Aug, shorter hours Sep to Jun

1911 **launch**. The gallery's windows are shaped like a ship's bow and overlook the *Titanic* slipway behind the museum.

Next, exhibits explore every detail of the *Titanic's* **fit-out**. The highlights are the audio-visual 'fly-through' from keel to bridge and the replica cabins of Titanic's first-, second-, and third-class passenger accommodation. Life aboard the ship is recreated with a walk on deck; look for touching family letters dispatched before the ship got into trouble, and a first-class dinner menu.

Tragedy Strikes

In a darkened corridor, the sinking of the *Titanic* is represented by the sounds of Morse code, the final messages sent to nearby ships and the stories of survivors. Exhibits include an **original lifejacket** from the ship.

The aftermath of the disaster is examined through witness testimonies given at the numerous enquiries. The 'Domino Effect' exhibit shows how a series of factors interacted to cause the disaster.

Finally, the **Ship of Dreams** gallery has a suspended scale model of the ship and a number of artefacts, including a violin belonging to the musician Wallace Hartley and a *Titanic* deckchair, recovered from the surface by a ship chartered to search for bodies after the sinking by the White Star Line. Titanic Belfast's policy is not to include artefacts recovered from the wreck, for ethical reasons.

SS Nomadic

Next to Titanic Belfast is the **SS *Nomadic*,** the last remaining vessel of the White Star Line. Built in Belfast in 1911, the little steamship ferried 1st- and 2nd-class passengers between Cherbourg Harbour and ocean liners that were too big to dock at the French port. On 10 April 1912, it delivered 172 passengers to the *Titanic*.

Nomadic was requisitioned during both world wars and ended up as a floating restaurant in Paris. In 2006, it was rescued from a breaker's yard and brought to Belfast for restoration.

The Slipways

Allow time to explore the massive slipways where the *Titanic* and her sister ship *Olympic* were built and launched, located behind the Titanic Belfast building. The size and location of each ship are indicated with blue lines, illuminated at night. Within the outline of *Titanic*, the promenade deck is inlaid in white stone, which indicates the position of the liner's lifeboats and funnels. Benches are positioned exactly where they were located on deck.

Within the outline of the *Olympic*, strips of lawn and decking of differing widths correspond to the numbers of people who died and survived. Divided into passenger class and crew, these offer a visual representation of how the proportion of survivors differed according to economic standing.

BUILDING DESIGN

The star attraction in the ongoing regeneration of the Titanic Quarter, Titanic Belfast opened in 2012, 100 years after the ship's tragic voyage.

According to the architects, the design of the Titanic Belfast building was inspired by the shape of water crystals as they freeze, icebergs, and the gantries used to build the ship. The layout of the interior is based on a maritime compass rose.

TOP TIPS

● Follow the story of several real-life *Titanic* passengers around the exhibition; look for panels telling their tales at each stage of the journey.

● Begin your visit at the Titanic Experience, then look around SS *Nomadic* (included in admission). If you are visiting late in the day, start at SS *Nomadic*, which closes earlier.

● Book tickets online in advance for a small discount and to avoid ticket-office queues. Discounted morning tickets and late saver tickets are available at certain times.

● Don't miss the other neighbourhood *Titanic* sites, including Thompson graving dock (where the *Titanic* was fitted out) and pump house, now Titanic Distillers (p506).

A WATERFRONT WALK THROUGH THE TITANIC QUARTER

Explore Belfast's maritime history on this walk through the Titanic Quarter, where the former shipyards have been transformed.

START	END	LENGTH
Lagan Weir footbridge	Titanic Distillers	3km; 2 hrs

From **1** **Lagan Weir** (p503), cross the footbridge to Queen's Quay. Turn left (north) and follow the riverbank path to **2** **Odyssey Complex**.

Continue past Abercorn Basin, a working marina, then cross the footbridge to Hamilton Dock and **3** **SS Nomadic** (p509), which ferried *Titanic* passengers from Cherbourg Harbour to the ship. Cross the footbridge to the 1867 **4** **pump house**, which was used to drain Hamilton Dock.

Now the gleaming, angular structure of **5** **Titanic Belfast** (p508) comes into full view. To the right of the Titanic Belfast building are the drawing offices where *Titanic* was designed, now the **6** **Titanic Hotel** (p529).

Behind Titanic Belfast are the **7** **slipways** from which *Titanic* and its sister ship *Olympic* were launched. Walk to the far end of the slipways to get a sense of the ships' size. From here, there is a good view of the yellow Harland & Wolff cranes, known as Samson and Goliath.

Continue along the waterside, with **8** **Titanic Studios** to your right, to reach the **9** **Great Light**, a former lighthouse lens, and on to Alexandra Dock, home to **10** **HMS Caroline**.

Behind it is the pump house used to drain the water from Thompson Dry Dock, where the *Titanic* was fitted out. The building is now **11** **Titanic Distillers** (p506).

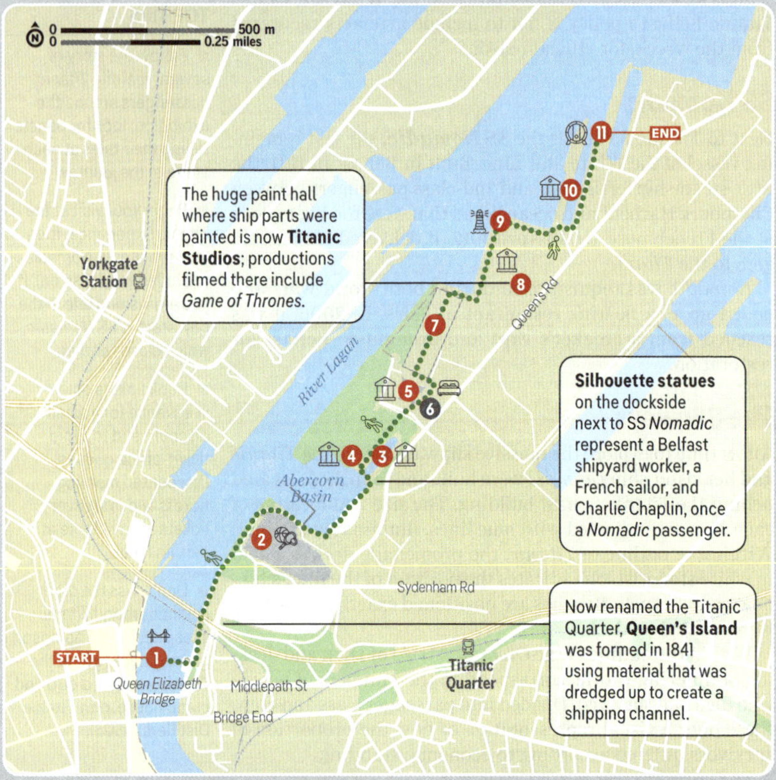
0 500 m
0 0.25 miles
The huge paint hall where ship parts were painted is now **Titanic Studios**; productions filmed there include *Game of Thrones*.
Yorkgate Station
River Lagan
Queen's Rd
Abercorn Basin
Silhouette statues on the dockside next to SS *Nomadic* represent a Belfast shipyard worker, a French sailor, and Charlie Chaplin, once a *Nomadic* passenger.
Sydenham Rd
Now renamed the Titanic Quarter, **Queen's Island** was formed in 1841 using material that was dredged up to create a shipping channel.
START
END
Queen Elizabeth Bridge
Middlepath St
Bridge End
Titanic Quarter

WWI Royal Navy Cruiser
On board HMS *Caroline*

The UK's last surviving WWI Royal Navy cruiser, **HMS *Caroline*** (nmrn.org.uk; adult/child £11/9), is now a floating museum at Alexandra Dock. Scheduled guided tours take in the captain's quarters, officers' cabins, marine mess, sick bay and galley kitchen, with interactive exhibits and a film dramatisation of HMS *Caroline*'s role in the 1916 Battle of Jutland. The engine room has been preserved as it was when it was an active warship. There are also interactive displays that simulate firing a torpedo and steering the ship. Allow at least an hour here.

Belfast Giants Ice Hockey Team
Catch them in action at SSE Arena

At the **Odyssey Complex**, a sports and entertainment complex, the **SSE Arena** (ssearenabelfast.com) is home to the Belfast Giants. This ice hockey team has won the UK's Elite Ice Hockey League multiple times. The season runs from September to April. See fixture dates and buy tickets at belfastgiants.com.

Northern Ireland's Parliament Building
Visit Stormont

The white neoclassical facade of **Stormont** (niassembly.gov.uk) is one of Belfast's most iconic. Built in 1932 to house Northern Ireland's parliament, the building occupies a dramatic hilltop position reached by a 1.5km tree-lined avenue.

Following the Good Friday Agreement of 1998, Stormont became home to the Northern Ireland Assembly, the devolved legislative body. Free, 45-minute guided tours (book online in advance) of the Great Hall, Assembly and Senate Chambers give an informative overview of the power-sharing political system and the Good Friday Agreement on which it is based.

Walking trails through the grounds pass through woodland areas and by several sculptures. Don't miss the bronze cast of the piece *Reconciliation* by Josefina De Vasconcellos; three further casts are located in Berlin, Coventry and Hiroshima.

Local Enterprise
Visit Boundary Brewery and Banana Block

On Newtownards Rd in East Belfast, the **Portview Trade Centre** is the location of a cluster of exciting local enterprises, neighbourhood arts projects and community spaces.

BEST FOR KIDS IN BELFAST

W5: This hands-on, interactive science discovery centre at the Odyssey Complex in the Titanic Quarter has a range of exciting exhibits for kids.

Colin Glen: Woodland area in West Belfast with ziplines (including the 700m River Rapid, suitable for children aged 10 and over), rope courses and a Gruffalo trail.

CS Lewis Square: At this East Belfast square, bronze statues by Irish artist Maurice Harron depict figures from *The Lion, The Witch and The Wardrobe*.

Titanic Boat Tours: River tours aboard the Lady of the Lagan sail past Titanic's slipway and Thompson Dry Dock; you might even spot seals.

Lagan Adventures: Cycle on the River Lagan on a hydrobike, suitable for children aged eight and up.

DRINKING IN TITANIC QUARTER & EAST BELFAST: COFFEE SHOPS

Dock Cafe: The tea, coffee and snacks at this Titanic Quarter cafe are offered in return for a voluntary donation in the honesty box. *11am-4pm Tue-Sat*

Native: Coffee and pastries at open-air tables on Titanic Quarter's Queen's Quay, with views of the harbour. *8am-4pm Mon-Fri, 9am-4pm Sat, 10am-4pm Sun*

Root & Branch: Coffee roasters and brew bar, where you can see the beans roasting behind the counter as you sip. *8.30am-3pm Mon-Fri*

General Merchants: Locally-roasted coffee, plus masala chai and matcha lattes. A popular spot for brunch. *8am-5pm Mon-Sat, 9am-5pm Sun*

VAN MORRISON'S EAST BELFAST

Belfast is a tangible presence in many of Van Morrison's songs, which are full of nostalgic references to his childhood in East Belfast. After achieving some success with the band Them, Morrison embarked on a solo career and released his hit song 'Brown Eyed Girl' in 1967. His affectionate portrayal of Belfast has made him popular in his hometown.

Neighbourhood sights referenced in Morisson's lyrics, include the Hollow (immortalised in 'Brown Eyed Girl'), an area by Conn's Water next to the historic Conn O'Neill stone bridge.

Another sight is leafy Cypress Ave. In the eponymous song, Morrison recalls walking down the tree-lined street in typically wet and windy Belfast weather, but says the sun broke through when his love appeared.

Comber Greenway

Here you can visit **Boundary Brewery** *(boundarybrewing. coop; tours £25)*, a cooperative that produces highly rated ales and lagers onsite. Head to the tap room to sample the range, or book a two-hour brewery tour and guided tasting, held on Saturdays. Coffee roaster Root & Branch (p511) also has its roastery and an espresso bar here; pop in for coffee or to pick up some beans.

Banana Block *(bananablock.org)* is an innovative commercial and community events space in a former linen mill. Look out for events including yoga classes, drag brunches and plant-care workshops, and check the date of the next East Block Bazaar, a monthly Sunday-afternoon artisan market.

East Belfast by Bike

Cycle the Comber Greenway

The **Comber Greenway** is an 11km path along a former railway line to the village of Comber in County Down. The traffic-free greenway begins at the car park at Ravenscroft Ave near Holywood Rd in East Belfast. Starting your cycle in the city centre or Titanic Quarter you can follow the Sustrans route along quiet residential streets to reach the greenway.

The flat tarmacked path leads east through the city, passing close to Stormont (p511) before emerging into the countryside. At the end of the greenway, you can extend your cycle to explore the shores of Strangford Lough.

EATING IN TITANIC QUARTER & EAST BELFAST: OUR PICKS

Flout!: Pizzeria on Newtownards Rd that's highly regarded by critics and punters; arrive early. *noon-2pm Wed & Thu, noon-2pm & 5pm-close Fri, noon-3pm Sat* ££

Drawing Office Two: Former Harland & Wolff drawing offices at Titanic Hotel, now an airy space serving bar meals and drinks. *9am-9.30pm* ££

Bistro Este: Intimate, family-run bistro serves classic dishes; come before 6.30pm for the earlybird menu. *5-8pm Wed & Thu, to 9.30pm Fri & Sat, 1-5pm Sun* £££

Cyprus Avenue: Family-friendly bistro in Ballyhackamore. *10am-9.30pm Mon-Thu, 10am-10.30pm Fri, 9.30am-10.30pm Sat & Sun* ££

Holywood

RESTAURANTS, MUSEUMS AND A BEACH

The nearest beach to Belfast is in the upmarket eastern suburb of Holywood, on the County Down coast. Easy to reach from the city centre by train or car, Holywood is a desirable place to live (houses here are some of Northern Ireland's most expensive), and the town makes a worthwhile day trip from Belfast. In recent years, Holywood has become one of the region's best places to eat out, with a vibrant food scene. Lining the High St are delis packed full of produce from local organic farms, bakeries, cafes and restaurants, alongside independent art shops, design stores and fashion boutiques.

Just east of Holywood, in Cultra, the Ulster Folk Museum has period buildings from all over the country, reconstructed on site to form an open-air museum; it makes a great day out for kids. Nearby is the Ulster Transport Museum, with steam engines, vintage motorbikes and cars.

Open-Air Museum Celebrating Local Traditions

Visit the Ulster Folk Museum

At the **Ulster Folk Museum** *(ulsterfolkmuseum.org; adult/child £12/7.45)*, a collection of heritage buildings has been relocated to recreate a typical Irish town and rural community of years gone by. The museum makes a fun day out for families. It's 3km east of Holywood, in Cultra.

Start by exploring the town, where you can watch the intricate printing process at Baird's Print Shop, see red-brick terraces from 19th-century Belfast and Dromore, and stop by the Picture House, a silent cinema that was housed in a County Down hayloft from 1909 to 1931. There's even a corner shop dating from 1889 selling sweets from glass jars.

From here follow Mill Rd to visit farmhouses, a rural school and the blacksmiths at Spade Mill, passing farm animals along the way.

The route is 2.4km long. Count on spending at least three hours here.

GETTING AROUND

Holywood is on the Belfast to Bangor train line. It's a 20-minute journey from Grand Central Station, stopping at Botanic, Lanyon Place, and Titanic Quarter. From Holywood Station, you can walk to the shops, restaurants and beach.

The nearest station to the Ulster Transport Museum and Ulster Folk Museum is Cultra, two stations east of Holywood.

You can also take buses 1, 2 or 502a from Lanyon Place Station.

From Belfast city centre, it's a 15-minute journey by car to Holywood – 20 minutes to the area's museums.

☑ TOP TIP

Iif you want to swim, head 7km east to Helen's Bay (p552); the beach is 10 minutes' walk south of Helen's Bay train station. You could walk there via the coastal path (8km, around two hours).

HOLYWOOD

HIGHLIGHTS
1. Holywood Seapark
2. Ulster Folk Museum
3. Ulster Transport Museum

SLEEPING
4. Culloden Hotel

EATING
5. Fontana
6. Frae
7. Lynchpin
8. Noble

SHOPPING
9. Epicurean Deli
10. Fox Boutique
11. Oscar & Joy
12. Roco & Coco
13. Yard Gallery

TRANSPORT
14. Holywood Train Station

DeLorean DMC prototype, Ulster Transport Museum

Historic Steam Trains & Vintage Cars
All aboard the Ulster Transport Museum

Across the road from the Ulster Folk Museum, the **Ulster Transport Museum** *(ulstertransportmuseum.org, adult/child £12/7.45, closed Monday)* is great for kids and transport enthusiasts, with steam locomotives, motorcycles, trams, buses and cars.

You can climb aboard the steam train *Meadb*, a 1939 Irish locomotive. The highlight of the car collection is the stainless-steel-clad prototype of the ill-fated DeLorean DMC, made in Belfast in 1981. The car was a commercial disaster but achieved everlasting fame in the *Back to the Future* films. Allow around two hours at the museum.

Beach Time & Coastal Walks
Visit Holywood Seapark

The sandy beach, grassy park and a large children's playground at **Holywood Seapark** make the perfect setting for a picnic on a sunny day. It's a beautiful spot at sunset.

Holywood Seapark is also the starting point for the **North Down Coastal Path**, which continues for 25km east to Bangor and beyond (p552).

BEST INDEPENDENT SHOPS IN HOLYWOOD

Epicurean Deli: Filled with Irish cheeses, freshly-baked sourdough and all kinds of local produce, this fantastic deli is a destination in itself.

Oscar & Joy: Homewares and design store selling items like fold-away bags and tea towels, as well as locally-made soaps.

Yard Gallery: This gallery sells a range of paintings and prints by local artists, as well as woodturning and ceramics.

Fox Boutique: The womenswear and handbags for sale here include colourful pieces in vibrant prints. Also sells gifts.

Roco & Coco: Womenswear boutique with a curated collection of different brands in sophisticated, mostly muted shades.

 EATING IN HOLYWOOD: BEST RESTAURANTS

Lynchpin: Standout vegan restaurant, serving brunches that include international street-food inspired dishes. Opens Friday nights from 7pm for themed supper clubs. *8am-4pm Wed-Sat* **££**

Noble: Tiny upstairs restaurant with an intimate feel. Serves dishes bursting with flavour; daily specials are written on the blackboard. *noon-3pm & 5-10pm Thu-Sat, 1-6.30pm Sun* **£££**

Frae: Chic neighbourhood restaurant and wine bar, serving dishes like Achill Island oysters, local mackerel with fennel, and Irish cheeses. *5-11pm Wed & Thu, noon-11pm Fri & Sat* **£££**

Fontana: Modern European restaurant serving local aged steak and homemade focaccia bread, plus two-course Sunday lunches. *noon-2.30pm & 5-9.30pm Wed-Sat, noon-4pm Sun* **£££**

Queen's Quarter & South Belfast

LEAFY CAMPUS AND RIVERSIDE NATURE

GETTING AROUND

From Donegall Sq E, Metro buses 8A to 8C run along Bradbury Pl and University Rd to Queen's University, then south along Malone Rd. Bus 8D goes down Stranmillis Rd (near the Lagan Towpath). Buses 9A to 9C go down the Lisburn Rd.

Botanic Station has train services to Belfast Grand Central, Bangor and Larne.

Sustrans Route 9 is a traffic-free bike path along the riverbank from Belfast to Lisburn (20km). There are several Belfast Bikes docking stations in Queen's Quarter and South Belfast.

☑ TOP TIP

For a scenic walk or ride from Queen's Quarter to the city centre, stroll or cycle through Botanic Gardens to reach Stranmillis Embankment and then follow the riverside path north for 3km along the west bank of the Lagan to Queen's Bridge, just east of the city centre.

South of the city centre are the leafy streets and student bars of the Queen's Quarter, which takes its name from Queen's University. Academic life extends beyond the campus to the neighbouring Ulster Museum, located in the Botanic Gardens, Belfast's prettiest park. Nearby are coffee shops, independent bookstores and boutiques.

This is Belfast's most ethnically diverse area; in addition to international students, it is where many members of the city's growing Chinese, South Asian and other minority communities live. In August, Belfast Mela celebrates global cultures with a festival of music and dance held in the Botanic Gardens.

Further south, Cutter's Wharf is one of several access points for the Lagan Towpath. Located at the centre of a designated Area of Outstanding Natural Beauty, the towpath passes through a variety of wetlands, tree-fringed riverside meadows and mixed woodlands and is a tranquil place for walking and cycling.

Leafy Park & Greenhouses   MAP P517

A stroll around Botanic Gardens

When the sun is out, Belfast's prettiest park, **Botanic Gardens** *(belfastcity.gov.uk/botanicgardens; free)*, fills with people. Students read on benches, lovers lounge on lawns and families stroll between fragrant flowerbeds and mature trees.

The showpiece of this city oasis is the **Palm House**, a cast-iron and curvilinear glass greenhouse designed by Charles Lanyon. The gardens were founded in 1828 at a time when plant hunting was all the rage, and it was soon decided that a glasshouse was needed for the exotic species gathered from around the globe. Work began on the structure in 1839, but the birdcage dome was not added until 1852. Look out for details such as rosettes in the structure's ironwork.

A second greenhouse, the red-brick **Tropical Ravine**, was added in 1889 to house tropical ferns, orchids, lilies and banana plants in a sunken glen. Inside, a raised walkway overlooks some 190 plant species housed in temperate and tropical zones.

QUEEN'S QUARTER

★ HIGHLIGHTS
1 Botanic Gardens
2 Maggie Mays
3 Queen's University
4 Ulster Museum

● SIGHTS
5 Palm House
6 Tropical Ravine

● SLEEPING
7 Botanical Backpackers
8 Global Village Backpackers
9 Harrison Chambers of Distinction
10 Regency House
11 Tara Lodge
12 The Malone
13 Vagabonds

● EATING
14 Bo Tree Kitchen
15 Deanes at Queen's
16 Holohan's Pantry

● DRINKING & NIGHTLIFE
17 Botanic Inn
18 Hatfield House
19 Lavery's
20 Town Square

● ENTERTAINMENT
see 22 Belfast Book Festival
21 Belfast Empire
22 Crescent Arts Centre
23 Mandela Hall
24 Queen's Film Theatre

● SHOPPING
25 No Alibis
26 Ulster Museum Shop

● TRANSPORT
27 Botanic Station

BEST ENTERTAINMENT VENUES

Queen's Film Theatre: A major venue for the Belfast Film Festival, this two-screen art-house cinema is close to Queen's University.

Crescent Arts Centre: Hosts a range of concerts, plays, workshops, literary events and dance classes. Most **Belfast Book Festival** events are held here.

Lyric Theatre: Overlooking the River Lagan, the Lyric is a full-time producing theatre (it produces its own plays and many cover local themes).

Belfast Empire: Live-music venue in a converted late-Victorian church. Look out for stand-up comedy and quiz nights too.

Mandela Hall: Venue at the Queen's Student Union, hosting live music, DJs, comedy and spoken word events.

Palm House (p516), Botanic Gardens

Notable plants include a Japanese fibre banana tree dating from 1904 and tree ferns thought to be 150 years old. Count on spending at least an hour here.

Architecture & Campus Grounds MAP P517

The buildings of Queen's University

Next to the Botanic Gardens and Ulster Museum, take a look at the striking architecture of **Queen's University**, for which the neighbourhood is named.

Architect Charles Lanyon designed what is now called the Lanyon building, an eye-catching Tudor Revival in red brick and honey-coloured sandstone built in 1849; he based the design of the central tower on the 15th-century Founder's Tower at Oxford University's Magdalen College. Just inside the main entrance is a Welcome Centre, with visitor information, maps of the grounds and a souvenir shop.

Ceremonial Earthwork

Visit the Giant's Ring MAP P520

From the east bank of the Lagan, south of Minnowburn car park, a signposted pedestrian trail leads through undulating farmland to **Giant's Ring** (also accessible by road). Built in

 EATING IN QUEEN'S QUARTER: OUR PICKS MAP P517

Maggie Mays: Popular with students, Maggie Mays serves comfort food and all-day breakfasts, including Ulster Fries. *8am-8.30pm Mon-Fri, 9am-8.30pm Sat & Sun* £

Bo Tree Kitchen: Authentic Thai curries, stir fries and street food made with herbs and spices imported from Thailand. *noon-2pm & 5-9pm Mon-Sat* ££

Holohan's Pantry: A good place to try boxty, a traditional savoury potato pancake. *noon-11pm Mon-Tue, 5-11pm Wed, noon-11.30pm Thu-Sat, 1-9.30pm Sun* ££

Deanes at Queen's: Local ingredients like Mourne lamb feature on the menu of this bright bistro. *noon-3pm & 5.30-9.30pm Wed-Fri, noon-10pm Sat, 1-7pm Sun* £££

TOP EXPERIENCE

Ulster Museum

The Ulster Museum is packed with fascinating treasures in galleries spread over five floors. You could spend hours exploring and there's plenty to keep children entertained, too. Highlights include the Armada room, which contains the spoils of the Spanish galleon *Girona*, and Takabuti, a 2500-year-old Egyptian mummy unwrapped in Belfast in 1835.

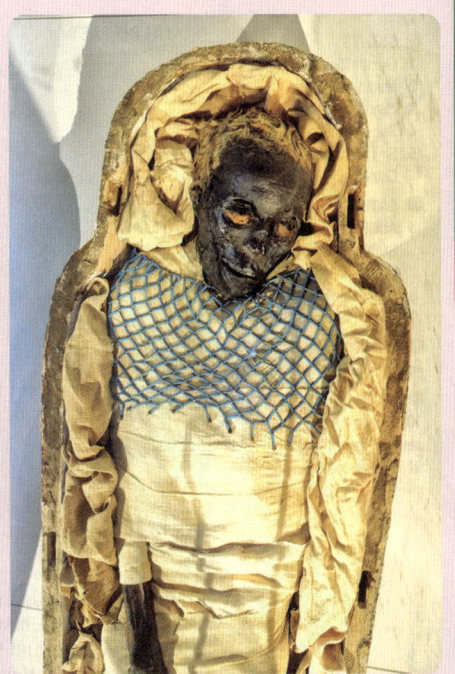

Takabuti

Art Galleries & Nature Zone

Start in the art galleries at the top of the building and spiral down through the levels. Works to look out for include Turner's 1841 *Dawn of Christianity (The Flight Into Egypt)*.

The kid-friendly, interactive Nature Zone on the 2nd floor covers geological time, evolution and natural history; highlights include the *Snapshot of an Ancient Sea Floor*, a fossilised portion of a 200-million-year-old seabed with jumbled ammonite shells and petrified driftwood.

History Galleries

One gallery displays the Egyptian mummy Takabuti, as well as items buried with her. Another highlight is the Armada room, which houses treasures recovered from the wreck of the *Girona*, a Spanish galleon that sank off the north Antrim coast in 1588.

On the ground floor an overview of local history from 1500 onward includes exhibits on the formation of the Society of United Irishmen and the Rebellion of 1798 against British rule in Ireland. Look for a letter from Theobald Wolfe Tone.

The Troubles and Beyond gallery explores Northern Ireland's emergence from years of conflict, representing the nuances of how the period is differently understood and remembered through a diverse range of memorabilia. One evocative item is a bomb disposal robot; such robots were developed in 1972 to allow bombs to be disarmed remotely.

TOP TIPS

● The Museum Map is available in 14 different languages. Request them from the ground-floor information desk.

● Children and adults are welcome to stop and sketch in the 5th-floor Discover Art room. Check out the views across Belfast to Cave Hill.

PRACTICALITIES

● ulstermuseum.org
● 10am-5pm Tue-Sun
● Free ● Map p517

- **SIGHTS**
1 Giant's Ring
2 Lagan Gateway
3 Minnowburn
4 Shaw's Bridge
5 Sir Thomas & Lady Dixon Park
- **EATING**
6 Ability Cafe at the Stables
7 Cutters Wharf
8 Lock Keeper's Inn
9 Lyric Theatre Café
- **ENTERTAINMENT**
see 9 Lyric Theatre
- **SHOPPING**
10 Arcadia
see 10 Maven
11 The Vineyard

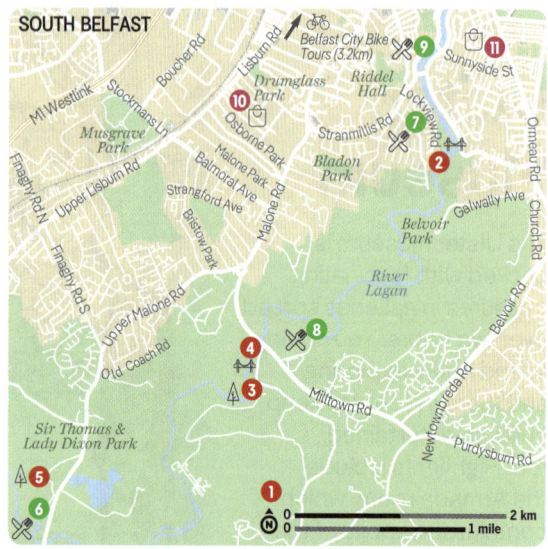

around 2000 BCE during the late Neolithic or early Bronze Age period, this prehistoric ceremonial earthwork is nearly 200m in diameter and has a stone passage grave in the centre. The views west towards the Belfast hills are particularly beautiful in the golden early evening light.

Riverside Walks & Wildlife Watching MAP P520

Exploring the Lagan Towpath

The River Lagan was once used to transport linen from the mills near Lisburn to Belfast for export. Now the wetlands, riverside meadows and mixed woodland on its banks are a haven for wildlife.

One of the best ways to explore the area is by bike, following the 20km Route 9 traffic-free path south along the riverbank from Belfast to Lisburn, where you can catch a train back to Belfast. **Belfast City Bike Tours** *(p492; belfastcitybike tours.com; from £20 per day)* offers 'bike and brew tours' *(four hours £55)* along the towpath to Hilden Brewery in Lisburn and bike rental. You can also explore shorter sections of the

---

 DRINKING IN QUEEN'S QUARTER: BEST BARS MAP P517

Town Square: On Botanic Ave, this friendly bar serves speciality coffee as well as cocktails, beer and other drinks. Has outdoor tables. *10am-1am Sun-Thu, to 2am Fri & Sat*

Hatfield House: Ormeau Rd pub with original timber and brass bar fixtures and ornate ceiling mouldings. Live music includes acoustic and folk. Popular with students. *noon-1am*

Lavery's: Vast, multilevel, boozing emporium, crammed with drinkers young and old. In the family since 1918. *noon-12.30am Mon-Thu, to 1.30am Fri & Sat, 1pm-12.30am Sun*

Botanic Inn: Longstanding Malone Rd bar, with sports screens, pool tables and club nights. *5pm-1am Mon-Thu, noon-1am Fri & Sat, 1pm-1am Sun*

towpath on foot. Along the way, keep a lookout for kingfishers, grey herons and speckled wood butterflies.

Just south of Cutter's Wharf at Stranmillis, the Lagan Towpath extends south from the **Lagan Gateway** pedestrian and cycle bridge. From here, the towpath winds along the west bank of the Lagan.

Cross the bridge at Mickey Taylor's lock to explore **Moreland's Meadow**, an island created by the canal that allowed barges to avoid the bend in the river.

Return to the towpath and continue south to reach **McLeave's Lock**. Here the old lock and stone bridge remain intact, and the lock-keeper's cottage has been preserved as a small museum. Nearby is Lock Keeper's Inn, a cafe with tables overlooking the river.

Beyond Clement Wilson park is **Shaw's Bridge**, a 300-year-old stone bridge. Cross over to follow the path along the east bank to **Minnowburn**, an area of meadowland and woodland. Trails lead through tall beech trees and up to Terrace Hill Garden, with views across the river to Malone House. The tables here are a picturesque spot for a picnic.

Back at the river, continue south to Gilchrist Bridge and cross back to the west bank. From here, the river snakes south through open farmland to reach **Sir Thomas & Lady Dixon Park**. Take time to explore the walled garden, meadow and woodland trails, and the spectacular **Rose Garden**, in bloom from mid-July. From the park, it's a further 8km to Lisburn.

BEST SHOPS IN QUEEN'S QUARTER & SOUTH BELFAST

Arcadia: A deli on the Lisburn Rd crammed with local produce, including Fermanagh Black Bacon and SD Bell coffee.

No Alibis: Small, independent bookshop specialising in crime fiction, on Botanic Avenue in Queen's Quarter; hosts regular poetry readings and book signings.

The Vineyard: Specialist wine, spirit and beer shop on the Ormeau Rd, stocking drinks from the region's distilleries and craft breweries.

Maven: On the Lisburn Rd, this beautiful furniture and design shop in a former bank is run by two sisters; it stocks international brands and local designers.

Ulster Museum Shop: Books on art and local history, as well as gift items related to the exhibitions, toys, local crafts, and jewellery.

 EATING IN SOUTH BELFAST: RIVERSIDE CAFES & BARS — MAP P520

Lock Keeper's Inn: Cafe on the Lagan Towpath. Grab a sandwich, cake and a coffee to eat outside. *9am-4pm Mon-Fri, to 4.30pm Sat & Sun* £

Lyric Theatre Café: Contemporary red-brick Lyric building houses a bright cafe with river views; serves pastries, sandwiches and soup. *10am-3pm Tue-Sun* £

Ability Cafe at the Stables: Social enterprise that employs people with disabilities at Sir Thomas & Lady Dixon Park, serving simple meals. *9am-4pm* £

Cutters Wharf: The large waterside terrace here is a lovely spot for a drink or bar meal after a towpath walk. *noon-7.30pm Sun-Tue, to 8.30pm Wed-Sat* ££

West & North Belfast

COMMUNITY CULTURE AND HILLTOP WALKS

GETTING AROUND

The G1 glider bus runs along Falls Rd and Divis St to City Hall, connecting the city centre with most of the West Belfast sights.

For Crumlin Road Gaol, take Metro bus 57 or 12B (Monday to Saturday); on Sunday take bus 12A and walk from Carlisle Circus.

To get to Belfast Castle and Cave Hill Country Park, take Metro bus 1 to Strathmore Park stop on Antrim Road. The route to the castle is signposted.

Divis and Black Mountain is best reached by car.

☑ TOP TIP

So-called peace lines still separate some of Belfast's Catholic and Protestant communities. The longest section divides Falls Rd and the Shankill in West Belfast. Its steel gates are generally open during the day. It is best to avoid the area at night and during times of heightened tensions.

West and North Belfast are largely residential areas extending as far as the Belfast hills, where walking trails offer fabulous views of the city and beyond. Though scarred by decades of conflict during the Troubles, West Belfast is a compelling place to visit. Here, a series of murals charts the history of the conflict and current political themes.

West Belfast developed with the linen mills that propelled the city into late-19th-century prosperity. It was an area of low-cost, working-class housing, and even in the Victorian era was divided along religious lines. These sectarian divisions became yet more entrenched from the early 1970s, as paramilitary groups ramped up their campaigns of armed conflict. But despite the area's violent past, there is a spirit of optimism and hope for the future. These days it's safe and visitors are welcome; in August, the Féile an Phobail festival celebrates West Belfast's community and culture.

History of the Republican Struggle

Visit the Eileen Hickey Irish Republican History Museum

At the Conway Mill complex, the **Eileen Hickey Irish Republican History Museum** *(eileenhickeymuseum.com; free)* houses artefacts related to the Republican struggle. The collection was started by Eileen Hickey, who was imprisoned at the Armagh Gaol from 1973 to 1977. At the entrance to the museum is a recreation of the Armagh Gaol cell in which Hickey was held, including her bed, personal photographs and an original cell door. The main exhibition space has handicrafts made by Republican prisoners, such as harps and intricate model caravans. Other items include rubber and plastic bullets, and a collection of weapons. The museum is run by Hickey's family members, who are happy to talk about the exhibits and what they represent. It is only open 10am to 2pm Tuesday to Saturday. Allow around 30 minutes here.

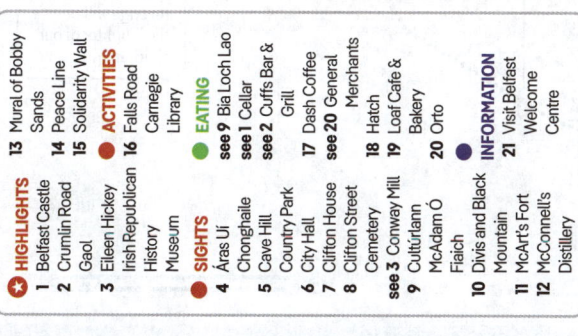

WEST & NORTH BELFAST

★ **HIGHLIGHTS**	**13** Mural of Bobby Sands
1 Belfast Castle	**14** Peace Line
2 Crumlin Road Gaol	**15** Solidarity Wall
3 Eileen Hickey Irish Republican History Museum	● **ACTIVITIES**
	16 Falls Road Carnegie Library
● **SIGHTS**	● **EATING**
4 Áras Uí Chonghaile	see **9** Bia Loch Lao
5 Cave Hill Country Park	see **1** Cellar
6 City Hall	see **2** Cuffs Bar & Grill
7 Clifton House	**17** Dash Coffee
8 Clifton Street Cemetery	see **20** General Merchants
see **3** Conway Mill	**18** Hatch
9 Cultúrlann McAdam Ó Fiaich	**19** Loaf Cafe & Bakery
10 Divis and Black Mountain	**20** Orto
11 McArt's Fort	● **INFORMATION**
12 McConnell's Distillery	**21** Visit Belfast Welcome Centre

THE GUIDE

BELFAST WEST & NORTH BELFAST

A WANDER THROUGH WEST BELFAST

Falls Rd is the main thoroughfare of Republican West Belfast, sometimes called the Gaeltacht (Irish-speaking) Quarter.

START	END	LENGTH
Solidarity Wall	Áras Uí Chonghaile	3.5km; 1½ hours

Start at the 1 **Solidarity Wall** on the corner of Divis St and Northumberland St. The collection of murals here expresses Republican sympathies with the Palestinian and Basque peoples, among others. One pays tribute to abolitionist Frederick Douglass, an advocate of the Irish independence movement in the 19th century. Continue on Northumberland St to reach the 2 **Peace Line** separating Catholic and Protestant communities; the gate here is closed at night. Return to Divis St, which becomes Falls Rd. Continue west, then turn right onto Conway St to reach 3 **Conway Mill**, a restored 19th-century flax mill that now houses artists' studios and work spaces for local enterprises. At the same complex is the Eileen Hickey Irish Republican History Museum (p522).

Back on Falls Rd, walk west, passing 4 **Falls Road Carnegie Library**; don't miss the angel carvings at the entrance. Next, look for the 5 **Mural of Bobby Sands**, who led the 1981 hunger strikes in which he and nine others died. Walk west to 6 **Cultúrlann McAdam Ó Fiaich.** Housed in a red-brick former Presbyterian church, this cultural centre is the focus for West Belfast community activity. Continue west to reach 7 **Áras Uí Chonghaile** (James Connolly Visitor Centre). Outside is a statue of Connolly himself.

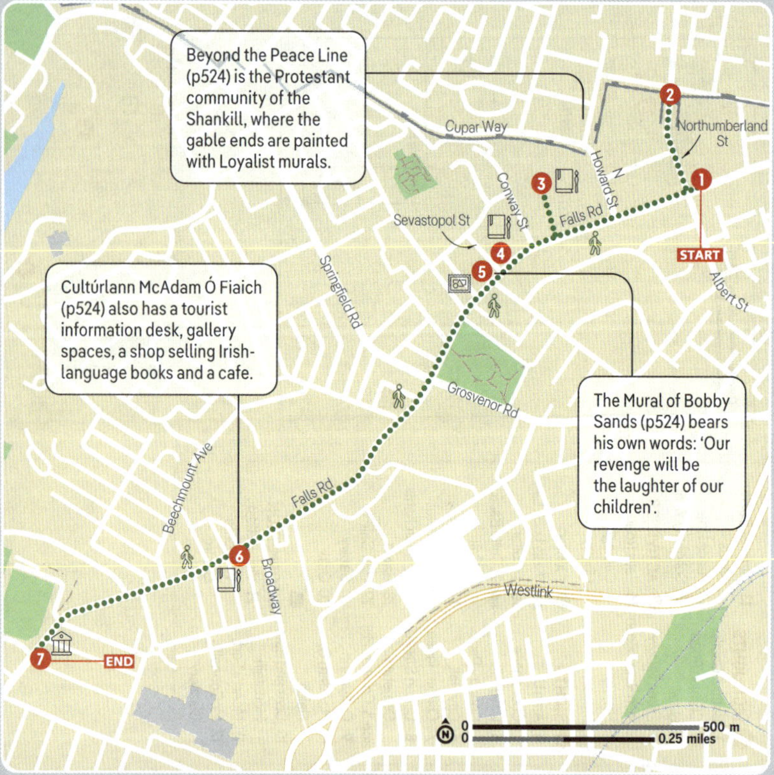
Beyond the Peace Line (p524) is the Protestant community of the Shankill, where the gable ends are painted with Loyalist murals.
Cultúrlann McAdam Ó Fiaich (p524) also has a tourist information desk, gallery spaces, a shop selling Irish-language books and a cafe.
The Mural of Bobby Sands (p524) bears his own words: 'Our revenge will be the laughter of our children'.
Cupar Way
Northumberland St
N Howard St
Conway St
Falls Rd
Sevastopol St
Springfield Rd
Albert St
Grosvenor Rd
Beechmount Ave
Broadway
Westlink
START
END
0 500 m
0 0.25 miles

Learn about James Connolly
Visit Áras Uí Chonghaile

James Connolly was a trade unionist and political activist who was executed for his role in the 1916 Easter Rising. Learn all about his life and work at the **James Connolly Experience** (*arasuichonghaile.com; adult/concession £10/7.50*), an interactive exhibition on the ground floor of **Áras Uí Chonghaile** (James Connolly Visitor Centre).

A 25-minute audioguide narrates key moments in Connolly's life, from his childhood in Edinburgh, through to his time as a union organiser and socialist writer and lecturer in the USA, to his return to Ireland in 1910. Connolly's family lived on the Falls Rd, where their house became a hub for revolutionary politics; Connolly would travel back and forth to Dublin. Finally, the exhibition covers the writing of the Proclamation of the Irish Republic, the Easter Rising, and Connolly's subsequent execution, with touching video footage of his daughter Nora recalling her final visits with her father at the jail in Dublin Castle.

See Political Murals from a Cab
Take a black taxi tour

Black taxi tours of West Belfast's murals are offered by a number of taxi companies and local cabbies, stopping to see the **Solidarity Wall**, the Bobby Sands mural and the murals of the Shankill. Tours can vary in quality and content, but in general, they are an intimate and entertaining way to see the sights. Be aware that these tours often reflect the personal experiences of the driver, and the recounting of historical events is likely to be coloured by his or her background. The discussion of violence during the Troubles may be distressing for some people.

The Visit Belfast (p499) tourist information office on Donegall Sq can help arrange a black taxi tour. Troubles-themed black taxi tours are also offered by Crumlin Road Gaol (p527). Tours last between one and two hours and cost around £70 for two people.

Nature & Panoramic Views
Walks at Divis and Black Mountain

In West Belfast, the trails at **Divis and Black Mountain** (*nationaltrust.org.uk/visit/northern-ireland/divis-and-the-black-mountain; free*) offer views extending over much of

THE 1792 BELFAST HARP FESTIVAL

The 1792 Belfast Harp Festival was perhaps the most important event in the history of Irish music. Organised by local radicals, including Henry Joy (the uncle of Mary Ann and Henry Joy McCracken), it aimed to document and revive the music of a dying art form.

After the festival, a young representative, Edward Bunting, travelled around Ireland making note of the traditional harp music in different regions. This was published in 1840 in a series of works collectively known as the *Ancient Music of Ireland*. Without this work, it is possible that much of Ireland's traditional harp music would have been lost.

While in Belfast, Bunting stayed at the family home of Mary Ann McCracken, who was left with a lifelong love of traditional Irish music.

 EATING IN WEST BELFAST: OUR PICKS

Loaf Cafe & Bakery: Social enterprise supporting young people with learning disabilities and autism. Offers breakfast and lunch. *8am-3.30pm Mon-Fri* £

Dash Coffee: Come here for coffee and a range of tempting cakes and sweet and savoury pastries. *7am-4pm Mon-Fri, 8am-4pm Sun* £

Hatch: Serves popular cooked breakfasts, then chicken wings, wraps and loaded fries later on. *8am-5pm Mon-Wed, to 7pm Thu & Fri, 9am-7pm Sat, 9am-5pm Sun* £

Bia Loch Lao: The restaurant at Cultúrlann McAdam Ó Fiaich (p524) serves excellent breakfasts, scones, sandwiches and soups. *9am-7pm Sun-Thu, to 9pm Fri & Sat* ££

MARY ANN MCCRACKEN

Mary Ann McCracken (1770–1866) was born into a middle-class Presbyterian family. She was educated at a progressive, co-ed school and became a fiercely independent social activist and philanthropist.

She was the only family member to accompany her brother Henry Joy McCracken, one of the founding members of the Society of United Irishmen, to the scaffold when he was executed for his role in the 1798 Rebellion.

Throughout her life, McCracken worked tirelessly at the Belfast Poor House to help educate children and provide employment opportunities. She was also a life-long abolitionist, and a statue outside City Hall (p493) depicts her with an anti-slavery leaflet in hand.

McCracken died aged 96, and is buried in Clifton Street Cemetery (p528).

View from Black Mountain (p525)

the north of Ireland, including Lough Neagh and the Sperrin Mountains to the west; on clear days it's possible to glimpse Sliabh Sneacht in Donegal. The views are particularly beautiful at dusk, when the lough water glows in the light of the setting sun.

The 5km summit trail (a challenging climb) and 7km ridge trail (a moderate hike) lead over open heath and exposed blanket bog protected by boardwalk; the trails connect to form a longer walk. There is a cafe and plenty of picnic tables. Come prepared for changeable weather.

Georgian Poor House

Visit Clifton House, home of the Belfast Charitable Trust

Opened in 1774, **Clifton House** *(cliftonbelfast.com; tours £10)* is Belfast's finest surviving Georgian building, with a pointed clock tower and ornamental gates. It was originally built as a poor house by the Belfast Charitable Society, with the involvement of Robert Joy (United Irishman Henry Joy McCracken's uncle). The building is open to the public on Friday and Saturdays for hour-long guided tours (book ahead), during which you'll learn about the history of the poor house and the political atmosphere of the time; many of the people

EATING IN NORTH BELFAST: OUR PICKS

General Merchants: Bright coffee and brunch spot near Cave Hill. Try the buttermilk fried chicken or miso mushrooms. *8am-5pm Mon-Sat, 9am-5pm Sun* ££

Orto: Large, family-friendly pizzeria on the Antrim Rd. Eat in or order to take up to Cave Hill. *8.30am-9pm Mon-Sat, noon-8pm Sun* ££

Cuffs Bar & Grill: Restaurant in the basement of Crumlin Road Gaol, serving burgers, scampi and roasts. *11am-6pm Sun, Mon & Thu, 11am-8pm Fri & Sat* ££

Cellar: At Belfast Castle, this restaurant serves lunchtime burgers and bigger meals, with fabulous views. *noon-7pm Tue-Thu, to 8pm Fri & Sat, to 6pm Sun* ££

TOP EXPERIENCE

Crumlin Road Gaol

Designed by Charles Lanyon, who based his plans on London's Pentonville prison, Crumlin Road Gaol was a working jail and prison from 1846 to 1996. These days the sombre Victorian buildings can be explored on self-guided tours, during which holograms of actors playing guards and inmates tell stories from different times in the jail's history. Allow up to 90 minutes for the visit.

Belfast's Notorious Jail

The visit includes an eerie descent into the tunnel beneath Crumlin Rd, built in 1850 to convey prisoners from the courthouse across the street, and continues through to the echoing halls of the Gaol Circle and C-Wing. Here the cramped cells are set up to convey the stories of prisoners from different eras in the jail's history, including a young woman held in 1846, a child jailed during the Victorian era, and political prisoners who served time in the Crum during the 1970s and 1980s. The most chilling of all is the execution chamber; the jail was the scene of the executions of 17 men between 1854 and 1961.

Former Inmates

During your tour you'll hear about historical figures detained in the Crum over the years. In 1914 suffragettes Dorothy Evans and Madge Muir were taken to the Crum for possession of explosives after a series of arson attacks. In 1924 Éamon de Valera, then leader of Sinn Féin, was imprisoned for illegally entering Northern Ireland; he was held in solitary confinement for a month. And in 1966, Ian Paisley served time in the Crum for unlawful assembly; his supporters rioted outside in protest.

TOP TIPS

● Book ahead for guided tours, with colourful stories of jailbreaks and prison life.

● Check for upcoming events, including concerts, the North Block Bazaar monthly craft market, and paranormal tours.

● Book a tour of McConnell's Distillery (p528) on the same site.

PRACTICALITIES

● crumlinroadgaol.com
● admission including self-guided tour adult/child £14.50/8 ● guided tour £19.50 ● 10am-5.30pm, last admission 4pm

CAVE HILL HISTORY

Evidence suggests that people lived on Cave Hill as far back as the Stone Age: a stone cairn on the summit dates from the Neolithic period 4500–2500 BCE. Flint arrowheads from the period have also been discovered nearby; they can be seen in Belfast Castle.

There are several raths (defensive earthen ringforts) dating from early Christian times (400–1200 CE), including **McArt's Fort**, an earthwork fortification on a high rocky outcrop. It was here that members of the United Irishmen looked down over the city in 1795 and pledged to fight for Irish independence.

Between 1840 and 1896 limestone was extracted from Cave Hill for use in the shipping industry. You can see the remains of a limestone quarry on the hills southern slopes.

---

involved in the Belfast Charitable Society were also active in the call for the abolition of slavery and with other social and political causes of the time.

Nearby on Henry Pl is **Clifton Street Cemetery**, which can be seen on a 90-minute guided tour *(£12.50)*. Guides point out the McCracken family grave, which marks the final resting place of Henry Joy McCracken and his sister, the abolitionist, philanthropist and social reformer Mary Ann McCracken.

Whiskey Distillery at a Former Jail
Take a tour of McConnell's Distillery

We can only imagine what the inmates of the notorious Crumlin Road Gaol (p527) would have thought about the jail being used to distil whiskey. But a beautifully renovated wing of the former jail is now the site of **McConnell's Distillery** *(mcconnellsirishwhisky.com)*.

McConnell's Irish Whiskey dates from 1776, but was out of production for decades until it was relaunched by the Belfast Distillery Company in 2020; McConnell's Distillery opened its doors to visitors four years later. Standard 50-minute distillery tours *(adult/child £25/15)* include a whiskey tasting for over 18s.

A Hike up Cave Hill
Belfast Castle and Cave Hill Country Park

Cave Hill (368m) is a North Belfast landmark and the site of **Belfast Castle** (1870). Run by Belfast City Council, the castle is used as a wedding venue. If there is no function scheduled, you may be able to look inside the turreted ground-floor rooms, with fabulous views; ask at the information desk. In the castle basement, there's a restaurant (Cellar, p526) and a few displays on the history of Cave Hill. Be sure to look around the beautiful gardens.

From Belfast Castle car park, halfway up the hill, walking and mountain-biking trails traverse **Cave Hill Country Park** *(belfastcity.gov.uk)*. The 7km **Cave Hill walking trail** (allow around 2½ hours) emerges through woodland to cross heath and meadowland, with views across Belfast Lough. In spring the air is perfumed with the scent of gorse and wildflowers, and is full of colourful butterflies, including the meadow brown, ringlet and common blue. Scramble up to take a closer look at the caves for which the hill is named on the ascent to McArt's Fort at the summit. Pause to take in the views across the city to the docks and south to the Mourne Mountains; the coast of Scotland is often visible, too.

The basalt cliffs at McArt's Fort are hunting grounds for peregrines, ravens and kestrels. In the forested areas, listen out for skylarks and meadow pipits.

Places We Love to Stay

£ Budget ££ Midrange £££ Top End

City Centre MAP p494

Flint ££ Suites here have a small kitchen and a table for eating or working. Located right by City Hall.

Room2 Belfast Hometel ££ This eco-conscious hotel has mid-century modern decor; loft rooms and suites have kitchenettes.

Ten Square £££ Service is first rate, and rooms are decorated with contemporary art at this stylish Donegal Sq hotel.

Fitzwilliam Hotel £££ Strikes all the right style notes with its use of designer fabrics, cool colours and mood lighting.

Bullitt Hotel £££ Designed with modern convenience in mind, rooms at the Bullitt have comfy beds and fast wi-fi; close to nightlife.

Malmaison Hotel £££ Housed in restored Italianate warehouses. Bedrooms have glamorous decor, with velvet headboards; some rooms have roll-top baths big enough for two.

Europa Hotel £££ Next door to the Grand Opera House, Belfast's most famous hotel (at one time Europe's most bombed) now exudes a plush but businesslike air.

Grand Central £££ Rooms are well-equipped and neutrally decorated, with floor-to-ceiling windows. The Observatory Bar is on the 23rd floor.

Hilton £££ This hotel's biggest selling point is the river views, especially from rooms on the higher floors.

Cathedral Quarter MAP p501

The Foundry ££ Stylish boutique hotel for people in Belfast to party. Located right in the middle of the neighbourhood's nightlife (don't expect a quiet night's sleep).

Merchant Hotel £££ Luxury hotel occupying the palatial former Ulster Bank head office, with opulent furnishings and a spa. Rooms are decorated in either Victorian or art deco style.

Holywood MAP p514

Rayanne House ££ In a 1883 manor house adjoining Holywood golf club; some rooms have balconies and views of Belfast Lough.

Culloden Hotel £££ Luxury hotel and spa in an 18th-century former Bishop's palace, set in beautifully-landscaped grounds on the shores of Belfast Lough.

Titanic Quarter MAP p507

Titanic Hotel Belfast (p510) £££ Located in the Harland & Wolff shipping company's old headquarters; the hotel's interior design references the city's shipbuilding past.

Queen's Quarter MAP p517

Vagabonds £ Within walking distance of the city centre, this popular, well-run hostel has dorms, private rooms and common areas for socialising.

Global Village £ This hostel has high ceilings, period features, an outdoor area and a bright cheery decor; has dorms and private rooms with shared bathrooms.

Botanical Backpackers £ Near Queen's University, this small but cosy hostel has dorm rooms and the friendly feeling of a home.

Tara Lodge ££ In a great location on a side street off Botanic Ave, with 34 good-value, tastefully-decorated rooms and excellent breakfasts.

The Malone ££ The centrepiece of a tree-lined Victorian terrace, the Malone has large, comfortable rooms, including family rooms and suites.

Regency House £££ On Upper Crescent, this five-star boutique hotel has luxurious suites overlooking Crescent Gardens (with record players and a vinyl library), plus smaller rooms, all in beautifully restored Georgian terrace houses.

Harrison Chambers of Distinction £££ Boutique hotel in a period building on Malone Rd, with creatively decorated themed rooms; some have four-poster beds.

Left: Mourne Mountains (p541); right: Grey Abbey (p550)

Down & Armagh

COASTLINE, MOUNTAINS AND LEGENDS

Follow in St Patrick's footsteps, from the site of his first church to his grave, passing scenic coastal landscapes and mountains steeped in legend.

Close to Belfast, the upmarket commuter villages of County Down have a cosmopolitan vibe and some excellent restaurants. Menus name-check local ingredients such as Comber potatoes, Kilkeel crab and Mourne lamb.

Further south, the Mourne Mountains occupy one of the most beautiful corners of the North, with a distinctive landscape of grey granite, yellow gorse and whitewashed cottages. The lower slopes of the hills are latticed with a neat patchwork of drystone walls cobbled together from huge, rounded granite boulders. The area is now part of the Mourne Gullion Strangford UNESCO global geopark, and the Mournes, Strangford Lough and the Ring of Gullion are all designated areas of outstanding natural beauty.

The recognition of the geological and cultural significance of the Ring of Gullion is long overdue. This area of South Armagh, which during the Troubles was known for its army watchtowers and IRA roadblocks, is now celebrated for its natural beauty and Celtic heritage.

And while the conveniences of modern life are never far away in Down and Armagh, the area has some fascinating historical sites to discover, including Neolithic passage tombs and dolmen, and an enigmatic Iron Age monument at Navan Fort. There are a number of sites related to St Patrick's missions in the area, while several grand country house estates offer a window into more recent history.

THE MAIN AREAS

NEWCASTLE
Where the Mournes meet the sea. **p536**

ARMAGH CITY
Ireland's ecclesiastical capital. **p553**

Find Your Way

Down and Armagh are small with good roads, making car journeys easy and quick. It's possible to make day trips from Belfast, but it's worth staying overnight on the coast or in the hills.

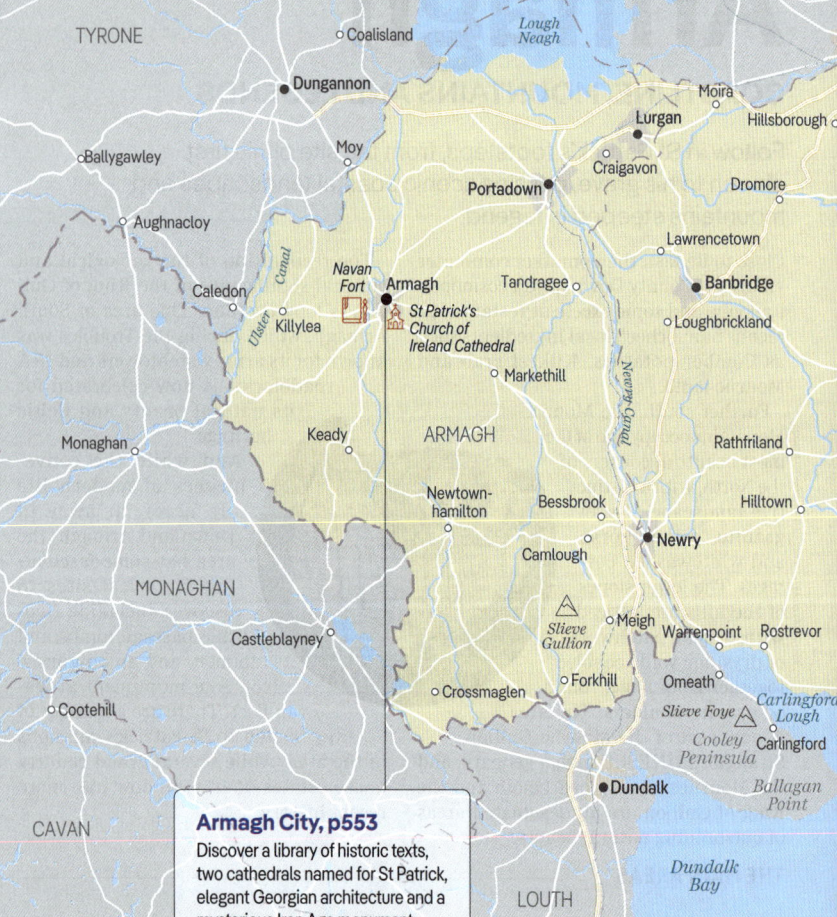

Armagh City, p553
Discover a library of historic texts, two cathedrals named for St Patrick, elegant Georgian architecture and a mysterious Iron Age monument.

CAR
The easiest way to get around Down and Armagh is by car, especially in rural areas where public transport is infrequent. Most places in the two counties are less than an hour by car from Belfast.

BUS
Ulsterbus services connect Belfast with most towns and villages in counties Down and Armagh. Key routes include bus 237 to Newcastle, bus 215 to Downpatrick, bus 270 to Armagh city, and bus 238 to Newry via Hillsborough and Banbridge.

BICYCLE
Sustrans (sustrans.org.uk) cycle routes pass through both counties: the off-road route 99 connects Belfast to Comber, connecting with the Strangford Lough Trail and continuing to Newcastle, and route 9 follows the towpath from Belfast to Newry, linking up with route 91 to Armagh city.

Newcastle, p536

The seaside town at the foot of the Mournes has a long sandy beach and trails through forests and into the hills.

Plan Your Time

With numerous pretty villages to discover and a wealth of walking and cycling trails to explore, allow time to travel at a slower pace, with plenty of stops at beauty spots along the way.

Ballywalter Beach (p552)

Pressed for Time

● With limited time, focus on the area around Newcastle. Here you can hit the hills, climbing **Slieve Donard** (p539), walking along the river and through the trees in **Tollymore Forest Park** (p539) or exploring the **Mournes by bike**. Next, relax on the beach in Newcastle or at **Murlough National Nature Reserve** (p542) in nearby Dundrum. Feast on seafood in one of **Dundrum's restaurants** (p543), then return to Newcastle to try the local beer.

● Book well in advance if you want to play golf at **Royal County Down Golf Club** (p538) in Newcastle. For further hiking or mountain biking, drive along the coast to Rostrevor and hit the trails of **Kilbroney Park** (p543), followed by a trad or folk music session in one of the village pubs.

Seasonal Highlights

Spring wildflowers, bright summer days, autumn leaves and frosty winters: this region is beautiful year-round. Be prepared for rain.

MARCH
The start of spring brings brighter days, but expect plenty of rain. On 17 March, **St Patrick's Festival** (p544) is celebrated with events in Armagh and parades in Downpatrick and Newry.

MAY
In early May the apple orchards of rural Armagh are awash with pink blossom, while the Down countryside is scented with the sweet coconut aroma and brightened by the vibrant yellow flowers of gorse.

JUNE
The longest day of the year is best spent outside, where the daylight lasts until 10pm. The strawberry season begins and the fruit is ready to harvest at County Down's farms.

Three-Day Adventure

- After exploring Newcastle and the Mournes, spend a day at Strangford Lough. Stop for breakfast or lunch at **Fodder in the Woods** (p548) on your way to **Castle Ward** (p548). Allow time to explore the house and grounds, including the walking and cycling trails, then take the ferry from **Strangford** to **Portaferry** (p549). Continue to **Mount Stewart** (p550) to take in the lough views from the house and gardens.

- On your third day, drive to **Armagh** (p553), stopping along the way to take a scenic walk at **Slieve Gullion Forest Park** (p557) or do the **Game of Thrones Studio Tour** (p544) near Banbridge. Spend the afternoon exploring Armagh city's historic buildings, making sure to fit in a tour of **Navan Fort** (p555) on the outskirts of town.

Five Days to Explore

- With time to spare, allow several days to fully explore the Mournes, taking supplies with you for a **scenic picnic** (p550). From Newcastle, take a day trip to **Downpatrick** (p547) to visit sites associated with Ireland's patron saint.

- Next, go for a morning walk along the **Newry Canal Towpath** (p544) then spend an afternoon in **Hillsborough** (p545) to visit the castle and grounds. Time your visit to include lunch or dinner in one of Hillsborough's pubs.

- After exploring the Ards Peninsula, head to the **North Down coast** (p552). Consider stopping at one of County Down's **distilleries** (p547), located on the Ards Peninsula, in the Mournes, and by Strangford Lough, to learn about the production of local gin and whiskey.

THE GUIDE

DOWN & ARMAGH

JULY
The school holidays start and accommodation gets booked up; reserve ahead. Warm weather brings families to the beach and walkers to the hills. Folk musicians gather in Rostrevor for the **Fiddler's Green Festival** (p544).

AUGUST
At **Navan Fort** (p555) the festival of Lughnasa (honouring the Celtic Sun God Lugh) is marked by setting fire to a 10m tall Wickerman. Wild blackberries are in season; pick them from hedgerows.

SEPTEMBER
Thousands of light-bellied Brent geese begin to arrive in Strangford Lough from the Arctic; spot them at **Castle Espie Wetland Centre** (p550). The apple harvest gets into full swing in the orchards of Armagh.

DECEMBER
There are Christmas trails at **Hillsborough Castle** (p545) and a Christmas market at **Castle Ward** (p548). Visit Santa onboard a heritage train at **Downpatrick & County Down Railway** (p548). The Mournes can be coated with snow.

Newcastle

MOUNTAIN HIKES | SANDY BEACHES | GOLF LINKS

Located in a spectacular coastal setting at the foot of the Mournes, Newcastle is a pleasing combination of cheery seaside town with ice cream shops and games arcades, faded Victorian holiday resort and vibrant community centre. At the northern end of town, the Royal County Down Golf Course has topped lists of the best and most beautiful courses in the world; it sits next to the landmark red-brick Slieve Donard hotel. From here, contemporary sculptures dot the 1km-long seafront promenade.

The town's main attraction is the beach, which stretches northeast to a nature reserve. The little harbour at the south end of town once served the stone boats that exported Mourne granite from the quarries of Slieve Donard. Wherever you are in Newcastle, the Mourne Mountains dominate the horizon, inviting walkers to scale their rolling peaks. From town, trails lead along former smuggling tracks into the hills.

Coastal Sculptures & Views
Exploring the seafront

Newcastle Promenade is a scenic place to stroll in the shadow of the Mournes.

At the northern end of town is the red-brick facade of the **Slieve Donard Resort & Spa**. In the grounds, the **Percy French Sculpture** pays tribute to the poet and songwriter who wrote 'The Mountains of Mourne'. The sculpture is inscribed with lyrics from the song which is in the form of a letter to a loved one expressing one man's longing to return to the place where the Mourne Mountains meet the sea.

From the hotel, the promenade extends south. Pass the **Tails of Flight Sculpture**, which commemorates Harry Ferguson's 1910 airplane flight along the sea front, then look for another tribute to Percy French, this time a sculpture featuring a silhouette of the poet.

GETTING AROUND

You can explore Newcastle on foot. Cycling is a handy way to reach nearby beaches and walking trails; **Bike Mourne** (bikemourne.com) rents bikes.

There are regular **Ulsterbus** express buses to Belfast (1¼ hours). In summer, the **Mourne Rambler** bus runs a circular route from Newcastle around the Mournes. Alternatively, the **Mourne Shuttle Service** (facebook.com/MourneShuttleService; 07516 412 076) runs a timetabled route linking several walkers' car parks, allowing for linear hiking routes; book ahead.

☑ TOP TIP

The Mourne Way is a 40km, two-day walking trail through the foothills of the Mourne Mountains from Newcastle to Rostrevor. Signage is patchy, so bring a map and compass.

NEWCASTLE

★ HIGHLIGHTS
1. Royal County Down Golf Club
2. Slieve Donard
3. Tollymore Forest Park

● SIGHTS
4. Cone of Light Sculpture
5. Global Journeys Sculpture
6. Newcastle Promenade
7. Percy French Sculpture
8. Silent Valley Reservoir
9. Spelga Dam
10. Tails of Flight Sculpture

● ACTIVITIES
11. Bloody Bridge
12. Glen River Trail

● SLEEPING
13. Enniskeen Country House Hotel
14. Enniskeen Estate
15. Hutt Hostel
16. Slieve Donard Resort & Spa
17. The Donard
18. Tollymore Forest Park

● EATING
19. Birch
20. Brunel's Restaurant
21. Great Jones
22. Morelli's Ice Cream
23. Olive Bizarre
24. Piccolo Kitchen
25. Railway Street
26. Villa Vinci

● DRINKING & NIGHTLIFE
27. Macken's Bar
28. Quinns Bar
29. Tap Room
30. Wild Hare

● SHOPPING
31. Candles & Plants
32. Donard Wines
33. Fish & Farm
34. Painted Earth

● INFORMATION
35. Newcastle Visitor Information Centre

● TRANSPORT
36. Bike Mourne
37. Carrick Little Car Park

WHY I LOVE NEWCASTLE & THE MOURNES

Isabel Albiston, writer

Though I have known the area since I was a child, I always catch my breath at the first glimpse of the Mournes on the drive into Newcastle. The combination of sparkling sea, sandy beaches and rolling mountains is truly beautiful, but more than that, it feels welcoming, as if the Mournes are waiting to embrace me. It's a place that will always hold fond memories for me, of splashing in the river with friends and camping in the hills. There is a freshness in the air that makes me feel renewed. These days one of my favourite places to walk is Kilbroney Park in Rostrevor, emerging from the forest to views over Carlingford Lough.

Slieve Donard Resort & Spa (p536)

After crossing the footbridge over the Shimna River, look for the **Global Journeys Sculpture**, a mirrored sphere that reflects the mountains and sea. At the southern end of the promenade, the **Cone of Light Sculpture** aligns with the peak of Slieve Donard.

Golf at Royal County Down

Tee-off at a world-renowned links course

Widely considered one of the world's best golf courses, **Royal County Down Golf Club** (*royalcountydown.org, Championship Links £450 per round; Annesley Links £120 per round*) is set along the shore of Dundrum Bay within Murlough Nature Reserve, amid flowering heather and gorse. The challenging **Championship Links** features narrow fairways that thread through the dunes. Course highlights include the scenic 4th hole, surrounded by gorse with views of the Mournes, and the much photographed 9th hole, where the elevated tee lines up with Slieve Donard's peak. The **Annesley Links** is a shorter course with similarly beautiful views. Visitors can play on certain days of the week from April to October, but you'll need to book several months in advance.

EATING IN NEWCASTLE: BEST RESTAURANTS

Piccolo Kitchen: Good value wood-fired pizzas and pasta dishes to eat in or take away. *5-9pm Mon & Tue, to 10pm Wed-Fri, 4-10pm Sat & Sun* **£**

Great Jones: Generous portions of holiday favourites, like fish and chips, steaks and burgers. *5-9pm Wed, noon-9pm Thu, noon-9.30pm Fri & Sat, noon-8pm Sun* **££**

Villa Vinci: Family-friendly restaurant with a long menu featuring Mediterranean-style mains, salads, pizzas and pasta dishes. Outdoor tables for sunny days. *noon-10pm* **££**

Brunel's Restaurant: Beautifully presented plates of contemporary European dishes, including Chateaubriand to share. *noon-2.30pm & 5-9.30pm Thu-Sat, 12.30-8pm Sun, 5-9pm Mon & Tue* **£££**

Birdwatching at Bloody Bridge
Coastal walk to Bloody Bridge River
Drive or cycle 5km south of town to Bloody Bridge car park to access the coastal path to **Bloody Bridge**, named for the killing of prisoners here in 1641. The rugged coastline has interesting rock formations formed from tilted upturned shale seabeds. A 1.6km linear trail leads through wildflowers, gorse and bell heather to the stone bridge crossing Bloody Bridge River, which cascades into natural pools, perfect for a refreshing dip. Look out for fulmars, black guillemots and herring gulls that nest in the cliffs here. There is a scenic picnic area, and toilets at the car park.

Woodland Walks at Tollymore Forest Park
Stepping stones and forest trails
Scenic **Tollymore Forest Park** *(nidirect.gov.uk/articles/tollymore-forest-park; car park £5)*, 3km west of Newcastle town centre, offers lovely walks and bike rides along the River Shimna and across the Mournes' northern slopes. At the river there is a hermitage, five stone bridges and stepping stones to explore. You can also take a dip in the river's natural rock pools.

Longer trails lead further into the hills through fragrant pine forest (look out for red squirrels), emerging onto mountain slopes with views out to the coast. There are picnic tables and charcoal barbecues are permitted. Count on spending a few hours here.

For a longer, more scenic walking route to Tollymore from Newcastle town centre, follow the first section of the Mourne Way trail from Newcastle Visitor Information Centre (p540; 5.7km). Upload a trail guide and map at walkni.com.

Climb Slieve Donard
Dramatic granite peak
The summit of Northern Ireland's highest hill, **Slieve Donard** (852m), can be reached from several starting points in and around Newcastle. It is a fairly steep hike; wear walking boots and bring a rain jacket.

The shortest route to the top is via the River Glen from Newcastle. The well-marked trail begins at **Donard Park car park**, at the edge of town. At the far end of the car park,

THE KINGDOM OF MOURNE

The crescent of low-lying land on the southern side of the mountains is known as the Kingdom of Mourne. Cut off for centuries (the main overland route passed north of the hills), it developed a distinctive landscape and culture. Until the coast road was built in the early 19th century, the only access was on foot or by sea.

Smuggling provided a source of income in the 18th century. Boats carrying French liquor landed at night and packhorses carried the casks through the hills to the inland road, avoiding the excise men at Newcastle. The Brandy Pad, a former smugglers' path from Trassey (just west of Tollymore Forest) to Bloody Bridge is a popular walking route today.

DRINKING IN NEWCASTLE: BEST PUBS

Tap Room: Beers on tap include Maggies Leap, an IPA brewed in nearby Kilkeel. Live jazz on Sundays. *11.30am-11pm Sun-Fri, to 1am Sat*

Quinns Bar: This traditional pub, housed in a wood-panelled former grocer's shop and bar, still has many original features. *11.30am-late Mon-Sat, noon-late Sun*

Macken's Bar: In business for over 200 years, Macken's is Newcastle's oldest pub; hosts trad sessions most Fridays plus regular live music. *7pm-midnight Wed, noon-midnight Thu-Sun*

Wild Hare: Cocktail bar and pub with a contemporary interior and a beer garden. In winter get a seat by the fire. *2pm-late Wed-Fri, noon-late Sat & Sun*

Slieve Donard (p539), see from Slieve Commedagh

BEST SHOPS IN NEWCASTLE

Painted Earth: Jewellery, prints and original artworks by local designers and makers, including plenty of scenes of the Mournes and coast.

Candles & Plants: Sells hand-poured soy wax candles by the Bearded Candle Makers, plus a range of plants.

Fish & Farm: Deli and fishmonger selling locally-sourced produce as well as freshly-prepared lasagnes, pies, chowder and sausage rolls.

Newcastle Visitor Information Centre: Sells Ordnance Survey maps of the Mournes and other useful resources for hiking trips.

Donard Wines: Independent off-licence stocking craft beers from Mourne Mountains Brewery in Rostrevor and Beer Hut Brewing in Kilkeel, among others.

continue through the gate into Donard Park and follow the way-marked **Glen River Trail** into Donard Forest. The path leads up the River Glen valley, crossing the river three times via pretty stone bridges before climbing to the saddle between Slieve Donard and Slieve Commedagh. From here, turn left (east) to follow the Mourne Wall to the summit. Return by the same route (round-trip 10km; allow around five hours). An alternative, less busy route to the summit starts at Bloody Bridge (p539) on the coast and follows the river up to the Mourne Wall (round-trip 10km). You could climb up one way and return via the alternative route, but you would need to arrange transport to or from Bloody Bridge (it's 5km south of town; the seasonal Causeway Rambler bus stops here). **Walk NI** *(walkni.com)* has detailed descriptions of both routes.

On a clear day, the view from the top extends to the hills of Donegal, the Wicklow Mountains, the coast of Scotland, the Isle of Man and even the hills of Snowdonia in Wales. At the summit, look for the prehistoric **Great Cairn**, a passage tomb dating from around 3000 BCE. About 200m northeast, overlooking Newcastle, is the Bronze Age **Lesser Cairn**. The mountain is named for St Donard, who retreated here to pray in early Christian times; he is believed to have used the cairns as a hermitage until his death in 506 CE.

EATING IN NEWCASTLE: BEST CAFES & ICE CREAM PARLOURS

Olive Bizarre: Come to this cheery cafe for locally roasted coffee, home-baked cakes, breakfast, brunch and lunch, including plenty of vegetarian and vegan options. *9am-5pm* £

Birch: A vegetarian and vegan cafe and speciality coffee shop serving soup and sourdough toasties, plus granola, pastries and cakes. *8am-4pm Mon-Sat, 9am-4pm Sun* £

Railway Street: This speciality coffee shop also offers light brunch bites (granola, açai bowls, sourdough toast) as well as pastries. *8.30am-4.30pm* £

Morelli's Ice Cream: When the sun comes out, head to Morelli's for a cone, milkshake or an ice cream sundae. *8am-5pm* £

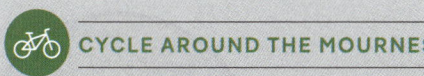

CYCLE AROUND THE MOURNES

This loop along quiet roads takes in some of the Mournes' most beautiful scenery. Bike Mourne (p536) rents e-bikes (book ahead).

START	END	LENGTH
Newcastle Harbour	Newcastle Harbour	46km; 4hr

From Newcastle, head south along Central Promenade, passing the harbour. Continue south along Kilkeel Rd, which hugs the coast as it steadily climbs. Stop at ❶ **Bloody Bridge** (p539) car park to spot sea birds from the trail, then continue pedalling south. In Glasdrumman village, turn right onto Quarter Rd. From here the road gently climbs into the foothills of the Mournes, passing grazing sheep as you cycle towards rolling mountain peaks.

Follow the bend in the road left onto Head Rd. Soon you'll reach ❷ **Carrick Little Car Park,** the start point for hikes up Slieve Binnian. Back on Head Rd, continue west to reach the entrance to ❸ **Silent Valley Reservoir** (p550) where the River Kilkeel was dammed in 1933 to supply Belfast and County Down with water. Cycle up to the water's edge to take in the views.

Return to Head Rd and continue west, then turn right onto Moyad Rd. From here there are views of Carlingford Lough to the south. Cycle through peaceful mountain terrain, passing ❹ **Spelga Dam** (p550); pull over at the roadside viewpoint for a better look.

At the fork, turn right onto Slievenaman Rd and continue to ❺ **Tollymore Forest Park** (p539). If you still have power in your legs, enter the park to explore the forest trails. Return to Newcastle via Bryansford Rd.

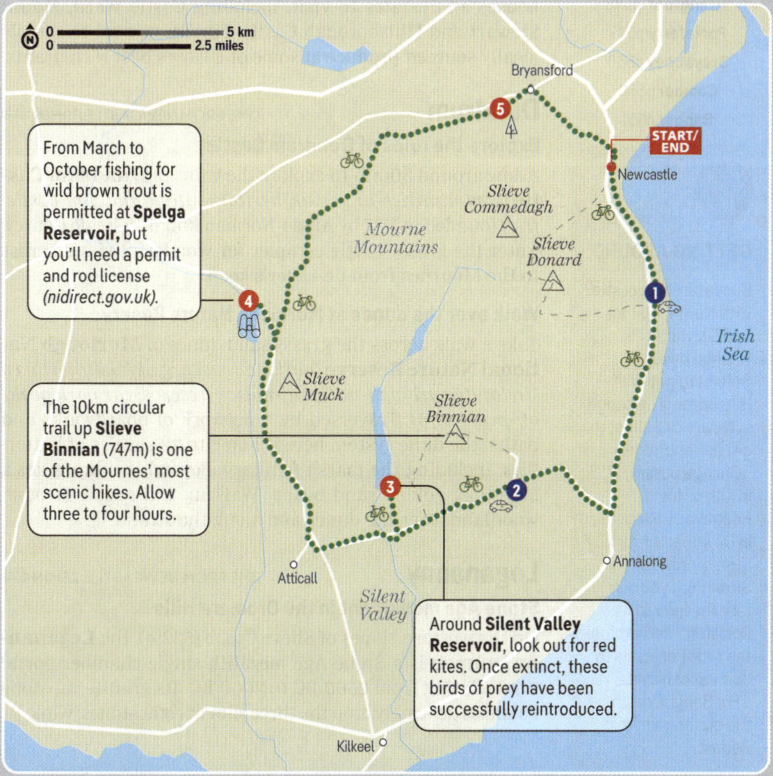

From March to October fishing for wild brown trout is permitted at **Spelga Reservoir,** but you'll need a permit and rod license (nidirect.gov.uk).

The 10km circular trail up **Slieve Binnian** (747m) is one of the Mournes' most scenic hikes. Allow three to four hours.

Around **Silent Valley Reservoir,** look out for red kites. Once extinct, these birds of prey have been successfully reintroduced.

Beyond Newcastle

From walks in the Mourne Mountains to birdwatching at Strangford Lough, you'll want to spend some time exploring County Down.

Places

Dundrum p542
Legananny p542
Rostrevor p543
Newry p544
Banbridge p544
Hillsborough p545
Downpatrick p547
Strangford p548
Portaferry p549
Greyabbey p550
Comber p550
Bangor p551

GETTING AROUND

Buses link Newcastle with Newry, Belfast and Downpatrick. Change buses in Belfast to get to Hillsborough. Change in Newry or Belfast to get to Banbridge.
Change buses in Kilkeel for Rostrevor. Change in Downpatrick for Strangford. From Strangford you can take the ferry to Portaferry and explore the Ards Peninsula by bus, car or bicycle.
For Bangor, catch the bus or train from Belfast.

There is no shortage of attractions in the area beyond Newcastle. Options for activities abound, from walks in the Mournes and through ancient woodland to boat rides in Strangford Lough, an area rich in wildlife. Some of Ireland's best mountain-biking trails traverse the forested hillsides of Kilbroney Park; afterwards, stop for a pint in Rostrevor, a village known for its folk music festival.

When the sun comes out, the area's beautiful sandy beaches are where you'll want to be. County Down also has some grand houses and estates to visit, including Castle Ward, Mount Stewart and Hillsborough Castle. Finally, be sure to sample locally sourced produce at some of Ulster's best restaurants.

Dundrum

TIME FROM NEWCASTLE: **10MIN**

Explore the ruins of Dundrum Castle

Allow around 30min to explore the ruins of **Dundrum Castle** *(communities-ni.gov.uk/heritage-sites/dundrum-castle; free)* founded in 1177 by Anglo-Norman knight John de Courcy. Enter the grassy castle complex for wonderful views across to the Mournes from de Lacey's keep.

Walk over the dunes at Murlough Nature Reserve

Take a walk across the grassy sand dunes of **Murlough National Nature Reserve** *(nationaltrust.org.uk/visit/northern-ireland/murlough-national-nature-reserve; car park peak/off-peak £7/5)*. Traversed by a network of boardwalks and paths, the dune system here is home to 22 species of butterflies, including the marsh fritillary. Beyond the dunes lies a 6km-long golden sand beach. Walking trails lead through woodland, over the dunes and along the strand.

Legananny

TIME FROM NEWCASTLE: **25MIN**

Stone Age monument in the Dromara Hills

On the western slopes of Slieve Croob (532m), the **Legananny Dolmen** is a Stone Age megalith single-chamber portal tomb, dating from 2500 BC to 2000 BC. Its granite capstone balances delicately atop the three slim upright stones, while its elevated position gives it an impressive view of the Mournes. Make a quick 10-minute stop to see the dolmen.

Rostrevor

TIME FROM NEWCASTLE: **35MIN**

Walk through the forest that inspired CS Lewis

Southeast of Rostrevor village, the forested hills of **Kilbroney Park** *(visitmournemountains.co.uk; car park £5)* can be explored on foot, by bike or by car.

There is a sense of magic to the place; CS Lewis once said that the part of Rostrevor that overlooks Carlingford Lough was his idea of Narnia. Dip your toe into the enchanted forest with a walk along the 1.2km **Fairy Glen Walk**, which follows the Kilbroney River from the village, connecting with other trails further into the park. Continue east to reach the 1km **Narnia Trail**, a children's woodland path dotted with sculptures of characters from *The Lion, the Witch and the Wardrobe*.

The main Kilbroney trailhead and car park is 1km east of the village. For a scenic, 4km circular hike, take the waymarked **Cloughmore Trail.** It follows the Glen River up to the Cloughmore Stone, a 30-tonne granite boulder inscribed with Victorian-era graffiti, from where there are superb views over the lough. It's also possible to reach the stone by car via the forest drive; it's a 10-minute walk from the upper car park. Plan on spending at least two to three hours exploring the park.

Hit Rostrevor's mountain-biking trails

Some of Ireland's best mountain-biking trails are through the forests of Kilbroney Park, including the 27km red trail, a loop trail that begins with an ascent up Slievemartin and has views over Carlingford Lough on the descent, and the 19km black trail, which follows the same trail uphill but takes a more technically-challenging route down.

Mountain-bike hire and an uplift service is offered by **Bike Mourne** *(bikemourne. com; three hours from £34.50; book ahead)*.

BIKE RIDES IN THE MOURNES

As well as cycling at Kilbroney Park, you can explore the trails at **Tollymore Forest Park** (p539), or explore further into the Mournes along quiet roads on a circular route from Newcastle (p541).

MOURNE WALL

The spectacular drystone Mourne Wall extends across the summits of 15 surrounding peaks, including the highest, Slieve Donard (852m). It was constructed with granite from the nearby quarries. You can walk the 2m-high, 1m-thick, 30km-long wall's entire length (a challenging hike beginning and ending at Carricklittle car park), or just a short section.

The wall was built in 1922 to stop livestock reaching the water catchment area of the Rivers Kilkeel and Annalong. Since 2017 the wall has been undergoing repairs as part of a major restoration project, but in 2025 the 145km/h winds of Storm Éowyn caused the wall to collapse in 63 different places. However, most of the damage was to sections of the wall that had not yet been repaired.

EATING IN AND AROUND DUNDRUM: BEST FOR SEAFOOD

Scopers: Hot food bar serving freshly-prepared local produce, including mussel popcorn with kimchi mayo and pickled seaweed. *noon-3pm & 5-9pm Thu & Fri, 10am-9pm Sat & Sun* **££**

Meghara Inn: Located in the village of Meghara; known for its seafood chowder. *noon-9pm Mon-Thu, to 9.30pm Fri & Sat, to 8.30pm Sun* **££**

Mourne Seafood Bar: Serves fresh fish, oysters, crab and langoustines, depending on the days' catch. *12.30-3pm & 5-9pm Wed-Thu, 12.30-3pm & 5-9.30pm Fri, 12.30-9.30pm Sat, 12.30-6pm Sun* **£££**

Buck's Head: The menu features oysters, Kilkeel crab and market fish, as well as Mourne lamb. *noon-3pm & 5.30-8.30pm Thu, to 9.30pm Fri & Sat, 1-8pm Sun* **£££**

BEST FESTIVALS IN COUNTY DOWN

St Patrick's Festival: On 17 March, colourful St Patrick's Day parades take place in Downpatrick, near the saint's grave, and in Newry.

Blues on the Bay: In late May, Warrenpoint offers a packed schedule of live music, including blues jams and jazz.

Fiddler's Green Festival: In July, folk musicians arrive in Rostrevor to perform in this long-running, five-day festival.

Open House Festival: Held throughout August in Bangor, featuring literature talks, art walks and live music, including folk on a boat.

Eats & Beats: This free festival in Newcastle takes place in September, with cooking demonstrations, food stalls and live music.

Catch a trad session

Rostrevor is known for the weeklong Fiddler's Green Festival, but you can also catch live folk and trad music in Rostrevor most nights throughout the year.

Crawford's Bar in Rostrevor Inn hosts songs and stories nights on Wednesdays, as well as trad sessions at weekends and regular folk music nights. Nearby, the Old Killowen Inn hosts impromptu trad music and set sessions on Saturdays. As well as regular live folk music, the Cloughmór Inn has trad sessions on Sunday afternoons and Thursday nights; musicians are welcome to join in.

Listen out for the song 'The Town of Rostrevor' by late folk singer Tommy Makem.

Walk through ancient woodland at Mourne Park

Take a stroll through a 73-hectare area of ancient woodland at **Mourne Park** *(woodlandtrust.org.uk; free)*, 12km east of Rostrevor. A 4.5km trail loops around Whitewater River (allow 1½ hours); look out for otters, pine martens and red squirrels. Come in spring to see the bluebells.

Newry
TIME FROM NEWCASTLE: **40MIN**

Discover the Newry Canal Towpath

The **Newry Canal Towpath** meanders through peaceful rolling countryside from Portadown to Newry (32km). Both towns are on the Belfast to Dublin train line, so it's possible to cycle or walk one way and get the train back.

The canalside **Hollie Berrie at the Tearooms** in Scarva is a good place to stop for cake or lunch. Just south of Scarva, the towpath passes **Lough Shark**, where it's possible to spot an array of wildlife, including whooper swans in winter.

Banbridge
TIME FROM NEWCASTLE: **30MIN**

Behind the scenes of Game of Thrones

Fans of *Game of Thrones* can learn how the blockbuster HBO series was made on a behind-the-scenes **Game of Thrones Studio Tour** *(gameofthronesstudiotour.com; adult/youth/child £29.50/12/5)* at Linen Mill Studios, where much of the series was filmed. A shuttle bus runs to the studio from the car park at Boulevard shopping mall near Banbridge.

EATING IN ROSTREVOR: OUR PICKS

Synge & Byrne: In Kilbroney park, this branch of the local cafe chain serves pies, pastries, baked goods, salads, sandwiches, smoothies and coffee. *9am-5pm* **£**

Feast: This standout restaurant serves refined breakfast and lunch plates made with seasonal local ingredients, such as Kilkeel crab, as well home-baked madeleines. *9am-4pm Thu-Sun* **££**

Rostrevor Inn: Generous portions of local fish and seafood, burgers and other mains. *5.30-9pm Wed, 12.30-3pm & 5.30-9pm Thu-Sat, 12.30-8pm Sun* **££**

Old School House: Offers cooked breakfasts and lengthy lunch and dinner menus, including burgers and wood-fired pizzas. *9am-4pm Mon & Thu, to 8pm Fri & Sat, to 6pm Sun* **££**

Game of Thrones Studio Tour

The high-tech self-guided tours recreate the drama of the series from the offset, with smoke and blasts of cold air as screens open to reveal Westeros. There are plenty of original props, costumes and scenery to see: highlights include the Winterfell great hall (which remains on the exact site where it was originally built and filmed), the Dragonstone map table, the map courtyard at King's Landing and the throne room.

Displays explain how the show was produced, including examples of the art department's storyboards and models, and filmed interviews with costume designers. The behind-the-scenes look at the prosthetic department includes the eerie Hall of Faces, for which the team made 600 unique face masks. Interactive screens allow you to see yourself as Thrones characters, and see your image projected onto the Hall of Faces. You can also pose for a photo on the Iron Throne. Thrones fans should allow two to three hours to tour the exhibition.

Hillsborough

TIME FROM NEWCASTLE: **40MIN**

Visit a royal residence

In the pretty village of Hillsborough, just 20 minutes' drive south of Belfast, is **Hillsborough Castle** *(hrp.org.uk, adult/child £20.80/10.40)*, the official home of the Secretary of State for Northern Ireland and a royal residence that is open to the

GAME OF THRONES LEGACY

For more than ten years, Northern Ireland was a filming location for all eight seasons of *Game of Thrones*. The large-scale production brought wide-ranging job opportunities, from costume making to work as a bearded extra in battle scenes, and helped establish the region within the film and TV industry. When production wrapped in 2019, local screen agency Northern Ireland Screen estimated that *Game of Thrones* had added £251 million to the local economy, while Tourism NI has said that some 350,000 people come to Northern Ireland each year just to visit *Thrones* sights.

Filming locations in County Down include Tollymore Forest Park (p539), Castle Ward (p548) and Inch Abbey (p547). **Game of Thrones Tours** *(gameofthronestours.com)* offers tours to filming locations from Belfast or Dublin.

 DRINKING IN ROSTREVOR: BEST PUBS

Crawford's Bar: The best bar in town for local craft beers, ciders and spirits, including Killowen and Mourne Dew whiskeys and gins, distilled nearby. *3pm-late*

Old Killowen Inn: Traditional village pub with nautical decor, warming fires on cold days and a beer garden for sunny weather. *11.30am-midnight*

Cloughmór Inn: Cosy pub with fires in winter and regular trad sessions. Serves a good pint of Guinness. *11am-11pm Sun-Fri, to midnight Sat*

Kilbroney: Traditional family-run pub with live music on weekends. *4pm-11pm Mon-Thu, 12.30pm-1pm Fri, 11.30am-1am Sat, 11am-11pm Sun*

Hillsborough Fort

HILLSBOROUGH HISTORY

Hillsborough Castle has been the stage for some important moments in history. In 1771 Benjamin Franklin made a visit to the Hill family home to meet with Wills Hill, who was Britain's Secretary of State for the Colonies; Franklin later led the charge for American independence.

In 1985, the castle was where British Prime Minister Margaret Thatcher and Irish Taoiseach Garret Fitzgerald signed the Anglo-Irish Agreement. In 1998, further peace talks were held here, paving the way for the Good Friday Agreement. And in 2009, the first meeting of the British and Irish heads of state took place when Irish president Mary McAleese met the Queen.

In 2021, the village was awarded royal status and its name was changed to Royal Hillsborough.

public for guided tours (around 45 minutes). The main entrance and car park are accessed from the A1 dual carriageway; if you are arriving on foot or by bus there is a pedestrian entrance on Main St in the village.

Hillsborough Castle is not a castle but a late-18th-century mansion house. It was bought by the British government in 1925. Book a tour to see the throne room, state drawing room and dining room, and Lady Grey's study where, in 2003, Tony Blair and President George W Bush held talks on Iraq. Don't miss the castle gardens; highlights include the lime-tree walk and the restored 18th-century walled garden. Plan to spend around two to three hours at the site. Look out for events in the castle grounds, such as concerts, food festivals and gardening workshops, and Christmas garden trails.

The castle was built as the family home of the wealthy Hill family, who had previously lived in **Hillsborough Fort**, which now sits at the edge of **Hillsborough Forest Park**. From the pedestrian entrance to the castle, cross Main St and go through the gates next to the Plough Inn to view the fort (the interior is closed to the public), then take a walk around the lake in the forest park. There is an excellent children's playground amid the trees, plus a sculpture trail to explore.

 EATING IN AND AROUND NEWRY & BANBRIDGE: OUR PICKS

Hollie Berrie at the Tearooms (p544): Scarva cafe serving homemade cakes and lunches, with outdoor tables by the towpath. *8am-5pm Tue-Fri, to 4pm Sat* **£**

Finegan & Son: Newry's best cafe serves speciality coffee, locally sourced breakfast, lunch dishes, plus small plates and natural wine. *9am-6pm Mon-Fri, to 4pm Sat & Sun* **££**

Blend & Batch: Banbridge cafe serving brunch until 4pm, burgers and evening meals, as well as coffee and cake. *8am-10pm Mon-Sat, to 5pm Sun* **££**

Wine & Brine: It's worth a detour to Moira to feast on exquisite plates of local produce. *noon-2.30pm & 5.30-9.30pm Thu-Sat, noon-6pm Sun* **£££**

Downpatrick

TIME FROM NEWCASTLE: **20MIN**

Learn the life story of St Patrick

St Patrick's mission to spread Christianity in Ireland began and ended in Downpatrick, where there are a number of sights connected to the saint.

Begin at the **Saint Patrick Centre** *(saintpatrickcentre.com; adult/child £9.75/7.75)*, where a multimedia exhibition tells the life story of Ireland's patron saint in his own words, from his childhood in Roman Britain to his abduction into slavery, his time in Ireland tending sheep, his escape and perilous journey back to Britain, and his decision to return to Ireland to found a church. The exhibition is based on Patrick's *Confession*, written in Latin around the year 450. At the end is a spectacular widescreen film that takes you on a swooping, low-level helicopter ride over the landscapes of Ireland. Allow around 45 minutes to view the exhibition.

See St Patrick's grave at Down Cathedral

From the Saint Patrick Centre, a path leads uphill to **Down Cathedral** *(downcathedral.org; free)*. In the churchyard, look for a slab of Mourne granite placed here in 1900 to mark the traditional site of **St Patrick's grave**.

Next, take a look inside the cathedral; don't miss the stained-glass window depicting scenes from St Patrick's life. The cathedral's elevated pipe organ is considered one of Ireland's finest; if you're lucky you might catch a recital by one of the skilled organists who travel to Downpatrick for the pleasure of playing it.

Visit a former jail turned museum

Walk up English St to the **Down County Museum** *(visitmournemountains.co.uk/museums/down-county-museum; free)* to see the 10th-century **Downpatrick High Cross**.

The museum is housed in Downpatrick's 18th-century jail. A former cell block at the back has models of some of the prisoners once incarcerated there, and details of their sad stories. United Irishman Thomas Russell was executed in the jail courtyard for his role in the failed rising of 1803. It's closed Mondays.

Take the train to Inch Abbey

In an atmospheric setting beside the marshes of the River Quoile, the unmanned ruins of **Inch Abbey** *(free)* are worth visiting for their attractive location and views across the river

DISTILLERY TOURS IN COUNTY DOWN

Echlinville Distillery: Farm distillery on the Ards Peninsula, where barley is grown, malted and distilled into whiskey, gin and poitín. *(echlinville.com)*

Shortcross Distillery: Learn how whiskeys and gins are made, followed by a tasting. Located near Crossgar village. *(rademonestatedistilleryshop.com)*

Copeland Distillery: Hear stories of local smugglers and taste whiskey, rum and gin at this Donaghadee distillery. *(copelanddistillery.com)*

Hinch Distillery: This distillery east of Hillsborough offers a range of tours, including inside the warehouse where the whiskey matures. *(hinchdistillery.com)*

Killowen Distillery: Produces small batch whiskeys and gins using traditional methods (flame-heated pot stills and traditional worm tub condensers). Located in the Mournes. *(killowendistillery.com)*

EATING IN HILLSBOROUGH: BEST PUBS & RESTAURANTS

Parson's Nose: A snug downstairs bar leads to a bright restaurant serving refined pub food and pizza. *noon-8.30pm Sun & Mon, to 9.30pm Tue-Sat* ££

Plough Inn: Has a beer garden and a maze of wood-panelled nooks and crannies; serves excellent bistro food. *noon-11pm Sun-Wed, to 12.30am Thu, to 1am Fri & Sat* £££

Pheasant: In the countryside 8km east of the village. Menu includes steaks cooked on the wood-burning grill. *noon-8pm Sun & Tue-Thu, to 9pm Sat & Sun* £££

Hillside: This pub specialises in real ale. The restaurant menu features scampi and Mourne lamb. *noon-9pm Mon-Thu, to 9.30pm Fri & Sat, 12.30pm-8pm Sun* £££

to Down Cathedral. Open 24 hours, most of the ruins are just foundations and low walls, but illustrated panels show how the abbey once looked and how the monks lived.

The abbey was built by John de Courcy for the Cistercians in 1180 on an existing monastic site. A monk was commissioned to rewrite the legends of St Patrick; it's possible that the story of St Patrick banishing the snakes from Ireland was written here.

A fun way to reach Inch Abbey from Downpatrick is onboard a vintage train; the **Downpatrick & County Down Railway** *(downrail.co.uk; adult/child £10.50/8.50)* offers return trips. Trains usually run on Saturdays in August and at Christmas and Easter; check the schedule online.

On the trail of St Patrick

In the rolling farmland surrounding Downpatrick are three peaceful sites connected to the saint.

First, drive or cycle to a secluded glen 3km east of Downpatrick to visit **Struell Wells**, where St Patrick is said to have spent the night immersed in what is now the drinking well. Between the bathhouses and the ruined chapel stands the eye well, whose waters are said to cure eye ailments.

Continue 4km north to reach **Saul Church**, a replica 10th-century church and round tower built in 1932 to mark the 1500th anniversary of St Patrick's arrival. It is located at the site where St Patrick is said to have founded his first church in 432. The church is kept unlocked during the day and open to visitors.

To the east is **Slieve Patrick** (120m), a hill with stations of the cross along the path leading to a 10m-high statue of St Patrick at the summit, with views of the drumlins, Strangford Lough and the Mournes.

Strangford
TIME FROM NEWCASTLE: **40MIN** 🚗

Discover Castle Ward House and grounds

Castle Ward *(nationaltrust.org.uk; adult/child £14/7)* is a country house estate overlooking Strangford Lough with all kinds of historic buildings, gardens, woodland areas and meadows to explore via a series of walking and cycling trails.

Start with a tour of **Castle Ward House**, a remarkable building of two halves. The front facade was designed in a neoclassical style, to suit the architectural tastes of Lord Bangor, while the rear facade is Gothic, to suit his wife. The

---

ST PATRICK'S WAY

Downpatrick is the final stop on **St Patrick's Way**, a 132km signposted pilgrim walk from Armagh city, linking sites related to St Patrick. Starting at Navan Fort (p555), the walk passes along the Newry canal towpath (p544) from Scarva to Newry, then on to Rostrevor (p543) and across the Mourne Mountains to Newcastle on the way to Downpatrick. You can pick up a free Pilgrim's Passport at the Navan Centre (p555) and tourist offices and collect stamps along the way; upload a free, 28-page *Pilgrim's Guide* at visitarmagh.com.

If walking doesn't appeal, pick up a map for the **St Patrick's Trail** (also available on visitarmagh.com) which highlights St Patrick-related and other Christian sights on a driving route from Armagh to Bangor.

 EATING IN AND AROUND DOWNPATRICK: OUR PICKS

Oakley Fayre: Cafe serving coffee, sandwiches, salads, pancakes and baked goods to eat in, plus deli produce to take away. *9am-4pm Mon-Sat* **£**

Garden Cafe: The upstairs cafe at the St Patrick Centre offers simple breakfasts and lunches, as well as tray bakes and snacks. *9.30am-4pm* **£**

Fodder in the Woods: Finnebrogue Dexter beef and homegrown salads served in a wonderful woodland cafe, with a farm shop and forest trails. *9am-4pm Tue & Thu-Sat, 10am-4pm Sun* **££**

Denvir's Restaurant: At this historic pub, the menu features seafood chowder, burgers and Denvir's pie of the day. *noon-8pm Sun-Thu, to 9pm Fri & Sat* **££**

Struell Wells

differing styles continue inside; don't miss the incredible fan vaulting of Lady Bangor's Gothic boudoir. Taxidermy on display includes a tableau of boxing squirrels and a bear holding a drinks tray.

You could spend all day here exploring the gardens and grounds, on foot or by bike – hire one at the **Stableyard** *(adult/child £7.50/5 for 2 hours)*. The 3km **Shore Trail** follows the lough's edge to **Audley's Castle**, a 15th-century gatehouse. Take the 4km **Farm Trail** to see the **Temple Water** lake and avenue of lime trees.

The estate was used as a filming location for *Game of Thrones*. At the shore, **Clearsky Adventure** *(clearsky-adventure.com)* rents mountain bikes for self-guided Westeros cycle tours around the grounds, and offers *Game of Thrones*–inspired archery sessions at Winterfell Castle; book ahead.

Portaferry

TIME FROM NEWCASTLE: **50MIN**

Take the ferry across the Narrows

Take the **Strangford Car Ferry** *(nidirect.gov.uk/articles/strangford-ferry-timetable; car £7.70, foot passenger adult/child £1.30/0.70)* from the pretty fishing village of Strangford to Portaferry on the Ards Peninsula, the finger of land to the

GEOGRAPHY OF STRANGFORD LOUGH

Almost landlocked, Strangford Lough (Loch Cuan) is connected to the open sea by a 800m-wide strait, the Narrows, between the towns of Portaferry and Strangford. At the Narrows, the tidal currents are some of the fastest flowing in the world, moving at up to eight knots. There are several swirling tidal pools here, including the Routen Wheel, a series of whirlpools caused by pinnacles of rock on the seabed.

The lough's western shore is fringed by drumlins – submerged mounds of boulder clay left behind by ice sheets at the end of the last ice age. On the eastern shore, the drumlins have been broken down by the waves into piles of boulders that form shallow tidal reefs, known locally as 'pladdies'.

 EATING IN STRANGFORD: OUR PICKS

Cake Room: Cute cafe serving a range of homemade pies, cakes and tray bakes, as well as sandwiches, pastries and scones. *10am-4pm* **£**

Lobster Pot: Cosy restaurant serving seafood (including lobster) and other dishes. *noon-11pm Mon-Thu, to 1.30am Fri & Sat, to midnight Sun* **££**

Artisan Cookhouse: High-end plates such as local smoked haddock and tempura cod. *10am-8pm Tue-Thu, to 9pm Fri & Sat, to 7pm Sun* **£££**

Cuan Restaurant: The restaurant at the Cuan specialises in seafood, including beer-battered scampi and cod. *8am-7.45pm Sun-Thu, to 8.45pm Fri & Sat* **£££**

BEST SCENIC PICNIC SPOTS

Castlewellan Forest Park: Forest walks, mountain-bike trails, paddleboarding on the lake and a peace maze to explore. Barbecues permitted.

Scrabo Tower & Country Park: Take in panoramic views over Strangford Lough and beyond from Scrabo Tower, visible for miles around; near Newtownards.

Spelga Dam: Roadside picnic spot with views over Spelga Reservoir and the Mournes; has a car park and toilets.

Crawfordsburn Country Park: Pack a picnic to eat by the beach. A 5km-trail leads through woodlands and meadows past a railway viaduct.

Silent Valley Reservoir: Peaceful spot in the heart of the Mournes, with picnic benches looking out to the mountains.

east of Strangford Lough. Ferries make the 10-minute journey every 30 minutes.

In Portaferry, explore the neat huddle of streets and medieval tower house, which looks across the Narrows to a matching tower in Strangford. Then take a walk along minor coastal roads north for 2.5km to **Ballyhenry Island** (accessible on foot at low tide) or south for 6km to the nature reserve at **Ballyquintin Point**. Both sites are free to access and good for birdwatching and seal spotting.

Greyabbey

TIME FROM NEWCASTLE: **1HR 10MIN**

Explore the ruins of Grey Abbey

In the village of Greyabbey, stop to look at the remains of **Grey Abbey** *(friendsoftheabbey.co.uk; free)*, a Cistercian abbey founded in 1193 by Affreca, wife of John de Courcy. Don't miss the **physic garden**, full of medicinal herbs once cultivated by the monks.

A small visitor centre explains Cistercian life and houses a sandstone effigy, possibly depicting Affreca. Even if the visitor centre is closed, the ruins are well labelled with informative signs. Be sure to look at the elaborate stonework of the church's **west door**.

Mount Stewart

Just north of Greyabbey on the shore of **Strangord Lough** sits **Mount Stewart** *(nationaltrust.org.uk; adult/child £15/7.50)* a magnificent 18th-century stately home. Take a tour to learn the story of the house and its contents. Treasures include the painting of racehorse *Hambletonian* (1800) by George Stubbs, one of the most important paintings in Ireland.

The house overlooks formal gardens filled with subtropical plants and eccentric topiary. Walking trails through the grounds lead around a lake and to a woodland hide for spotting red squirrels. Don't miss the 18th-century Temple of the Winds, a classical Greek style summer house built on a high point above the lough. Count on spending at least two hours at the site.

Comber

TIME FROM NEWCASTLE: **50MIN**

Birdwatching at Castle Espie

One of the best places to bird spot is **Castle Espie Wetland Centre** *(wwt.org.uk; adult/child £9.45/6.13)* on the western shore of Strangford Lough. The grounds are dotted with

EATING AROUND STRANGFORD LOUGH: BEST PUBS AND RESTAURANTS

Dufferin Arms: Behind a bright pink facade, the Dufferin serves typical Irish pub food, like fish and chips and lasagne. *noon-9pm Mon-Sat, to 8pm Sun* **££**

Poacher's Pocket: Historic pub with a menu featuring local produce, such a Portavogie scampi. *noon-8pm Mon-Wed, to 9pm Fri & Sat, 9.30am-9pm Sat, 9.30am-8pm Sun* **£££**

Balloo House: Country pub near Killinchy with a restaurant specialising in steak; excellent desserts too. *noon-8pm Mon-Wed, to 9pm Thu-Sun.* **£££**

No 14 Georgian House: Elegant Comber restaurant serving beautifully presented dishes made with quality local produce. *9.30am-5pm Mon-Wed, to 9pm Thu-Sat, to 8pm Sun* **£££**

Pickie Funpark

birdwatching hides and are great for fledgling naturalists, with family bird-feeding sessions and an adventure playground.

Strangford Lough is a designated marine nature reserve that's home to porpoises, seals and otters, as well as flocks of nesting seabirds. One of the great birdwatching spectacles of Ireland is the autumn arrival of vast flocks of light-bellied brent geese (75% of the world population). Around 30,000 geese come here during winter, as well as knots and redshanks. It's also possible to see peregrines, merlins and the short-eared owl.

Bangor

TIME FROM NEWCASTLE: 1HR

Visit the museum and gardens at Bangor Castle

Located on the site of what was once a thriving early-Christian monastery, **Bangor Castle** is now the City Hall. In the former stable block is the **North Down Museum** *(andculture. org.uk; free)*; pop inside to see a recreation of a monk's cell and the Bangor Bell, a 9th-century bronze handbell. Look out, too, for the sugar-cube model of the castle. The museum is closed Mondays.

Next, walk through the castle grounds to explore the beautiful **Bangor Castle Walled Garden** *(free)*; concerts and events are held here during August's Open House Festival (p544).

BEST FOR KIDS IN COUNTY DOWN

Pickie Funpark: Swan-shaped pedal boats, a ride-aboard miniature train and mini golf by the sea in Bangor.

Ark Open Farm: Farm near Newtownards with animals to pet (goats, donkeys, alpacas and ponies, among others), a fairytale forest and tractor rides.

Ballyburren Outdoor Escapes: Book an alpaca trek (a walk along a woodland trail with an alpaca in tow); near Ballynahinch.

Strangford Lough Activity Centre: Wildlife-spotting tours around Strangford Lough in a rigid inflatable boat; full moon night trips available.

Exploris Aquarium: Discover the marine life of Strangford Lough, as well as tropical fish, at this Portaferry aquarium and seal sanctuary.

EATING IN BANGOR: OUR PICKS

Guillemot: Opposite Bangor marina, this cafe does all-day breakfasts, gourmet sandwiches, soups, salads and homemade cakes. *9am-5pm* £

Underground Dining: Opt for a range of small tasting plates or classic European main dishes. *noon-2.30pm & 5-8.30pm Tue-Thu, to 9.30pm Fri & Sat* ££

Jamaica Inn: On the seafront, with indoor and outdoor tables. Serves an all-day menu of snacks and meals, including burgers and fish and chips. *noon-9pm* ££

Tuk Tuk Asian Bistro: Serves a range of curries and stir fries from Thailand, Indonesia and Malaysia. *4.30-9.15pm Wed & Thu, 1-9.15pm Fri-Sun* ££

BEST BEACHES IN COUNTY DOWN

Ballyholme Beach: This beach in Bangor is backed by a promenade; there's a children's playground here too.

Helen's Bay Beach: Sandy beach on the north Down coast that's popular with swimmers; it can be reached by train from Belfast.

Ballywalter Beach: On the east coast of the Ards Peninsula, this sandy beach has rock pools to explore.

Cranfield Beach: An inclusive beach with accessible facilities and beach wheelchairs and other equipment available; at the mouth of Carlingford Lough.

Tyrella Beach: A wide sandy beach backed by dunes, 10km south of Downpatrick. Lifeguards on duty in summer.

Helen's Bay Beach

Sweat in a woodland sauna

Book a shared or private session in the wood-fired **Sudor Sauna** *(sudorsauna.co.uk; per person from £15)*, set among the trees at Quarries Farm. Alternate time in the heat with dips in the cold plunge pool. You can also book a Sudor sauna in the grounds of Castle Ward (p548).

Hike the North Down Coastal Path

The **North Down Coastal Path** follows the shore from Holywood on Belfast's northeastern edge to Bangor Marina (14.5km), and continues east to Orlock Point (10.5km).

The Belfast to Bangor train line runs along the coast, making it possible to walk a linear section of the path on a day trip from Belfast. The most accessible and scenic section is between Bangor and Helen's Bay (6km), which has a train station and a lovely beach for swimming.

Armagh City

HISTORIC CATHEDRALS | APPLE CIDER | CELTIC MYTHS

The small-town atmosphere of Armagh city these days belies its importance as a religious centre steeped in history and legend. Excavations at Navan Fort on the city's outskirts suggest the site was once occupied by royalty or high priests of great importance, who more than 2000 years ago may have brought animals from as far away as Africa. The site is mythologised in the Ulster Cycle of legends as the court of King Conchobar mac Nessa, uncle of the great warrior Cúchulainn. Little wonder then that in the 5th century, St Patrick chose a nearby hill as the site of his first church, at the location of what is now St Patrick's Church of Ireland Cathedral.

Armagh remains the ecclesiastical capital of Ireland, the seat of both the Anglican and Roman Catholic archbishops of Armagh. Their two cathedrals look across at each other from their respective hilltops.

St Patrick's Roman Catholic Cathedral (p554)

GETTING AROUND

Armagh's hilly city centre is small enough to explore on foot. Traffic can move slowly on Upper English St and along the narrow roads around the Church of Ireland Cathedral. The closest car parks to the city centre are at the Mall Shopping Centre and Linenhall St. On street parking (including disabled spaces) is also available but can be hard to come by.

There are several buses a day to Belfast (the 251 Express) and Newry (bus 40). Navan Fort is 4km west of Armagh city; take bus 73 from the bus centre.

ARMAGH CITY

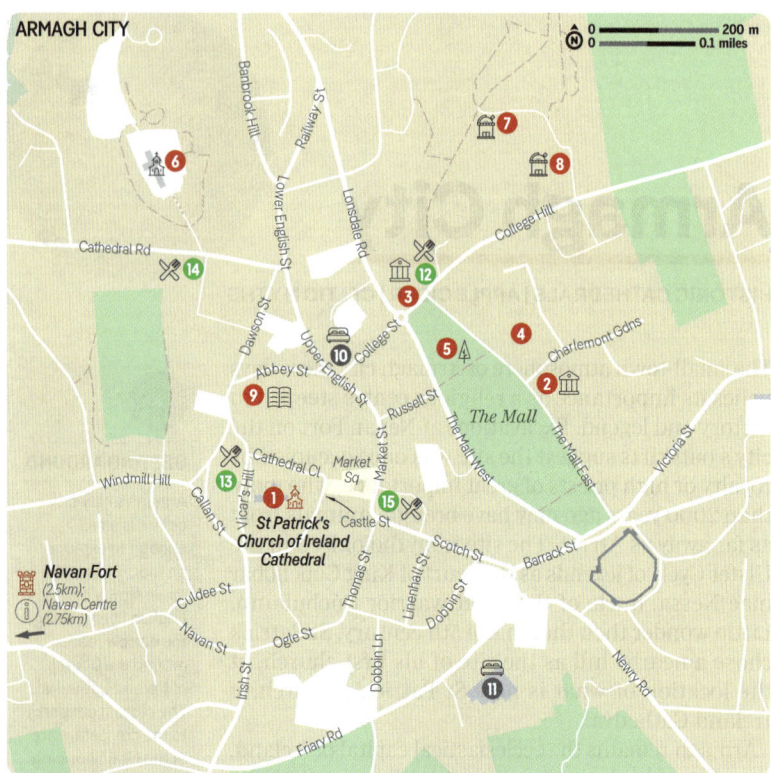

HIGHLIGHTS
1 St Patrick's Church of Ireland Cathedral

SIGHTS
2 Armagh County Museum
3 Armagh Courthouse
4 Charlemont Place
5 Mall
6 St Patrick's Roman Catholic Cathedral

ACTIVITIES
7 Armagh Observatory
8 Armagh Planetarium
9 Armagh Robinson Library

SLEEPING
10 7 Houses
11 Armagh City Hotel

EATING
12 4C Coffee House & Kitchen
13 Gathering Rooms
14 Mulberry Bistro
15 Uluru Bar & Grill

☑ TOP TIP

If you are interested in looking at any particular specialist books or resources from the vast **Armagh Robinson Library** collection, you can search the online catalogue at armaghrobinsonlibrary.co.uk and contact the library with your request. Library staff will endeavour to have it ready for you when you visit.

Armagh's Two Cathedrals

Site of St Patrick's main church

Inside **St Patrick's Church of Ireland Cathedral** *(st patricks-cathedral.org; adult/child £4/free)* look for the **Tandragee Idol**, a 3000-year-old stone carving believed to represent the Irish king Nuadhe. Look inside the **crypt**, built in 1268 and open to visitors on request, for more fascinating pre-Christian **stone carvings**, including one that probably represents the sun god Lugh, and three dogs possibly carved by the sculptor of the Tandragee Idol.

Gazing across at the cathedral from a neighbouring hill are the Gothic-revival twin towers of **St Patrick's Roman Catholic Cathedral** *(armaghparish.net; free)*. Look inside to see the walls and ceilings covered in beautiful coloured mosaics.

Celtic History at Navan Fort
Enigmatic Iron Age monument

Perched atop a drumlin on the outskirts of Armagh, **Navan Fort** is Ulster's most important archaeological site. It was probably a site of rituals and ceremonies, and was an important centre from around 330 BCE to 330 CE. These days you can climb the grassy mounds and enjoy views towards the cathedrals of Armagh.

To better understand the site, start your visit at the **Navan Centre** *(visitarmagh.com; tours adult/child £12.50/8.50; closed Mon)* which offers guided tours and living history experiences that place the fort in its historical and mythological context. Costumed actors portray Celtic life in a re-creation of an Iron Age settlement. A good option for children is the **Meet the Warriors** experience, with face painting and storytelling. The **Legendary Navan Fort Tour** includes a guided walk to the site. The actors are on site Tuesday to Sunday during the summer and weekends only at other times; book in advance.

A 500m interpretative trail leads from the centre to Navan Fort. Allow time to explore the circular earthwork enclosure, which is 250m in diameter, with two smaller earth mounds on the hilltop. Excavations of the larger mound revealed the remains of an intriguing structure that is believed to be a temple with a roof supported by concentric rows of wooden posts, constructed around 95 BCE and set on fire as part of a ritual. At the Navan Centre, look for a charred wooden **temple post,** carbon dated to 95 BCE and believed to be a remnant from the ceremonial temple burning. Allow around two hours for a tour, plus time to explore the centre and site.

Navan Centre holds events celebrating traditional Celtic festivals including Lughnasa in August, marked by the burning of a giant **Wickerman.**

THE LEGENDS OF EMAIN MACHA

Navan Fort appears in early literature as Emain Macha, the court of mythical King Conchobar mac Nessa. The Ulster Cycle is a series of legends set in the heroic age of the distant past, and one of four cycles in Irish mythology. The central tale, Táin Bó Cúailnge (The Cattle Raid of Cooley), tells the story of a raid by the army of Queen Medbh of Connacht. The hero of the Ulster Cycle tales is Cúchulainn, a great warrior. During the *táin,* the men of Ulster were weakened by a curse after the pregnant goddess Macha was forced to race against a horse-drawn chariot. Only Cúchulainn, who was born outside Ulster, was unaffected by the curse, leaving him to defend Ulster alone.

EATING IN ARMAGH CITY: OUR PICKS

Gathering Rooms: This cafe employs and trains young people with autism. It serves delicious cakes and lunches at indoor and outdoor tables. *9am-4pm Mon-Thu* **£**

Mulberry Bistro: Welcoming bistro serving cooked breakfasts, coffee and cake, and a lunchtime menu of sandwiches, burgers, lasagne and more. *9am-3pm Sun-Fri, 8am-3pm Sat* **££**

Uluru Bar & Grill: An Australian-style restaurant specialising in chargrilled meats (including kangaroo) cooked on the Josper grill, plus local beers and ciders. *noon-8pm Tue-Sun* **££**

4C Coffee House & Kitchen: Quirky cafe and restaurant overlooking the Mall; come for breakfast, lunch or dinner, or coffee and cake. *7am-8pm Mon-Sat, 7.30am-6pm Sun* **££**

A WALK AROUND ARMAGH'S HISTORIC CITY CENTRE

Armagh's architectural highlights underline the city's historical importance as a centre of religion and learning.

START	END	LENGTH
St Patrick's Cathedral	Armagh Observatory	1.5km; 2hr

Start at ❶ **St Patrick's Church of Ireland Cathedral** (p554), on the site of St Patrick's original stone church. A plaque on the exterior marks the burial place of Brian Ború, the Irish king who died in a 1014 battle against the Vikings.

Walk down Vicar's Hill to reach the ❷ **Armagh Robinson Library** (p554), founded in 1771. It houses the Archbishop's personal collection, including a first edition of *Gulliver's Travels* (1726), annotated by Jonathan Swift himself and on display in the library's long room.

Continue along Abbey St and College St to reach the ❸ **Mall**, a long grassy park created under the direction of the Archbishop. It's overlooked by ❹ **Armagh Courthouse** (1809). On the eastern side of the mall, look at the five late-Georgian houses of ❺ **Charlemont Place** (1830), now council offices. Next to them, a 1834 school now houses ❻ **Armagh County Museum**.

Retrace your steps along the Mall and walk up Robinson Dr to reach ❼ **Armagh Observatory**, founded by Archbishop Robinson in 1789 and still a leading astronomical research institute. Take a look at the observatory's elegant architecture (the building's interior is closed to the public), then follow trails through the grounds to see a scale model of the solar system and the hill of infinity, demonstrating distances in space.

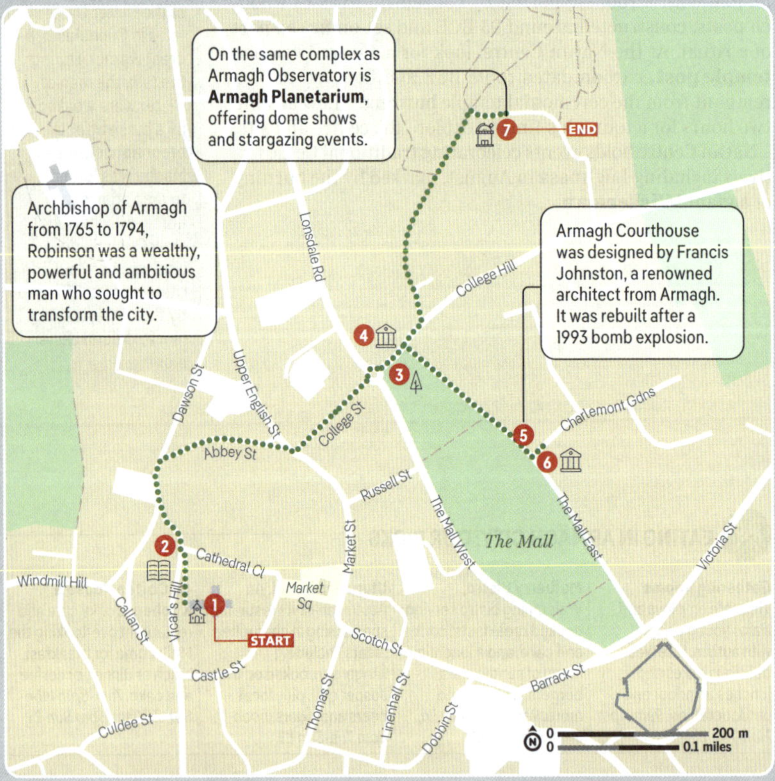

On the same complex as Armagh Observatory is **Armagh Planetarium**, offering dome shows and stargazing events.

Archbishop of Armagh from 1765 to 1794, Robinson was a wealthy, powerful and ambitious man who sought to transform the city.

Armagh Courthouse was designed by Francis Johnston, a renowned architect from Armagh. It was rebuilt after a 1993 bomb explosion.

Beyond Armagh City

With tranquil hill walks and peaceful bird-watching spots, County Armagh offers natural beauty without the crowds.

The area between Armagh city and the southern shore of Lough Neagh is apple orchard country, where Armagh Bramleys are grown and turned into cider. Apple-growing conditions are improved by a slight microclimate effect created by the lough. At the lough, birdlife thrives; the various habitats at Oxford Island offer wonderful wildlife-watching opportunities.

In South Armagh, the Ring of Gullion is an unusual geographical landform that is now part of the Mourne Gullion Strangford UNESCO Geopark. At the centre of a circle of hills stands Slieve Gullion, a seemingly magical place linked to several Celtic legends, and the place where the mythical warrior Cúchulainn got his name.

Places
Oxford Island p557
Ring of Gullion p557

Oxford Island
TIME FROM ARMAGH: **30MIN**

Birdwatching & lakeside nature trails

Oxford Island *(visitarmagh.com; free)* nature reserve is not an island but a peninsula of land on Lough Neagh's southern edge. Here you can explore a range of habitats, including woodland, wet grassland (meadows that are important breeding grounds for butterflies) and reedy shoreline, traversed by walking and cycling trails. There are several birdwatching hides; look out for grey herons, great crested grebes, little grebes, coots, moorhens goldeneye and reed buntings. Follow the tree trail to see 20 different native species. The loughside **Lough Neagh Discovery Centre** has information on the reserve's flora and fauna and is free to enter and has free parking.

Ring of Gullion
TIME FROM ARMAGH: **20MIN**

Explore Slieve Gullion Forest Park

The Ring of Gullion is a string of rugged hills encircling Slieve Gullion (573m) in an unusual 60-million-year-old geological formation known as a ring dyke. Begin exploring at **Slieve Gullion Forest Park** *(visitmournemountains.co.uk; car park £5)*. Here Slieve Gullion Courtyard (an area with an information point, cafe and car park) is the starting point for **Fionn's Giant Adventure**, a magical forest trail for children, with hidden fairy doors and play equipment in the trees. From here, follow the 10km scenic drive to a parking and picnic

GETTING AROUND

National cycle route 9 links Newry with Slieve Gullion Courtyard via minor roads (15km).

Oxford Island is also connected to Newry and Belfast via cycle route 9. The 180km signposted Loughshore Trail cycle route encircles Lough Neagh via a series of quiet country roads and traffic-free paths.

The nearest bus stop to Oxford Island is Island View Lane, 3km south of Lough Neagh Discovery Centre, served by the 352 bus from Lurgan.

View of Carlingfor Lough from Slieve Gullion Forest Park (p557)

LOUGH NEAGH EELS

The eels of Lough Neagh are believed to have been eaten by locals since the Bronze Age, and are still caught and sold today by members of the Lough Neagh Fishermen's Cooperative. Indeed, Lough Neagh Eels have PGI (Protected Geographical Indicator) status. However, in 2025 the fishing season was suspended due to the poor quality of the catch (the eels had a low fat content), a problem attributed to environmental changes.

At Oxford Island (p557), look for the sculpture *Eel Retreat* by Trudi Entwistle, which captures the motion of eels swimming through water. The eels' remarkable 6000km migration from the spawning grounds of the Sargasso Sea to Lough Neagh was the inspiration for Seamus Heaney's poem 'A Lough Neagh Sequence'.

area, from where you can hike to the summit (1.3km). The mountain heath is carpeted with purple heather in summer.

At the top, look for a **Neolithic burial chamber** which aligns with the setting sun of the winter solstice; it is Ireland's highest surviving passage tomb. From here, there are outstanding views of the outer hills that form the Ring of Gullion. Continue north along the mountain path to reach a small lake. Legend has it that Calliagh Berra (who lived in the South Cairn passage tomb) tricked the giant Finn McCool into diving into the bottomless lake to retrieve her ring.

Turn a Celtic wooden bowl

On the first Saturday of the month, you can create your own Celtic wooden bowl during a full-day woodturning experience at **Bluebell Lane** *(bluebell-lane.com; £145 including lunch)*, a 26-acre woodland with over 20,000 native trees. Book in advance.

EATING IN COUNTY ARMAGH: OUR PICKS

Groucho's: Characterful pub and restaurant in Richhill. Local ingredients on the menu include Armagh pork. *4-11pm Thu, noon-11pm Thu & Fri, 10am-11pm Sat, 10am-10pm Sun* ££

Sally McNally's: Low-key country restaurant serving excellent food; located 5km south of Portadown. *4-8pm Thu, noon-8.30pm Fri, noon-9pm Sat, 12.30-7.30pm Sun* ££

Gullion at Killeavy: Gourmet meals made with produce from the Killeavy Castle Estate farm; near Miegh in the Ring of Gullion. *6-9pm Thu-Sat, 12.30-8pm Sun* £££

Yellow Heifer: Bar and bistro serving steak, lamb shanks and burgers. In Camlough in the Ring of Gullion. *11am-8pm Thu, to 8.30pm Fri & Sun, to 9pm Sat* £££

Places We Love to Stay

£ Budget ££ Midrange £££ Top End

Newcastle MAP p537

Hutt Hostel £ In a renovated Victorian townhouse by the beach, this hostel has shared dorms and excellent amenities.

Tollymore Forest Park £ Camping sites for tents and caravans (with or without electricity) in attractive surroundings. Open year-round.

The Donard ££ This hotel's 19 bedrooms include good-value triple and family rooms. Located in town.

Enniskeen Estate £££ On the edge of Tollymore Forest, the cabins at this luxurious glamping retreat are really special, with private wood-fired hot tubs under the stars.

Enniskeen Country House Hotel £££ Traditional 19th-century manor house hotel, 2km northwest of town, with mountain and sea views.

Slieve Donard Resort & Spa (p536) £££ This magnificent red-brick hotel has been a local landmark since 1898. The interior is just as elegant.

Mourne Mountains

Mourne Lodge £ Appealing, purpose-built hostel with dorms and private rooms, a kitchen and a cosy living room. Located near Silent Valley.

Carrick Little Glamping ££ These three basic pods at the foot of Slieve Binnian have breathtaking views; each has a private fire pit.

Rostrevor

Kilbroney Caravan Park £ Camping sites for tents and caravans; close to the trails and walking distance from the village.

Rostrevor Inn ££ The seven contemporary rooms here include a family room with a Narnia theme. Rates include a hearty breakfast.

Hillsborough

Arthur's of Hillsborough £££ Boutique hotel in the village; the rooms have velvet headboards and creative interior decor.

Downpatrick

Denvir's Hotel ££ Old coaching inn dating from 1642. Rooms in the original inn have period features; those in the mews have contemporary decor.

Strangford & Castle Ward

Castle Ward Caravan Park £ Castle Ward Estate has a campsite with pitches for tents and caravans and basic glamping huts.

Downpatrick Gate Lodge £££ Romantic self-catering cottage, with a wood-burner and loft bedroom, in the grounds of Castle Ward Estate.

Cuan £££ In the village of Strangford, the Cuan has nine rooms decorated by a local interior designer.

Portaferry

Portaferry Hotel ££ Elegant waterfront hotel and restaurant in a converted row of 18th-century terrace houses.

Strangford Lough

Dufferin Coaching Inn ££ The Dufferin has plush rooms, some with four-poster beds; the lounge was once Killyleagh's village bank.

Bangor

Cairn Bay Lodge ££ Family-run guesthouse in an Edwardian home in Bangor, with creative decor and sea views.

Old Inn £££ In operation since 1614, this historic inn in Crawfordsburn has a bar with log fires and luxurious rooms.

Clandeboye Lodge Hotel £££ Luxury hotel in a rural setting on the outskirts of Bangor, with woodland trails and a drinks terrace.

Armagh City MAP p554

7 Houses ££ This guesthouse has bright, contemporary rooms with period features and comfy beds; located right in the city centre.

Armagh City Hotel £££ Large, modern hotel in Armagh city with excellent amenities, including a pool; deluxe rooms have cathedral views.

Ring of Gullion

Bluebell Lane ££ Stay in a safari tent, a shepherd's hut or a pod in beautiful surrounds near Slieve Gullion.

Killeavy Castle Estate £££ In the forested grounds of a listed castle in the Ring of Gullion, this 45-room hotel has two restaurants and a spa.

Researched by
Isabel Albiston

Derry & Antrim

HOME OF THE CAUSEWAY COAST

This dramatic coastline of basalt cliffs, hexagonal rocks and sandy beaches is backed by rolling hills and farmland.

Counties Derry and Antrim's remarkable landscape of cliffs, glens and caves form part of the Antrim Plateau: the entire area between Cave Hill in Belfast and the north coast, extending west as far as Binevenagh Mountain, is formed of basalt rock and layers of limestone. The most striking natural features, such as the U-shaped valleys of the Antrim Glens, were formed during the Ice Age, around 20,000 years ago.

As you head north through County Antrim you may notice that the regional accent has a Scottish lilt. This corner of Ireland has long had strong cultural connections with its closest neighbour (there is just 20km of sea between Antrim's Torr Head and the Scottish Mull of Kintyre). During the 16th century, the Scottish MacDonnell clan took control of several castles on the north coast, including Dunluce.

These days the Causeway Coast is home to a number of independent producers of artisan goods. There are waves to surf, paths to hike and excellent cafes and restaurants to enjoy. Little wonder, then, that the area has become an increasingly popular place to live.

To the west, the walled city of Derry sits alongside a broad sweep of the River Foyle. Though Derry's turbulent history forms part of the city's fabric, it also has a thriving arts and music scene, and hosts some of Ireland's best festivals.

SERGII FIGURNYI/SHUTTERSTOCK

THE MAIN AREAS

DERRY CITY
Historic walled city. **p566**

BUSHMILLS
Whiskey and the Giant's Causeway. **p575**

BALLYCASTLE
Seaside town on the Antrim coast. **p584**

For places to stay in Derry and Antrim, see p593

Left: Giant's Causeway (p581); right: Carrick-a-Rede (p588)

DERRY & ANTRIM

Bushmills, p575
Known for its whiskey distillery, Bushmills is walking distance from the Giant's Causeway on one of Ireland's most beautiful stretches of coastline.

Derry City, p566
Walled city on the River Foyle with a thriving arts and cultural scene. Museums provide context to the city's fascinating but turbulent history.

Find Your Way

Derry and Antrim's biggest attractions are located on or near the coast. To see them, follow the coastline from Belfast to Derry, allowing plenty of time for detours and hikes along the way.

Ballycastle, p584

The seaside town of Ballycastle has a lively trad music scene and is perfectly located for trips to Rathlin Island and the Antrim Glens.

CAR & BICYCLE

Having your own wheels is the easiest way to get around. Roads are generally good in both counties. Sustrans cycling route 93 extends all the way from Derry to Larne, including several traffic-free sections.

BUS

Coastal buses are handy for getting back from one-way hikes and avoiding car park fees. Services are limited or nonexistent to out-of-the-way places. The Belfast to Derry express bus takes the fastest inland route.

TRAIN

The Derry to Coleraine train journey is one of Ireland's most scenic, following the River Foyle out of the city then hugging the coastline alongside Benone strand, with views of Binevenagh to the south.

Plan Your Time

You'll want to hit the Causeway Coast's major sights, but allow time to take walks and spot wildlife in the spaces in between.

Two Days on the Causeway Coast

● Begin with a bracing walk over **Carrick-a-Rede Rope Bridge** (p588), then hike west across the sands of **White Park Bay** (p582) and along the cliffs to the **Giant's Causeway** (p581), to see the iconic hexagonal stones. Then take an afternoon tour and whiskey tasting at the **Old Bushmills Distillery** (p575).

● The next day, drive west towards Derry, stopping in **Downhill** (p573) on the way to walk the trails and take photos at Downhill Demesne. Walk around **Derry's city walls** (p569) and pop into the **Guildhall** (p566). Cross the Peace Bridge and head to **Ebrington Square** (p570) and have a craft beer at **Walled City Brewery** (p571), then spend the evening listening to live music in one of the **city's pubs** (p568).

Walled City Brewery (p571)

Seasonal Highlights

This popular region draws crowds in summer, when there is a cheery holiday atmosphere on the coast. Come in winter for peace and solitude.

MAY
Wildflowers bloom along the cliffs of the Causeway Coast and puffins arrive at Rathlin Island and the Gobbins. The region's sunniest month. The **North West 200** (p579) motorcycle races are held in Portstewart and Portrush.

JUNE
Puffins and their chicks can be seen on the cliffs of **Rathlin Island** (p587). On the summer solstice, the sun stays bright late into the night, finally dipping below the horizon at 10pm.

JULY
The weather is mild and coastal sights and beaches are busy; book accommodation well in advance. The best time for sea bathing and camping. Locally-grown raspberries and strawberries are in season.

Five-Day Loop from Belfast

- Book a morning guided walk at the **Gobbins** (p589) cliff path, then drive to Ballycastle via the **Antrim Glens** (p590), stopping at Cushendun and Cushendall.

- Spend the following day on **Rathlin Island** (p587). Start at the **West Light Seabird Centre** (p587) to spot puffins and other nesting seabirds, then spend the afternoon hiking the island's trails. Back in **Ballycastle** (p584), catch a trad session in one of the town's pubs.

- Next, drive west to Portrush, stopping at the **Giant's Causeway** (p581) and **Dunluce Castle** (p580). In Portrush, take a **surf lesson** (p579) or relax on the beach. Continue west to **Derry** (p566) for a day. Finally, stop at **Seamus Heaney Home Place** (p572) on the drive back to Belfast.

Week-Long Break

- Start in **Derry** (p566) to learn the history of the **Bogside** (p568) through murals and museums.

- Next, head east to **Benone Strand** (p573) to surf, hike along the sand to **Downhill** (p573) or take in the views from **Binevenagh** (p573). Continue to **Portstewart** (p578) for more beach time and an evening sauna.

- Golfers are tantalisingly close to the links courses of **Royal Portrush** (p579); book a visitor slot in advance to play.

- Continue east along the Causeway Coast – stopping at **Dunluce Castle** (p580), **Old Bushmills Distillery** (p575) and the **Giant's Causeway** (p581) – to **Ballycastle** (p584). Take a boat trip to spot sea birds and seals off **Rathlin Island** (p587), or take in **Kinbane Castle** (p588) and **Carrick-a-Rede Rope Bridge** (p588) from the water.

AUGUST
Purple heather coats the hills, including **Binevenagh** (p573) and on Rathlin Island. Ballycastle's long-running **Ould Lammas Fair** (p584) takes place on the last weekend in August, with horse trading and folk music.

SEPTEMBER
The school holidays are over and tourist numbers drop, meaning fewer crowds at popular sites such as the **Giant's Causeway** (p581). In early September the sea temperature is the warmest it gets all year.

OCTOBER
The autumn sunsets are often some of the most beautiful of the year, particularly around the Giant's Causeway, where the stones glow in the light. Derry celebrates **Halloween** (p571), with concerts, parades and street parties.

DECEMBER
Winter swells bring surfers to Portrush, Downhill and Benone. The Northern Lights are sometimes visible from the north coast, including **Dunluce Castle** (p580). Pubs have warming fires and trad sessions to pass the longer, colder nights.

Derry City

CITY WALLS | HISTORY | FOYLE VIEWS

☑ TOP TIP

The Derry Urban Greenways are cycling and walking paths on either side of the River Foyle. From the Peace Bridge, the Foyle Valley Greenway extends south along the west bank, continuing inland to Strabane. The Waterside Greenway runs north from the Peace Bridge along the east bank to Foyle Bridge.

The artistic and cultural hub of Ireland's northwest, Derry has a complicated history that continues to seep into its present. The city's very name is a source of conflict: while nationalists prefer Derry, many unionists insist on Londonderry. Attempts by the local council to change the city's official name to Derry were foiled by a UK ruling that the city's legal name could only be changed by legislation or royal prerogative. Most people, regardless of political persuasion, call it Derry in everyday speech.

The city was depicted in the series *Derry Girls* (2018–22). Set in the 1990s, the series uses humour to show everyday life for teenagers during the final years of the Troubles, amid the religious and political divisions of the time. Today, these divisions can still be seen in the city's layout: the Bogside is a Catholic neighbourhood while the Fountain remains a Protestant area. Across the Foyle, the Waterside is home to both Catholics and Protestants.

Look inside the Guildhall

Architecture and stained-glass windows

Standing just outside the city walls, the neogothic **Guildhall** *(guildhallderry.com; free)* was originally built in 1890, then rebuilt after a fire in 1908.

Inside, the highlights are the stained-glass windows and the mahogany-panelled main hall. On the 1st floor, look for

---

GETTING AROUND

Buses and trains arrive at the North West Hub on the Waterside. There is also a large park-and-ride car park here. A greenway links the hub with the city centre (1km) via the Peace Bridge. Buses to Derry City Airport leave from the Foyle St bus centre, stopping at the North West hub on the way.

Derry's main attractions can be reached on foot or by bike; **Far and Wild** *(farandwild.org)* offers rentals. Avoid driving within the walled city, where streets are narrow and traffic slow.

BEST SHOPS

Cool Discs Music: Independent record shop with a wide selection of music by Irish artists old and new.

Craft Village: A handful of craft shops sell Derry crystal, handwoven cloth, ceramics, jewellery and other items.

Derry Designer Makers: Sells pieces by a collective of artists and craftspeople, who take turns staffing the shop at the Craft Village.

Smart Swag: Come here for original pieces, like jewellery made from vinyl records, upcycled furniture, screen-printed T-shirts and illustrations of Derry.

Foyle Books: Small independent bookstore with floor-to-ceiling shelves packed full of secondhand and antiquarian tomes.

---

a display cabinet containing John Hume's Nobel Peace Prize and other awards. The nationalist politician and civil rights activist from Derry was one of the key architects of the Good Friday Agreement in 1998; he and the unionist politician David Trimble were jointly awarded the Nobel Prize the same year.

From St Colmcille's Monastery to Derry Girls
Visit Derry's Tower Museum

Housed inside a replica 16th-century tower house near the Magazine Gate is the **Tower Museum** (*towermuseumcollections.com; adult/child £6/3*). Here, the **Story of Derry** exhibition depicts the city's history from the founding of the monastery of St Colmcille (Columba) in the 6th century to the Battle of the Bogside in the late 1960s. The museum highlight is the **Derry Girls Experience**, an interactive exhibition featuring original costumes and props from the television series; check to see if the experience is ongoing (the props are not part of the museum's permanent collection, but there is no confirmed exhibition end date).

In 2027, the museum is set to move to Ebrington Square, where the new **DNA Museum** will house the Tower Museum's current exhibitions, the **Armada Shipwreck** exhibition (in storage until the new museum opening) and other new exhibitions.

Learn the Poignant History of the Bogside
Visit the Museum of Free Derry and the Peacemakers Museum

To the west of the walled city, the Bogside district is the predominantly Catholic residential area where Derry's most notorious and tragic event took place. On 30 January 1972, 13 civilians were shot dead by the British Army during a Civil Rights march, on a day that became known as Bloody Sunday.

The **Museum of Free Derry** (*museumoffreederry.org; adult/child £9/free*) chronicles the history of the Bogside, the Northern Ireland Civil Rights Association and the events of Bloody Sunday through photos, newspaper reports, film clips, interactive displays and accounts of firsthand witnesses. Items on display include original Civil Rights banners and posters, and rubber bullets used by the police against protesters.

Most moving are the funeral cards of those killed on Bloody Sunday, and the jackets worn that day by Michael McDaid and Jim Wray, with holes from the bullets that killed them. Look

---

DRINKING IN DERRY: BARS WITH LIVE MUSIC

Peadar O'Donnell's: Atmospheric Irish pub with rowdy trad sessions every night and sometimes afternoons as well. *11.30am-1.30am Mon-Sat, 10.30am-1.30am Sun*

Sandino's Cafe-Bar: This poster-covered cafe-bar has a relaxed vibe, with regular live music, club nights and gigs. *12.30pm-1.30am Mon-Sat, to 1am Sun*

Guildhall Taphouse: Craft beers and cocktails in a wooden-beamed, 19th-century building. Nightly performances by local musicians. *noon-1am Mon-Thu, to 1.30am Fri & Sat, to 12.30am Sun*

Bennigans Bar: Live jazz on Saturday afternoons, plus a range of folk, blues, rock and soul performers. *4pm-12.30am Wed, to 1am Thu-Sat, to 10pm Sun*

A WALK AROUND DERRY'S CITY WALLS

The best way to get a feel for Derry's layout and history is to walk the circumference of the city's walls.

START	END	LENGTH
The Diamond	The Diamond	1.5km; one hour

Start at the ① **Diamond**, Derry's central square. Head west on Butcher St, where the town's butchers used to be, to ② **Butcher's Gate**, and climb the steps to the top of the city walls. Stroll downhill to ③ **Magazine Gate**. Inside the walls is the modern O'Doherty's Tower, housing the Tower Museum (p566); outside the walls stands the Guildhall (p566). Pass ④ **Shipquay Gate,** then follow the walls southwest and climb to Newgate Bastion. Pause to look back at the ⑤ **Derry Girls Mural**, depicting the five main characters from the series. Continue to ⑥ **Ferryquay Gate**, where the apprentice boys barred the gate at the start of the Great Siege of 1688–89.

Stroll around the southern stretch of the wall to see the cannons of the ⑦ **Double Bastion.** The next section of wall is known as the ⑧ **Grand Parade**, and offers an excellent view of the murals painted by the Bogside Artists (p570). An empty plinth on ⑨ **Royal Bastion** marks the former site of a monument to the Reverend George Walker, joint governor of the city during the Great Siege; it was blown up by the IRA in 1973. A little further along is the ⑩ **Apprentice Boys' Memorial Hall** and the adjoining Siege Museum. From here you can return to the Diamond.

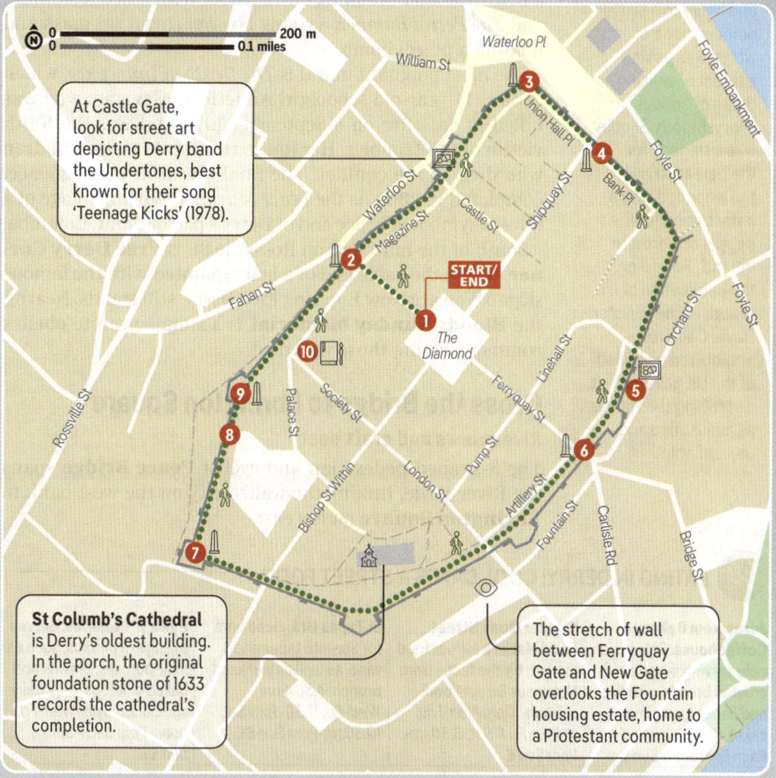

At Castle Gate, look for street art depicting Derry band the Undertones, best known for their song 'Teenage Kicks' (1978).

St Columb's Cathedral is Derry's oldest building. In the porch, the original foundation stone of 1633 records the cathedral's completion.

The stretch of wall between Ferryquay Gate and New Gate overlooks the Fountain housing estate, home to a Protestant community.

THE BLOODY SUNDAY INQUIRY

Longstanding dissatisfaction with the 1972 Widgery investigation, which had failed to find anyone responsible for the events of Bloody Sunday, led to the Bloody Sunday Inquiry, headed by Lord Saville. Its report was published in 2010.

Lord Saville found that 'The firing by soldiers of 1 PARA [1st Battalion, Parachute Regiment] on Bloody Sunday caused the deaths of 13 people and injury to a similar number, none of whom was posing a threat of causing death or serious injury. Bloody Sunday was a tragedy for the bereaved and the wounded, and a catastrophe for the people of Northern Ireland.' Following the publication of the report, Prime Minister David Cameron apologised on behalf of the UK government, describing the killings as 'unjustified and unjustifiable'.

too for the white handkerchief waved by local priest Father Daly as he led a group of men carrying the body of Jackie Duddy. Allow at least an hour at the museum.

The story is picked up 10 minutes walk away at the **Peacemakers Museum** *(peacemakersmuseumderry.com; adult/concession £8/7)*, 600m south of the Museum of Free Derry. Housed in a former gasworks, the museum explores the path to peace from 1972 to 2007, focusing on the role of three men from the Bogside: John Hume, Martin McGuinness and Mitchel McLaughlin. You'd need two to three hours to read all of the exhibition's text-dense panels in full. Videos summarise events in the words of residents and activists; their personal recollections of key moments in the peace process give an insight into how an agreement was reached and implemented.

See the Murals of the People's Gallery
Exploring the Bogside

Father Daly's handkerchief features in the Bloody Sunday mural, one of the **People's Gallery** of 12 murals by the **Bogside Artists** that decorate the gable ends of houses along Rossville St, outside the Museum of Free Derry (p568). Mostly painted between 1997 and 2001, the murals commemorate key events in the Troubles. Look for *Operation Motorman*, showing a British soldier breaking down a door with a sledgehammer and *The Petrol Bomber*, a young boy wearing a gas mask and holding a petrol bomb.

The most poignant mural is *The Death of Innocence*, which depicts 14-year-old schoolgirl Annette McGavigan, who was killed in crossfire on 6 September 1971, and was the 100th victim of the Troubles. Her image represents all the children who died in the conflict. The final mural in the sequence, completed in 2004, is the *Peace Mural*, a swirling image of a dove, a symbol of peace and of Derry's patron saint, Columba.

South of the museum, on Rossville St, is **Free Derry Corner**, where the gable end of a house painted with the famous slogan 'You are Now Entering Free Derry' still stands. Nearby, the **Bloody Sunday Memorial** is a simple granite obelisk commemorating those who died.

Cross the Bridge to Ebrington Square
River views and craft beer

The S-shaped pedestrian and cyclist **Peace Bridge** spans the River Foyle, linking the walled city on the west bank to **Ebrington Square** on the east.

EATING IN DERRY: COOL CAFES & STREET FOOD

Jerusalem Bakery & Coffeehouse: Palestinian cafe serving sesame-crusted breads, pastries and *harisa* (semolina cake). *8am-5pm Wed-Fri, 9am-5pm Sat & Sun* £

Clipper Quay Street Food Market: Indoor food market; try the tacos from Notorious Street Food. *8.30am-10pm Mon-Thu, to 11pm Fri & Sat, 8.30am-9pm Sun* £

El Tapas Grá: Head here for Spanish tapas and wine, as well as weekend brunch. *4.30-9pm Wed-Fri, 12.30-9pm Sat, 10.30am-9pm Sun* ££

Pyke 'n' Pommes: Serves a range of *pintxos,* such as mini-burgers, prawns and baked scallops, plus daily specials. *5-9pm Wed-Fri, noon-9pm Sat, 1-8pm Sun* ££

Peace Bridge

Access the bridge from the riverbank near Guildhall (p566) and cross to the west bank, from where there are views of the Guildhall's clock tower, modelled on London's Big Ben.

Ebrington Square was a British Army base; the former parade ground now serves as a public square. Walk across the square to Walled City Brewery, a craft brewery and gastro-pub. On Saturdays you can book a 45-minute brewery tour and tasting *(walledcitybrewery.com; £20)*.

Derry Halloween
Europe's biggest Halloween Festival

The people of Derry city put on their spookiest fancy dress for **Derry Halloween** *(derryhalloween.com)*, a four-night street festival with live music, a walled-city Halloween trail, a carnival parade and fireworks. What started out some forty years ago as a pub fancy dress party has evolved into Europe's biggest Halloween festival; book accommodation in advance.

In fact, Halloween's roots go back to the ancient Celtic festival of Samhain (p443), the moment at which it was believed the veil between this world and the other world was at its thinnest, allowing spirits to pass through. People lit bonfires and wore costumes to disguise themselves from the spirits and avoid harm.

BEST ARTS VENUES

Centre for Contemporary Art: Showcases the work of emerging artists from Ireland in three gallery spaces; admission is free.

Void Art Centre: Contemporary arts space exhibiting local and international artists. Also hosts poetry and music open mic events.

Nerve Centre: An arts space that supports young creatives, with a performance space and an arthouse cinema.

Playhouse: Community arts centre staging music, dance and theatre by local and international performers; housed in beautiful former school buildings.

Millennium Forum: A major venue for dance, drama, concerts, opera and musicals, with seating for 1,000 people.

EATING IN DERRY: BEST RESTAURANTS

Mekong: Gets rave reviews for its Vietnamese and Thai dishes, including Pad Thai and Vietnamese curried cauliflower. *5-9pm Tue & Wed, 3-9pm Thu-Sat* £££

Artis by Phelim O'Hagan: Fine-dining restaurant at the Craft Village offering a la carte and tasting menus. *5-9pm Wed & Thu, noon-2.30pm & 5-9pm Fri & Sat* £££

Walled City Brewery: Dishes include Donegal cod, sea bass, burgers and steak, plus Sunday roasts. *4.30-8pm Mon-Thu, 1-3pm & 5-9pm Fri & Sat, 1-5pm Sun* £££

Browns Bonds Hill: This Waterside restaurant is a Derry institution, serving creative dishes made with fresh local ingredients. *hours vary* £££

Beyond Derry City

To the east of Derry, the coast is lined with broad sandy beaches with surfing breaks and ancient dunes.

Places
Bellaghy p572
Benone p573
Downhill p573

GETTING AROUND

Trains run along the coastal line between Derry and Coleraine, with connections to Portrush.

Bus services connect the coastal towns, including Downhill, Portstewart and Portrush.

Cycle Route 93 links Derry and Coleraine via quiet inland roads, taking a scenic route over Binevenagh Mountain. However, the easiest way to get around is by car.

You can take the **Lough Foyle Ferry** *(loughfoyleferry. com)* to the Inishowen Peninsula in Donegal from Magilligan Point.

There is some outstanding scenery in the areas surrounding Derry. The basalt mountain of Binevenagh dominates the landscape in the Roe Valley and at the coast near Downhill and Benone. The triangle of land at the mouth of Lough Foyle is mostly taken up by a firing range and is also home to a prison. Still, it's worth a visit for its vast sandy beaches. Surfers should head to Benone, Downhill and Portrush.

South of Derry, the newly improved A6 road to Belfast climbs over the Sperrin Mountains at the Glenshane Pass. North of Lough Neagh, the Seamus Heaney Home Place museum and arts centre in the village of Bellaghy is worth a detour.

Bellaghy

TIME FROM DERRY: **45MIN**

Hear poetry by Seamus Heaney

Nobel Prize–winning poet Seamus Heaney's home town is the location of **Seamus Heaney Home Place** *(seamus heaneyhome.com; adult/child £12/7.50)*, an exhibition and arts centre dedicated to the poet and his work. Bellaghy is near the main road from Belfast to Derry, and about halfway between the two cities.

References in Heaney's poetry to the local landscape, everyday village life and the people who influenced him are highlighted in a creatively laid-out exhibition, which places his work in the context of his home and surroundings. Audio guides allow you to listen to poems read by Heaney himself, bringing his words to life. On display are personal items, including Heaney's duffle coat and his old school bag.

Visit the poet's grave

From Home Place, take a walk north along William St to St Mary's Church to visit Heaney's grave; his simple gravestone reads 'Walk on air against your better judgement.'

Also in the village is *The Turfman* (2009), a sculpture by David Annand that represents the poem 'Digging'.

Landscapes that inspired poetry

Follow signs to **Lough Beg** nature reserve, 3km south of Bellaghy, a wildfowl refuge and a landscape described in Heaney's poignant poem 'The Strand at Lough Beg'. A boardwalk leads along the shoreline (the strand) and loops around Longpoint Wood, with views of Church Island. Stop at the post looking out across the water to the distant church spire to hear a recording of Heaney reading his poem, which was written in response to the death of his cousin in a shooting during the Troubles.

Birds to look out for include curlews, redshanks and snipe; listen out for the 'peewit' call of lapwings, too. In autumn, whooper swans arrive from Iceland to spend winter at the lough.

Benone

TIME FROM DERRY: **40MIN**

Beach walks at Benone Strand

Backed by grassy dunes, behind which Binevenagh Mountain looms, the broad sandy beach at **Benone Strand** is a spectacular spot.

From the Benone Strand carpark, a boardwalk leads east over the dunes, through marram grass and colourful wildflowers including harebells, kidney vetch and lady's bed straw, as well as orchids and wild strawberries.

Follow the boardwalk onto the sand, from where you can walk along the beach all the way to **Downhill Strand** (4km), passing a waterfall and taking in the wild natural beauty of the often windswept coastline.

Bask in the beauty of Binevenagh

From Downhill, the signposted Binevenagh Scenic Drive leads up Bishop's Rd to the **Gortmore Viewpoint** and picnic area, from where there are views over Lough Foyle to Donegal.

A small car park on Leighery Rd is the starting point for a 4.5km circular walk up **Binevenagh**. It begins with a gentle ascent along a forest track, then passes a lake to reach the cliff edge, with spectacular views. The trail returns down a steep, rough trail through the forest. See walkni.com for details of the route; allow 1½ hours. In August the hills are covered with purple heather and butterflies.

Downhill

TIME FROM DERRY: **45MIN**

Discover Downhill Demesne

Perched on a grassy cliff overlooking Downhill Strand is one of the iconic sights of the northern coastline. It is part of **Downhill Demesne** *(nationaltrust.org.uk; free)*, the National Trust–owned grounds that from 1774 were the home of the bishop of Derry. There are two entrances to the site:

SEAMUS HEANEY'S POETRY

Widely considered to be one of the most important poets of the 20th century, Seamus Heaney (1939-2013) grew up in rural County Derry and studied English at Queen's University Belfast.

Heaney said that while studying at Queen's he learnt that rather than being irrelevant to the modern world, his childhood experiences in Derry could be trusted. The landscapes of his homeland feature in many of his poems, and are vividly described in 'Death of a Naturalist'. In 'Blackberry-Picking', Heaney recalls picking the fruit during childhood summers, while 'Digging' compares his father's use of a spade to dig up potatoes with the poet's use of a pen. He also wrote poems about the Troubles.

In 1995, Heaney was awarded the Nobel Prize for Literature.

DRINKING NEAR BENONE AND DOWNHILL: OUR PICKS

Sea Shed Coffee & Surf: Beachside coffee shop selling single-origin coffee, cold brews, hot chocolate, teas and pastries. *10am-4pm*

Al's Coffee: At the Lion's Gate entrance to Downhill Demesne, Al's coffee bar uses quality beans; good tray bakes too. *10am-4.30pm*

Sea Shed Downhill: By Downhill Forest, this cafe serves coffee, smoothies and pastries, with outdoor seating beneath the trees; peacocks roam the garden. *10am-4pm*

Point Bar: This pub at Magilligan Point with roaring open fires serves a great pint of Guinness, plus meals like burgers, chowder and fish and chips. *noon-9pm Wed-Sun*

Mussenden Temple

ACTIVITIES AROUND BENONE

Dan Lavery, founder of **Long Line Surf School**, shares his tips. *@longlinesurf*

Surfing: We rent out 8ft longboards at the Sea Shed Coffee & Surf (p573) at Benone, where there are good beginner waves. The surf gets bigger towards Downhill.

Hotbox Sauna: Sweat it out in the wood-fired Finnish sauna in a trailer on Benone Strand (*hotboxseasauna.com*), then run into the sea.

Stand-up Paddleboarding: Paddle down the River Roe, with views of Binevenagh. You might spot kingfishers and otters. Rent gear and access the river at **Swanns Bridge Glamping**. Long Line (*longlinesurfschool.co.uk*) offers 90-minute guided trips.

Beach walks: From Benone, you can walk west along the beach for 11km to Magilligan Point. The Point Bar (p573) there does a good pint of Guinness by the fire.

the main car park *(£10)* is reached via the magnificent **Lion's Gate**, topped with restored stone leopards, while free on-street parking is possible by the **Bishop's Gate** entrance, if there is space.

The grand manor house the bishop built for himself is now in ruins, but the collonaded, dome-capped **Mussenden Temple** – the bishop's private library – remains intact. Mussenden Temple's interior is not generally open to the public, but is sometimes used as a wedding venue and to host occasional events such as intimate concerts. From here, the views across the coast are spectacular. Allow around two hours to snap photos and explore the trails through the grounds.

NORTH COAST SURF SPOTS

In addition to Benone and Downhill, **Portrush** (p579) is another popular north coast surfing spot; the best beach breaks are at Portrush East Strand. There are several surfboard hire shops and surf schools in the town.

Bushmills

WHISKEY DISTILLERY | LOCAL CRAFTS | GIANT'S CAUSEWAY

The name Bushmills is widely known thanks to its famous whiskey, produced at the world's oldest licensed distillery using water from a tributary of the River Bush. Surrounded by rolling farmland, Bushmills has a privileged location as the nearest village to the region's star sight, the Giant's Causeway. The famous coastline of hexagonal basalt columns lies just 3km north of Bushmills by road.

During the 17th century, the settlement known as Portcaman expanded and became known as Bushmills, reflecting its role as a centre for the production of flax, corn and whiskey. Historical records suggest there were once some seven working mills on the river Bush. Many of the town's pretty listed buildings date from the Victorian era, when the Giant's Causeway became a popular tourist destination and an innovative hydro-electric railway was constructed to transport passengers between Bushmills and the coast.

The village is home to a predominantly Protestant community and you will see Union flags here in July.

Whiskey at the Old Bushmills Distillery
The world's oldest licensed distillery

Old Bushmills Distillery *(bushmills.eu)* occupies a large lot at the southern end of the village. Book ahead to join a one-hour guided distillery tour *(adult/child £15/6)* to learn about the whiskey-making process, take in the sounds and smells of the mash house and still house, and see the mashing process, fermentation tanks and condensers in action. Bushmills single-malt whiskey is made with Irish malted barley and water from St Columb's Rill, a tributary of the River Bush, triple-distilled in copper pot stills, and matured in a variety of barrels. After the tour, you can try a sample of your choice from the Bushmills' range (included in the tour price).

You can also book tours that include guided tastings of three reserves of different ages *(1½ hours; £35)*, or six whiskeys including a 21-year old reserve *(2½ hours; £50)*.

GETTING AROUND

Bushmills is a small village and easy to navigate on foot. There are two large free public car parks in the village, at Dundarave Pk and Staid Rd; consider leaving your car and taking the bus to busier sites along the coast (such as the Giant's Causeway and White Park Bay), where parking is limited. There is a large car park at the Old Bushmills Distillery.

You can also cycle around Bushmills village and to nearby sites. Cycle route 93 includes an off-road section from Bushmills to Runkerry Strand (the nearest beach) and the Giant's Causeway.

HIGHLIGHTS
1 Designerie
2 Old Bushmills Distillery

SLEEPING
3 Bushmills Hostel
see 5 Bushmills Inn Hotel
see 3 Bushmills Townhouse

EATING
4 Bistro at the Courthouse
5 Bushmills Inn Bar
6 Lorna's Kitchen
7 Tartine

TRANSPORT
8 Giant's Causeway & Bushmills Railway

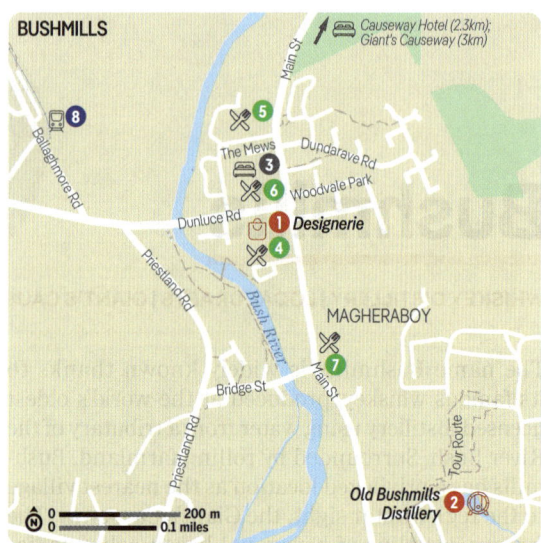

TOP TIP
Take a walk or cycle along the railway-side path from Bushmills railway station to the Giant's Causeway. The 5km trail follows the River Bush and passes Runkerry Beach on its way to the Causeway headland.

Alternatively, skip the tour and sip Bushmills at the **1608 Bar**, decorated with distillery memorabilia. You can buy personalised bottles of the distillery reserve (a 12-year-old malt), as well as other whiskeys and merchandise, at the gift shop.

Train Ride to the Causeway
All aboard the narrow-gauge heritage railway

A fun way to reach the Giant's Causeway is by train. Brought from a private line on the shores of Lough Neagh, the narrow-gauge line and diesel locomotive **Giant's Causeway & Bushmills Railway** *(facebook.com/GCBRNI; adult/child £8/6)* follows the route of a 19th-century tourist tramway for 3km from Bushmills to the station below the Giant's Causeway Visitor Centre. Trains run daily in July and August, and at weekends only in June and September.

The Giant's Causeway was a popular attraction during Victorian times. The original tramway opened in 1883 to transport passengers from Portrush to Bushmills; the section that is currently in use from Bushmills to the Causeway was added later.

EATING IN BUSHMILLS: OUR PICKS

Lorna's Kitchen: This cafe serves good-value cooked breakfasts and lunch dishes, such as soup, baked potatoes and sandwiches. *8.30am-3pm Mon-Sat* £

Bushmills Inn Bar: A reliable choice for local classics, such as beer-battered haddock and chips, and Bushmills Irish stew. *noon-4pm & 5-8pm* ££

Bistro at the Courthouse: Uses local ingredients to create plates such as all-day breakfasts and slow-braised pulled pork. *10am-3pm Mon & Tue, 10am-3pm & 5-9pm Thu-Sat, 12.30-3pm Sun* ££

Tartine: At the Distillers Arms, this restaurant serves refined dishes made with local ingredients. Book ahead. *5-9pm Wed-Sat, 12.15-2.30pm & 5-9pm Sun* £££

Giant's Causeway & Bushmills Railway

Shop for Locally Made Crafts
Meet the designer-makers

In a renovated courthouse building, the **Designerie** *(the designerie.co.uk)* sells handcrafted ceramics, soaps, art and textiles by Irish designer-makers. There are some fine pieces to be found here, including soft leather bags, glass sculptures and handwoven blankets. Shop for seaweed-infused face oil and seaweed bath salts from Wasi Seaweed Ltd, scented candles from Só Soy, and art prints of the Causeway Coast by various local artists.

Head upstairs to see the studio spaces of local designers and makers, who are happy to discuss their work.

THE LEGEND OF FINN MCCOOL

The Giant's Causeway (p581) gets its name from the legend about how these rock formations were formed.

The story goes that the Irish giant Finn McCool built the Causeway so he could cross the sea to fight his rival, the Scottish giant Benandonner. When Benandonner pursued Finn back across the Causeway, Finn disguised himself as a baby and hid in a giant cradle. Fearing an encounter with the parents of such a large child, whom he assumed to be even bigger, Benandonner fled back to Scotland, ripping up the Causeway as he went. All that remains are its ends – the Giant's Causeway in Ireland, and the island of Staffa in Scotland, which has similar rock formations.

Beyond Bushmills

An extravaganza of sea stacks, beaches, cliffs and caves, the Causeway Coast is one of the most beautiful places in Ireland.

Places
Portstewart p578
Portrush p579
White Park Bay p582

Bushmills is surrounded by a wealth of sights, of which the Giant's Causeway is the most famous. For hundreds of years, travellers have come to view the geological marvel of the hexagonal basalt columns; these days visitors continue to arrive by the coachload. Visit the Causeway in the early morning or late evening to avoid the crowds.

There is a holiday atmosphere in the neighbouring seaside towns of Portstewart in County Derry and Portrush in County Antrim. Portstewart has a beautiful sandy beach, backed by dunes, while Portrush is a major surfing spot and home to the Royal Portrush Golf Course. The towns are linked by a scenic coastal road, along which motorcycles race during the North West 200.

GETTING AROUND
The Ulsterbus 402 Causeway Rambler service connects Coleraine and Ballycastle via Portrush, Dunluce Castle, Bushmills, the Giant's Causeway and White Park Bay.

To get to Portstewart, take the 140 bus from Coleraine or Portrush.

From Portstewart, the coastal path leads 10.5km to Whiterocks, 3km east of Portrush.

Cycle route 93 runs west from Bushmills to Portrush, Portstewart and beyond, and east to the Giant's Causeway, continuing along an inland route to Ballycastle.

Portstewart
TIME FROM BUSHMILLS: **20MIN**

Take a dive to see underwater wrecks
The waters around Portstewart abound with marine life and shipwrecks, offering fantastic diving. Based in Portstewart, **Aquaholics** *(aquaholics.co.uk)* offers dives to nearby sites, including a Skerries cavern with walls covered in soft coral, and the wreck of HMS *Drake* near Rathlin Island.

If you'd rather stay above water, you can book a boat trip along the Causeway Coast, with views of Dunluce Castle, the Skerries and the Giant's Causeway itself.

Hit the beach
There are lovely walks through the ancient dunes of **Portstewart Strand** *(www.nationaltrust.org.uk/portstewart-strand)* to the west of town, where the sand extends west to the mouth of the River Bann. Cars are permitted to park on the sand here *(per car summer/winter £8.50/4)*, but there is a car-free stretch of beach that is patrolled by lifeguards in July and August. You can take a surfing lesson or hire gear from **Sub 6** *(sub6life.com; lessons from £40)*. Afterwards, ease your muscles with a sauna session with **Sauna & Sea** *(saunaandsea.co.uk; per person from £20)*.

Portstewart Strand is an inclusive beach, with accessible facilities and a free beach equipment loan scheme; book beach wheelchairs at least 72 hours in advance through the Mae Murray Foundation *(maemurrayfoundation.org)*.

Portstewart Strand

Try the North West 200

Motorcycle racing fans won't want to miss the **North West 200** *(northwest200.org; grandstand tickets £45)* in May, run on a 14km road circuit taking in Portrush, Portstewart and Coleraine. More than 85,000 spectators watch riders zip by at speeds of over 200mph (322kmph). Race Week events include nine races as well as vintage and classic bike displays.

Portrush

TIME FROM BUSHMILLS: **10MIN**

Surfing

Portrush Strand is one of Ireland's top surfing centres. Book a lesson with **Troggs Surf School** *(troggssurfschool.co.uk; lessons from £40)* at the **East Strand**. It also offers surfboard and wetsuit rental, and can provide surf reports and general advice. The surf is fairly reliable, but can be flat in summer (when the beach is often busy, too). Waves are biggest in winter.

Golf at Royal Portrush

For golfers, one of the Causeway Coast's biggest draws is **Royal Portrush Golf Club** *(royalportrushgolfclub.com; green fees per person Dunluce Links £420, Valley Links £200)*. Founded in 1888, Royal Portrush is spectacularly situated alongside the Atlantic at the town's eastern edge. It has two

THE OPEN AT ROYAL PORTRUSH

The world's oldest golf competition, the Open Championship, was first held at Royal Portrush in 1951, when it became the first course outside England and Scotland to host the event.

The Open returned to Portrush in 2019, when 237,750 spectators looked on as Ireland's Shane Lowry clinched victory with a display of brilliance; the crowd responded by singing his name and serenading him with Irish folk songs.

In 2025 the Open was held in Portrush once again. This time the crowd's support was firmly behind County Down-born, former world number one Rory McIlroy, who was given a standing ovation after a day of thrilling golf during the third round. However, in the end Scottie Scheffler from the United States won an emphatic victory.

 EATING IN PORTSTEWART: OUR PICKS

Morelli's: Founded by Italians and serving its own ice cream since 1911. Its sundaes are legendary. *9am-9pm Sun-Thu, to 10pm Sat & Sun* **£**

Lost & Found: This cafe with sea views is a local favourite for its brunches and flat whites. *8.30am-4.30pm Sun-Thu, to 8pm Fri & Sat* **£**

Harry's Shack: Situated right on Portstewart Strand, Harry's serves local seafood with ocean views. *12.30-8.30pm* **££**

Lir: Located on the banks of the River Bann in Coleraine, 6km south of Portstewart, this standout restaurant specialises in sustainable local seafood. *9am-9pm Tue-Sat* **£££**

Dunluce Castle

HISTORY OF DUNLUCE CASTLE

Dunluce Castle was built between the 15th and 17th centuries and was once one of the finest castles in the region. The round towers and outer walls date from 1480 and were part of a chain of defensive forts built by the MacQuillan clan.

In 1565, the castle was seized by chieftain Sorley Boy MacDonnell, whose son Randal built a grand Jacobean mansion on the site. In 1642 the settlement was attacked, and Dunluce was abandoned soon after.

According to local legend, in 1639 the castle's kitchen buildings collapsed into the sea during a dinner party, taking seven people with them. However, paintings from the early 19th century show the building intact, suggesting the kitchen fell later, when the castle was no longer occupied.

links courses: the Dunluce, with its water's-edge White Rock (5th) and ravine-set Calamity Corner (16th) holes, and the Valley. Visitor bookings for both courses are permitted at certain times; book well in advance.

Royal Portrush first hosted the Open Championship in 1951. To the delight of local golf fans, the Open returned to Portrush in 2019 and again in 2025.

The ruins of Dunluce Castle

Perched precariously atop sheer basalt cliffs, 5km east of Portrush, the ruins of **Dunluce Castle** *(adult/child £6/4)* are truly atmospheric. A narrow bridge leads from the mainland across a dizzying gap to the main part of the fortress, from where the views are sublime.

After exploring the ruins of the gatehouse (look for hexagonal stones from the Giant's Causeway in the walls), inner and outer ward and the Renaissance-style manor house, don't miss the path that leads down to the Mermaid's Cave beneath the castle crag. Allow up to an hour at the castle.

For spectacular castle views (and photos), stop at Magheracross car park and picnic site, 750m west of Dunluce on the main road.

EATING IN PORTRUSH: OUR PICKS

Arcadia: 1920s art deco pavilion housing a breezy beach cafe, serving breakfasts, fresh juices, pastries, salads and home-made sausage rolls. *9.30am-4.30pm Wed-Sun* £

Follow Coast: Serves overnight oats, sourdough sandwiches, pancake stacks and slow-cooked brisket bagels, along with coffee made with locally-roasted Fidela beans. *9am-5pm* £

Shanty: Serves dishes like burgers and fish and chips; the terrace has sunset views. Try a glass of Shanty's own gin. *10am-6pm Mon-Wed, to 8.30pm Fri & Sat, to 8pm Sun* ££

Bailiú Restaurant: Dunluce Lodge's fine-dining restaurant creates dishes such as Lough Neagh eel tart, north coast scallops, and Lisdergen flax-fed beef. *noon-3pm & 6-8.30pm* £££

TOP EXPERIENCE

Giant's Causeway

Equally exhilarating when cloaked in mist as when bathed in sunshine, the Giant's Causeway is one of Ireland's most atmospheric landscape features. Uneven stacks of tightly packed hexagonal columns stand in neat clusters along the water's edge, forming a causeway that inspired the legend that the stones were put in place by a giant.

Visitor Centre

The geological phenomenon of the rocks and the legends associated with them are explained in the National Trust's **Giant's Causeway Visitor Centre**. Visiting the Causeway is free of charge, but you pay to use the car park on a combined ticket with the visitor centre; parking-only tickets aren't available. Admission includes an audio guide to listen to as you explore the rocks. There are also hourly tours down to the rocks with a storytelling guide from the visitor centre.

Exploring the Causeway

From the visitor centre, it's a gentle 10- to 15-minute walk downhill to the Causeway itself, where you can walk out onto the stones as the ocean laps around you. You can also take the shuttle bus from the visitor centre to the causeway (£1).

The lower coastal path leads east as far as the **Amphitheatre viewpoint**, passing impressive rock formations including the **Organ**, a stack of 60 vertical basalt columns resembling organ pipes.

From here, you can retrace your steps west to the **Shepherd's Steps**, and climb to the clifftop path and walk west to return to the visitor centre, or head east past the Chimney Stacks headland as far as Dunseverick or beyond.

TOP TIPS

● Book visitor centre admission and car parking spaces online in advance, especially in summer.

● Visitor centre admission prices are reduced at off-peak times, from 9am-11am and 3pm-5pm daily.

● To visit the Causeway for free, park in Bushmills and walk or take the bus.

PRACTICALITIES
● nationaltrust.org.uk/giants-causeway
● adult/child £15/7.50 9am-6pm
● Causeway free, open dawn to dusk

BEST GAME OF THRONES FILMING LOCATIONS

Dark Hedges: Gnarled, entwined beech trees that doubled as the Kingsroad; located 14km southwest of Ballycastle.

Ballintoy Harbour: This Causeway Coast location was Lordsport on the Iron Island of Pyke, where Theon and Yara Greyjoy are reunited.

Larrybane Quarry: Near the Carrick-a-Rede Rope Bridge, this was Renly Baratheon's camp in the Stormlands.

Downhill Strand: This beach in County Derry was used as a filming location for scenes set on Dragonstone Island.

Binevenagh: This hill overlooking Lough Foyle was used to film the Dothraki Sea in season 5.

White Park Bay

White Park Bay

TIME FROM BUSHMILLS: **10MIN**

Listen to sand hum

The 5km-long sweep of sand backed by ancient dunes at **White Park Bay** is a special spot. The remains of Neolithic huts have been found here, suggesting the bay was home to some of Ireland's earliest communities.

Access the beach at the western end, driving down a steep lane just north of the A2 Whitepark Rd to reach a free National Trust car park that's open dawn to dusk. From here, follow the path down to the beach. Listen carefully; the sand here is so fine that when the wind blows it makes a low humming sound. Note that due to strong currents, the sea here is not suitable for swimming.

You might spot otters splashing about here. In the dunes, look out for colourful wildflowers, butterflies and rabbits. From time to time, cows belonging to a local farmer have been known to wander onto the beach.

 DRINKING ON THE CAUSEWAY COAST: OUR PICKS

Bothy Coffee: This White Park Bay cafe buys Colombian beans direct from the farm to roast in-house; also serves breakfast pancake stacks, sandwiches and cake. *9am-5pm Mon-Sat*

Two Twenty: This cafe east of Portrush has a wood-burning stove; serves locally-roasted coffee as well as breakfast, sandwiches and homemade sausage rolls. *9am-4pm Mon-Sat*

Kiwi's Brew Bar: Portrush bar serving a wide range of craft beers, including beers from local brewery Lacada. *1pm-1am Mon-Fri, noon-1am Sat & Sun*

Eldon's: The bar at the Elephant Rock Hotel in Portrush offers a long list of cocktails made with local spirits and served in chic surroundings. *noon-late*

HIKE THE CAUSEWAY COAST WAY

The scenic day hike from Carrick-a-Rede to the Giant's Causeway is one of the finest coastal walks in Ireland.

START	END	LENGTH
Carrick-a-Rede Rope Bridge	Giant's Causeway	16.5km; five to six hours.

After testing your nerve on the 1 **Carrick-a-Rede Rope Bridge** (p588), take the path from Larrybane car park along a clifftop with views of Sheep Island. At Ballintoy church, turn right and follow the road down to 2 **Ballintoy Harbour**.

Continue along the shoreline past a series of conical sea stacks and arches, and scramble around the foot of a limestone crag to reach the sandy sweep of 3 **White Park Bay**; time your hike so you reach the beach at low tide. At the far end of the bay, hike over rocks and boulders at the bottom of a high limestone cliff for 250m (slippery in places) to 4 **Portbradden**.

Beyond Portbradden, white limestone gives way to black basalt, and the path threads through a natural tunnel in the rocks before weaving around several rocky coves. At tiny 5 **Dunseverick Harbour**, follow a minor road for 200m before descending steps on the right. The path then wanders along the grassy foreshore, rounds a headland and passes a waterfall before reaching 6 **Dunseverick Castle**.

Continue along the cliff path. Near Benbane Head, a wooden bench marks the viewpoint known as Hamilton's Seat. Soak up the spectacular panorama of 100m-high sea cliffs, stacks and pinnacles, before you set off on the final stretch. Descend the 7 **Shepherd's Steps** to reach the 8 **Giant's Causeway** (p581).

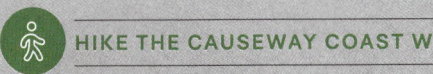

0
0
5 km
2.5 miles
Now an atmospheric basalt ruin, **Dunseverick Castle** is the site of an ancient fort dating back to the Iron Age.
Atlantic Ocean
Sheep Island
START
Carrick-a-Rede Island
END
Port Reostan
Croyer Hill
White Park Bay
Ulster Way
BALLINTOY
Whitepark Rd
Causeway Rd
DUNSEVERICK
Ballinlea Rd
BLACKROCK
Bush Bay
Whitepark Rd
The **Causeway Coast Way** stretches for 53km from Portstewart to Ballycastle; the full hike can be done in two days.
Note that at high tide it is not possible to access **White Park Bay** at the eastern and western ends of the beach.

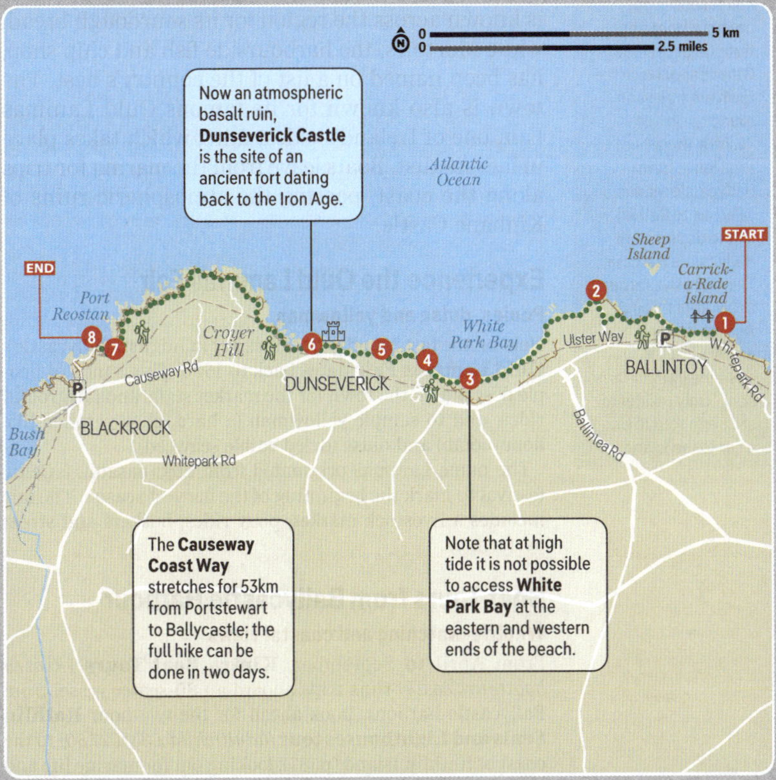

Ballycastle

TRAD MUSIC | COASTAL VIEWS | BOAT TRIPS

GETTING AROUND

Ballycastle town is small enough to cover on foot or by bike.

The large car parks at the harbour and marina cost 50p per hour from April through September. Other car parks in the town are free year-round.

Kintra Tours boat trips leave from Ballycastle marina.

Ferries to Rathlin Island depart from Ballycastle Harbour. There are five ferries a day April through August (fewer in winter). Book in advance *(rathlin-ferry. com)*. Only residents are permitted to bring a car to the island.

Ballycastle is a seaside town with a thriving trad music scene, a broad sandy beach, and views of nearby Rathlin Island and Fair Head. The town's main street has as many small family-run businesses as big-name chain stores, and you'll find more pubs here than might be expected for a town of this size. It's the kind of place where locals know the name of their butcher and the deli counter cheese comes from a nearby farm. In fact, Ursa Minor Bakehouse is known across the region for its sourdough bread, while Morton's, the harbourside fish and chip shop, has been named on a list of the country's best. The town is also known for its famous Ould Lammas Fair, one of Ireland's oldest fairs, which takes place in late August. Boats leave from the marina for trips along the coast, passing the atmospheric ruins of Kinbane Castle.

Experience the Ould Lammas Fair
Ponies, dulse and yellowman

Held on the last Monday and Tuesday in August, Ballycastle's **Ould Lammas Fair** dates back to 1606. Thousands of people descend on the town for the market stalls and fairground rides, and to sample yellowman (a hard, chewy, toffee-like honeycomb) and dulse (dried edible seaweed).

The name Lammas originated from Lughnasadh, a Celtic festival to mark the beginning of the harvest season. The fair includes a livestock market, pony rides, buskers and street performers.

Boat Tours from Ballycastle Harbour
Wildlife-watching and coastal views

From April to September, **Kintra Boat Tours** *(kintra boattours.co.uk)* runs trips aboard an 80-seater vessel from Ballycastle harbour. Book ahead for the two-hour **Rathlin Seals and Lighthouses tour** *(adult/child £33/£27.50)* to the coast of Rathlin Island (p587), looking out for marine life and

BALLYCASTLE

★ HIGHLIGHTS
1. House of McDonnell
2. Sea Haven Therapy
3. Ursa Minor Bakehouse

● SIGHTS
4. Ballycastle Strand

● ACTIVITIES
5. Ballycastle Golf Club
6. Kintra Boat Tours

● SLEEPING
7. An Caislean Guesthouse
8. Marine Hotel
9. Salthouse Hotel

● EATING
10. Anzac Restaurant
11. Morton's Fish & Chips
12. Thyme & Co

● DRINKING & NIGHTLIFE
13. Boyd Arms
14. O'Connor's Bar
15. Tessie's

● ENTERTAINMENT
16. Ould Lammas Fair

● SHOPPING
17. McLister's

---

seabirds (including puffins) at the sea stacks by the West Lighthouse, the East Lighthouse and Rue Point; or the 90-minute **Carrick-a-Rede Cliffs, Caves and Waterfalls tour** (adult/child/infant £25/19/4), which heads west along the coast as far as the Carrick-a-Rede Rope Bridge (p588), with views of Kinbane Castle (p588) along the way. The boat has indoor and outdoor seating; you remain on board throughout the tour.

You might spot dolphins and basking sharks, which, as filter feeders, swim open-mouthed just beneath the surface. Orca sightings are rare, but they have been spotted off the coast of Rathlin.

☑ TOP TIP

If you want to pack a picnic, the family-owned general store and delicatessen **McLister's** is a good place to pick up supplies, including local cheeses. The shop at Ursa Minor Bakehouse has a small selection of deli produce as well as bread and baked goods.

🍴 EATING IN BALLYCASTLE: OUR PICKS

Ursa Minor Bakehouse: Some of Ireland's best sourdough and flakiest pastries are baked here; the cafe serves breakfast and lunch. *9am-4pm Tue-Sat* £

Morton's Fish & Chips: Fish and chips don't come fresher: local boats unload their daily catch right alongside this harbourside hut. *3-8pm Mon-Wed, 12.30-8pm Thu-Sun* £

Thyme & Co: Cafe serving breakfast and soups, quiches, pastries and cake; Saturday is pizza night. *9.30am-3.30pm Mon-Tue & Thu-Sat, plus 5.30-8pm Sat, 9.30am-2pm Sun* £

Anzac Restaurant: Bright restaurant known for its steak and panfried fillet of hake; book ahead. *5-9pm Wed-Sat, 1-7pm Sun* £££

BEST BALLYCASTLE ACTIVITIES

Fair Head: The dolerite crag at Fair Head is considered the greatest expanse of climbable rock in Ireland.

Causeway Coasteering: Scramble over rocks, jump into the water and swim into sea caves at various locations along the Causeway Coast.

Broughgammon Farm: Join a foraging walk, take a butchery course, or learn to make Christmas mince pies at this sustainable farm, which specialises in goat meat.

Ballycastle Golf Club: It's not the most famous golf course on the Causeway Coast, but this quirky course has wonderful views.

Sea Swimming: In summer lifeguards patrol Ballycastle Strand, a 1.2km-long sandy beach with views of Fair Head. The water here is chilly year-round.

Yellowman sweets at Ould Lammas Fair (p584)

Take a Seaweed Bath

Relax in hand-harvested seaweed

If hiking on the Causeway Coast has left you feeling tired and achy, immerse yourself in a relaxing natural seaweed bath (good for muscular aches, joint pain and circulation) while enjoying views of Rathlin Island and beyond, at **Sea Haven Therapy** *(seahaventherapy.com; 30-min seaweed bath £30)*. You can also book a massage.

It's next to the Rathlin Island ferry terminal at Ballycastle Harbour.

DRINKING IN BALLYCASTLE: TRADITIONAL PUBS

House of McDonnell: Historic pub with views of the hills from garden. Live music Sunday nights, plus trad sessions some Saturdays. *5pm-midnight Thu & Fri, 2pm-1am Sat & Sun*

O'Connor's Bar: Behind a cheery green and gold facade, O'Connor's is a good place to hear live music, with trad sessions every Thursday. *11.30am-1.30am*

Boyd Arms: Locals say this wood-panelled pub serves Ballycastle's best pint of Guinness. The interior feels like a living museum. *11.30am-1.30am*

Tessie's: The sign says Anglers Arms, but this harbour-side pub is known locally as Tessie's; there's a beer garden at the back. *noon-11pm*

Beyond Ballycastle

Ballycastle is the perfect launchpad for jaunts along the Antrim coast, hikes through the Glens and ferry trips to Rathlin Island.

One of Ballycastle's biggest draws is its proximity to Rathlin Island, where in spring and early summer puffins can be spotted at the nesting seabird colonies. Rathlin is also a good place to see harbour seals, which can be spotted basking on rocks and splashing in the water. The island can be visited by ferry as a day trip or for an overnight stay.

South of Ballycastle, the Antrim Coast and Glens is a designated Area of Outstanding Natural Beauty, with rolling hills to hike and waterfalls to discover.

Near Belfast, the railway town of Whitehead is worth visiting for its coastal walks to Blackhead Lighthouse and along the Gobbins coastal path at nearby Islandmagee.

Rathlin Island

TIME FROM BALLYCASTLE: 30–40MIN

Spot seabirds from an upside-down lighthouse

From Church Bay, you can cycle, hike or take the Puffin minibus (it waits at the pier for ferries to arrive; *adult/child £6/4 cash only*) 7km to the **Rathlin West Light Seabird Centre** *(rspb.org.uk; adult/child £9/5)* for views of a thriving seabird colony at a nearby sea stack. Every year, thousands of seabirds return here to breed, including puffins, guillemots, razorbills, kittiwakes and fulmars.

At the centre, Royal Society for the Protection of Birds staff and volunteers can help you identify birds and show you where to look for puffins and their chicks using telescopes and binoculars. It's open from April to the end of August. The best times to see puffins are mid-May (when the birds gather on the cliffs), mid-June (when chicks begin hatching) and late July (when puffins prepare to return to sea).

The viewing platforms are at the base of Rathlin's upside-down west lighthouse, which houses the seabird centre. The building is unusual because the light is at its base and not at its top. Built into the cliff face, it was a feat of engineering when completed in 1919. The lighthouse tower now contains exhibits on Rathlin's marine life and history; don't miss the recreated lighthouse keeper's bedroom.

Count on spending around an hour watching birds and exploring the lighthouse.

Places

Rathlin Island p587
Kinbane Head p588
Carrick-a-Rede p588
Islandmagee p589
Whitehead p592
Slemish Mountain p592

GETTING AROUND

It's possible to reach sights near Ballycastle by public transport, but it's easier by car.

The 402 Causeway Rambler service stops at Carrick-a-Rede Rope Bridge. The 162 bus links Ballycastle with Cushendun and Cushendall.

There are trains from Belfast to Whitehead and Ballycarry (for the Gobbins).

Cycle route 93 takes in glorious scenery on the way from Larne to Ballycastle.

Rathlin Island is 6km north of Ballycastle and reachable by ferry; book in advance *(rathlin-ferry.com; adult/child/bike £8/4/2.20)*.

WHY I LOVE RATHLIN ISLAND

Isabel Albiston, Lonely Planet writer

The first time I disembarked at Rathlin pier, I noticed that several of the nearby rocks were occupied by sunbathing seals. It felt like the short ferry journey had brought us to a different world. Rathlin's rugged beauty is instantly beguiling, and its size is just right: small enough to get around on foot, but large enough for longer hikes. In August, the island is covered with purple heather.

But for me, the biggest draw is the noisy seabird colony on the western sea stacks, where the birds return to mate each year. When I finally saw a pair of puffins among the squawking seabirds, watching them was just as special as I hoped it would be.

Wildlife-watching & windswept walks

Rugged, L-shaped Rathlin Island has a number of walking trails, which are wonderful for wildlife-watching. At Church Bay, the **Boathouse Visitor Centre** has maps, as well as displays on the island's history. You might spot seals on the small beach here, or basking on rocks by the harbour.

From here, take the signed trail to **East Lighthouse** (3.2km round-trip). The route is also suitable for cycling. Beneath the East Lighthouse, and only accessible by sea, is the cave where Scottish King Robert the Bruce is said to have been inspired by a spider. Bruce had fled to the island following a defeat in 1306, but after watching the tenacious spider spinning its web, he was encouraged to return to fight for his crown.

In the south of the island, the clifftop **Roonivoolin walking trail** (6.5km) is a good place to spot meadow pipits, rock pipits and wheatear, hear the singing of skylarks and see Irish hares.

Kinbane Head
TIME FROM BALLYCASTLE: **10MIN**

Clamber over coastal castle ruins

Five kilometres west of Ballycastle harbour, the photogenic ruins of **Kinbane Castle** sit on a limestone headland jutting out from the basalt cliffs, with incredible views of Rathlin Island and Scotland. From the car park, there are 140 steep steps down to the shore. From there, a rough path and more steps lead up to the ruins. Take care as you clamber around the headland, with nothing but sheer cliff face between you and the crashing waves below.

The Castle was built in 1547 by Colla MacDonnell, brother of legendary chieftain Sorley Boy. The view back to the shoreline from here is timeless, with few visible signs of 21st-century life. Allow around 40 minutes to explore.

Carrick-a-Rede
TIME FROM BALLYCASTLE: **10MIN**

Wobble across a rope bridge

Fishers once slung a rope bridge over the chasm between the sea cliffs and the little island of Carrick-a-Rede to allow them access to migrating salmon; these days a sturdier, 20m-long, 1m-wide bridge of wire rope sways 30m above the rock-strewn water. To cross the **Carrick-a-Rede Rope Bridge** *(nationaltrust.org.uk/carrick-a-rede; adult/child £15/7.50)* you must book a time slot in advance online. Count on spending around 1½ hours here.

From the car park and ticket office, a 1km coastal trail leads over the cliffs to the bridge, with the Atlantic on the left and

---

 EATING AND DRINKING ON RATHLIN ISLAND

McCuaig's Bar: Rathlin Island's pub and beer garden overlooks the harbour, an idyllic spot for a pint on a sunny day. *11am-11pm*

Rathlin Co-op Shop: The island's small shop has basic staples and some local produce for sale. *11am-4pm Mon-Sat, noon-4pm Sun*

Ebb & Flow: Adjacent to McCuaig's serves bar meals like fish and chips, scampi and burgers. Eat at outdoor tables overlooking the bay. *12.30-5pm* **£**

Manor House: Serves light lunches (sandwiches, salads) and fuller dinners. Pre-order lobster from the Rathlin coast. *noon-3pm & 6-7.30pm Mon-Sat, noon-7pm Sun* **£££**

windswept farmland on the right; look out for butterflies, rabbits and hares. Soon you'll reach a set of steps cut into the cliff face, leading down to the rope bridge.

Crossing the bridge is perfectly safe, but frightening if you don't have a head for heights. Dare to look down and you might spot basking sharks, dolphins and porpoises. From the island, views take in Rathlin Island and Fair Head to the east. Peer over the cliffs to spot seabirds, including kittiwakes and guillemots.

On the island, look for a whitewashed fisher's cottage, abandoned after dwindling salmon stocks put an end to fishing in 2002.

Islandmagee

TIME FROM BALLYCASTLE: 1HR 15MIN

Dramatic cliff walk at the Gobbins

At the **Gobbins** (*thegobbinscliffpath.com; adult/child £22.75/16.50*), tubular bridges, rocky surfaces, tunnels, caves and narrow crevices form a dramatic cliff path at Islandmagee, the slender peninsula that runs parallel to the coastline between Whitehead and Larne. The Gobbins coastal path is accessible on 2½-hour guided tours (book ahead). A good level of fitness, a minimum height of 1.2m and suitable footwear are essential.

Tours leave from the visitor centre, from where it's a five-minute bus ride to the path. The most strenuous part of the 5km walk is the return climb up the steep access path; otherwise, the path is not physically demanding. Guides explain the history of the Gobbins and highlight geological and natural features of the coastline. As well as spectacular views out to the Irish Sea, you might spot dolphins and puffins on the walk. Above the Gobbins path, a viewing platform and clifftop path are free to access without booking a tour. In 2025, tours were suspended following rock fall; check online to see if the path has reopened.

HIKE THE CAUSEWAY COAST

From Carrick-a-Rede, the Causeway Coast Way continues west all the way to Portstewart. A shorter section takes you as far as the **Giant's Causeway** (p581).

A FEAT OF ENGINEERING

The Gobbins first opened as a tourist attraction in 1902, when the new railway made the area accessible to visitors from Belfast. It was created by local engineer Berkeley Deane Wise, who saw the potential of the Antrim coastline as a tourist attraction.

The path was closed in the 1930s and fell into disrepair; a £7.5 million investment saw the attraction reopen in 2016.

The basalt cliffs at the Gobbins are at the eastern edge of a basalt structure that stretches from Cave Hill in Belfast to Binevenagh in County Derry. The rock was created by volcanic eruptions 65 million years ago, during which time the hexagonal columns of the Giant's Causeway were also formed by quick-cooling pools of lava.

EATING IN THE ANTRIM GLENS: OUR PICKS

Village Tearooms: Lunch dishes include sandwiches and homemade seafood chowder; eat in the pretty garden. *9.30am-3pm Mon-Fri, to 3.30pm Sat & Sun* £

Mary McBride's: Cushendun pub serves bar meals and more refined plates in upstairs restaurant, the Little Black Door. *noon-6.30pm Sun-Wed, to 9.30pm Thu-Sat* £££

Glenarm Castle Tea Room: Produce from the estate farm and kitchen garden feature on the menu, such as Glenarm shorthorn beef burger, plus homemade cakes. *9am-5pm* ££

Harry's Restaurant: With its cosy lounge-bar, Harry's is a Cushendall institution; the menu features steaks and seafood. *noon-8.30pm Mon-Sat, to 8pm Sun* ££

ROAD TRIP

The Antrim Glens

Scenic roads traverse the northeastern corner of Antrim, a high plateau of black basalt lava overlying beds of white chalk. Along the coast, between Cushendun and Glenarm, the plateau has been dissected by a series of glacier-gouged valleys known as the Glens of Antrim. This driving route from Ballycastle to Glenarm takes in woodland waterfalls and breathtaking cliff-top views. Bring walking boots for hikes on the way.

❶ Fair Head

Branching off from the A2 4.5km east of Ballycastle, the single-track **Torr Head Scenic Route** is an alternative route to Cushendun. It's not for the faint-hearted, as it clings to steep slopes high above the sea. The first turnoff from Torr Head Rd leads to Fair Head (p586), where there is a car park and walking trails. The 4km **Perimeter Walk** follows the line of the cliff edge, with views of the famous **Rathlin Wall** climbing site below.

The Drive: Choose between returning to the A2 for a more straightforward drive to Cushendun, or continuing along the precarious and narrow road via Torr Head to the village. Both are scenic drives.

❷ Cushendun

This charming village has interesting architecture and caves to explore. Park in the car park at **Cushendun Beach** and walk south through the dunes to the village. Take a look at the distinctive Cornish-style

Ess-Na-Larach Waterfall

cottages, which were designed by Clough Williams-Ellis and built in 1912.

The Village Tearooms (p589) serves breakfast and lunch.

The Drive: Follow Knocknacarry Rd south then bear left onto the minor Layde Rd. Continue until you reach Layd Church (signposted).

3 Cushendall

The ruins of **Layd Old Church** occupy a picturesque site on the cliffs above Cushendall. It was once part of a Franciscan friary, founded in the 13th century. Near the gate stands an ancient, weathered cross. There are picnic tables here with sea views.

The Drive: Head south through Cushendall town, passing the 1817 Curfew Tower, then follow the B14 through beautiful Glenballyeamon. After 10km, look for the left turn onto A43 (signed Glenariff Forest Park).

4 Glenariff

At the head of the Glenariff Valley is **Glenariff Forest Park**, where the main attraction is Ess-Na-Larach Waterfall, an 800m walk from the visitor centre. Look out for red squirrels and Irish hares.

The Drive: Take the A43 east through Glenariff to Waterfoot, then drive south along the coastal road, right along the water's edge.

5 Glenarm

The village is home to **Glenarm Castle & Walled Garden**, the family seat of the McDonnell family. The castle interior can be seen on guided tours; check the website for times and dates. Take a look at the walled garden, with herbaceous borders and water features.

Head through the village to **Glenarm Forest**, where the 3.5km river trail offers great views of the castle.

ST PATRICK'S TIME AT SLEMISH

Slemish Mountain is an important site due to its connections with St Patrick. It is believed that Patrick was kidnapped as a 16-year-old boy from his home on the west coast of Roman Britain and taken to Ireland. For the following six years, he herded sheep for a local chieftain on the slopes of Slemish.

In his writings, Patrick described how during this period of isolation and deprivation he would pray throughout the day and night and was visited by a vision of an angel who helped him escape captivity onboard a ship to the European continent. After returning to Britain, Patrick felt called to go back to Ireland to set up his mission.

The Gobbins (p589)

Whitehead

TIME FROM BALLYCASTLE: **1HR 10MIN**

Coastal walk to Blackhead Lighthouse

The 3.5km round-trip walk to **Blackhead Lighthouse** begins from Whitehead car park on Old Castle Rd. It follows the shoreline (look out for seals, basking on rocks), then ascends up stone steps to the lighthouse (not open to the public). Steps on the other side take you back down to sea level. Here the highlight is the walkway under the cliffs, from where you can see dark swirling water underfoot. Allow around 1½ hours.

Slemish Mountain

TIME FROM BALLYCASTLE: **50MIN**

Follow in St Patrick's footsteps

The skyline to the east of Ballymena is dominated by the distinctive craggy peak of **Slemish Mountain** (438m). The hill is one of many sites in the North associated with Ireland's patron saint. The young St Patrick is said to have tended sheep on its slopes.

On St Patrick's Day, hundreds of people make a pilgrimage to the summit; the rest of the year it's a pleasant climb, though steep and slippery in wet weather, rewarded with fine views of Lough Neagh, the Antrim coast and Scotland. There is a toilet block and picnic tables at the car park but no shop or cafe. Allow one hour to make the 1.5km trip there and back.

Places We Love to Stay

£ Budget ££ Midrange £££ Top End

Derry City

Rose Park House ££ Good-value B&B in the Rosemount neighbourhood, a 15-minute walk west of the city centre.

Shipquay Hotel £££ Boutique hotel in a historic building in the centre of town; Prosecco is served at breakfast.

Bishop's Gate Hotel £££ Rooms have period features at this hotel inside Derry's city walls; good bar and restaurant.

Ebrington Hotel £££ Luxury hotel and spa in a 19th-century former army barracks. Rooms at the front have views of the Foyle.

Benone & Downhill

Benone Holiday & Leisure Park £ This family-friendly campsite adjacent to Benone Strand has sites for tents and caravans, and basic glamping huts.

Burrenmore Nest £££ At Downhill, these luxurious forest lodges on stilts have hot tubs and views of the trees. There's a sauna, fire pit and barbecue on site.

Bushmills

Bushmills Hostel £ Modern, purpose-built hostel with dorms and private rooms; has a kitchen, laundry and bike shed.

Bushmills Inn Hotel £££ An old coaching inn, complete with a secret library and round tower, with warm, professional service and well-appointed rooms.

Bushmills Townhouse £££ The suites here have roll-top bathtubs and their own private terrace or garden areas.

Causeway Hotel £££ Located at the Giant's Causeway, this hotel is ideal for exploring the coast before the crowds arrive.

Portstewart

Cul-Erg House ££ Family-run B&B near the Portstewart seafront, with an onsite cafe serving homemade cake.

Cromore Retreat £££ Luxury bubble domes in the trees of the Cromore Estate, with views of the stars. Located 2km south of Portstewart seafront.

Portrush

Elephant Rock Hotel £££ Boutique hotel in a Victorian terrace in Portrush, with sea views and bold interior decor.

Dunluce Lodge £££ Golfers will love the suites here, located alongside the fairway of Royal Portrush Golf Club. Excellent restaurant, too.

Portrush Adelphi £££ This luxurious Marine and Lawn golf-themed hotel is beautifully decorated with themed memorabilia and high-end fittings.

White Park Bay & Ballintoy

Sheep Island View Hostel £ Independent hostel in Ballintoy with dorms and private rooms. There's a kitchen and laundry.

Whitepark Bay Hostel £ Dorms, private rooms, a kitchen, and a lounge positioned to soak up the view. White Park Bay beach is a short walk through the dunes.

Ballycastle

An Caisleán Guesthouse ££ Well-run B&B located a short walk from the town and beach, with a large guest lounge.

Marine Hotel ££ Family-friendly hotel with spacious rooms, some with sea views. Bike hire and yoga mats available.

Salthouse Hotel £££ Luxury hotel on the outskirts of town with outstanding sea views, two restaurants and a spa.

Rathlin Island

Rathlin Glamping Pods ££ These simple pods look directly at the ocean. They have fire pits, attached bathrooms and small kitchenettes.

Manor House ££ Rathlin's 18th-century manor house is now a guesthouse and restaurant, with views across Church Bay.

Antrim Glens

Watertop Farm £ Camping pitches on a family-run farm, 10km east of Ballycastle on the road to Cushendun.

Ballyeamon Barn £ Near Glenariff Forest Park, this barn has hostel accommodation and hosts regular storytelling and music sessions.

Researched by
Isabel Albiston

Fermanagh & Tyrone

ANCIENT LANDSCAPE OF LAKELANDS AND HILLS

Hidden in the loughs and waterways of Fermanagh and the boggy hills of Tyrone are intriguing historical remains and an array of wildlife.

Life in Fermanagh revolves around the water. The summer boat traffic on Lough Erne hearkens back to a time when the waterways were the main thoroughfares across an Ireland covered in thick and treacherous woodland. Islands such as Devenish were chosen as strategically located, accessible sites for monasteries that were the important religious, cultural and political centres of their time. As recently as the 1950s, the islands were home to a substantial community; these days, they are virtually uninhabited and have become an important area for birds, particularly breeding waders. The islands are also used to graze livestock, which are transported in special boats.

Tyrone's three largest towns – Omagh, Dungannon and Cookstown – form a triangle across its centre, but the county's biggest draw lies in the largely untouched wildness of the Sperrin Mountains, whose southern foothills are scattered with prehistoric sites. The area encompassing Davagh Forest and the Beaghmore Stone Circles is now a designated dark-sky park, with an observatory and astronomy-related walking trails. It's a magical place, and there is a sense of timelessness in the views of the Milky Way above the forest treetops in Davagh. It's possible that the intriguing stone circles of Beaghmore were laid out to reflect the sky; so fitting, then, that the site is once more a place for stargazers to gather.

THE MAIN AREAS

ENNISKILLEN
An island town. **p598**

Left: St Mary's Abbey (p603); right: Ceoldán the Stargazer (p609), Davagh Forest

FERMANAGH & TYRONE

THE GUIDE

Find Your Way

County Fermanagh is known as the lakelands for a reason: it's about one-third water. Between the loughs (lakes, long narrow bays or arms of the sea), the terrain is rugged and hilly. Small, rural County Tyrone is home to the Sperrin Mountains.

CAR
Driving is the most convenient way to get around because public transport is patchy outside the main towns. Some rural roads are single track, particularly around the Sperrin Mountains in County Tyrone.

BOAT
Lough Erne's islands can be reached by boat, kayak or canoe. Self-drive motor boats are available for hire (no experience required). Taxi boats and tours also take passengers out onto the water.

Enniskillen, p598
The island town has museums and a country house to discover, plus adventures to be had in the surrounding waters.

Upper Lough Erne (p607)

Plan Your Time

You'll want to get out onto the water and explore the loughs and islands, but there are land-based attractions to visit too. Allow time for walks in the hills.

Pressed for Time

- Start at **Enniskillen Castle** (p598), then take a boat trip to **Devenish Island** (p602) to see the remarkable round tower and monastic ruins. The next day, drive to the **Cuilcagh Boardwalk Trail** (p606) and hike to the viewing platform, and then descend down to **Marble Arch Caves** (p605). Finally, drive to **OM Dark Sky Park** (p608) and stay until nightfall to see the stars.

Four Days to Travel Around

- After the first itinerary, head to **Castle Archdale** (p603) and hire a kayak and paddle out to White Island. Stop at **Caldragh Cemetery** (p604) before returning to Enniskillen to walk or ride to **Castle Coole** (p600). Spend a morning at **Florence Court** (p606), then head to Crom and explore **Upper Lough Erne** (p607).

SEASONAL HIGHLIGHTS

SPRING
Catch the **Bluegrass Omagh** (p610) festival. Mayfly season begins, the best time for trout fishing on Lough Erne.

SUMMER
July and August are the busiest months at the Fermanagh lakes. The long days are ideal for **hillwalking** (p608) in the Sperrin Mountains.

AUTUMN
The leaves turn russet and gold in the forested grounds of **Florence Court** (p606) and **Crom Estate** (p607), and on the islands.

WINTER
Long winter nights mean more time for **stargazing** at the **OM Dark Sky Park and Observatory** (p608).

Enniskillen

MONASTIC SITES | LAKE VIEWS | WATERSPORTS

GETTING AROUND

Enniskillen town centre is small enough to explore on foot. Enniskillen Castle has a large car park. Several buses a day go to Belfast and Dublin from the **bus station**.

To get out onto the water, hire a kayak or canoe from **Blue Green Yonder** *(bluegreenyonder. com)* or a self-drive boat from Erne Boat Hire (p602), both at the Blueways Water Activity Zone, or book a trip with Erne Water Taxi (p602). Erne Tours (p602) boat trips to Devenish Island leave from the Round O Jetty.

The Kingfisher Trail is a long-distance bike trail from Enniskillen.

☑ TOP TIP

Enniskillen Castle and Castle Coole are connected by the 4.5km Castle to Castle trail. The route is 90% traffic free and suitable for walking or cycling. It links up with the Kingfisher Trail cycling route, which has great views of the river.

On the banks of the River Erne between Upper and Lower Lough Erne, Enniskillen is surrounded by water: the town centre is an island, accessed at either end by bridge. Enniskillen Castle guards the island's western end, its twin-turreted Watergate looming over passing fleets of cabin cruisers. Boating and watersports are a way of life here, and it's easy to get out onto the water in a kayak or a self-drive boat.

Oscar Wilde and Samuel Beckett were pupils at the Portora Royal School, now called Enniskillen Royal Grammar School. Wilde's connection to Enniskillen is celebrated with 150 gold-leaf swallow sculptures, mounted on buildings around town in reference to his story *The Happy Prince*.

The town's name is also prominent in the history of the Troubles. On Remembrance Sunday in 1987, an IRA bomb killed 11 people during a service at Enniskillen's war memorial.

Learn about Fermanagh's Past at Enniskillen Castle

Museums in former Maguire stronghold

On the banks of the River Erne, **Enniskillen Castle** was a former fortress of the 16th-century Maguire chieftains. These days, the **Enniskillen Castle Museums** *(enniskillencastle. co.uk; adult/child £6/4.50)* complex houses the Fermanagh County Museum, with displays on the county's history, archaeology, landscape and wildlife.

Start in the galleries of **Barrack Coach House**. On the ground floor, look for the 1000-year-old 16kg block of bog butter, unearthed by a Fermanagh farmer in 1980. It was probably buried in the bog to preserve it for consumption during winter.

Upstairs, the **Lakelands Gallery** has fascinating displays dedicated to the history of Fermanagh's waterways. It includes local stone heads, fragments of crosses and a model of the Devenish Island round tower. Don't miss the River Erne Horn, a medieval instrument uncovered during the dredging of the river.

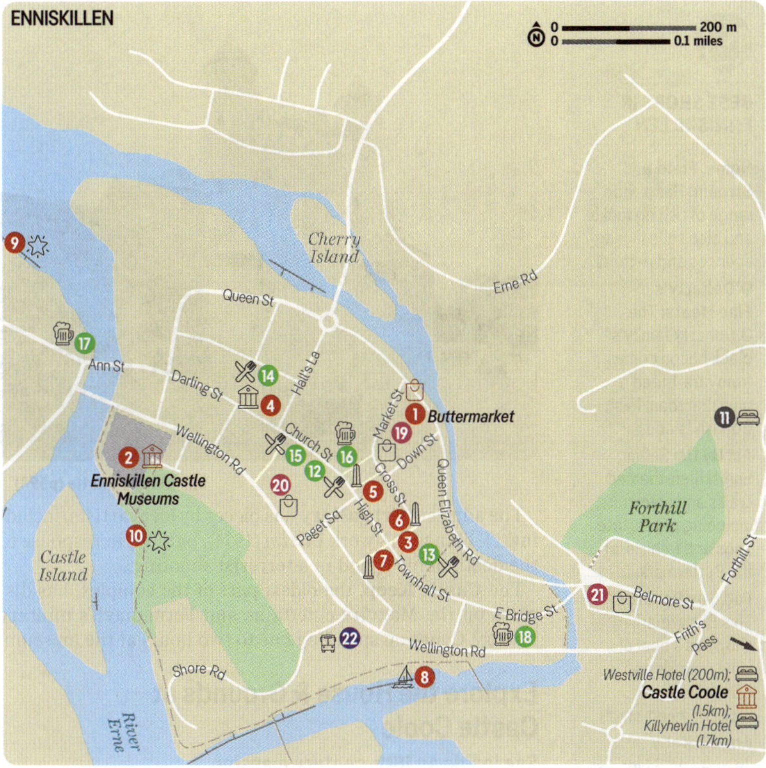

ENNISKILLEN

- **HIGHLIGHTS**
  1 Buttermarket
  2 Enniskillen Castle Museums

- **SIGHTS**
  3 Clock Tower
  4 Headhunters Barber Shop & Railway Museum
  5 Now We're Suckin' Diesel
  6 The Happy Prince
  7 Trad Session

- **ACTIVITIES**
  8 Erne Boat Hire
  9 Erne Tours
  10 Erne Water Taxi

- **SLEEPING**
  11 Enniskillen Hotel

- **EATING**
  12 28 at the Hollow
  13 Dollakis
  14 Jolly Sandwich Bar
  15 The Toastery

- **DRINKING & NIGHTLIFE**
  see 12 Blakes of the Hollow
  16 Charlie's Bar
  17 Lough Inn
  18 Magee's Spirit Store

- **SHOPPING**
  19 Angela Kelly Jewellery
  see 19 Art By Us
  see 19 Fall Guy Records
  20 Home, Field & Stream
  21 O'Doherty's Fine Meats

- **TRANSPORT**
  22 Bus Station

EATING IN ENNISKILLEN: OUR PICKS

The Toastery: Head here for speciality coffee, gourmet sourdough toasties made with local produce and cake. *8am-5pm Mon-Sat* £

Jolly Sandwich Bar: Divine house-baked cakes and pastries, plus salads and sandwiches; order to eat in or take away. *9am-3pm Tue-Sat* £

Dollakis: Family-run Greek restaurant serving small mezze plates and daily specials cooked on a charcoal grill. *noon-9pm Wed-Sat* ££

28 at the Hollow: Beneath Blakes of the Hollow, chef Glen Wheeler creates innovative fine-dining plates. *5.30-9pm Wed & Thu, noon-2pm & 5.30-9pm Fri & Sat* £££

BEST SHOPS IN ENNISKILLEN

Home, Field & Stream: Has a wide range of fishing tackle and also sells fishing licences and permits.

O'Doherty's Fine Meats: The O'Doherty family's black bacon comes from rare-breed pigs that roam Inish Corkish Island.

Art By Us: Selling Enniskillen-themed crafts and souvenirs, including prints, tote bags and t-shirts, at the Buttermarket.

Fall Guy Records: This Buttermarket shop has a host of vinyl records and CDs, as well as rock-themed t-shirts.

Angela Kelly Jewellery: Silver jewellery with Celtic designs, made with Irish gemstones and rocks, at the Buttermarket.

Enniskillen Castle (p598)

The adjacent **art gallery** has pieces by local artists, including TP Flanagan's work *Victim* (1974), painted in response to the death of his friend in a terrorist shooting.

The **Castle Keep**, the oldest part of the complex, has displays on the Maguire chieftains and Fermanagh's military history. Count on spending one to two hours at the museum.

Explore the House & Grounds at Castle Coole

See inside an 18th-century mansion

Located 2.5km southeast of Enniskillen town centre, **Castle Coole** *(nationaltrust.org.uk; adult/child £13/6.50)* is a National Trust–owned neoclassical country house, which sits on 600 hectares of parkland traversed by walking trails. The house is open for tours from March to October; the grounds are open year-round. Allow at least two hours to explore the house and trails.

Take a guided tour to see the house's double cantilever staircase, Italian marble fireplaces, Regency furniture and basement servants' quarters. When King George IV visited Ireland in 1821, a state bedroom was specially prepared at Castle Coole in anticipation of his visit. Though the king never showed up, the bedroom, draped in red silk and decorated with paintings depicting *A Rake's Progress*, is one of the highlights of the tour.

DRINKING IN ENNISKILLEN: BEST PUBS

Blakes of the Hollow: Historic bar with a gorgeous interior, folk music and trad nights. Stocks local spirits and pours a good pint of Guinness. *11.30am-1am*

Charlie's Bar: Traditional pub with live music Thursday to Saturday and a trad session on Sunday. *11.30am-11pm Mon-Wed, to 1am Thu-Sat, 12.30-11.30pm Sun*

Magee's Spirit Store: Locals often end their nights at Magee's. Live music Friday to Wednesday. *5pm-1.30am Mon-Fri, noon-1.30am Sat, noon-12.30am Sun*

Lough Inn: This pub has a beer garden with views over the water, making it a good choice on a sunny day. *noon-1.30am Mon-Sat, to midnight Sun*

A STROLL AROUND THE ISLAND TOWN

This walk around Enniskillen's central island gives a taste of local life and culture.

START	END	LENGTH
Buttermarket	Enniskillen Castle Museums	750m; 45min

Start at the 1 **Buttermarket**, where the restored buildings of the old marketplace house craft shops and artists' studios. Walk southeast down Cross St and then turn right onto Water St. On the right, look for a mural of 2 **The Happy Prince**, a story penned by former Enniskillen schoolboy, Oscar Wilde, who was inspired to write the tale by the view of Cole's Monument from his dormitory window. On the left is the town hall, with its 1901 3 **Clock Tower** watched over by two stone soldiers, representing the town's military history.

Cross Townhall St to the Diamond to see more street art, this time a 4 **Trad Session** featuring the late Fermanagh musician John McManus on the fiddle. Continue northwest on Townhall St. At Charlie's Bar, look for a mural of *Line of Duty* actor Adrian Dunbar, who was born in Enniskillen; it features his character's catchphrase 5 **Now We're Suckin' Diesel**.

Next, pop inside 6 **Blakes of the Hollow** (p600), a pub that has barely changed since 1887, with a marble-topped bar, sherry casks and wood panelling. Continue on Townhall St to reach 7 **Headhunters Barber Shop & Railway Museum**, which displays a collection of railway memorabilia and is open for haircuts. From here, continue to Castle St and then head south to reach 8 **Enniskillen Castle Museums** (p598).

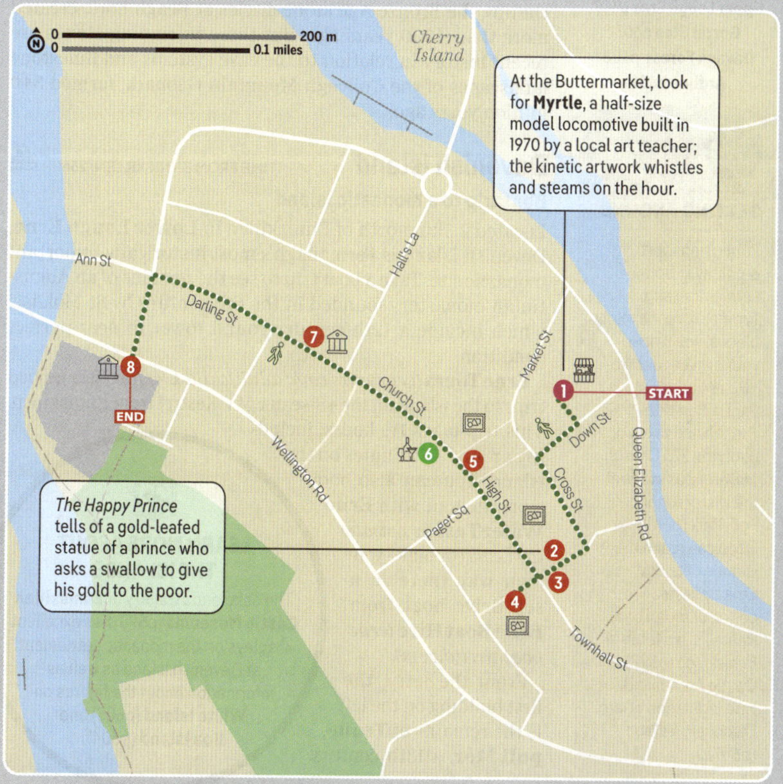
0 200 m
0 0.1 miles
Cherry Island
At the Buttermarket, look for **Myrtle**, a half-size model locomotive built in 1970 by a local art teacher; the kinetic artwork whistles and steams on the hour.
Ann St
Darling St
Hall's La
Market St
Church St
Down St
Cross St
Queen Elizabeth Rd
High St
Paget Sq
Wellington Rd
Townhall St
START
END
The Happy Prince tells of a gold-leafed statue of a prince who asks a swallow to give his gold to the poor.

Beyond Enniskillen

The loughs and hills surrounding Enniskillen offer adventures on water and land, with ancient stone figures and wildlife to spot.

Places

Devenish Island p602
Castle Archdale p603
Boa Island p604
Castle Caldwell Forest p604
Belleek p604
Lough Navar Forest p604
Cuilcagh Lakelands p605
Upper Lough Erne p607
Gortin Glen p607
Davagh Forest p608
Ardboe p609

GETTING AROUND

Public transport is patchy in both Fermanagh and Tyrone. To reach many places, you'll need your own car or bike.

Bus 94 connects Enniskillen with Omagh and takes one hour; the 273 Omagh to Derry bus stops at the Ulster American Folk Park (p610).

You can reach the islands of Lough Erne by kayak, canoe or motorboat. Rental is available in Enniskillen (p598), Castle Archdale Boat Hire (right) and Share Discovery Village (p607).

The town of Enniskillen is the perfect launchpad for day trips by boat or kayak around the inlets and islands of Lough Erne. This waterway was an important pilgrimage route during early Christian times, and today you can visit the remains of a thriving monastic community on Devenish Island. Less is known about the mysterious stone figures on nearby Boa and White Islands.

Going back further in time, the southern slopes of Tyrone's Sperrin Mountains are dotted with ancient monuments, including the Bronze Age stone circles at Beaghmore, created more than 4000 years ago. But these intriguing stones are recent history in relation to the cave systems and limestone landscapes of the Cuilcagh Mountain Geopark, formed 340 million years ago.

Devenish Island

TIME FROM ENNISKILLEN: 25MIN

Boat trip to a monastic island

Located 2.5km north of Enniskillen in **Lower Lough Erne**, Devenish Island is Fermanagh's most historically important monastic site. Take a boat trip to see the remains of an Augustinian monastery founded in the 6th century by St Molaise, which include a 12th-century round tower in near-perfect condition.

Erne Tours *(ernetours.com; adult/child £14/10)* offers guided trips to the island on the 48-seater MV Kestrel from Enniskillen. This trip takes 1½ hours, including around 45 minutes on the island. You can also book a private tour with **Erne Water Taxi** *(ernewatertaxi.com)* or make your own way there in a self-drive boat from **Erne Boat Hire** *(erneboathireltd.com)*.

From the jetty, the first building on the left is the remains of **Teampull Mór**, a 13th-century

LEARN MORE ABOUT THE ISLANDS

The Lakelands Gallery at **Enniskillen Castle Museums** (p598) has excellent displays on the monastic settlement at Devenish Island as well as information about the figures on **White Island** (p603) and **Boa Island** (p604).

church that had a regular congregation right up to the 17th century. Take time to look at the unusual carved headstones in the graveyard. Inside the church is a medieval stone coffin known as St Molaise's Bed. Local folklore has it that lying in the stone bed and turning over three times will cure ailments, but it's a tight squeeze.

The next structure you'll pass is the 12th-century **St Molaise's House**, which was built as a shrine to house the saint's remains. Ahead is the magnificent **Round Tower**, built as a bell tower, a watch tower and a place of refuge. It's not usually open to the public.

The final building is the remains of **St Mary's Abbey**, built in the 12th century. To the south of the abbey is a well-preserved **15th-century cross**. Go around to the back (western side) of the abbey and look for the carved stone head over the arch. Climb up the narrow stone steps of the tower to see the vaulted ceiling and views out over the island.

Back at ground level, walk up to the fence behind the abbey for views of the ruins, the tower and the water; it's a good spot for photos.

Castle Archdale

TIME FROM ENNISKILLEN: 20MIN

Discover the enigmatic figures of White Island

Of all the stone carvings at Lough Erne, the **White Island** figures are the strangest and most evocative. Finding a way to reach the island is all part of the adventure. One option is to hire a kayak and paddle from the Castle Archdale marina on the eastern shore of Lough Erne. **Castle Archdale Boat Hire** (castlearchdaleboathire.com) rents **kayaks** (one/two hours £15/20), two-person **canoes** (one/two hours £25/40) and **motorboats** (half-/full-day £90/130).

From the marina, the paddle out by kayak takes around 30 minutes. Near the jetty at the eastern tip of the island are the ruins of a small 12th-century church surrounded by grass. Inside are eight extraordinary stone figures lined up along the wall. Possibly dating from the 9th century, the age and interpretation of these figures have been the subject of much debate. Look for the figure with a grimacing face with puffy cheeks, thought to represent lust, and the hooded figure with a staff that is likely to be a bishop or abbot.

Back at **Castle Archdale Country Park**, you can walk or cycle the forest trails.

A PLACE OF PILGRIMAGE

In early Christian times when overland travel was difficult, Lough Erne was an important waterway between the Donegal coast and inland Leitrim. At this time, the lough was the route taken by pilgrims travelling via Devenish Island to Lough Derg in Donegal and there are records of people from all over Europe staying on the island.

Devenish Island was raided by Vikings in 837 and again in 923, but by the 12th century, Devenish was a large and important community of up to 1000 monks. The stonemasons and builders responsible for the round tower were some of the most skilled craftsmen of their day, and Devenish continued to thrive as a centre of learning and arts until the 16th century.

EATING AROUND LOWER LOUGH ERNE: OUR PICKS

Thatch Coffee Shop: Inside a little thatched cottage in Belleek, this cafe serves breakfast, lunchtime soups and sandwiches, plus cakes and scones. *9am-5pm Mon-Sat* £

Lodge Bar and Restaurant: On Lusty Beg Island, the Lodge serves burgers and seafood by an open fire or on the terrace. *12.30-3.45pm & 5-9pm* ££

Lasair: The restaurant at Finn Lough serves a menu of small plates made with local seasonal ingredients, organised around flavours. *1-4pm & 6-9pm* £££

Catalina Restaurant: Fine-dining at Lough Erne Resort, serving a five-course menu (beginning with Irish oysters) and four-course Sunday lunch. *6.30-9pm Mon-Sat, 1-3pm Sun* £££

Boa Island

TIME FROM ENNISKILLEN: **35MIN**

Intriguing Caldragh Cemetery

At the end of a short country lane off the main road through Boa Island, the atmospheric **Caldragh Cemetery** contains two intriguing stone figures, surrounded by a muddle of gravestones and long grass. The most intriguing of the statues is the larger, Dreenan Figure, thought to date from the early Christian period. Nearby is a smaller figure, brought here from Lusty More island.

Boa Island is connected to the mainland by road; a 10-minute stop is enough time to see the figures.

Castle Caldwell Forest

TIME FROM ENNISKILLEN: **35MIN**

Birdwatch from Loughside Forest Trails

One of the best places to spot Lough Erne's abundant birdlife is Castle Caldwell Forest. Here, the 4km **Rossergole Point Trail** is the longest of three trails, following the shoreline of a narrow peninsula to Rossergole Point and returning through beech woodland. Allow 1 hour 20 minutes for the walk.

The islands of Lower Lough Erne form part of a **Royal Society for the Protection of Birds (RSPB)** reserve, and are an important habitat for breeding waders (curlew, snipes, lapwings and redshank), as well as a colony of breeding Sandwich terns (a mostly white bird with a black cap on its head, a black bill with a yellow tip and a forked tail). Garden warblers arrive in summer.

Belleek

TIME FROM ENNISKILLEN: **35MIN**

See how Belleek Pottery is made

The world-famous **Belleek Pottery** *(belleekpottery.ie)* founded in 1857, can be found in an imposing grey building in the village of Belleek. You can see the pottery being made on 30-minute guided tours *(adult/child £10/8)* of the factory floor, which include the mould-making process and the delicate task of handcrafting flowers and baskets. Pieces are available to buy in the shop.

Lough Navar Forest

TIME FROM ENNISKILLEN: **30 MINS**

Take in the views on a scenic drive

On the western edge of Lower Lough Erne, **Lough Navar Forest Park** extends over 2,600 hectares of bog, heath and woodland traversed by walking trails. Give your legs a rest and take the 10km scenic drive to the **Magho Viewpoint** at the 300m-high Cliffs of Magho, a limestone escarpment above the forest.

The panorama from the Magho clifftop is one of the finest in Ireland. It looks out over the shimmering expanse of lough and river to the Blue Stack Mountains, the sparkling waters of Donegal Bay and the sea cliffs of Sliabh Liag.

MYSTERIOUS ORIGINS OF THE CALDRAGH CEMETERY FIGURES

The exact origins and meanings of the figures at Caldragh Cemetery remain unclear. The Dreenan Figure, which has been in the graveyard since at least 1841, was believed for many years to date from the pagan Iron Age and was thought to be 2000 years old. Though it was long referred to as a Janus (multifaced) figure, it is actually two separate figures placed back to back. It is now thought to date from the early Christian period, from 500 to 1000 CE. Experts have proposed that the figure might represent Badhbh, a frightening war goddess in local folklore.

Seamus Heaney wrote the poem 'January God' about the statue, referencing the Roman deity Janus, whom the figure was then believed to represent.

Belleek Pottery

Sample gin at Boatyard Distillery

Located on the lough shore (get here by car or by boat), **Boatyard Distillery** *(boatyarddistillery.com; tours £55)* produces gins and vodka found in some of the world's best bars. Book ahead for an immersive **distillery tour**, offered Wednesday to Sunday, which includes tastings of the spirits, both neat and in cocktails. You'll hear the distillery's history and learn about Boatyard Double Gin, made with organic wheat and eight botanicals, including Sweet Gale from the family farm.

Cuilcagh Lakelands   TIME FROM ENNISKILLEN: 25MIN

Discover the subterranean world of Marble Arch Caves

Southwest of Lower Lough Erne lies a limestone plateau, where Fermanagh's abundant rainwater has carved out a network of subterranean caverns, the largest of which is known as the **Marble Arch Caves** *(marblearchcaves.co.uk; adult/child £16/8; book ahead)*. You can explore 1.5km of show cave passages on a guided tour that takes 60 to 75 minutes.

When water levels are high enough, tours begin with a short boat trip along the waters of the underground River Cladagh to Junction Jetty, where three subterranean streams meet up. You then continue on foot to a tunnel leading into the New

BEST ACTIVITIES IN FERMANAGH & TYRONE

Elements Spa Trail: A private two-hour open-air spa trail through loughside flotation pools, saunas and steam rooms at Finn Lough.

Water Park: An inflatable children's obstacle course of slides, bridges and platforms at Share Discovery Village on Upper Lough Erne.

An Creagán: Book a guided foraging experience in the grounds of An Creagán to search for berries and herbs used by early settlers.

Hydrobikes: Get out onto the water on a pedal-powered raft. Suitable for children over eight. Hire them at Castle Archdale or Enniskillen.

Lusty Beg Island: Activities include archery, clay pigeon shooting, kayaking, cycling and trips in a RIB (rigid inflatable boat).

EATING IN COUNTY TYRONE: OUR PICKS

An Creagán Restaurant: Restaurant with courtyard near the Beaghmore Stone Circles serving breakfast, lunch (soup, salad, sandwiches), traybakes and scones. *10am-3pm* **£**

The Kitchen: Chic brunch spot in Omagh serves tempting plates of tacos, pancake stacks and French toast. *9am-4pm Mon-Thu, to 5pm Fri & Sat, 10am-4pm Sun* **££**

Brewer's House: This cosy pub in Donaghmore village has open fires and serves creative modern dishes. *5-8.30pm Wed & Thu, 5-9pm Fri, 3-9.30pm Sat, 3-8.30pm Sun* **£££**

Grants Restaurant: Omagh restaurant with timber booths serving steak and other classic dishes. *5.15-8.30pm Thu, 5-9.30pm Fri, 4.30-9.30pm Sat, 1.15-8pm Sun* **£££**

WHY I LOVE LOUGH ERNE

Isabel Albiston, Lonely Planet writer

In my childhood memories it's always sunny at Lough Erne. I picture us outside watching the water turn pink and gold as the sun sets late into the night. I remember kayaking out to Inish Rath and the smell of wild garlic in the woods as we walked up from the jetty.

I have always been attracted to the sense of adventure and the romance of paddling out to the lough's islands. Out on the water, no two days are the same. There is magic in the play of light on the lough's surface, the rolling mists, and the peacefulness of being alone with nature. The monastic ruins and intriguing stone figures add to the allure.

Chamber and through the Moses Walk, a walled pathway sunk waist-deep into the river. The reflections of the formations in the water are evocative and otherworldly. If the water levels of the river are too low (or too high) for a boat trip, a walking tour is offered instead. Note that there are 150 steps to the caves. Wear sturdy shoes and bring an extra layer (the caves are around 10 degrees cooler than the temperature outside).

Book in advance for 'Earth Yoga' classes, which take place in the show cave one Saturday per month.

Hike the Cuilcagh Boardwalk Trail

Known as the 'stairway to heaven', the photogenic **Cuilcagh Boardwalk Trail** up its namesake mountain has become one of Fermanagh's most popular walks. It leads 6km to a viewing platform at the edge of the mountain plateau, which has breathtaking views of Lough Erne and beyond. The trail begins 500m east of the turnoff to Marble Arch Caves. Allow three to four hours for the hike.

The first 4km of the trail follow a gravel path through limestone grasslands with grazing sheep. Soon the landscape begins to change to blanket bog, coated with white bog cotton in spring and purple moor grass in late summer. It's here that the boardwalk begins. It was not constructed with the convenience of walkers in mind, but instead to protect the delicate blanket bog beneath it.

The final ascent is via a series of steps over boulders and streams to a platform with a fantastic view of the drumlins of Upper Lough Erne. The trail is 6km each way; allow around three or four hours.

Beyond the platform, a rough mountain path traverses the summit plateau to reach a Bronze Age cairn. The summit plateau is a breeding ground for golden plovers and is rich in rare plants such as alpine clubmoss. Unless you have a map and compass, it's best to turn back once you reach the end of the boardwalk; mist can roll in quickly, and it's easy to get lost.

Explore the country estate at Florence Court

Florence Court *(nationaltrust.org.uk; £14/7)* is a grand baroque country house in a superb setting, surrounded by parkland and woodland and with views of Benaughlin Mountain.

Take a house tour to see the famous rococo plasterwork and antique Irish furniture. In the drawing room are three large paintings of Fermanagh from the 1730s; Devenish Island looks almost the same today. One of the tour highlights is viewing the downstairs servants' quarters.

EATING AROUND CUILCAGH AND UPPER LOUGH ERNE: OUR PICKS

Little Orchard Tea Room: The cafe at Crom Estate serves soup, sandwiches, house-baked brownies and cakes. Cash only. *11am-5pm* £

Kissin Crust: Lisnaskae coffee shop stacked with house-baked pies, quiches and scones; serves lunchtime soup and sandwiches. *9am-4pm Tue-Sat* £

Dog & Duck Inn: Serves a seasonal menu. Specialises in independent beers and craft spirits, some from the onsite micro distillery. In Lisbellow. *5-11pm Thu & Fri, 1-11pm Sat* £££

Tully Mill Restaurant: Friday night tapas, Saturday night dinners and Sunday lunch made with local ingredients; near Florence Court. *5-9pm Fri & Sat, 12.30-4pm Sun* £££

Cuilcagh Boardwalk Trail

Hire a bike at the visitor centre to explore the 9km-long red trail through the landscaped grounds and woodland, passing an ancient Irish yew tree. Don't miss the large walled garden and restored kitchen garden, with glasshouses used for growing food.

Upper Lough Erne

TIME FROM ENNISKILLEN: 25MIN

Wildlife watching from the water

Upper Lough Erne is not so much a lake as a spectacular watery maze of islands, inlets, reedy bays and meandering backwaters. The area is home to an array of wildlife.

Hire a kayak, canoe or stand-up paddleboard at **Share Discovery Village** *(sharevillage.org)* to get out onto the water. The route from Share to Crom is a lovely half-day paddle. It takes you past **Inish Rath** *(krishnaisland.org)*, an island with a Hare Krishna temple. On Sundays, visitors are welcome to join the community for worship and lunch.

Allow at least an hour or two to explore on land at **Crom Estate** *(nationaltrust.org.uk; adult/child £9/4.50)*, a National Trust–managed property with a large area of natural woodland and thriving wildlife. From the visitor centre, you can follow a 5.6km walking trail past old castle ruins, a walled garden and gnarled yew trees, enjoying views over the reed-fringed lough. Castle Crom itself is privately owned and closed to the public.

Crom Estate is a haven for pine martens, bats and many species of birds. Flocks of whooper swans and goldeneyes overwinter here, while great crested grebes nest in the spring.

Gortin Glen

TIME FROM ENNISKILLEN: 50MIN

Walks in Gortin Glen Forest Park

Originally planted for timber production, the coniferous woods of **Gortin Glen Forest Park** are traversed by a series of way-marked walking trails. The 2km **Pollan Trail** follows the

GEOLOGY OF THE CUILCAGH LAKELANDS

On account of its important geology, the area around Cuilcagh Mountain forms part of the **Cuilcagh Lakelands UNESCO Global Geopark**. The landscape is rich in limestone, which was formed 340 million years ago by layers of lime-rich mud and the remains of sea creatures on what was then the seabed. Cuilcagh Mountain is made from layers of sandstone on top of limestone, and its slopes are coated with rare limestone grasslands and blanket bog.

The Geopark's biggest attractions are the Cuilcagh Boardwalk Trail (p606) and the nearby Marble Arch Caves (p605). The water in the caves runs down Cuilcagh Mountain, so if you hike the boardwalk trail before descending into the caves, you will be tracing the water's path.

GIANTS OF THE SPERRINS

The **Giants of the Sperrins** is a series of sculptures made with recycled materials and wood by Danish artist Thomas Dambo. **Nowanois the Storyteller** is depicted talking to his younger self, bridging the gap between past and future. It's located 2km east of Cranagh village, off Glenelly Rd.

Darach the Guardian, who watches over the present, stands atop Mullaghcarn Mountain with her arms outstretched towards the landscape she protects. She is encircled by a ring of stones, which reference the ancient stone circles found in Tyrone. She can be reached via a walking trail through Gortin Glen Forest Park (p607).

At Davagh Forest (p608), **Ceoldán the Stargazer** looks towards the future. He kneels between poles depicting the constellations of the zodiac.

path of the Pollan Burn (stream), passing small waterfalls; you might spot red squirrels and even pine martens along the way. The **Mullaghcarn Trail** climbs to the summit, where you can see Darach, one of the Giants of the Sperrins (p608), and take in far-reaching views. Allow three hours to make the seven-kilometre round trip.

There's also an 8km scenic forest drive, graded mountain-biking trails, a large children's playground and a picnic area.

Davagh Forest

TIME FROM ENNISKILLEN: 1HR 25MIN

Stargaze at OM Dark Sky Park

In the sparsely populated Sperrin Mountains, the starry night skies above Davagh Forest and the ancient stone circles of Beaghmore are now an official International Dark Sky Park. At Davagh Forest, the **OM Dark Sky Park and Observatory** *(omdarksky.com; guided tour £6/3.90)* houses telescopes and an exhibition.

Book an observatory tour to learn about astronomy, look through telescopes and see the night sky using a virtual reality headset. For a chance to look through the observatory's 355mm LX600 Meade telescope, look out for regular stargazing events. Remember that in June, it stays light until after 10pm, but in December, the sun sets as early as 4pm. The park remains open all night, even when the observatory is closed. There are toilets in the lower car park. Check the website for regular scheduled events, such as full moon lunar observations, sun observations (using a special lens), sunset bat walks and a summer solstice guided walk to the Beaghmore Stone Circles (p608).

Walk to the Beaghmore Stone Circles

From the OM observatory, a 3.4km **Solar Walk** trail leads to the **Beaghmore Stone Circles**. Along the way, an information board for each planet in the solar system is positioned at a distance relative to its distance from the sun in space. Much of the trail is over boardwalk (built to protect the delicate bogland), with views of the rolling hills of the Sperrins along the way.

At Beaghmore, the intriguing cluster of seven stone circles, ten rows of stones and 12 cairns dates from 2500 to 500 BCE. It is believed they might also be related to astronomy and could have been created to chart lunar, solar and stellar events.

Beaghmore is a beautiful spot at sunset. After dark, it's sometimes possible to see the northern lights from here, too.

Mountain-biking and walking trails

Davagh Forest provides some of the best mountain biking in Ireland, ranging from family-friendly green and blue trails along a wooded stream to 16km of red trails leading to the top of Beleevenamore Mountain, with several challenging rock slabs and drop-offs on the descents. Before hitting the **trails** *(midulstercouncil.org/davaghforest; free)*, you can practice switchbacks, rock rolls and log rides in the skills park and pump track. Access them from the lower car park, watched

Beaghmore Stone Circles

over by **Ceoldán the Stargazer**, one of three Giants of the Sperrins (p608). There are bike washing facilities here, but no bike rental services in the immediate area.

Davagh's walking trails give you more time to enjoy this landscape of rolling hills and sweeping forests. A 3km loop trail takes in the forests and red-hued stream.

Ardboe

TIME FROM ENNISKILLEN: 1HR 20MIN

See the Ardboe High Cross

A 6th-century monastic site on the western shores of Lough Neagh is the evocative location of the **Ardboe High Cross**, one of Ireland's best-preserved and most elaborately decorated Celtic stone crosses. The 10th-century cross has 22 carved panels depicting Old and New Testament scenes, including Christ's entry into Jerusalem. It's located 16km east of Cookstown.

ANGLING IN FERMANAGH

The lakes of Fermanagh are renowned for both coarse and game fishing. Lough Erne has pike, perch, rudd, bream, roach, salmon and brown trout.

The Lough Erne salmon- and trout-fishing season runs from the beginning of March to the end of September. The mayfly season usually lasts a month from the second week in May.

To fish in Northern Ireland, you need a rod licence and a permit or day tickets, which can be purchased from Home, Field & Stream (p600) in Enniskillen. See the government website **NI Direct** *(nidirect.gov.uk)* for angling season dates, limits and permit information.

In May, anglers compete to reel in the biggest catch during the **Fermanagh Classic Fishing Festival** *(fermanaghomagh. com)*.

TOP EXPERIENCE

Ulster American Folk Park

In the 18th and 19th centuries, more than two million people left Ulster to forge a new life across the Atlantic. Their story is told at the Ulster American Folk Park, where exhibits are split into Ulster cottages and American log cabins, with guides in period costume on hand to bring the stories to life. The museum is 8km north of Omagh.

Musicians at the Ulster American Folk Park

TOP TIPS

- Much of the museum is open air, so come prepared for the weather.

- Take in the rural scenery from the viewpoint beyond the Mellon Homestead.

- In May the museum hosts the **Bluegrass Omagh** festival, with musicians from around the world performing on four different stages.

Life in Ulster

The experience begins with a journey through Ulster. Here a mixture of replica and original buildings (removed from their original locations and rebuilt onsite) include a blacksmith's forge, a weaver's thatched cottage, a Presbyterian meeting house and a schoolhouse.

The only building in its original place is the Mellon Homestead, around which the park was built. Thomas Mellon, who was born in the farmhouse in 1813, emigrated to Pennsylvania as a child and went on to become the founder of Mellon Bank. There is usually a costumed guide in the house making soda bread on the griddle; be sure to try it.

Journey to America

The two parts of the park are cleverly linked by passing through a mock-up of an emigrant ship. In the American section of the park, you can visit a genuine 18th-century stone cottage and a log house, both shipped across the Atlantic from Pennsylvania, along with other buildings.

Bad Bridget Exhibition

PRACTICALITIES

- ulsteramericanfolkpark.org
- adult/child £13/8
- 10am-5pm Tue-Sun

In the main museum building, the innovative Bad Bridget exhibition looks at the struggles and temptations faced by Irish immigrants in America using comic-style illustrations, stories, sounds and smells.

Places We Love to Stay

£ Budget ££ Midrange £££ Top End

Enniskillen MAP p599

Enniskillen Hotel ££ This modern, centrally located hotel has 14 budget motel rooms (doubles from £80 per night) and 35 more stylishly decorated hotel rooms.

Westville Hotel ££ Offers a central location, spacious rooms and good breakfasts. Staff are friendly and helpful.

Killyhevlin Hotel ££ Lakeside resort 1.5km south of town with hotel rooms, self-catering lodges with hot tubs, a spa and a restaurant.

Castle Archdale

Castle Archdale Caravan Park £ A popular loughside site with pitches for tents and caravans, as well as basic glamping pods.

Boa Island

Lusty Beg Island (p605) **£££** Island retreat reached by ferry from Boa Island, with self-catering chalets and B&B rooms. Has a spa, bikes, kayaks and archery.

Finn Lough £££ Stay in a transparent forest bubble dome, an indoor suite or a lakeside cottage at this wonderful complex with an outdoor spa.

Lough Navar Forest

Lough Erne Resort £££ Luxury hotel and golf resort with extensive grounds and a spa, on the western shores of the lough.

Cuilcagh Lakelands

Tully Mill Cottages ££ These neat self-catering cottages are right by the Florence Court estate; good for families. Excellent restaurant on site.

Arch House ££ Traditional B&B with good breakfasts; well located for visiting Florence Court and Marble Arch Caves.

Rose Cottage £££ Two-bedroom self-catering cottage overlooking an apple orchard in the grounds of Florence Court; built in 1840 for the estate's head gardener.

Upper Lough Erne

Crom Campsite £ Camping and glamping are available in the peaceful grounds of the National Trust's Crom Estate.

Share Discovery Village £ Tent pitches, glamping pods and self-catering chalets on the loughshore, plus an indoor pool.

Omagh

Silverbirch Hotel ££ This hotel in Omagh, 9km south of the Ulster American Folk Park (p610), has friendly staff, spacious rooms (though the decor is a little dated), a bar and a restaurant.

Tattykeel House ££ B&B accommodation in a large Georgian house with spectacular gardens. It's 5km south of Omagh town centre.

Gortin Glen

Gortin Glen Glamping ££ Nicely furnished, spacious glamping pods with private hot tubs and fire pits, plus a shared indoor kitchen and dining area.

Davagh Forest

Sperrinview Glamping ££ These glamping pods near Davagh Forest have bathrooms, kitchenettes and large windows looking out to the night sky; some have hot tubs.

An Creagán Cottages £££ Well-equipped, self-catering cottages in an idyllic setting in the foothills of the Sperrins, 10km west of Davagh Forest. Forest trails and a cafe on site.

TOOLKIT

Bike repair, Ardara (p417)
NICOLAS D'HOEDT/LONELY PLANET

TOOLKIT

The chapters in this section cover the most important topics you'll need to know about in Ireland. They're full of nuts-and-bolts information and valuable insights to help you understand and navigate Ireland and get the most out of your trip.

Arriving
p614

Getting Around
p615

Money
p616

Accommodation
p617

Family Travel
p618

Health & Safe Travel
p619

Food, Drink & Nightlife
p620

Responsible Travel
p622

LGBTIQ+ Travellers
p624

Accessible Travel
p625

Drive the Wild Atlantic Way
p626

Nuts & Bolts
p627

Language
p628

Arriving

Dublin is the main point of entry for most travellers to Ireland. Dublin Airport is located 10km north of the city centre. It has two interconnected terminals with ATMs, restaurants and convenience shops. Buses connect Dublin Airport with towns and cities across Ireland. You can also fly to Belfast, Shannon and Cork, and smaller airports including Knock and Kerry.

SIM Cards

SIM cards for unlocked phones can be purchased from WHSmith in the arrivals hall of both terminals at Dublin Airport, and at the Spar convenience shop in Terminal 2. The airport has free wi-fi.

Ferry

Car ferries from Liverpool in England, Holyhead in Wales and Cherbourg in France arrive at Dublin Ferry Port, 5km east of the city centre. Belfast has ferry connections to Scotland and England.

Duty Free

Duty-free prices are available to people travelling from the Republic of Ireland to countries outside the European Union, including Britain. They are not available for journeys from Northern Ireland to the EU or Britain.

US Preclearance

When travelling from Dublin or Shannon airports to the US, passport and immigration formalities are done at US Preclearance before boarding; allow extra time. When you arrive in the US, your flight is then treated as a domestic arrival.

Transport from Airport to City Centre

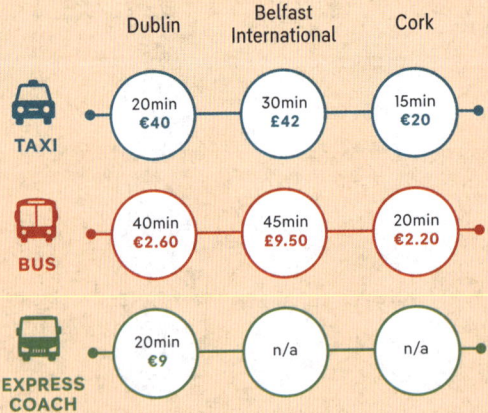

	Dublin	Belfast International	Cork
TAXI	20min €40	30min £42	15min €20
BUS	40min €2.60	45min £9.50	20min €2.20
EXPRESS COACH	20min €9	n/a	n/a

ENTRY REQUIREMENTS

Ireland and Britain are part of the Common Travel Area (CTA). The Republic is in the EU, but is not a member of Schengen, and is not planning to implement ETIAS *(European Travel Information and Authorisation System; travel-europe.europa.eu/etias_en)*, launching in late 2026. No UK ETA is required for the Republic. Northern Ireland, as part of the UK (but no longer the EU post-Brexit), requires visa-exempt visitors to obtain a UK ETA *(Electronic Travel Authorisation; gov.uk/eta)*, whether arriving directly to or from the Republic. While the 'soft' border between the Republic and Northern Ireland means there are no passport controls, visitors still require a UK ETA for any Northern Ireland travel.

Getting Around

Exploring Ireland's wildest and most beautiful corners is easiest by car. Keep your camera and walking boots handy for impromptu stops along the way.

TRAVEL COSTS

Car hire
From €30/day

Petrol
Approx €1.76 per litre

EV charging
€10–30 for a full charge

Tolls
€1.70–13

Bus

Private buses compete with **Bus Éireann** *(buseireann.ie)* in the Republic and also run where national buses are irregular or absent. Few bus journeys last longer than five hours. Bus Éireann bookings can be made online. Book early to get the lowest fares.

Train

Ireland's rail network is limited, but trains are a good option for some intercity routes, including Belfast to Dublin and Dublin to Cork. Services are operated by **Iarnród Éirean/Irish Rail** *(irishrail.ie)* in the Republic and **NI Railways** *(translink.co.uk)* in Northern Ireland. For the best fares, book in advance.

TIP

Download Transport for Ireland's (TFI) app, **TFI Live** *(transportforireland.ie)*, to plan bus, train and tram trips using real-time departure information.

RURAL ROAD HAZARDS

Ireland's rural roads can be steep, narrow and winding. Single-track roads with blind bends can be challenging, even without the hazard of wandering sheep and deer. If you see an oncoming vehicle, look for a passing place to pull into. The etiquette is for the car nearest to a passing place to reverse; thank the driver with a wave. Be aware, too, that mist can roll in quickly at the coast and on the hills, reducing visibility.

Hiring a Car

Cars can be hired in every major town and city, but book in advance, especially during the summer when demand sometimes outstrips supply. Most cars are manual; automatic cars are more expensive. You need to be aged 25 or over to hire a car from most companies.

Travel Cards

In Dublin, the **Leap Visitor Card** *(leapcard.ie)* covers all Dublin Bus, Luas tram, DART and commuter train travel for one, three or seven days. The **Irish Explorer Rail Pass** *(irishrail.ie)* covers five days of unlimited rail travel in the Republic within 15 consecutive days.

Toll Roads

Ireland has 11 toll roads, 10 of which have conventional barrier-toll plazas where you pay at the cashier's booth. Dublin's **M50** *(eflow.ie)* toll plaza is barrier-free; pay online before 8pm the following day. Peak rates are charged on weekday mornings (€13) and evenings (€12) at the Dublin Port Tunnel.

DRIVING ESSENTIALS

Drive on the left.

Speed limits are in kilometres per hour in the Republic and miles per hour in Northern Ireland.

.05
The legal alcohol limit is 0.05%.

Money

CURRENCY: IRELAND: EURO (€) NORTHERN IRELAND: POUND (£)

Credit Cards

Nearly all businesses take cards. In many cases, card payment is preferred, and some restaurants and tour companies only accept card payment. Most accommodation options, including campsites, require credit card details or advance payment to secure a reservation. A few rural guesthouses and campsites accept cash only.

Taxes & Refunds

Most goods come with a value-added tax (VAT) of 23% (20% in Northern Ireland), which non-EU residents can claim back under the Retail Export Scheme. The scheme is also available in Northern Ireland. The goods must be taken out of the EU within three months of the purchase date.

Contactless Payments

Card payments for amounts up to €50 (£100 in Northern Ireland) are usually contactless. Pay by tapping your card on the machine.

Digital Payment

Payments using digital wallets on mobile phones have become increasingly popular in Ireland. They can be used anywhere that accepts contactless card payments.

HOW MUCH FOR A...

Surfboard rental **€20**

Museum entry **€14**

Bike rental **€20**

Dublin–Cork bus ticket **€14**

HOW TO... Save Some Euros

Many attractions offer discounted rates if you buy tickets online in advance. You can also buy visitor passes, such as **Go City Dublin** (gocity.com), that include entry to a number of attractions. The **Heritage Card** (heritageireland.ie) includes free entry to all sites managed by the Office of Public Works; it can be a good deal, depending on how many you plan to visit.

TIPPING ETIQUETTE

Ireland does not have a tipping culture, and tipping isn't necessary in most situations.

Accommodation Hotel porters €1–2/£1–2 per bag; cleaning staff at your discretion. Not expected in small B&Bs.

Pubs Only if there's table service, then €1–2/£1–2 per round of drinks. If you're dining, tip as you would in a restaurant.

Restaurants Check whether your bill includes a service charge. For decent service 10%; up to 15% in more expensive places.

Cafes/coffee shops Not expected; many have an optional tip jar on the counter.

Taxis Round up to an even amount.

Toilet attendants Loose change; no more than €0.50/50p.

LOCAL TIP

If you are offered a choice of currencies when paying by card, choosing to pay in the local currency invariably offers a better rate than selecting payment in your home currency.

Accommodation

Lighthouses

A number of Ireland's iconic lighthouses are available to rent as holiday lets. You might have to climb some stairs, but the wild scenery and sea views are unbeatable. The **Irish Landmark Trust** (irishlandmark.com) preserves buildings of special historical interest and rents them as holiday accommodation. Properties include Wicklow Head Lighthouse and lightkeepers' houses at Blackhead Lighthouse in County Antrim and St John's Point in County Donegal.

Castles

If you've dreamed of staying in a castle, Ireland might be the place to experience it. Some of Ireland's grandest castles are now luxury hotels, including Ashford Castle in County Mayo, Lough Eske Castle in County Donegal and Ballynahinch Castle in County Galway. Castles are usually set in magnificent locations, often with extensive grounds and woodland to explore.

Glamping Pods & Yurts

Camping in Ireland always carries the risk of a washout, but swapping your tent for a timber pod raises the comfort level and reduces the risk of leaks. Glamping pods range from basic huts with bunks (bring your own bedding) to cabins with attached bathrooms and kitchenettes. Alternatively, book a stay in a proper bed in a luxurious glamping yurt. These are often spectacularly located, with gorgeous views.

Tree Houses & Bubble Domes

Some of Ireland's most atmospheric accommodation is hidden in the woods. In County Fermanagh, the transparent forest bubble domes at **Finn Lough** (finnlough.com) offer views of the night sky. Across the country, you'll find beautifully designed tree houses in which you can spend a night in the woods, such as **Burrenmore Nest** (burrenmore-nest.com) in County Derry.

HOW MUCH FOR A NIGHT IN A...

Camping pitch
€30

B&B
€130

Castle hotel
€350+

Cabin Cruises & Canal Barges

One way to experience Ireland's inland waterways is to hire a live-aboard motorboat or canal barge. A number of companies offer self-drive, liveaboard cabin cruisers for exploring the **Shannon–Erne Waterway** (p445). You can also rent a narrowboat or barge and cruise the Grand Canal and River Barrow. No previous boating experience is required.

THE HOUSING CRISIS

The relocation of a number of multinational companies to Dublin is one factor that has contributed to the city's housing crisis. Rents have soared, and housing is scarce. In 2025 the Department of Housing reported that there were more than 10,925 homeless people living in the city.

In some popular tourist areas of the country, such as the Dingle Peninsula in County Kerry, a shortage of affordable housing is partly because of properties being bought up as holiday homes and landlords choosing to rent properties on short-stay accommodation platforms such as Airbnb.

CLOCKWISE FROM TOP LEFT: JANUSZ PIENKOWSKI/SHUTTERSTOCK, SERGIY NIGERUK/SHUTTERSTOCK, ASIER ROMERO/SHUTTERSTOCK, MPACHENKO/SHUTTERSTOCK

Family Travel

From interactive museums to cycling paths, nature trails and beaches, Ireland has plenty to keep the kids entertained. The country's small size, mild climate and relative safety make it an easy place for families to explore.

Where to Sleep

Nearly all hotels provide cots, but reserve ahead, especially during holiday periods. Many hotels have interconnecting rooms and offer babysitting services. In summer, look for kids' clubs and other activities. Glamping in pods has become increasingly popular in Ireland. Most sleep four to six people and are perfect for families. Some guesthouses do not accept young children, so check before booking.

Seeing the Sights

Most of Ireland's museums, wildlife centres and other visitor attractions cater to kids as much as they do to adults, and they offer reduced-price admission for families. Many visitor experiences feature activities for children, especially during the school holidays, and most attractions have playgrounds and picnic tables. Activity centres offer kids' programmes for all ages.

KID-FRIENDLY PICKS

Beyond the Trees
Explore treetop walkways, a forest viewing-tower and a giant slide at Avondale Forest Park in County Wicklow. (p122)

Spike Island
Visit the former prison island in County Cork. (p199)

Irish National Heritage Park
Learn about 9000 years of Irish history at this open-air museum in Wexford. (p147)

Waterford Greenway
Cycle this family-friendly trail from Waterford city to Dungarvan. (p160)

W5
Head to this interactive science discovery centre in Belfast. (p511)

Eating

Restaurants generally have high chairs, children's menus and baby-changing facilities. Fine-dining restaurants might not be suitable for kids. Pubs do not allow under 15s after 9pm. Supermarket meal deals (sandwich, drink and snack) offer good-value lunches on the go.

On the Road

Public transport is free for children under eight in the Republic of Ireland, and for children under four in Northern Ireland. If you're driving, child seats are mandatory for young children (check requirements). Car-hire companies can provide them; book in advance.

LAND OF GIANTS & FAIRIES

Irish folklore is full of tales of giants and mischievous fairies. Far from being friendly wish-granting creatures, the fairies were troublesome entities that humans took great care not to disturb or annoy. As for the giants of Irish mythology, the Fomorians were sea monsters that were the archenemies of the Tuatha dé Danann, the ancient tribe of Ireland. Legend has it the **Giant's Causeway** (p581) was built by Finn McCool.

The myths are brought to life on Fionn's Giant Adventure trail at **Slieve Gullion Forest Park** (p557) in County Armagh, where an innovative storybook forest trail passes fairy houses and the discarded belongings of a giant.

Health & Safe Travel

INSURANCE

Travel insurance is not required to enter Ireland, but comprehensive insurance is highly recommended to cover theft and loss as well as any medical problems. EU citizens carrying a free European Health Insurance Card (EHIC) are covered for most emergency medical care but not for nonemergencies or emergency repatriation.

Midges

These little biting insects are most active between May and September, particularly in the boggy areas of Connemara and Donegal. They often appear in swarms around dusk. Luckily they don't carry diseases, and the windiness of the Irish climate helps keep them at bay. Locals use Avon's Skin So Soft moisturiser to prevent bites.

Theft & Fraud

Crime levels in Ireland are low, and it is a relatively safe country for travellers. Nearly all crimes against tourists happen in Dublin, and they mostly consist of pickpocketing, bag snatching and theft from cars. Don't leave anything visible through the windows of your car when you park, and try to find secure parking areas.

BEACH SAFETY

Rip currents are the leading hazard for beachgoers. If lifeguards aren't present, ask locals whether the water is suitable for swimming.

SWIM SAFELY

Red and yellow flag
A lifeguarded area; the safest place to swim.

Black and white chequered flag
An area for surfing, kayaking and other non-powered craft. Do not swim here.

Red flag
Danger. Do not enter the water.

Reporting a Crime

The best place to report an incident is the nearest *garda* (Irish Republic police) station, or Police Service of Northern Ireland (PSNI) station in Northern Ireland. Ask for an incident report, for insurance claims and emergency documents. The Irish Tourist Assistance Services (ITAS) provides free help and support to people who are victims of crime while travelling in Ireland.

NORTHERN IRELAND

Sectarian conflict is unlikely to cause problems for travellers these days, but it's a good idea to keep an eye on the news. Avoid any areas where there are riots or clashes with the police. Though rare, this kind of violence does occasionally flare up. However, such clashes do not usually pose a safety threat or cause widespread disruption.

Food, Drink & Nightlife

When to Eat

Breakfast (7–10am) During the week, Irish people usually eat toast, cereal or porridge. Cooked breakfasts are more often eaten at weekends.

Lunch (12.30–2pm) Often soup and a sandwich, or something light.

Dinner (5–9pm) Also called tea, this is the main meal of the day. Sometimes followed by a dessert (pudding) of something sweet such as apple pie.

MENU DECODER

Starter An appetiser dish eaten at the start of the meal.

Main course The main dish of the meal (known as an entree in the US).

Dessert A sweet pudding, cake or ice cream eaten at the end of the meal.

Cheese board A plate of cheese and crackers sometimes offered on dessert menus.

Early bird/Pre-theatre menu A fixed-price, two- or three-course menu served in the early evening; often good value for money.

Tasting menu A fixed menu of specially prepared small plates.

Wine pairings A glass of specially selected wine with each course.

Sunday roast Roast beef, chicken or lamb served with roast and mashed potatoes, vegetables and gravy.

Chips Like potato fries but fatter and fluffier. Crisps are potato snacks sold in packets (known as chips in the US).

Where to Eat

Cafes The best Irish cafes serve house-made soups, salads, sandwiches, baked potatoes and cakes.

Coffee shops Specialist coffee shops sell lattes, flat whites and drip coffees, plus pastries.

Restaurants Irish restaurants range from family-friendly bistros to Michelin-starred fine-dining establishments.

Pubs Most pubs also offer meals, usually generous portions of comfort food such as fish and chips.

Food trucks Sometimes parked in particularly scenic places, food trucks serve everything from lobster rolls to Thai food.

HOW TO... Order Drinks in a Pub

If you're in a pub with friends, it's usual for people to take turns buying a round of drinks for the group. When it's your turn, announce your intentions by saying, 'My round.' Ask everybody in your party what they would like and then order and pay at the bar. If you're with a large group or on a tight budget, don't fret: it's not always necessary to get a round, and you can just order your own drink.

Draft beer and Guinness are served by the pint and half-pint; specify the quantity when you order. In Ireland, a standard measure of spirits is 35.5mL; you can order a single or a double (70mL). Tipping the person behind the bar is not expected, but you may wish to do so, especially if you're ordering a round.

VENGEROF/SHUTTERSTOCK

HOW MUCH FOR A...

Pint of Guinness
€6

Takeaway fish and chips
€14

Bowl of seafood chowder
€12

Flat white
€4

Glass of wine
€7

Gourmet dinner
€70

Ice cream
€4

Full Irish/Ulster fry
€10

HOW TO... Pack a Perfect Picnic

The practice of bringing food on an outdoor excursion to eat in scenic surroundings has been popular across Europe since the French Revolution, when French aristocrats fled their homeland and brought their fondness for picnicking with them. In Ireland, picnics have long been an integral part of summer family outings to the beach, the hills or even the local park.

For a typical Irish picnic, you'll need a blanket. This can be laid out on the grass or sand, with the food placed in the middle, or draped over the top of a picnic table. As for the picnic food, these days the options extend far beyond the traditional ham sandwiches on white sliced bread. Instead, look for freshly baked sourdough in an artisan bakery. Next, stop at a deli to pick up Irish cheeses, quiches and pies. Sausage rolls (sausage meat wrapped in flaky pastry) are also ideal for a picnic. Look out for punnets of local strawberries, sometimes sold at the roadside when they're in season. For a truly authentic Irish picnic experience, bring a flask of tea. (It will help keep you warm if the temperature drops.) Most importantly, don't forget to buy several bags of Tayto crisps.

If it starts pouring with rain and you end up eating your sandwiches in the car, take solace in the fact that this is an Irish picnicking tradition.

Gourmet Picnic Hampers

If packing a picnic sounds like too much effort, a number of hotels and guesthouses offer luxury picnic experiences, where they prepare a gourmet hamper for you to bring on an excursion to a nearby beauty spot.

FARM TO TABLE

Farm-to-table and farm-to-fork dining are terms used for restaurants that source their ingredients directly from local farmers, fishing boats and artisan suppliers, with a focus on seasonal and organic produce. At the forefront of this movement in Ireland is **Ballymaloe House**, a restaurant in County Cork where the daily menu is based on what has been cultivated on-site and at nearby farms. While they have used house-grown produce since the 1960s, this sustainable practice is now gaining traction in Ireland.

Menus at farm-to-table restaurants are based on whatever seasonal produce is currently available; this usually changes day by day. In addition to being more sustainable, fresh ingredients taste better, so the philosophy of many farm-to-table chefs is to let the flavours shine through in deceptively simple dishes.

Foraging is also undergoing a revival in Ireland. These days, it's common to see foraged herbs on restaurant menus, and several farms offer foraging trips to help identify edible wild berries, mushrooms, elderflower, samphire, wild garlic and sorrel. Edible seaweeds, which have long been foraged on Ireland's shores, have recently become fashionable again for their health benefits.

If you have self-catering accommodation, you can create your own farm-to-table experience by shopping for ingredients at a farmers market; find them listed on *bordbia.ie* and *nigoodfood.com*. To take your farm-to-table cooking skills to the next level, enrol in a course at **Ballymaloe Cookery School** – Darina Allen's County Cork establishment – where ingredients are sourced from their organic farm and gardens.

Responsible Travel

Climate Change & Travel

It's impossible to ignore the impact we have when travelling; Lonely Planet urges all travellers to engage with their travel carbon footprint, which will mainly come from air travel. While there often isn't an alternative, travellers can look to minimise the number of flights they take, opt for newer aircrafts and use cleaner ground transport, such as trains. One proposed solution – purchasing carbon offsets – unfortunately does not cancel out the impact of individual flights. While most destinations will depend on air travel for the foreseeable future, for now, pursuing ground-based travel where possible is the best course of action.

The **UN Carbon Offset Calculator** shows how flying impacts a household's emissions

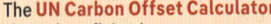

The **ICAO's carbon emissions calculator** allows visitors to analyse the CO2 generated by point-to-point journeys

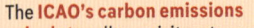

Save the Seals

Visit the seals and help support the work of **Seal Rescue Ireland** in County Wexford. Volunteers rescue and rehabilitate orphaned and injured seals, plant trees, and raise awareness of marine conservation issues.

Accessible Gardens

The **Delta Sensory Gardens** in Carlow include a five senses garden, a musical fountain and a sculpture garden. Proceeds go to the adjacent Delta Centre for adults with disabilities, for whom the gardens were designed.

Pick up litter with other volunteers on a community beach cleanup organised by **Clean Coasts** (cleancoasts.org).

Organic Trust (organictrust.ie) has a list of certified organic farm shops and organic produce vendors.

REWILDING

The rewilding movement aims to restore Ireland's native forests. Pick up Eoghan Daltun's book *An Irish Atlantic Rainforest: A Personal Journey into the Magic of Rewilding* (2022) to learn about his efforts to rewild an area of the Beara Peninsula.

WIND-POWERED HOTEL

The **Salthouse Hotel** in County Antrim has an on-site wind turbine and solar panels that supply renewable energy to both the hotel and the car park EV chargers. Air-source heat pumps are used for heating.

Buy Local Arts & Crafts

Design Ireland *(designireland.ie)* highlights the work of independent Irish designers and makers, and Design Ireland artists also host workshops and demonstrations in their studios. **Craft NI** *(craftni.org)* does the same in Northern Ireland and has a shop in Belfast.

Brigit's Garden

This not-for-profit garden in Galway is themed around Celtic festivals. It was established to help people get in touch with nature and learn about Celtic traditions. There is also a focus on herbs and their healing properties.

Burren Ecotourism

The **Burren Ecotourism Network** *(burren.ie)* has brought together more than 70 local businesses to create a community model for sustainable tourism in the Burren and Cliffs of Moher Geopark.

Bogland Boardwalks

Boardwalk trails have been constructed to protect areas of delicate blanket bog, including the **Cuilcagh Boardwalk Trail** in County Fermanagh. Stick to the paths to avoid damaging the bogs.

Walkinstown Green Social Enterprises

WALK *(walk.ie)* provides training, employment and community for people with disabilities. Support them by eating at the social enterprise cafe, Green Kitchen and Garden Shop, in Dublin.

In Dublin, get your coffee from one of three branches of **Mug Shot Café**. These cafes are owned and managed by PACE, a social enterprise that creates jobs for people who have experienced prison.

The **Irish Wildlife Trust** *(iwt.ie)* campaigns for the protection of Ireland's wildlife and manages a number of wildlife reserves. Get involved by joining one of the events hosted at branches around the country.

TOOLKIT — RESPONSIBLE TRAVEL

15.7 million tonnes

The amount of waste produced by people in Ireland each year. The Circular Economy is a set of measures designed to ensure that raw materials remain in use for as long as possible through reuse and recycling.

RESOURCES

sustainabletourismnetwork.ie
Has a list of tourism providers that meet the criteria of sustainable tourism.

iwt.ie
The Irish Wildlife Trust's website, with information on current campaigns.

allirelandsustainability.com
Educates on biodiversity, a circular economy and reducing carbon footprints.

LGBTIQ+ Travellers

Ireland is generally welcoming to LGBTIQ+ travellers, and it is unusual to encounter hostility at hotels or other accommodation. Out-dated attitudes persist, though, and Ireland's LGBTIQ+ community continues to face discrimination and harassment, but travellers are not usually the targets. Dublin and Belfast have the most well-established gay scenes.

Pride

Pride celebrations take place across the country. Ireland's biggest LGBTIQ+ event is Dublin Pride, which kicks off in June and culminates in a huge parade through the capital on the last Saturday of the month. Belfast Pride is held in late July, with more than 150 events across 10 days. A weeklong festival takes place in Cork city in late July and early August, and in Galway in August. Smaller events and parades are held in Wexford in May; Mayo and Inishowen in June; Carlow and Limerick in July; and Derry (Foyle Pride) and Waterford in August.

THE SCENE

Dublin has plenty of community-friendly bars and clubs, including the George. In Belfast, the scene is centred on Union St in the Cathedral Quarter. Dublin's **Outhouse** *(outhouse.ie)* is an LGBTIQ+ resource centre and cafe. It's a great place to meet people and find out what's on. The website has listings.

Trans-Fusion

Held in Dublin in late May/early June, this weeklong arts festival celebrates Ireland's trans community with poetry, storytelling, spoken word, comedy, history and music events. One of the festival's aims is to show how shared performance spaces and the arts can boost self-esteem and lead to positive mental health outcomes.

LGBTIQ+ IRELAND

In line with a troubling trend across Europe, the number of reported hate crimes against the LGBTIQ+ community in Ireland has risen. Homophobic or transphobic harassment and violence are crimes and can be reported to the police. You can also call the LGBT Helpline on 1800 929 539.

POLITICS

Leo Varadkar became Ireland's first openly gay head of government when he was first appointed Taoiseach (prime minister) in 2017. He had come out publicly in 2015, in the lead-up to the referendum in which Ireland voted to change the constitution to recognise same-sex marriage. Varadkar expressed support for the trans community, acknowledging in a 2022 interview that it was 'extraordinarily difficult to be trans in Ireland today'.

Béar Féile

This four-day bear event in Dublin features DJs, parties, bear bingo, a bear *céilidh* (session of traditional music and dancing) and a Mr Bear Ireland competition. The events are at bars and clubs in the city centre in March.

Accessible Travel

Ireland still has accessibility issues, but efforts are made to improve public spaces – with ramps, lifts and other facilities – and create a welcoming environment for people who have learning disabilities or are neurodiverse.

Autism-Friendly Towns

Clonakilty in West Cork was named Ireland's first autism-friendly town by the charity AsIAm. The accreditation involved training staff in local businesses, becoming service-dog friendly and introducing quiet spaces. Maynooth, Waterford city, Killarney and Drumcondra have followed.

Airport

Passengers with reduced mobility can request airport assistance. Ask at least 48 hours in advance through your airline. You can also prebook assistance at Dublin Airport through an app, **PRM Assist Mobile** (prmassist.com).

Accommodation

Hotels built after 2010 should have lifts, ramps and other facilities. Urban chain hotels are most likely to have fully accessible rooms. Other accommodation such as B&Bs, private rentals and historic hotels may not be accessible.

ACCESSIBLE ATTRACTIONS

The **Cliffs of Moher** (p298) have wheelchair-friendly paths, as does the **Burren** (p290). **Titanic Belfast** (p508) and **Guinness Storehouse** (p80) are fully wheelchair accessible.

Inclusive Beaches and Wheelchairs

In Northern Ireland, **Inclusive Beaches**, run by the **Mae Murray Foundation** (maemurrayfoundation.org), offers free loans of beach wheelchairs at several locations, including Portstewart Strand in County Derry, which also has accessible parking, and disabled toilet and shower facilities.

On beaches.ie, search for beaches with beach wheelchairs and disabled access in the Republic. The **Disability Federation of Ireland** (disability-federation.ie) has a list of contacts for reserving beach wheelchairs.

SENSORY ROOMS

A number of hotels have adapted rooms with projectors and special lighting for people with autism; some also have sensory playrooms for children. Hotels with adapted rooms include the Pillo Hotel in Ashbourne and the Radisson in Sligo.

RESOURCES

Disability Federation of Ireland (disability-federation.ie) advocates for people with disabilities in the Republic of Ireland.

Disability Action (disabilityaction.org) is the equivalent body in Northern Ireland.

Enable Ireland (enableireland.ie) is a national disability services provider for adults and children.

AsIAm (asiam.ie) provides details of autism support groups.

Transport for Ireland (transportforireland.ie) has information on accessibility for public transport users as well as contact information for wheelchair-accessible taxis.

JAM Card

Designed to be used by people with learning disabilities or autism, the **JAM Card** (jamcard.org) can be downloaded onto your phone, or you can request a physical card. It is used to discreetly ask for 'just a minute' when you need more time.

Drive the Wild Atlantic Way

The Wild Atlantic Way (Slí an Atlantaigh Fhiáin) is an official waymarked driving route that extends 2500km along Ireland's western coastline, from the Inishowen Peninsula in Donegal to Kinsale in West Cork. Along the way are plenty of places to stop and take in views of jagged cliffs, crescent strands and sheep-studded hills, as well as towns where you can catch a trad session in a pub or dine on freshly caught local seafood.

The Route

The route is split into 14 stages spread across nine counties: Donegal, Leitrim, Sligo, Mayo, Galway, Clare, Limerick, Kerry and Cork. It's marked by signposts featuring a blue wave and the direction of travel (N for north and S for south).

You can drive the route in either direction, but if you drive from south to north, you're on the side of the road that's closest to the sea, giving passengers even better views. Highlights along the route are marked with 'discovery point' signs; these are good places to stop along the way.

Cycle

Cycling the Wild Atlantic Way is a challenge. It's hilly, and the roads can be busy with cars, especially in summer. The full route takes six or seven weeks by bike, so most cyclists choose just one section of the route to cover. The prevailing wind is southerly, so south to north should be easier (even though the wind can't really be relied on to cooperate).

Resources

Fáilte Ireland's designated **Wild Atlantic Way** *(wildatlanticway.com)* website has maps and up-to-date information about the route.

Route Highlights

The entire route is a highlight in itself; allow plenty of time for stops.

Slieve League Cliffs (Sliabh Liag; p414), County Donegal: Ireland's highest sea cliffs (and some of the highest in Europe); intrepid travellers can walk the nerve-testing 6km-long One Man's Path.

Inishcrone, County Sligo: Sweeping white-sand beach stretching 3km between Inishcrone and the Moy Estuary.

Clew Bay (p371), County Mayo: Croagh Patrick, Ireland's most sacred peak, has spectacular views over the 365 islands in Clew Bay, next to Westport.

Kylemore Abbey (p334), County Galway: Crenelated, neogothic country house (later an abbey) perched photogenically on the shores of Pollacapall Lough.

Cliffs of Moher (p298), County Clare: Ireland's most famous cliffs are especially dramatic when viewed from the water on a cruise.

Drombeg Stone Circle (p209), County Cork: Superbly atmospheric, Drombeg's 17 standing stones are oriented towards the winter solstice sunset.

Cahergal (p241), County Kerry: One of two extraordinary stone ringforts, Cahergal dates from the 10th century; it's located just outside Cahersiveen on the Ring of Kerry.

WILD ATLANTIC ISLANDS

Along the route, a number of islands make for interesting detours. In Donegal, you can catch a trad session and meet a community of artists on Tory Island, or explore the walking trails of wild Arranmore. In County Mayo is Achill Island, which can be reached by a causeway from the mainland. Take your pick of three Aran Islands in Galway, which can be accessed by ferry; each one gives the feeling of living at the edge of the world. At the tip of the Beara Peninsula in Cork is Dursey Island, which can be reached by cable car.

Nuts & Bolts

OPENING HOURS

Shops 9am–6pm Monday to Saturday, noon–6pm Sunday; in cities and larger towns, some shops stay open late to 9pm on Thursday

Museums 9am–5pm; outside cities and larger towns, some may close during the winter months

Pubs 10.30am–11.30pm Monday to Thursday, to 12.30pm Saturday, to 11pm Sunday (30 minutes 'drinking up' time allowed); closed Christmas Day

Off-licences 10.30am–10pm Monday to Saturday, 12.30–10pm Sunday

Restaurants noon–2pm and 5–9pm; many close one day a week (usually a Monday or Tuesday)

Cafes 8am–5pm (often opening earlier and closing later in cities and larger towns)

Mobile Phone Coverage

Mobile phones in Northern Ireland use UK networks. If you have a European SIM card, you might be charged different rates in Northern Ireland and the Republic. Some rural areas do not have mobile phone coverage, so download maps before taking car journeys.

Weights & Measures
The metric system is used except for beer, which comes in pints.

Smoking
It is illegal to smoke indoors, except for private residences.

GOOD TO KNOW

Time Zone
GMT; GMT+1 late March through October

Country Code
+353 (Republic); +44 (Northern Ireland)

Emergency Number
999

Population
7.2 million

Electricity 230V/50Hz

Type G

PUBLIC HOLIDAYS

New Year's Day
1 January

St Brigid's Day 1st Monday in February (Republic of Ireland only)

St Patrick's Day
17 March

Easter Monday
March/April

Easter Tuesday
March/April (Northern Ireland only)

May Bank Holiday
1st Monday in May

Spring Bank Holiday
Last Monday in May (Northern Ireland only)

June Bank Holiday
1st Monday in June (Republic of Ireland only)

The Twelfth 12 July (Northern Ireland only)

August Bank Holiday
1st Monday in August (Republic of Ireland only)

Summer Bank Holiday Last Monday in August (Northern Ireland only)

October Bank Holiday Last Monday in October (Republic of Ireland only)

Christmas Day
25 December

St Stephen's Day (Boxing Day)
26 December

Language

Irish (Gaeilge) is the country's official language. In 2003 the government introduced the Official Languages Act, whereby all official documents, street signs and official titles must be either in Irish or in both Irish and English

Basics
Hello. Dia duit. *deea gwit*
Hello (reply). Dia is Muire (duit). *deeas mwira dit*
Good morning. Maidin mhaith. *mawjin wah*
Good night. Oíche mhaith. *eeheh wah*
Goodbye. Slán leat. *slawn lat*
Yes. Tá. *taw*
It is. Sea. *shah*
No. Níl. *neel*
It isn't. Ní hea. *nee hah*
Thank you (very much). Go raibh (míle) maith agat. *goh rev (meela) mah agut*
Excuse me. Gabh mo leithscéal. *gamoh lesh scale*
I'm sorry. Tá brón orm. *taw brohn oruhm*
I don't understand. Ní thuigim. *nee higgim*
Do you speak Irish? An bhfuil Gaeilge agat? *on vwil gwaylge oguht*
Cad é seo? What is this? *kod ay shoh*
Cad é sin? What is that? *kod ay shin*
I'd like to go to... Ba mhaith liom dul go dtí... *baw wah lohm dull go dee...*
I'd like to buy... Ba mhaith liom... a cheannack *bah wah lohm... a kyanukh...*
another/ one more. ceann eile. *kyown ella*
nice. go deas. *goh dyass*

Signs
Fir. Men. *fear*
Gardaí. Police (plural). *gardee*
Leithreas. Toilet. *lehrass*
Mná. Women. *mnaw*
Oifig An Phoist. Post office. *iffig ohn fwisht*

Days of the Week
Monday. Dé Luaín. *day loon*
Tuesday. Dé Máirt. *day maart*
Wednesday. Dé Ceádaoin. *day kaydeen*
Thursday. Déardaoin. *daredeen*
Friday. Dé hAoine. *day heeneh*
Saturday. Dé Sathairn. *day saherin*
Sunday. Dé Domhnaigh. *day downick*

Today. inniu. *inyuv*
Tomorrow. amárach. *am-oar-uck*
Yesterday. inné. *innay*

Emergencies
Help! Cabhrú! *cowroo*
Go away! Imigh leat! *imig lat*
I'm ill. Tá tinis orm. *Taw tinis urum*
Call ...! Glaoch ar...! *Glay-uck air...*
    ...a doctor an dochtúir *on ducktoor*
    ...the police an garda siochana/ na gardaí *on gorda she-uck-awna/ na gardee*

NUMBERS	
1	**haon** *hayin*
2	**dó** *doe*
3	**trí** *tree*
4	**ceathair** *kahirr*
5	**cúig** *cooig*
6	**sé** *shay*
7	**seacht** *shocked*
8	**ocht** *hukt*
9	**naoi** *nay*
10	**deich** *jeh*

DONATIONS TO ENGLISH

Whiskey, galore (from Irish *go leor*), banshee, smithereens (from *smiodar*, meaning 'debris'), Tory (from Irish *toraí*, meaning 'outlaw')

Cúpla Focal

Here are a few phrases *as Gaeilge* (in Irish) to help you impress the locals.

Tóg go bog é. Take it easy. *tohg ay gobogay*

Ní féidir é! Impossible! *nee faydir ay*

Ráiméis! Nonsense! *rawmaysh*

Go huafásach! That's terrible! *guh hoofawsokh*

Sláinte! Your health!/Cheers! *slawncha*

Táim go maith. I'm fine. *thawm go mah*

Nollaig shona! Happy Christmas! *nuhlig hona*

Go n-éirí an bóthar leat! Bon voyage! *go nairee on bohhar lat*

Gaeltachts

Despite its official status, Irish is really only spoken in pockets of rural Ireland known as the Gaeltacht, the main ones being Cork (Corcaigh), Donegal (Dún na nGall), Galway (Gaillimh), Kerry (Ciarraí) and Mayo (Maigh Eo).

Dialects

Irish has three main dialects: Connacht Irish (in Galway and northern Mayo), Munster Irish (in Cork, Kerry and Waterford) and Ulster Irish (in Donegal).

WHO SPEAKS IRISH?

As well as the Gaeltachts listed above, there are also a number of Neo-Gaeltachts including the Gaeltacht Quarter in Belfast, parts of west County Clare and south County Derry.

PRONUNCIATION

Irish divides vowels into long (those with an accent) and short (those without) and also distinguishes between broad (a, á, o, ó, u) and slender (e, é, i and í), which can affect the pronunciation of preceding consonants. Other than a few odd-looking clusters, such as mh and bhf (both pronounced as w), consonants are generally pronounced as they are in English.

The 2022 census reported almost two million Irish speakers in the Republic and 6000 in Northern Ireland.

THE IRELAND
STORYBOOK

Our writers delve deep into different aspects of Irish life.

A History of Ireland in 15 Places
Throughout Ireland's history, invaders have been met with resistance and rebellion.
Isabel Albiston
p632

Meet the Irish
The famous Irish charm is more complex than many think.
Fionn Davenport
p636

Gaelic Games: More than Sport
Gaelic games encapsulate Irishness like nothing else.
Fionn Davenport
p638

William Butler Yeats
Learn about Yeats, one of Ireland's best-known poets.
Brian Barry
p641

Ireland's Red Deer
Once on the brink of extinction, indigenous red deer are making a slow comeback.
Brian Barry
p644

Donegal Castle (p420)

A HISTORY OF IRELAND IN
15 PLACES

Ireland's history has been marked by invasions from the Vikings, the Normans and the English, whose long period of Irish domination was met with resistance and rebellion. These 15 places are linked to key moments in Irish history, offering snapshots ranging from Neolithic ceremonies to recent political conflicts. By Isabel Albiston

THE EARLIEST EVIDENCE of humans in Ireland is a butchered bear bone found in a cave in County Clare that was carbon-dated to 10,500 BCE. In fact, Ireland's prehistoric period is both rich and intriguing: early standing stone arrangements are believed to relate to astrology; mysterious ceremonial sites align with the sun at key moments of the year; and the time before the arrival of the Celtic tribes is associated with the mythical fairy folk of the Tuatha dé Danann.

The beginnings of Christianity in Ireland heralded a period in which the country's earliest monasteries became important centres of learning, though these monastic centres would soon have to fend off attacks from the Vikings.

However, Ireland's darkest and most turbulent history relates to its fractured and complicated relationship with its close neighbour, England. Ever since the invasion of the Anglo-Normans in the 12th century, Ireland has suffered under various iterations of English dominance and occupation. Even after Ireland's hard-won independence, the country was left divided, creating a precarious political situation in the North.

Through it all, Ireland's folk traditions and literary output have thrived, reflecting the themes of rebellion and resistance that run through its history.

1. Céide Fields
WORLD'S OLDEST STONE-WALLED FIELDS
Preserved beneath the blanket bogs of County Mayo are a series of dwelling areas, tombs and fields that date from around 3700 BCE. These stone-walled fields are the oldest – and some of the largest – such enclosures to have been uncovered in the world. The rectangular plots of this Stone Age farming site indicate a system of community farming, which, by this period, had replaced hunting in Ireland. In the 1930s, a local teacher came across the stone walls buried beneath the bogs, but he failed to pique the interest of the experts he wrote to; excavation did not begin until 1969.

For more on the Céide Fields, see p375.

2. Brú na Bóinne
PREHISTORIC PASSAGE TOMBS
Located at a bend in the River Boyne in County Meath are the burial tombs of Newgrange, Knowth and Dowth, which date from around 3200 BCE. The remarkable complex is one of the most important Neolithic sites in the world, and the ceremonial structures also contain a large collection

of megalithic art. Newgrange's passage leads to a central chamber that directly aligns with the sunlight of the winter solstice, and it was a place of ritual. In 2020 analysis of the DNA of a man buried in Newgrange revealed that his parents were closely related, suggesting he could have been royalty.

For more on Brú na Bóinne, see p460.

3. Navan Fort
MYSTERIOUS MOUND STEEPED IN LEGEND

Near Armagh city, the intriguing Iron Age monument of Navan Fort is believed to have been occupied by royalty or high priests. Excavations suggest that the largest structure was once a temple and probably a site of rituals and ceremonies, but the precise details remain a mystery. Navan Fort is referenced in Irish legends as Emain Macha, the court of a mythical Irish king. The significance of the site as a centre of power and spirituality could be one reason why St Patrick later chose to build his first stone church on a nearby hill – where St Patrick's Cathedral stands today.

For more on Navan Fort, see p555.

Wooden cross on Slemish Mountain (p592)

4. Slemish Mountain
THE LEGEND OF ST PATRICK

At age 16, Ireland's patron saint was kidnapped from his home in 5th-century Roman Britain and brought to Ireland. It was during his hours of solitude tending sheep on Slemish Mountain in County Antrim that Patrick dreamed of his escape from Ireland on board a ship. After a difficult journey, Patrick made it back to Britain but later felt called by a vision to return to Ireland to spread Christianity. Though Patrick was not the first Christian missionary in Ireland, his mission was hugely influential. St Patrick's death date, 17 March, is celebrated across Ireland with parties and parades.

For more on Slemish Mountain, see page p592.

5. Clonmacnoise
EARLY CHRISTIAN MONASTERY

The monastery established on the banks of the River Shannon by St Ciarán in 548 was once an influential centre of learning, attended by monks from all over Europe. It was one of Ireland's earliest monastic settlements, and its strategic location further increased its prominence. The monks were the scholars of their day, as well as skilled builders who designed and constructed the round stone towers found at Clonmacnoise and other monastic sites. The site fell into decline in the 12th century, and what remained was reduced to ruins by the English in 1552.

For more on Clonmacnoise, see p530.

6. Waterford City
VIKING SETTLEMENT

Vikings settled in what is now Waterford city from as early as 914 CE, naming the town Vadrarjfordr. The Vikings chose the site because of its easily defended location on the River Suir, and they established settlements in Dublin and Wexford for the same reason. Today their legacy lives on in the oldest part of the city, Waterford's Viking Triangle, which contains a giant replica Viking chessboard. By the 12th century, the Anglo-Normans had arrived, adding medieval buildings and constructing city walls. These days, Waterford's walls are the canvas for a vibrant street-art scene.

For more on Waterford city, see p154.

7. Clare Island
IRELAND'S PIRATE QUEEN

Born into a powerful seafaring family on the Mayo coast, Grace O'Malley (Gráinne ní Mháille or Granuaile, c 1530–1603) took to waylaying cargo vessels at Galway port and demanding payment for safe passage. If they refused, she would have them looted. She soon controlled Mayo's Clew Bay and settled on Clare Island, though she continued marauding around the Irish and Scottish coasts. After O'Malley's piracy caught the attention of the English, she ended up meeting Queen Elizabeth I, who offered her a pardon and a title; O'Malley replied that she was already the Queen of Connacht. She is thought to be buried on Clare Island.

For more on Clare Island, see p364.

8. Donegal Castle
FLIGHT OF THE EARLS

In 1607, after years of fighting against the English in Ulster, the Gaelic earls Hugh O'Neill and Rory O'Donnell boarded a ship in Rathmullan and left Ireland for good, an event known as the Flight of the Earls. It's believed that as an act of defiance against the English, O'Donnell torched his own castle in Donegal before fleeing. The Flight of the Earls marked the end of the rule of Irish chieftains and left Ulster open to English rule and to the Plantation policy, in which the land of the Gaelic earls was confiscated and redistributed to British settlers.

For more on Donegal Castle, see p420.

9. Belfast Entries
THE SOCIETY OF UNITED IRISHMEN

In 1791 Theobald Wolfe Tone was invited to Belfast to attend the inaugural meeting of the Society of United Irish Men at a tavern in Crown Entry in the Belfast Entries – a series of narrow alleyways in the city centre. Inspired by the French Revolution, the society's initial aims were religious equality and parliamentary reform. In the face of British attempts to suppress the society, it was forced underground and soon planned an armed rebellion with the help of the French. It was ultimately unsuccessful, and the rebels were arrested and the leaders sentenced to execution. Today, the historic events that occurred in the Belfast Entries are referenced in the street art that can be seen down their narrow passageways.

For more on the Belfast Entries, see p497.

10. Dunbrody Famine Ship
FAMINE AND EMIGRATION

As a result of the Great Famine (1845–51), it's estimated that up to one million people died and some two million emigrated from Ireland. Though the immediate cause was the failure of the potato crop, the British government insisted that food exports from Ireland continue throughout the Famine, leaving Irish people to starve. New Ross in County Wexford was a departure point for the 'coffin ships' that left Ireland for North America. Today, an experience aboard a replica ship tells of the harrowing journey across the Atlantic, which countless passengers didn't survive.

For more on the Dunbrody Famine Ship, see p152.

11. Butter Market
CORK'S FOODIE HERITAGE

An 1855 butter-weighing implement known as the Firkin Crane bears testament to the days when Cork had the largest butter market in the world. It was here, outside the Old Butter Market, that butter was weighed and packed for export. The nearby Cork Butter Museum displays a slab of butter that was buried in the peat bogs, where it remained preserved for 1000 years.

The city's foodie history can also be experienced at the English Market, established in 1788 by the Protestant or 'English' corporation that then controlled the city; these days, it showcases some of Cork's best produce.

For more on the Butter Market, see p194.

12. Sweny's Pharmacy
WHERE LEOPOLD BLOOM BOUGHT SOAP

Of all the writers and poets who have contributed to Ireland's rich literary heritage, James Joyce (1882–1941) was arguably the most influential. His modernist novel *Ulysses* (1922) takes place in Dublin over the course of a single day, 16 June 1904. In the book, the protagonist Leopold Bloom visits a number of real-life locations, including

Sweny's Pharmacy (p62)

Sweny's Pharmacy, where he buys a bar of lemon soap. The pharmacy, which was established in 1847, has been preserved as it was in Joyce's day; today it hosts literary events and sells soap and books. Joyce's *Ulysses* notebooks can be seen in the Museum of Literature Ireland.

For more on Sweny's Pharmacy, see p62.

13. General Post Office
HQ OF THE 1916 EASTER RISING

In an armed uprising that aimed to overthrow British rule, a group of republicans seized Dublin's General Post Office on Easter Monday 1916 and announced the formation of an Irish republic. After less than a week of fighting, the rebels surrendered. But the subsequent execution of the 15 rebellion leaders garnered sympathy for the cause among Irish people, and the Easter Rising marked the beginning of the revolution that led to the War of Independence and the creation of the Irish Free State in 1921 – though six of Ireland's 32 counties would remain part of the UK.

For more on the General Post Office, see p86.

14. The Bogside
BLOODY SUNDAY

In Derry on 30 January 1972, on what is known as Bloody Sunday, a peaceful civil rights protest ended with the killing of 14 unarmed civilians by British paratroopers. The shootings occurred in the Bogside neighbourhood, near Free Derry Corner, where the events are commemorated with wall murals and memorials, and at the Museum of Free Derry. In 2010, following a years-long inquiry into the day, British Prime Minister David Cameron apologised on behalf of the British government for the 'unjustified and unjustifiable' killings. It was a tragic event that only exacerbated the years of violent conflict in Northern Ireland that followed.

For more on the Bogside, see p568.

15. Stormont
END OF THE TROUBLES

On 10 April 1998, the Good Friday Agreement was signed at Belfast's Parliament Buildings, known as Stormont. This marked the end of the 30 years of armed political conflict that was known as the Troubles. It included a clause that granted people from Northern Ireland the right to identify as Irish, British or both. The public voted in favour of the agreement in referendums in the North and South, leading to the establishment of a power-sharing Northern Ireland Assembly at Stormont. However, the complexities of the power-sharing system and various political scandals have led to the suspension of the assembly for extended periods.

For more on Stormont, see p511.

MEET THE IRISH

Charming, affable and quick-witted: the Irish have a very positive reputation. While usually genuine, Irish charm cloaks a deeper, more complex character. FIONN DAVENPORT tries to unravel the Irish psyche.

THE KEY TO understanding the Irish is knowing that we go to great lengths to never appear to take ourselves too seriously, even when we are deadly earnest. We put a premium on self-deprecation and the outward appearance of modesty.

Ireland's best-loved sons and daughters are skilled at marrying excellence with humility, and nothing will endear you more to the Irish than being incredibly good at something while making it clear that success hasn't changed you at all. Olympic gold? That's great, so long as your mother's home-cooked meals are still the best prize of all.

This form of modest self-deprecation is traditionally characterised as *an béal bocht*, or 'putting on the poor mouth' – letting on that you're worse off than you really are. It's an attribute born out of centuries of struggling Irish tenants exaggerating the difficulty of their circumstances to elicit the forbearance of (English) landlords in a system where any material improvement would risk an increase in rent. Times may have changed, but undoing the mores that are hardwired into Ireland's cultural DNA is a slow burn.

Yet recent prosperity and the unique brand of self-awareness of millennials and Gen Z Irish are going a long way towards doing that. Like their peers across the West, younger Irish have a heightened sense of identity and a clearer sense of their place in the world. Rather than hide their candle under a bushel as previous generations did, they loudly celebrate their strengths and accomplishments. They are also more vocal in their support of one another – partly a reaction to constantly grappling with the pitfalls of the digital world's never-ending feedback loop.

The same tensions inform the Irish sense of humour, which is infused with sarcasm, irony and the mastery of the deadpan understatement. Where else would you refer to WWII as 'the Emergency' and 30 years of sectarian violence in Northern Ireland as 'the Troubles'?

Dark humour is stock-in-trade. Whether to deal with poverty and political unrest or a housing crisis that puts starter homes beyond the reach of most young people, finding laughter in grim situations serves as a coping mechanism, and transforms potentially debilitating situations into moments of shared resilience. We diminish the power of adversity by laughing at it.

'Slagging' is the Irish art form of teasing. It might seem caustic to unfamiliar ears, but your ability to 'take a slagging' in good spirits is the ultimate test of how grounded you are, and a truer measure of the strength of a friendship than a cheaply paid compliment. Making humorous light of yourself acts as a social lubricant and a way of connecting with others on an equal footing. You know we love you; just don't expect us to tell you.

People

In 2025, the Republic of Ireland's population was 5.3 million and 1.9 million people lived in Northern Ireland. The urban/rural divide was 65/35, and 79% of the population used social media.

STORYBOOK

HOME IN MY IRISH SKIN

I was born in Dublin, in a mother-and-child home, as my birth mother got pregnant as a teenager at a time when having a baby out of wedlock was a societal no-no. As luck would have it, I was adopted by an Irish father and an Italian mother, which meant I grew up bilingual and – crucially – spent all of my summers in Italy until I left school.

As a result, I always had a feeling of 'otherness', my sense of Irishness tempered by a strong attachment to my mum's Italian heritage and a disavowal of the narrow-minded Catholicism that dominated Irish society for all of my youth.

In the early 1990s, I joined the Irish diaspora and moved to the US. The country I returned to at the dawn of the millennium was almost unrecognisable from the one I left, its gaze no longer inward but outward as it sought to remould a more inclusive society. Twenty-five years later, I'm more home than ever.

GAELIC GAMES: MORE THAN SPORT

Enshrined in ancient tales, Gaelic games are a unifying community force, and essential to Irish culture. By Fionn Davenport

MORE THAN MUSIC and literature – more than Guinness and perhaps more than the Irish language itself – Gaelic games encapsulate Irishness like nothing else. They are enmeshed in the fabric of Irish life and act as a useful shorthand for the best qualities of Irish culture. Their governing body, the Gaelic Athletic Association (GAA), is therefore more than a sporting organisation; it is the custodian of the identity, heritage and community spirit of the Irish people.

That's a lot of heavy lifting for some games. There are four of them, and the most popular by far is Gaelic football, followed by hurling, camogie (the women's version of hurling) and handball, which is a lot like American handball and is played in various formats, including one-wall, three-wall and four-wall versions. Handball's adherents are passionate but few; in truth, when talking about Gaelic games, most people stick to Gaelic football, hurling and camogie.

The Rules

Both Gaelic football and hurling are played by two teams of 15 players whose aim is to get the ball through what resembles rugby goal posts: two long, vertical posts joined by a horizontal bar, below which is a soccer-style goal protected by a goalkeeper.

Goals (where the ball is sent below the crossbar) are worth three points, whereas a point (where the ball sent is over the crossbar) is worth one point. Scores are shown as 1-12, meaning one goal and 12 points, giving a total of 15 points.

Gaelic football is played with a round, soccer-sized ball, and players are allowed to kick it or handpass it (as in AFL football in Australia). Hurling is played with a flat stick or bat known as a hurley or *camán*. The small leather ball, called a *slíotar*, is hit or carried on the hurley; a well-struck ball can travel over 100m at 150km/h. Both games are played over the course of 70 action-filled minutes.

The Majesty of Hurling

If Gaelic football is the most popular game, hurling is the more revered. It's also one of the world's oldest field games and is mentioned in the epic tales of Irish mythology. In the last decades of the 19th century, the newly established GAA gave pride of place to hurling as the most Irish of Irish sports: an ancient game that not only puts a premium on skill and athleticism but also enshrines the values of courage and fair play that resonated deeply with the Gaelic Revival – the intellectual and cultural movement that underpinned Ireland's march towards independence.

STORYBOOK

Gaelic Football

Gaelic football is much younger than hurling, and today's version was developed in the latter half of the 19th century, mostly by blending a variety of rudimentary field games with the newer games of rugby and soccer, resulting in a uniquely Irish style of football. At its core, the GAA sought to instil pride in Irishness at a time when British rule had significantly impacted the cultural landscape, but Gaelic football was as much a nod to modernity as it was a recognition of the growing popularity of 'English' games.

A National Obsession

The games are played at club level throughout the country, and the best players are selected to play for their respective counties. It's the ultimate ambition of every player to represent their county in an All-Ireland Final at Dublin's Croke Park stadium; it's the climax of a knockout championship that is played first at provincial and then inter-provincial level.

Almost every county in Ireland plays Gaelic football, with Kerry and then Dublin by far the most successful. The exceptions are Kilkenny, Limerick, Waterford, Clare and Tipperary, where hurling is king and football a mere afterthought. A handful of other counties – Cork, Dublin, Galway, Offaly and Wexford – put serious effort into both games.

Strictly Amateur

Perhaps the most striking feature of Gaelic games is their steadfastly amateur status. Players play for their hometown clubs and, if they're good enough, their county. Even the best players don't receive salaries and often balance rigorous training with full-time jobs or study.

At its best, the amateur ethos fosters a unique sense of purity, camaraderie and grassroots enthusiasm. Clubs become tight-knit communities, and players are deeply connected to local identities, only ever moving from their hometown clubs for work or study (and even then, county players will only ever play for their home county).

Unlike most professional sports leagues, the majority of GAA clubs are volunteer-driven. Whether it's a tiny village in County Kerry or a busy Dublin suburb, the local GAA club is the cornerstone of the community, and its busy calendar of events serves to raise funds and reinforce that community connection.

The Politics of Irish Sport

Politically, the GAA has served as a unifying force, albeit with complexities. It was founded as a nationalist institution, and many of its members fought for Irish independence: Croke Park's Hogan Stand is named after one of the victims of an atrocity committed by British soldiers in 1920.

For much of the GAA's existence, players were barred from playing soccer or rugby under penalty of exclusion, but this prohibition was finally lifted in 1971.

> **IF GAELIC FOOTBALL IS THE MOST POPULAR GAME, HURLING IS THE MORE REVERED.**

Although Gaelic games in Northern Ireland are still played almost exclusively in nationalist communities, efforts have been made to bridge the sectarian divide: one of the most visible results was the 2002 establishment of a Gaelic club for members of the Police Service of Northern Ireland (PSNI).

The (Slow) March Towards Greater Inclusivity

Women's participation in Gaelic games has seen a recent surge. There are more than 500 camogie clubs throughout Ireland, while Ladies Gaelic Football (to give it its proper name) is one of the fastest-growing participation sports in Europe.

Having struggled to access grounds, training facilities and equipment (players threatened to go on strike in 2023, and it was only in 2025 that camogie players were permitted to wear shorts instead of the hybrid skirt/shorts known as skorts), the Camogie Association and Ladies' Gaelic Football Association are finally set for full integration with the GAA in 2027.

WILLIAM BUTLER YEATS

Irish mysticism, a Nobel Prize and thwarted love – it's no wonder William Butler Yeats is one of Ireland's best-known poets. By Brian Barry

WIDELY REGARDED AS one of the most significant figures of 20th-century literature, WB Yeats was greatly influenced by Ireland's rich cultural heritage and his country's natural beauty – particularly that of his mother's home county of Sligo. Awarded the Nobel Prize in Literature in 1923 largely for his work as a playwright, Yeats went on to write some of his most famous poetry later in his career. It's as a poet rather than as a playwright that he is now best remembered.

Beginnings

William Butler Yeats was born in Dublin in 1865. His mother, Susan, came from a prosperous Sligo family and his father, John, studied law but abandoned his legal career to pursue his ambitions of becoming a landscape and portrait painter. The family moved to London so John could follow his dreams of becoming an artist, but Yeats spent large parts of his boyhood in Sligo, and the county's landscape would have a profound impact on his work.

Irish Mysticism & Identity

Yeats liked to say that by age 24 (in 1889) he'd read 'most, if not all, recorded Irish folk tales'. His writings, whether poetry, prose or plays, celebrated Celtic legends and myths. He firmly believed that the Irish could emerge from English domination and create their own purely Irish identity by revelling in the ancient Celtic myths still commonly recounted across the island. In 1888 Yeats collaborated on the landmark *Fairy and Folk Tales of the Irish Peasantry*. Four years later, he wrote the children's book *Irish Fairy Tales*. In these works he codified many of the most common Irish myths, characters and legends, including fairies, leprechauns and banshees.

The Abbey Theatre

At the turn of the 20th century, Yeats showed an increased interest in theatre, and in the summer of 1897 he stayed at the estate of Lady Gregory in County Galway. The Gregory house and estate offered him some sanctuary from the stress of an increasingly public life in both Ireland and Britain. During this stay, he, Lady Gregory and Edward Martin conceived the idea of a Celtic theatre, which would become the Irish Literary Theatre. Seeking to support the resurgence of Irish literature and cultural traditions, the theatre put on its first show in Dublin in May 1899. Until his death, Yeats continued to be involved in the theatre

– which grew into the Abbey Theatre – as both board member and playwright.

Never to Be: Maud Gonne

Maud Gonne was an English heiress and a committed Irish nationalist whom Yeats met in 1889. He quickly became infatuated with Gonne, and she would have a lasting influence on his work and life. He proposed to her in 1891 and again in 1899, 1900 and 1901, but she always refused his offers. Much to his dismay, she married Irish nationalist Major John MacBride in 1903. Yeats was distraught at having lost his muse to another man and set about ridiculing MacBride in his letters and poetry. Gonne's marriage was a disaster, and eventually she and MacBride separated. Yeats and Gonne later spent one night together, but she wrote to him afterwards to say that their relationship could not continue. She would write further letters highlighting the advantage to artists of remaining chaste. Yeats wrote about his night with Gonne in his poem 'A Man Young and Old' (1928).

Poetry

Yeats' most famous poems demonstrate his deep-rooted love of the Irish landscape as well as his interest in Irish mysticism and his awareness of early-20th-century political turmoil.

'The Wild Swans at Coole' (1916–17) lyrically describes the natural world:

Upon the brimming water among the stones
Are nine-and-fifty swans

He then contrasts it with an awareness of human decline:

All's changed since I, hearing at twilight,
The first time on this shore,
The bell-beat of their wings above my head,
Trod with a lighter tread.

Written just after WWI, 'The Second Coming' (1919) blends a Christian sensibility with the horror of global catastrophe:

And what rough beast, its hour come round at last,
Slouches towards Bethlehem to be born?

The later 'Sailing to Byzantium' (1928) is also concerned with age and decline: 'That is no country for old men'. Later still, 'Under Ben Bulben' (1939) sums up the poet's major concerns of Irish mysticism, the Sligo landscape (punctuated by the mountain of Benbulben) and humankind's struggle for spiritual meaning:

Many times man lives and dies
Between his two eternities,
That of race and that of soul,
And ancient Ireland knew it all.

A Nobel Laureate

When Yeats was awarded the Nobel Prize in Literature in December 1923 'for his always inspired poetry, which in a highly artistic form gives expression to the spirit of a whole nation', he was aware of the platform he had been given to highlight Ireland's newfound independence. The symbolic value of an Irish writer winning the prize was enormous. Yeats answered many letters of congratulations with, 'I consider that this honour has come to me less as an individual than as a representative of Irish literature; it is part of Europe's welcome to the Free State'.

A Poet to the Last

In 1939, after a short illness, Yeats died at the age of 73 in the French Riviera town of Roquebrune. In line with his wishes, he was buried in Drumcliff, County Sligo. His grave is marked by a simple gravestone engraved with an epitaph from 'Under Ben Bulben':

Cast a cold eye
on Life, on death.
Horseman, pass by!

> YEATS WAS GREATLY INFLUENCED BY IRELAND'S RICH CULTURAL HERITAGE AND HIS COUNTRY'S NATURAL BEAUTY

IRELAND'S RED DEER

Present in Ireland since the Neolithic period, indigenous red deer have been endangered by habitat loss, overhunting and interbreeding with non-native species. By Brian Barry

IRELAND'S MAJESTIC RED deer are thought to have been present in the country since the end of the last ice age. Brought to the country by Neolithic people, they roamed freely until habitat destruction and overhunting caused their numbers to decline sharply. At the turn of the 20th century, there were more than 1500 red deer in Killarney, County Kerry, but this number had fallen to as few as 60 by 1960. Populations have steadily increased in recent years thanks to conservation efforts, and an estimated 1000 native red deer now live in the woodlands and mountains around Killarney National Park.

Stags, Hinds & Fawns

As their name suggests, Ireland's native red deer have a rich red coat that changes to a darker greyish brown in winter. Stags can be as tall as 120cm at the shoulder and weigh up to 190kg. Hinds (females) are up to 110cm tall at the shoulder and weigh up to 110kg.

Red deer, Killarney National Park (p226)

Stags' antlers, with a soft skin covering called velvet, grow from spring until late summer. Antlers most commonly have 14 to 16 tines (points), but a dominant male's antlers can have up to 20 tines. Ahead of the autumn rutting (mating) season (when stags use their antlers to spar with each other), the stags' velvet dies off (or is scraped off on trees), they grow thick manes on their throats, their aggression increases and their neck muscles swell.

Hinds begin breeding at around 18 months old. For two weeks after they're born, fawns will remain hidden when the mother goes out to graze. A young fawn found on its own has not been abandoned and should not be moved or touched.

Outside the breeding season, stags and hinds live separately.

Herd size depends on the deer's habitat. Larger herds form when the deer live in open country, and herds remain smaller in woodland areas. The deer graze year-round but also eat moss, lichen, heather shoots and mat-grass through the winter months.

> **AN ESTIMATED 1000 NATIVE RED DEER NOW LIVE IN THE WOODLANDS AND MOUNTAINS AROUND KILLARNEY NATIONAL PARK**

Red deer, Wicklow Mountains (p114)

Seeing Deer in the Wild

The best time to see stags is during the rut in late September and early October. (Take care not to approach them, as males can be aggressive.) The main herds can be found in the lowlands of Killarney National Park in County Kerry and the surrounding Cores, Torc and Mangerton Mountains. These animals are direct descendants of the Scottish red deer that were introduced to Ireland more than 5000 years ago.

Red deer can also be found in County Wicklow in the Glendalough Valley and at Turlough Hill, but these herds have crossbred with Sika deer, a Japanese breed that was introduced to Powerscourt in County Wicklow in 1860 and to Killarney in 1865. There are wild red deer in Connemara in County Galway and Glenveagh National Park in County Donegal, but these deer were introduced from Scotland in the late 19th century.

Protection & Conservation

Red deer are a protected game species in Ireland, and a licence from the National Parks & Wildlife Service is required to hunt them. Stag-hunting season is from 1 August to 30 April, and hinds may be hunted from 1 November to 31 March. The hunting of all red deer in County Kerry, where the last native herd is located, is strictly prohibited.

In the 1980s a number of red deer were transported by helicopter to Inishvickillane, a private island in County Kerry, to prevent interbreeding with Sika deer. The island herd flourished, but because of the harsh Atlantic conditions and limited feeding, the deer are much smaller in size.

Red deer have had no natural predator since wolves were eradicated from Ireland more than 200 years ago. The biggest threat to Killarney's native red deer is genetic contamination through crossbreeding with Sika deer, though this has not yet been recorded in the national park. Scientists are closely monitoring, as it is vital that the genetic purity of Ireland's last remaining indigenous herd of red deer is maintained.

INDEX

A

abandoned villages 370, 419
Abbeyleix 436
accessible travel 18, 578, 622, 625
accommodation 617, 618
Achill Island 367-71, 391, **368**
Achill-Henge 371
activities 42-5, **44-5**, *see also individual activities*
Adare 268-9, 285
Ahakista 218, 219
air shows 125-6
airports 402, 614
Alcock, John 339, 343, 345
alcohol limit 615
Allen, Myrtle 200
alpacas 406
amusement parks 477
An Port 419
animals 10-11, *see also individual animals*
Antrim 560-5, 575-93, **562-3**
 itineraries 564-5
 navigation 562-3
 travel seasons 564-5
 travel within Antrim 562-3
Antrim Glens 590-1, 593
Aran Islands 348-52, 353, **349**
architecture, *see also* Georgian architecture
 Tudor Revival 269, 518
 Victorian era 495, 496
Ardara 417-18
Ardboe High Cross 609
Ardfert 256-7
Ardmore 164
Ards Forest Park 408-9
Arigna 447
Arkle 132
Armagh 531-5, 553-9, **532-3**
 accommodation 559
 itineraries 534-5

 navigation 532-3
 travel seasons 534-5
 travel within Armagh 532-3
Armagh city 553-6, 559, **554, 556**
Armagh Observatory 556
Arranmore Island 402-3
art museums
 Butler Gallery 175
 Gallery 23 195
 Golden Thread Gallery 498
 GOMA 158
 Icon Factory 74-5
 Irish Museum of Modern Art 82
 Lewis Glucksman Gallery 191
 National Gallery of Ireland 54-5
 Royal Hibernian Academy of Arts 67-8
 Visual Centre for Contemporary Art 167
 Waterford Gallery of Art 158
arts & cultural centres 147, 388, 505, 512, 571, 572
Athlone 428-32, 453, **429**
aurora borealis 406-7
Avoca 124
Avoca Handweavers 118, 125
Avondale 122-3

B

Baile Átha Luain, *see* Athlone
Ballina 380-1
Ballintoy 593
Ballintoy Harbour 582
Ballitore 134-5
Ballybunion 257
Ballycastle 29, 584-6, 593, **585**
Ballyconneely 345-6
Ballyhack 153
Ballyhenry Island 550
Ballyhoura 271
Ballyjamesduff 478
Ballyliffin 411
Ballymaloe House 200, 219
Ballymastocker Bay 408
Ballyvaughan 313
Baltimore 206-9, 219
Banba's Crown 406
Banbridge 544-5, 546
Bangor 551-2, 559
Bantry 26, 210-13, 219, **211**

Bantry Blueway 212
Barrow Way 169
basking sharks 405
beach safety 619
beaches 14-15, 44
 Achill Island 367, 369
 Ardmore 164
 Ballinskelligs Beach 236
 Ballydonegan Beach 217
 Ballyquin Beach 164
 Banna Strand 256-7
 Benone Strand 573
 Clonea Strand 164
 Coumeenoole Beach 252
 Culdaff Beach 411
 Derrynane Beach 236
 Dooks Beach 236
 Down 552
 Downhill Strand 573
 Dugort Beach 369
 Dunmore East 159
 Easkey Beach 381
 East Strand 579
 Enniscrone Beach 377
 Eyrephort Beach 341
 Glassillaun 336
 Inch Strand 251
 Inchydoney 204
 Keem Bay Beach 367
 Lenan Beach 411
 Lettergesh Beach 336
 Malin Beg Beach 416
 Narin 420
 Portstewart Strand 578
 Renvyle Beach 336
 Rosslare Strand 150
 Rossnowlagh Beach 422
 Shroove Beach 411
 St Finian's Bay 236
 Strandhill 382
 Streedagh Strand 389-90
 Stroove 411
 Tramore 160
 Trawmore Beach 367, 369
 Tullan Strand 421
 White Park Bay 582
 White Strand 236
Beaghmore Stone Circles 608
beauty pageants 255
Beggars Bush Barracks 102
Belfast 30, 486-529, **488-9**, **494, 501, 507, 514, 517, 520, 523**, *see also individual neighbourhoods*
 accommodation 529

 Cathedral Quarter 500-5, 529, **501**
 entertainment 518
 Holywood 513-15, 529, **514**
 itineraries 490-1, 496, 503, 510, 524, **496, 503, 510, 524**
 LGBTIQ+ travellers 624
 navigation 488-9
 Queen's Quarter & South Belfast 516-21, **517, 520**
 tours 520
 travel seasons 490-1
 travel within Belfast 489
 West & North Belfast 522-8, **523**
Belfast Entries 634
Bellaghy 572-3
Belleek 604
Belmullet 374
Belvedere House 448-9, 453
Benbaun 333
Benbulben Mountain 389-90
Benone 573, 593
bicycle hire
 Achill Island 367
 Aran Islands 348
 Bantry 210
 Belfast 489, 492, 506
 Burren, the 290
 Cahersiveen 240
 Clifden 337
 Cork city 188
 Derry 566
 Dingle 244
 Doolin 290
 Dublin 77, 95, 100
 Erris Head 375
 Florence Court 607
 Galway 320
 Glen of Aherlow 281
 Glenveagh National Park 396
 Graiguenamanagh 180
 Killarney town 226
 Kinvara 290
 Limerick city 264
 Loop Head Peninsula 307
 Newcastle 536
 Strangford 549
 Tralee 253
 Westport 363
Big Houses 169, *see also* country houses & manors
Binevenagh 573, 582

646

birdwatching 42
  Bloody Bridge 539
  Castle Caldwell Forest 604
  Castle Espie 550-1
  Cliffs of Moher 299
  Inishtrahull 413
  Lough Ree 433
  Rathlin Island 587
  Wexford 151
  Wild Nephin National Park 373
Birr 434-5, 453
Black Head 295
Black Hill 280
black pudding 204
Blarney Castle 200
Blarney Stone 200
Blasket Islands 249-50
Blessington 127
Bloody Sunday 570, 635
blowholes 374
Boa Island 604, 611
boat hire 212, 413, 445-6, 602, 603
boat tours, *see also* ferries
  Arranmore Island 403
  Ballycastle 584-5
  Belfast 511
  Blackwater Eco Tours 163
  Cliffs of Moher 299
  Clonmacnoise 432
  Cork 208
  Devenish Island 602
  Dingle 244, 246
  Dunmore East 160
  Galway city 323
  Gap of Dunloe 230-1
  Great Blasket 250
  Inchagoill 328
  Killary Harbour 335
  Kilrush 312
  Kinsale 195
  Lough Corrib 323
  Lough Leane 232
  Lough Ree 433
  Lower Lough Erne 602
  New Ross 152
  Shannon-Erne Waterway 446
  Slieve League Cliffs 415
bodhráns 346
Bog of Allen Nature Centre 135
Bogside district 568, 570, 635
Book of Kells 58
book shops 72, 74
books 39
  Angela's Ashes 267
  Guinness Book of Records 147
  McCarthy's Bar 215
  Road to Glenlough, The 419
borders 482
Boyle 445
Boyne Valley Camino 469, **469**
Bray 125-6, 137

breweries
  Boundary Brewery 512
  Dungarvan Brewing Company 162
  Guinness Storehouse 80-1
  Highbank Orchards 179
  Killarney Brewing & Distilling Co 233
  Rising Sons 193
  Treaty City Brewery 267
  Urban Brewing 89
  Wicklow Brewery 124
Brigid of Kildare 136
Brogan Carroll Bothy 374
Brown, Arthur 339, 343, 345
Brú na Bóinne 30, 460-5, 632-3, **461**
bubble domes 617
budgeting 615, 616, 617, 621
Buncrana 412
Bundoran 421-2
Bunratty 304-5
Burren, the 290-6, **291**
bus travel 615
Bushmills 575-7, 593, **576**
business hours 68, 627
busking 299
Butter Market 634

cabin cruises 617
cable cars 216
Caherdaniel 235-6
Cahersiveen 239, 240-1
Cahill, Martin 127
Cahir 285
Callery, Jim 441
camogie 175, 640
camping 206, 400
canal barges 617
candles 178
canoeing, *see* kayaking & canoeing
Cape Clear Island 208-9
car hire 615
car racing 134
Carlingford 471-2, 485
Carlingford Lough 471
Carlow 138-43, 165-70, **140-1**
  accommodation 181
  itineraries 142-3
  navigation 140-1
  travel seasons 142-3
  travel within Carlow 140-1
Carlow town 34, 165-7, **166**
Carrauntoohil 232-3
Carrick-a-Rede 588-9
Carrick-a-Rede Rope Bridge 588-9
Carrickmacross 482-3, 485
Carrick-on-Shannon 445-6, 453
Carrowkeel Megalithic Complex 384

Carrowmore Megalithic Cemetery 383
Cashel 35, 272-6, 285, **273**
Castle Archdale 603, 611
Castle Caldwell Forest 604
Castle Espie Wetland Centre 550
Castle Ward 559
Castlebar 363
Castlegregory 251
Castlepollard 451
castles 16-17
  accommodation 617
  Athlone Castle 428
  Aughnanure Castle 327
  Ballybunion Castle 257
  Barryscourt Castle 198
  Belfast Castle 528
  Belleek Castle 380-1
  Birr Castle 434-5
  Bunratty Castle 304-5
  Cahir Castle 277
  Carlow Castle 166
  Castle Coole 600
  Classiebawn Castle 385-6
  Clifden Castle 341
  Clough Oughter Castle 480
  Doe Castle 408
  Donegal Castle 420-1, 634
  Dublin Castle 55, 60
  Dún na Séad Castle 207
  Dunboy Castle 215
  Dundrum Castle 542
  Dungarvan Castle 162
  Dunluce Castle 580
  Dunsany Castle 477
  Dysert O'Dea Castle 304
  Easkey Castle 381
  Enniscorthy Castle 149
  Enniskillen Castle 598, 600
  Glenveagh Castle 397
  Grace O'Malley's Castle 371
  Hillsborough Castle 545-6
  Johnstown Castle 146-7
  Kearney's Castle 272
  Kilkenny Castle 172
  Kinbane Castle 588
  King John's Castle 264
  Leap Castle 435
  Listowel Castle 257
  Loughmore Castle 280
  Roscommon castle 444
  Ross Castle 229
  Slane Castle 470-1
  Trim Castle 474-5
Castletownbere 215-17, 219
Cathedral Quarter 500-5, 529, **501**
Cavan 455-9, 478-80, **456-7**, **479**
  accommodation 478, 485
  itineraries 458-9
  navigation 456-7
  travel seasons 458-9
  travel within Cavan 456-7
Cavan Burren 484

Cave Hill 528
caves
  Aillwee Cave 290, 292
  Caves of Keash 383-4
  Crag Cave 258
  Doolin Cave 296
  Dunmore Cave 177
  Marble Arch Caves 605-6
  Oweynagat Cave 443
Céide Fields 375, 376, 632
Celbridge 133-4, 137
cemeteries 99, 104, 117, 390, 604
Ceoldán the Stargazer 608, 609
ceramics 178, 272, 346, 604
cheese 41, 504
chess 156
children, travel with, *see* family travel
chocolate 294, 305
chowder 412
CHQ Building 89
churches & cathedrals
  Ardfert Cathedral 256
  Carlow Cathedral 166
  Cathedral of St Peter & St Paul 120
  Cathedral of Sts Mary & Senan 311
  Cathedral of the Most Holy Trinity 157
  Christ Church 70, 72
  Christ Church Cathedral 157
  Corcomroe Abbey 295
  Down Cathedral 547
  Dunlewey Church 402
  Dysert O'Dea Church 304
  Kilmalkedar Church 248
  Reefert Church 120
  Rock of Cashel 274-5
  Saul Church 548
  Selskar Abbey 144
  St Anne's Cathedral 500
  St Anne's Church 194
  St Audoen's Catholic Church 84
  St Audoen's Church of Ireland 84
  St Canice's Cathedral 174
  St Colman's Cathedral 199
  St Declan's Church 164
  St Feichin's Church 450
  St Fin Barre's Cathedral 193
  St Kevin's Kitchen 120
  St Patrick's Cathedral 77-8
  St Patrick's Church of Ireland Cathedral 554
  St Patrick's Roman Catholic Cathedral 554
  St Peter's Church of Ireland 466
  St Peter's Roman Catholic Church 466
  Teampall na Naoimh 326
  Teampall Phádraig 326

cinemas 75, 98, 106, 518
City Centre (Belfast) 492-9, **494**
  accommodation 529
  drinking 494, 498
  food 495, 497
  shopping 495, 499
city halls 63, 279, 493
Claddagh rings 329
Clara Bog Nature Reserve 436
Clare 286-313, **288**
  accommodation 313
  itineraries 289
  navigation 288
  travel seasons 289
  travel within Clare 288
Clare Island 364, 634
Cleggan 343
Clew Bay 371
Clifden 337-42, 353, **338**
Cliffs of Moher 26, 298-9
Clifton House 526
climate 36-7, 622-3
Cloghane 251
Clonakilty 33, 202-4, 219, **203**
Clonmacnoise 35, 430-1, 633
clothes 38
coal mines 447
coasteering 586
Cobh 198-200, 219
coffee 40, 270, 271, 623
Cois na hAbhna 302
Collins, Michael 60, 203, 204
Comber 550-1
Connemara National Park
  330-3, **331**
Connemara Railway 336
Connolly, James 525
Connor Pass 250-1
Conolly, William 133
cooking courses 200
Coomanaspig 237
Cork 183-219, **184-5**
  accommodation 219
  camping 206
  festivals & events 186-7
  food 191
  itineraries 186-7
  navigation 184-5
  travel seasons 186-7
  travel within Cork 184-5, 198
Cork city 33, 188-94, 634, **189**
  accommodation 219
  drinking 191
  festivals and events 191
  food 190, 192
  shopping 193
  travel within Cork city 188

Map Pages **000**

Corlea Trackway 434
Corslieve 372-3
costs 615, 616, 617, 621
country code 627
country houses & manors 16-17
  Adare Manor 269
  Avondale House 123
  Bantry House & Garden
    210-11
  Belvedere House 448-9
  Bishop's Palace 157
  Borris House 169
  Castle Ward 548-9
  Castletown House 133-4
  Curraghmore House &
    Gardens 161
  Daniel O'Connell House –
    Derrynane House 235-6
  Emo Court 438
  Florence Court 606-7
  Fota House, Arboretum &
    Gardens 198
  Kells Bay House & Gardens
    241
  Killarney House 226-7
  Kilruddery House &
    Gardens 126
  Lissadell House 390
  Mount Congreve House &
    Gardens 158
  Mount Juliet 179
  Mount Stewart 550
  Mount Vernon 292
  Muckross House 227, 229
  Powerscourt House 117
  Russborough House 127
  Strokestown Park 439-40
  Tullynally Castle & Gardens
    451
courses 84, 162, 416, 505
Crag Cave 258
credit cards 616
Creevykeel Court Tomb 386
Croagh Patrick 365
Croaghaun Cliffs 371
Crom Estate 607
Cromwell, Oliver 468
Croppies' Acre 97
Crown Entry 498
Crumlin Road Gaol 527
crystal 154, 156
Cuilcagh Lakelands 605-7, 611
culture 636-7
currachs 246, 346
Curragh Racecourse 128-9
Curraghmore 161
currencies 616
Cushendall 591
Cushendun 590-1
Custom House 91
customs 614
cycling 43, 45, 65, 68, *see
  also* greenways, mountain
  biking
  Belfast 520
  Belleek Woods 381

Bog Rd 347, **347**
Burren, the 292
Castle Ward 549
Comber Greenway 512
Derry Urban Greenways 566
Florence Court 607
Gap of Dunloe 230-1, **231**
Glen of Aherlow 283, **283**
Glenveagh National Park
  399-400
Graiguenamanagh 180
Loop Head Heritage Trail
  308-9
Lough Boora Discovery
  Park 436
Mournes, the 541, **541**
Muckross Lake 234, **234**
Newry Canal Towpath 544
North Down Coastal
  Path 515
Sky Road Loop 340-1, **341**
Tory Island 404
tours 65, 68

Dalkey 106-7
Darach the Guardian 608
Dark Hedges 582
dark sky reserves 238-9,
  373-4, 608
Davagh Forest 608-9, 611
Deerpark – Virginia 484
DeLorean DMC 515
Derrigimlagh 343, 345
Derry 560-74, 593, 635,
  562-3
  itineraries 564-5
  navigation 562-3
  travel seasons 564-5
  travel within Derry 562-3
Derry city 29, 566-71, 593,
  567, 569
Derry Girls 566, 568, 569
Devenish Island 602-3
Devil's Bit 278, 280
Diamond Hill 331-2
Dingle 26, 244-7, 259, **245**
dinosaurs 240
discount passes 93, 156, 462
discounts 616
distilleries 83, *see also* whiskey
  Ballykeefe Distillery 179-80
  Blackwater Distillery 163
  Boatyard Distillery 605
  Clonakilty Distillery 204
  Copeland Distillery 547
  Dingle Distillery 247
  Echlinville Distillery 547
  Fore Distillery 451
  Highbank Orchards 179
  Hinch Distillery 547
  Jameson Distillery 97-8
  Jameson Midleton Distillery
    Experience 197

Killarney Brewing & Distilling
  Co 233
Killowen Distillery 547
McConnell's Distillery 528
Old Bushmills Distillery
  575-6
Pearse Lyons Distillery 84
Powerscourt 118
Rebel City Distillery 193
Roe & Co 84-5
Shortcross Distillery 547
Slane Irish Whiskey 471
Teeling 83
Titanic Distillers 506
Tullamore D.E.W. 436
diving & snorkelling 43, 251,
  352, 578
Divis & Black Mountain 525-6
Docklands 100-2, 109, **101**
dolmens 170, 296, 383
  Calf House 479
  Legananny 482-3
dolphins 244, 246, 312
Donegal 393-423, **394**
  accommodation 423
  itineraries 395
  navigation 394
  travel seasons 395
  travel within Donegal 394
Donegal Airport 402
Donegal town 420-1
Donore 134
Doolin 294-6, 299, 313
Doolough Valley 366
Dorinish Island 371
Down 531-52, 559, **532-3**
  accommodation 559
  festivals & events 544
  itineraries 534-5
  navigation 532-3
  travel seasons 534-5
  travel within Down 532-3
Downhill 573-4, 582, 593
Downhill Demesne 573-4
Downpatrick 547-8, 559
Dowth 460-1
drinks 620-1, *see also* coffee,
  tea, whiskey
driving 615
Drogheda 462, 466-70,
  485, **461**
Dromineer 306
Drumcliff 390
drumlins 483, 549
Drummully Salient 482
drums 346
Dublin 31, 48-109, **50-1,
  56-7, 71, 79, 87, 96, 101, 104,
  107**, *see also individual
  neighbourhoods*
  accommodation 109
  Docklands 100-2, 109, **101**
  festivals & events 52, 61,
    64, 69, 82
  food 66
  history 83

itineraries 52-3
LGBTIQ+ travellers 624
navigation 50-1
Northern suburbs 103-5, 109, **104**
Smithfield 95-9, 109, **96**
Southern suburbs 106-8, 109, **107**
Stoneybatter 95-9, 109, **96**
tickets 89
tours 65, 67, 68, 72, 73
travel within Dublin 50-1
Dún an Rí 484
Dún Briste 376
Dún na mBó 374
Dunbrody Famine Ship 634
Duncannon 153
Dundrum 542, 543
Dunfanaghy 409
Dungarvan 33, 162, 164
Dunlewey Church 402
Dunlewey Lough 402
Dunmore Cave 177
Dunmore East 159-60
Dunquin 249-50
Durrow 436
Dursey Island 216
duty-free shopping 614
Dysert O'Dea 304

Easkey 381
East Belfast, see Titanic Quarter & East Belfast
eels 558
ÉIRE' signs 310, 406
electricity 627
Ellis Wood 332
Emerald Park 477
emergency number 627
English Market 192
Ennis 301-3, 313, **302**
Enniscorthy 149
Enniscrone 377-9, 391, **378**
Enniskillen 28, 598-601, 611, **599, 601**
Ennistimon 313
environmental issues 207
Equiano, Olaudah 497
Erris Head 374
etiquette 38, 616
events, see festivals & events

Fahan Beehive Huts 252
Fair Head 590
family travel 43, 136, 511, 551, 618
Fanad Peninsula 408-9
farms
  Broughgammon Farm 586
  Highbank Orchards 179
  Joe's Farm 198

Joyce Country Sheepdogs 335
Killary Sheep Farm 335
King's Yard 284
Muckross Creamery 233
Muckross Traditional Farms 227, 229
Newgrange Farm 462
Rostellan Farm 198
Top of the Rock Pod Páirc 206
Fastnet Rock 209
Fermanagh 594-607, 609, 611, **596**
  itineraries 597
  navigation 596
  travel seasons 597
  travel within Fermanagh 596
ferries 614
  Aran Islands 348
  Arranmore Island 403
  Cape Clear Island 209
  Clare Island 364
  Glengarriff 217
  Kilrush 311
  Portaferry 549-50
  Rosslare Europort 150
  Saltee Ferry 151
  Tory Island 404
  Valentia Island 240
  Whiddy Island 211-12
festivals & events 37, see also film festivals, food festivals, literary festivals, music festivals
  All Together Now 161
  Ballina Salmon Festival 380
  Bealtaine Fire Festival 452
  Calves Week 217
  Cat Laughs Comedy Festival 176
  Clifden Arts Festival 339
  Comedy Festival 64
  Derry Halloween 571
  Féile Lúghnasa 251
  Galway International Arts Festival 324
  Halloween 571
  Harvest Festival 157
  Imagine Arts Festival 157
  IMMA Outdoors 82
  Kilkenny Arts Festival 176
  Lisdoonvarna Matchmaking Festival 293
  Lughnasa 419
  Mayo Dark Sky Festival 374
  National Heritage Week 452
  North West 200 579
  Ould Lammas Fair 584
  Púca Festival 475
  Spraoi 157
  St Patrick's Festival Kilkenny 176
  Summer in the City 157
  Westival 361
  Wexford Fringe Festival 147

Wexford Spiegeltent Festival 147
Winterval 157
Yulefest 176
Fethard 278, 279, 285, **279**
Fethard-on-Sea 153
film festivals 61, 217
film locations
  Bad Sisters 107
  Banshees of Inisherin 370
  Crown, The 385
  Field, The 335
  Game of Thrones 544-5, 549, 582
  Harry Potter & the Half-Blood Prince 299
  Normal People 390
  Quiet Man, The 327, 328
  Spy Who Came in from the Cold, The 97 *Star Wars: The Force Awakens* 240
  Star Wars: The Last Jedi 240, 407
films 39, see also film locations
Fionn's Stone 381
fishing 232, 347, 433, 480, 609
Fitzpatrick, Jim 308
flora 294
food 40-1, 620-1, see also individual locations, food festivals
  courses 505
  family travel 618
  pizza 63
  Sligo 390
  tours 69, 191, 323, 498
food festivals 41
  Baltimore Seafood & Wooden Boat Festival 208
  Blas na Bealtaine 324
  Cork on a Fork Fest 191
  Dingle Food Festival 247
  Eats & Beats 544
  Galway International Oyster & Seafood Festival 324
  Savour Kilkenny 176
  Taste of Dublin 64
  Taste of Wicklow Food Festival 123
  Waterford Festival of Food 162
foraging 123, 162, 236, 586, 605
Fore 450-1
Fore Valley 450
forest parks 484
Fort Dunree 410-11
forts
  Charles Fort 196
  Dún Aonghasa 350
  Dún Chonchúir 352
  Elizabeth Fort 193
  Fort Dunree 410-11
  Grianán of Aileach 410
  McArt's Fort 528
  Navan Fort 555, 633
fossils 240

Foxford Woollen Mill 381
Foynes 270
fraud 619
Friel, Brian 419, 420
fudge 350
Fungie 246

GAA 105, 278, 638-40
Gaeilge language 628-9
Gaelic Athletic Association 105, 278, 638-40
Gaelic football 638, 640
Gaeltacht 629
galleries, see museums & galleries
Galtee Mountains 281-3, **282**
Galtees, the 281-3, **282**
Galtybeg 284
Galtymore 284
Galway 315-53, **316-17**
  accommodation 353
  festivals & events 318-19
  itineraries 318-19
  navigation 316-17
  travel seasons 318-19
  travel within Galway 316-17
Galway city 27, 320-4, 353, **321**
Game of Thrones 544-5, 549, 582
gaols 85, 190, 527
Gap of Dunloe 230-1
Gap of Mamore 412
gardens, see parks & gardens
gay travellers 624
genealogy 472
General Post Office 86, 635
Geokaun 240
geology 296, 483
Georgian architecture
  Bantry 210
  Belfast 526, 528
  Belvedere House 448-9
  Carrickmacross 482
  Celbridge 133-4
  Dublin 55, 61, 63, 66, 90-1, 99
  Laois 436
  Limerick town 267
  Listowel 257
  Powerscourt Estate 117
  Strokestown 439-40
  Waterford city 157-8
  Westport 360
Georgian Dublin 54-69, **56-7**
  accommodation 109
  drinking 62, 64, 65, 66, 67, 69
  food 54, 60, 62, 67, 68
  shopping 66
  travel within Georgian Dublin 54
ghost towns 370, 419
giants 618
Giant's Causeway 29, 576, 577, 581

649

Giants of the Sperrins 608
Gillespie, Christy 419
glamping 617
Glassillaun 336
glassware 154, 156, 178
Glen of Aherlow 281-4, 285, **282**
Glenarm 591
Glencolmcille 416
Glendalough 31, 119-21
Glengarriff 217, 219
Glenties 419
Glenveagh National Park 28, 396-400, 423, **397**
Gobbins 589
Goldsmith, Oliver 438
golf 42
  Adare Manor Golf Club 269
  Ballybunion Golf Club 257
  Ballycastle Golf Club 586
  Ballyliffin Golf Club 411-12
  Carton House 134
  Castle Course 300
  Golf Course at Adare Manor 269
  Greencastle Golf Club 412
  Lahinch Golf Club 297, 300
  Old Course 300
  Old Head Golf Links 197
  Open Championship 579
  Powerscourt Golf Club 118
  Rosslare Golf Club 150
  Royal Portrush Golf Club 579-80
  Waterville Golf Links 236
Gonne, Maud 642
Gortin Glen 607-8, 611
Gortin Glen Forest Park 607-8
Gortmore 346
Grace O'Malley 634
Graiguenamanagh 180
Grand Canal 447
Grand Opera House 495
Grange stone circle 269
Great Blasket 249-50
Great Famine
  Carrickmacross 482-3
  Doolough Valley memorial cross 366
  Dunbrody Famine Ship 152, 634
  Famine sculpture 90
  Famine Summer School 441
  Jeanie Johnston 89, 441
  National Famine Memorial 365

National Famine Museum 440-1
National Famine Way 441
Skibbereen 206
Skibbereen Heritage Centre 205
Great Sugarloaf 116
greenways 160
  Comber Greenway 512
  Connemara Greenway 336
  Derry Urban Greenways 566
  Great Western Greenway 364-5
  Listowel to Limerick Greenway 258
  South East Greenway 152, 160
  Tralee to Fenit Greenway 258
  Waterford Greenway 160
Greyabbey 550
Greystones 126
Grianán of Aileach 410
Guevara, Che 308
Guildhall 566, 568
Guinness 80-1
Guinness, Arthur 130
Guinness Book of Records 147
Guinness Storehouse 77, 80-1

Halloween 571
Ha'penny Bridge 73
Harp Festival 525
health 619
Heaney, Seamus 572, 573
Hederman Smoke House 198
Hellelil & Hildebrand, the Meeting on the Turret Stairs 55
Henrietta St 91
highlights 6-7, 8-21
hiking 18-19, 42-3, 45, *see also* walking, walking tours
  Achill Island 370-1
  Bangor Trail 373
  Benbaun 333
  Black Hill 280
  Boyne Valley Camino 469, **469**
  Burren National Park 293-4
  Camaderry Mountain 120
  Carrauntoohil 232-3
  Cavan Way 479-80
  Cave Hill 528
  Caves of Kesh 384
  Connemara National Park 331-2
  Copper Mine Trail 216-17
  Croagh Patrick 365
  Cuilcagh Boardwalk Trail 606
  Devil's Bit 278, 280
  Divis & Black Mountain 525-6
  Dursey Island Loop 216
  Galtees, the 284

Glenveagh National Park 398-9
Glounaclohy Walk 206
Inisheer 351, **351**
Knocknarea Cairn 382-3
Lake Muskry 282
Loop Head Lighthouse 310
Malin Head Trail 405-6
Miners' Way 118
Miners Way & Historical Trail 447
Mt Brandon 249
Mt Errigal 401-2
National Famine Way 441
Omey Island 344, **344**
Slieve Donard 539-40
Slieve League Cliffs 414-15
Spinc 120
St Patrick's Way 548
Wicklow Mountains 116-17, 118
Wicklow Way 117
Wild Nephin National Park 373
Wormhole 350
Hill of Slane 470
Hill of Tara 476-7
Hill of Uisneach 451-2
Hillsborough 545-6, 547, 559
Hillsborough Castle 546
history 8-9, 632-5
  1798 rebellion 150
  1916 Easter Rising 85, 86, 94, 99
  Aran Islands 352
  Battle of the Boyne 467
  Belfast 502
  borders 482
  Caldragh Cemetery 604
  Cashel 276
  Cavan 480
  Cave Hill 528
  Clonmacnoise 431
  Cobh 199
  Cork city 190
  Derry 570
  Drogheda 468
  Dungarvan Castle 162
  Forty Foot 107
  General Post Office 86
  Hillsborough Castle 546
  harp music 525
  independence 97
  Inisfallen 232
  Killarney town 229
  Kingdom of Mourne 539
  Liberties, the 84
  Limerick city 266
  Powerscourt Estate 117
  punk rock 502
  Tara 477
  Temple Bar 74
  Trinity College Dublin 64
  Troubles, the 525, 570, 598, 635
  whiskey 83
  WWII 310

HMS *Caroline* 511
Holy Island 305
Holywood 513-15, 529, **514**
Hook Head 153
hookers 326
Horn Head 409
horse racing 128-9, 135, 161, 324
horse riding 43, 235, 345-6
horse studs 131-1, 278
horse-drawn buggies 227
horses 278
housing crisis 617
Howard-Bury, Charles Kenneth 449
Howth 105
hurling 175, 638
hydrobikes 511, 605

ice hockey 511
Ilnacullin – Garinish Island 217
Inchagoill 326, 328
Inchcleraun 433
Inisfallen 232
Inisheer 351, **351**
Inishmaan 352
Inishmore 350, 352
Inishowen Peninsula 28
Inish Rath 607
Inishtrahull 412-13
Inistioge 178-9
Inniskeen 481-2
insurances 619
Irish coffee 270, 271, 436
Irish language 628-9
Islandmagee 589
itineraries 26-35, **27**, **29**, **31**, **32-3**, **35**, *see also individual locations*

jails 85, 190, 527
Jameson Distillery 97-8
jaunting cars 227
Jeanie Johnston 89-90, 441
jewellers 175
John Mulligan's 62
Joyce, James 62, 90, 108, 634-5
Joy's Entry 498

karst 296
Kavanagh, Patrick 482
kayaking & canoeing 42, *see also* watersports
  Barrow Way 169
  Castle Archdale 603
  Dingle 246
  Dublin 100-1
  Limerick city 266

Lough Hyne 206
Lough Leane 229
Lough Oughter 480
Trim 475
Upper Lough Erne 607
Kenmare 235, 238
Kennedy, Patrick 152
Kerry 220-59, **222-3**
 accommodation 259
 festivals & events 224-5
 itineraries 224-5
 navigation 222-3
 travel seasons 224-5
 travel within 222-3
Kilbroney Park 543
Kildare 34, 111-13, 128-37, **112**, **129**
 accommodation 137
 itineraries 113
 navigation 112
 travel seasons 113
 travel within Kildare 112
Kildare town 137
Kilfenora 313
Kilkee 307, 308, 309, 313
Kilkenny 138-43, 171-80, **140-1**
 accommodation 181
 itineraries 142-3
 navigation 140-1
 travel seasons 142-3
 travel within Kilkenny 140-1
Kilkenny Castle 172
Kilkenny city 34, 171-6, 181, **173**
Killarney National Park 226-34, **228**
Killarney town 226-33, 259, **228**
 drinking 233
 festivals & events 233
 food 227, 228
 shopping 227
 travel within Killarney town 226
Killary Harbour 335
Killinthomas Wood 131-2
Killykeen 484
Killykeen Forest Park 480
Kilmacthomas 164
Kilmainham 77-85, **79**
 accommodation 109
 drinking 82
 food 78, 83
 shopping 78
 travel around Kilmainham 77
Kilmore Quay 32, 151-2
Kilrush 311-12
Kinbane Head 588
King family 445
Kingdom of Mourne 539
Kings of Tory Island 404
Kinsale 195-7, 219
Kinvara 328-9, 353
knit garments 350, 352, 381
Knocknarea Cairn 382-3
Knowth 463-5
Kylemore 334-5
Kylemore Abbey 334, 335
Kylemore Castle 335

lacemaking 482
Lagan Towpath 520-1
Lahinch 297, 300, 313
Lake Muskry 282
Lanesborough 433-4
languages 39, 479, 628-9
Laois, see Midlands, the
Larrybane Quarry 582
Ledwidge, Francis 468
Leenane 335, 353
Legananny 542-3
legends 577
Leitrim, see Midlands, the
Lennon, John 371
leprechauns 93
Letterfrack 332, 353
Lewis, CS 543
LGBTIQ+ travellers 624
Liberties, the 77-85, **79**
 accommodation 109
 drinking 81, 82
 food 78, 83
 history 84
 shopping 78, 83
 travel within the Liberties 77
libraries 58-9, 66, 78, 497, 554
Liffey Bridge 73
lighthouses
 accommodation 617
 Blackhead Lighthouse 592
 Blacksod Lighthouse 375
 Dunmore East 159
 Fanad Lighthouse 408
 Hook Head 153
 Inishtrahull 413
 Loop Head Lighthouse 309-10
 Poolbeg Lighthouse 101
 Rathlin Island 588
 Valentia Island Lighthouse 240
Limerick 261-71, 285, **262**
 itineraries 263
 navigation 262
 travel seasons 263
 travel within Limerick 262
Limerick city 35, 264-7, 285, **265**
Linen Hall Library 497
Liscannor 313
Lisdoonvarna 293
Lismore 163, 164
Lissadell 390
Listowel 257-8
literary festivals
 Belfast Book Festival 518
 Cúirt International Festival of Literature 324
 Dublin International Literature Festival 61
 Kavanagh Weekend 482
 Listowel Literary Festival 258

Town of Books 180
West Cork Literary Festival 217
literary museums
 Chester Beatty 60
 Francis Ledwidge Museum 468
 James Joyce Centre 90
 Joyce Tower Museum 108
 Kerry Writers' Museum 257
 Museum of Literature Ireland 61-2
 Oscar Wilde House 63
literature 20, see also literary festivals, individual writers
 Dublin Literary Pub Crawl 64-5
 museums 61-2, 63, 257-8
Little Skellig 243
live music 73, 82, 470-1, 504, 518, see also music, traditional music
Londonderry, see Derry city
Longford, see Midlands, the
Loop Head Peninsula 307-10, 313, **309**
Lough Beg 572-3
Lough Corrib 323
Lough Curra 284
Lough Derg 306, 313, **306**
Lough Erne 603
Lough Gur 269
Lough Hyne 205-6
Lough Key Forest Park 445
Lough Leane 229, 232
Lough Murree 292
Lough Navar Forest 611
Lough Navar Forest Park 604
Lough Neagh 557, 558
Lough Oughter 480
Lough Ree 433, 453
Lough Shark 544
Lough Tay 116
Loughcrew 471
Louisburgh 364
Louth 455-9, 462, 466-70, 471-2, 485, **456-7**
 accommodation 485
 itineraries 458-9
 navigation 456-7
 travel seasons 458-9
 travel within Louth 456-7
Lower Lough Erne 602, 603
Lullymore 135-6
Lullymore Heritage & Discovery Park 136

MacGill Summer School 419
Mahon family 440
Malin Head 405-9, 423, **407**
mansions, see country houses & manors
Marconi, Guglielmo 343

marine environment 236
markets
 Ardmore 164
 Bantry 211
 Belfast 499
 Boyle 445
 Castletownbere 215
 Clifden 337-8
 Clonakilty 202
 Cobh 198
 Cork 191, 192
 Dublin 73, 83, 85, 91, 92
 Dungarvan 162, 164
 Galway city 324
 Howth 105
 Kilkee 309
 Kilmacthomas 164
 Kinsale 198
 Limerick 266
 Lismore 164
 Midleton 198
 Rathdrum 123
 Stradbally 164
matchmaking 293
Maynooth 137
Mayo 354-76, 391, **356-7**
 accommodation 391
 festivals & events 359
 itineraries 358-9
 navigation 356-7
 travel seasons 358-9
 travel within Mayo 356-7
McCool, Finn 577
McCourt, Frank 267
McCracken, Mary Ann 526
Meath 455-65, 470-1, 473-7, **456-7**
 accommodation 485
 itineraries 458-9
 navigation 456-7
 travel seasons 458-9
 travel within Meath 456-7
midges 619
Midlands, the 424-53, **426**
 accommodation 453
 itineraries 427
 navigation 426
 travel seasons 427
 travel within the Midlands 426
Midleton 197, 219
Military Road 114-15
Minaun Heights 371
Mizen Head 214-15
mobile phones 627
Moll's Gap 238
Monaghan 455-9, 481-4, **456-7**
 accommodation 485
 itineraries 458-9
 navigation 456-7
 travel seasons 458-9
 travel within Monaghan 456-7
Monaghan town 483-4, 485
Monasterboice 470

monastic sites
- Augustinian Priory 268
- Black Abbey 174
- Boyle Abbey 445
- Clonmacnoise 430-1, 633
- Duiske Abbey 180
- Dunbrody Abbey 153
- Ennis Friary 301-2
- Glendalough 119-21
- Grey Abbey 550
- Holy Island 305
- Hore Abbey 275
- Inch Abbey 547-8
- Jerpoint Abbey 178
- Kells Priory 178
- Kylemore Abbey 334, 335
- Monasterboice 468, 470
- Moyne Abbey 383
- Mt Melleray Abbey 163
- Old Mellifont Abbey 468
- Our Lady's Island 150
- Skellig Michael 243
- Slane Abbey 470
- Sligo Abbey 387
- St Declan's Monastery 164
- St Dominick's Priory 273
- St Mary's Abbey 603
- St Mullins Monastery 170
- Tintern Abbey 153
- Toureen Peakaun 284

Mondello Park 134
money 616
monuments & memorials 124, 129-30, 340, 365, 366, 570
Moore, Thomas 124
Morrison, Van 512
motorcycle racing 579
Mount Stewart 550
mountain biking 271, 435, 543, 608-9, *see also* cycling
mountain climbing 43
Mountbatten, Lord Louis 386
Mountmellick 436
Mountshannon 305
Mourne 539
Mourne Mountains 559
Mourne Wall 543
Mt Brandon 249
Mt Croaghaun 371
Mt Errigal 401-2
Mt Slievemore 370-1
Muckross Lake 234, **234**
Mullaghmore 293, 385-6, 391, **386**
Mullaghmore Head 385
Mullet Peninsula 374

Munster 276
murals 502, 525, 601, *see also* street art
Murrisk 365
museums & galleries 21, *see also* art museums, literary museums
- 14 Henrietta Street 90-1
- Allihies Copper Mine Museum 216
- Carlow County Museum 166
- Cavan County Museum 478
- Clonakilty Black Pudding Visitor Centre 204
- Cobh Heritage Centre: The Queenstown Story 199
- Connemara Heritage & History Centre 334
- Cork Butter Museum 194
- County Carlow Military Museum 167
- DNA Museum 568
- Down County Museum 547
- Eileen Hickey Irish Republican History Museum 522
- Enniskillen Castle Museums 598, 600
- EPIC The Irish Emigration Museum 88-9
- Foynes Flying Boat Museum 270
- GAA Museum 105
- Galway City Museum 323-4
- GPO Witness History 86
- Horse Country Experience 278
- Hunt Museum 265
- Irish Agricultural Museum 146
- Irish Horse Museum 131
- Irish Jewish Museum 99
- Irish Museum of Time 156
- Irish National Heritage Park 147-8
- Irish Silver Museum 156
- Irish Wake Museum 156
- Irish Whiskey Museum 65
- James Connolly Experience 525
- Jameson Midleton Distillery Experience 197
- Kerry Bog Village 239
- Kerry County Museum 253-4
- Kilmainham Gaol 85
- King House 445
- Lár na Páirce Museum 278
- Little Museum of Dublin 55
- Medieval Mile Museum 171
- Medieval Museum 156
- Michael Collins Centre 203
- Michael Collins House 203
- Millmount Museum 466
- Monaghan County Museum 483-4
- Músaem Chorca Dhuibhne – West Kerry Museum 252

- Museum of Free Derry 568, 570
- Museum of Natural History 62
- Museum of Style Icons 132
- Nano Nagle Place 194
- National 1798 Rebellion Centre 149
- National Design & Craft Gallery 175
- National Leprechaun Museum 93
- National Museum of Ireland – Archaeology 61
- National Museum of Ireland – Country Life 363
- National Museum of Ireland – Decorative Arts & History 95, 97
- National Print Museum 102
- North Down Museum 551
- Oh Yeah Music Centre 502, 504
- Old Head Signal Tower 196-7
- Peacemakers Museum 570
- Photo Museum Ireland 74
- Project Arts Centre 73-4
- Quakers in Ireland 134
- Roscommon County Museum 444
- Station House Museum 338-9
- Titanic Belfast 508-9
- Tower Museum 568
- Ulster Museum 519
- Ulster Transport Museum 515
- Valentia Island Heritage Centre 240
- Valentia Transatlantic Cable Station 240

music 39, 100, 101
music festivals
- Bluegrass Omagh 610
- Blues on the Bay 544
- Clonakilty International Guitar Festival 203
- Cork city 191
- Cork Jazz Festival 37
- Doolin FolkFest 294
- Dunmore East Bluegrass Festival 160
- Eats & Beats 544
- Ennis Trad Festival 303
- Fiddler's Green Festival 544
- Fleadh Nua 37, 302
- Forbidden Fruit 61
- Harvest Time Blues Festival 484
- Jim Dowling Uilleann Pipe & Trad Festival 217
- Kilkenny Roots Festival 176
- Kilkenny Tradfest 176
- West Cork Chamber Music Festival 217
- Wexford Festival Opera 147

Nancy's Barn 412
naomhóg 246
Narin 420
national parks & nature reserves 44
- Ards Forest Park 408-9
- Ballyteigue Burrow Nature Reserve 151
- Burren National Park 290, 293-4
- Clara Bog Nature Reserve 436
- Connemara National Park 330-3
- Glenveagh National Park 28
- Killarney National Park 226-34, 645, **228**
- Knockomagh Wood Nature Reserve 206
- Lough Beg Nature Reserve 572-3
- Murlough National Nature Reserve 542
- Oxford Island 557
- Páirc Náisiúnta na Mara, Ciarraí 250
- Slieve Bloom Nature Reserve 435
- Wicklow Mountains National Park 114-21, **115**
- Wild Nephin National Park 372-4

nature 10-11
New Ross 152
Newbridge 132
Newcastle 30, 536-41, 559, **537**
Newgrange 463-5, 467
Newport 364-5
Newry 544, 546
North Belfast, *see* West & North Belfast
North City Centre 86-94
- accommodation 109
- drinking 89, 92-3
- food 88, 91
- shopping 94
- travel within North City Centre 86
northern lights 406-7
Northern Suburbs (Dublin) 103-5, 109, **104**
Nowanois the Storyteller 608
nuns 335

obelisks 326, 337
O'Brien, Edna 305
O'Connell, Daniel 237
O'Connell St (Dublin) 86-94
- accommodation 109
- drinking 92, 93

Map Pages **000**

food 88, 91
safe travel 88
shopping 94
travel within O'Connell St 86
O'Connor, Sinéad 125
Offaly, see Midlands, the
O'Hara, Maureen 270
Oileán Acaill, see Achill Island
Old Head Signal Tower 196-7
Omagh 611
O'Malley, Grace 364, 371
Omey Island 344, **344**
open-air museums 276, 305, 416, 513, 610
opening hours 627
O'Sullivan, Maureen 445
Oughterard 326, 327, 328
Our Lady's Island 150
Oxford Island 557

Páirc Náisiúnta na Mara, Ciarraí 250
parks & gardens 16
 Altamont Gardens 168
 Bangor Castle Walled Garden 551
 Bantry House & Garden 210-11
 Belvedere House 449
 Botanic Gardens (Belfast) 516, 518
 Crom Estate 607
 Delta Sensory Gardens 168, 622
 Duckett's Grove 168
 Fota House, Arboretum & Gardens 198
 Garden of Remembrance 94
 Glenveagh Castle 398
 Hardymount Gardens 168
 Holywood Seapark 515
 Huntington Castle & Gardens 169
 Iveagh Gardens 64
 Japanese Gardens 131
 Johnstown Castle Gardens 147
 Kells Bay House & Gardens 241
 Kilbroney Park 543
 Killiney Hill Park 107
 Kilmacurragh Botanic Gardens 125
 Mount Usher Gardens 125
 Mourne Park 544
 National Botanic Gardens 104-5
 Parnell National Memorial Park 124
 Phoenix Park 103-4
 Powerscourt Estate 117
 Rothe House & Garden 174
 St Stephen's Green 55

Strokestown Park 439-40
Tollymore Forest Park 539
Tullynally Castle & Gardens 451
Vandeleur Walled Garden 311-12
War Memorial Gardens 83
Woodstock Gardens & Arboretum 179
Parnell, Charles Stewart 123
passage tombs
 Brú na Bóinne 460, 463-5, 632-3
 Calf House Dolmen 479
 Carrowkeel Megalithic Complex 384
 Carrowmore Megalithic Cemetery 383
 Dowth 460-1
 Hill of Tara 476-7
 Knowth 463-4
 Legananny Dolmen 542-3
 Loughcrew Megalithic Cemetery 471
 Newgrange 463-5
 Ring of Gullion 558
 Slieve Donard 540
 Sligo 382
 Tullygobban 479
Peace Bridge 570-1
Peace Line 524
Pearse, Pádraig/Patrick 346
people 636-7
People's Gallery 570
perfumeries 294
photography 74, 295
picnicking 550, 621
pilates 505
pitch & putt courses 379
pizza 63
planning 38-9, 66
podcasts 39
police 619
ponies 339, 345-6
population 636-7
Portaferry 549-50, 559
portal tombs, see passage tombs
Portarlington 436
Portlaoise 438
Portnoo 420
Portrush 579-80, 593
Portstewart 578-9, 593
Portview Trade Centre 511-12
Pottinger's Entry 498
Powerscourt Estate 31, 117-18
prehistoric sites, see also passage tombs
 Aran Islands 352
 Beaghmore Stone Circles 608
 Brú na Bóinne 460-5, 632-3
 Carrowkeel Megalithic Complex 384
 Carrowmore Megalithic Cemetery 383

Cavan Burren Park 478-9
Céide Fields 375, 376, 632
Creevykeel Court Tomb 386
Dunbeg Fort 252
Giant's Ring 518, 520
Hill of Tara 476-7
Knowth 463-5
Loughcrew Megalithic Cemetery 471
Newgrange 463-5
Poulnabrone Dolmen 295, 296
Rath of Mullaghmast 134-5
Rathcroghan 442-3
Rathcroghan Mound 443
Slieve Gullion Forest Park 558
Tullygobban 479
Pride 61, 191, 624
Priest's Leap 212-13
prisons 85, 190, 527
pub crawls 64, 73, 320
public holidays 627
pubs & bars 12-13, 68, 620
 Cobblestone 99
 Crown Liquor Saloon 492
 De Barra's 202
 Farren's Bar 407
 Hacienda 92-3
 Hackett's Bar 214
 Harbour Bar 126
 Jim O' the Mills 280
 John Mulligan's 62
 Kytelers Inn 174
 MacCarthy's Bar 215
 Matt Molloy's 360
 McCarthy's 278
 Mick Doyle's 180
 O'Connor's Famous Pub 325-6
 Power's Bar 159
 Sean's Bar 429, 432
 Strand Inn 159
 Temple Bar 73
 Whelan's 65
punk rock 502

Queen Maeve 382, 444
Queen's Quarter & South Belfast 516-21, **517**, **520**
Quiet Man Bridge 327
Quiet Man, The 327, 328

R

R2D2 road sign 407
Ramelton 408
Rath of Mullaghmast 134-5
Rathcroghan 442-3
Rathcroghan Mound 443
Rathdrum 123-5, 137
Rathlin Island 587-8, 593

Rathlin West Light Seabird Centre 587
red deer 399, 400, 644-5
Renvyle 336
responsible travel 622-3
rewilding 622
Ring of Gullion 557-8, 559
Ring of Kerry 236, 237, 238-9, 241, **239**
ringforts 241, 443
River Barrow 169-70
River Boyne 464, 475
River Lagan 520-1
River Shannon 432, 480
road trips
 Antrim Glens 590-1, **591**
 Carlow Garden Trail 168
 Dingle Peninsula 252, **252**
 Doolough Valley 366
 Fanad Peninsula 408-9, **409**
 Gap of Mamore 412
 Glengesh Pass 418
 Lough Corrib 327, **327**
 Lough Derg 306, **306**
 Military Road 114-15
 Ring of Kerry 238-9, **239**
 Sheep's Head Peninsula 218, **218**
 Skellig Ring 236-7
 Sligo Food Trail 390
 St Patrick's Trail 548
 Waterford 163, **163**
 Wexford 153, **153**
 Wild Atlantic Way 626
 Yeats Trail 389
Robinson, Tim 345
rock climbing 402, 586
Rock of Cashel 274-5
Rock of Dunamase 438
Rooney, Sally 59
rope courses 511
Roscommon, see Midlands, the
Roscommon town 444
Rosslare 150
Rossmore 484
Rossnowlagh 422
Rostrevor 543-4, 544, 545, 559
Roundstone 346, 353
rowing 246
Royal Canal 447
rugby 267
rural roads 615

S

safe travel 88, 615, 619
salmon 323, 380
Salt Lake 342
Saltee Islands 151-2
Salthill 325-6
Samhain 443
saunas 296, 364, 552, 574, 578, 605
Scattery Island 311

653

Scéal 126
Schull 214
sculptures
 Big Fish 503
 Dragon Slayer Sword 156
 Eel Retreat 558
 Famine 90
 Giants of the Sperrins 608
 National Famine Memorial 365
 Newcastle 536, 538
 Permanent Present, The 502
 Spire 93
 Strongbow & Aoife 157
 Turfman The 572
seals 622
seaweed 41, 236
seaweed baths 150, 164, 295, 378-9, 586
Shandon 194
Shannon 432, 480
Shannon Pot 480
Shannonbridge fortifications 437, **437**
Shannon-Erne Waterway 445
Share Discovery Village 605, 607
sheepdogs 389
Sheep's Head Peninsula 218, **218**
Shergar 131
silverware 69, 132, 156
SIM cards 614
skateboarding 505
Skellig Islands 240, 242-3
Skellig Michael 240, 242-3
Skellig Ring 236-7
Skibbereen 205-6, 219
Slane 470-1, 485
Slane Castle 470-1
Slemish Mountain 592, 633
Sliabh Liag, see Slieve League Cliffs
Slieve Bloom Nature Reserve 435
Slieve Donard 539-40
Slieve Donard Resort & Spa 536
Slieve Gullion Forest Park 557-8
Slieve League Cliffs 27, 414-16, 423, **415**
Slieve Patrick 548
Slieve Roe 293
Slievemore 370
Sligo 354-9, 377-91, **356-7**
 accommodation 391
 itineraries 358-9

navigation 356-7
travel seasons 358-9
travel within Sligo 356-7
Sligo town 387-8
Smithfield 95-9, 109, **96**
smoked salmon 198, 293, 345
Sneem 238
snorkelling 342, see also diving & snorkelling
Solidarity Wall 525
solstice 464
sound therapy 505
South Belfast, see Queen's Quarter & South Belfast
Southern Suburbs 106-8, 109, **107**
Spanish Arch 323
spas 164, 295-6, 378-9, 605
speed limits 615
Spike Island 199-200
Spire 93
Split Rock 381
sports venues
 Aviva Stadium 101
 Croke Park Stadium 105
 Nowlan Park 175
 Odyssey Complex 511
 Semple Stadium 278
 SSE Arena 511
 Thomond Park Stadium 267
SS Nomadic 509
stand-up paddleboarding 43, 246, 574, 607
stargazing 373, 608
St Brendan 257
St Brigid 136
St Ciarán 430, 431
St George's Market 499
St Mullins 169-70
St Patrick 470, 471, 547, 548, 592
St Patrick's Cathedral 77-8
St Patrick's Festival 37, 61, 176, 233, 544
stone circles 209, 383
Stoneybatter 95-9, 109, **96**
Stormont 511, 635
storytelling 209, 505
stout 40
Stradbally 164
Straffan 137
Strandhill 382-3
Strangford 548-9, 559
Strangford Lough 549, 550-1, 559
street art 75, 98, 156, 497-8
Strokestown 439-41, 453, **440**
Strongbow 72
Struell Wells 548
surfing 43, 45
 Achill Island 369-70
 Aileen's 300
 Benone 574
 Bundoran 421
 Easkey 381
 Enniscrone 377, 379
 Inchydoney 204

Lahinch 300
Louisburgh 364
Portrush 579
Portstewart 578
Rossnowlagh Beach 422
Strandhill 382
Tramore 160
sustainable travel 622-3
Sweny's Pharmacy 62, 634-5
swimming
 Ballycastle 586
 Belmullet 374
 Forty Foot 107
 Kilkee 308
 safety flags 619
 Salt Lake 342
 Vico Bathing Place 107
Swiss Cottage 277
Synge, John Millington 352

Tara 476-7
taxes 616
tea 40
television 39
Temple Bar (area) 70-6, **71**
 accommodation 76, 109
 drinking 74
 food 72
 shopping 72, 74, 75
 travel within Temple Bar 70
Temple Bar (pub) 73
tetrapods 240
theatres
 Belfast 495, 502, 518
 Carlow town 167
 Derry city 571
 Dublin 74, 92, 101
 Sligo town 388
 Tralee 254
 Wexford town 147
theft 619
Thomastown 178
Thomond kingdom 301-2
Thurles 278, 280
tickets 89
Timahoe 436
time zones 627
Tipperary 261-3, 272-85, **262**
 itineraries 263
 navigation 262
 travel seasons 263
 travel within Tipperary 262
tipping 616
Titanic 199, 500, 508-9
Titanic Belfast 508-9
Titanic Quarter & East Belfast 506-12, **507**
 accommodation 529
 drinking 511
 food 512
 tours 510
 travel within Titanic Quarter & East Belfast 506

toll roads 615
Tollymore Forest Park 539
Tory Island 404
tours, see also cycling, road trips, walking tours
 Bantry 216
 Belfast 498, 503, 510, **503, 510**
 Belfast murals 525
 Brú na Bóinne 460
 Dublin Musical Pub Crawl 73
 food 69, 323, 498
 Kilkenny city 174
 marine environment 236
town halls 63, 279, 493
traditional music 12-13, see also music festivals
 Ardara 418
 Belfast 504
 Brú Ború Heritage Centre 276
 Clonakilty 202
 Doolin 295
 Dublin 61
 Dungarvan 164
 Ennis 302
 Galway 320
 Rostrevor 544
 Westport 360-1
train travel 158, 336, 548, 576, 615
Tralee 253-5, 259, **254**
Tralee Bay Wetlands 254
Tramore 160-1
transatlantic flight 343
travel cards 615
travel seasons 36-7
travel to/from Ireland 614
travel within Ireland 615
tree houses 617
treetop walks 43, 122-3, 445
Trim 473-5, 485, **474**
Trim Castle 474-5
Trinity College (Dublin) 54-69, **56-7**
 accommodation 109
 drinking 62, 64, 65, 66, 67, 69
 food 54, 60, 62, 67, 68
 shopping 66
 travel within Trinity College area 54
Trinity College Dublin 58-9, 64
Troubles, the 525, 570, 598, 635
Tullamore 436
Tullynally Castle & Gardens 451
Tulsk 442-3
tweed 417-18
Twelve Bens 333
Twelve Pins 333
Tyrone 594-7, 605, 607-11, **596**
 itineraries 597
 navigation 596
 travel seasons 597
 travel within Tyrone 596

U

Ulster American Folk Park 610
Ulster Museum 519
Ulysses 39, 61, 90, 108, 634-5
UNESCO sites
 Brú na Bóinne 460-5
 Burren, the 293
 Cliffs of Moher 293
 Copper Coast 161
 Cuilcagh Lakelands 607
 Skellig Michael 242-3
 Sligo 382
universities 58-9, 64, 190-1, 518
Upper Lough Erne 606, 607, 611
Upperchurch 280
US travellers 614

V

Vale of Avoca 125
Valentia Island 237, 240
Vandeleur family 312
Ventry 248
Vikings 65, 75-6, 156, 633
Vinegar Hill 149

W

walking 42-3, 45, see also greenways, hiking, walking tours
 Ardmore 164
 Arranmore Island 402-3
 Aughris Head 383
 Ballybunion 257
 Belleek Woods 381
 Benbulben Loop 389
 Benone 574
 Binevenagh 573
 Bothy Loop 373
 Boyne Valley Camino 469, **469**
 Bray cliff walk 125
 Burren, the 292
 Calf House Dolmen Trail 479
 Castle Ward 549
 Cliffs of Moher 299
 Connemara National Park 330
 Derry Urban Greenways 566
 Dunmore East Coastal Walk 160
 Eamonn an Chnoic (Ned of the Hill) Loop 280
 Enniscrone 377-8
 Erris Head Loop 374
 Fionn's Giant Adventure 557
 Flaggy Shore Loop 292
 Glenveagh National Park 398-9
 Gortin Glen Forest Park 607-8
 Graiguenamanagh 180
 Helvick Head Walking Trail 164
 Howth 105
 Inishmaan 352
 Inniskeen 482
 Kavanagh Trail 482
 Kerry Cliffs 237
 Kilbroney Park 543
 Kilkee Cliff Walk 307-8
 Killinthomas Wood 131-2
 Knockomagh Wood Nature Reserve 206
 Lagan Towpath 520-1
 Letterkeen Loop 373
 Lough Boora Discovery Park 436
 Lough Gur 269
 Lough Key Forest Park 445
 Malin Head Trail 405-6
 Mourne Park 544
 Mullaghmore Head Loop 385
 Nore Linear Park 176
 Nore Valley Walk 176, 178
 North Down Coastal Path 552
 Raghly Cliff Walk 383
 Rathlin Island 588
 Roguey Cliff Walk 422
 Saints Road 248
 Scilly Walk 196
 Slieve Bloom Nature Reserve 435
 St Fechin's Way 451
 St Patrick's Way 548
 Tollymore Forest Park 539
 Tory Island 404
 tours 69, 90
 Upper Lake 121
 Whiddy Island Loop Walk 211
 Wild Nephin National Park 372-3
walking tours
 Achill Island 369
 Armagh city 556, **556**
 Belfast 496, **496**
 Carrickmacross 482
 Causeway Coast Way 583, **583**
 Derry city 569, **569**
 Dublin 65, 69, 97
 Enniskillen 601, **601**
 Fethard 279, **279**
 Galway 322, **322**
 Gobbins 589
 Inisheer 351, **351**
 Kinsale 195
 Limerick city 267
 Muckross Lake 234, **234**
 Shannonbridge fortifications 437, **437**
 Titanic Quarter 510, **510**
 West Belfast 524, **524**
 Westport 362, **362**
 Wexford 146
 Youghal 201, **201**
water parks 160, 605
waterfalls 116, 117-18, 163, 347, 418
Waterford 138-43, 154-64, **140-1**
 accommodation 181
 itineraries 142-3
 navigation 140-1
 travel seasons 142-3
 travel within Waterford 140-1
Waterford city 32, 154-8, 181, 633, **155**
Waterford Crystal 154, 156
watersports
 Achill Island 369-70
 Ardmore 164
 Arranmore Island 403
 Castlegregory 251
 Dingle 246
 Dunmore East 160
 Graiguenamanagh 180
Waterville 236-7, 239
weather 36-7, see also individual counties
weaving 125, 417
Wellesley, Arthur 475
West & North Belfast 522-8, **523**
 food 525, 526
 tours 524, **524**
West Clare Railway 303
Westmeath, see Midlands, the
Westport 27, 360-2, 391, **361**
wetlands 254
Wexford 138-81, **140-1**
 accommodation 181
 itineraries 142-3
 navigation 140-1
 travel seasons 142-3
 travel within Wexford 140-1
Wexford town 32, 144-8, 181, **145**
Whiddy Island 211-12
whiskey 40, 83, 197, see also distilleries
 Irish Whiskey Museum 65
 Jameson Midleton Distillery Experience 197
White Island 603
White Park Bay 582, 593
Whitehead 592
Wicklow 111-27, **112**
 accommodation 137
 itineraries 113
 navigation 112
 travel seasons 113
 travel within Wicklow 112
Wicklow Mountains National Park 114-21, **115**
 accommodation 117, 137
 food 116
 shopping 118
 travel within Wicklow Mountains National Park 114
Wicklow Way 117
Wild Atlantic Way 626
Wild Nephin National Park 372-4
Wilde, Oscar 63, 598
wildflowers 294
wildlife 623, see also individual animals
wildlife-watching 151, 332-3, 406, see also birdwatching
Windmill Lane 100
windmills 255
Winecellar Entry 498
winter solstice 464, 465
witchcraft 174
Wittgenstein, Ludwig 99
woodturning 178, 558
Wormhole 350
WWII 310

Y

Yeats, WB 388, 389, 390, 641-3
yoga 505
Youghal 201, **201**
yurts 617

Z

ziplines 511
zoos 104, 127, 197-8, 247

Be awed by the rugged, unspoilt beauty of the northern-most tip of mainland Ireland at Malin Head (p405).

Nestled at the foot of Mt Errigal, at the entrance to the Poisoned Glen, is the stunning ruin of Dunlewey Church (p402).

All rights reserved. No part of this publication may be copied, stored in a retrieval system, or transmitted in any form by any means, electronic, mechanical, recording or otherwise, except brief extracts for the purpose of review, and no part of this publication may be sold or hired, without the written permission of the publisher. Lonely Planet and the Lonely Planet logo are trademarks of Lonely Planet and are registered in the US Patent and Trademark Office and in other countries. Lonely Planet does not allow its name or logo to be appropriated by commercial establishments, such as retailers, restaurants or hotels. Please let us know of any misuses: lonelyplanet.com/legal/intellectual-property.

Mapping data sources:
© Lonely Planet
© OpenStreetMap http://openstreetmap.org/copyright

THIS BOOK

The 17th edition of Lonely Planet's Ireland guidebook was written and researched by Isabel Albiston, Fionn Davenport, Kathy Donaghy, Catherine Le Nevez and Neil Wilson. The previous edition was written by Isabel Albiston, Brian Barry, Fionn Davenport, Noelle Kelly, Catherine le Nevez and Neil Wilson. This guidebook was produced by the following:

Destination Editors
Amy Lynch, James Smart

Production Editor
Barbara Delissen

Image Editor
Nicolas D'Hoedt

Cartographer
Julie Dodkin

Assisting Cartographers
Anita Banh, Mark Griffiths, Valentina Kremenchutskaya

Coordinating Editor
Shauna Daly

Assisting Editors
Liana Cafolla, Felicity Hughes, Karyn Noble, Maja Vatrić

Cover Researcher
Valeria Suasnavas

Thanks Sofie Andersen, Janet Austin, Michelle Bennett, Melanie Dankel, Kevin Ebbutt, Saralinda Turner

Paper in this book is certified against the Forest Stewardship Council™ standards. FSC™ promotes environmentally responsible, socially beneficial and economically viable management of the world's forests.

Published by Lonely Planet Global Limited
CRN 554153
17th edition – May 2026
ISBN 978 1 83869 806 5
© Lonely Planet 2026 Photographs © as indicated 2026
10 9 8 7 6 5 4 3 2 1
Printed in China